D1452136

"*A Nation in God's Hands* is the most complete and convincing explanation to date about how Adventism became Adventism in the midst of the American Civil War. This trailblazing study, thoughtfully and attractively written, reveals with exceptional clarity the prophetic role of Ellen White during this terrible and bloody conflict. Lake, in his highly readable style, fills a necessary void within Adventist studies and reflects the very best in Adventist scholarship."—*Michael W. Campbell, associate professor of Adventist studies, Adventist International Institute of Advanced Studies*

"*A Nation in God's Hands* is a thoroughly researched and elegantly written historical commentary on Ellen White's Civil War visions and writings. Jud Lake analyzes each of Ellen White's Civil War predictions and interpretations and meticulously compares them with the historical evidence. In the process, he provides a fascinating and richly detailed portrayal of the historical era in which the Adventist Church became an organized body. The pages are studded with literally hundreds of memorable quotes from a wide range of contemporary sources, including Abraham Lincoln, other political leaders, military officers from both North and South, journalists, and many other participants and eyewitnesses. A must-read for students of Ellen White, early Adventism, and the Civil War."—*Jerry Moon, professor of church history, Andrews University*

"This volume is a unique and thought-provoking look at our great national conflict of 1861–1865. It should appeal to historians as well as Civil War enthusiasts. Adventists familiar with Mrs. White's visions will find many new insights provided by Dr. Lake's in-depth research."—*Myron House, professor emeritus, University of West Georgia*

"In *A Nation in God's Hands*, Jud Lake provides an exhaustively researched historical commentary on Ellen White's Civil War visions. The writing is clear and easy to follow, and Lake sprinkles fascinating historical quotes and anecdotes throughout the book. Additionally, he provides a balanced handling of the Union and Confederate sources and actions. If you want to understand Ellen White's Civil War statements in their immediate and larger historical context, then this is the book for you."—*Brian E. Strayer, professor emeritus of history, Andrews University*

JUD LAKE

The Robert Arthur Williams Library

A NATION IN GOD'S HANDS

Pacific Press®
Publishing Association
Nampa, Idaho | Oshawa, Ontario, Canada
www.pacificpress.com

OTHER BOOKS BY JUD LAKE

Ellen White Under Fire: Identifying the Mistakes of Her Critics

Cover design by Gerald Monks
Cover design resources from iStock_29551604 / traveler1116

The author assumes full responsibility for the accuracy of all facts and quotations as cited in this book.

Unless otherwise mentioned, all Scripture quotations are from the King James Version.

Scripture quotations marked ESV are from the Holy Bible, English Standard Version®. Copyright © 2001 by Crossway Bibles, a publishing ministry of Good News Publishers.

Scripture quotations marked NASB are taken from the NEW AMERICAN STANDARD BIBLE®, Copyright © 1960, 1962, 1963, 1968, 1971, 1972, 1973, 1975, 1977, 1995 by The Lockman Foundation. Used by permission. www.lockman.org.

Scripture quotations marked NCV are taken from the New Century Version®. Copyright © 2005 by Thomas Nelson, Inc. Used by permission. All rights reserved.

Additional copies of this book are available by calling toll-free 1-800-765-6955 or by visiting www.AdventistBookCenter.com.

Library of Congress Cataloging-in-Publication Data

Names: Lake, Judson Shepherd, author.
Title: A nation in God's hands : Ellen White and the Civil War / Jud Lake.
Description: Nampa : Pacific Press Publishing, 2017.
Identifiers: LCCN 2016051085 | ISBN 9780816362585 (pbk.)
Subjects: LCSH: White, Ellen Gould Harmon, 1827-1915—Prophecies. | United States—History—Civil War, 1861-1865—Prophecies.
Classification: LCC BX6193.W5 L3535 2017 | DDC 286.7092--dc23 LC record available at https://lccn.loc.gov/2016051085

March 2017

DEDICATION

TO PASTOR RONALD R. NEALL (1930–2014)
SPIRITUAL MENTOR AND CIVIL WAR ENTHUSIAST

ACKNOWLEDGMENTS

I owe a great deal of gratitude to several groups of individuals. First, the following professional historians read through the manuscript and offered helpful critiques and suggestions: Douglas Morgan (professor of history, Washington Adventist University), Ben McArthur (professor of history, Southern Adventist University), Dennis Pettibone (professor emeritus of history, Southern Adventist University), Brian E. Strayer (professor emeritus of history, Andrews University), Nicholas Miller (professor of church history, Andrews University), Myron House (professor emeritus, University of West Georgia), Eric Anderson (retired professor of history and former president of Southwestern Adventist University), and George C. Rable

(Charles Summersell, professor of Southern history, University of Alabama).

Second, the following Ellen White scholars also read through the manuscript and suggested helpful and important nuances to my interpretation of the Ellen White material: Jim Nix (director, Ellen G. White Estate), Denis Fortin (professor of theology, Andrews University), Jerry Moon (professor of church history, Andrews University), Michael W. Campbell (associate professor of Adventist studies, Adventist International Institute of Advanced Studies), and Benjamin Baker (managing editor, *Encyclopedia of Seventh-day Adventists*, General Conference of Seventh-day Adventists).

Third, Kevin Morgan (pastor and author of *Journeying to the Same Heaven: Ellen G. White, the Civil War, and the Goal of Post-Racialism*) and Kevin Burton (doctoral student and former researcher at the Center for Adventist Research) extended my arms of research and fortified this book with their excellent skills of fact-finding. Burton especially aided me by enhancing the information in several chapters. Star Stevens (resource secretary, School of Religion, Southern Adventist University) offered her services of copyediting and, as with my former book, cleaned up the manuscript in its various stages of completion. Distinguished Adventist historian George R. Knight (professor emeritus of church history, Andrews University) read the manuscript and wrote the foreword, for which I am grateful.

Finally, what would any contemporary researcher in nineteenth-century history do without the digitization projects at Google and the Internet Archive? Because of these projects, I was able to access many primary-source, original publications for free at the click of a mouse. Additionally, McKee Library at Southern Adventist University was especially patient and allowed me to keep scores of books for several years without returning them. Then there is the Center for Adventist Research at Andrews University, managed by the capable Merlin Burt. This excellent facility once again proved helpful in my research into nineteenth-century Adventism.

Ultimately, God alone was the revitalizing presence that sustained me through the long years of completing this book. "Commit your works to the Lord and your plans will be established" (Proverbs 16:3, NASB).

CONTENTS

How can such a small topic demand such a large book? The small topic is not the American Civil War, which has been the focus of more than sixty thousand books, pamphlets, and Internet resources. Rather, the smallness relates to Ellen White's writings on the subject. Her works reflect only four visions and/or testimonies on the war; all were contained in thirty pages of her writings,[1] and all occurred during the first half of the war. She is totally silent after January 1863 on what is undoubtedly the most important event in the post-Revolutionary history of the United States. And in her published and unpublished writings, we find not one mention of Abraham Lincoln during the conflict—the name that was on everybody's lips for more than four years. Nor does she even mention Gettysburg, or any other battle by name except First Manassas (Bull Run). The same can be said regarding the great generals of the day. In short, her response to the war was almost total silence. Yet that does not mean that what she had to say was unimportant or insignificant.

To the contrary, Jud Lake, in his comprehensive and fast-flowing treatment, indicates that her views, when seen against the backdrop of contemporary events, were both insightful and pertinent. Unfortunately, as historian Eric Anderson pointed out, both Ellen White's "critics and her followers have distorted her statements" about the war. Her comments too often "have been wrested from any appropriate historical context and conscripted into the service of such polemical purposes as proving either that she was a 'false prophet' or a truly inspired one."[2]

Jud Lake's purpose moves away from both of those approaches. Working on the well-substantiated historical understanding in both the North and the South that the Civil War was an event permeated by religious motivations and meanings, Lake's purpose "is to set White's war visions in their historical context and provide a theological interpretation of the war through her prophetic lens." The volume "is first and foremost a *religious interpretation* of the American Civil War." Lake is not unique in focusing on a religious interpretation. There are many volumes by leading historians on the topic. And as Lake demonstrates in his last chapter, even Lincoln's understanding of the significance of the war in his second inaugural address is a religious interpretation.

Lake's intention is not to rehash the understandings of others but to set forth Ellen White's interpretations in the light of her statements and viewed in their historical context during the onward flow of the war. And in that purpose, he delivers a unique perspective and makes a valuable contribution. In the process of achieving that purpose, he provides what in many cases turns out to be almost a line-by-line commentary of her most insightful and/or controversial remarks. It might be added that Lake's aim is not primarily to contextualize Ellen White's remarks; but while examining her interpretation of the war, he does an excellent job of contextualizing.

It is safe to say that in all the literature related to Ellen White, there is no parallel to this extensive treatment. We are looking at a new genre in the world of Ellen White studies, but one that points the direction for many other possible and needed investigations. While on the topic of new approaches to exploring the significance of Ellen White and her work, it should be noted that we are witnessing not a mere renaissance in books about Ellen White but, more important, new approaches to the topic. One only has to think of Gilbert Valentine's *The Prophet and the Presidents* (2011) and Alberto Timm and Dwain Esmond's edited volume titled *The Gift of Prophecy in Scripture and History* (2015). Jud Lake's approach in *A Nation in God's Hands* is an important contribution to the new world of Ellen White studies. And an exciting aspect of that new world is that it is a child of the past decade. My hope is that the coming years will see continuing dynamism in this important field of research and publishing.

It should be noted that Lake is not a newcomer to the field of Ellen White studies. In 2010, he published *Ellen White Under Fire: Identifying the Mistakes of Her Critics*.

While the field of apologetics regarding her work was not new, his approach was. And in that he made a major contribution in producing a must-read book reflecting intense research and clear writing. Lake's new book joins his earlier one as an imaginative and informative contribution to our understanding of Ellen White and her world. Needless to say, I highly recommend this book not only to students of Adventism and Ellen White but also to Civil War buffs of all flavors.

George R. Knight
Professor Emeritus of Church History
Andrews University

---

1. Ellen G. White, *Testimonies for the Church,* vol. 1 (Oakland, CA: Pacific Press®, 1885), 253–268, 355–368.

2. Eric Anderson, "War, Slavery, and Race," in *Ellen Harmon White: American Prophet*, ed. Terrie Dopp Aamodt, Gary Land, and Ronald L. Numbers (New York: Oxford University Press, 2014), 262.

INTRODUCTION

The rattle of musketry fire tore through the atmosphere with a loud ripping sound. Cannons boomed and roared in the background as billows of white smoke puffed into the sky. The wide field was speckled with Union and Confederate soldiers firing their weapons at one another, charging, screaming, shouting, and falling to the ground. It was the 150th anniversary reenactment of the Battle of First Manassas, and I was there, taking in every moment.

This experience was the beginning of my research into the American Civil War, which has culminated in this volume before you. Fortunately for me, the sesquicentennial celebration of this war (2011–2015) coincided with the writing of this book. The many commemorations, conferences, books, exhibits, reenactments of battles, and other public events during these four years, which continue to the present time, were an asset to my research and testify to the profound influence of this epic war between the North and the South from 1861 to 1865.[1]

This "American Iliad"[2] was a defining event unlike any other in American history. While the American Revolutionary War of 1775–1783 created the United States, the Civil War preserved it and shaped it into the modern nation it is today. "Before 1861 'United States' was a plural noun: The United States *have* a republican form of government. Since 1865 'United States' is a singular noun: The United States *is* a world power. The North went to war to preserve the *Union*; it ended by creating a *nation*."[3]

The Civil War settled two fundamental, festering issues left unresolved by the revolution: "whether the United States would endure as one nation, indivisible; and whether slavery would continue to mock the ideals of liberty on which the republic was founded."[4] By the war's end in 1865, the unity of the United States was secure, and the institution of slavery had met its demise through the Emancipation Proclamation, the end of the Confederacy, and the Thirteenth Amendment to the Constitution. America was now theoretically consistent with its Declaration of Independence that states "all men are created equal."[5]

But these victories did not come without a heavy price. The tragedies of human suffering and death took their toll on the nation. According to the latest research, some 750,000 soldiers, plus an unknown number of civilians, lost their lives in the war,[6] not to mention the countless wounded soldiers who lived on with significant physical disfigurements. The emotional toll at the home front was also enormous as families mourned the loss of their sons, and the population on both sides suffered four long years of deprivation. The Civil War was an event of large-scale destruction that left the great cities of the South in utter ruin and decimated its socioeconomic foundations.

Seventh-day Adventists lived through these difficult years and experienced all the anxiety and deprivation that come with a nation being at war. Like most other Northerners, they eagerly read the news of the war and followed the rise and fall of the Union armies on the battlefields.[7] Although they had no sympathy for the South in its practice of slavery, neither were they happy with the United States (U.S.) government in its many compromises with the South. These Adventists felt fortunate, however, that they found a source of insight and encouragement in the visions of Ellen White. By the time the war began, she was in her seventeenth year of prophetic ministry to the Adventist people.

Ellen White's Civil War visions

Between the years 1858 and 1862, Ellen White witnessed several visions about slavery and the Civil War. In March 1858, she experienced her comprehensive great controversy vision in which she beheld the entire plan of redemption—from Satan's rebellion in heaven to the earth made new—specifically from the perspective of the cosmic battle between Christ and Satan. Part of that vision dealt with God's anger about chattel slavery in America, and White published it in the fall of 1858 in

Spiritual Gifts, volume 1.[8] It is a vehement condemnation of slavery and a warning of imminent divine punishment coming to the nation.

Parkville vision. White's first Civil War vision took place on January 12, 1861, while she was visiting the church in Parkville, Michigan. After the vision, she explained to an attentive audience that the secession of South Carolina was the beginning of many states that would secede from the Union and that this would result in a "terrible war." She described the booming of the cannons and the massive carnage on the battlefields. Church leader John N. Loughborough, who was present at the meeting, recorded her words as she described what she had seen in the vision. Years later, in 1892, he published his account of the vision for the first time in his book *Rise and Progress of the Seventh-day Adventists*.[9]

Roosevelt vision. On August 3, 1861, while in Roosevelt, New York, nearly two weeks after the first major battle of the Civil War at Manassas, Virginia, Ellen White experienced her second war vision. Later she wrote about this experience and published it in the August 27, 1861, issue of the *Advent Review and Sabbath Herald*, titled "Communication From Sister White."[10] She announced that God was punishing both the North and the South for the sin of slavery; yet, He "has the destiny of this nation in his hands."[11] A notable feature of this vision was her depiction of an angel that descended in the heat of battle at First Manassas and initiated the sudden retreat of the Federal troops. This supernatural intervention was an assurance that God would involve Himself in the battles of the war. Based on this angelic intervention, White forecast the pattern of Union victories and losses throughout the entire war.

Battle Creek vision of January 1862. The third war vision occurred in Battle Creek, Michigan, on January 4, 1862, and was published as *Testimony for the Church, No. 7* the following month.[12] This document was based on a rather comprehensive vision that Ellen White received about the philosophy behind the war, the way it was being prosecuted, the national fasts, the conflict with England, and the protracted struggle ahead.

Battle Creek vision of November 1862. White didn't give a specific date for when this fourth war vision occurred, but the most likely candidate was her November 5 vision—the last one in 1862.[13] The war part of the vision was published in the first section of *Testimony for the Church, No. 9* in January 1863.[14] It dealt with the challenge of conscription that the young church faced and provided counsel on how to navigate through the crisis. It also addressed problems in the Union army that were protracting the war, such as proslavery influences in the military and officers who sought guidance from Spiritualist mediums. This was White's last vision about the war.

In 1885, the first twenty-eight pamphlet-sized *Testimonies* were published in four volumes, which grew into nine volumes toward the end of Ellen White's life.[15] She chose to republish the Roosevelt vision and the Parkville vision with the Battle Creek vision of January 1862 in *Testimony for the Church, No. 7*, which was later republished in *Testimonies for the Church*, volume 1.[16] *Testimony for the Church, No. 9* was also republished in the same volume.[17] Thus, all four of White's Civil War visions can be read in *Testimonies for the Church*, volume 1. It should be pointed out, however, that these visions were not only about the war. Other subjects, based on these same war visions, were written out and published in *Testimony for the Church, No. 7* and *Testimony for the Church, No. 9* as well.[18] It was not uncommon in White's early experience for a single vision to cover multiple subjects.[19]

It should also be mentioned that White's claim in predicting the coming of the Civil War was not unique. Quaker Joseph Hoag, for example, reportedly experienced a vision in 1803 and prophesied "a civil war" in which "an abundance of human blood was shed in [the] course of the combat" and that the "Southern States" would lose "their power" and slavery would be banished "from their borders." This vision circulated widely in manuscript form during the decade before the Civil War and was first published by Frederick Douglass in 1854.[20] After the war, the vision circulated among the Adventists and was published in the *Review and Herald*.[21]

In 1832, the Mormon prophet Joseph Smith predicted a coming war that would begin with South Carolina.[22] The radical Southern secessionist Edmund Ruffin foretold secession, civil war, and Southern independence in his *Anticipations of the Future* (1860).[23] Although Ruffin never claimed the prophetic gift, he "acted like a prophet and appeared as one to friends, foes, and even himself."[24] The Spiritualist Emma Hardinge also claimed that she had "fearful and mysterious visions of death and desolation" prior to the war, as did other Spiritualists.[25]

The uniqueness of White in the midst of this visionary milieu was that she provided *theological* commentary on the war as it unfolded.[26] She addressed specific events during the conflict and alluded to others, while providing her readers with theological and biblical insights and perspectives. But she never conceived of herself as a lecturer to the North or as a prophetic voice to the nation. There was nothing in her career to suggest that she sought national publicity. She only sought to mentor her church members and brace them for the trials ahead during the national calamities.[27] The main purpose in all her war essays was to prepare her readers for the second coming of Christ.[28]

Purpose and organization of this book

The purpose of this book is to set White's war visions in their historical context and provide a theological interpretation of the war through her prophetic lens. Presently, more than sixty thousand books, pamphlets, and Internet resources have been written on the Civil War since the guns ceased firing more than a century and a half ago. This book will tell the story of this war again but from the unique perspective of White's visions. As such, it is first and foremost a *religious interpretation* of the American Civil War and is best understood and appreciated in that framework.[29] In his significant *God's Almost Chosen Peoples: A Religious History of the American Civil War*, distinguished historian George C. Rable demonstrated that Americans, both North and South, interpreted the events of the war theologically.[30] This volume is a study of one such American who believed she had the prophetic gift and interpreted the war out of that framework.

The book is organized according to Mrs. White's visions, in the order that she received them, as the table of contents shows. Starting with the decades before the war and how White became a prophet to the Adventist people, the book moves through the war years and analyzes the visions in relation to their historical and religious settings. The last chapter of the book will reveal a link between the message of White at the beginning of the war and President Lincoln at the end of the war. Her theological message was fully anticipatory of his second inaugural address.

The overarching argument throughout the book is that White comprehended the issues of the war extraordinarily well and provided a nuanced theological interpretation of this major conflict for the Adventist people. She insisted that God was angry with the nation, that the war was God's punishment on both the North and the South for the sin of slavery, that the Union military was weakened by proslavery forces working against the war effort, and that the Union forces would not have ultimate success in the war until emancipation of the slaves became the dominant purpose. But in the midst of her grim prognosis, White gave hints that the Union would ultimately prevail over the South in God's time and the slaves would be free.

Most important, White provided a theologically nuanced view of God's providence and care for America that gave hope to her readers. At the outset of the conflict, she stated twice that God "has the destiny of the nation in His hands."[31] This assertion came within two weeks of the first major Union disaster at the Battle of First Manassas. When Adventists and all other Northerners feared the fate of the nation during this hour, White assured the Adventists that God had this nation in His hands and was in control of its future. But she made this assertion in the midst of her condemnation of the nation for the sin of slavery. So by saying that America's destiny was in God's hands in the midst of the national crisis, she was not only stating that divine providence would preserve the nation but that it would allow disaster and ruin to occur for moral correction. This concept is at the core of White's writings on the Civil War and functions as a major theme throughout this book.

Adventists had mixed feelings about their country. They believed it was the greatest nation on earth and a model republic because of its principles of political and religious liberty. But they also viewed America as the beast power of Revelation 13:11–18 that was lamblike in its principles of liberty but dragonlike in its potential threat to religious freedom. They especially believed that America was marred by the South's institution of slavery.[32] Their only hope was that God had their church *and* the nation in His hands. Ellen White provided this hope for them and for all others who desire God's providence in this nation's affairs.

Practical matters

Several practical matters should be mentioned. For those who are not familiar with the American Civil War and want to gain a better understanding, the appendix contains suggestions for further reading. Also, each chapter is summarized in a paragraph or two after its conclusion. This feature is ideal for those who want to see the main argument of a chapter in a nutshell. Additionally, as the reader will notice in the comprehensive endnotes, many sources were used in the writing of this book. While I have carefully listened to primary sources, the secondary sources by Civil War historians were most useful in telling the story of the war. Consequently, I have drawn from these sources and let them speak on the historical setting for White's visions. I am most grateful for the research of those who have specialized in the

Civil War. Their research and writing on the battles, politics, and narrative of this epic war is a wonderful legacy for all students.

I encourage the reader to keep the text of Ellen White's war visions close for reference during the reading of this book. One can use the hard-copy text in volume 1 of *Testimonies for the Church* or the iPhone app, with of all White's published writings, which can be downloaded for free from the official Ellen G. White Estate Web site. Additionally, there is the *Ellen G. White Writings Comprehensive Research Edition* CD-ROM.[33]

Finally, a word on the reading audiences of this book: For the Adventist audience who, in general, embraces Ellen White's prophetic ministry, this book will open up the riches of the Civil War era and place her writings in that context. Her perceptive insights and keen theological interpretations will be explained in their historical setting as the book moves through the story of the war. This book will also touch on the organization and birth of the Seventh-day Adventist Church during the perilous war years and spotlight how Adventists reacted to the war and the issue of slavery in the pages of the *Review and Herald*, the church's official publication. Battles, generals, and especially President Abraham Lincoln will feature prominently throughout some chapters of this book. In many ways, Lincoln was central to the story of the Civil War.

I have also kept in mind those outside of the Adventist community who may not share my view that White possessed supernatural endowment. In recent years, she has been recognized as a significant figure in American religious history,[34] and her largely overlooked war "Testimonies"[35] are primary sources of how one contemporary writer of that era interpreted this epic conflict as it unfolded. Students and enthusiasts of the Civil War will find in her war writings many statements reflective of the contemporary religious milieu but cast in the unique framework of her Seventh-day Adventist faith and sense of prophetic calling. This book will give an explanation of White's war writings from that faith perspective and thus provide an example of how one religious group has interpreted the American Civil War historically and presently.

A personal reflection

Prior to the research for this book, I had only general knowledge of the great human interest stories of the war about Lincoln, Lee, Grant, Sherman, Sheridan, and others, but I never really knew in any great detail the context of the war and its profound drama. Now, after immersing myself in the literature over the last several years to write this book, the American Civil War—its drama and excitement, its sadness and suffering, its battlefields and conflicts, and its profound life lessons—has captured my imagination and touched my heart. It has also significantly enhanced my appreciation of this period as a historical framework for early Adventist history. As I have often said to my students in the classroom, my research into the life and teachings of Ellen White has led me into adventures I never could have imagined. The study of the Civil War, without a doubt, is one of the greatest of these adventures.

1. For those who want to gain a basic working knowledge of the American Civil War, the sources listed below are a good place to start.

2. Charles P. Roland, *An American Iliad: The Story of the Civil War*, 2nd ed. (Lexington, KY: University Press of Kentucky, 2002).

3. James McPherson, *The War That Forged a Nation: Why the Civil War Still Matters* (New York: Oxford University Press, 2015), 6 (emphasis in original).

4. James McPherson, *Drawn With the Sword: Reflections on the American Civil War* (New York: Oxford University Press, 1996), viii.

5. America had other steps to take in future years regarding equal rights for black Americans.

6. J. David Hacker, "A Census-Based Count of the Civil War Dead," *Civil War History* 57, no. 4 (December 2011): 307–348.

7. In Letter 6a, July 26, 1861, Ellen White wrote her friends at home about reading the "war news" while James had two teeth filled. Ellen G. White to "Friends at Home," Letter 6a, Eagle Harbor, New York, July 26, 1861, in Ellen G. White Writings, accessed November 2, 2016, https://m.egwwritings.org/en/book/3018.2000001#1.

8. Ellen G. White, *Spiritual Gifts*, vol. 1 (Battle Creek, MI: James White, 1858), 189–193.

9. John N. Loughborough, *Rise and Progress of the Seventh-day Adventists* (Battle Creek, MI: General Conference Association of Seventh-day Adventists, 1892), 236, 237.

10. Ellen G. White, "Communication From Sister White," *Advent Review and Sabbath Herald*, August 27, 1861, 101. (The *Advent Review and Sabbath Herald* will be referred to as the *Review and Herald* hereafter.)

11. Ellen G. White, *Testimonies for the Church*, vol. 1 (Oakland, CA: Pacific Press®, 1885), 264.

12. Ellen G. White, *Testimony for the Church, No. 7* (Battle Creek, MI: Steam Press of the Seventh-day Adventist

Church, 1862).

13. On page 48 of the January 6, 1863, edition of the *Review and Herald*, it was announced that *Testimony for the Church, No. 9* "will be ready in a few days." The only recorded vision prior to this time was her November 5, 1862, vision, which she makes several references to in Letter 11, 1862; Letter 23, 1862; and MS 10, 1862. (The letters and manuscript can be read in their entirety at the Ellen G. White Writings Web site; see https://m.egwwritings.org/en/folders/553.) The content in these communications thematically corresponds to the material in *Testimony for the Church, No. 9*. Although Ellen G. White does not specify when she received the vision relating to the war in *Testimony for the Church, No. 9*, the November 5, 1862, vision is thus the most likely candidate.

14. Ellen G. White, *Testimony for the Church, No. 9* (Battle Creek, MI: Steam Press of the Seventh-day Adventist Church, 1863).

15. Ellen G. White, *Testimonies for the Church*, 9 vols. (Mountain View, CA: Pacific Press®, 1885–1948).

16. White, *Testimonies for the Church*, 1:253–270.

17. Ibid., 1:355–368.

18. Ibid., 1:270–302; 368–389.

19. See Denis Fortin, "Visions of Ellen G. White," in *The Ellen G. White Encyclopedia*, ed. Denis Fortin and Jerry Moon (Hagerstown, MD: Review and Herald®, 2014), 1249.

20. See *Frederick Douglass' Paper*, July 6, 1854; for a discussion of the background and dating of Hoag's vision, see Hugh Barbour et al., eds., *Quaker Crosscurrents: Three Hundred Years of Friends in the New York Yearly Meetings* (Syracuse, NY: Syracuse University Press, 1995), 190, and the Hoag documents at Swarthmore College: "Joseph Hoag Family Papers, 1813–1864," Swarthmore College, accessed November 2, 2016, http://www.swarthmore.edu/library/friends/ead/5199joho.xml.

21. "Joseph Hoag's Vision," *Review and Herald*, April 9, 1867, 210. Before printing the entire vision, the editor, Uriah Smith, provided readers with a caveat: "In compliance with repeated requests we now give it to our readers; we do not say it is not what it purports to be; but with it would yet request all to receive such documents with caution, remembering that this is an age of deceptions and counterfeits." The vision received attention by Adventists in later years because Hoag predicted a "National religion" at the end of time; see "Joseph Hoag's Vision," *Review and Herald*, October 15, 1867, 280; "Joseph Hoag's Vision," *Review and Herald*, January 31, 1899, 75; "Prophecy of Joseph Hoag," *Signs of the Times*, August 8, 1900, 6.

22. Joseph Smith, *The Doctrine and Covenants* (Salt Lake City, UT: Church of Jesus Christ of Latter-day Saints, 1949), sec. 87:1–8, accessed November 2, 2016, https://www.lds.org/scriptures/dc-testament/dc/87.

23. Edmund Ruffin, *Anticipations of the Future, to Serve as Lessons for the Present Time* (Richmond, VA: J. W. Randolph, 1860).

24. Jason Phillips, "The Prophecy of Edmund Ruffin: Anticipating the Future of Civil War History," in Ben Wright and Zachary W. Dresser, eds., *Apocalypse and the Millennium in the American Civil War Era* (Baton Rouge, LA: Louisiana State University Press, 2013), 14.

25. Emma Hardinge, *Modern American Spiritualism* (New York: Emma Hardinge, 1870), 490. For other Spiritualist predictions, see Mark A. Lause, *Free Spirits: Spiritualism, Republicanism, and Radicalism in the Civil War Era* (Chicago: University of Illinois Press, 2016), 48, 49.

26. In contrast, the "spirits" provided political commentary on the war through their mediums; see Lause, *Free Spirits*, 59–63.

27. See Lee Ellsworth Eusey, "The American Civil War: An Interpretation" (master's thesis, Andrews University, 1965), 119.

28. On the dominance of this theme in Ellen White's writings, see Denis Fortin, "The Theology of Ellen G. White," in Fortin and Moon, *The Ellen G. White Encyclopedia*, 277, 278, and Norman Gulley, "Second Coming of Christ," in *The Ellen G. White Encyclopedia*, 1140, 1141.

29. For a discussion on different Christian interpretations of the Civil War during the first century after it ceased, see William A. Clebsch, *Christian Interpretations of the Civil War* (Philadelphia, PA: Fortress Press, 1969).

30. George C. Rable, *God's Almost Chosen Peoples: A Religious History of the American Civil War* (Chapel Hill, NC: University of North Carolina Press, 2010).

31. White, *Testimonies for the Church*, 1:264, see also 267.

32. See Douglas Morgan, *Adventism and the American Republic: The Public Involvement of a Major Apocalyptic Movement* (Knoxville, TN: University of Tennessee Press, 2001), 20. See pages 11–26 for a discussion on the shaping of Seventh-day Adventist apocalypticism. See also Douglas Morgan, "United States in Prophecy," in Fortin and Moon, *The Ellen G. White Encyclopedia*, 1237–1241; and Jonathan M. Butler, "Adventism and the American Experience," in Edwin Scott Gaustad, ed., *The Rise of Adventism: A Commentary on the Social and Religious Ferment of Mid-Nineteenth Century America* (New York: Harper & Row, 1974), 181, 182, 185.

33. See White, *Testimonies for the Church*, vol. 1; the Ellen G. White Estate Web site at http://www.whiteestate .org; and *Ellen G. White Writings Comprehensive Research Edition* CD-ROM (Silver Spring, MD: Ellen G. White Estate, 2008).

34. See "The 100 Most Significant Americans of All Time," *Smithsonian* (Spring 2015): 72, 73, and Terrie Dopp Aamodt, Gary Land, and Ronald L. Numbers, eds., *Ellen Harmon White: American Prophet* (New York: Oxford University Press, 2014).

35. For what a "Testimony" is and how it functioned in Ellen White's writings, see Graeme Sharrock, "Testimonies," in Aamodt, Land, and Numbers, *Ellen Harmon White: American Prophet*, 52–73.

PART I

BEFORE THE WAR (MARCH 1858):
"HIS ANGER BURNS AGAINST THIS NATION"

Ellen White, about 1864
(egwwritings.org)

CHAPTER 1

ELLEN G. WHITE: A PROPHET TO THE ADVENTIST PEOPLE

Ellen Gould Harmon White was a Yankee—born above the Mason-Dixon Line, raised with New England values, and sympathetic to the antislavery cause—a Northerner to the core.[1] She received her prophetic calling in Maine, the northeasternmost part of Yankee New England. Her Yankee parents, Robert and Eunice Harmon, had resided in Maine for many years and were loyal New England Methodists. She married a Yankee from Maine, James White, and raised her children in Yankee Michigan. Her prophetic ministry thus began in Yankee territory, but it would one day extend beyond the Mason-Dixon Line to the Deep South and to the rest of the world.

The first three decades of Ellen's life (1827–1857) were part of a fascinating and turbulent period in American history known as "antebellum America" (literally, "before the war").[2] Historians often date this period from Andrew Jackson's victory at the Battle of New Orleans in 1815 to the Civil War in 1861.[3] It was characterized by chaotic social, theological, territorial, and political forces that repeatedly clashed with each other and caused an antagonistic sectional rift between the North and the South. By the end of 1860, this intense ideological conflict had established a national psychological mind-set that inevitably led to open hostilities in the Civil War. This period was also a time of unprecedented social reforms and spiritual revivals that swept across the American landscape. Ellen White, like all other Americans during this era, was impacted by these events. This chapter will provide the historical framework for the story of how Ellen White became a prophet to the Adventist people.

The Missouri Compromise of 1820

Seven years before Ellen's birth in 1827, her home state of Maine entered the Union as a result of the Missouri Compromise of 1820. This significant political event was the nation's first major crisis over slavery and is recognized by historians as planting the seeds for the Civil War that occurred forty years later. During the years of 1802 through 1819, as new states joined the Union, they did so essentially in pairs: one free state from the North, and another slave state from the South. By the close of 1819, the sectional divide over slavery in America was geographically evident in the twenty-two states: eleven slave, and eleven free. This balance was disrupted with the application of Missouri, a slave state, for admission to the Union.

The controversial aspect of Missouri's admission to statehood was that it would mean the first slave state completely west of the Mississippi River. Slavery had existed in North America for more than 150 years before the ratification of the Constitution in 1788 and was legal in every one of the thirteen colonies. The North had developed a more diverse economy that was not dependent on slavery and gravitated away from it as fundamental to its society. The South had, in contrast, organized its entire economic and social life on human bondage; the slave states "were not merely societies with slaves but 'slave societies' " themselves.[4] Politically, the issue of slavery proved to be volatile with regard to congressional representation. Because of the growing populations in the Northern free states, the North had more votes in Congress than the Southern slave states, so the South constantly fought for an equal vote.

It was in this context that the free state of Maine applied for statehood in the Union and complicated the concern over slavery and freedom in Missouri. The debate was intense, but the compromise ultimately admitted Missouri into the Union as a slave state and prohibited any more slave states to be admitted from the Louisiana Purchase north of Missouri's southern border, the latitude 36°30'. In this context, Maine entered the Union as a free state and maintained the balance between the free states and the slave states.[5] The compromise of 1820 was passed through the House, and nationalists on both the North and South sides accepted the settlement.

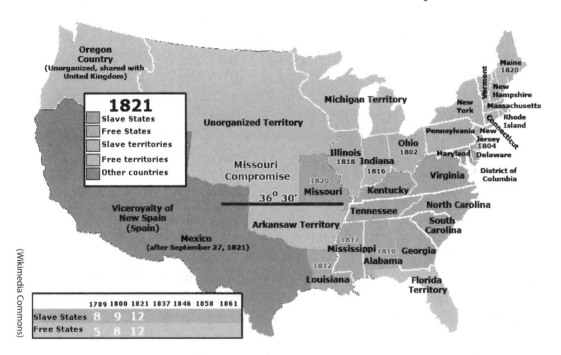

On April 22, 1820, the aged Thomas Jefferson wrote to John Holmes of Maine that the Missouri Compromise, "like a fire bell in the night, awakened and filled me with terror. I considered it at once as the knell of the Union." The idea of "a geographical line, coinciding with a marked principle, moral and political, once conceived and held up to the angry passions of men, will never be obliterated; and every new irritation will mark it deeper and deeper."[6] These words would ring true with almost prophetic accuracy. Each debate over the issue of slavery would deepen the geopolitical division in the country. When the Missouri Compromise was repealed years later in 1854, many in the country saw it as a call to war. Historian Robert Pierce Forbes believed that the Missouri Compromise is best understood "as a flash of lightning that illuminated the realities of sectional power in the United States and ignited a fire that smoldered for a generation" and then, when circumstances were right, "burst into flame."[7] Such was the politically charged atmosphere into which Ellen White was born.

Religious and reform movements

Americans in general were optimistic during this antebellum period, especially since the War of 1812 had placed them in the family of nations and provided a hero in the person of Andrew Jackson, who was a symbol of progress and individualism. With social and technological developments, an expansion of the territory, and religious freedom, Americans looked at their country and wondered at "what hath God wrought."[8] This climate of optimism helped spawn the many reform movements that sought to help America fulfill its destiny and usher in the millennium. Temperance, education, women's rights, abolitionism, and other issues all became part of the reform movements in America during that time; each with its own leaders and societies.

Because of America's democratic stance, its soil was ripe for the birth of numerous religious movements. During Ellen White's childhood years in the 1830s, America experienced a great revival. From approximately 1790 to the mid-1840s, a Great Awakening, sometimes referred to as the Second Great Awakening,[9] swept through the United States and became the most influential revival of Christianity in American history.[10] From approximately 1825 to the late 1830s, the revival found its momentum in Charles Grandison Finney, the Presbyterian turned Congregationalist who, according to historian Mark A. Noll, "may have had a greater impact on the public life of antebellum America than any of the nation's politicians."[11]

Finney developed his own style of revival that impacted the masses as he traveled from place to place.[12] Because he taught that slavery was a national sin and was against God's moral law, abolitionist activity increased dramatically after his revival campaigns. Although Finney never participated directly in the abolitionist movement, his preaching provided the theological foundation for antislavery views. He believed that converting souls through revival, rather than political activism, would bring about abolitionism. His message of holiness and perfection in this life encouraged the antislavery activists to believe that they could perfect society and usher in Christ's millennial reign.[13] This postmillennial understanding (that Christ would return after the millennium) was characteristic of Protestant theology in antebellum America and fueled the many reform efforts of that era.

Outside of evangelical churches, utopian communities, such as the Shakers and Oneida Perfectionists, endeavored to perfect American society with their unique religious beliefs. Universalists, with their benevolent view of God, and Unitarians, with their focus on the nature and rationality of humankind, both cast their presence across the New England landscape. Spiritualism, with its birth in 1848 at the home of Kate and Maggie Fox, proliferated into a significant presence in America by the time of the Civil War. Mormonism, with a theocracy centered in its prophet, Joseph Smith, was a constant controversial presence in antebellum America. Finally, the restorationists and Millerites, more biblically oriented than the others, were seminal influences on the founders of Seventh-day Adventism.[14]

On a more intellectual level was the influential Transcendentalist movement that put emphasis on the inherent goodness of man. "Innately present in each individual," said the Transcendentalists, "is a spiritual principle that, of itself, without any external stimuli, allows one to distinguish between right and wrong, good and bad, God and Satan, and it supersedes any outward laws or injunctions."[15] Leaders of the movement, such as Ralph Waldo Emerson, Theodore Parker, and Henry David Thoreau, viewed slavery as inherently wrong and thus participated in the abolitionist movement.[16] The spiritually charged atmosphere created by all these movements impacted Americans, including the family of the young Ellen Harmon.

Tumultuous events of 1831

The year that Ellen turned four years old, 1831, was a year full of tumultuous events that would influence America's destiny.[17] On January 1, William Lloyd Garrison published the first issue of *The Liberator* and emerged as the most outspoken and radical abolitionist in the antebellum United States. "I am in earnest," Garrison declared in his opening editorial, "I will not equivocate—I will not excuse—I will not retreat a single inch—*and I will be heard*."[18] Prior to this, abolitionists advocated for a gradual emancipation of slavery in the United States. But Garrison launched what would come to be known as "immediate emancipation"—a new movement in abolitionism that would agitate the slavery issue in the United States. The next chapter will look at the movement of abolitionism in more detail as the context to understand Ellen White's strong antislavery stance better.

February 12, 1831, was a day many Americans anticipated with a sense of impending danger. It was heralded by the media as the "Great Eclipse of 1831" and would be the darkest day in the history of the United States, and the day the earth would "tremble on its axis." When the fateful day finally arrived, Americans searched the heavens to witness the solar eclipse, but the day passed and the spectacle was rather unimpressive. Nevertheless, preachers capitalized on the event and preached on the "signs in the sun" from Luke 21:25.[19]

In Southampton County, Virginia, one preacher saw the February 12 eclipse as a sign to begin an insurrection.[20] Nat Turner had escaped from slavery in 1821 but returned to his former plantation to plot and plan a slave revolt. As a preacher, he was allowed to speak at different plantations and used this opportunity to rally other slaves to his cause. Turner interpreted the eclipse as a sign to begin his rebellion, and he watched for the opportune day. On August 22, he launched the revolt, and after slaying some sixty whites, his followers were apprehended; though Turner himself escaped capture until October 30. Turner was sentenced to death and hanged on November 11. On November 25, Turner's attorney published *The Confessions of Nat Turner*.[21] American slavery historian Eugene Genovese suggested that "Turner's revolt was a turning point in the movement towards the United States Civil War because it stiffened the resolve of both abolitionists and proslavery advocates."[22]

Falling of the stars in 1833

On November 13, 1833, while young Ellen slept through the night, many Americans again watched another spectacle in the sky. This one was much more impressive than the solar eclipse of 1831. On this night, the stars fell from the sky. One eyewitness wrote, "No language, indeed, can come up to the splendor of that magnificent display; . . . no one who did not witness it can form an adequate conception of its glory. It seemed as if the whole starry heavens had congregated at one point near the zenith, and were simultaneously shooting forth, with the velocity of lightning, to every part of the horizon; and yet they were not exhausted—thousands swiftly followed in the tracks of thousands, as if created for the occasion."[23] Another described the display throughout the night: "The meteors began to attract notice by their unusual frequency or brilliancy, from nine to twelve o'clock in the evening, were most striking in their appearance, from two to five, arrived at their maximum, in many places, about four o'clock, and continued till rendered invisible by the light of day."[24]

A young Frederick Douglass, the escaped slave who would become the most famous black abolitionist and civil-rights activist in nineteenth-century America, awoke that morning and peered into the sky. "I witnessed this gorgeous spectacle, and was awe-struck," he later recalled. "The air seemed filled with bright descending messengers from the sky. It was about daybreak when I saw this sublime scene. I was not without the suggestion, at the moment, that it might be the harbinger of the coming of the Son of Man; and, in my then state of mind, I was prepared to hail Him as my friend and deliverer. I had read, that the 'stars shall fall from heaven'; and they were now falling."[25] Interestingly, years later, Ellen White wrote in *The Great Controversy* that the falling of the stars on November 13, 1833, directed the attention of many people "to the fulfillment of prophecy, and many were led to give heed to the warning of the second advent."[26]

Rise of the Millerites

The falling of the stars provided credibility to one preacher in particular. William Miller, a former military officer in the War of 1812, concluded, after an intense study of the Scriptures from 1816 to 1818, that Christ was coming back around 1843. This successful farmer and abolitionist was reluctant to share his views, but he finally began preaching and publishing his message in 1831.[27] Throughout the rest of the 1830s, Miller heralded the soon return of Christ; this message of the premillennial return of Christ was in stark contrast to the postmillennialism of the day. Preachers welcomed Miller because he was a church-growth agent; wherever he went, revival ensued.[28] In 1839, Joshua V. Himes, the dynamic preacher and radical abolitionist at the Chardon Street Chapel in Boston, took up the Second Advent cause and provided momentum for Miller's ideas by organizing giant camp meetings and Second Advent conferences, landing Miller in the large cities. Eventually, Miller's message swelled into a national movement, and he became one of the greatest evangelistic influences in the northeastern United States between 1840 and 1844.[29]

It was during this time that young Ellen first heard William Miller preach. "In March, 1840, William Miller visited Portland, Maine," she recalled, "and gave a course of lectures on the second coming of Christ." She remembered vividly how "Mr. Miller traced down the prophecies with an exactness that struck conviction to the hearts of his hearers. He dwelt upon the prophetic periods, and brought many proofs to strengthen his position. Then his solemn and powerful appeals and admonitions to those who were unprepared, held the crowds as if spellbound."[30]

Struck by the contrast of Miller's message with what she had heard in her own church, Ellen pondered, "I had been taught that a temporal millennium would take place prior to the coming of Christ in the clouds of heaven; but now I was listening to the startling announcement that Christ was coming in 1843, only a few short years in the future."[31] Again, two years later in 1842, she heard Miller preach in Portland and was stirred. These meetings and a series of other events led to Ellen's conversion, and she rejoiced in the soon return of Christ.[32]

Miller never set a specific date for Christ to come. Instead, he was always approximate, "about the year 1843." After this time period passed uneventfully, one of his followers, Samuel S. Snow, convincingly demonstrated in August 1844 that the fulfillment of the 2,300-day prophecy of Daniel 8:14 would take place in the autumn of 1844. Specifically, Snow showed that Daniel's prophecy about the cleansing of the sanctuary in Daniel 8:14 would meet its completion on the Jewish Day of Atonement—the tenth day of the seventh month of the Jewish year (Leviticus 23:27). That day in 1844 was October 22. Christ's coming was just two months away![33]

For the teenaged Ellen, this was a time of glad expectation. She remembered the revival that took place in the believers' hearts during this time: "We assembled in the orchards and groves to commune with God and to offer up our petitions to Him, feeling more fully in His presence when surrounded by His natural works. The joys of salvation were more necessary to us than our food and drink. If clouds obscured our minds, we dared not rest or sleep till they were swept away by the consciousness of our acceptance with the Lord."[34] Ellen, along with tens of thousands of Millerites on that chilly day of October 22, 1844, searched the skies, looking for the coming King. But the time "passed unmarked by the advent of Jesus," she recalled. "It was a bitter disappointment."[35]

Meanwhile, the rest of the country was focused on the national presidential campaign during the fall of 1844. The Democratic nominee, James K. Polk, ran on a platform that supported territorial expansion, later known as "manifest destiny"—America's right to expand its territory and destiny. Polk supported the annexation of Texas, which was a hot issue during the campaign, and the Whig nominee, Henry Clay, opposed it. James Gillespie Birney ran as the antislavery Liberty Party nominee; Joseph Smith, the Mormon prophet, ran as an independent, but his campaign ended abruptly when he was killed in a jail riot on June 27. On December 4, Polk won the presidency in a very close election,[36] and his victory would be significant in terms of America's territorial expansion—an issue that would inflame the slavery question in the 1850s.

Ellen White's visions and the rise of Sabbatarian Adventism

Also in December of 1844, two months after the Great Disappointment, seventeen-year-old Ellen received her first vision, which she published later in *The Day-Star*, a Second Advent periodical, on January 24, 1846. "The Holy Ghost fell upon me," she recounted,

> I raised my eyes, and saw a straight and narrow path, cast up high above the world. On this path the Advent people were traveling to the city, which was at the farther end of the path. They had a bright light set up behind them at the beginning of the path, which an angel told me was the midnight cry. This light shone all along the path and gave light for their feet so that they might not stumble. If they kept their eyes fixed on Jesus, who was just before them, leading them to the city, they were safe. But soon some grew weary, and said the city was a great way off, and they expected to have entered it before.[37]

This inaugural vision captured the essence of the 1844 experience for the believers and provided confidence in God's leading through that time. The "midnight cry" represented the 1844 message, and the vision assured that it was a genuine prophetic message.

According to Adventist historian George R. Knight, this vision tells us a great deal about Ellen Harmon's seventy-year prophetic ministry:

> First and foremost it points us to her lifelong passion—the soon return of Jesus and God's care for His children. Beyond that, it presents a dual emphasis that runs throughout her 70-year ministry.
>
> The first aspect of that emphasis is that something of great importance took place in heaven on October 22, 1844, and that Adventists should never forget their place in prophetic history. . . .
>
> The second aspect of her dual emphasis was that individuals must keep their eyes focused on Jesus, their Savior.[38]

After her initial vision in December of 1844, Ellen Harmon shared her other early visions with various audiences. In 1846, she married James White, who shared her convictions on the prophetic nature of the Millerite movement. This was also a time of foment for the remaining Millerites, and several movements emerged from the fallout.[39] Over time, one of those movements evolved into the Sabbatarian Adventists, the forerunner of Seventh-day Adventism. During the years 1848–1850, the Sabbatarian Adventists met together in what they called "Sabbath Conferences" and consolidated their doctrinal positions.[40]

By 1850, the basic teaching of what would eventually become Seventh-day Adventism had taken a unique doctrinal shape. The leaders of the movement had accepted the Bible alone as their rule of faith and practice; the law of God as immutable, including the obligation to observe the fourth commandment, the Sabbath; the cleansing of the heavenly sanctuary, with the antitypical day of atonement beginning on October 22, 1844; the personal, visible, premillennial return of Christ; the validity of the gift of prophecy as manifested in Ellen White's visions; and the conditional immortality of the soul. All of these beliefs were integrated into two biblical ideas: the sanctuary and the three angels' messages of Revelation 14:6–12.[41] In November 1850, James White released the first issue of the *Second Advent Review and Sabbath Herald*, the premier journal that proved to be a unifying and fortifying force to the scattered Sabbatarian believers.[42] It should also be pointed out that, from its beginning, Adventism was characterized by a strong antislavery stance, due in part to the New England heritage of its early adherents and to its interpretation of Scripture.

Manifest destiny and the war with Mexico

While the Sabbatarian Adventists were focused on building their doctrinal base, America was absorbed in its "manifest destiny," the popular idea, as noted earlier, that the nation was destined by God and history to expand its boundaries over a vast area. The enthusiasm for this idea reached its zenith during President Polk's administration and reopened the painful controversy over slavery. The annexation of Texas and Oregon heightened the issue of slave states versus free states. In addition to the slavery question was the problem with Mexico. Tensions over borders and debts escalated into violence, inciting President Polk to declare war in May 1846.[43]

At the outset of the war with Mexico, the debate over the future of slavery in the newly conquered territories had divided Congress. To help resolve the issue, Pennsylvania Democrat David Wilmot introduced an amendment to an army finance bill that banned slavery from any territory acquired from Mexico. Although ultimately voted down, the Wilmot Proviso, as it was called, proved to be explosive. It foreshadowed the Northern opposition to extending slavery in the West and deepened the Southern resentment toward the blockage of their right to take their slave property into the West. Consequently, it intensified the sectional divide between the North and the South. As such, the Wilmot Proviso is considered by historians as another early event that helped move the nation toward Civil War.[44] Ralph Waldo Emerson, a founder of Transcendentalism, correctly predicted that "the United States will conquer Mexico, but it will be as the man swallows the arsenic, which brings him down in turn. Mexico will poison us."[45]

The "poison" of Mexico was already evident in the mixed feelings Americans had about the war. Some felt that it was an excellent opportunity to take all of Mexico and expand America's manifest destiny. Slave owners viewed Mexico as an opportunity to extend slavery. Others believed that the United States was robbing Mexico of her territory. A tall, lanky thirty-eight-year-old congressman named Abraham Lincoln stood up in Congress and criticized President Polk for starting the war and not knowing how to end it.[46] Ulysses S. Grant believed this war was "one of the most unjust ever waged by a stronger against a weaker nation."[47] Sea captain Joseph Bates condemned the war and called the United States a "heaven-daring, soul-destroying, slave-holding, neighbor-murdering country!"[48] In the end, American soldiers fought their way to Mexico City, to "the halls of Montezuma," and won the war in 1848.

It is an interesting irony that the American soldiers who fought side by side in the Mexican-American War would later fight *against each other* in the Civil War. Classic examples were Robert E. Lee, the future general of the Confederate army; and Ulysses S. Grant, the future general of the Union army. Neither of them realized at the time that the Mexican-American War was a training ground for the not-too-distant war of friend against friend and brother against brother.

A Word to the "Little Flock"

In May 1847, a year before the American war with Mexico ended, James White published *A Word to the "Little Flock."* That document, which is very important to Seventh-day Adventist history, presented "a snapshot in time that recaptures the thoughts and interactions of the three founders of Seventh-day Adventism in the spring of 1847"—James White, Ellen White, and Joseph Bates.[49] One of the major emphases in the publication was the prophetic ministry of Ellen White.[50] In the preface to the written account of his wife's first vision, James set forth the relationship of the modern gift of prophecy to the Bible. "I am well aware of the prejudice in many minds on this subject," he acknowledged, but this was due to "the lack of a correct view of this subject."

Then James White presented what he believed to be the correct view of his wife's vision: "The bible is a perfect, and complete revelation. It is our only rule of faith and practice. But this is no reason, why God may not show the past, present, and future fulfilment of his word, in these last days, by dreams and visions; according to Peter's testimony. True visions are given to lead us to God, and his written word; but those that are given for a new rule of faith and practice, separate from the bible, cannot be from God, and should be rejected."[51]

This important statement helped lay the foundation for a better understanding of Ellen's future prophetic ministry in relationship to the Bible. Although it would take several years before her visionary experience would be widely accepted in the Sabbatarian ranks, James set things in motion for that to happen. Thus, Ellen was well on her way to becoming established as a *prophet to the Adventists*—the then-developing Seventh-day Adventist Church.

As the decade of the 1840s came to a close, Americans were proud of the vast new lands they had acquired from Mexico. They were poised for westward expansion and greatness, but few realized how those territories would become a major point of controversy between proslavery and antislavery forces. The heart of the controversy that was about to begin was whether or not slavery would be extended into those areas. The American republic was on the verge of a great crisis and "knew it not."

The Compromise of 1850

During the spring and summer of 1850, while Sabbatarian Adventists were engaged in refining their basic doctrines, members of the Thirty-First United States Congress debated questions of great importance to the Union—questions that, if not handled delicately, would divide the country and marshal it into war. It was "America's Great Debate," as Fergus M. Bordewich appropriately called it,[52] with emotions running high and tempers running short. At this perilous moment in America's history, Henry Clay, the aged and eminent senator from Kentucky, proposed a plan of compromise to settle the differences between the North and the South. It would later be known as the Compromise of 1850, yet another one of America's great compromises with slavery.

The driving issue in the debate was this: what should be done with the vast territories obtained from Mexico in 1848? The South wanted to expand slavery into these areas, while the North wanted to make them free soil. The spark that ignited the debate was California. Since James W. Marshall's discovery of gold at John Sutter's mill in January 1848, prospectors, known as "forty-niners," had poured into California for the gold rush of 1849. By 1850, the sizable population in this region requested statehood, with a constitution that prohibited slavery. If California entered the Union as a free state, then free states would outnumber the slave states, and the South would lack equal power in the Senate. The question of California thus became a "touchstone of Southern rights and power."[53] The atmosphere was so emotionally charged that several fistfights broke out in Congress; one senator even pulled a revolver on a colleague on the Senate floor, but, fortunately, the weapon was pried from his fingers before he could fire it.[54] The "great debate" was a crisis of the first order for the republic.[55]

After months of long debate, five measures passed the Senate and were signed into law by President Millard Fillmore. Among the measures were the admission of California as a free state, a concession to the North; and a more stringent Fugitive Slave Law, a major concession to the South.[56] While the Compromise of 1850 brought temporary relief on the issue of slavery in a similar way that the Missouri Compromise of 1820 had done, it really laid the foundation for more intense conflict in the decade ahead. Rather than solve the issue of slavery in the territories, the compromise only prolonged the conflict. No one really knew how to end slavery and still hold the North and South together. Thirty years earlier, Thomas Jefferson put it vividly when he said of slavery: "We have the wolf by the ears, and we can neither hold him, nor safely let him go."[57]

The Fugitive Slave Law

The measure that proved to be the most controversial and explosive was the revised Fugitive Slave Law. The first Fugitive Slave Act, passed by Congress in 1793, had empowered the slave owner with the right to "seize or arrest" the fugitive slave and, through the legal process, return the fugitive "to the State or Territory from which he or she fled."[58] Over the years, the antislavery sentiment in the North led to the passage of personal liberty laws, which protected free blacks living within the borders of a Northern state. In short, the North was unwilling to yield to Southern demands for the strict enforcement of the Fugitive Slave Law. This issue was a constant cause of tension between the North and the South. By the 1840s, the original force of the 1793 law had been significantly diminished as more and more slaves were escaping into the North.

The new Fugitive Slave Law remedied this problem by tightening up the old one and adding new measures. For the first time, the federal government was on the side of the slaveholders to help them hunt down their human property. What upset Northerners, especially the abolitionists, the most about the new Fugitive Slave Law was that it empowered the slave-catching marshals to enter the Northern states and not only legally seize runaway slaves but also force free-state citizens or bystanders to join their posse (*posse comitatus*).[59] Resistance meant heavy penalties and imprisonment. Regardless of one's antislavery convictions, a person could be compelled to join in the chase and capture of a fugitive slave.

Northerners reacted strongly. In a speech given on August 11, 1852, before a large convention, Frederick Douglass condemned the "hell born enactment" of the Fugitive Slave Law. "This vile, infernal law," he roared, "makes it criminal . . . for you, sir, to carry out the principles of Christianity. It forbids you the right to do right—forbids you to show mercy—forbids you to follow the example of the good Samaritan."[60] In the pages of the *Review and Herald*, Adventists also condemned the Fugitive Slave Law. One contributor referred to it as an "atrocious bargain," the "foulest stain that ever blotted the history of any nation."[61] Another Sabbatarian referred to it as "a damning feature of this our vaunted free government; and the foul stain extending to the very doors of the capitol."[62]

Uncle Tom's Cabin

The most significant and far-reaching Northern reaction to the Fugitive Slave Law of 1850 was found in Harriet Beecher Stowe's writings.[63] Raised a Yankee in the home of a Congregational clergyman, Stowe developed antislavery sympathies in her youth and nurtured them as an adult. Upset with the Fugitive Slave Law, like many other Northerners, she responded by writing a narrative about two families of slaves and their fates in the world of slavery. The story was first published through installments in the abolitionist newspaper *National Era* during 1851–1852 and then later published in 1852 as a novel.[64] *Uncle Tom's Cabin; or, Life Among the Lowly*, as it was titled, is considered to be the most influential book ever written by an American.[65] It became an instant bestseller in its time, selling three hundred thousand copies the first year,[66] and it continues to be read and valued today.

Through the unforgettable characters of *Uncle Tom's Cabin*—Uncle Tom, Little Eva, Topsy, Simon Legree, and others—Stowe endeavored to make the horrors of slavery a living, dramatic reality.[67] The violent death of the Christlike Uncle Tom at the end of the book, for example, depicted the brutality of slavery in a way that no other abolitionist writings had done before. These vivid portrayals of the slave as a human being in the plight of human bondage moved tens of thousands of Northern readers to tears. When the editor of the *New-York Daily Tribune* and supporter of the Compromise of 1850, Horace Greeley, read through the book on a train ride from Boston to Washington, DC, he wept so profusely that when the train stopped in Springfield, "he had to get off the train and spend a night to compose himself."[68] Thus, the stiff Northern resistance to antislavery reform began to soften.

The reaction in the South was quite different. Since Southerners viewed slavery as "a natural, biblically sanctioned institution,"[69] they believed Stowe's book was a direct attack on their institutions, social system, and way of life. Most Southern states discouraged the sale of *Uncle Tom's Cabin*, and some even criminalized it. One example of the South's vehemence was when the editor of the *Southern Literary Messenger* referred to Stowe as "the vile wretch in petticoats who could write such a volume."[70] Within a month of the publication of *Uncle Tom's Cabin*, proslavery novels were released in the South that portrayed slavery in a positive light; by the time of the Civil War, at least twenty-nine anti-Tom novels had been published. None of these novels, however, even came close to the success of *Uncle Tom's Cabin*. Through reactionary poetry, song, and literature, the South attempted to refute Stowe's novel and vent its bitterness at the North.[71]

Uncle Tom's Cabin thus galvanized the attitudes of both the North and the South on the issue of slavery. Within a decade of its publication, the novel had sold more than two million copies in the United States,[72] a staggering figure for that day, and was a major contributing factor in widening and deepening the divide between the North and the South. An illustration of its impact is the story, passed along by Stowe's family, about an interview she had with Abraham Lincoln on or around Thanksgiving Day 1862, in which Lincoln greeted her with the following words:

" 'Why, Mrs. Stowe, right glad to see you!' Then with a humorous twinkle in his eye, he said, 'So you're the little woman who wrote the book that made this great war!' "[73]

Ellen White's reaction to the Fugitive Slave Law

In 1859, Ellen White spoke out boldly against the Fugitive Slave Law in one of her *Testimonies*. Clearly grasping the specifics of the law, she declared, "When the laws of men conflict with the word and law of God, we are to obey the latter, whatever the consequences may be. The law of our land requiring us to deliver a slave to his master, we are not to obey; and we must abide the consequences of violating this law. The slave is not the property of any man. God is his rightful master, and man has no right to take God's workmanship into his hands, and claim him as his own."[74]

In the literary context of this statement, she is not encouraging disobedience to all laws of the land: "We have men placed over us for rulers, and laws to govern the people. Were it not for these laws, the condition of the world would be worse than it is now," she declared. "I saw that the Lord still has something to do with the laws of the land."[75] So while respecting the laws of government in general, she condemned the Fugitive Slave Law in particular as a fundamental violation of moral principle.

In the historical background to this statement, two controversial cases over the Fugitive Slave Law had captured the attention of the nation in 1859. In Wisconsin, *Ableman v. Booth* made it to the Supreme Court and confirmed the constitutionality of the 1850 law. For several weeks in Ohio, the Oberlin-Wellington Rescue case spotlighted the strong resistance to the law and the powerful forces supporting it.[76] A year earlier, the *Review and Herald* had reported on the following case: "Judge Leavitt, in his charge to the jury in the case of Conelly, tried at Cincinnati for harboring fugitive slaves, said that 'Christian charity was not within the meaning or intent of the Fugitive Slave law, and it would not therefore answer as a defense for violating the law.' This is an admission which shows the infamous nature of that law in a clearer light than any of its enemies have ever depicted it."[77] These highly publicized cases accented the consequences of disobeying the Fugitive Slave Law, and this context may have been what prompted Ellen White to speak against it in 1859—nine years after its initial passage.

Lincoln-Douglas senatorial debates

In the fall of 1858, one of the most important senatorial contests in American history took place. The politically influential Stephen A. Douglas defended his senatorial position against the challenger Abraham Lincoln, a successful lawyer and part-time politician in Illinois. The two met in a series of debates that received wide coverage throughout the nation. Because of Douglas's prominence and the issue of slavery's extension into the territories, the newspapers took notice of the contest and considered it to be of supreme importance.

The debates illuminated the sharp differences between Lincoln and Douglas: Lincoln declared slavery as a moral, social, and political wrong, whereas Douglas avoided the moral questions. For Douglas, whether or not to allow slavery in the Western territories should remain a local decision. Lincoln took a moderate position when he said that he would respect slavery in the South as constitutional, though morally wrong. But he said that Congress should have the power to bar it from the Western territories. In the end, Douglas won the election by a narrow margin, but the debates propelled Lincoln into the top rungs of the Republican Party.[78]

John Brown's raid on Harpers Ferry

One of the most fascinating and enigmatic characters of the 1850s is John Brown, whose life mission as a radical abolitionist came to an end in Harpers Ferry, West Virginia (originally Virginia) in 1859. After his role in the "Bleeding Kansas" affair—the fighting between the antislavery and proslavery forces in the Kansas territory during the mid-1850s[79]—he lay low and planned an attack on slavery on a much grander scale. His target was the federal arsenal and armory at Harpers Ferry, the ideal place to secure enough weapons for an army of slaves. Financed by six leading members of the abolitionist movement (later known as the "Secret Six") and armed with Sharps carbines and rifles, called "Beecher's Bibles" (inspired by the New England abolitionist and minister Henry Ward Beecher, the brother of Harriet Beecher Stowe), Brown led thirteen white men and five black men into Harpers Ferry on the evening of October 16, 1859. The strategy was simple: arm local slaves, who Brown hoped would join them, then head south and rally other slaves to their cause, thus depleting the South of its slaves, one county after another.

Initially, the raid went well, but then shots were exchanged, and things went downhill. The local slaves hadn't joined the raid, and Brown and his small party took refuge in the armory's engine house. Soon the Virginia militia and Federal troops—marines under the command of Colonel Robert E. Lee—surrounded the structure and demanded Brown's surrender. When he refused, the troops stormed the building and captured the rebels. Ten of the raiders were killed; several escaped; and the rest were taken prisoner, including the badly wounded John Brown.[80]

The raid had been a complete failure, and Brown, along with his followers, was tried by the state of Virginia and sentenced to hang. In the weeks before his execution, Brown spent his time in jail writing letters to family, associates, newspaper editors, and strangers who wrote to him expressing their support. Knowing that much of what he wrote would be published in newspapers, he carefully explained and justified his actions at Harpers Ferry.[81] He found comfort in reading the Bible, and he believed that his impending execution would be a "testimony for God and humanity."[82] Brown died by hanging on December 2, 1859, surrounded by fifteen hundred soldiers and a large audience of onlookers. According to various eyewitness accounts, he died with a peace and dignity that impressed more than a few.[83]

The impact of Brown's death on the country was profound. On the day of his execution, organized expressions of sympathy could be found taking place over much of the North: bells tolled, minute guns fired, prayer meetings assembled, and memorial resolutions were adopted. In the weeks following Brown's death, the Transcendentalists hailed him as a martyr and likened him to Christ. Ralph Waldo Emerson, for example, wrote that Brown would "make the gallows as glorious as the cross." Henry David Thoreau declared, "He is not Old Brown any longer; he is an angel of light." Abolitionist William Lloyd Garrison wrote in his *Liberator* that Brown's execution should be "the occasion of such a public moral demonstration against the bloody and merciless slave system as the land has ever witnessed."[84]

Not everyone in the North was captivated with Brown, however. Leading moderate Republican politicians, such as Abraham Lincoln and William H. Seward, endeavored to distance themselves from him. The day after Brown's execution, Lincoln said in a speech: "Old John Brown has just been executed for treason against a state. We cannot object, even though he agreed with us in thinking slavery wrong. That cannot excuse violence, bloodshed, and treason. It could avail him nothing that he might think himself right."[85] Lincoln's view represented the minds of many in the North who did not favor the abolitionist movement. A year later, during the campaign for the presidency, the Republican platform would denounce the Harpers Ferry affair and any other similar invasions as "among the gravest of crimes."[86]

Southerners learned about all the public affirmation of Brown and were shocked.

For them, he was the devil incarnate—an abolitionist seeking to incite a slave insurrection. They found it especially appalling when they learned, during the course of Brown's trial, that several influential Northern abolitionists, the Secret Six, had provided financial support to Brown's raid.[87] This was the white Southerner's worst nightmare: Northerners orchestrating a slave insurrection that would spread death and destruction across the South. It was worse than Nat Turner's 1831 rebellion because Turner was black, but these were Northern white people plotting against Southern white people.

After Brown's trial and execution, Southerners viewed themselves as isolated and alone. They adopted the attitude that "those who are not for us are against us."[88] William W. Blackford, who would serve in the Confederacy, typified the response of many in the South. "After the John Brown affair," he later recalled, "I was so firmly convinced that there might be trouble that I took active steps to raise a cavalry company in Washington County."[89] Thus, "communities all over the South raised companies of armed men for defense against further insurrectionary attacks," explained historian Elizabeth R. Varon, "and they passed resolutions warning the North against further provocations."[90] As a result of the John Brown affair, the South braced itself for invasion.

Shortly before John Brown was taken to the gallows for hanging, Brown wrote his last words on a scrap of paper and handed it to the jail's guard. The cryptic, prophetic words read, "I John Brown am now quite certain that the crimes of this guilty land: will never be purged away, but with Blood." These ominous words would be "long remembered," according to historian Robert E. McGlone: "For knowledgeable observers, it harkened back to the familiar words of Paul: 'Almost all things are by the law purged with blood; and without shedding of blood is no remission' (Hebrews 9:22). But Brown's statement was not so much an appeal to biblical authority as a stark warning, a chilling jeremiad. Brown had cautioned the South in the aftermath of his capture that despite his defeat the slavery question would not go away. Now he made that warning a prophecy: slavery, he was saying, would end only with bloodshed."[91]

McGlone reflected, "John Brown did not cause the Civil War. But he hastened its coming. His real legacy to his 'guilty land' may have been to make war thinkable if subserved to a Godly purpose. For thousands and tens of thousands in the North, John Brown's 'martyrdom' sanctified his cause and war itself."[92]

Conclusion

As the 1850s came to a close, the nation was more divided than ever before. Although Americans were not yet ready to take up arms, they were at a point where only a straw would break the camel's back. That straw would be the upcoming presidential election of 1860—the most fateful presidential campaign in U.S. history—and the secession of Southern states thereafter.

On November 24, 1859, a little over a month after John Brown's Harpers Ferry raid, the *Review and Herald* printed an extract from the Radical Republican journal *Independent* that captured the state of the country at the end of the decade and that resonated with Adventists. Because of the slavery issue in the United States, the article reasoned, the nation is like a huge volcano about to blow. "God himself is about to uncap the volcano, if an insensate, hardened people persist in the violation of his law."[93] The volcano did explode, but first we must understand the greatest reform movement of antebellum America—abolitionism—and where Ellen White and the Adventist people stood in relationship to it.

Chapter in a nutshell

Ellen White was born in Yankee Maine and raised with New England values. She grew up during a fascinating and turbulent period in American history known as antebellum America (1815–1860). This period was a time of unprecedented social reforms and spiritual revivals that swept across the American landscape. It was also a time in which many social and political events occurred that deepened the antagonistic, sectional rift between the North and the South. The inflammatory issue behind the conflict was slavery and whether or not it should extend into the new territories acquired from America's war with Mexico. White grew into adulthood during this time and was impacted by these events, as were all other Americans. After the Compromise of 1850, the conflict worsened due to Northern reactions to the Fugitive Slave Law, continual agitation over the slavery issue, and John Brown's raid on Harpers Ferry. It was during this time that the Sabbatarian Adventists embraced White's prophetic gift and accepted her as a prophet. She and her fellow Adventists reacted to the events happening around them and took a strong stance against slavery. By the end of the 1850s, the nation was significantly divided, and tensions were higher than they had ever been. America was on the verge of an epic crisis and did not realize it.

1. These characteristics were basic to the term *Yankee* in the early nineteenth century. The term took on negative connotations during the Civil War when Confederates used it as a contemptuous epithet for Union soldiers. For a discussion on the changing definitions of the term, see Martin J. Manning, "Yankees," in *The Encyclopedia of New England*, ed. Burt Feintuch and David H. Watters (New Haven, CT: Yale University Press, 2005), 811–813.

2. *Antebellum* is a Latin term: *ante* = before + *bellum* = war, hence "before war." Thus, antebellum America was the period in American history preceding the Civil War.

3. Some historians date the antebellum period from 1800 to 1860, others from 1820 to 1860, and still others from 1784 to 1861. The end of the War of 1812, with Andrew Jackson's victory at the Battle of New Orleans in 1815, seemed to begin the real mood of the antebellum period with its Jacksonian outlook. A good argument could be made, however, to begin the antebellum period in 1820 with the Missouri Compromise. Suffice it to say, that while the beginning date of the antebellum period is debatable, its ending date—with Lincoln's election, the secession, and the Civil War—has a wide consensus.

4. Elizabeth R. Varon, *Disunion! The Coming of the American Civil War, 1789–1859* (Chapel Hill, NC: University of North Carolina Press, 2008), 17.

5. Ronald F. Banks, *Maine Becomes a State: The Movement to Separate Maine From Massachusetts, 1785-1820* (Middletown, CT: Wesleyan University Press, 1970), 184–204.

6. Thomas Jefferson to John Holmes, Monticello, April 22, 1820, in *The Works of Thomas Jefferson,* ed. Paul Leicester Ford, vol. 12, Federal ed. (New York: G. P. Putnam's Sons, 1905), 158, accessed November 2, 2016, http://oll.libertyfund.org/titles/jefferson-the-works-vol-12-correspondence-and-papers-1816-1826#lf0054-12 _head_064.

7. Robert Pierce Forbes, *The Missouri Compromise and Its Aftermath: Slavery and the Meaning of America* (Chapel Hill, NC: University of North Carolina Press, 2007), 5.

8. See Gary Land, "Ideas and Society," in *The World of Ellen G. White*, ed. Gary Land (Hagerstown, MD: Review and Herald®, 1987), 209–213; and Daniel Walker Howe, *What Hath God Wrought: The Transformation of America, 1815–1848* (New York: Oxford University Press, 2007).

9. Recent scholarship has concluded that the term *Second Great Awakening* is misleading because, after the initial revivals in the mid-1700s, there was a continual undercurrent of revival up through the early 1800s in America. According to the historian Thomas S. Kidd, "There was simply no clear break between the First and Second Great Awakenings." Thomas S. Kidd, *The Great Awakening: The Roots of Evangelical Christianity in Colonial America* (New Haven, CT: Yale University Press, 2007), 321; see also John Wolffe, *The Expansion of Evangelicalism: The Age of Wilberforce, More, Chalmers and Finney* (Downers Grove, IL: InterVarsity Press, 2007), 45–70.

10. For detailed coverage on this period of the Great Awakening, see Mark A. Noll, *A History of Christianity in the United States and Canada* (Grand Rapids, MI: Eerdmans, 1992), 165–190; and Wolffe, *The Expansion of Evangelicalism*, 71–94.

11. Noll, *A History of Christianity*, 170.

12. For details on Finney's evangelistic style, see ibid., 174–178.

13. Dianne Wheaton Cappiello, "Finney, Charles Gradison (1792–1875)," in *Encyclopedia of Antislavery and Abolition*, eds. Peter Hinks and John McKivigan (Westport, CT: Greenwood Press, 2007), 1:254, 255.

14. For overviews of each movement with selected writings, see Edwin S. Gaustad and Mark A. Noll, eds., *A Documentary History of Religion in America to 1877*, 3rd ed. (Grand Rapids, MI: Eerdmans, 2003), 252–270, 328–370.

15. Philip F. Gura, *American Transcendentalism: A History* (New York: Hill and Wang, 2007), 11.

16. Ibid., 240–266.

17. For detailed coverage of the major events in America during this year, see Louis P. Masur, *1831: Year of Eclipse* (New York: Hill and Wang, 2001).

18. William Lloyd Garrison, "To the Public," *The Liberator*, January 1, 1831, 1 (emphasis in the original).

19. Masur, *1831*, 3–8.

20. Ibid., 9–21.

21. Nat Turner, *The Confessions of Nat Turner, the Leader of the Late Insurrection in Southampton, Virginia* (Baltimore: Thomas R. Gray, 1831).

22. Eugene Genovese, quoted in Jennifer J. Pierce, "Turner, Nat (1800–1831)," in Hinks and McKivigan, *Encyclopedia of Antislavery and Abolition*, 2:688; for a well-researched and engaging narrative, see also Stephen B. Oates, *The Fires of Jubilee: Nat Turner's Fierce Rebellion* (New York: Harper Perennial, 1990).

23. F. Reed, *Christian Advocate and Journal*, December 13, 1833.

24. Denison Olmsted, "Observations on the Meteors of Nov. 13th, 1833," *American Journal of Science and Arts* 25, no. 2 (January 1834): 386.

25. Frederick Douglass, *My Bondage and My Freedom*, in *Douglass: Autobiographies,* Library of America (New York: Literary Classics of the United States, 1994), 245. *My Bondage and My Freedom* was originally published in 1855.

26. Ellen G. White, *The Great Controversy* (Mountain View, CA: Pacific Press®, 1950), 334.

27. See Sylvester Bliss, *Memoirs of William Miller*, Adventist Classic Library, ed. George R. Knight (Berrien Springs, MI: Andrews University Press, 2005), 98–100; on 1831 as the date of Miller's first sermon, see David L. Rowe, *God's Strange Work: William Miller and the End of the World* (Grand Rapids, MI: Eerdmans, 2008), 98, 99.

28. For the definitive study on Millerite history, see George R. Knight, *William Miller and the Rise of Adventism* (Nampa, ID: Pacific Press®, 2010); see also Everett N. Dick, *William Miller and the Advent Crisis*, ed. Gary Land (Berrien Springs, MI: Andrews University Press, 1994).

29. Knight, *William Miller and the Rise of Adventism*, 20, 76, 77; and Everett N. Dick, "The Millerite Movement, 1830-1845," in Gary Land, ed., *Adventism in America: A History*, rev. ed. (Berrien Springs, MI: Andrews University Press, 1998), 27.

30. Ellen G. White, *Life Sketches of Ellen G. White* (Mountain View, CA: Pacific Press®, 1943), 20.

31. Ibid., 21.

32. Ibid., 26–28. See Merlin D. Burt, "Ellen G. Harmon's Three-Step Conversion Between 1836 and 1843 and the Harmon Family Methodist Experience" (research paper, Andrews University Theological Seminary, 1998).

33. See George R. Knight, *A Brief History of Seventh-day Adventists*, 2nd ed. (Hagerstown, MD: Review and Herald®, 2004), 21–23.

34. White, *Life Sketches*, 60.

35. Ibid., 61.

36. For a discussion of the complexities of this presidential campaign, see James Brewer Stewart, *Holy Warriors: The Abolitionists and American Slavery*, rev. ed. (New York: Hill and Wang, 1997), 107–110, and Paul F. Boller Jr., *Presidential Campaigns: From George Washington to George W. Bush* (New York: Oxford University Press, 2004), 78–83.

37. Ellen G. White, *Early Writings* (Washington, DC: Review and Herald®, 1945), 14.

38. Knight, *A Brief History*, 35, 36.

39. For a discussion on the different branches of the Millerites after the Disappointment and the rise of Seventh-day Adventism, see Knight, *William Miller*, 209–276.

40. For details on the birth of Seventh-day Adventism, see Richard W. Schwarz and Floyd Greenleaf, *Light Bearers: A History of the Seventh-day Adventist Church* (Nampa, ID: Pacific Press®, 2000), 51–99; on the Sabbath Conferences, see Knight, *A Brief History*, 52–55.

41. For more detail on Seventh-day Adventist doctrinal development, see Godfrey T. Anderson, "Sectarianism and Organization, 1846–1864," in Land, *Adventism in America*, 30–33; especially P. Gerard Damsteegt, *Foundations of the Seventh-day Adventist Message and Mission* (Berrien Springs, MI: Andrews University Press, 1977); and Alberto R. Timm, *The Sanctuary and the Three Angels' Messages: Integrating Factors in the Development of Seventh-day Adventist Doctrines*, Adventist Theological Society Dissertation Series, vol. 5 (Berrien Springs, MI: Adventist Theological Society, 1995).

42. For a discussion on James White's publishing efforts prior to November 1850, see George R. Knight, "Historical Introduction," in *Earliest Seventh-day Adventist Periodicals*, Adventist Classic Library, ed. George R. Knight (Berrien Springs, MI: Andrews University Press, 2005), vii–xxxiii.

43. For details on manifest destiny and the war with Mexico, see Howe, *What Hath God Wrought*, 701–836, and James McPherson, *Battle Cry of Freedom: The Civil War Era* (New York: Oxford University Press, 2003), 47–77.

44. See McPherson, *Battle Cry of Freedom*, 52–58.

45. Edward W. Emerson and Waldo E. Forbes, eds., *Journals of Ralph Waldo Emerson*, vol. 7 (Boston: Houghton Mifflin, 1912), 206, quoted in McPherson, *Battle Cry of Freedom*, 51.

46. *The Collected Works of Abraham Lincoln*, ed. Roy Basler (New Brunswick, NJ: Rutgers University Press, 1953), 1:431-441.

47. Ulysses S. Grant, *Memoirs and Selected Letters: Personal Memoirs of U. S. Grant, Selected Letters, 1839–1865*, Library of America (New York: Literary Classics of the United States, 1990), 41.

48. Joseph Bates, *Second Advent Way Marks and High Heaps; or, A Connected View of the Fulfilment of Prophecy by God's Peculiar People* (New Bedford, MA: Press of Benjamin Lindsey, 1847), 48.

49. Knight, "Historical Introduction" in *Earliest Seventh-day Adventist Periodicals*, xxxii.

50. Two other emphases in this twenty-four-page pamphlet were end-time events and the eschatological significance of the Sabbath. For a detailed analysis of its contents, see Merlin D. Burt, "The Historical Background, Interconnected Development, and Integration of the Doctrines of the Sanctuary, the Sabbath, and Ellen G. White's Role in Sabbatarian Adventism From 1844-1849" (PhD diss., Andrews University, 2002), 308–323. For a concise overview of its contents, see Knight, "Historical Introduction," in *Earliest Seventh-day Adventist Periodicals*, xxiv–xxvi.

51. James White, *A Word to the "Little Flock"* (Brunswick, ME: James White, 1847), 13, quoted in Knight, *Earliest Seventh-day Adventist Periodicals*. For details on how the early Adventist came to accept Ellen White's prophetic gift, see Theodore Levterov, *Accepting Ellen White: Early Seventh-day Adventism and the Gift of Prophecy Dilemma* (Nampa, ID: Pacific Press®, 2017).

52. For an excellent and engaging narrative of the Compromise of 1850, see Fergus M. Bordewich, *America's Great Debate: Henry Clay, Stephen A. Douglas, and the Compromise That Preserved the Union* (New York: Simon & Schuster, 2012).

53. James McPherson and James K. Hogue, *Ordeal by Fire: The Civil War and Reconstruction*, 3rd ed. (New York: McGraw-Hill, 2000), 71.

54. For a description that captures all of this event's drama and the implications for the debate, see Bordewich, *America's Great Debate*, 219–221.

55. See a concise discussion of the issues leading up to the Compromise of 1850 in McPherson and Hogue, *Ordeal by Fire*, 70–76; see also Holman Hamilton, *Prologue to Conflict: The Crisis and Compromise of 1850* (Lexington, KY: University Press of Kentucky, 1964), for a definitive study on this subject; and David M. Potter, *The Impending Crisis: America Before the Civil War, 1848–1861*, ed. Don E. Fehrenbacher (New York: Harper Perennial, 2011), 90–120.

56. The Compromise included five measures passed from mid-August to mid-September of 1850: (1) the admission of California as a free state; (2) the organization of Texas and New Mexico, with the provision that when admitted as states, they "shall be received into the Union with or without slavery, as their constitution may prescribe at the time of their admission"; (3) the establishment of the Utah territory with the same provisions as Texas and New Mexico; (4) an amendment to the original Fugitive Slave Law of 1793 that made it much more stringent; and (5) the abolition of the slave trade in the District of Columbia. See Hamilton, appendix D to *Prologue to Conflict*, 201–208, for the entire text of the Compromise. The original source is *The Statutes at Large and Treaties of the United States of America*, vol. 9 (Boston: Little, Brown and Co., 1862), 446–458, 462–465, 467, 468.

57. Thomas Jefferson to John Holmes, Monticello, April 22, 1820.

58. For the original document, see "Fugitive Slave Act of 1793," USHistory.org, accessed November 9, 2016, http://www.ushistory.org/presidenthouse/history/slaveact1793.php.

59. See Hamilton, *Prologue to Conflict*, 206, on section 5 of the Compromise.

60. Frederick Douglass, "Let All Soil Be Free Soil," in John W. Blassingame, ed., *Speeches, Debates, and Interviews,* vol. 2, *1847–54,* Frederick Douglass Papers, Series 1 (New Haven, CT: Yale University Press, 1982), 391.

61. E. R. Seaman, "The Days of Noah and the Son of Man," *Review and Herald*, June 13, 1854, 157.

62. Joseph Clarke, "You Will Vote at Our Spring Election, Won't You," *Review and Herald*, April 23, 1857, 198.

63. For the definitive biography on Stowe, see Joan D. Hedrick, *Harriet Beecher Stowe: A Life* (New York: Oxford University Press, 1994).

64. Cindy Weinstein, introduction to *The Cambridge Companion to Harriet Beecher Stowe*, ed. Cindy Weinstein (Cambridge: Cambridge University Press, 2004), 2.

65. For helpful discussions on the impact of *Uncle Tom's Cabin* and its author, see McPherson, *Battle Cry of Freedom*, 88–91; and especially David S. Reynolds, *Mightier Than the Sword: Uncle Tom's Cabin and the Battle for America* (New York: W. W. Norton, 2011).

66. McPherson, *Battle Cry of Freedom*, 88.

67. Harriet Beecher Stowe, *Uncle Tom's Cabin* (New York: Everyman's Library, 1994), 488.

68. David Goldfield, *America Aflame: How the Civil War Created a Nation* (New York: Bloomsbury Press, 2011), 80.

69. Reynolds, *Mightier Than the Sword*, 151.

70. McPherson, *Battle Cry of Freedom*, 90.

71. Reynolds, *Mightier Than the Sword*, 150–161, provides a detailed account of the South's reaction to *Uncle Tom's Cabin*.

72. McPherson, *Battle Cry of Freedom*, 89.

73. Charles E. Stowe and Lyman B. Stowe, *Harriet Beecher Stowe: The Story of Her Life* (Boston: Houghton Mifflin, 1911), 201-203.

74. Ellen G. White, *Testimonies for the Church*, vol. 1 (Mountain View, CA: Pacific Press®, 1948) 201, 202.

75. Ibid. The larger context of the testimony is the issue of Christians taking oaths in legal proceedings. "If there is anyone on earth who can consistently testify under oath, it is the Christian" (ibid., 202). But in the case of slavery, the Christian cannot take an oath to uphold the law with regard to the runaway slave.

76. See Stanley W. Campbell, *The Slave Catchers: Enforcement of the Fugitive Slave Law, 1850–1860* (Chapel Hill, NC: University of North Carolina, 1970), 159–161, 164–167; and Douglas Morgan, "Ellen White, Slavery and Politics—II," *Peace Messenger* (blog), April 25, 2008, http://adventistpeace.typepad.com/peacemessenger/2008/04/ellen-white-sla.html.

77. *Review and Herald*, June 3, 1858, 24.

78. Thanks to Gary W. Gallagher for this insight from his lectures on the Civil War years. Gary W. Gallagher, *The History of the United States, Lectures 37–48,* 2nd ed., The Great Courses (Chantilly, VA: Teaching Co., 2003), 27–30.

79. See Nicole Etcheson, *Bleeding Kansas: Contested Liberty in the Civil War Era* (Lawrence, KS: University Press of Kansas, 2004).

80. The most detailed accounts of Brown's Harpers Ferry raid are found in his better biographies: see Stephen B. Oates, *To Purge This Land With Blood: A Biography of John Brown* (Amherst, MA: University of Massachusetts Press, 1984), 229–306; Tony Horwitz, *Midnight Rising: John Brown and the Raid That Sparked the Civil War* (New York: Henry Holt and Co., 2011), 127–187; David S. Reynolds, *John Brown, Abolitionist: The Man Who Killed Slavery, Sparked the Civil War, and Seeded Civil Rights* (New York: Alfred A. Knopf, 2005), 309–333; and Robert E. McGlone, *John Brown's War Against Slavery* (New York: Cambridge University Press, 2009), 1–6. The literature on Brown and his raid is extensive and will not all be listed here because of space. These four books and several others mentioned below have been found to be the most helpful.

81. Jonathan Earle, *John Brown's Raid on Harpers Ferry: A Brief History With Documents* (Boston: Bedford/St. Martin's, 2008), 88–103. This book provides easy access to several of Brown's letters written while he was awaiting execution.

82. See Louis A. DeCaro Jr., *"Fire From the Midst of You": A Religious Life of John Brown* (New York: New York University Press, 2002), 271, 272. DeCaro gives great insight and documentation into the spirituality of John Brown. Brown has often been portrayed as a violent fanatic, but this work and the other recent works on Brown in note 80 provide a different view of him in the religious and social context of antebellum America.

83. An especially interesting and detailed depiction of Brown's execution is provided in Horwitz, *Midnight Rising*, 248–257.

84. For details and these quotations with their references, see Potter, *The Impending Crisis*, 378, 379.

85. Basler, *The Collected Works of Abraham Lincoln*, 3:502; see also pages 538–540.

86. See "Republican National Platform, 1860," Central Pacific Railroad Photograph History Museum, accessed November 7, 2016, http://cprr.org/Museum/Ephemera/Republican_Platform_1860.html.

87. For details on the Secret Six, see Edward J. Renehan Jr., *The Secret Six: The True Tale of the Men Who Conspired With John Brown* (Columbia, SC: University of South Carolina, 1997).

88. For more specifics on the South's negative reaction to the Brown affair, see Potter, *The Impending Crisis*, 383; see pages 380–384.

89. William W. Blackford, *War Years With Jeb Stuart* (New York: Charles Scribner's Sons, 1945), 13.

90. Varon, *Disunion!*, 329, 330.

91. McGlone, *John Brown's War*, 327.

92. Ibid., 328.

93. "Our Country's Future," *Review and Herald*, November 24, 1859, 4.

Frederick Douglass about 1847–1852
(Art Institue of Chicago)

CHAPTER 2

AN ABOLITIONIST AT HEART

O h! be warned! be warned!" thundered the black abolitionist Frederick Douglass to his all-white audience perched on the edge of their seats in Rochester's Corinthian Hall on July 5, 1852. "A horrible reptile is coiled up in your nation's bosom; the venomous creature is nursing at the tender breast of your youthful republic; *for the love of God, tear away,* and fling from you the hideous monster, and *let the weight of twenty millions crush and destroy it forever!*" With these vivid, picturesque words, Douglass captured the essence of the abolitionist message to antebellum America: tear the horrible reptile of slavery away from the heart of this nation and crush it forever.[1]

The nineteenth-century American abolitionists have rightfully been called "a dissenting minority," "holy warriors," and "prophets of protest."[2] Their resolve was firm and their passion intense—slavery was an evil that must be destroyed. But the ways in which to accomplish this goal were not always clear, and the movement took many complex twists and turns. This chapter will provide a concise overview of the abolitionists' story and place the antislavery sentiments of Ellen White and Sabbatarian Adventists in that context. In particular, it will examine Ellen White's antebellum writings about slavery in the context of the abolitionist message.

Understanding abolitionists

Simply put, abolitionists in antebellum America were individuals who wanted to "abolish" slavery.[3] They viewed slavery as morally wrong, a violation of the natural rights of humankind, and inconsistent with the Declaration of Independence. During the Revolutionary War period, various antislavery societies were formed in such places as Pennsylvania, Virginia, Connecticut, Rhode Island, Maryland, Delaware, New York, and New Jersey. The Quakers were especially influential in their uncompromising battle against slavery. By the end of the eighteenth century, the Northern states had generally abolished the practice of slavery, but, to the chagrin of the abolitionists, the Southern states continued its practice.

Early in the nineteenth century, abolitionists began to advocate a mode of operation called "gradualism," or "gradual, compensated emancipation." According to historian Merton L. Dillon, although the abolitionists vehemently condemned slavery and slaveholders, "they seldom proposed drastic, immediate change in master-slave relations." Consequently, "they were more likely to regard slavery as an evil to be ameliorated and very gradually ended through slow and painless changes than as a sin to be abandoned immediately."[4] Part of making the process as painless as possible was to compensate the slaveholders financially for their loss.

Immediate abolitionism

By 1830, the abolitionists were fed up with gradual emancipation and the American Colonization Society, founded in 1816, with its plan to transport free blacks out of the country and back to Africa.[5] Neither of these programs had really dealt with the problem of racial prejudice, and America had become a great slaveholding republic. At this point, a new form of abolitionism known as "immediatism" was introduced and would dominate the movement up to the Civil War. Our earlier definition of an abolitionist can now be expanded to mean those individuals who, between 1830 and the Civil War, "agitated for immediate, unconditional, and universal abolition of slavery in the United States."[6]

Four basic arguments of the immediate abolitionists

Immediate abolitionists used four basic arguments in their campaign against slavery.[7] In the first argument, they used moral suasion to assert that the Bible actually condemned slavery and that it is morally wrong—a sin against God and humanity. The second argument labeled slavery as outdated, a thing of the past, and a throwback to the old European feudal system when the aristocracy owned all of the land and the peasant class was forced to work the land. The United States, argued the abolitionists, was built upon "life, liberty, and the pursuit of happiness" for all people, and no one group of people should permanently rule another.[8]

The third argument rested on a political platform: the Declaration of Independence stated that "all men are created equal, that they are endowed by their Creator with certain unalienable Rights, that among these are Life, Liberty and the pursuit of Happiness." The abolitionists argued that slavery violated this egalitarian ideal embodied in the Declaration. Slaveholders were perverting the original intent of the Founding Fathers, who envisioned a land of freedom for all people when they created the United States. Slavery should be abolished because it is un-American.[9]

The fourth argument abolitionists used was based on humanitarianism. By its nature, slavery was cruel and inhumane. Slaveholders were unkind to their slaves in general, and there were too many cases in which slaveholders beat, tortured, and killed their slaves. There was also the rape of slave girls, which created the dilemma of half-white babies who were still considered slaves because they were born to slave mothers. Slave families were often broken up, tearing screaming children from their mothers' arms. Slavery was thus an inhumane system that abused helpless men, women, and children.[10]

Slaveholders, of course, responded to these arguments levied against them. They attempted to answer each abolitionist argument and, over time, developed their most sophisticated arguments during the 1850s based on new quasi-scientific racial theories and changing socioeconomic conditions.[11] The best of these arguments may be found in a compendium published in 1860 by E. N. Elliott of Mississippi: *Cotton Is King, and Pro-slavery Arguments: Comprising the Writings of Hammond, Harper, Christy, Stringfellow, Hodge, Bledsoe, and Cartwright, on This Important Subject.*[12]

They argued, for example, that the Bible endorsed slavery, because the great men of God in the Old Testament were themselves slave owners. In the New Testament, Paul also endorsed the system of slavery when he said, "Slaves, obey your masters" (Ephesians 6:5, NCV; Colossians 3:22, NCV). The Bible thus recognized that slavery was an accepted institution. This argument, of course, missed the overall teaching of the Bible about the dignity and equality of all human beings before God. In 1863, the *Review and Herald* printed an eleven-part article series, titled "The Bible No Refuge for Slavery," which addressed the arguments used by slaveholders to justify their practice of slavery from the Bible.[13]

Of all the arguments that the proslavery apologists used, their legal interpretation of the U.S. Constitution was the only one that proved irrefutable. The Supreme Court had always upheld the idea that slaves were property and were not subject to the rights of citizens. It was not until the Thirteenth Amendment was passed that this argument could be successfully overturned.[14]

It was not easy to be an abolitionist in antebellum America. They were small in number compared to the rest of Northern society, and they faced significant obstacles, especially during the 1830s. The greatest obstacle was racial prejudice. While not favorable to slavery as an institution, most Northern whites believed in the inferiority of blacks and preferred that they remain in the South. When the abolitionists called for the equality of these blacks in America, abundant wrath fell upon them.[15]

Types of abolitionists

Abolitionists were complex characters, and their splintering groups are difficult to categorize in terms of their varying beliefs and practices; but for purposes of clarity and discussion, several groupings can be identified in America between 1830 and the Civil War.[16] Understanding these different groupings will provide insight into the nature of Ellen White's abolitionism.

The most prominent grouping was the Garrisonians. This cluster of abolitionists derived their name from William Lloyd Garrison (1805–1879), who became one of the most outspoken white abolitionists in antebellum America.[17] Garrison started his abolitionist career by supporting the American Colonization Society and gradual emancipation but, through various influences, shifted to immediatism and rejected the teaching of the American Colonization Society. He began publishing his newspaper, *The Liberator*, on January 1, 1831, and called for immediate emancipation without compensation to the slaveholder and for no more colonization of the freedmen. Garrison became a rallying point for other abolitionists, and in December 1833, he and fifty others founded the American Anti-Slavery Society. Abolitionists connected with Garrison at the beginning were Frederick Douglass, Theodore Dwight Weld, Gerrit Smith, Arthur Tappan, Lewis Tappan, and James G. Birney.

Following Garrison's lead, the Garrisonians championed women's rights, grew critical of orthodox Christianity, rejected political parties, and promoted the doctrine of nonresistance, which condemned any governmental use of force. They eventually denounced the U.S. Constitution as a proslavery document and advocated that the North should dissolve the Union in order to terminate its sinful and criminal support of slavery in the South.[18] Garrison also condemned other abolitionists when they disagreed with him. By the mid-to-late 1830s, a division occurred in the Garrisonian ranks due to Garrison's rejection of political activity and organized religion, his advocacy of women's rights, and his questioning of the Bible's inspiration. By 1840, a major schism occurred, and the anti-Garrisonians left Garrison and his followers to establish other forms of abolitionism.

From this schism emerged a grouping of abolitionists who turned to politics. Feeling frustrated that the Garrisonians' moral suasion had not worked to end slavery, these political abolitionists rejected Garrison's nonresistance and his contention against the Constitution. In contrast, they embraced third-party politics and formed the Liberty Party, which nominated for president of the United States the reformed slaveholder and abolitionist James G. Birney in 1840 and 1844. They believed that the U.S. Constitution made slavery illegal in the United States when interpreted in light of the Bible and natural law.[19]

Another grouping of abolitionists who left Garrison were the evangelicals. They found their model in Lewis Tappan, the son of a Northampton, Massachusetts, storekeeper and a founding father of the American and Foreign Anti-Slavery Society (AFASS).[20] Originally supportive of the Garrisonians' moral suasion and nonresistance, Tappan maintained a strong evangelical faith at the core of his abolitionism, which he received from the influence of the revivalist Charles G. Finney. Due to Garrison's repudiation of organized evangelical churches, his advocacy of women's rights, and his questioning of evangelical tenets, such as the inspiration of the Bible, evangelicals like Tappan seceded to form their own society—the AFASS. Initially cautious of political involvement, the AFASS eventually embraced political abolitionism and supported the Liberty Party. Nevertheless, its main focus was to keep the moral and religious aspects of the cause at the center of its abolitionist activity.

A small but more extreme grouping of abolitionists found their identity in John Brown, who resorted to violence in his campaign against slavery. Most abolitionists, especially the Garrisonians, abhorred violence and had always advocated pacifism.

William Lloyd Garrison about 1850
(Metropolitan Museum of Art)

But by the time of Brown's Harpers Ferry raid in 1859, many were frustrated that their universal methods to end slavery—moral suasion, nonresistance, and political action—had not worked. Gerrit Smith, for example, had financially supported Brown's exploits in Kansas and was a lead conspirator in the Harpers Ferry plan, although he later regretted his involvement.[21] Other evangelical abolitionists condemned Brown's use of violence. On the whole, though, abolitionists hailed Brown as a martyr after his execution.

One grouping of abolitionists in antebellum America did not belong to any antislavery organization but were known in their respective communities and states as outspoken critics of slavery. While some of them spoke out on abolitionist platforms, all of them testified in behalf of freedom in their daily callings.[22] These community abolitionists were made up of church leaders from various denominations and included physicians, lawyers, Transcendentalist intellectuals, and even poets, such as John Greenleaf Whittier, the beloved Quaker poet of Amesbury, Massachusetts; and William Cullen Bryant, the great romantic poet of New York.

Women also played a significant role in the abolitionist movement, as noted by Frederick Douglass when he reflected on his long career in abolitionism and made "emphatic mention" of the contribution of women to the abolitionist cause:

When the true history of the anti-slavery cause shall be written, women will occupy a large space in its pages; for the cause of the slave has been peculiarly woman's cause. Her heart and her conscience have supplied in large degree its motive and mainspring. Her skill, industry, patience, and perseverance have been wonderfully manifest in every trial hour. Not only did her feet run on "willing errands," and her fingers do the work which in large degree supplied the sinews of war, but her deep moral convictions, and her tender human sensibilities, found convincing and persuasive expression by her pen and her voice.[23]

Douglass then described the contributions of such women abolitionists as Lucretia Mott, Lydia Maria Child, Sarah Grimké, Angelina Grimké, Abby Kelley, and Harriet Beecher Stowe.[24] Intimately connected with women abolitionists was the women's rights movement, which Douglass and Garrison both advocated. Especially powerful were the careers of former female slaves, such as Sojourner Truth, who was well known on the abolitionist speech circuit; and Harriet Tubman, a self-emancipated woman and conductor on the Underground Railroad—the secret avenues of escape for runaway slaves from South to North.[25]

Perhaps the most unique grouping of abolitionists were the Spiritualists. Robert K. Nelson argued effectively that "spirit politics," a "preoccupation with disembodied spirituality" and the "formulation of its social implications" running "through antebellum radical reform," significantly impacted the major abolitionists.[26] Several radical abolitionists "sympathetically investigated or actively practiced Spiritualism,"[27] such as William Lloyd Garrison,[28] Henry C. Wright,[29] Thomas Wentworth Higginson,[30] and Sojourner Truth.[31] The Spiritualist movement in general expressed a strong antislavery sentiment and argued for the removal of slavery from the country.

Such were the various abolitionist groupings in antebellum America. Although they overlapped and differed in many areas, abolitionists were all united in the belief that slavery was wrong and should end immediately. With this background in mind, we turn to the abolitionism of the Millerites and Sabbatarian Adventists and the immediate context for Ellen White's abolitionism.

Millerite abolitionism

That William Miller was an abolitionist and helper on the Underground Railroad is noted by his biographer, David L. Rowe, in *God's Strange Work: William Miller and the End of the World*.[32] Although Miller agreed with William Lloyd Garrison, he was unimpressed when he attended a meeting of the American Anti-Slavery Society in 1840. This was during the time that the Garrisonians were experiencing a division over their principles and procedures, as noted above. "They are in trouble," Miller reported, "divided, split in two, scattered, and weakened by their uneasy designing and master spirits." For Miller, this meant "that all earthly things are passing away" and "the year of Jubilee to the poor slave is not near if man is the cause." It is only God who "can & will release the captive. And to him alone we must look for redress."[33]

Joshua V. Himes, the primary Millerite leader after Miller, was a great reformer in temperance, education, and especially abolitionism. He was one of Garrison's earliest supporters, and the two became lifelong friends. Consequently, the Millerite movement attracted many abolitionists, such as the evangelical Charles Fitch, who was well known in abolitionist circles and who became an important Millerite leader;[34] Joseph Bates, the sea captain who would become one of the key founders of Seventh-day Adventism;[35] Elon Galusha[36] and Gerrit Smith,[37] both active political abolitionists; and Angelina Grimké,[38] a well-known female abolitionist. Thus, one could find among the Millerites representative abolitionists from the various groups discussed above.[39]

Sabbatarian abolitionism

Since Sabbatarian Adventists, the pioneers of Seventh-day Adventism, emerged out of the Millerite movement, it should be no surprise that they were against slavery. Joseph Bates, for example, was originally a supporter of the American Colonization Society but later became an immediatist and helped to form the Fairhaven Antislavery Society in the early 1830s.[40] John Byington, who would become the first president of the Seventh-day Adventist General Conference, grew up in an antislavery home and condemned slavery from the pulpit as a young Methodist minister, calling it "an outrage" and a "sin." Recent evidence has confirmed that his homestead was a stop on the Underground Railroad to Canada.[41] William Gifford also helped to operate a stop on the Underground Railroad. Even some slaves who escaped on the Underground Railroad later became Seventh-day Adventists, such as Louise McElroy.[42]

Uriah Smith and James White, as editors of the *Review and Herald*, took a decided stance against slavery and printed editorials, articles, and opinions against it. As noted in the last chapter, the Adventists were very aware of the escalating conflict over slavery throughout the 1850s and frequently commented on major events. They also cited excerpts from articles and speeches by the antislavery Radical Republicans.

One reader of the *Review and Herald* considered it to be an "auxiliary" support to the "antislavery cause" but questioned Uriah Smith's position against taking political action to emancipate the slaves. Smith responded that the primary goal is to point the slave "to the coming of the Messiah as his true hope," rather than working for "slavery emancipation," which should be "at most but secondary."[43] Thus, because of their belief that the imminent return of Christ was the only hope for emancipation of the slaves, the editors of the *Review and Herald* were abolitionist in principle rather than action. Such was the immediate context for Ellen White's abolitionist stance.

Ellen White—an abolitionist at heart

One of the most powerful denunciations of slavery in the antebellum period came from the pen of Ellen White. From her appeal to divine law and the equality of all human beings to her condemnation of the entire nation and all Christians who tolerate racism and slavery, Ellen White spoke in the tradition of the immediate abolitionists. Unlike the later Garrisonians, however, she never rejected the U.S. Constitution, devalued the Bible, or encouraged the North to separate from the South. She also abstained from the political activism of the Liberty Party and its successors. Neither did she seek to work within the structure of the churches, as did the evangelical abolitionists, or accept violence as the way to deal with the slavery problem. She clearly rejected any form of Spiritualism.

In one sense, Ellen White does not fit into any of the abolitionist groupings. Her assertion that God had given her specific visions about the nation and slavery was unique among abolitionists. She was also distinct from the Spiritualist abolitionists, who claimed that the spirits of dead Americans spoke to them about the wrongs of slavery. In another sense, though, themes from the immediate abolitionists' message echo through her antebellum writings, such as the moral suasion of the Garrisonians, the righteous indignation of the evangelicals, and the compassion of the women abolitionists. Because she didn't belong to any antislavery organization and was an outspoken critic of slavery in her own community, White is best understood as a community abolitionist who expressed her antislavery sentiments in the context of her Seventh-day Adventist faith. But she was also a woman, and like her fellow women abolitionists, she powerfully and eloquently articulated her moral convictions about the evils of human bondage.

Now that Ellen White's abolitionist activity has been identified in the context of the abolitionist movement, we turn to her antebellum writings about slavery. She addressed the issue three times during that period.

The pious slave vindicated and the wicked master confounded

First, in a letter to Joseph Bates in 1847—Ellen White's earliest statement about slavery—she set forth the future of the "pious slave" and the "wicked master." After describing the final events immediately preceding the second coming of Christ, she announced, "I saw the pious slave rise in triumph and victory, and shake off the chains that bound him, while his wicked master was in confusion, and knew not what to do."[44]

Published about the same time was the proslavery essay "The Duties of Christian Masters," in which its author, Reverend A. T. Holmes, argued, among other things, that the Bible supports slavery, slaveholding is not inconsistent with devotion to Christ, and masters are good persons who should not be condemned by other nonslaveholding Christians.[45] But for Ellen White, as well as for other abolitionists, slaveholding was a grievous sin, and nowhere in the Bible is it condoned. When seen with this background, her view of slaveholders as "wicked" was true to most abolition sentiments about slavery.

Ellen White's use of the word *pious* to describe the slave was also relevant to the period. According to Peter Kolchin, a noted historian of American slavery, "By the late antebellum period, evangelical Christianity had emerged throughout the South as a central feature of slave life." Significantly, "most mid-nineteenth-century slaves, unlike their ancestors a century earlier, were devoutly Christian."[46] For Ellen White, then, the "pious slave" will rise in the resurrection, whereas the "wicked" master will be left "in confusion" on the day of Christ's coming.

The fact that Christ didn't come during antebellum America, when there were pious slaves and wicked masters, raises a question on the fulfillment of this vision. Ellen White lived many years after slavery disappeared in the United States. In response to the charge that her early visions on the Second Coming were never fulfilled, she responded, "It is true that time has continued longer than we expected in the early days of this message. Our Saviour did not appear as soon as we hoped. But has the word of the Lord failed? Never! It should be remembered that the promises and threatenings of God are alike conditional."[47] Prior to this statement, she quoted several passages in the New Testament that speak of the imminent coming of the Lord. The heart of her argument was that the Lord could have come but chose to delay His coming. Another way she and others of her day resolved this issue was noting the fact that the book of Revelation indicated that slavery will exist at the second coming of Christ (Revelation 6:15; 18:13; 19:18).[48]

The Fugitive Slave Law and the higher law

Second, she spoke out boldly against the Fugitive Slave Law passed in 1850, as noted in the last chapter. As the basis of her defiance of this law, she stated, "When the laws of men conflict with the word and law of God, we are to obey the latter, whatever the consequences may be."[49] As such, she appealed to the higher-law argument used by William Henry Seward, Charles Grandison Finney, and William Lloyd Garrison.[50] Although there were different nuances to this argument, Ellen White clearly understood the higher law to be that which is found in the Bible—the law of God. Since the Decalogue and the rest of Scripture teach the value and dignity of all human beings, she called for her community to defy the Fugitive Slave Law and obey the law of God instead.

Indictment against slavery and professed Christians

Third, White's most significant antebellum discussion on human slavery was a strong indictment of professed Christians who either supported the institution or actually engaged in it. This 1858 essay, "The Sins of Babylon," is chapter 33 in volume 1 of her book *Spiritual Gifts* and requires a more extensive discussion.[51] The larger context for this chapter is important.

The great controversy theme. In March of 1858, Ellen White received what scholars of her works call "the great controversy vision,"[52] in which she beheld through prophetic revelation the entire plan of salvation, from Satan's rebellion in heaven to the earth made new, specifically from the perspective of the cosmic battle between Christ and Satan. She saw the events of biblical times all culminating in Christ's decisive victory over Satan at Calvary, and Satan's continuing deception over the many centuries until the Second Coming, at which time he is cast into the bottomless pit (Revelation 20:3) to await final judgment and punishment after the thousand years.

After this major vision in the spring of 1858, Ellen White spent the rest of her life writing on the great controversy between Christ and Satan—the overarching theme in her writings.[53] Her first presentation of it was published six months after the vision in *Spiritual Gifts*, volume 1. The second, expanded presentation was in the series known as the *Spirit of Prophecy*, which she wrote during the years 1870–1884. Her final and most expanded presentation of this theme was in the five-volume set known today as the Conflict of the Ages series: *Patriarchs and Prophets, Prophets and Kings, The Desire of Ages, The Acts of the Apostles,* and *The Great Controversy,* which was written during the last two decades of her life.[54]

Volume 1 of *Spiritual Gifts*, then, is Ellen White's first presentation of the great controversy theme, written and published in 1858 during the latter antebellum period. Chapters 1 through 21 cover the fall of Satan, the life of Christ, the apostolic period, and church history up to the Reformation period. Chapters 22 through 33 present Ellen White's prophetic insights on the rise of the Millerite movement and Sabbatarian Adventists during the period from 1830 to 1858. The remaining chapters address end-time events up to the Second Coming and the earth made new. With this larger context in mind, we now turn to the specifics of chapter 33 in *Spiritual Gifts*.

Sins of Babylon. The title of chapter 33 in *Spiritual Gifts*, "The Sins of Babylon," reflected the thinking of Ellen White and Sabbatarian Adventists in 1858 about the great controversy between Christ and Satan. They understood their Millerite experience to be a fulfillment of the prophecies of Daniel and Revelation, and they placed special emphasis on the three angels' messages of Revelation 14:6–12, which they believed to be the last messages proclaimed to the world before the Second Coming. The first angel's message, in verses 6 and 7, was viewed as a symbol of the Advent message—the proclamation of Christ's second coming—and an announcement of the judgment hour.[55] The second angel's message, in verse 8, announced the fallen nature of mystical Babylon, believed at that time to be all corrupt Christianity, as found in the Protestant churches, particularly those who rejected the Millerite message of the first angel.[56] The third angel's message of verses 9–11 was seen as the solemn warning against receiving the mark of the beast, enforced by the two-horned beast (the United States) in union with the ten-horned beast (the papacy) as described in Revelation 13:1–18.[57]

In light of this background, Ellen White began the chapter thus: "I saw the state of the different churches since the second angel proclaimed their fall." Here she referred to the autumn of 1844, when the Millerite message experienced its greatest persecution and was rejected by the popular churches. Since that time, the churches "have been growing more and more corrupt." Thus, over the period from 1844 to 1858, the churches, according to this first paragraph, had grown worldlier, even to the point that "Satan has taken full possession of the churches as a body." The reason for this strong indictment is the hypocrisy that "very many, who profess to be Christians, have not known God" and are, instead, "Satan's own faithful servants, notwithstanding they have assumed another name."[58]

In the next paragraph, her language intensifies as it transitions into the subject of slavery, to which the rest of the chapter is devoted: "I saw great iniquity and vileness in the churches; yet they profess to be Christians. Their profession, their prayers and their exhortations, are an abomination in the sight of God. Said the angel, God will not smell in their assemblies. Selfishness, fraud and deceit are practiced by them without the reproving of conscience. And over all these evil traits they throw the cloak of religion."[59]

White's jeremiad against slavery. So far in the first half of chapter 33 of *Spiritual Gifts*, Ellen White has indicted the Protestant churches, the corrupt mystical Babylon, for rejecting the first angel's message and for the escalating worldliness and selfishness in their midst. These are part of the "sins of Babylon" that culminate in the worst sin of all—human bondage. It is best to view this chapter as a *jeremiad*, a term that derives from the Old Testament prophet Jeremiah, who called the people of Israel out for their abandonment of the covenant with Jehovah and their return to pagan idolatry. He attributed their calamities to disobedience, denounced their religious and moral iniquities, and called for repentance and reformation in order that Jehovah might restore them to His favor. Thus, a *jeremiad* is a type of rhetoric that condemns a social or spiritual evil and calls for repentance and reformation. Jeremiads were typical in the American religious tradition and often took the form of sermons, speeches, and written articles.[60] Technically, all of White's writings about slavery and the Civil War were her jeremiads against the nation for its participation in the evils of slavery.

As a lead-in to the sin of slavery, she declared concerning the churches:

Jesus and the angels looked upon them [nominal Christians] in anger. Said the angel, Their sins and pride have reached unto heaven. Their portion is prepared. Justice and judgment have slumbered long, but will soon awake. Vengeance is mine, and I will repay, saith the Lord. The fearful threatenings of the third angel are to be realized, and they will drink the wrath of God. An innumerable host of evil angels are spreading themselves over the whole land. The churches and religious bodies are crowded with them. And they look upon the religious bodies with exultation; for the cloak of religion covers the greatest crimes and iniquity.[61]

Then, at the heart of her jeremiad, White articulated in two paragraphs one of the strongest indictments against slavery in the antebellum period:

All heaven beholds with indignation, human beings, the workmanship of God, reduced to the lowest depths of degradation, and placed on a level with the brute creation by their fellow men. And professed followers of that dear Saviour whose compassion was ever moved as he witnessed human woe, heartily engage in this enormous and grievous sin, and deal in slaves and souls of men. Angels have recorded it all. It is written in the book. The tears of the pious bond-men and bond-women, of fathers, mothers and children, brothers and sisters, are all bottled up in heaven. Agony, human agony, is carried from place to place, and bought and sold. God will restrain his anger but a little longer. His anger burns against this nation, and especially against the religious bodies who have sanctioned, and have themselves engaged in this terrible merchandise. Such injustice, such oppression, such sufferings, many professed followers of the meek and lowly Jesus can witness with heartless indifference. And many of them can inflict with hateful satisfaction, all this indescribable agony themselves, and yet dare to worship God. It is solemn mockery, and Satan exults over it, and reproaches Jesus and his angels with such inconsistency, saying, with hellish triumph, *Such* are CHRIST'S *followers!*

These professed Christians read of the sufferings of the martyrs, and tears course down their cheeks. They wonder that men could ever possess hearts so hardened as to practice such inhuman cruelties towards their fellow-men, while at the same time they hold their fellow-men in slavery. And this is not all. They sever the ties of nature, and cruelly oppress from day to day their fellow-men. They can inflict most inhuman tortures with relentless cruelty, which would well compare with the cruelty papists and heathens exercised towards Christ's followers. Said the angel, It will be more tolerable for the heathen and for papists in the day of the execution of God's judgment than for such men. The cries and sufferings of the oppressed have reached unto heaven, and angels stand amazed at the hard-hearted, untold, agonizing, suffering, man in the image of his Maker, causes his fellow-man. Said the angel, The names of such are written in blood, crossed with stripes, and flooded with agonizing, burning tears of suffering. God's anger will not cease until he has caused the land of light to drink the dregs of the cup of his fury, and until he has rewarded unto Babylon double. Reward her even as she rewarded you, double unto her double according to her works: in the cup which she hath filled, fill to her double.[62]

A NATION IN GOD'S HANDS

This significant statement followed in the tradition of the evangelical abolitionists who believed slavery to be a great sin against God. These two paragraphs, coupled with her later essays on the sin of slavery during the war years, reflected the similar sentiments of Lewis Tappan, who also believed God would punish the nation for the sin of slavery.[63] But White wrote from the basis of her prophetic visions on the subject of slavery. As such, this jeremiad is unique in antebellum abolitionist literature, because no major abolitionist leader claimed to possess the biblical prophetic gift.

Several observations on these two paragraphs are in order. *First, her vivid depiction of the cruelty and suffering caused by professed Christian slaveholders was historically accurate.* By the late 1850s, the proslavery Southern apologists had developed a somewhat sophisticated defense of the institution through law, racial theory, and the Bible.[64] The South's religious leaders and clergy were themselves slaveholders and claimed the Bible's support for this practice. Moreover, they argued that God ordained the institution of slavery, that Christian masters treated their slaves humanely, that whites were the guardians of the helpless black race, and that blacks preferred to be enslaved. Eugene D. Genovese and Elizabeth Fox-Genovese, scholars of Southern slavery, have demonstrated that the slaveholders had deceived themselves and were not in touch with reality.[65]

The proslavery argument, for example, that slaves were treated humanely and that cases of cruelty were rare exceptions, did not fit the many eyewitness testimonies.[66] Historian Kenneth M. Stampp asserted,

> The exact truth will never be known, because surviving records are fragmentary and sometimes hint only vaguely at conditions. There is no way to discover what went on in the "voiceless solitudes" where no records were kept, or on hundreds of plantations where visitors were unwelcome and the proprietors were in residence only part of the year. ... Even so, the public and private records that do survive suggest that, although the average slaveholder was not the inhuman brute described by the abolitionists, acts of cruelty were not as exceptional as proslavery writers claimed.[67]

Frederick Douglass in his first autobiography, *Narrative of the Life of Frederick Douglass, an American Slave*, vividly depicted the hypocrisy among professed Christian slaveholders in the South:

I assert most unhesitatingly, that the religion of the south is a mere covering for the most horrid crimes,—a justifier of the most appalling barbarity,—a sanctifier of the most hateful frauds,—and a dark shelter under which the darkest, foulest, grossest, and most infernal deeds of slaveholders find the strongest protection. Were I to be again reduced to the chains of slavery, next to that enslavement, I should regard being the slave of a religious master the greatest calamity that could befall me. For of all slaveholders with whom I have ever met, religious slaveholders are the worst. I have found them the meanest and basest, the most cruel and cowardly, of all others.[68]

Douglass then related the story of the Reverend Rigby Hopkins, a minister of the "Reformed Methodist Church," who whipped his slaves for the "smallest offences."

Mr. Hopkins could always find some excuse for whipping a slave. It would astonish one, unaccustomed to a slaveholding life, to see with what wonderful ease a slaveholder can find things, of which to make occasion to whip a slave. A mere look, word, or motion,—a mistake, accident, or want of power,—are all matters for which a slave may be whipped at any time. . . . Mr. Hopkins could always find something of this sort to justify the use of the lash [and was feared by slaves everywhere]. And yet there was not a man any where round, who made higher professions of religion, or was more active in revivals,—more attentive to the class, love-feast, prayer and preaching meetings, or more devotional in his family,—that prayed earlier, later, louder, and longer,—than this same reverend slave-driver, Rigby Hopkins.[69]

Second, Ellen White's strong words targeted not only the Southern churches but the Northern ones as well. "His anger burns against this nation and especially against the religious bodies who have sanctioned, and have themselves engaged in this terrible merchandise," she declared. The Northern churches were guilty because they were generally racist. As previously noted, the abolitionists repeatedly faced racism in the North. In fact, the abolitionists' call to leave the popular churches, known as "come-outerism,"[70] was due in part to the racist attitudes in the North. Frederick Douglass stated it pointedly in his first speech given during the fall of 1841, when he was a freedman living in the North: "Prejudice against color is stronger north than south; it hangs around my neck like a heavy weight. It presses me out from among my fellow men."[71]

Historian Leon F. Litwack provided a vivid description how the white Northern churches expressed their belief in the inferiority of their black parishioners:

> In white society, the church possessed great social as well as spiritual importance. To preserve proper decorum, church officials assigned an inconspicuous position to their colored parishioners. When attending services, Negroes found themselves segregated, either in an "African corner," a "Nigger Pew," seats marked "B.M." (Black Members), or aloft in "Nigger Heaven." The Sabbath schools also provided separate quarters for Negro and white children. Religious bodies which offered the Lord's Supper generally compelled Negroes to wait until the whites had partaken of the bread and wine. "Who would have believed it?" a French traveler asked. "Ranks and privilege in Christian churches!"[72]

Of such professed Christians, Ellen White wrote, "Their profession, their prayers and their exhortations, are an abomination in the sight of God." Thus, her jeremiad spared no racist or slaveholder in the religious bodies of the North or South.

Third, the chapter climaxed with the warning of coming retribution to America. "God's anger will not cease until he has caused the land of light to drink the dregs of the cup of his fury, and until he has rewarded unto Babylon double. Reward her even as she rewarded you, double unto her double according to her works: in the cup which she hath filled, fill to her double." This statement, based on Revelation 18:6, completed this fiery jeremiad with the foreshadowing of punishment to America: "the land of light to drink the dregs of the cup of his fury." The latter sentence indicated a double punishment on Babylon, the religious bodies who "sanctioned" and "engaged in" human bondage. The word *double* could also be a reference to punishment on both the North and South. With such a declaration, White spoke in the biblical prophetic tradition and announced the visitation of divine wrath on the nation. Three years later when the war was underway, she asserted that God had "the destiny of this nation in his hand" but was punishing it for the sin of slavery.[73]

Fate of lost slaves

The final paragraph of this chapter is a unique statement about slaves and their masters:

> I saw that the slave-master would have to answer for the soul of his slave whom he has kept in ignorance; and all the sins of the slave will be visited upon the master. God cannot take the slave to heaven, who has been kept in ignorance and degradation, knowing nothing of God, or the Bible, fearing nothing but his master's lash, and not holding so elevated a position as his master's brute beasts. But he does the best thing for him that a compassionate God can do. He lets him be as though he had not been; while the master has to suffer the seven last plagues, and then come up in the second resurrection, and suffer the second, most awful death. Then the wrath of God will be appeased.[74]

To some readers, it doesn't seem fair that God would keep the poor slaves out of heaven when it was their masters who kept them from a knowledge of the Bible. To others, the idea that these slaves will not be resurrected seems to contradict Scripture, in which "all" will come forth either in the resurrection of the saved or in the resurrection of the lost (John 5:28, 29). Finally, some wonder how this statement fits with the fact that not all slaves were ignorant about God; many knew and loved Him.

These concerns are important and deserve answers. But they tend to overlook the main focus of the passage—God's judgment on the wicked slave masters and His compassion on the poor ignorant slaves. A brief analysis of these two themes will help resolve the three concerns above.

First, the passage is the climax of God's judgment on the sin of slavery. In the previous paragraphs, White has indicted the churches in both the North and South for the sin of slavery. This final paragraph of the chapter places the spotlight on the slave masters. Accordingly, it is the slave master who will "answer for the soul of his slave," who kept the slave "in ignorance and degradation, knowing nothing of God, or the Bible." God's justice is satisfied when all of the slaves' sins are "visited upon the master." Consequently, "the master has to suffer the seven last plagues, and then come up in the second resurrection, and suffer the second, most awful death." "The wrath of God will be appeased" when the slave masters are punished for their own sins and the sins of the slaves. Thus, the wrath of God falls on the original perpetrators of slavery—the slave masters themselves.

The context does not address all slave masters but only those who were especially cruel and treated their slaves like "brute beasts." During the late antebellum years, when this statement was published, the vast majority of slave owners had concluded that religion made their slaves more docile and obedient.[75] There is also testimony of slave owners who treated their slaves humanely and allowed them to practice their religion.[76] Thomas "Stonewall" Jackson, the famous Confederate general, for example, treated his own slaves with kindness and even created a Sunday School for the slave community so that he could teach them the basics of Christianity.[77] But many recorded slave testimonies describe slave masters who were brutal and cruel.[78] Also, during the earliest years of slavery in America, slave masters viewed Christianity as a bar to slaveholding and effective slave management and thus kept their slaves from experiencing any religion.[79]

Neither does the context address all slaves but only those who experienced such intense, systematic, and demonic cruelty from their masters that they were devastated spiritually and were consequently kept from a knowledge of God. Many slaves embraced evangelical Christianity, and Ellen White saw that many of them will be resurrected at the Second Coming.[80] But for those slaves under discussion, the fact that many of their cruel owners had professed to be Christians intensified their judgment in White's understanding.[81]

Second, the passage is a revelation of God's compassion toward these slaves. The statement "God cannot take the slave to heaven" seems harsh when taken by itself. But in its context, God's mercy is inseparable from His justice: The "best thing" God can do as a "compassionate God," and still remain just ("the wages of sin is death" [Romans 6:23]), is to let the lost slave, spiritually ruined by his master, "be as though he had not been." This unique statement about these eternally lost slaves is best comprehended in the framework of White's understanding of the final events associated with the millennium mentioned in Revelation 20.[82] Because these slaves were kept from a saving knowledge of Christ, they will not be raised in the first resurrection of the righteous at the Second Coming (before the millennium; verses 5, 6). But neither will they be raised in the second resurrection of the wicked to experience the "second death" (after the millennium; verse 6).

So the "best thing" God does for these slaves is an act of compassion. Although they have been "kept in ignorance and degradation, knowing nothing of God,"[83] they are still recipients of God's pity and mercy. He does not add more affliction to their lives of suffering by putting them through the painful experience of the second death after the second resurrection. The first death is their final one, and they will not experience God's wrath against sin but will "be as though" they "had not been." This scenario fits within the framework of White's conditional-immortality, annihilationist understanding.[84]

Some may object that this some-slaves-not-resurrected exception cannot be found in Scripture. True; there is no text in the Bible that specifically teaches that a certain class of people will not be resurrected. But there are, however, departures from the two general resurrections in Scripture. Examples are the special resurrection of the righteous Moses (Jude 9) and a special resurrection of the wicked who crucified Christ (Matthew 26:64).[85] In light of these exceptions, then, there is no reason on scriptural grounds to deny the possibility that God will make a unique exception for the slaves under discussion and show compassion on them while still being just.

Furthermore, the Bible's writers often used inclusive language. For example, Jesus said that when He is lifted up on the cross, He would "draw all men" unto Himself (John 12:32). The word *all* here is inclusive in the general sense that it embraces all humans on the planet. But this inclusive language did not rule out the fact that not everyone has yielded to the drawing influence of Christ. So also, when Jesus said, "Do not marvel at this, for an hour is coming when all who are in the tombs will hear his voice and come out, those who have done good to the resurrection of life, and those who have done evil to the resurrection of judgment" (John 5:28, 29, ESV), He used inclusive language, which doesn't necessarily rule out exceptions that He and the Father could make.

To culminate the theological issues in this paragraph, Ellen White set forth an exception to the two general biblical resurrections (John 5:28, 29; Revelation 20:5, 6), in which God will leave in the grave a specific class of slaves who were so overwhelmed by the cruel treatment from their masters that they were never able to come to a knowledge of Christ. In His divine justice, God cannot take these slaves to heaven without their sins transferred vicariously to Christ (Romans 3:23–26). But neither does God punish the slaves for their own sins, according to White. Rather, He transfers the guilt of their sins to the slave masters, who receive double punishment for their own sins and that of their slaves.[86] Because the slaves' sins were transferred to their slave masters rather than to Christ, who alone can impute His righteousness in return to save them (Romans 3:22; 2 Corinthians 5:21; Philippians 3:9), and they never entered into a saving relationship with Christ, which involves a fitness for heaven (John 15:4, 5, 10; 17:3; Ephesians 2:8–10; Philippians 3:8–10),[87] God does the best thing that "a compassionate God can do"—He leaves them in the grave after the first death, as though they had "not been,"[88] and thus exempts them from the second resurrection and punishing "second death" (Revelation 20:14).

It is important to note that God's compassion on these poor oppressed slaves is at the heart of the paragraph. This scenario shows how God is merciful to this abused class of people, and yet remains just in the theological framework of the Bible's teaching on salvation in Christ.[89]

Conclusion

Ellen White was an outspoken abolitionist who gave strong testimonies against human chattel before her Sabbatarian Adventist community. She never joined any of the abolitionist societies nor worked alongside any of the major abolitionist groups, such as the Garrisonians or the political, evangelical, or violent abolitionists. But she did echo many of their sentiments against slavery and did so as a woman with a unique prophetic voice.

After the Civil War, she continued the abolitionist spirit, fighting for the rights of African Americans in the Adventist Church. According to Delbert Baker, a scholar of black Adventist history, "Ellen White can rightfully be called the initiator of the Black work. No person had a greater impact on the inclusion and status of Black people in the Adventist church; it is impossible to talk about Black Adventist history without constantly referring to her contributions."[90] To the end of her life in 1915, White remained an abolitionist at heart and held true to this conviction penned in 1891: "The black man's name is written in the book of life beside the white man's. All are one in Christ. Birth, station, nationality, or color cannot elevate or degrade men."[91]

Three months before the Civil War officially commenced in the spring of 1861, Ellen White received a vision of war in which she heard the cannons booming and saw the massive death toll. The next section will unpack the details of this vision.

Chapter in a nutshell

Abolitionists were outspoken people in antebellum America who wanted slavery abolished from the land. Their resolve was firm and their passion intense, but they often disagreed on the details of how to end slavery. At first, they advocated "gradualism," a method that would gradually end slavery and compensate the slaveholders. By 1830, the abolitionists were fed up with gradual emancipation and began to call for immediate, unconditional, and universal abolition of slavery in the United States. Several groupings of abolitionists can be identified during the years leading up to the Civil War: Garrisonian abolitionists, political abolitionists, evangelical abolitionists, violent abolitionists, community abolitionists, women abolitionists, and Spiritualist abolitionists. Millerite and Sabbatarian Adventist abolitionism was the immediate context for Ellen White's abolitionist stance.

Because Ellen White didn't belong to any antislavery organization and was an outspoken critic of slavery in her own community, she is best understood as a community abolitionist who expressed her antislavery sentiments as a woman; like her fellow women abolitionists, she powerfully and eloquently articulated her moral convictions about the evils of human bondage. White addressed slavery several times before the Civil War and condemned it in no uncertain terms. Her most significant discussion was a strong indictment of professed Christians who either supported or actually engaged in slavery. In this jeremiad, she accurately depicted the cruelty and suffering of slaves caused by professed Christian slaveholders, condemned the Northern churches as well as the Southern ones, and warned of coming retribution to America. She emphasized God's judgment on the slaveholders and His mercy on the slaves. White remained an abolitionist at heart for the rest of her life and believed that all human beings, regardless of color, are created equal before God and one in Christ.

1. Frederick Douglass, "What to the Slave Is the Fourth of July?: An Address Delivered in Rochester, New York, on 5 July 1852," in Blassingame, *Speeches, Debates, and Interviews*, 2:383, 384 (emphasis in original).

2. As reflected in the titles of three respected books on the abolitionists: Merton L. Dillon, *The Abolitionists: The Growth of a Dissenting Minority* (DeKalb, IL: Northern Illinois University Press, 1974); Stewart, *Holy Warriors*; and Timothy Patrick McCarthy and John Stauffer, eds., *Prophets of Protest: Reconsidering the History of American Abolitionism* (New York: New Press, 2006).

3. See Dillon, *The Abolitionists*, 3–139.

4. Ibid., 11.

5. For a concise overview of the society, see Jerome L. Clark, *Social Movements*, vol. 2 of *1844* (Nashville, TN: Southern Publishing Association, 1968), 35–39.

6. James McPherson, *The Struggle for Equality: Abolitionists and the Negro in the Civil War and Reconstruction*, 2nd ed. (Princeton, NJ: Princeton University Press, 1995), 3.

7. This section is drawn from T. Adams Upchurch, *Abolitionist Movement,* Landmarks of the American Mosaic (Santa Barbara, CA: Greenwood, 2011), 57–65.

8. Upchurch, *Abolitionist Movement*, 59.

9. Ibid.

10. Ibid., 59, 60.

11. Ibid., 60.

12. E. N. Elliott, *Cotton Is King, and Pro-slavery Arguments: Comprising the Writings of Hammond, Harper, Christy, Stringfellow, Hodge, Bledsoe, and Cartwright, on This Important Subject* (Augusta, GA: Pritchard, Abbott & Loomis, 1860), available at Google Books.

13. See Luther Lee, "The Bible No Refuge for Slavery," *Review and Herald*, 1863: February 3, 73, 74; February 10, 81–83; February 24, 97, 98; March 3, 105, 106; March 10, 113, 114; March 17, 121–123; March 24, 129, 130; April 7, 145, 146; April 21, 161–163; April 28, 169, 170; May 5, 177, 178.

14. Upchurch, *Abolitionist Movement*, 64. See also Paul Finkelman, "United States Constitution and Antislavery," in Hinks and McKivigan, *Encyclopedia of Antislavery and Abolition*, 2:715–718.

15. Dillon, *The Abolitionists*, 77.

16. This section has been drawn from the following sources: Ronald G. Walters, *The Antislavery Appeal: American Abolitionism After 1830* (New York: W. W. Norton, 1978); Stanley Harrold, *American Abolitionists* (New York: Pearson Education, 2001); Dillon, *The Abolitionists*; Stewart, *Holy Warriors*; and McPherson, *The Struggle for Equality*, 3–8. Several of these works have identified various groupings of the abolitionists and used various titles to describe them.

17. For the definitive biography on Garrison, see Henry Mayer, *All on Fire: William Lloyd Garrison and the Abolition of Slavery* (New York: W. W. Norton, 1998).

18. Harrold, *American Abolitionists*, 35, 36.

19. Ibid., 65.

20. For the definitive biography of Tappan, see Bertram Wyatt-Brown, *Lewis Tappan and the Evangelical War Against Slavery* (New York: Atheneum, 1971).

21. John Stauffer, "Smith, Gerrit (1797–1874)," in Hinks and McKivigan, *Encyclopedia of Antislavery and Abolition*, 2:637.

22. McPherson, *The Struggle for Equality*, 7.

23. Frederick Douglass, *Life and Times of Frederick Douglass*, in *Douglass: Autobiographies* (New York: Library of America, 1994), 903.

24. Ibid., 903–908. For an excellent analysis of women's antislavery activism, see Julie Roy Jeffrey, *The Great Silent Army of Abolitionism: Ordinary Women in the Antislavery Movement* (Chapel Hill, NC: University of North Carolina Press, 1998). See also Anna M. Speicher, *The Religious World of Antislavery Women: Spirituality in the Lives of Five Abolitionist Lecturers* (Syracuse, NY: Syracuse University Press, 2000).

25. For bibliographies on both of these remarkable women, see the following two articles: Iris Hunter, "Truth, Sojourner (c. 1797–1883)," and Nadine Hunt, "Tubman, Harriet (c. 1825–1913)," in Hinks and McKivigan, *Encyclopedia of Antislavery and Abolition*, 2:681–684. For a discussion on her relationship to Seventh-day Adventists, see also "Sojourner Truth," in Denis Fortin and Jerry Moon, *The Ellen G. White Encyclopedia*, 2nd ed. (Hagerstown, MD: Review and Herald®, 2013), 528–530.

26. Robert K. Nelson, "Spirit Politics: Radical Abolitionists and the Dead End of Spiritualism," in Ben Wright and Zachary W. Dresser, eds., *Apocalypse and the Millennium in the American Civil War Era* (Baton Rouge, LA: Louisiana State University Press, 2013), 34ff.

27. Ibid., 39. For a discussion on Spiritualism and the antislavery insurgency of the Free Democrats and Republicans, see Mark A. Lause, *Free Spirits: Spiritualism, Republicanism, and Radicalism in the Civil War Era* (Chicago: University of Illinois Press, 2016), 23–43.

28. Mayer, *All on Fire*, 465, 466, 621, 622; and Ann Braude, *Radical Spirits: Spiritualism and Women's Rights in Nineteenth-Century America*, 2nd ed. (Bloomington, IN: Indiana University Press, 2001), 17n16, 207, 208.

29. For documentation of Wright's activity in Spiritualism, see Braude, *Radical Spirits*, 17, 65, 66, 74, 169.

30. See Tilden G. Edelstein, *Strange Enthusiasm: A Life of Thomas Wentworth Higginson* (New Haven, CT: Yale University Press, 1968), 130; Braude, *Radical Spirits*, 28, 66, 73.

31. See Margaret Washington, *Sojourner Truth's America* (Chicago: University of Illinois Press, 2009), 278–280.

32. Rowe, *God's Strange Work*, 154, 155.

33. Ibid.

34. For a discussion on Fitch's split with Garrison and his conversion to Millerism, see Knight, *William Miller*, 88–94.

35. See George R. Knight, *Joseph Bates: The Real Founder of Seventh-day Adventism* (Hagerstown, MD: Review and Herald®, 2004), 52–54.

36. For a discussion of Galusha's Millerite experience, see Douglas M. Strong, *Perfectionist Politics: Abolitionism and the Religious Tensions of American Democracy* (Syracuse, NY: Syracuse University Press, 1999), 111–113.

37. For a discussion of Smith's Millerite experience, see John Stauffer, *The Black Hearts of Men: Radical Abolitionists and the Transformation of Race* (Cambridge, MA: Harvard University Press, 2001), 105–107.

38. For a discussion of Grimké's Millerite experience, see Speicher, *The Religious World of Antislavery Women*, 133–136.

39. For further discussion of Millerite abolitionism, see Ronald D. Graybill, "The Abolitionist-Millerite Connection," in *The Disappointed: Millerism and Millenarianism in the Nineteenth Century*, ed. Ronald L. Numbers and Jonathan M. Butler (Knoxville, TN: University of Tennessee, 1993), 139–152.

40. See Knight, *Joseph Bates*, 52–54.

41. See "John Byington," in Fortin and Moon, *The Ellen G. White Encyclopedia*, 333; and Don F. Neufeld and Julia Neuffer, et al., *Seventh-day Adventist Encyclopedia*, 2nd rev. ed., Commentary Reference Series, vol. 10 (Hagerstown, MD: Review and Herald®, 1996), s.v. "John Byington." For recent evidence on Byington's homestead and the Underground Railroad, see the forthcoming biography on John Byington by Brian E. Strayer.

42. On William Gifford, see "Brief Sketch of a Review and Herald Centenarian," *Review and Herald*, January 14, 1902, 19; for Louise McElroy, see her obituary, *Review and Herald*, October 28, 1909, 23.

43. Anson Byington and Uriah Smith, "From A. Byington," *Review and Herald*, March 10, 1859, 124. For a helpful and concise coverage of this exchange between Anson Byington, brother of John Byington, and Uriah Smith, see Douglas Morgan, "An Abolitionist Urges Adventist Action," *Peace Messenger* (blog), accessed November 8, 2016, http://adventistpeace.typepad.com/peacemessenger/2008/01/an-abolitionist.html.

44. This statement was part of a letter to Joseph Bates in which Ellen White described a vision given at Topsham, Maine, on the subject of end-time events, such as the Sabbath, the mark of the beast, the time of trouble, and the Second Coming. It was first published as a broadside in 1847, "April 7, 1847, a Vision." Shortly thereafter, it was published in *A Word to the "Little Flock*," 20; then in 1851, it appeared in *A Sketch of the Christian Experience and*

Views of Ellen G. White (Sarasota Springs, NY: James White, 1851), 18; also in *Spiritual Gifts*, vol. 1 (Hagerstown, MD: Review and Herald®, 2001), 206; and later *Early Writings*, 35.

45. A. T. Holmes, "The Duties of Christian Masters," in Holland N. McTyeire, C. F. Sturgis, and A. T. Holmes, *Duties of Masters to Servants: Three Premium Essays* (Charleston, SC: Southern Baptist Publication Society, 1851), 131–151.

46. Peter Kolchin, *American Slavery, 1619–1877* (New York: Hill and Wang, 1993), 143. Kolchin's work is considered a definitive study of American slavery.

47. Ellen G. White, *Selected Messages*, bk. 1 (Washington, DC: Review and Herald®, 1958), 67.

48. For studies on Ellen White and the delay of Christ's coming, see Ralph E. Neall, *How Long, O Lord?* (Hagerstown, MD: Review and Herald®, 1988), and Arnold Wallenkampf, *The Apparent Delay: What Role Do We Play in the Timing of Jesus' Return?* (Hagerstown, MD: Review and Herald®, 1994).

49. White, *Testimonies for the Church*, 1:201, 202.

50. For a helpful summary of the concept of higher law during the antebellum years, see Neil Brody Miller, "Higher Law and Antislavery," in Hinks and McKivigan, *Encyclopedia of Antislavery and Abolition*, 1:327–330.

51. See White, *Spiritual Gifts*, 1:189–193.

52. See Michael W. Campbell, "Great Controversy Vision," in Fortin and Moon, *The Ellen G. White Encyclopedia*, 853, 854.

53. See Denis Fortin, "The Theology of Ellen G. White," in Fortin and Moon, *The Ellen G. White Encyclopedia*, 266–268; and Herbert E. Douglass, "Great Controversy Theme," in Fortin and Moon, *The Ellen G. White Encyclopedia*, 850–853.

54. For a fuller explanation of the development of the great controversy theme in White's writings, see George R. Knight, "Conflict of the Ages Series," in Fortin and Moon, *The Ellen G. White Encyclopedia*, 730, 731; and Jud Lake, *Ellen White Under Fire* (Nampa, ID: Pacific Press®, 2010), 211, 212.

55. Timm, *The Sanctuary*, 180, 181.

56. John Nevins Andrews, "Thoughts on Revelation XIII and XIV," *Review and Herald*, May 19, 1851, 81. Throughout the 1850s, Andrews and James White debated over whether or not "Babylon" included the papacy. By 1868, White had moved to Andrews' side that both corrupt Protestantism and the papacy were part of mystical Babylon. See Timm, *The Sanctuary*, 182, 183; and Damsteegt, *Foundations of the Seventh-day Adventist Message and Mission*, 179.

57. For an explanation, see Timm, *The Sanctuary*, 187–191.

58. White, *Spiritual Gifts*, 1:189, 190.

59. Ibid., 1:190.

60. See Donna M. Campbell, "Forms of Puritan Rhetoric: The Jeremiad and the Conversion Narrative," Literary Movements, accessed November 10, 2016, http://public.wsu.edu/~campbelld/amlit/jeremiad.htm; and Sacvan Bercovitch, *The American Jeremiad* (Madison, WI: University of Wisconsin Press, 1978).

61. White, *Spiritual Gifts*, 1:191, 192.

62. Ibid. (emphasis in original).

63. At the time of this writing, the only online version of Lewis Tappan's pamphlet "The War: Its Cause and Remedy" is found at the Web site of the Sons of Union Veterans of the Civil War: http://suvcw.org/pr/art043.htm.

64. For original documents, see Elliott, *Cotton Is King*; and Paul Finkelman, ed., *Defending Slavery: Proslavery Thought in the Old South, a Brief History With Documents* (Boston: Bedford / St. Martin's, 2003); and Drew Gilpin Faust, ed., *The Ideology of Slavery: Proslavery Thought in the Antebellum South, 1830–1860* (Baton Rouge, LA: Louisiana State University Press, 1981).

65. Eugene D. Genovese and Elizabeth Fox-Genovese, *Fatal Self-Deception: Slaveholding Paternalism in the Old South* (New York: Cambridge University Press, 2011).

66. See the slave testimony in Theodore Dwight Weld, *American Slavery as It Is: Testimony of a Thousand Witnesses* (New York: American Anti-Slavery Society, 1839); Norman R. Yetman, ed., *Voices From Slavery: 100 Authentic Slave*

Narratives (Mineola, NY: Dover Publications, 2000); and James Mellon, ed., *Bullwhip Days: The Slaves Remember* (New York: Grove Press, 1988).

67. Kenneth M. Stampp, *The Peculiar Institution: Slavery in the Antebellum South* (New York: Alfred A. Knopf, 1969), 181.

68. Frederick Douglass, *Narrative of the Life of Frederick Douglass, an American Slave*, in *Douglass: Autobiographies*, 68.

69. Ibid., 69, 70. For a discussion of the daily cruelties of plantation life, such as repeated floggings, see John W. Blassingame, *The Slave Community: Plantation Life in the Antebellum South*, rev. and enl. ed. (New York: Oxford University Press, 1979), 293–303.

70. See Dianne Wheaton Cappiello, "Come-Outerism," in Hinks and McKivigan, *Encyclopedia of Antislavery and Abolition*, 1:174, 175.

71. Frederick Douglass, "I Have Come to Tell You Something About Slavery: An Address Delivered in Lynn, Massachusetts, in October 1841," in John W. Blassingame, ed. *Speeches, Debates, and Interviews,* vol. 1 *1841–46,* The Frederick Douglass Papers, Series 1 (New York: Yale University Press, 1979), 5.

72. Leon F. Litwack, *North of Slavery: The Negro in the Free States, 1790–1860* (Chicago: University of Chicago Press, 1961), 196.

73. White, *Testimonies for the Church*, 1:264.

74. White, *Spiritual Gifts*, 1:193. A complementary theological analysis of this controversial paragraph can be found in Moon, "Slaves, Fate of Lost," in Fortin and Moon, *The Ellen G. White Encyclopedia*, 1171–1174; for discussion of White's Amalgamation statements, see Jud Lake and Jerry Moon, "Current Science and Ellen White: Twelve Controversial Statements" in Fortin and Moon, *The Ellen G. White Encyclopedia*, 231–233.

75. Kolchin, *American Slavery*, 148.

76. For a personal narrative of both humane and cruel slave masters, see Solomon Northup, *Twelve Years a Slave* (Auburn, NY: Derby & Miller, 1853).

77. S. C. Gwynne, *Rebel Yell: The Violence, Passion, and Redemption of Stonewall Jackson* (New York: Scribner, 2014), 154–157.

78. See the sources of slave testimony in note 66.

79. See Jon Butler, *Awash in a Sea of Faith* (Cambridge, MA: Harvard University Press, 1990), 132, 133.

80. White, *Early Writings*, 35.

81. White, *Spiritual Gifts*, 1:190–193.

82. At the time Ellen White wrote this statement, her understanding of the final events were penned in volume 1 of *Spiritual Gifts*, chaps. 37, 40, and 41, and were significantly expanded in the 1911 edition of *The Great Controversy* (Mountain View, CA: Pacific Press®, 1911), chaps. 38–42.

83. White, *Spiritual Gifts*, 1:193.

84. For a discussion of White's understanding on annihilation, see Edwin E. Reynolds, "Wicked, Fate of the," in Fortin and Moon, *The Ellen G. White Encyclopedia*, 1265, 1266.

85. Ellen White wrote about three eschatological resurrections, with a special resurrection followed by the two general resurrections. See Edwin E. Reynolds, "Resurrection," in Fortin and Moon, *The Ellen G. White Encyclopedia*, 1082–1084.

86. In a similar way, White wrote about all the sins of the righteous being "transferred to Satan" in the great judgment as he is thrown into the lake of fire. "He is made to suffer not only for his own rebellion, but for all the sins which he has caused God's people to commit. His punishment is to be far greater than that of those whom he has deceived." White, *The Great Controversy*, 673. See also *Spiritual Gifts*, 1:218. In this context, however, this transaction occurs after the sins of the righteous have already been vicariously transferred to Christ in His death on the cross. Satan now bears responsibility for all the sins he caused Christians to commit. See Frank B. Holbrook, *The Atoning Priesthood of Jesus Christ* (Berrien Springs, MI: Adventist Theological Society Publications, 1996), 126–129.

87. Jerry Moon focuses on the fitness-for-heaven aspect behind White's statement on lost slaves in his article,

"Slaves, Fate of Lost," in Fortin and Moon, *The Ellen G. White Encyclopedia*, 1171–1174.

88. The idea behind this unique phrase is most likely not that God forgets who they were as persons, but that He forgets their life of sin.

89. Some might wonder about those who come to a knowledge of God without the Bible, as in Romans 1. But this class of people were not oppressed and kept from a knowledge of God like some of the slaves in antebellum America.

90. Delbert W. Baker, "In Search of Roots: Exploring the History of Adventist African-Americans in the United States, Part 1," *Adventist Review*, February 4, 1993, 14. This statement is based on Baker's conclusion in his doctoral dissertation, *The Dynamics of Communication and African-American Progress in the Seventh-day Adventist Organization: A Historical Descriptive Analysis* (Ann Arbor, MI: University Microfilms International, 1993).

91. Ellen G. White, "Our Duty to the Colored People," November 4, 1889, MS 6, 1891, Ellen G. White Estate, accessed November 9, 2016, https://m.egwwritings.org/en/book/7244.2000001#17; see also Ellen G. White, *Selected Messages*, vol. 2 (Washington, DC: Review and Herald®, 1958), 342.

PART II

PARKVILLE VISION (JANUARY 1861):
"A MOST TERRIBLE WAR"

CHAPTER 3

THE PREDICTION

There is not a person in this house who has even dreamed of the trouble that is coming upon this land," declared Ellen White to her stunned audience on the cold winter morning of January 12, 1861, in Parkville, Michigan. "People are making sport of the secession ordinance of South Carolina, but I have just been shown that a large number of States are going to join that State, and there will be a most terrible war."[1] Most of the audience sat motionless, while some shook their heads in disbelief. The idea of the nation entering into a long, drawn-out war with massive casualties was beyond their comprehension. This was Ellen White's first Civil War vision, and over time, its prediction became a horrible reality.

The Parkville vision

The story of this vision was first published by the Adventist pioneer and historical chronicler John N. Loughborough in his 1892 book *Rise and Progress of the Seventh-day Adventists*.[2] "On the 12th of January, 1861," he wrote, "the Seventh-day Adventist meeting-house in Parkville, Mich., was dedicated."[3] The church had been started through the evangelistic work of John Nevins Andrews and John N. Loughborough in 1859. After the meetinghouse was built, an announcement of dedication

John N. Loughborough
(egwwritings.org)

services, which were set for January 11 and 12, 1861, appeared in the *Review and Herald* and invited church leaders to attend, "and as many more as can come."[4] Thus, on January 12, the top Sabbatarian Adventist officials were present for the dedication, which included James White, Ellen White, J. H. Waggoner, Uriah Smith, and Loughborough himself. After J. H. Waggoner preached the sermon, James White offered the dedicatory prayer and made several remarks.[5] Then, according to Loughborough, Ellen White stood to speak:

Mrs. White gave a stirring exhortation, after which she took her seat in a chair. In this position she was taken off in vision. The house was crowded with people, and it was indeed a solemn place. After coming out of the vision, she arose, and looking about the house, said:—

"There is not a person in this house who has even dreamed of the trouble that is coming upon this land. People are making sport of the secession ordinance of South Carolina, but I have just been shown that a large number of States are going to join that State, and there will be a most terrible war. In this vision I have seen large armies of both sides gathered on the field of battle. I heard the booming of the cannon, and saw the dead and dying on every hand. Then I saw them rushing up engaged in hand-to-hand fighting [bayoneting one another].[6] Then I saw the field after battle, all covered with the dead and dying. Then I was carried to prisons, and saw the sufferings of those in want, who were wasting away. Then I was taken to the homes of those who had lost husbands, sons, or brothers in the war. I saw there distress and anguish."

Then looking slowly around the house she said, "There are those in this house who will lose sons in that war."[7]

The dramatic nature and timing of this vision is at once apparent to the student of the Civil War. January 12, 1861, was three months to the day before the war began with the shelling of Fort Sumter on April 12, 1861. It is considered by some Adventist writers to be a most stunning prediction and one of Ellen White's "great visions."[8] The story as told by Loughborough in his 1892 book has been used by these and other Adventist writers to validate Ellen White's prophetic ministry.[9] But the story faces one major problem for historians—it lacks contemporary confirmation outside of Loughborough. No one else who was present during the vision corroborated Loughborough's account in writing.

Loughborough himself first recognized this problem and attempted to verify the prediction while he was preparing his 1892 book. In 1891, he obtained a testimony from Martha V. Ensign, who was not part of the Adventist community in 1861 but who had heard about the vision through her neighbors. In January 1891, she wrote out what had lingered in her memory for thirty years and signed an affidavit attesting to the veracity of Loughborough's account. The statement made its way into *Rise and Progress of the Seventh-day Adventists*:

As a confirmation of the above fact, and that the prediction was made on the day stated, and as an illustration of how the congregation understood it and circulated it, the following testimony is given:—

"This certifies that I was living in St. Joseph Co., Mich., in January, 1861, about six miles from Parkville. I was not an Adventist. On the 12th day of that month, a number of my neighbors went to Parkville to attend meetings. When they came home, they told me that there was a woman at the meeting that was in a trance, and who said that there was a terrible war coming on the United States; that large armies were going to be raised on both sides, in the South as well as in the North, and there would be many who would suffer in prisons; and pinching want would be felt in many families in consequence of losing husbands, sons, and brothers in the war; and that there were men in the house who would lose sons in that war." Signed, "Martha V. Ensign, Wild Flower, Fresno Co., Cal., Jan. 30, 1891."[10]

Loughborough added another testimony that related to the Parkville prediction of sons being lost in the war:

As to the prediction concerning the men in the Parkville meeting-house losing sons in the war, I will simply state, that in the autumn of 1883, I met the elder of the Parkville church, who was also the elder in January, 1861, when the vision was given, and asked him if he remembered the above expression made by Mrs. White in relating the vision concerning the war. "Yes," said he, "I do." "Will you tell me how many you know who were in the house that day who lost sons in the war?" He at once recalled the names of five who were present on that occasion, and had lost sons in this way, and said, "I know these were there, and that they lost sons in the war; and if I were at home, where I could talk with my people, I could give you more names. I think," he continued, "there were five more, besides these that I have mentioned."[11]

No direct evidence for the vision

For Loughborough, the two testimonies above provided evidence for his readers that White's prediction actually occurred on January 12, 1861. For contemporary researchers, however, these testimonies are problematic. Not only was Martha Ensign's testimony published thirty years after the event, she was not even present during the vision and reported what her neighbors told her. Loughborough's interview with the elder of the Parkville church also took place twenty-two years after the event and then wasn't published for another nine years. If Loughborough remembered the words of the elder, why didn't he list the names of those who lost sons in the war? This kind of evidence is inconclusive. Additionally, Loughborough told his readers in the book's preface that he had kept a diary of "daily occurrences" since November 1853 and based the narrative of his book on that diary.[12] Many of these diaries are available for research, but, unfortunately, the ones from 1860 to 1866 are no longer extant, and, therefore, the vision cannot be documented from this source.[13]

Consequently, the Parkville vision is lacking in terms of direct testimonial evidence, and this is a concern for serious researchers. It is puzzling that Ellen White, James White, Uriah Smith, and others who were reported as present at the dedication of the Parkville church on January 12, 1861, never gave any written testimony to this dramatic prediction. Nevertheless, the story of the Parkville vision has been passed down to the present generation, unquestioned by Adventist writers such as Arthur White, Roger Coon, and Herbert Douglass.[14]

Because of Loughborough's status as a church pioneer and his firsthand witness of events in Adventist history and of Ellen White's prophetic ministry, his testimony has received great weight in the Advent movement. His lively stories and interpretations of events have been influential in Adventist historiography well into the twentieth and early twenty-first centuries and accepted as correct and factual. Research has shown, however, that in some areas of interpretation and presentation of facts Loughborough was inaccurate and thus not always the best guide in the historical details.[15]

Overall, though, Loughborough's telling of Adventism's story was accurate.[16] It is highly unlikely that he fabricated the story of Ellen White's Parkville vision: he was never known to be dishonest,[17] and his repeated telling of the Parkville story was never challenged by those who were at that church on the morning of January 12, 1861. But he may have been confused on some of the details and unintentionally distorted what Mrs. White really said about the coming war. After all, his account was published thirty years after the vision. While we can assume he wrote down what she said word for word in his diary, this cannot be confirmed, since his diary from that period is lost.

Indirect evidence for the vision

The lack of direct evidence for the Parkville vision does not necessarily mean that Loughborough's account can't be supported, however. Recent research has revealed several pieces of circumstantial evidence that indirectly support the actual occurrence of the vision.[18] Although direct evidence is the strongest proof in a court of law, the inferences drawn from circumstantial, indirect evidence are often sufficient to prove a case. The following pieces of circumstantial evidence for Loughborough's account of the Parkville vision, therefore, are worthy of consideration.

First, the head elder of the Parkville church publicly invited church leaders in the December 18, 1860, issue of the *Review and Herald* to come and hold a conference: "We wish to say through the *Review* that the brethren and sisters at Parkville, Mich., request a conference at their place commencing Jan. 11, at 6 p. m. We invite brethren J. N. Loughborough, J. H. Waggoner, J. White, J. Byington, and as many more as can come to labor with us."[19] Referring back to the meetings in the January 15, 1861, issue of the *Review and Herald*, James White gave a brief report of the conferences he and his wife had attended, which included Parkville: "We have just returned from the Conferences at Monterey, Wright and Parkville, in usual health, and greatly revived and encouraged."[20] On February 23, 1861, Ellen White referenced her vision in Parkville: "While at Parkville your case was presented before me in vision."[21] Although the war vision on January 12 was not mentioned in these references, they confirm that the conference at Parkville did occur the weekend of January 11–12, 1861; that James White, Ellen White, John N. Loughborough, and other key church leaders were present; and that Ellen White had a vision there.

Second, the loss of Parkville's sons in the war can be documented. The statement by Harvey Keeney, the elder Loughborough spoke to in 1883, that numerous sons of Parkville died in the war can be confirmed in the *History of St. Joseph County, Michigan.*[22] Michigan supplied to the Union army thirty regiments consisting of thousands of men from all over the state; men who fought and died in essentially every major campaign of the Civil War. Men from the Parkville and surrounding regions are listed among those killed,[23] and, at the time of this writing, at least one can be linked to the Parkville church.[24]

Third, Loughborough later recalled returning to Parkville a year after the vision: "One year from that time, I spoke in the same house," and "my subject was spiritual gifts. In illustration of the gift, as manifest by Sister White, I referred to the vision of January 12, 1861."[25] This meeting was corroborated in the *Review and Herald* on February 11, 1862, by M. E. Cornell, who attended the January 25–26, 1862, meetings with Loughborough: "The subjects presented were the Christian's hope, spiritual gifts, necessity of the whole armor, the three [angels'] messages, and the signs of the times."[26] For those who were present during the vision on January 12, 1861, in the Parkville church, Loughborough's reference to the Civil War vision and how it had been fulfilled over the last year would certainly have been impactful. Significantly, Cornell noted, "Several testified that their doubts in regard to sister White's visions were now all removed."[27]

Fourth, in 1866, the year after the war ended, Uriah Smith, the editor of the *Review and Herald*, asked John N. Loughborough to "write out some of the fulfillments of the visions" that he had witnessed. One of the "fulfillments" was an event associated with the Parkville vision. Loughborough recalled,

I saw a noted Spiritualist and mesmerizer present once, when she [Ellen White] had a vision at Parkville, Michigan. He had given out before she came that if she should have a vision there, as it was nothing but mesmerism, he could bring her out of it. When he saw her in vision he came forward where she was, but instead of trying to bring her out, he went staggering toward the door, saying to the congregation, "She don't breathe," and declaring that he did not know what it was, turned deadly pale and left the room.[28]

The fact that Uriah Smith, who was present in the Parkville church on January 12, 1861,[29] published this story in the church paper indicated that he believed it to be true. Loughborough also later related the story in chapter 9, "Fresh Tokens of Divine Guidance," in *Rise and Progress of the Seventh-day Adventists*.[30]

Fifth, a year after the Parkville conference, in February 1862, Ellen White published a vision in *Testimony for the Church, No. 7* that was similar in content to Loughborough's 1892 account. Notice the two side by side:

Loughborough's account (1892)	Ellen White's account (1862)
There is not a person in this house who has even dreamed of the trouble that is coming upon this land. People are making sport of the secession ordinance of South Carolina, but I have just been shown that a large number of States are going to join that State, and there will be a most terrible war. In this vision I have seen large armies of both sides gathered on the field of battle. I heard the booming of the cannon, and saw the dead and dying on every hand. Then I saw them rushing up engaged in hand-to-hand fighting [bayoneting one another]. Then I saw the field after battle, all covered with the dead and dying. Then I was carried to prisons, and saw the sufferings of those in want, who were wasting away. Then I was taken to the homes of those who had lost husbands, sons, or brothers in the war. I saw there distress and anguish.[31]	I saw greater distress in the land than we have yet witnessed. I heard groans and cries of distress, and saw large companies in active battle. I heard the booming of the cannon, the clash of arms, the hand-to-hand fight, and the groans and prayers of the dying. The ground was covered with the wounded and the dead. I saw desolate, despairing families, and pinching want in many dwellings. Even now many families are suffering want, but this will increase. The faces of many looked haggard, pale, and pinched with hunger.[32]

In his master's thesis, Lee Eusey explained that Ellen White's 1862 document "gave written form to verbal statements she had made at the Parkville vision."[33] As one can see above, there are similar statements in both documents, such as the cannon fire, armies clashing into one another on the field, and the carnage and death. But there are also significant differences, such as the details about South Carolina, secession, and the prisons found only in Loughborough's 1892 account. Loughborough's document is contextualized to January 1861, on the eve of secession, and White's document is contextualized to February 1862, long after secession was over and shortly before the war kicked into high gear in the spring. If Eusey is right, then Ellen White's 1862 document provides confirmation for Loughborough's 1892 document.

It should be noted that Mrs. White never gave any explanation on the origin of her 1862 forecast, and it appears to stand alone as a prediction of what was ahead from that point in the war. On occasion, she did recycle material from earlier published visions,[34] but that is not the case here. There is no *published* antecedent to this vision. All we have is Loughborough's account, published years later in 1892. Nevertheless, White's 1862 prediction appears to be a recasting of the 1861 Parkville vision in her own pen.

Sixth, Ellen White endorsed the second edition of Loughborough's book. In 1899, Loughborough had heard a rumor that Mrs. White was unhappy with his *Rise and Progress of the Seventh-day Adventists*, and he wrote Willie, her son, asking if it was true. "As regards the question you ask about Mother's views and feelings about your book," wrote Willie, "I can say that I have often heard her speak of this book, but I have never heard her express the opinion that its publication was a mistake, or that it ought not to have been written." But, he added, "I have heard her say that she was sorry that you made her so prominent in the work."[35] Her complaint was that Loughborough had given her a greater role in the early years of Adventism than she felt she deserved. Obviously, she had not read the book until after it was published.

In 1902, when the plates for Loughborough's 1892 *Rise and Progress of the Seventh-day Adventists* were destroyed in the Review and Herald fire, the demand for the popular book by Adventist youth, literature evangelists, and ministers called for the production of an updated edition.[36] While Loughborough was working on the new edition in 1903, Ellen White wrote Elder G. I. Butler on June 1 and commented on it: "The record of the experience through which the people of God passed in the early history of our work must be republished. Many of those who have since come into the truth are ignorant of the way in which the Lord wrought. The experience of

William Miller and his associates, of Captain Joseph Bates, and of other pioneers in the Advent message should be kept before our people. Elder Loughborough's book should receive attention. Our leading men should see what can be done for the circulation of this book."[37]

On July 12, 1903, she wrote, "I certainly think that it would be well if Elder Loughborough's book could be given a larger circulation."[38]

Significantly, when an early draft of the manuscript was completed, Loughborough brought it to Ellen White to discuss the contents with her. "Elder Loughborough came today, bringing with him the manuscript for his new book," Ellen White wrote to Willie on February 15, 1904. "He wishes to call my attention to some points. I could do nothing about the matter today, but will try to go over the points with him tomorrow."[39] Although there is no documentation of this meeting, we can assume that it took place with regard to the forthcoming book.

That summer when the final draft of the manuscript was finished, Loughborough published the news about the forthcoming book in the *Review and Herald*:

> I have not been idle during the past winter, but have written a book to take the place of "Rise and Progress," which was written thirteen years ago. Since writing that book I have been able to obtain many interesting facts concerning the advent movement which I did not then have in hand, and the record comes down thirteen years later than when that book was written. The new book takes a world-wide view of the advent movement of the years 1833-44. I have entitled the book "The Great Second Advent Movement; Its Rise and Progress."[40]

The significance of this information for the Parkville vision is that Ellen White gave Loughborough's *The Great Second Advent Movement* her full endorsement as a reliable record of Adventist history and called for "leading men" in the church to promote its "circulation."[41] Yet, as Brian Strayer, Loughborough's biographer, noted, *The Great Second Advent Movement* was not a scholarly history book. Rather, it focused on the "supernatural origin" of the Advent movement.[42] It was apparently in this sense that Ellen White endorsed the book.

We don't know which specific parts of the book Loughborough discussed with Mrs. White; the Parkville vision may or may not have been one of them. But it is significant that the narrative of the January 12, 1861, vision remained essentially unchanged in the 1905 publication. This suggests that White was satisfied with Loughborough's 1892 account. For those who know Ellen White and her writings, it is hard to imagine that she would have allowed falseness or error to be associated with any of her visions.

The preceding six points of circumstantial evidence do not prove conclusively that the Parkville vision occurred on January 12, 1861, in the way that Loughborough narrated it. But they do provide a framework of indirect evidence that suggests that the vision did occur and that White believed it should be repeated for future generations, along with the rest of the contents in *The Great Second Advent Movement*. Although the details in Loughborough's account of the vision cannot all be corroborated at this time, White apparently had no problem with them. It is in this framework that I accept that Ellen White experienced a vision on January 12, 1861—three months to the day before Fort Sumter was shelled—in which she saw the secession of many states and a most terrible war.

The essence of Loughborough's account can be summed up in two parts: (1) a "large number of States" will follow South Carolina in seceding from the Union, and (2) "there will be a most terrible war." The rest of this chapter will focus on the first part and present the historical context of the vision, with emphasis on the main events that transpired before and after January 12, 1861.

A "large number of States" will follow South Carolina

The South had worked itself up into a frenzy over the election of Republican Abraham Lincoln on November 6, 1860. Rumors of slave insurrections and of terrible things that would happen if a Republican won the office had swept across the South and created a climate of hysteria. Lincoln had promised that, although he would not allow slavery to extend into the new Western territories, he would leave it alone in the South. Nonetheless, many Southerners thought that a Republican president would mean the end of their way of life and refused to believe anything Lincoln said. The day after his election, the palmetto flag was raised in defiance in Charleston, South Carolina. "The tea has been thrown overboard," stated the *Charleston Mercury* on November 8. "The revolution of 1860 has been initiated."[43]

A correspondent of the *London Times* wrote from Charleston: "There is nothing in all the dark caves of human passion so cruel and deadly as the hatred the South

Carolinians profess for the Yankees."[44] In this frame of mind, the South Carolina legislature called a convention to discuss the secession; the convention began on December 17 and concluded on December 20. In a vote of 169–0, the people of South Carolina voted to secede from the Union[45] and declared "that the Union now subsisting between South Carolina and other States under the name of the United States of America is hereby dissolved."[46]

The formal signing took place in Institute Hall during the evening of December 20 while all of Charleston celebrated. "Placards announced the news, church bells rang, cannons roared, the governor and public officials appeared." Edmund Ruffin, a Virginia secessionist who was present, wrote that when the signing was complete and South Carolina was declared "to be a free and independent country, the cheers of the whole assembly continued for some minutes, while every man waved or threw up his hat, & every lady waved her handkerchief." In the streets, he observed "demonstrations of joy, from early in the afternoon. Some military companies paraded, salutes were fired, & as night came on, bonfires, made of barrels of rosin, were lighted in the principal streets, rockets discharged, & innumerable crackers fired by the boys." According to another observer, "The whole heart of the people had spoken." One pro-Union citizen of Charleston, however, warned, "I tell you there is a fire; they have this day set a blazing torch to the temple of constitutional liberty, and, please God, we shall have no more peace forever."[47]

E. B. Long described the situation best when he wrote that "South Carolina had broken the dam of events; now the waters would begin to rush."[48] One of the first events of these rushing waters was the occupation of federal property in Charleston Harbor. On December 26, 1860, Major Robert Anderson transferred his small garrison from Fort Moultrie on the shoreline of Charleston Harbor to Fort Sumter—a small island in the harbor itself. He made this move based on what he felt was evidence that Fort Moultrie would be seized by South Carolinians, which happened the next day. By December 30, 1860, South Carolina troops had seized the federal arsenal at Charleston and had occupied all other federal property in the area except Fort Sumter. Other Southern states began to seize federal forts and arsenals as well.[49]

Early in the new year three other states seceded from the Union: Mississippi on Wednesday, January 9, Florida on Thursday, January 10, and Alabama on Friday, January 11.[50] Each state's vote was accompanied by cheering, clapping, and patriotic celebrations in the streets. "It was not entirely clear," wrote Bruce Catton, "just where all of the marching and singing and voting would take people. Secession was real, voted by men deeply in earnest—and yet there might still be room for an arrangement; the people of the North might yet give way when they understood that the people of the South really meant what they said."[51] The following day, Saturday, January 12, at the dedication of the Parkville church, Ellen White experienced her vision that South Carolina's secession was the beginning of many states that would secede and then a terrible war.

Seven days after the vision, Georgia seceded from the Union on January 19. Like the previous four states, there was celebration in the streets, thundering of cannons, and loud cheering at the newfound freedom from federal control. Without any armed clash, the federal forts and arsenals in these cotton states were seized and put under state control. "The sheer sweep of dramatic events carried many men along," Catton explained. "There was a rising sense of identification with a powerful movement; no one knew quite where the Southern states were going, but at least they were on the march and it was exciting to be a part of it."[52]

On January 21, five senators from Florida, Alabama, and Mississippi gave farewell speeches and left the chamber of the U.S. Senate forever, indicating the Southern resolve to secede. Senator Jefferson Davis from Mississippi, the future president of the Confederacy, gave the last speech. "Mr. President, and Senators," he concluded, "having made the announcement which the occasion seemed to me to require, it remains only for me to bid you a final adieu." It was an unforgettable scene in the Senate.[53] "Inexpressibly sad," Mrs. Davis said of her husband, "he left the chamber, with but faint hope."[54] Five days later Louisiana seceded, and then Texas on February 1. Thus, by February 1, 1861, seven of the fifteen slave states had left the Union.[55]

National mind-set on war

Why was it that no one seated in that newly built church in Parkville, Michigan, on January 12, 1861, could imagine a prolonged civil war that would take the lives of more than seven hundred thousand soldiers? First of all, the magnitude of the blood and carnage Ellen White described was beyond the imagination of any American living at the time.

Another reason was the probable influence of the Republican Party in the audience. Michigan was a Republican stronghold,[56] and not surprisingly, Loughborough noted that "leading men in the Republican Party" were in the audience.[57] The issue was that the Republican Party had, in general, failed to apprehend the serious nature of the secession crisis in the South. Since its founding in 1854, the party had "learned to discount all evidences of Southern discontent, and now eminent Republican leaders—as well as members of the rank and file—seemed unresponsive to the events of secession."[58] To these Republicans, the recent actions of South Carolina were nothing more than "another temper tantrum."[59]

Noted poet and Republican William Cullen Bryant, for example, believed that only "silly people" expect Southern secession to create disunion in the United States.[60] Other Republican leaders viewed the Southern "howl and rave" as "all a humbug."[61] Even the Republican president-elect, Abraham Lincoln, initially perceived the Southern threats as no danger to the Union. According to his friend and law partner, William H. Herndon, Lincoln "could not in his heart believe that the South designed the overthrow of the Government."[62]

Furthermore, "not only in the Republican party," noted historian David Potter, "but throughout the North in general, the public was very slow to perceive that the Southern movement was more than another episode in the sham battle of party warfare."[63] As such, the perceived "theatrical ring"[64] to the Southern threats most likely influenced the thinking of those in the audience who heard Ellen White recount her vision of secession and war on January 12. It is no wonder that, as Loughborough reported, some men in the audience shook their heads in disbelief while she related the vision.[65]

Others in the North, however, felt that if the Union were dissolved, war would be the result. Several weeks before South Carolina's secession, for example, the influential *New York Times* stated, "If South Carolina is determined upon secession, she should make the plunge with her eyes open. She must face all the consequences,—and *among them all, the most unquestionable is War*."[66] After South Carolina's secession, the *Times* pessimistically noted that people everywhere were saying, "Civil war is imminent—peace is impossible."[67] According to Walt Whitman, "nine-tenths of the people of the free States look'd upon the rebellion, as started in South Carolina, from a feeling one-half of contempt, and the other half composed of anger and incredulity."[68]

The same mixed feelings on the possibility of war existed in the South as well during this time. Following Lincoln's election, numerous secessionists' papers denied that secession means war. "Everything considered," explained an Alabama paper on January 10, "we cannot believe there will be much fighting." The *Atlanta Daily Intelligencer* declared on January 28, "So far as civil war is concerned, we have no fears of that in Atlanta." On November 15, Georgia's *Albany Patriot* had promised to insure with a postage stamp "the life of every southern man" killed in a war against the North.[69] The most dramatic statement against a war resulting from the secession was made by South Carolina's Senator James Chesnut, who "offered to drink all the blood shed as a consequence of secession." Consequently, a common saying circulated in the South during Secession Winter: "A lady's thimble will hold all the blood that will be shed."[70]

Other Southerners, however, felt that war was certain. In early January, Little Rock's *Arkansas State Gazette* stated, "The conflict between the sections of the country becomes more and more intense. The wisest men in the land can see no peaceful solution to our difficulties, nor are we sanguine enough to hope for any good results from them—or indeed anything but disaster and dire calamity and distress."[71] North Carolina's *Salisbury Daily Banner* grimly predicted that "fire and sword will devastate the land" and military despotism would result.[72]

Such was the national mind-set when Ellen White predicted a terrible civil war on January 12, 1861. Her narrative of a war resulting from the secession, while unthinkable to her immediate audience, was contemplated by others in the nation. The unique aspect of her vision, however, was the magnitude of its descriptions: a "large number" of states to secede and a "most terrible war."

Making sport of the secession ordinance of South Carolina

Loughborough's account noted that people were, as White stated in her vision, "making sport of the secession ordinance of South Carolina." Some Northerners, as noted above, took South Carolina very seriously, while others were "making sport." To give evidence of White's statement, Loughborough noted that "many of the leading journals said, 'If a few old women with broomsticks should go down to South Carolina, they could quickly quell all the rebellion there is there.' "[73] This was apparently a popular abolitionist saying that circulated during and after the war.[74] Other statements were published that Loughborough didn't mention, such as the following sarcastic dispatch in the *New-York Daily Tribune* on December 21, 1860, the day after South Carolina's secession: "The agony is over, *parturiunt montes nascitur ridiculus mus*. South Carolina is out of the Union. No earthquake or terrible subterranean convulsion has followed her Secession. At 3 o'clock this afternoon a dispatch was received in the House informing the United States that they are minus one. But as astonishing and almost incredible as it may appear to the Seceders, the news created no excitement whatever. . . . The stars and stripes still float over the capitol of the nation; none of them will be eradicated."[75]

The Latin phrase originated from a poem by Phaedrus in one of Aesop's Fables, "The Mountain in Labour." In English it reads, "Mountains will labour: what's born? A ridiculous mouse!"[76] The story is about a mountain that went into labor and, after much pain and groaning, produced a little mouse. Accordingly, the phrase refers to those who make big talk but produce little results. Such was the initial opinion of some over South Carolina's secession.

Formation of the Confederacy

Within a month of January 12, when White had forecast that a large number of other states would join South Carolina in seceding from the Union, the South made a dramatic move to create a confederacy. Emory Thomas explained, "By February 1, 1861, seven Southern states had reenacted, they believed, the revolutionary 'secession' of the Founding Fathers. In the process, Southerners had been preoccupied with a political philosophy whose end was revolution and with radical agitation whose goal was dissolution of the Union. . . . [The work of] rending a nation was past; the time for making a nation from independent republics had arrived."[77] Whereas secession was a "negative process," the creation of the Confederate States of America was a creative and positive process. Thus, on February 4, representatives from six seceded states gathered in Montgomery, Alabama, to form a new nation. (Texas had not completed the secession process, and her delegates arrived later.)[78] Although seven states were not as many as the leaders had hoped for, "they were regarded as sufficient for a viable new confederation."[79]

The leadership was good, and the delegates were well organized and motivated. Within four days of assembling, they adopted a constitution for the provisional government of the Confederate States. The delegates used the U.S. Constitution as their model, which enabled them to complete their work quickly. Unlike the Founding Fathers of the U.S. Constitution in 1787, this group had a blueprint from which to work.[80] On February 8, the day after the preliminary constitution was adopted, Jefferson Davis was elected as the provisional president of the Confederacy, and Alexander

Stephens was named vice president. On February 18, Davis was inaugurated, and on March 11, "the Confederate Congress unanimously adopted the Constitution of the Confederacy."[81] Thus, "in just thirty-five days, less than half the time it took the Founding Fathers to write the U.S. Constitution, the delegates had laid the foundation of the Southern Confederacy."[82]

It is important to note that while the final draft of the Confederate Constitution was a slightly altered version of the U.S. Constitution, its small changes were significant. These changes reflected the state rights and proslavery concerns that had ignited secession in the first place. Slavery was specifically mentioned and given constitutional protection. For instance, article I, section 9.4, stated, "No . . . law denying or impairing the right of property in Negro slaves shall be passed."[83] Shortly after the adoption of the permanent constitution, Vice President Stephens declared to an audience in Savannah, Georgia, that the Confederate government's "foundations are laid, its corner-stone rests, upon the great truth that the negro is not equal to the white man; that slavery, subordination to the superior race, is his natural and normal condition."[84]

Thus, a new nation was born in the early spring of 1861, a nation with slavery as its "cornerstone." Ellen White would declare, based upon future visions, that this "cornerstone" would be the downfall of the Confederacy. (This will be discussed in later chapters.)

The new Southern Confederacy had a problem, however. Eight slave states in the Upper South still remained in the Union: Missouri, Kentucky, Maryland, Delaware, Arkansas, Tennessee, North Carolina, and Virginia. Without those states, the seven-state Confederacy was not a strong republic, and they knew it.

Hopes of a Southern republic demolished

During December and January, secessionists had experienced an uninterrupted series of successes as one state after another in the Deep South seceded from the Union. This all came to a screeching halt on February 4, however, when Virginians voted against secession. After such "an unbroken string of victories" following Lincoln's election, "it seemed a great turning point when Virginia, with all her prestige as the 'mother of states,' the cultural capital of the South, and the most populous and economically important of the southern states, dealt the secessionists such a smashing blow."[85] Northerners were hopeful that this would bring an end to a Southern republic. A correspondent wrote to William H. Seward and assured him, "The Gulf Confederacy can count Virginia out of their little family arrangement—she will never join them."[86] Pennsylvania Congressman Thaddeus Stevens remarked, "Well, well, well, old Virginia has tucked her tail between her legs and run, and thus ends the secession farce."[87]

Over the next month, Tennessee, Arkansas, North Carolina, Missouri, Kentucky, Maryland, and Delaware—state after state of the Upper South—followed Virginia's lead and rejected immediate secession from the Union.[88] As historian David Potter noted, the "late winter of 1860–1861 proved as depressing for the secessionists as the early winter had been exhilarating." The month of February that "witnessed the birth of a seven-state confederacy also saw the hopes of a united southern republic completely demolished."[89]

For the time being, it looked like the threat of an imminent war was off again. Those who heard Ellen White's predictions on January 12 and noted the secession of states must have wondered what had happened to her forecast of a "most terrible war."

Abraham Lincoln's strategy to avert war

Originally, Lincoln had believed that there was a strong enough Unionist sentiment in the Lower South to extinguish secession. But when the seven Southern states seceded, he changed his focus to the upper states and felt that they would never join the Deep South states in secession. He had friends from those states and believed that they would become the leaders and avert secession. Only seven states were gone from the Union, Lincoln and other Republicans thought, so the other eight should remain. Their strategy was to wait a while and hope the whole thing would work to their advantage. When these eight Upper South states[90] chose not to secede from the Union, Lincoln and the other Republicans watched and waited for a Union majority to assert itself and, hopefully, bring the Deep South back into the Union.

Thus, Lincoln's strategy was to wait and let things cool down, hoping that the "better angels" of human nature would bring the two sections back together again in the Union.[91] In spite of Lincoln's brilliant eloquence and diplomacy, however, "off stage, unseen, not yet even in existence but surely fated to exist very soon, waited the terrible armies of unknowing boys who would presently be tramping their way across the bewildered country."[92]

Fort Sumter crisis

Since the January 5–9 crisis when the unarmed vessel *Star of the West* was sent to reinforce and resupply Major Robert Anderson and was then repelled by South Carolina artillery, Fort Sumter had become an important symbol to both the North and the South.[93] Most in the North believed it was federal property and thus belonged to the United States. Republicans, especially, were adamantly opposed to yielding the fort to the South. But the South was just as adamant about keeping Fort Sumter. It's in Charleston Harbor and a part of South Carolina, they argued, and therefore belonged to the Confederacy.

After his inauguration, Lincoln was under pressure to do something. Major Anderson had sent word on March 5 to the newly installed president that if supplies were not sent, he could not hold out and would have to surrender the fort. It was a very fine line, for if Lincoln committed any aggressive act to occupy the fort, he might upset the states that still remained in the Union and sympathized with the South, such as Virginia and North Carolina, and cause them to join the Confederacy.

Knowing that the strong Northern opinion would not tolerate giving up the fort, Lincoln devised a plan in harmony with the principles of "no invasion," which he had enunciated in his inauguration speech a month earlier. To avoid making the North look like the aggressor, he sent word to the governor of South Carolina that he was sending an unarmed vessel "with provisions only." With cautious wording, Lincoln made it clear that "if such an attempt be not resisted, no effort to throw in men, arms, or ammunition will be made."[94]

Now the president of the Confederacy, Jefferson Davis, and his cabinet were placed in a difficult position. "Lincoln had maneuvered them into the position of having either to back down on their threats or else to fire the first shot of the war. What was worse, in the eyes of the world, that first shot would be fired for the immediate purpose of keeping food from hungry men."[95] But Davis was under intense political pressure to hold Fort Sumter. If he allowed Lincoln to supply the fort, then it would remain in federal hands.

Davis decided that he had no choice but to order Anderson to surrender the fort. Anderson refused, and at 4:30 A.M. on April 12, 1861, Confederate artillery, under the command of General Pierre Gustave Toutant Beauregard, fired on Fort Sumter. For thirty-six hours, Confederate forces shelled the beleaguered fort. Crowds of people watched the spectacular display from rooftops and other vantage points around the harbor. One teenager described the shelling as "a perfect sheet of flame flashed out, a deafening roar, a rumbling deadening sound, and the war was on."[96] On April 13, Major Anderson surrendered Fort Sumter to the Confederates. Miraculously, none of the Federal soldiers were killed during the intense bombing of the fort.[97]

The immediate trigger event

Technically, the war was on between the North and the seven-state Confederacy. But without the Upper South and Border States, the weaker Confederacy didn't really have a fighting chance of winning a war against the stronger North. The possibility of Ellen White's "terrible war" still appeared less likely until Lincoln called for seventy-five thousand volunteers on April 15. This call for troops was the immediate trigger event that set things in motion for a terrible war with large armies on both sides. The Upper South slave states still in the Union refused to supply Lincoln troops from their states. How could they let their own Southern men fight against their brethren in the Deep South? The secession dam once again burst open, and the second wave of secession surged forward.[98]

Beginning in April, the following Upper South states seceded from the Union and joined the Confederacy: Virginia on April 17, Arkansas on May 6, North Carolina on May 20, and Tennessee on June 8.[99] The first three states were a trio that would be central to the Confederate war effort. They contained more than half of the manufacturing resources of all the South. They contained the top military leaders, such as Robert E. Lee and Stonewall Jackson, and other key commanders who would serve in both the eastern and western theaters. They contained more than half of all the food crops needed for the Confederate armies. And they contained nearly half of the South's mules and horses, crucial to waging mid-nineteenth-century warfare.[100]

"In other words," explained historian Gary Gallagher, "these three states of the Upper South that left after Lincoln called for volunteers" would "be absolutely central to the Confederate war effort. Without them on the side of the Confederacy, it's very difficult to imagine the war lasting four years or being as destructive of physical and human resources as it was. It's absolutely unthinkable that the seven Deep South states by themselves could have mounted the kind of resistance that the Confederacy would mount over the next four years."[101] To honor Virginia and its importance, the capital of the Confederacy was moved from Montgomery, Alabama, to Richmond,

Virginia. Now the Confederacy had eleven states with far more resources and far more people than they had before—and now it was a dangerous threat to the United States.

Shots had been fired at Fort Sumter; the North had rallied together and raged with war fever, and on May 6, the Confederacy officially declared a state of war between the United States of America and the Confederate States of America. Now war was really on! Hopes of navigating through the perilous difficulties and finding a peaceful solution were gone. It was just a matter of time before the serious fighting would begin. But few envisioned how terrible the war would be.

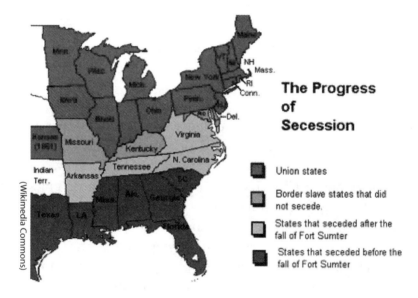

The Progress of Secession

■ Union states

■ Border slave states that did not secede.

■ States that seceded after the fall of Fort Sumter

■ States that seceded before the fall of Fort Sumter

(Wikimedia Commons)

Fulfillment of the vision

Those who heard Mrs. White relate her vision on January 12, 1861, must have watched the ebb and flow of political events with great interest: the secession of state after state during the early winter, the failed attempts at compromise and peace talks, the formation of the seven-state Confederacy, the Upper South's rejection of secession during the late winter, the inauguration of President Abraham Lincoln, the rising tension at Fort Sumter, the shelling of Fort Sumter, the president's call for seventy-five thousand troops, the further secession of the important Upper South states, the enlarged size of the Confederacy, the war fever in the North, and the

Confederacy's declaration of war on the United States. Such were the calamities that befell the Union in the four months following the Parkville vision.

Yet, even with all this, only the first half of the vision (the secession of "a large number of States") had come to pass. The other half of the vision—the "most terrible war" with the "booming of the cannon," the "dead and dying on every hand," the charging and "hand-to-hand fighting," the battlefields covered with "the dead and dying," the prisons with "the sufferings of those in want," the "homes of those who had lost husbands, sons, or brothers in the war," and the "distress and anguish" had not yet occurred.

Conclusion

In one of his later narratives of the Parkville vision, Loughborough mentioned by name the men who shook their heads in disbelief at Ellen White's warning of a coming war and described his encounter with them some years later:[102]

> In the room, and near the stand, sat Police Judge [Nathan] Osborne [Osborn], whose wife was a Sabbath-keeper. By his side sat Mr. Shelhouse [Schell-hous], owner of a large woolen factory in the place. His father was elder of the Seventh-day Adventist Church at Colon, about six or more miles away. These men were leading men in the Republican Party. They looked at me and shook their heads when Sister White told what was coming. I, in turn, looked at them, and nodded assent to what she was saying. This seemed to surprise them. Little did they realize that when she said, "There are men in this house that will lose sons in the war," they were among the number.
>
> One year from that time,[103] I spoke in the same house. These two men sat together, in the same seat. My subject was spiritual gifts. In illustration of the gift, as manifest by Sister White, I referred to the vision of January 12, 1861. As I referred to what she said about the war, there was no shaking of the heads of these two men, but instead their faces were in their handkerchiefs, and they [were] sobbing bitter tears. Alas! One had lost his only adopted son in the war.[104] The other had lost one son on the battle-field, and another was at that time a prisoner in a Southern prison.[105]

A year after she received the Parkville vision, Ellen White reaffirmed what she had seen and published it for the first time.[106] The next chapter will pick up the flow of events after the shelling of Fort Sumter and address the second part of the Parkville vision in relationship to a most terrible war.

Chapter in a nutshell

According to John N. Loughborough in his 1892 book, *Rise and Progress of the Seventh-day Adventists*, Ellen White had a vision in Parkville, Michigan, on January 12, 1861, and declared to an attentive audience that many states would follow South Carolina's secession from the Union and that there would be a "most terrible war." In this vision, White described scenes of battle and great loss of life, including Parkville's sons, three months to the day before the war began with the shelling of Fort Sumter. The only account of this prediction is from Loughborough's book, published thirty years after the vision, with no other written corroboration by anyone else present. This lack of direct testimonial evidence, however, does not necessarily mean that Loughborough's account can't be supported.

Recent research has revealed several pieces of circumstantial evidence that indirectly support the actual occurrence of the vision. First, the Parkville conference, with key church leaders in attendance on January 11–12, 1861, was confirmed in the *Review and Herald* in 1861. Second, the loss of Parkville sons in the war can be documented in Michigan's records. Third, Loughborough's reference to the vision a year later during a spiritual gifts seminar can be corroborated in the *Review and Herald* in 1862. Fourth, Uriah Smith, who was also present at the Parkville vision, printed Loughborough's account of an occurrence during the Parkville vision soon after the war ended in 1866. Fifth, a year after the Parkville conference, Ellen White published a vision in *Testimony for the Church, No. 7* that was similar in content to Loughborough's 1892 account. Sixth, Ellen White endorsed the second edition of Loughborough's book, and there was no change in the narrative of the Parkville vision. These six points of circumstantial evidence do not conclusively prove that the vision occurred on January 12, 1861, in the way that Loughborough described it. But they do provide a framework of indirect evidence that suggests that the vision did occur and that Ellen White believed it should be repeated for future generations of Adventists.

Those who heard Mrs. White on January 12, 1861, must have watched with great interest the flow of political events and noted the fulfillment of the vision over the next four months: the secession of state after state, the formation of the Confederacy, the rising tension over Fort Sumter, the shelling of Fort Sumter, President Lincoln's call for seventy-five thousand troops, the second wave of secession, and the Confederacy's declaration of war on the United States.

1. John N. Loughborough, *Rise and Progress of the Seventh-day Adventists* (Battle Creek, MI: General Conference Association of Seventh-day Adventists, 1892), 236.

2. After *Rise and Progress*, Loughborough published his account of the vision in the following sources listed chronologically: John N. Loughborough, "The Study of the Testimonies—No. 4," *Review and Herald Extra: Daily Bulletin of the General Conference*, January 31–February 1, 1893, 61; John N. Loughborough, "All This Came," *Review and Herald*, November 14, 1899, 730, 731; John N. Loughborough, *The Great Second Advent Movement: Its Rise and Progress* (Nashville, TN: Southern Publishing Association, 1905), 337, 338; John N. Loughborough, *The Prophetic Gift in the Gospel Church* (Mountain View, CA: Pacific Press®, 1911), 80, 81; and John N. Loughborough, "Sketches of the Past—No. 121," *Pacific Union Recorder*, March 7, 1912, 1, 2. The wording is essentially the same in the 1892, 1893, 1899, and 1905 publications, but it is slightly changed in the 1911 publication and significantly changed in the 1912 publication, although the content is essentially the same.

3. Loughborough, *Rise and Progress*, 236.

4. *Review and Herald*, December 18, 1860, 40.

5. For a discussion on the background of the Parkville Seventh-day Adventist Church and this gathering, see Roger W. Coon, *The Great Visions of Ellen G. White* (Hagerstown, MD: Review and Herald®, 1992), 77.

6. Loughborough added the bracketed interpolation as an explanation.

7. Loughborough, *Rise and Progress*, 236, 237.

8. See, e.g., Herbert E. Douglass, *Dramatic Prophecies of Ellen White: Stories of World Events Divinely Foretold* (Nampa, ID: Pacific Press®, 2007), 13–16; and Coon, *The Great Visions of Ellen G. White*, 76–82.

9. Significantly, William C. White told the story and used it to verify his mother's prophetic gift in "Sketches and Memories of James and Ellen G. White: XXXVIII—The Civil War Crisis," *Review and Herald*, November 26, 1936, 6. He referenced Loughborough's *The Great Second Advent Movement* as the source to find "further details of this vision and of the accuracy of its fulfillment." William C. White, "Sketches and Memories," 6.

10. Loughborough, *Rise and Progress*, 237.

11. Ibid., 238, 239.

12. Ibid., iii.

13. Loughborough's extant diaries can be accessed in the Center for Adventist Research at Andrews University. For a discussion of Loughborough's diary, see Brian Strayer, *J. N. Loughborough: The Last of the Adventist Pioneers*

(Hagerstown, MD: Review and Herald®, 2014), 402–404.

14. Arthur White, *Ellen G. White,* vol. 1, *The Early Years, 1827–1862* (Washington, DC: Review and Herald®, 1985), 462–464; Coon, *The Great Visions of Ellen G. White,* 76–82; and Douglass, *Dramatic Prophecies of Ellen White,* 13–16.

15. For discussion on this, see Strayer, *J. N. Loughborough,* 329.

16. Ibid.

17. See ibid.

18. See Kevin L. Morgan, *Journeying to the Same Heaven: Ellen G. White, the Civil War, and the Goal of Post-racialism,* 2nd ed. (Millers Creek, NC: Honor Him Publishers, 2015), 146–149.

19. H. Keeney and A. Hafer, *Review and Herald,* December 18, 1860, 40.

20. James White, "Brief Report," *Review and Herald,* January 15, 1861, 72.

21. Ellen G. White to Friend William, Letter 2, February 23, 1861, in Ellen G. White Writings, accessed November 13, 2016, https://m.egwwritings.org/en/book/3027.0.

22. *History of St. Joseph County, Michigan* (Philadelphia: L. H. Everts & Co., 1877), 58, 59, 70, 71, 80–82, 89, 106, 107, 125–127, 133, 134, 148, 149, 163, 164, 176, 177, 186, 187, 192, 197, 198, 203, 204, 211, 212, 218, 226, and 227, lists many sons of St. Joseph County who died in the war. Page 218 specifically mentions Parkville men who died in the war.

23. See H. G. Cutler, ed., *History of St. Joseph County, Michigan,* vol. 1 (Chicago: Lewis Publishing, 1911), 240, 241. See also Morgan, *Journeying to the Same Heaven,* 148n28.

24. In 1899, Loughborough stated that ten fathers in the Parkville church had sons who fought and died in the war. Loughborough, "All This Came," 730n2. The only one of these sons documented at the time of this writing is Frank A. Osborn, the adopted son of Nathan Osborn and biological son of Rebecca Adler Foster Osborn (Sabbath-keeper at the Parkville church), who enlisted in Parkville, Michigan, on August 18, 1862, in Company C, 17th Michigan Infantry. He was killed in action on October 4, 1862, in Middleton, Maryland. See Morgan, *Journeying to the Same Heaven,* 22, 23, 149n33–36.

25. John N. Loughborough, "Sketches of the Past—No. 122," *Pacific Union Recorder,* March 14, 1912, 1.

26. M. E. Cornell, "Report of Meetings," *Review and Herald,* February 11, 1862, 85. See Morgan, *Journeying to the Same Heaven,* 149n31, for an explanation of the background to this article.

27. Cornell, "Report of Meetings."

28. John N. Loughborough, "Remarkable Fulfillments of the Visions," *Review and Herald,* December 25, 1866, 30.

29. See Loughborough, *Rise and Progress,* 236.

30. Ibid., 97, 98.

31. Ibid., 236, 237.

32. White, *Testimonies for the Church,* 1:260.

33. Lee Ellsworth Eusey, "The American Civil War: An Interpretation," (MA thesis, Andrews University, 1965), 18.

34. See, e.g., White, "Slavery and the War," in *Testimonies for the Church,* 1:264–268, dated August 3, 1861, that was first published in the *Review and Herald,* August 27, 1861, 100. Paragraphs 2 and 3, however, are recycled from *Spiritual Gifts,* 1:191, 192.

35. William C. White to John N. Loughborough, Cooranbong, Australia, November 20, 1899, in W. C. White Letter Books, Center for Adventist Research.

36. See Strayer, *J. N. Loughborough,* 391.

37. Ellen G. White to G. I. Butler, Letter 105, 1903, "Elmshaven," St. Helena, California, June 1, 1903, in Ellen G. White, *Manuscript Releases,* vol. 17 (Silver Spring, MD: Ellen G. White Estate, 1993), 344.

38. Ellen G. White to W. C. White, Letter 141, "Elmshaven," St. Helena, California, July 12, 1903, in Ellen G. White Writings, accessed November 13, 2016, https://m.egwwritings.org/en/book/10314.2000001.

39. Ellen G. White to W. C. White, Letter 87, 1904, "Elmshaven," St. Helena, California, February 15, 1904, in Ellen G. White Writings, accessed November 13, 2016, https://m.egwwritings.org/en/book/9021.2000001.

40. John N. Loughborough, "Report From Elder Loughborough," *Review and Herald*, June 9, 1904, 18.

41. Ellen G. White to G. I. Butler, Letter 105.

42. Strayer, *J. N. Loughborough*, 393, 394.

43. Quoted in E. B. Long, *The Civil War Day by Day: An Almanac, 1861–1865* (Garden City, NY: Doubleday, 1971), 3, 4.

44. W. H. Russell, quoted in Frank Moore, ed., *The Rebellion Record: A Diary of American Events*, vol. 1 (New York: G. P. Putnam, 1861), 315.

45. Long, *The Civil War Day by Day*, 13.

46. *Journal of the Congress of the Confederate States of America, 1861–1865*, vol. 1 (Washington, DC: Government Printing Office, 1904), 7.

47. Long, *The Civil War Day by Day*, 13.

48. Ibid., 20.

49. Ibid., 15–17.

50. For details, see Ralph A. Wooster, *The Secession Conventions of the South* (Princeton, NJ: Princeton University Press, 1962), 26–79.

51. Bruce Catton, *The Coming Fury*, Centennial History of the Civil War (New York: Simon & Schuster, 1961), 190.

52. Ibid., 189.

53. For a gripping account of this scene, see Shelby Foote, *The Civil War: A Narrative*, vol. 1, *Fort Sumter to Perryville* (New York: Random House, 1958), 3–5, where this speech by Davis is quoted at length.

54. Mrs. Jefferson Davis, quoted in Long, *The Civil War Day by Day*, 28, 29.

55. For a day-by-day discussion of the states seceding in chronological order, see Long, *The Civil War Day by Day*; and Wooster, *The Secession Conventions of the South*.

56. Roy E. Finkenbine, "A Beacon of Liberty on the Great Lakes," in *The History of Michigan Law*, eds. Paul Finkelman and Martin J. Hershock (Athens, OH: Ohio University Press, 2006), 83–107.

57. Loughborough, "Sketches of the Past—No. 122," 1. For a discussion on who these men were, see Morgan, *Journeying to the Same Heaven*, 22, 148n28.

58. David M. Potter, *Lincoln and His Party in the Secession Crisis* (New Haven, CT: Yale University Press, 1962), 77ff.

59. Potter, *The Impending Crisis*, 517.

60. William Cullen Bryant to his brother, November 29, 1860, Bryant Papers, New York Public Library, quoted in Kenneth M. Stampp, *And the War Came: The North and the Secession Crisis, 1860–1861* (Baton Rouge, LA: Louisiana State University Press, 1970), 14.

61. Benjamin F. Wade to Lyman Trumbull, November 14, 1860, Sumner Papers, Widener Library, Harvard University, quoted in Stampp, *And the War Came*, 14.

62. William H. Herndon and Jesse W. Weik, *Herndon's Lincoln*, eds. Douglas L. Wilson and Rodney O. Davis (Chicago: Knox College/University of Illinois Press, 2006), 284.

63. Potter, *Lincoln and His Party in the Secession Crisis*, 76.

64. Potter, *The Impending Crisis*, 517.

65. Loughborough, "Sketches of the Past—No. 122," 1.

66. "The President and Disunion," *New York Times*, December 1, 1860, quoted in Stampp, *And the War Came*, 28 (emphasis in the original).

67. *New York Times*, December 21, 1860, quoted in Stampp, *And the War Came*, 69.

68. Walt Whitman, *Specimen Days and Collect* (New York: Dover Publications, 1995), 22.

69. *Clarke County Democrat*, January 10, 1861; *Atlanta Daily Intelligencer*, January 28, 1861; *Albany Patriot*,

November 15, 1860; quoted in Donald E. Reynolds, *Editors Make War: Southern Newspapers in the Secession Crisis* (Carbondale, IL: Southern Illinois University Press, 2006), 174.

70. Merton Coulter, *The Confederate States of America, 1861–1865* (Baton Rouge, LA: Louisiana State University Press/University of Texas, 1950), 15, quoted in McPherson, *Battle Cry of Freedom*, 238.

71. *Arkansas State Gazette*, January 5, 1861, quoted in Reynolds, *Editors Make War*, 167.

72. *Salisbury (NC) Daily Banner*, quoted in Reynolds, *Editors Make War*, 167.

73. Loughborough, *Rise and Progress*, 236.

74. The earliest published account of this statement found so far is from the *Plymouth Democrat*, December 26, 1861, 9, which stated that the abolitionists had declared, "The North could whip the South before breakfast,— that a few old women with broomsticks could quell the rebellion." Loughborough apparently paraphrased the statement, which is also found in the *Weekly Republican*, May 26, 1864, 10, and the *Athens Post*, August 7, 1868, 5. Researcher Kevin Burton first discovered these statements and brought them to my attention, for which I am grateful. Loughborough also wrote in *Rise and Progress* that "Horace Greeley, in the *Tribune*, about December, 1860, compared the secession of South Carolina to the little Scotch boy who was breaking through the hedge into a gentleman's garden, and was accosted by the owner with the words, 'Where are you going, sonte?' The lad at once quickly responded, 'Going back agin.' So, he said, with those trying to get out of the Union; as soon as sharply spoken to for their rebellion, they would say, 'Going back again' " (236). Years later, in his article "Sketches of the Past—No. 121," in the *Pacific Union Recorder*, for March 7, 1912, Loughborough told the same story and said it came from the "first week in January, 1861" of the *Tribune*. To date, neither I nor other researchers have been able to locate this citation from Greeley in the issues Loughborough mentioned. Neither have we been able to locate it in other issues of the *Tribune* during the approximate time period. It appears that with the lapse of time Loughborough may have been confused as to where he actually read the statement. Loughborough's biographer, Brian Strayer, noted that scholarly referencing was not important to the pioneer, a frustration to researchers today. Strayer, *J. N. Loughborough*, 327–329, 393–395.

75. "From Washington," *New-York Daily Tribune*, December 21, 1860, 4.

76. See Wikipedia contributors, "The Mountain in Labour," *Wikipedia*, accessed November 13, 2016, http://en.wikipedia.org/wiki/The_Mountain_in_Labour.

77. Emory M. Thomas, *The Confederate Nation, 1861–1865* (New York: Harper Perennial, 2011), 38.

78. Ibid.

79. Allan Nevins, *The Emergence of Lincoln*, vol. 2, *Prologue to Civil War, 1859–1861* (New York: Charles Scriber's Sons, 1950), 417.

80. Gary W. Gallagher, *The American Civil War*, The Great Courses (Chantilly, VA: Teaching Co., 2000), 44.

81. Long, *The Civil War Day by Day*. For specifics on what happened on each of these days, see E. B. Long, *The Civil War Day by Day*.

82. Thomas, *The Confederate Nation*, 63.

83. See Charles Robert Lee Jr., *The Confederate Constitutions* (Westport, CT: Greenwood Press, 1963), 182.

84. Alexander Stephens, quoted in Moore, *The Rebellion Record*, 1:45. This is known as Stephens's "Cornerstone" speech. Ibid., 1:44–49.

85. Potter, *The Impending Crisis*, 508.

86. W. D. Moss to William H. Seward, Moundsville, Virginia, February 6, 1861, in Frederick Bancroft, *The Life of William H. Seward* (New York: Harper & Bros., 1900), 2:533, 534, quoted in ibid.

87. Thaddeus Stevens, quoted in Daniel W. Crofts, *Reluctant Confederates: Upper South Unionists in the Secession* (Chapel Hill, NC: University of North Carolina Press, 1989), 153.

88. For details, see Potter, *The Impending Crisis*, 510; and Wooster, *The Secession Conventions of the South*, 139–255.

89. Potter, *The Impending Crisis*, 510.

90. For discussion on the division of the South, see William W. Freehling, *The South Vs. the South: How Anti-*

Confederate Southerners Shaped the Course of the Civil War (New York: Oxford University Press, 2001), 17–32, where he uses the terms *Lower South* for the seven-state Confederacy; *Middle South* for Arkansas, Tennessee, North Carolina, and Virginia; and *Border South* for Missouri, Kentucky, Maryland, and Delaware. I use the terms *Deep South, Upper South*, and *Border States*, most commonly used by historians. Missouri, Kentucky, Maryland, and Delaware were the "Border States," the four slave states that stayed in the Union throughout the war.

91. Ibid., 271.

92. Catton, *The Coming Fury*, 246.

93. Gallagher, *The American Civil War*, 66.

94. Basler, *The Collected Works of Abraham Lincoln*, 4:323.

95. Foote, *The Civil War*, 1:47.

96. Long, *The Civil War Day by Day*, 57.

97. For interesting and helpful narratives on the Fort Sumter crisis and bombing, see Maury Klein, *Days of Defiance: Sumter, Secession, and the Coming of the Civil War* (New York: Vintage Books, 1997); and David Detzer, *Allegiance: Fort Sumter, Charleston, and the Beginning of the Civil War* (New York: Harcourt, 2001).

98. Foote, *The Civil War*, 1:52.

99. See Wooster, *The Secession Conventions of the South*, 139–203.

100. Gallagher, *The American Civil War*, 69.

101. Ibid.

102. I have corrected some of Loughborough's errors in the spelling of the names and the timing of the conversation.

103. Loughborough must have been confused on the dates of his visits to Parkville because the son of Nathan Osborn (Frank A. Osborn) died in the war on October 4, 1862. Morgan, *Journeying to the Same Heaven*, 22, 23. So Loughborough would not have had a conversation with his father in January 1862 about his son's death. The likely date for this conversation was when Loughborough returned again to Parkville after Osborn's son had died, which occurred in January 1863. "Report From Bro. Loughborough," *Review and Herald*, January 20, 1863, 60. Because of a lack of data, this is only a working hypothesis. The research on these sons continues and future discoveries may change our conclusions yet again. As noted earlier, Loughborough was not always accurate in the details of his narratives.

104. This would have been Osborn's adopted son, Frank A. Osborn. See Morgan, *Journeying to the Same Heaven*, 22, 23.

105. Loughborough, "Sketches of the Past—No. 122," 1. These sons have not been documented at the time of this writing.

106. White, *Testimonies for the Church*, 1:260.

CHAPTER 4

THE REALITY

After the war began with the shelling of Fort Sumter in the spring of 1861, many Americans in both the North and the South believed that it would be short, decided by one or two major battles. One Alabama soldier believed that the next year would bring peace, "because we are going to kill the last Yankee before that time if there is any fight in them still. I believe that J. D. Walker's Brigade can whip 25,000 Yankees. I think I can whip 25 myself."[1] The Northern poet Walt Whitman remembered "a couple of companies of the Thirteenth Brooklyn, who rendezvoused at the city armory, and started thence as thirty-days' men, were all provided with pieces of rope, conspicuously tied to their musket barrels, with which to bring back each man a prisoner from the audacious South, to be led in a noose, on our men's early and triumphant return!"[2]

John N. Loughborough also recalled seeing a company of Union soldiers starting out at Battle Creek. "A jolly company they were too," he wrote, "as full of glee and hilarity as though going to a picnic; and as the train pulled out from the station, with waving hats and handkerchiefs they shouted, 'Good-by, boys, we'll all be back in six weeks.' "[3] On May 4, the *Harper's Weekly* concluded that "if Abraham Lincoln is equal to the position he fills, this war will be over by January, 1862."[4] And on May

6, Ulysses S. Grant wrote to his father: "My own opinion is that this War will be but of short duration."[5]

Such thoughts of a short war were in sharp contrast to Ellen White's January 1861 Parkville forecast of a "most terrible war." Even those leaders in the North and the South who did not share the popular view of a short war failed to comprehend the bloody reality depicted in her initial vision. According to Civil War historian James McPherson, these leaders "could not foresee the kind of conflict this war would become—a total war, requiring total mobilization of men and resources, destroying these men and resources on a massive scale, and ending only with unconditional surrender."[6] As Lee Eusey put it, "That there would be four years of blood-packed warfare, thousands of casualties, numerous fresh cemeteries, public and private debts as common as rainwater, and endless personal tragedies for both Northerners and Southerners, was frankly beyond the ken of most Americans."[7]

Reality of the Parkville vision

During the early summer of 1861, several military engagements took place, some of which were considered to be great battles at the time. But it was clear that the biggest fight would take place in Virginia, and many in the North hoped that this battle would end the war before winter. By mid-July, the Federal forces, led by General Irvin McDowell, moved westward from the Potomac toward Centreville and Manassas, Virginia, to face off with the Confederate forces around Manassas Junction, which were commanded by P. G. T. Beauregard. The combined Union forces converging on Manassas had about 28,450 soldiers, and the Confederates had about 32,230.[8] The Union would name this the First Battle of Bull Run ("First" because there was a second battle there in 1862), after the creek in the area, whereas the Confederates would name it the Battle of First Manassas, after the city.[9]

The battle began early on the morning of July 21 and lasted until about four-thirty in the afternoon. It was a hot day, and the fighting was intense. In the end, "it was the momentous fight of the amateurs, the battle where everything went wrong, the great day of awakening for the whole nation."[10] The Union troops were seized with sudden confusion and retreated back toward Washington, while the Confederates were unable to pursue them. It was a decisive tactical victory for the Confederates in the sense that the battle postponed any further Union efforts to invade the Virginia heartland for eight months.[11] For the Northerners, it was a shameful loss. "We are utterly and disgracefully routed, beaten, whipped," wrote a New Yorker upon hearing the news.[12] And Washington was seized with fear of a Confederate attack, which never came.[13]

The *New York Times* believed the fight was "the greatest battle ever fought on this continent."[14] It had more casualties than any previous battle and seemed like a terrible bloodletting to the Northern people. But in the context of the entire Civil War, the First Battle of Bull Run was no more than a moderately sized battle. Nevertheless, it was, as Walt Whitman described it, a "terrible shock" to the nation.[15] Each side realized that the dream of a short, glorious, and bloodless war was over.

For the first time, the nation was beginning to come to grips with what Ellen White had forecast more than six months earlier in Parkville, Michigan, as a "most terrible war." Her words in that little church on January 12, 1861, must have come to the minds of those who heard her. Perhaps they assumed that the vision was now fulfilled in this first "great" battle by Bull Run.

On August 3, about two weeks after the battle, however, Mrs. White experienced her second Civil War vision at Roosevelt, New York, and published it in the August 27, 1861, edition of the *Review and Herald*. She reminded her readers that the war was far from over: "I was shown that many realize not the extent of the evil which has come upon us. They have flattered themselves that the national difficulties would soon be settled, and confusion and war end; but all will be convinced that there is more reality in the matter than was anticipated. Many have looked for the North to strike a blow, and the controversy be ended."[16] Clearly, she wanted her people to understand that this first great battle at Manassas was only the beginning of an inescapably long and terrible war.

Hope of a short war renewed

While the Southern home front celebrated its victory, "the shock of defeat jolted the North into reality," and a "mood of grim determination replaced the incandescent optimism of the spring."[17] The day after the battle, Lincoln signed a bill for the enlistment of 500,000 three-year men, and three days later he signed a second bill authorizing another 500,000.[18] He also relieved General Irvin McDowell, put General George B. McClellan in command of the Army of the Potomac, and later made him general-in-chief of the U.S. Army upon Winfield Scott's retirement. McClellan had been a bright cadet at West Point, fought with distinction in the Mexican-American

War, experienced several minor victories early in the present war, and was charismatic in personality. When he took command of the incoming recruits around Washington, they were much disorganized, and he was just what they needed. A master organizer, McClellan took hold with a firm hand and reorganized the troops.[19] By the end of September, "he'd built the Army of the Potomac into a formidable force of more than 100,000 well-equipped and well-trained men."[20] The press "hailed McClellan as the man to save the country,"[21] and hope was renewed in the North. "The army was beginning to be an army, and the slapdash informality of the militia days was gone. The capital took heart."[22]

As the country transitioned into the winter months, however, McClellan's well-trained army made no major offensive, and Lincoln and the country grew impatient. They were still looking for a decisive battle to crush the Southern rebels, and McClellan's "magnificent army" was not moving.[23] Even McClellan's own soldiers were growing impatient. Elisha Hunt Rhodes, among them, wrote home on January 31, 1862: "I want to see service and have the war over so that I can go home."[24] During the month of February 1862, the *Atlantic Monthly* printed a poem by Julia Ward Howe. The inspiring words were not forgotten and were soon transported into the song "The Battle Hymn of the Republic." This moving hymn inspired Northern hearts and rekindled hope "that the 'swift sword' would become truly swift and strike home."[25]

The Parkville vision reaffirmed

It was in this setting that Ellen White published what was apparently a reaffirmation of the Parkville vision, along with a warning that the war would continue and that death, carnage, and suffering would increase. In *Testimony for the Church, No. 7*, published in February 1862, she wrote, "I saw greater distress in the land than we have yet witnessed. I heard groans and cries of distress, and saw large companies in active battle. I heard the booming of the cannon, the clash of arms, the hand-to-hand fight, and the groans and prayers of the dying. The ground was covered with the wounded and the dead. I saw desolate, despairing families, and pinching want in many dwellings. Even now many families are suffering want, but this will increase. The faces of many looked haggard, pale, and pinched with hunger."[26]

The language of this forecast is similar to that in the Parkville vision as related by Loughborough. Lee Eusey concluded from his research that Ellen White recast the 1861 Parkville vision in the context of the 1862 winter, when both sides were waiting for the armies to move. He thus observed, "A year had elapsed since her Parkville statements, and up to early 1862 it would seem that reality had not reached her initial concept of the war's immensity."[27] Accordingly, White wanted her readers to understand that the full force and fury of the war was about to commence.

Since White never gave any explanation as to the origin of this "greater distress in the land" vision, it is also possible to view it as a part of her third war vision (the Battle Creek vision of January 1862) that reaffirmed what she had seen in the Parkville vision. In the context of *Testimony for the Church, No. 7*,[28] for instance, it follows the January 1862 Battle Creek vision.[29] The opening sentence, "I saw greater distress in the land than we have yet witnessed," could have indicated a new revelation that contextualized the contents of the Parkville vision to the winter of 1862. What they had "yet witnessed" was the 1861 summer and fall battles of First Bull Run, Wilson's Creek, and Ball's Bluff. Each battle had its own death and carnage, with the First Battle of Bull Run being the greatest. But the prediction noted that there was to be "greater distress" than was associated with the 1861 battles.

Readers of *Testimony for the Church, No. 7* probably noted that she was stating information that everyone already knew from the carnage of the previous battles—the booming of the cannon, the clash of arms, and so on. But White's point was that greater trouble was ahead, that the "groans and cries of distress" in the nation would occur in an epic proportion previously unknown. The language of the 1862 prediction thus described an *intensification* of that which had already taken place in the early phase of the war. The *reality* of a "most terrible war" with unprecedented casualties was about to strike the nation.

This forecast of greater war ahead was part of the larger vision that dealt with other war issues and especially spiritual preparation. "God alone can be our shield and strength in this time of our national calamities," she penned. "Greater perils are before us, and yet we are not awake."[30] Above all, her great concern was to prepare her people for the return of Christ. "There is no help for us but in God; in this state of earth's confusion we can be composed, strong, or safe, only in the strength of living faith; nor can we be at peace, only as we rest in God and wait for His salvation."[31]

The following sections will discuss phrases in White's forecast in relation to what happened in the war after the winter of 1862: large companies, wounded and the dead, groans and prayers of the dying, suffering families, and prisons.

Large companies

At the time of the Parkville vision in January 1861, the U.S. Army was small, with approximately 16,000 officers and men, and it decreased in size when Southerners left to join the Confederacy in the spring. The size of the Union army increased dramatically, however, after Lincoln's call for 75,000 men on April 15, 1861, to serve ninety days and then another call for 42,035 army volunteers to serve for three years, unless discharged sooner. Within days of the defeat at the First Battle of Bull Run in Manassas, Virginia, on July 21, "Lincoln signed two bills authorizing the enlistment of one million additional men for three years," as noted earlier. By the end of the war, approximately 2.2 million men served the Union armies, and the Confederacy was able to generate between 750,000 and 850,000 soldiers for their military force.[32] Thus, approximately 3 million soldiers fought in the Civil War.[33]

This created the numbers for the "large companies" that gathered on the fields of battle throughout the war. The First Battle of Bull Run on July 21, 1861, involved 60,680 forces (Union 28,450; Confederate 32,230).[34] Two months after Ellen White published the account of "greater distress" coming to the land in *Testimony for the Church, No. 7* (February 1862), about 110,053 men (Union 65,085; Confederate 44,968) clashed in the woods of Tennessee at the Battle of Shiloh (April 6–7, 1862). This was a battle almost twice the size of the forces engaged at the First Battle of Bull Run.[35] Shiloh caused more casualties than all of America's previous wars combined at that time and was "the first battle on a scale that became commonplace during the next three years."[36]

Shiloh shattered all hopes of a quick end to the war. "Up to the battle of Shiloh," recalled Ulysses S. Grant, "I, as well as thousands of other citizens, believed that the rebellion against the Government would collapse suddenly and soon, if a decisive victory could be gained over any of its armies." But with no decisive victory at Shiloh, Grant concluded that the Union could only be saved by "complete conquest."[37] And this conquest could only be accomplished by an invasion into the Confederate heartland. The Confederacy also realized after Shiloh that a long and hard war was ahead. Thus, Ellen White's January 1861 depiction of a "most terrible war" and her February 1862 warning of "greater distress in the land than we have yet witnessed" became a *horrible reality* in the Battle of Shiloh and afterward, when the "war exploded into full-scale combat."[38]

Note the size of several major battles:

Antietam on September 16–18, 1862	131,000 forces engaged (Union 87,000; Confederate 45,000)
Fredericksburg on December 11–15, 1862	172,504 forces engaged (Union 100,007; Confederate 72,497)
Chancellorsville on April 30–May 6, 1863	154,734 forces engaged (Union 97,382; Confederate 57,352)
Gettysburg on July 1–3, 1863	165,620 forces engaged (Union 93,921; Confederate 71,699)
The Wilderness on May 5–7, 1864	169,920 forces engaged (Union 101,895; Confederate 61,025)
Spotsylvania Court House on May 8–21, 1864	152,000 forces engaged (Union 100,000; Confederate 52,000)
Cold Harbor on May 31–June 12, 1864	170,000 forces engaged (Union 108,000; Confederate 62,000)[39]

Not all forces were engaged on every day of a battle, but daily battles can clearly be described as "large companies in active battle." As such, Ellen White's forecast of large armies clashing into one another accurately reflected the major Civil War battles during the last three years of the war.

The wounded and the dead covering the ground

"Whether fired from artillery or small arms," explained Earl J. Hess, "millions of lethal projectiles filled the air on every Civil War battlefield." Often, lines of soldiers would go down in heaps from an intense barrage of missiles. "You have seen, in a bowling alley or the beach, a ball rolled into the pins and all but two or three fall," a Union soldier recalled, "so have I seen human beings fall around me and I left standing." The impact of these projectiles seriously "traumatized any part of their [soldiers'] bodies that chance allowed." Many soldiers recalled the sound of bullets and other projectiles striking human flesh and bone. "The noise could be poignant—'a thud, a sickening, dull cracking sound.' " Worst of all was the sight of a comrade's body ripped apart under the impact of artillery. One soldier "watched an infantryman's leg ripped off by a solid shot at Gettysburg. The limb 'whirled like a stone through the air, until it came against a caisson with a loud whack.' "[40] Such devastation caused the Civil War battlefields to be littered with the "wounded and the dead."

The writings of those who participated in the Civil War are replete with vivid descriptions of the dead and dying on the battlefields. Below are eyewitness accounts of the shock and awe generated by the sight of massive loss of life after the Battles of Shiloh, Antietam, Fredericksburg, and Gettysburg.[41]

Battle of Shiloh, April 6–7, 1862 (23,746 estimated casualties)
- After the first day of the Battle of Shiloh, one soldier remembered, "At midnight a heavy rain set in, accompanied by peal after peal of thunder, together with the roaring of the cannon and the bursting of shell. The flashes of lightning revealed the ghastly features of the dead. . . . Oh, what a night of horrors that was!"[42]
- William Tecumseh Sherman described the scene in a letter to his wife: "The scenes on this field would have cured anybody of war. Mangled bodies, dead, dying, in every conceivable shape, without heads, legs; and horses!"[43]
- Grant recalled the aftermath of the battlefield: "Shiloh was the severest battle fought at the West during the war, and but few in the East equalled it for hard, determined fighting. I saw an open field, in our possession on the second day, over which the Confederates had made repeated charges the day before, so covered with dead that it would have been possible to walk across the clearing, in any direction, stepping on dead bodies, without a foot touching the ground."[44]
- One Confederate soldier described the Union dead and dying: "They

Some of the dead covering the ground after the Battle of
Antietam on the Hagerstown Turnpike, north of the Dunker Church.
Photograph by Alexander Gardner

were mangled in every conceivable form. Some were in the last agonies of death. I could not pass a wounded man without saying 'God have mercy on him.' "[45]

Battle of Antietam, September 17, 1862 (22,717 estimated casualties)
September 17, 1862, at Antietam was the bloodiest day of battle in American history. On that day sixty-five hundred to seven thousand men were killed in action. According to one estimate, approximately "one man died every five or six seconds of the battle."[46] The intensity of the combat is incomparable in the annals of American military history.

According to historian James McPherson,

The number of casualties in one day at the battle of Antietam . . . was nearly four times the number of American casualties on D-Day, June 6, 1944. Twice as many people were killed and mortally wounded than were killed by the terrorist attacks on the United States on September 11, 2001. Indeed, the number of battle deaths in one day at Antietam exceeded the total battle deaths in all the other wars the United States fought in the nineteenth century; the War of 1812; the Mexican-American War; the Spanish-American war; and the Indian wars.[47]

- Lieutenant Elisha Hunt Rhodes of the Second Rhode Island Volunteers was startled by the carnage on the Antietam battlefield the day after: "I have never in my soldier life seen such a sight. The dead and wounded covered the ground."[48]
- The colonel of the Sixth Wisconsin described the Hagerstown turnpike as "indescribably horrible," and recalled that as he rode through the scattered corpses of men and animals, his horse "trembled in every limb with fright and was wet with perspiration."[49]
- "Union Lt. George F. Noyes spoke for many who witnessed the aftermath of the slaughter at Antietam: 'No matter in what direction we turned, it was all the same shocking picture, awakening awe rather than pity, benumbing the senses rather than touching the heart, glazing the eye with horror rather than filling it with tears.' "[50]
- Soldier and former *Harper's* correspondent, David H. Strother, remem-

bered that the dead bodies were gruesomely bloated and blackened: "Many were so covered with dust, torn, crushed and trampled that they resembled clods of earth and you were obliged to look twice before recognizing them as human beings."[51]

Battle of Fredericksburg, December 13, 1862 (17,929 estimated casualties)
- "*London Times* correspondent Francis Charles Lawley, who viewed the battle from the Confederate lines, reported victors' view of the terrible toll exacted on Union troops: 'Not for 50 years to come will that scene ever fade from the memory of those who saw it. There, in every attitude of death, lying so close to each other that you might step from body to body, lay acres of the Federal dead.' "[52]
- E. R. Hutchins walked around the perimeter of the Fredericksburg battlefield the night after the battle and observed "mangled forms, rent and tossed, as if maddened beasts of the arena had run riot among them. Limbs flung from their bodies, and half trampled in the mire. Grave faces, stark and stiff and deadly pale, looking like phantom lights. They looked like something neither dead nor living, with a fixedness that was more than stillness. There were open eyes that saw not, and hands still grasping muskets with a clutch that no living strength could loose. Horses, cannoneers, dismounted guns, crashed wheels, overturned gun carriages, the tongues upright in the air, and the yokes swinging like gibbets on high."[53]

Battle of Gettysburg, July 1–2, 1863 (51,112 estimated casualties)
The estimated casualties in battles during 1863 would peak at Gettysburg. The description of Robert Carter of the Twenty-Second Massachusetts, who saw the battlefields of Gettysburg immediately following the engagements, is most vivid: "In every direction among the bodies was the debris of battle—haversacks, canteens, hats, caps, sombreros, blankets of every shade and hue, bayonets, cartridge boxes—every conceivable part of the equipment of a soldier. . . . Corpses strewed the ground at every step. Arms, legs, heads, and parts of dismembered bodies were scattered all about, and sticking among the rocks, and against the trunks of trees, hair, brains, entrails and shreds of human flesh still hung, a disgusting, sickening, heartrending spectacle to our young minds."[54]

Many other testimonies of battlefields could be cited, such as the horrors of the Wilderness, Spotsylvania, and Cold Harbor in 1864. But perhaps the best summary of the fearful sights in a wide-angled view of a Civil War battlefield came from a Union cavalry officer who, after the Seven Days Battles, observed the slopes of Malvern Hill on July 2, 1862: "Our ears had been filled with agonizing cries from thousands before the fog was lifted, but now our eyes saw an appalling spectacle upon the slopes down to the woodlands half a mile away. Over five thousand dead and wounded men were on the ground, in every attitude of distress. A third of them were dead or dying, but enough were alive and moving to give to the field a singular crawling effect."[55]

Thus, Ellen White's brief depiction of the dead and dying on the Civil War battlefields vividly captured four years of horrific carnage. Shelby Foote observed "that casualties in Civil War battles were so far beyond anything we can imagine now. If we had 10 percent casualties in a battle today, it would be looked on as a bloodbath. They had 30 percent in several battles."[56] James McPherson estimated in 2015 that if the same percentage of Americans were to be killed in a war fought today as those killed in the Civil War (2.4 percent), the number of American war dead would be about 7.5 million.[57]

Groans and prayers of the dying

A most vivid account of the sound of those dying on the Civil War battlefield came from Joshua L. Chamberlain, at the time a lieutenant colonel with the Twentieth Maine Volunteers, who was stuck on the Fredericksburg battlefield, lying among the bodies the night after the battle. His retelling of that unforgettable night is haunting:

> But out of silence from the battle's crash and roar rose new sounds more appalling still; rose or fell, you know not which, or whether from the earth or air; a strange ventriloquism, of which you could not locate the source, a smothered moan that seemed to come from distances beyond reach of the natural sense, a wail so far and deep and wide, as if a thousand discords were flowing together into a key-note, weird, unearthly, terrible to hear and bear, yet startling with its nearness; the writhing concord broken by cries for help, pierced by shrieks of paroxysm; some begging for a drop of water; some calling on God for pity; and some on friendly hands to finish what the enemy had so horribly begun; some with delirious, dreamy voices murmuring love names, as if the dearest

were bending over them; some gathering their last strength to fire a musket to call attention to them where they lay helpless and deserted; and underneath, all the time, that deep bass note from closed lips too hopeless or too heroic to articulate their agony.[58]

Suffering families

"Even now many families are suffering want," White wrote in February 1862, "but this will increase. The faces of many looked haggard, pale, and pinched with hunger."[59] This depiction forecast the starvation of civilians during the Civil War, especially in the South. It is noteworthy that she observed "suffering want … will increase." This is precisely what happened when the Union forces invaded the South. According to Marilyn Mayer Culpepper in her *Trials and Triumphs: The Women of the American Civil War*, "The ravages of war left countless women (particularly Southerners) absolutely destitute." After the siege of Atlanta, for example, one Southern woman recalled:

I could not be oblivious to the fact that I was hungry, very hungry. And there was another [her mother], whose footsteps were becoming more and more feeble day by day and whose voice, when heard at all, was full of the pathos of despair, who needed nourishment that could not be obtained, and consolation, which it seemed a mockery to offer.

In vain did I look round for relief. There was nothing left in the country to eat. Yea, a crow flying over it would have failed to discover a morsel with which to appease its hunger.[60]

Another eyewitness described the devastation and deprivation in the South:

Well, the struggles of the war continued to rage till the South was famine stricken. The material for making clothing was all gone, the wolf was at the door of all those who had been independently wealthy and were reduced to the utmost poverty. There had been no crops raised for four years in the large part of the country. The fences had been burned, the houses had been destroyed and mules taken from the farms and many of the beautiful houses left in ashes. It was a discouraged, nearly broken people and many thousands felt that life was not worth living and gave up in despair.[61]

ANDERSONVILLE PRISON

AS SEEN BY

JOHN L. RANSOM,

AUTHOR AND PUBLISHER OF "ANDERSONVILLE DIARY, ESCAPE AND LIST OF THE DEAD,"

WASHINGTON, D. C.

1. Head Quarters,
2. Rebel Camp,
3. Hospital,
4. Cook House,
5. Death House,
6. Death Line,
7. The Island,
8. Sutler's Camp,
9. Police Quarters,

10. Hospitals along the Death Line,
11. Market Street,
12. Broad Street,
13. Inside Stockade,
14. Second Line Stockade,
15. Third Line Stockade,
16. Lieut. Head Quarters,
17. Washing Place,
18. Rifle Pits,
19. Some House Mess,

Civil War prisons

According to the Loughborough account of the Parkville vision, White stated that she saw prisons: "Then I was carried to prisons, and saw the sufferings of those in want, who were wasting away."[62] In *Testimony for the Church, No. 7*, several pages before the forecast of the worsening condition of the war, she wrote that the Civil War prisons at the time (in 1862) were "a fate more to be dreaded than death."[63]

When the war began, neither the United States nor the Confederacy possessed the facilities or the ability to house and care for the huge numbers of prisoners over four years. Confident that the war would be short lived, they failed to anticipate such circumstances. As the warring sides went off to battle, neither could foresee the grand scale of suffering attendant to Civil War prisons. Consequently, the prison systems in both the North and South initially functioned on a provisional basis until the numbers of prisoners got out of control. "This short-sighted approach to the treatment of prisoners led to one of the war's great horrors: tens of thousands of men corralled into unsanitary pens, often exposed to the elements, without the food, exercise, shelter, or clean water needed to sustain them."[64]

Civil War prisons have been appropriately described by one historian as "portals to hell."[65] Of the 150 prisons during the war, Elmira in the North (New York State) and Andersonville in the South (Georgia) stand out as especially terrible. Andersonville was more like a concentration camp and came to symbolize the horrors of Civil War prisoners. This stockade camp of sixteen acres, located in southwest Georgia, was originally designed for ten thousand prisoners. But by August 1864, it had been enlarged to twenty-six acres and packed with thirty-three thousand men, "an average of thirty-four square feet per man—without shade in a Deep South summer and with no shelter except what they could rig from sticks, tent flies, blankets, and odd bits of cloth."[66]

Within months of Andersonville's establishment, prisoners reported that upon entering the front gates, the sights and smell of the compound caused them to double over and vomit.[67] According to one historian, "the whole stockade reeked with an overpowering stench. In the absence of prison discipline, prisoners were very careless of sanitary practices, and men suffering from chronic diarrhea and others too sick to get to the latrines deposited human wastes all over the stockade."[68] Additionally, the main stream that ran through the prison and supplied water for washing and drinking was contaminated with human excrement. When the stream was swollen from rains, according to one medical professional, the lower part of the stockade was "overflowed by a solution of excrement, which, subsiding and the surface exposed to the sun, produces a horrible stench."[69] Worst of all, sick prisoners often laid "on the ground in their own excrements" and died.[70]

Another aspect of suffering found in Andersonville was "insufficiency of rations and inadequacy of wood for cooking." One prisoner described the starving conditions: "None will ever realize the suffering here but those that live to endure and live through it. . . . Men actually starve to death here for want of food. We are now getting scant rations of beef, some of the wormiest types I ever did see, and one-quarter ration of corn bread, one spoonful of salt a day and not one fifth wood enough to cook with." Resourceful prisoners "killed low-flying birds and ate them raw as soon as they were dead."[71]

One South Carolinian summed up Andersonville: "It is a singular sight to look down into this enclosure. The suffering within both mind and body is fearful, and one can only compare it to a Hades on Earth. The dirt, filth, and stench in and around the Stockade is awful. I frequently see the Yankees picking from their bodies lice and fleas."[72] It is no small wonder that, at its worst, approximately one hundred men died per day at Andersonville. Of the more than forty-one thousand men who found themselves there throughout its existence, thirteen thousand died.[73] Thus, Ellen White's view of men "wasting away" accurately described the fate of many prisoners in Andersonville and in the many other prisons of the Civil War, both North and South.

Conclusion

If the statements in the above January 1861 and January 1862 visions are considered to be genuine prophetic utterances and dated before the Civil War really got underway, then they can be explained as being uniformly vindicated in the events of the war itself. The broad strokes that Ellen White provided gave an ominous yet realistic portrayal of events that transpired in the course of the war. One of her most interesting insights into the war came after the First Battle of Bull Run, in which she saw in vision an angel descend and intervene in the battle, and then she forecast the outcome of the Union battles throughout the duration of the war, which the next section is devoted to.

Chapter in a nutshell

Early in the war, many Americans believed the conflict would be short, decided by one or two major battles. Even after the devastating battle of First Manassas on July 21, 1861, the hope of a short war renewed, especially in the North. In this setting, Ellen White published a warning that the war would linger on and that death, carnage, and suffering would increase. This vision, published in *Testimony for the Church, No. 7* in February 1862, was very similar to the contents of the winter 1861 Parkville vision. It appeared to be a recasting of this vision in the context of winter 1862. It could have been a new revelation that contextualized the contents of the Parkville vision to the winter of 1862. The language described an intensification of that which had already taken place in the early phase of the war. The reality of White's original January 1861 prediction of a "most terrible war" with unprecedented casualties officially began with the Battle of Shiloh. Her language in both the 1861 and 1862 accounts—large companies on the battlefield, the wounded and the dead covering the ground, the groans and prayers of the dying, suffering families, and prisons—forecast the events of the war from that time forward. The broad strokes that she provided to the Adventist audience gave an ominous yet realistic portrayal of the events that actually transpired.

1. Quoted in McPherson, *Battle Cry of Freedom*, 333.

2. Whitman, *Specimen Days and Collect*, 22.

3. Loughborough, *Rise and Progress*, 238. After this remembrance, Loughborough added, "But, poor fellows, many of them never returned."

4. "The War," *Harper's Weekly*, May 4, 1861, 274.

5. Ulysses S. Grant to Jesse Root Grant, May 6, 1861, quoted in Brooks D. Simpson, Stephen W. Sears, and Aaron Sheehan-Dean, eds., *The Civil War: The First Year Told by Those Who Lived It* (New York: Library of America, 2011), 348.

6. McPherson, *Battle Cry of Freedom*, 333.

7. Eusey, "The American Civil War," 16.

8. See "Bull Run," Civil War Trust, accessed November 13, 2016, http://www.civilwar.org/battlefields/bullrun.html?tab=facts; and Gallagher, *The American Civil War: Lectures 1–24,* 130, 131, for a similar estimate.

9. This was typical for naming the battles. The North generally chose a physical landmark nearest to the battle (Bull Run), whereas the Confederates chose the town they used for their base (Manassas). For some battles, the names were used interchangeably. See McPherson, *Battle Cry of Freedom*, 346n7.

10. Bruce Catton, *The Civil War* (New York: Mariner Books, 2004), 42.

11. McPherson, *Battle Cry of Freedom*, 346, 347.

12. Quoted in ibid., 347.

13. Ibid., 346.

14. H. J. R., "The Greatest Battle Ever Fought on This Continent," *New York Times*, July 22, 1861, in Harold Holzer and Craig L. Symonds, eds., *The "New York Times": Complete Civil War, 1861–1865* (New York: Black Dog & Leventhal Publishers, 2010), 94.

15. Whitman, *Specimen Days and Collect*, 22.

16. See also White, *Testimonies for the Church*, 1:264.

17. James McPherson and James K. Hogue, *Ordeal by Fire: The Civil War and Reconstruction*, 4th ed. (New York: McGraw-Hill Education, 2010), 232.

18. McPherson, *Battle Cry of Freedom*, 348.

19. McPherson and Hogue, *Ordeal by Fire*, 232. For the standard biography of McClellan, see Stephen W. Sears, *George B. McClellan: The Young Napoleon* (New York: Da Capo Press, 1999).

20. Gallagher, *The American Civil War: Lectures 1–24*, 192.

21. McPherson and Hogue, *Ordeal by Fire*, 233.

22. Catton, *The Civil War*, 54.

23. McPherson and Hogue, *Ordeal by Fire*, 234.

24. Elisha Hunt Rhodes, diary entry for January 31, 1862, in *All for the Union: The Civil War Diary and Letters of Elisha Hunt Rhodes*, ed. Robert Hunt Rhodes (New York: Vintage Books, 1992), 46.

25. Long, *The Civil War Day by Day*, 165. For discussion on the poem, see Terrie Dopp Aamodt, *Righteous Armies, Holy Cause: Apocalyptic Imagery and the Civil War* (Macon, GA: Mercer University Press, 2002), 81–86, 165, 166.

26. White, *Testimony for the Church, No. 7*, 11, 12; see also White, *Testimonies for the Church*, 1:260.

27. Eusey, "The American Civil War," 18.

28. White, *Testimonies for the Church*, 1:253–260.

29. Ibid., 1:253.

30. Ibid., 1:260.

31. Ibid., 1:262.

32. Margaret E. Wagner, Gary W. Gallagher, and Paul Finkelman, eds., *The Library of Congress Civil War Desk Reference* (New York: Simon & Schuster, 2002), 376; Gallagher, *The American Civil War: Lectures 1–24*, 77.

33. The Web site of the Civil War Trust gives the precise figure of 3,211,067. See "Civil War Facts," Civil War Trust, accessed November 14, 2016, http://www.civilwar.org/education/history/faq.

34. These figures are derived from "Bull Run," Civil War Trust, accessed November 14, 2016, http://www.civilwar.org/battlefields/bullrun.html?tab=facts.

35. These figures are derived from "Shiloh," Civil War Trust, accessed November 14, 2016, http://www.civilwar.org/battlefields/shiloh.html?tab=facts.

36. McPherson, *Battle Cry of Freedom*, 413.

37. Grant, *Memoirs and Selected Letters*, 246.

38. Wagner, Gallagher, and Finkelman, *Civil War Desk Reference*, 250.

39. These battle statistics are derived from "Civil War Battlefields," Civil War Trust, accessed November 14, 2016, http://www.civilwar.org/battlefields/.

40. Earl J. Hess, *The Union Soldier in Battle: Enduring the Ordeal of Combat* (Lawrence, KS: University Press of Kansas, 1997), 27, 28.

41. See "Civil War Battlefields," Civil War Trust, accessed November 14, 2016, http://www.civilwar.org/battlefields/ for casualty estimates used for each battle. For slightly different casualty estimates, see Wagner, Gallagher, and Finkelman, *Civil War Desk Reference*, 252, 266, 282, 306–308.

42. Quoted in Neil Kagan and Stephen Hyslop, eds., *Eyewitness to the Civil War: The Complete History From Secession to Reconstruction* (Washington, DC: National Geographic Society, 2006), 115.

43. William T. Sherman to Ellen Ewing Sherman, April 11, 1862, quoted in Stephen W. Sears, ed., *The Civil War: The Second Year Told by Those Who Lived It* (New York: Library of America, 2012), 166.

44. Grant, *Memoirs and Selected Letters*, 238, 239.

45. Quoted in Kagan and Hyslop, *Eyewitness to the Civil War*, 111.

46. Richard K. Kolb, "Antietam: America's Deadliest Day," *Veterans of Foreign Affairs*, September 2012, 38, http://digitaledition.qwinc.com/article/Antietam%3A_America's_Deadliest_Day/1135327/120990/article.html.

47. James McPherson, foreword to *The Library of Congress Civil War Desk Reference*, edited by Margaret E. Wagner, Gary W. Gallagher, and Paul Finkelman (New York: Simon & Schuster, 2002), xvii.

48. Rhodes, *All for the Union*, 73.

49. Quoted in Bruce Catton, *The Army of the Potomac: Mr. Lincoln's Army* (Garden City, NY: Doubleday & Company, Inc., 1962), 318.

50. Quoted in Kolb, "Antietam: America's Deadliest Day," 39.

51. Quoted in Bruce Catton, *Terrible Swift Sword* (Garden City, NY: Doubleday & Company, 1963, 458.

52. Quoted in Wagner, Gallagher, and Finkelman, *Civil War Desk Reference*, 273.

53. Quoted in Brent Nosworthy, *The Bloody Crucible of Courage: Fighting Methods and Combat Experience of the Civil War* (New York: Carroll & Graf, 2003), 228. Nosworthy considers this "one of the most vivid descriptions of the aftermath of a Civil War battle" (228).

54. Quoted in Hess, *The Union Soldier in Battle*, 37, 38.

55. William W. Averell, "With the Cavalry on the Peninsula," in *Battles and Leaders of the Civil War*, ed. Robert Underwood Johnson and Clarence Clough Buel (Secaucus, NJ: Castle, 1982), 2:432.

56. Shelby Foote, "Men at War: An Interview With Shelby Foote," in Geoffrey C. Ward, *The Civil War: An Illustrated History* (New York: Alfred A. Knopf, 1990), 273.

57. James McPherson, *The War That Forged a Nation: Why the Civil War Still Matters* (New York: Oxford University Press, 2015), 2.

58. Joshua L. Chamberlain, "Night on the Field of Fredericksburg," in Henry Steele Commager, *The Blue and the Gray: The Story of the Civil War as Told by Participants* (New York: Bobbs-Merrill, 1950), 247.

59. White, *Testimonies for the Church*, 1:260.

60. Marilyn Mayer Culpepper, *Trials and Triumphs: The Women of the American Civil War* (East Lansing, MI: Michigan State University Press, 1991), 199.

61. Virginia Norfleet, quoted in ibid., 205.

62. Loughborough, *Rise and Progress*, 237.

63. White, *Testimonies for the Church*, 1:255.

64. Wagner, Gallagher, and Finkelman, *Civil War Desk Reference*, 583.

65. Lonnie R. Speer, *Portals to Hell: Military Prisons of the Civil War* (Lincoln, NE: University of Nebraska Press, 2005).

66. McPherson, *Battle Cry of Freedom*, 796.

67. Speer, *Portals to Hell*, 259.

68. Ovid L. Futch, *History of Andersonville Prison*, rev. ed. (Gainesville, FL: University Press of Florida, 2011), 38.

69. Ibid.

70. Eliza Frances Andrews, *The War-Time Journal of a Georgia Girl, 1864–1865* (Lincoln, NE: University of Nebraska Press, 1997), 78.

71. Futch, *History of Andersonville Prison*, 37.

72. Ibid., 45. For other discussion on the history of Andersonville and its horrors, see Robert Scott Davis, *Andersonville Civil War Prison* (Charleston, SC: History Press, 2010), 53–6. For a firsthand account of a prisoner, see John L. Ransom, *John Ransom's Andersonville Diary: Life Inside the Civil War's Most Infamous Prison* (New York: Berkley Books, 1994).

73. Gallagher, *The American Civil War: Lectures 25-48* (Chantilly, VA: Teaching Co., 2000), 303; and McPherson, *Battle Cry of Freedom*, 796.

PART III

ROOSEVELT VISION (AUGUST 1861):
"GOD HAD THIS NATION IN HIS OWN HAND"

CHAPTER 5

AN ANGEL ON THE BATTLEFIELD

During the hot afternoon of July 21, 1861, in Manassas, Virginia, the first major battle of the Civil War came to a sudden end. The entire Union army commenced a universal retreat from the battlefield and fled all the way back to Washington, D.C. This was a victory "entirely unexpected by the rebels."[1] In the days following the disaster, the North was in despair and couldn't understand the sudden retreat of Federal troops from the battlefield. "The secret of that panic," according to the *New-York Daily Tribune*, "will perhaps never be known. All essay to explain it, and all fail."[2] Ellen White, however, provided her readers with a unique explanation of the battle's end: an angel caused the retreat.

The expectation that the war would be over in one major battle was shattered, and a season of public gloom cast its shadow over the North. In the columns of the *Review and Herald*, one writer cited the words of a friend who expressed the national sentiment: "Nothing but war, war, war, in every man's mouth!"[3] In the context of this national feeling, James and Ellen White left Michigan on a eastern tour and reached Roosevelt, New York. Two weeks after the battle in Manassas, on August 3, while attending a conference at the Roosevelt church, Ellen experienced her second war vision that brought encouragement to her fellow believers. Her insights gave these church members a sense of security and confidence in the midst of the recent loss. The Roosevelt vision addressed the philosophy of the war and the sin of slavery, but at its core, it was a description of the Battle of First Manassas, or Bull Run,[4] which pulled back the veil that hid the invisible world:

> I had a view of the late disastrous battle at Manassas, Va.[5] It was a most exciting, thrilling, distressing scene. The Southern army had everything in their favor, and were prepared for a dreadful contest. The Northern army was moving on with triumph, not doubting but that they would be victorious. Many were reckless, and marched forward boastingly as though victory were already theirs. As they neared the battle-field, many were almost fainting through weariness and want of refreshment. They did not expect so fierce an encounter. They rushed into battle and fought bravely, desperately. The dead and dying were on every side. Both the North and the South suffered severely. The Southern men felt the battle, and in a little [while] would have been driven back still further. Northern men were rushing on, although their destruction was very great. Just then an angel descended and waved his hand backward. Instantly there was confusion in their ranks. It appeared to the Northern men that their troops were retreating, when it was not in reality so; and a precipitate retreat commenced. This seemed wonderful to me. Then it was explained, that God had this nation in his own hand, and would suffer no victories to be gained faster than he ordained, and no more losses to the Northern men than in his wisdom he saw fit, to punish the North for their sin. And in this battle had the Northern army pushed the battle still further, in their fainting, exhausted condition, a far greater struggle and destruction awaited them, which would have caused great triumph in the South. God would not permit this, and sent an angel to interfere. The sudden falling back of the Northern troops was a mystery to all. They knew not that God's hand was in the matter.[6]

Of all Ellen White's comments on the Civil War, this one is the most outstanding. The point of this testimony is that God would control the battles of the oncoming war in such a way as to accomplish his purposes of punishing the nation, yet giving the North victory in the end. Lee Eusey, who made the first attempt to study this battle in relation to Ellen White's vision, posed the following questions in his 1965 master's thesis: "Is her account plausible? What evidence is there to support such a conception of the panic? Must one discard this as a theory not meriting consideration, or can it become a part of one's ponderable information?"[7] This chapter follows Eusey's work on the First Battle of Bull Run, updating it with the wealth of research on the battle since 1965.[8]

The contents of the vision can be summarized in the following points:

1. The Confederates had prepared to fight at this place.
2. The encounter was determined and hard fought, while the reckless Northerners expected a victory to be within their grasp.
3. The stampede occurred as the Southerners were about to withdraw.
4. The Federal troops would have suffered an awful decimation had they pressed their advances still deeper into the Confederate front.
5. At this critical moment, confusion struck the attacking regiments of the Union troops; they concluded that their front ranks were in retreat, when actually they had not been absolutely repulsed.
6. The assaulting forces broke into sudden confusion and abandoned the field.
7. God had this nation in His hand and would intervene in the battles.
8. Emancipation was at stake—victory would have to wait.
9. The sudden retreat was a mystery to all.[9]

With these introductory points in mind, an overview of the battle will set the context for a more detailed analysis afterward.

Overview of the battle

On Tuesday, July 16, 1861, Brigadier General Irvin McDowell finally moved his Federal army of approximately twenty-eight thousand men westward from the Potomac toward Centreville and Manassas, Virginia. His plan was to scatter or drive back General P. G. T. Beauregard's Confederate army of about twenty thousand from Manassas Junction and move on to Richmond.[10] At the same time, an army of eighteen thousand men under the command of Robert Patterson, positioned in the lower Shenandoah Valley, was to advance against the twelve thousand Confederates also in the same valley, commanded by Joseph Eggleston Johnston, and keep them from reinforcing Beauregard at Manassas. This would ensure McDowell's numerical advantage in the attack. "If everything went well as planned, Richmond might be taken within the month, and the war end . . . that is, if everything went as planned."[11]

But nothing went according to plan. The twenty-five-mile march to Centreville, the place from which the invasion would be launched, was a disaster and took twice as long as it should have. In the meantime, Beauregard had placed his twenty thousand men at fords or crossing sites along the southern bank of the Bull Run, which flowed southeast halfway between Centreville and Manassas Junction. Any army advancing toward Richmond must come through this area, and the Confederate army was prepared to block it. Once Beauregard was alerted to the advancing Northern army through the Washington newspapers and intelligence, he immediately began fortifying his forces and preparing them for the attack.

"The night of July 20, 1861," explained historian Charles P. Poland Jr., "saw commanders of both sides planning to attack the other the next day. Men in both moonlit camps anxiously pondered their fate."[12] McDowell planned to attack Beauregard on his left, hoping to outflank him and collapse his line on Bull Run, and Beauregard planned a similar move on McDowell's left. "If both had moved according to plan," wrote Shelby Foote, "the two armies might have grappled and spun round and round, like a pair of dancers clutching each other and twirling to the accompaniment of cannon. However, this could only happen if both moved on schedule."[13]

McDowell began the advance of his army at two-thirty in the morning on Sunday, July 21, hoping to surprise the Confederate left flank at seven o'clock in the morning. The troops stumbled through the darkness of night in a stop-and-go pace, bone tired from the lack of sleep and terribly behind schedule. The plan was for Brigadier General Daniel Tyler's division to provide a fake attack at the heavily guarded Stone Bridge and for Colonel I. B. Richardson's division to do the same at Blackburn's Ford, where an engagement had taken place three days before. This would draw attention away from the two divisions of Colonels David Hunter and Samuel P. Heintzelman, who were to make a turning movement to the north and cross the river at Sudley Springs Ford in order to turn the enemies' left.

The day dawned bright and clear. And the "listless stirring of the trees gave promise that the day would be hot. Dust lay thick upon the grass, the brush, and the uniforms of the men." At quarter past five that morning, the first shots of the battle began with a "thunderous roar of a big gun in the vicinity of the Stone Bridge."[14] This diversion created by Tyler's division initially drew the Confederates' attention away from the two divisions of Hunter and Heintzelman (approximately twelve thousand men) as they turned north at Cub Run Bridge and followed a narrow road to Sudley Springs Ford. Unfortunately for McDowell, the two divisions heading north were two and a half hours behind schedule.

From a high observation point within the Confederate defenses, the signal officer, E. P. Alexander, who, with spyglass in hand, had been scanning the horizon for any signs of a flanking movement, spotted the glistening bayonets and musket barrels in the vicinity of Sudley Springs Ford. He immediately signaled Colonel Nathan G. Evans, the commander at Stone Bridge: "Look out for your left; you are turned."[15]

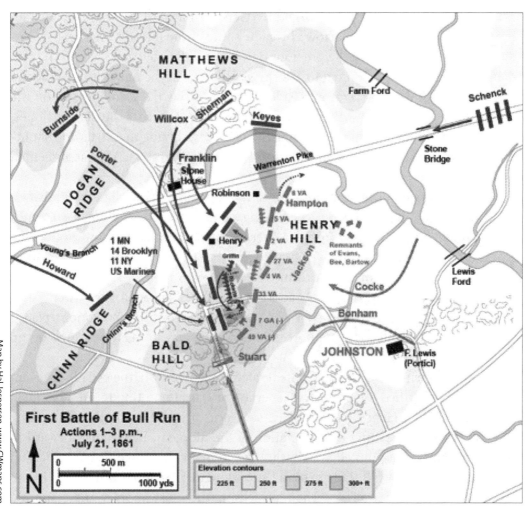

First Battle of Bull Run
Actions 1–3 p.m.,
July 21, 1861

Evans had already determined that Tyler's attack was a trick and had rapidly moved to counter the flanking column positioned on Matthews Hill. Thus began the shifting of Confederate strength from their right flank to their left flank.

The battle would be fought on three rolling hills known as Matthews Hill, Henry Hill, and Chinn Ridge, separated by Sudley Road and the Warrenton Turnpike, which form a giant cross on the terrain.[16] The two armies clashed on Matthews Hill around a quarter to ten in the morning, the official beginning of the First Battle of Bull Run.

After about an hour of intense engagement with the Union troops, Evans sent an urgent request for the aid of Brigadier General Barnard E. Bee's brigade, accompanied by Colonel F. S. Bartow's brigade, some of the interior lines from Johnston's army that had arrived the previous day. Bee and Bartow quickly moved from where they had been positioned to Matthews Hill to join the fight. Still having the advantage in numbers, McDowell's Federal troops drove the Confederates off the field. As they watched the scattered Confederates retreat across the distant slopes, McDowell and his staff "galloped among the brigades, waving their hats and shouting. . . . 'They are running! Victory! Victory! The day is ours!' "[17] At least, it seemed so at the time.

For the next two hours, from noon until two o'clock, McDowell believed that he had won the day and issued no orders, leaving eighteen thousand Union men standing around anxiously waiting to fight. There was sporadic combat but nothing of significance. The two-hour break from the Union attack gave Johnston and Beauregard time to bring in more reinforcements and reform their lines. By one o'clock, Brigadier General Thomas Jackson had formed a line of approximately twenty-five hundred men on the southeast edge of Henry Hill, with thirteen cannons placed in front of them. With more reinforcements on the way, things were looking up considerably for the Confederates.

Sometime during or after the Confederate retreat from Matthews Hill, an event transpired that birthed a legend. As General Bee was attempting to rally his men, he "glanced toward Henry Hill where he saw Jackson and his command standing bold and resolute. Catching the inspiration of the moment, Bee leaned forward in his stirrups and, with pointed sword, shouted to his men, 'Look! There is Jackson standing like a stone wall! Rally behind the Virginians!' " Such was the birth of the legendary name "Stonewall" for Thomas Jackson, the most popular and respected general in the Confederacy until his death at the Battle of Chancellorsville.[18]

To collapse the Confederate line, McDowell had to go over Henry Hill and hit them from behind, but his two-hour period of inaction cost him dearly. If he had acted sooner, his army could have driven the scattered Confederates off Henry Hill and collapsed their line, winning the battle. But it was too late, and during Mc-Dowell's attack on the hill between one-thirty and four o'clock, it became a place of pandemonium. Historian JoAnna McDonald provided a concise summary of the reasons for the confusing nature of the battle on Henry Hill:

> 1) Fifteen Union regiments and thirteen Confederate regiments charged and counterattacked so quickly that the action became a whirlpool of obscurity; 2) Afterwards, not even the participants could provide a clear account; 3) Many Union regiments fired only a few rounds before falling back; as another regiment replaced them, the retreating and charging men became intermingled; 4) As a result, several Union regiments became so disorganized that the soldiers fought in smaller, make-shift battalions; 5) Confederate units combined as well. Those that assailed Matthews Hill either joined with other regiments, battled in make-shift battalions, or rested behind lines. To add to the confusion, many Union regiments wore gray uniforms which created a distressing dilemma for Confederate and Union alike. The similarity of flags also contributed to officers mistaking enemy regiments for their own. Frequently, one could hear, "Stop firing; you are shooting at your friends."[19]

McDowell sent his forces up the slopes of Henry Hill in piecemeal fashion to break through Jackson's Confederate line. For two hours, the battle swayed back and forth and centered on the eleven Union guns (cannons) of Captain Charles Griffin and Captain James B. Ricketts sent up the slopes by McDowell. It was during this phase of the battle that several shells struck the Henry family's house, from which the hill was named. Ellen Henry and John Henry attempted to carry their elderly mother, Judith, out of her home and away from the danger. As the shells exploded all around them, they saw no other choice but to return to the house and put their mother back into her bedroom. The family cowered as the shells fell in and around the house. One cannonball crashed into Mrs. Henry's bedroom, and fragments hit her in the neck, side, and feet, nearly severing one foot. Later that day, when she died from her multiple wounds, her son went outside and hugged the ground, raising himself up occasionally to cry out, "They have killed my mother!" Judith Henry was the first civilian casualty of the Civil War.[20]

Around three-thirty, the entire tenor of the battle changed and went downhill rapidly for the North. McDowell put his last hopes in the two brigades of Colonel William T. Sherman and Colonel Oliver O. Howard. Sherman sent his brigade up the hill, regiment by regiment, and they broke into disorder and began to retreat. Soon Henry Hill was full of Union troops retreating from the field, some in orderly fashion and others in a wild panic.

Howard arrived on Chinn Ridge just as the fight on Henry Hill was winding down. His New England brigade clashed with the Confederate brigades and eventually fled in retreat like the Northern troops on Henry Hill.[21] By four-thirty, McDowell's entire army was in retreat. The Confederate brigades of Colonels Arnold Elzey and Jubal A. Early, aided by Jeb Stuart's cavalry, swept across the field after the Federals and pursued them for a short distance.[22] The Union army fled all the way back to Washington, D.C. The Confederates obtained a victory but were not sure what to do with it and never pursued the Union troops back to the capital.[23]

In light of the above overview, the remaining sections of this chapter will provide a commentary on the contents of White's vision and explain the historical situation behind each statement.

The march to the battle

"The Southern army had everything in their favor and were prepared for a dreadful contest."[24] Even though the Union had the advantage of greater numbers initially, several factors gave the Confederates the advantage in this battle. First, Beauregard's forces enjoyed what are called in military parlance "interior lines"—a situation in which a commander has the ability to reinforce his lines and employ them against the enemy faster than the enemy can counter his moves.[25] The Confederate troops were transported by the Manassas Gap Railroad, which enabled them to reinforce their forces faster than the Union army. Although McDowell gained the upper hand during the first part of the battle on Matthews Hill, his fatal two-hour delay before advancing to Henry Hill gave the Confederates the time they needed to put their final reinforcements in place. These reinforcements, particularly Thomas "Stonewall" Jackson's brigade (who arrived the day before the battle) and other brigades (who

arrived on the Union army's right flank that afternoon), posed a major threat to the North during the second part of the battle on Henry Hill.

Second, Beauregard's forces were bunkered down the night before the battle, whereas McDowell's army stumbled through dense forests and rough terrain most of the night and arrived on the battlefield exhausted—a point White observed. Third, the Confederates enjoyed a psychological advantage over their enemies, due to the fact that they were the defending force rather than the invading force. "Men tend to fight harder to defend their homes than they do to try to impose their will on others who are defending their homes," noted Gary Gallagher.[26] The Confederates were fighting for their own territory in Virginia and thus enjoyed a higher morale than the Union troops. This was probably one of the reasons that motivated them to prepare for a "dreadful contest."

"The Northern army was moving on with triumph, not doubting but that they would be victorious. Many were reckless and marched forward boastingly, as though victory were already theirs."[27] As the Union soldiers marched out of the Washington, D.C., area on July 16, they were jubilant and sang, "John Brown's body lies a-mouldering in the grave. His soul's marching on! Glory, Hally, Hallelujah!" among other marching songs.[28] "Never again in this war—or perhaps in any American war—would an army take the field so assured of its holy mission, so convinced that God's work was surely its own."[29] Victory was a sure thing in the Union soldier's mind. Even as they neared the battlefield, according to Elisha Hunt Rhodes, the soldiers maintained a "reckless" attitude: "We now took a side road that skirted a piece of woods and marched for some distance, the men amusing themselves with laughter and jokes, with occasional stops for berries."

And even as they marched onto the battlefield, Rhodes recalled, "One of our boys by the name of Webb fell off the fence and broke his bayonet. This caused some amusement, for even at this time we did not realize that we were about to engage in battle."[30] According to the brigade commander William T. Sherman, "The march demonstrated little save the general laxity of discipline; for all my personal efforts I could not prevent the men from straggling for water, blackberries, or anything on the way they fancied."[31]

"As they neared the battlefield, many were almost fainting through weariness and want of refreshment."[32] McDowell's army had good reason to feel exhausted as they fought on July 21, 1861. First, they had been marching since two-thirty in the

morning and were bone tired. Second, the day of the battle was hot and humid, which caused dehydration in the troops. Those brigades not involved in the morning fighting marched and waited in the hot sun for orders. As McDowell fed his troops to the battle throughout the day, exhaustion took its toll, and only the strong survived. Colonel Oliver O. Howard's brigade, for example, had been marching in the hot sun most of the day with canteens long emptied and "the dust from the road and the drifting battle smoke choking their lungs." Late in the day, they were ordered onto Chinn Ridge as a flanking move on the Confederates. But as they approached the battlefield, according to Howard, "many dropped out and fainted from exhaustion."[33] In fact, some of his companies that had started the day with about sixty men ended up with as few as eight men in the ranks.[34]

"*They did not expect so fierce an encounter.*"[35] The Northern soldier in general "did not expect so fierce an encounter" in this battle. According to historian Reid Mitchell, they "were convinced that the Confederate armies were composed of degraded, intimidated men . . . the dupes of a self-styled aristocracy."[36] "Armies composed of such poor timber could hardly be expected to put up much resistance when confronted by the true men in the ranks of Northern armies when they met in battle." Furthermore, Northerners didn't believe that secession had strong support among Southerners and that all they needed was a little punishment to make them recant.[37] "Not until the guns began to go off," however, "would the North realize that when men like Jefferson Davis talked about seceding from the Union they meant every word of it."[38]

The battle

The battle, as noted above, took place in three phases on three different hills:

> Phase 1: Matthews Hill
> Phase 2: Henry Hill
> Phase 3: Chinn Ridge

The following comments could apply to the fighting on any of these hills. But White is most likely describing what happened on Henry Hill, the second phase of the battle and the epicenter of the most intense fighting.

"*They rushed into battle and fought bravely, desperately. The dead and dying were on every side. Both the North and the South suffered severely.*"[39] This description certainly describes what took place between 2:00 and 4:00 P.M. on Henry Hill surrounding the cannons that Ricketts (ten-pounders) and Griffin (howitzers) placed on the field early in the afternoon. McDowell sent his forces up the slopes of Henry Hill in piecemeal fashion to break through Jackson's Confederate line. For two hours, the battle swayed back and forth, centering on the eleven Union cannons of Griffin and Ricketts. The casualties on both sides were highest during this period. Just after 3:00 P.M., it seemed that Jackson's Confederate line might disintegrate from a devastating volley fired into the left flank, but they recovered the cannons once again.

During the last hour of the battle, the Confederates held eight of the Union cannons, and the Northern soldiers lunged forward to retake them. According to one historian, "It was bedlam, a maelstrom of surging and retreating men, acrid smoke, rattling muskets, and exploding shells. Regiments came onto the field one by one, and generally went into position as each particular colonel saw fit. And then, once in the fight, trim and polished ranks quickly degenerated into seething mobs of frightened men—men who knew what they wanted to do, but who had little idea of how to go about doing it."[40]

The retreat

Now we have reached the part of White's testimony that is most unique. According to her vision, at a dramatic point in the battle when the Northern armies were charging under enemy fire, an angel descended and caused an immediate retreat.

"The Southern men felt the battle, and in a little while would have been driven back still further. The Northern men were rushing on, although their destruction was very great. Just then an angel descended and waved his hand backward. Instantly there was confusion in the ranks. It appeared to the Northern men that their troops were retreating, when it was not so in reality, and a precipitate retreat commenced. This seemed wonderful to me."[41] It should be noted at the outset that White's depiction was a snapshot of one scene on a large battlefield with numerous military maneuvers taking place in the midst of chaos and confusion. She gave no specific indication *when* the retreat occurred, although it was obviously the beginning of the end of the battle as "a precipitate retreat commenced." Neither did she specify *where* the retreat occurred, whether on Henry Hill or Chinn Ridge. (Retreats occurred on both hills.)

It is up to the researcher, therefore, to analyze the battle from the perspective of White's brief account and determine when, where, and how the retreat happened on the battlefield, if it happened at all like White said. Because the ending of the battle was plagued by chaos and confusion, as JoAnna McDonald noted above, this is not an easy task.

White used lay terminology to describe the military action she observed. The Northern men "rushing on" in "ranks" were the regiments organized in battle lines charging the enemy. "Confusion in their ranks" obviously referred to a scattering of these battle lines and total disorganization. The retreat itself was "precipitate," or sudden and immediate. After beholding the excitement of battle and supernatural intervention, White's reaction is not surprising: "This seemed wonderful to me." The experience was obviously an emotional one for her.

The angel. It was common knowledge that the entire Northern army retreated from the battlefield, a fact Ellen White acknowledged earlier in the testimony when she described the battle as "disastrous." Retreats had already occurred periodically throughout the afternoon on both sides of the battle. The uniqueness of White's contribution here lies not in stating that a retreat occurred on the battlefield, but in pinpointing the origin of the final retreat by the Union forces. To her, the origin of the retreat that ended the battle was a supernatural cause—"an angel descended and waved his hand backward." The result was instant "confusion" in the Northern "ranks" and the commencement of "a precipitate retreat."

None of the historical sources on the battle say anything about divine intervention by an angel. But the instant "confusion" and "precipitate retreat" were events that could be identified by those who witnessed the retreat on the battlefield. This analysis is therefore deeply interested in the critical moment when demoralization of the entire Union army struck.

Interpretation of the retreat

Fortunately, for researchers who want to study this critical moment, information concerning it is readily available. Many of the chief participants wrote and spoke afterward about their experience on the battlefield. The first "wave" of testimony appeared within days or weeks of the fight and was later recorded in the *Official Records of the Union and Confederate Armies.*[42] The second wave "crested" six months later when a Congressional committee investigated Union officers; the committee's findings were published in "Bull Run—Ball's Bluff," part 2 of the *Report of the Joint Committee on the Conduct of the War*.[43] The third wave "washed ashore"[44] later in the century and was published in volume 1 of the four-volume *Battles and Leaders of the Civil War*.[45] The most insightful of these testimonies came from the first wave, those reports written "hot from the field" by officers and soldiers in both armies.[46]

The secondary sources on the battle are numerous and also offer many helpful insights.[47] These studies, written by historians of the battle, have pieced together from the primary sources several narratives that have become the major interpretation of the Union retreat on Henry Hill and Chinn Ridge. These narratives attribute the retreat to several factors that culminated in Confederate advances that swept the Federals off the field into a massive retreat. One of the main contributing factors was the Confederate interior line, or fresh troops, that came onto the field during the afternoon and flanked the Federals on their right, reinforcing Jackson's line on the crest of Henry Hill. An atlas of the First Battle of Bull Run, such as Bradley M. Gottfried's *The Maps of First Bull Run*, will help readers to visualize the movement of the troops as discussed below.[48]

Manassas battlefield historian John Hennessy best articulated one of the dominant narratives on the beginning of the final Union retreat:

The fight for Henry Hill had begun as a battle for time—time that would allow the Confederate commanders to get additional troops on the field. Hampton, Jackson, Smith, Fisher, Bee and Bartow had bought that time, and though at the moment the Federals controlled Henry Hill, significant numbers of fresh Confederates were arriving at Portici, ready to enter the fight. Cocke's brigade arrived first, then Bonham's two regiments, the 2nd and 8th South Carolina, and Kemper's battery, which had hurried up from Mitchell's Ford. At about 3:30, when the fight for Henry Hill raged most fiercely, Arnold Elzey's brigade arrived, fresh off the trains at Manassas Junction. Following Elzey came Jubal Early. All told, between 3 and 4 o'clock probably 7,000 fresh Confederates arrived at Johnston's headquarters. Johnston lost no time in pushing them to the front.

The 8th and 18th Virginia of Cocke's brigade moved first—together only coincidentally. The 8th, commanded by Colonel Eppa Hunton of Warrenton, bore toward the north and came up on the right of what had been Jackson's line, near the Robinson house. Colonel Robert E. Withers' 18th moved toward the left of the line. As the Virginians neared Henry Hill, dozens of discouraged and wounded comrades streamed by, spreading tales of doom. Officers rode among these gloomsayers, trying to rally the healthy ones, and soon troops from a half-dozen states formed a ragged battalion and joined in the advance. Also, turning about were the exhausted remnants of the Hampton Legion. Captain Conner formed his regiment on Withers' right. The Lynchburg artillery offered support by unlimbering on the ridge east of Henry Hill and opening fire.

Without halting for speeches or realignment, the 8th and 18th Virginia swept across the top of the hill. Their charge rocked the 38th New York near Griffin's abandoned guns, and the surprised Federals hastily gave ground. Near the Henry House the 8th Virginia smashed into the 69th New York. "We suffered terribly," a member of the 69th recalled. The 69th resisted briefly, then withdrew to Sudley Road. The 13th New York, which had maintained its toehold on Henry Hill, about 200 yards from Mrs. Henry's riddled house, saw now that it was in an extremely precarious position. As the regiment began to retreat, it came under a raking Confederate fire. One man was knocked 10 feet by the explosion of a shell. "I thought I was dead," he wrote, "and shut my eyes—but finding myself still alive I got up and ran like thunder."

The Confederates surged past the Henry house and through the wreckage of Ricketts's battery—disabled caissons and limbers, dead horses, and the bodies of hundreds who had fought over the guns—to Sudley Road. The 13th, 38th and 69th New York offered no resistance and fled down the hill toward the Stone House. The 18th Virginia poured into the road, while the 8th Virginia seized the ground around the dying widow Henry's house.[49]

In this classic narrative, the charging Union regiments (Sixty-Ninth and Thirty-Eighth New York) were driven off the field by the countercharge of the Confederate regiments (Eighth and Eighteenth Virginia). Hennessy's interpretation of the crucial moments that climaxed the battle on Henry Hill is based on his careful research of primary sources and is the predominant interpretation of what happened.[50] White's version could fit within Hennessy's interpretation: as the Federals' ranks fell apart, "their destruction was very great." But as will be shown by the various eyewitness testimonies, another interpretation is possible, one that reconciles White's description of the fight with the battle account, with no major Confederate countercharge at the time the Union lines fell apart.

Before we get into the specific reports of the officers on the battlefield, note the basic facts most of the reports agree on: the Union advances were relatively successful until about three-thirty in the afternoon, when the regiments began to fall apart; the Confederate forces were, at times, on the verge of defeat; the universal retreat of the Union forces began around four o'clock; the Sixty-Ninth and Thirty-Eighth New York were the Union regiments advancing on Henry Hill from three-thirty to four o'clock; the Thirteenth New York remained in its precarious foothold until the retreat commenced; the Confederates on top of Henry Hill facing the advancing Union forces were Hampton's Legion, Cocke's Eighth and Eighteenth Virginia, reinforcements for Jackson's line; the breakup of the Sixty-Ninth New York seems to have been the beginning of the major retreat by the Union army; and as the fight on Henry Hill wound down, Howard's brigade marched onto Chinn Ridge and encountered the flanking brigades of Elzey and Early, eventually recoiled, and joined in on the rest of the Union retreat, which ended the battle.

The question at hand, then, is this: Do any of the reports of those on the battlefield acknowledge Ellen White's interpretation of sudden confusion in the advancing Northern ranks and a resulting "precipitate retreat" that commenced the end of the battle? The challenge is that the reports tend to be contradictory and lend themselves to more than one interpretation. The reason for the contradiction in the reports is the general chaos of the battle and because each participant viewed the battle from his own perspective, thus providing only a thin slice of the entire battle picture. There is some consensus, however, that supported White's version of the retreat, and these reports help to provide the full picture of what happened. We begin with the Union reports of the retreat.

Union reports of the retreat. The key officer opposing Jackson's line on Henry Hill that afternoon was William T. Sherman. His report of the crucial moment read: "Here, about 3.30 p. m. began the scene of confusion and disorder that characterized the remainder of the day. Up to that time all had kept their places, and seemed perfectly cool and used to the shells and shot that fell comparatively harmless all around us; but the short exposure to an intense fire of small-arms at close range had killed many, wounded more, and had produced disorder in all the battalions that had attempted to destroy it [the Confederate line on Henry Hill's plateau]. Men fell away talking and in great confusion."[51]

Here Sherman referred to the bloody charges across the plateau in front of the Henry home and around Ricketts' fallen batteries, the relative safety of the exhausted regiments as they rested under the brow of the hill and in the depressed road, and the commencement of the confusion about three-thirty.[52] In a letter to his wife about this final phase of the battle, he explained in more detail: "The volunteers up to that time had done well, but they were repulsed regiment by regiment, and I do think it was impossible to stand long in that fire. I did not find fault with them, but they fell into disorder—an incessant clamor of tongues, one saying that they were not properly supported, another that they could not tell friend from foe; but I observed the gradual retreat going on and did all I could to stop it. At last it became manifest we were falling back."[53]

When Sherman's official report is combined with the letter to his wife, it presents the picture that his men "fell into disorder" and "great confusion," similar to White's description of instant "confusion in the ranks." Sherman also observed that his men fell into "an incessant clamor of tongues," or had different opinions as to why they were retreating. The outcry "that they were not properly supported" could refer to the perception, as noted by White, "that their troops were retreating."[54] Apparently, Sherman "observed the gradual retreat going on." At any rate, the commander willingly acknowledged that the fatal demoralization began among his men.

The origin of the panic is identified in the report of Colonel Kelly of the Sixty-Ninth New York, who gave closer attention to some of the details than did Sherman, his superior officer. He explained as follows: "After sustaining and repelling a continuous fire of musketry and artillery, directed on us from the masked positions of the enemy, our regiment formed into line directly in front of the enemy's battery, charged upon it twice, were finally driven off, *owing principally to the panic of the regiment which preceded us*, and then, under a desperate fire, retired to the line from which we had advanced on the battery, and then endeavored to reform. *The panic was too general*, and the Sixty-ninth had to retreat with the great mass of the Federals."[55]

The "regiment which preceded us" is positively identified as being the root of the panic. According to Eusey, "this contaminating unit was the Seventy-Ninth New York under Colonel James Cameron. All of this prompts closer scrutiny of the actions around Henry House. In succession and separately, Sherman attacked Jackson with the Second Wisconsin, the Seventy-Ninth New York, and the Sixty-Ninth New York. The first two of these regiments, having each made repeated charges, fell back for cover under the crest of the hill, thus opening the way for the Sixty-Ninth New York to test their fortitude. Their courage, however, had been sapped by the demoralizing experiences of the Seventy-Ninth."[56]

The Seventy-Ninth New York had made several assaults against the Confederates but failed in the end. In the last attempt, their commander, Colonel James Cameron, started up the hill "waving his sword and crying to his men to follow." But, unfortunately, none of them followed him. The wounded Confederate Colonel Wade Hampton, lying in the Henry House yard directly in the path of the attacking regiments, observed the vain efforts of the fearless Union leader, and exclaimed to his companion: "Isn't it terrible to see that brave officer trying to lead his men forward and they won't follow him?" A few minutes later Cameron fell to the ground, fatally wounded.[57]

"After this tragedy," explained Eusey, Cameron's

men milled around in comparative safety below the hill, although fearing further calamities, imagining subsequent setbacks to the Sixty-Ninth to be major disasters, and transmitting their fears to their comrades of the Sixty-Ninth, who, looking on, apparently absorbed the jitters pretty well. Thus, when Kelly finally managed to propel his regiment a second time (alongside Farnsworth's Thirty-Eighth New York) up to the enemy's lines for a 15-minute slugging match, his men were too ready to *see things*. Suddenly, it appeared to them (because of their imbibed fearfulness, according to Kelly's version) that their ranks were being crushed, when in reality this was not true. Then, in an instant, the regiment became completely unnerved, fell into disorder, and ran as a unit from the field. Within moments, most of the other Federal units on and around the hill were also sucked into the scramble to the rear. The Bull Run debacle had been triggered.[58]

Captain Kelly's description of the disaster is enriched by contributions from other Union officers on or near Henry Hill. John Barnard of the Corps of Engineers remembered observing the "action on the heights [atop Henry Hill], where the enemy made his final and successful stand." He specifically recalled the crucial "moment when our lines finally gave way in front, upon the decisive point [Henry Hill]."[59] Colonel Addison Farnsworth of the Thirty-Eighth New York, who led his regiment in a charge up the center of Henry Hill simultaneously with Kelly's Sixty-Ninth New York, described the general panic:

> Another rally was then again made by my regiment, the gallant men readily responding to the orders of their officers. Advancing in double-quick time to the right and front towards a dense woods, in which the enemy had been concealed in large force during the day, and from which evidences of a retreat were now visible, my regiment, with detached portions of others of our force, became engaged in a sharp and spirited skirmish with the enemy's infantry and cavalry, and *we appeared for a time to have complete possession of the field.*
>
> This was the last rally made by my regiment. Suddenly and unexpectedly, the enemy, re-enforced by fresh troops, literally swarming the woods, poured in upon us a perfect shower of lead from his musketry; his batteries reopened upon us with terrible effect, and *a panic at this moment seeming to have taken possession of our troops generally*, a retreat was ordered, and my regiment in comparatively good order commenced its march towards Centreville.[60]

There is nothing in Ellen White's account of the crucial moment that indicates that the Federals were not being fired upon. In fact, she seems to suggest that when the retreat suddenly occurred, as the "Northern men were rushing on," their "destruction was very great."[61] Colonel Farnsworth's report noted the "panic" that took possession of "our troops generally," and *then* a retreat was ordered. His reference to an ordered retreat and his regiment's orderly march towards Centreville indicated that the retreat involved some order, at least with his regiment. Nevertheless, confusion and panic cannot be ruled out, as noted here and in other reports.

It is important to keep in mind when reading these accounts that they reflect a compression of the events that actually occurred that afternoon. In other words, the officers were describing the highlights of many events that happened from their own perspectives of the battle and skipped over many details.

Captain Daniel Woodbury of the Army Corps of Engineers confirmed the sudden confusion and disorder: "At 4 o'clock in the afternoon of the 21st there were more than twelve thousand volunteers on the battle-field of Bull Run [Henry Hill] who had entirely lost their regimental organizations. They could no longer be handled as troops, for the officers and men were not together. Men and officers mingled together promiscuously; and it is worthy of remark that this disorganization did not result from defeat or fear, for up to 4 o'clock we had been uniformly successful."[62]

Lieutenant Colonel Josias R. King remembered that the "situation and condition of affairs prevailing at this time began to impress me as being most peculiar and strange." He "could not understand or account for it"; as he tried to understand the situation, he became "more puzzled." Adding to the confusion already present after the initial retreat, when "pandemonium reigned supreme," he remembered the Confederates fired a volley into the Union mob, and "it was then 'Skiddoo,' every man for himself and the devil take the hindmost." After this, "there was nothing else to do but to get up and git out of the way; we could do nothing; it was an utter possibility to restore order."[63]

The Federal field commander, Irvin McDowell, observed that after three o'clock, the "enemy was evidently disheartened and broken." He then lamented:

It was at this time that the enemy's re-enforcements [Confederate interior lines] came to his aid from the railroad train (understood to have just arrived from the valley with the residue of Johnston's army). They threw themselves in the woods on our right [Elzey and Early's brigades with Stuart's Calvary], and opened a fire of musketry on our men [Howard's brigade on Chinn Ridge], which caused them to break and retire down the hill-side. This soon degenerated into disorder, for which there was no remedy. Every effort was made to rally them, even beyond the reach of the enemy's fire, but in vain.[64]

Interestingly, McDowell omitted from his report the "staggering prostration"[65] on Henry Hill, choosing instead to focus on the collapse of his army at Chinn Ridge, which occurred when his troops on Henry Hill were already in mass retreat. Nevertheless, he vividly captured the scene that many would long remember: "The plain was covered with the retreating groups, and they seemed to infect those with whom they came in contact. The retreat soon became a rout, and this soon degenerated still further into a panic."[66] Reflecting on the retreat from beginning to end, Colonel Samuel P. Heintzelman punctuated his report by blurting: "Such a rout I never witnessed before. No efforts could induce a single regiment to form after the retreat was commenced."[67]

Military historian Edward G. Longacre recently argued that "at the start, the Union withdrawal was a deliberate and, in the main, orderly affair. There was no widespread panic or chaos, for the army was not then threatened with a vigorous pursuit."[68] This is based on the narrative that the panic didn't really commence until later in the flight to Washington, when the retreaters felt threatened by a Confederate pursuit.[69]

One Michigan infantryman remembered, "As a matter of fact, I saw no running where the fight took place but the men fell back in a sullen, dogged manner until they had got away from the presence of the enemy."[70] This was evidently true for some of the troops on Henry Hill that afternoon. But some of the reports do affirm a Federal panic on the hill that resulted in a disorderly retreat, as already noted. Most likely, the large masses of Federal soldiers retreating that afternoon on Henry Hill were a combination of demoralized, confused, and panicked troops, some walking and some running. Again, the testimonies reflect what each participant saw from his own particular angle of vision rather than a wide view of the battle.

Confederate reports of the retreat. Now we will examine the Confederate reports of Colonels Eppa Hunton, Robert E. Withers, and Joseph B. Kershaw, who were on the attacking line at Henry Hill during the crucial moment of the Federal retreat. The key question for the Confederate reports is this: Was Jackson's line counter-charging the Federals when they began to retreat from the field?

Colonel Eppa Hunton of the Eighth Virginia Infantry remembered the climax of the battle on Henry Hill when his regiment was ordered "to the fight around Mrs. Henry's house, where the Eighth made a most gallant and impetuous charge, routing the enemy." This is generally understood to be the charge made simultaneously with the Eighteenth Virginia that swept the hill clean of the Sixty-Ninth and Thirty-Eighth New York around four o'clock. But after this charge, Hunton reported, "I then drew the men back to a ravine on the east side of the house, to shelter them from random shots, when I was ordered to take a position near our first [the location of their previous charge on Henry Hill], to meet what was then supposed to be an advancing column of the enemy, when it was found to be a retreat."[71] He was apparently describing another Federal column advancing up the hill that, when his infantry went to meet it, was "found to be a retreat."

If this interpretation is correct, then the previous charge that drove the Federals off the field was not their final retreat. They launched another advance (Sherman's Sixty-Ninth New York under the command of Colonel Kelly) and then apparently retreated for some reason other than a countercharge by the Confederates. Thus, Hunton's Eighth Virginia was in no thrusting combat move at the critical moment of the last Federal retreat. It is difficult to be absolutely sure based on the reports, because they reflect the confusion during this time.

Colonel Robert E. Withers of the Eighteenth Virginia Infantry ordered a charge that drove "back the enemy . . . beyond the hill" which, he recalled, was part of the "celebrated Sherman battery." After this, he reported "two other bodies of troops passing up the hill towards the [Henry] house." They fired upon them "from their own cannon," he remembered. "A few shots sufficed to drive all the enemy out of sight." From Withers' report, then, we learn again that during the final Federal advance, there was no thrusting line at the critical moment of retreat, only the firing of weapons. Specifically, he stated that after clearing the Federals from the field, "My regiment was then ordered by General Beauregard to push for the turnpike at stone bridge."[72]

Colonel John B. Kershaw of the Second South Carolina Infantry added important details to Colonel Withers' report. Marching his regiment north on the east side of Sudley Springs Road toward the battle on Henry Hill, he "perceived a regiment emerging from the wood on the left of Colonel Cash, and advancing in admirable order up the slope to the hill recently occupied by the forces of the enemy whom we had driven off." This most likely would have been the Sixty-Ninth New York and the Thirty-Eighth New York. Kershaw described what happened next:

I immediately advanced my whole command, moving my regiment by the right flank along the road, Colonel Cash in the field in line. Arriving on the face of the hill towards the enemy, I formed [a] line of battle to the left of the road. Here I found Colonel Withers' Virginia regiment on the hill to the right of [the] road, to whom I communicated my purpose to form [a] line and advance to the attack, and I asked his co-operation, to which he immediately acceded. With Colonel Withers' command I found also the remnant of Hampton's Legion, under Captain Conner, assisted by Captain Gary. Captain Conner reported to me and was assigned to my left.

> *As soon as the entire line was displayed evidences of movements became perceptible in the line of the enemy, and in a few moments they were in full retreat by the rear of their left flank.*[73]

Notice that when Kershaw's and Withers' line was "displayed," there was apparently no advance of the line yet. The beginning of the "full retreat" from Kershaw's vantage point, then, commenced in the "line of the enemy" before any Confederate advance.

Differing from these reports is that of the Confederate commander Joseph E. Johnston. He stated in his report that General Beauregard, who was commanding in the thick of the battle, "threw forward his whole line," and "the enemy was driven back from the long-contested [Henry] hill, and victory was no longer doubtful." He further explained that while the brigades of Elzey and Early were flanking the Union right, "a simultaneous charge was made by General Beauregard in front."[74] Thus, the entire Confederate line was thrust forward and swept the field clean of the Federals. General Beauregard reported a similar narrative of a "combined attack" by which he threw his entire line forward and drove the Federals off the field.[75] According to James McPherson, "Beauregard ordered a counterattack all along the line. As Confederate units surged forward, a strange, eerie scream rent the air. Soon to be known as the rebel yell, this unearthly wail struck fear into the hearts of the enemy then and later."[76] The Beauregard-Johnston explanation of the battle's climax continues to be one of the major narratives of the battle's end.

The most accurate battlefield narrative, however, is the one presented above by John Hennessy, in which the Confederate charges on the Federals were spottier, often two regiments at a time, rather than one unified charge by the entire Confederate line.[77] Additionally, the famous "rebel yell" most likely originated with Stonewall Jackson who, earlier in the battle, ordered his regiments to "yell like furies" when they charged.[78]

The heart of the issue in this discussion is timing. For Ellen White's view to be a possibility, the conditions had to be right. The Northern troops were charging under enemy fire but suddenly retreated before any major Confederate charge took place. Thus, the retreat she saw, a small piece of the entire battle picture, apparently took place *before* any major Confederate advance. As already noted, the most likely time for this to have occurred was during the climax of the fight on Henry Hill, when the Sixty-Ninth New York and Thirty-Eighth New York simultaneously charged up the hill towards the Confederate line, who, while firing, did not countercharge at that time. The major Confederate charge, according to this narrative, must have taken place following the retreat. It is important to keep in mind that charges and countercharges had occurred all afternoon, and the exact time when they took place cannot be determined.

Another important witness was Colonel Jubal A. Early, who also denied that a general forward movement of the Confederate line occurred before the Federal retreat. He reported viewing from atop a ridge the "enemy's troops in full retreat across and beyond the pike." Then he explained, "We were now on the extreme left of the whole of our infantry, and in advance of the main line. The only troops on our left of any description were the two companies of cavalry and Beckham's battery with Stuart. On my immediate right and a little to the rear was Elzey's brigade, and farther to the right I saw our line extending towards Bull Run [the Confederate line on Henry Hill], but I discovered *no indications of a forward movement*."[79]

Thus, Early reported very clearly that he saw the Federals in retreat *before* any major Confederate advancement of lines.

Interestingly, twenty-five years after his original report, General Beauregard added a significant detail in his recital of the final events of the battle, published in the first volume of *Battles and Leaders of the Civil War*: "Before the full advance of the Confederate ranks the enemy's whole line, whose right was already yielding, irretrievably broke, fleeing across Bull Run by every available direction."[80] Although the exact timing of the events of this battle is not always clear, this statement seems to fit the situation during the climax on Henry Hill. A Confederate soldier who was there on Henry Hill at this time remembered years later: "I stood not four rods from General Beauregard when that stampede [the Federal retreat] began. Beauregard had their cannons loaded with chain shot, and was about to fire. He looked toward the advancing host, and cried out: 'The Yanks are all retreating. Don't fire the guns.'" The old soldier pondered, "Had they fired that charge, they would have mowed everything down before them to the earth."[81]

The narrative of the Federal retreat that began before the Confederate advance fits several other testimonies describing the Confederates' complete surprise at the sudden Federal retreat. James B. Ricketts, for example, the Union commander of "Ricketts' guns," was taken prisoner to Richmond and later testified that while there,

Confederate officers he knew well, told him, "that at one time they [the Confederates] were giving away, and that our panic was perfectly unaccountable to them."[82] Corps of Engineers leader John Barnard added that the Confederate "victory seemed to them so unexpected and unaccountable, that they were quite incapable of following up, *or even understanding the first retreat of our line*; nor did they dare to make any serious effort to reap the advantage they might have reaped from their victory."[83] Federal officer Erasmus Keyes remembered, "As I retired, with ranks closed, towards the point where I was to descend to the crossing of Bull Run, I saw on the heights to the left a long line of Rebel infantry looking down upon us in what appeared to be a state of uncertainty. They did not fire upon us, although we were within range, and I joined the retreating mass a short distance in rear of General McDowell and his staff."[84]

Based on the testimonies above, while there was apparently no thrusting move by the Confederate line at the commencement of the Federal retreat, sometime later the Confederates did pursue their retreating enemy for a while.

Confederate Colonel William W. Blackford's testimony. Of all the eyewitness testimonies, Confederate Colonel William W. Blackford's description of the moment of retreat, published in his book *War Years With Jeb Stuart*, was the closest to Ellen White's version. Civil War historian Douglas S. Freeman, who edited and published Blackford's journal in 1945, set forth its significance in the book's introduction: "Every line of this narrative by Lieut. Col. William Willis Blackford has the 'feel' of the cavalry Corps of the Army of Northern Virginia. Authenticity is stamped on each paragraph. The historical evidence is that of an eye-witness. First as Adjutant of 'Jeb' Stuart's command and then as chief engineer and a member of the staff at cavalry headquarters, Blackford observed from his commander's side nearly all the operations of the mounted troops from June, 1861, to the end of January, 1864."[85]

According to Eusey, "Those who in 1945 remembered" Ellen White's description of Bull Run (written eighty-four years earlier) "were astonished when they compared his account with hers. Here was one who saw almost as she had seen and who wrote almost as she had written."[86]

After engaging in battle throughout the afternoon, Blackford found himself "almost perishing from thirst from the intense heat." He took his horse, Comet, and went toward the nearest stream. "In [the] rear of the enemy there was a small branch and to this I determined to venture," he recalled. This stream of water was

Young's Branch, a small stream on the northern side of Chinn Ridge. There he found "the enemy's wounded who had crawled there to drink, and many had died with their heads in the water, the dark blood flowing into and gradually mingling with the stream." After finding a clearing in the water, he and his horse drank. "It was, indeed, literally drinking the blood of our enemies, for the clearest of it was suspiciously tinted and flavored."[87]

The next sentence transported the reader immediately to the battle scene: "It was now about four o'clock and the battle raged with unabated fury. The lines of blue were unbroken and their fire as vigorous as ever while they surged against the solid walls of gray, standing immovable in their front." Due to the compressed nature of the narrative, Blackford didn't say whether he stayed in the valley by Young's Branch after drinking from the stream, in which case he would have seen Howard's brigades surging forward, or whether he trekked back up to the top of Chinn Ridge. But in the next sentence he made it clear that he was viewing the "lines of blue" on Henry Hill: "It was on that ridge earlier in the day Jackson won the name of Stonewall."[88]

Thus, around four o'clock, Blackford emerged atop Chinn Ridge sometime before Howard's brigades arrived, farther to the left and forward of Early's brigade. "He was on top of the battle cyclorama," for certain points on Chinn Ridge provided a broad view of the battlefield, and he was captivated by the scene: "the rallying Federal regiments on Matthews Hill, Sherman's milling men below the Henry House plateau and in the depressed Sudley Springs Road, and the uniformed grapplers struggling with each other on the edge of Henry Green. Blackford then recorded this moving picture as if he had a photographic memory:"[89]

But now the most extraordinary spectacle I have ever witnessed took place. I had been gazing at the numerous well-formed lines as they moved forward to the attack, some fifteen or twenty thousand strong in full view [the actual number of Union troops on the field was much less, around twelve thousand], and for some reason had turned my head in another direction for a moment, when some one exclaimed, pointing to the battlefield, "Look! Look!" I looked, and what a change had taken place in an instant. Where those "well dressed," well-defined lines, with clear spaces between, had been steadily pressing forward, the whole field was a confused swarm of men, like bees, running away as fast as their legs could carry them, with all order and organization abandoned.

In a moment more the whole valley was filled with them as far as the eye could reach.[90]

Notice how closely Blackford's account parallels White's account:

White	Blackford
The Northern **men were rushing on,** although their destruction was very great.	The lines of blue were unbroken and their fire as vigorous as ever while they **surged against the solid walls of gray**, standing immovable in their front.
Just then an angel descended and waved his hand backward. **Instantly there was confusion in their ranks.** It appeared to the Northern men that their troops were retreating, when it was not so in reality, and a **precipitate retreat commenced.** This seemed wonderful to me.	But now **the most extraordinary spectacle I have ever witnessed took place.** I . . . had turned my head in another direction for a moment, when some one exclaimed, pointing to the battlefield, "Look! Look!" I looked, and **what a change had taken place in an instant. . . . The whole field was a confused swarm of men, like bees, running away as fast as their legs could carry them, with all order and organization abandoned.**

Thus, it seems that the panic which touched off the retreat was accounted for by White but graphically detailed by Blackford. She spied the backward wave of the angelic hand; he sensed the electric effect of it. She described confusion in the ranks; he saw "a confused swarm of men, like bees." She observed a "precipitate retreat"; he was surprised at the complete loss of military organization as the army ran off the field.[91]

The above reports of both Union and Confederate officers viewed together affirm that there was no major Confederate countercharge,[92] that the break of the main Union columns attacking Jackson was instantaneous, and that there was dissolution of military organization. As such, these reports lend support to the instant confusion and "precipitate retreat" in Ellen White's narrative.

Potential flanking disaster for the Federals

And had the Northern army at this time pushed the battle still further in their fainting, exhausted condition, the far greater struggle and destruction which awaited them would have caused great triumph in the South.[93]

One other insight bears mentioning in White's narrative of the events that afternoon: "The Southern men felt the battle, and in a little while would have been driven back still further."[94] This sentence, appearing as it does at the beginning of the narrative about the angel's intervention in the battle, indicated that if God had not interfered in the battle, the Union troops would have driven the Confederates back on Henry Hill's plateau. Later, White followed up this statement: "And had the Northern army at this time pushed the battle still further in their fainting, exhausted condition, the far greater struggle and destruction which awaited them would have caused great triumph in the South."[95]

This statement is battlefield accurate, due to the Confederate's interior lines. As noted above, Johnston's reinforcements were continually arriving on the battlefield all afternoon. Had the Federals broken through Jackson's line, they would have been flanked from behind and destroyed. Although Oliver Howard's brigade and George Sykes' regulars were attempting to flank the Confederate's left, their units, as well as the others concentrated on Henry Hill, were, moment by moment, coming into deadly peril because of the enemies' interior lines. Confederates Early and Elzey's brigades, Stuart's cavalry, and Holmes' and Ewell's brigades, some of which were from Johnston's army fresh by train from Winchester, were concentrating heavy power in the area around Chinn Ridge.

These fresh troops intended to sweep down and overwhelm the Union flank and rear. The threat to the Union forces was thus very great. Beauregard himself confirmed this when he stated that "if the enemy had remained on the field till the arrival of Ewell and Holmes, they would have been so strongly outflanked that many who escaped would have been destroyed or captured."[96] According to Ellen White's supernatural perspective, "God would not permit this, and sent an angel to interfere."[97] From the human perspective, however, the Federal retreat was, according to Confederate General Edward P. Alexander, a great escape: "Never did an enemy make a cleaner escape out of such an exposed position after such an utter rout."[98]

The mystery of the retreat

The sudden falling back of the Northern troops is a mystery to all. They know not that God's hand was in the matter.[99]

As noted earlier, the sudden retreat of the Federals from the battlefield could not be explained and was a mystery to everyone. General Winfield Scott expressed the mystery in a letter dispatched at one o'clock in the morning on Monday, July 22, to General George McClellan: "After fairly beating the enemy, and taking three of his batteries, a panic seized McDowell's army, and it is in full retreat on the Potomac. A *most unaccountable transformation* into a mob of a finely-appointed and admirably-led army."[100] Federal officer Louis Blenker explained in his report that the Confederates "were retreating" and that the Northern retreat was "a panic, all at once. There was a panic which nobody can explain."[101]

According to Walt Whitman, the retreat and loss of the battle was a "terrible shock" to the North. "Each side supposed it had won," he pondered, "till the last moment. One had, in point of fact, just the same right to be routed as the other. *By a fiction, or series of fictions, the national forces at the last moment exploded in a panic and fled from the field.*"[102] By attributing the panicked retreat to "a fiction, or series of fictions," Whitman captured the unexplainable nature of the retreat. There were so many stories of what happened that it was best explained as a mystery.[103]

But to Ellen White and her audience, there was no mystery: "God's hand was in the matter."[104] Whereas most in the North thought it was a terrible defeat for the Federal army, she understood the retreat as deliverance. The angel had delivered the Northern army from total destruction and humbled them at the same time. They would live to fight again, for God "would not suffer victories to be gained faster than He ordained, and would permit no more losses to the Northern men than in His wisdom He saw fit, to punish them for their sins."[105]

Conclusion

The participants in the thick of the fight on Henry Hill did their best to describe what they saw, as it all came to a sudden end. Some of their reports support Ellen White's "precipitate retreat," while others offer a different version. Due to the conflicting nature of the reports and confusing nature of the battle's end, more than one interpretation is possible. Those who discount the supernatural attribute the sudden retreat of the Federals to natural causes in the ebb and flow of battle.[106] White's interpretation of the battle's end is strictly a supernatural one and is best understood and appreciated when viewed from that perspective. In the end, this chapter has argued that Ellen White's description of what she saw was a plausible explanation for the retreat on Henry Hill, and it harmonized with several reports of the participants on the battlefield.

To all Christians who accept God's intervening providence in the affairs of humankind, Ellen White's words—"God had this nation in His own hand"[107]—offer great encouragement. The meaning of this statement and how it played out in the battles of the Civil War are the subjects of the next chapter.

Chapter in a nutshell

The first major battle of the Civil War, at Manassas, Virginia, on July 21, 1861, came to a sudden end when the Union troops universally retreated from the battlefield and fled back to Washington, D.C. In the days following the disaster, the North was in despair and couldn't understand what happened to their troops. Approximately two weeks later, Ellen White experienced a vision in Roosevelt, New York, about this battle, in which she saw an angel descend and cause instant confusion in the Union lines and an immediate retreat. Is this account of sudden confusion and immediate retreat plausible? This chapter identified Henry Hill as the place of the retreat and its commencement at around four o'clock in the afternoon. Because of the chaos of the battle, the reports of the officers tend to be contradictory. There is some consensus, however, that support White's version of the retreat, and this chapter provides those various Union and Confederate reports. In particular, Confederate Colonel William W. Blackford's testimony published in his *War Years With Jeb Stuart* provided an account almost identical to White's but absent of the supernatural elements. In the end, while some of the reports support White's version of the retreat and others don't, her account is a plausible one. But it is strictly a supernatural one and best appreciated when viewed from that perspective.

---

1. John G. Nicolay, *The Outbreak of Rebellion* (Cambridge, MA: 1995), 196, 197. Nicolay was the private sec-

retary to President Lincoln.

2. "The War for the Union," *New-York Daily Tribune*, July 26, 1861, 6.

3. E. S. Walker, "The Day of the Lord," *Review and Herald*, August 13, 1861, 86.

4. See chapter 4 for the larger political context of this battle. For an explanation of the dual names of the battle, see note 9 in chapter 4.

5. Ellen G. White chose to identify the battle by the closest major city (like the Confederates) instead of the landmark—Bull Run (like the Federals). According to James McPherson, the names could be used interchangeably, which would account for White, a Yankee, using the Confederate name. See McPherson, *Battle Cry of Freedom*, 346n7.

6. Ellen G. White, "Communication From Sister White," *Review and Herald*, August 27, 1861, 101. This vision was edited and published in *Testimony for the Church, No. 7* in February 1862 and then later published in White, *Testimonies for the Church*, 1:266, 267.

7. Eusey, "The American Civil War," 26.

8. This chapter is an update of Eusey's work on the First Battle of Bull Run, chapter 3, "A Bull Run Ponderable," in his thesis. Eusey, "The American Civil War," 24–64.

9. Eusey, "The American Civil War," 26, provided this summary, and I have added points "7" and "9."

10. For a recent thorough treatment of the events that led up to the battle, see Edward G. Longacre, *The Early Morning of War: Bull Run, 1861* (Norman, OK: University of Oklahoma Press, 2014), 3–163.

11. John Hennessy, *The First Battle of Manassas: An End to Innocence, July 18–21, 1861,* rev. ed. (Lynchburg, VA: H. E. Howard, 1989), 5.

12. Charles P. Poland Jr., *The Glories of War: Small Battles and Early Heroes of 1861* (Bloomington, IN: Author-House, 2006), 57.

13. Foote, *The Civil War*, 1:76.

14. Francis F. Wilshin, *Manassas (Bull Run),* National Park Service Historical Handbook, Series No. 15 (Washington, DC: National Battlefield Park, 1961), 8.

15. Ibid., 10.

16. Poland, *The Glories of War*, 61. This giant cross can still be observed at the Manassas National Battlefield Park; visit the park's Web site at http://www.nps.gov/mana/index.htm.

17. Quoted in Hennessy, *The First Battle of Manassas,* 62. See also Daniel Tyler, quoted in *Report of the Joint Committee on the Conduct of the War*, pt. 2 (Washington, DC: Government Printing Office, 1863), 201.

18. Wilshin, *Manassas*, 12, 13. For the debate on what Bee actually said and meant, see Douglas S. Freeman, *Lee's Lieutenants: A Study in Command,* vol. 1, *Manassas to Malvern Hill* (New York: Scribner, 1970), 733, 734. Longacre, *The Early Morning of War*, 372–376, offers support that Bee's title was not an expression of praise and admiration.

19. JoAnna M. McDonald, *Give Them the Bayonet! A Guide to the Battle for Henry Hill, July 21, 1861,* A Walk in Time (Shippensburg, PA: Burd Street, 1999), vii, viii.

20. See ibid., 11; Gallagher, *The American Civil War: Lectures 1–24*, 134. For another version of the story, see Joseph Mills Hanson, *Bull Run Remembers: The History, Traditions and Landmarks of the Manassas (Bull Run) Campaigns Before Washington, 1861–1862* (Manassas, VA: National Capital Publishers, 1957), 88–90.

21. For details of the fight on Chinn Ridge, see Hennessy, *The First Battle of Manassas*, 109–115.

22. For the most detailed treatment of the Union rout and Confederate pursuit, see Longacre, *The Early Morning of War*, 439–476.

23. On the Confederate debate regarding the failure to pursue the Federals to Washington, see Longacre, *The Early Morning of War*, 477–482. For descriptions of the legendary retreat back to Washington, see William W. Blackford, *War Years With Jeb Stuart* (New York: Charles Scribner's Sons, 1945), 34; Erasmus D. Keyes, *Fifty Years' Observations of Men and Events: Civil and Military* (New York: Charles Scribner's Sons, 1884), 434, 435; and William Howard Russell, *My Diary North and South*, ed. Eugene H. Berwanger (Baton Rouge, LA: Louisiana State

University, 1988), 277. Russell's account is one of the most vivid and interesting depictions of the retreat from the perspective of a civilian; see 268–278.

24. White, *Testimonies for the Church*, 1:266.

25. Mark M. Boatner III, *The Civil War Dictionary* (New York: Vintage Books, 1991), 425.

26. Gallagher, *The American Civil War*, 80.

27. White, *Testimonies for the Church*, 1:266.

28. See Long, *The Civil War Day by Day*, 95. For background on the song "John Brown's Body," see Earle, *John Brown's Raid on Harpers Ferry*, 142, 143; and Aamodt, *Righteous Armies, Holy Cause*, 46. For the lyrics, see Aamodt, *Righteous Armies, Holy Cause*, 179.

29. William C. Davis, *Battle at Bull Run: A History of the First Major Campaign of the Civil War* (Baton Rouge, LA: Louisiana State University Press, 1977), 92.

30. Rhodes, diary entry, in Rhodes, *All for the Union*, 18.

31. William T. Sherman, *Memoirs of General W. T. Sherman* (New York: Library of America 1990), 198.

32. White, *Testimonies for the Church*, 1:266.

33. Oliver O. Howard, "Report of Col. Oliver O. Howard," in *The War of the Rebellion: A Compilation of the Official Records of the Union and Confederate Armies*, ser. 1, vol. 2 (Washington, DC: Government Printing Office, 1880), 418. See also Davis, *Battle at Bull Run*, 219, 220.

34. Hennessy, *The First Battle of Manassas*, 110.

35. White, *Testimonies for the Church*, 1:266.

36. Reid Mitchell, *Civil War Soldiers* (New York: Penguin Books, 1988), 32, 33.

37. Ethan S. Rafuse, *A Single Grand Victory: The First Campaign and Battle of Manassas* (Wilmington, DE: Scholarly Resources, 2002), 10, 11.

38. Catton, *The Civil War*, 23.

39. White, *Testimonies for the Church*, 1:266, 267.

40. Hennessy, *The First Battle of Manassas*, 99.

41. White, *Testimonies for the Church*, 1:267.

42. U.S. War Department, *The War of the Rebellion: A Compilation of the Official Records of the Union and Confederate Armies*, 128 vols. (Washington, DC: Government Printing Office, 1880–1902) 1, vol. 2.

43. "Bull Run–Ball's Bluff," *Report of the Joint Committee of the Conduct of the War, Part 2* (Washington, DC: Government Printing Office, 1863).

44. The wave metaphor is from Eusey, "The American Civil War," 35.

45. Robert U. Johnson and Clarence C. Buel, eds., *Battles and Leaders of the Civil War: The Opening Battles*, vol. 1 (Secaucus, NJ: Castle, 1982).

46. Eusey, "The American Civil War," 35.

47. The most helpful volumes are Davis, *Battle of Bull Run*; Hennessy, *The First Battle of Manassas;* Longacre, *The Early Morning of War;* and Rafuse, A Single Grand Victory.

48. Bradley M. Gottfried, *The Maps of First Bull Run: An Atlas of the First Bull Run (Manassas) Campaign, Including the Battle of Ball's Bluff, June–October 1861* (New York: Savas Beatie, 2009). See also Blaikie Hines, *The Battle of First Bull Run: Manassas Campaign—July 16–22, 1861* (Thomaston, ME: American Patriot Press, 2011).

49. Hennessy, *The First Battle of Manassas*, 106, 107.

50. Longacre, *The Early Morning of War*, 422, 423, follows Hennessy's basic framework with several different nuances. He believed that a multipronged Confederate assault swept the field clean of the Federals. Longacre, *The Early Morning of War*, 422.

51. William T. Sherman, quoted in *Official Records of the Union and Confederate Armies*, ser. 1, vol. 2, 370.

52. Eusey, "The American Civil War," 38.

53. William T. Sherman, *Home Letters of General Sherman*, ed. M. A. DeWolfe Howe (New York: Charles Scribner's Sons, 1909), 208.

54. White, *Testimonies for the Church*, 1:267.

55. James Kelly, quoted in *Official Records of the Union and Confederate Armies*, ser. 1, vol. 2, 372 (emphasis added).

56. Eusey, "The American Civil War," 39.

57. Hanson, *Bull Run Remembers*, 91.

58. Eusey, "The American Civil War," 40 (emphasis in original).

59. John G. Barnard, quoted in *Official Records of the Union and Confederate Armies*, ser. 1, vol. 2, 332.

60. Addison Farnsworth, quoted in *Official Records of the Union and Confederate Armies*, ser. 1, vol. 2, 414, 415; emphasis added. Both Kelly's and Farnsworth's testimonies of Union "general panic" on Henry Hill conflicted with Major General James B. Fry, who wrote years later that "there was no panic" initially in the retreat "until the retiring soldiers, guns, wagons, congressmen, and carriages were fired upon," and "the bridge over Cub Run" was "rendered impassable." James B. Fry, "McDowell's Advance to Bull Run," in Underwood and Buel, *Battles and Leaders of the Civil War,* 1:191. This narrative has been perpetuated over the years in spite of the recorded testimonies of those who were in the heat of the battle.

61. White, *Testimonies for the Church*, 1:267.

62. Daniel P. Woodbury, quoted in *Official Records of the Union and Confederate Armies*, ser. 1, vol. 2, 334.

63. Josias R. King, "The Battle of Bull Run: A Confederate Victory Obtained but Not Achieved," in *Glimpses of the Nation's Struggle*, vol. 6 (Minneapolis, MN: Aug. Davis, Publisher, 1909), 505, 506.

64. Irvin McDowell, quoted in *Official Records of the Union and Confederate Armies*, ser. 1, vol. 2, 320. See also *Report of the Joint Committee*, pt. 2, 39, 40.

65. Eusey, "The American Civil War," 43.

66. McDowell, quoted in *Official Records of the Union and Confederate Armies*, ser. 1, vol. 2, 320.

67. Samuel P. Heintzelman, quoted in *Official Records of the Union and Confederate Armies*, ser. 1, vol. 2, 404.

68. Longacre, *The Early Morning of War*, 436.

69. Davis, *Battle at Bull Run*, 237; and Longacre, *The Early Morning of War*, 448–476.

70. Quoted in Longacre, *The Early Morning of War*, 437.

71. Eppa Hunton, quoted in *Official Records of the Union and Confederate Armies*, ser. 1, vol. 2, 545.

72. Robert E. Withers, quoted in *Official Records of the Union and Confederate Armies*, ser. 1, vol. 2, 547, 548.

73. John B. Kershaw, quoted in *Official Records of the Union and Confederate Armies*, ser. 1, vol. 2, 523, 524 (emphasis added).

74. Joseph E. Johnston, quoted in *Official Records of the Union and Confederate Armies*, ser. 1, vol. 2, 476.

75. P. G. T. Beauregard, quoted in *Official Records of the Union and Confederate Armies*, ser. 1, vol. 2, 496.

76. McPherson, *Battle Cry of Freedom*, 344.

77. Historian Ethan Rafuse, in his *A Single Grand Victory*, followed the narrative of Hennessy but interpreted some of the details in the reports of Hunton and Withers differently: "As Hunton's men reclaimed the area around the Henry House [after a major charge that cleared the field of the Federals], Withers's men gained possession of the eight guns of Ricketts's shattered battery for the South and turned them on the Federals. Finding the Sudley Road no longer a safe haven, Sherman's and Willcox's men decided to abandon Henry Hill altogether and began falling back northward into the Young's Branch Valley. As Major George Sykes's battalion of regulars moved into the woods west of the Sudley Road to cover the Federal withdrawal from Henry Hill, Withers pushed his command down the slope from Ricketts's battery into the Sudley Road, where the men quickly became disorganized" (181, 182).

78. Hennessy, *The First Battle of Manassas*, 97.

79. Jubal A. Early, *Jubal Early's Memoirs: Autobiographical Sketch and Narrative of the War Between the States* (Baltimore, MD: Nautical & Aviation Publishing Company of America, 1989), 25 (emphasis added). See also Jubal A. Early, quoted in *Official Records of the Union and Confederate Armies,* ser. 1, vol. 2, 557.

80. P. G. T. Beauregard, "The First Battle of Bull Run," in Underwood and Buel, *Battles and Leaders of the Civil War*, 1:215.

81. Brother Johnson, quoted in John N. Loughborough, "Sketches of the Past—No. 123," *Pacific Union Recorder*, March 21, 1912, 10. This statement comes from a former Confederate soldier who was at the Battle of First Manassas and shared his experience with Loughborough at Prescott, Arkansas, in 1895.

82. *Report of the Joint Committee*, pt. 2, 245.

83. John G. Barnard, *The Confederate States Army and Bull Run* (New York: D. Van Nostrand, 1862), 111; emphasis added.

84. Keyes, *Fifty Years' Observation of Men and Events*, 434.

85. Douglas S. Freeman, introduction to *War Years With Jeb Stuart*, ix.

86. Eusey, "The American Civil War, 58.

87. Blackford, *War Years With Jeb Stuart*, 33, 34.

88. Ibid., 34.

89. Eusey's remarks before quoting Blackford. Eusey, "The American Civil War," 58.

90. Ibid. In *The Early Morning of War*, Longacre, 433, cited the latter part of this statement from Blackford and interpreted it as taking place during the last phase of the battle on Chinn Ridge. Thus, Blackford would have seen "the fields beyond Chinn Ridge" filled with the confused men fleeing "like bees," instead of the confused ranks on Henry Hill. If Blackford's account is taken in its entirety as accurate, however, he specifically identified the ridge he was eyeing as the one where "Jackson won the name of Stonewall," which was Henry Hill. Blackford, *War Years With Jeb Stuart*, 34.

91. See Eusey, "The American Civil War," 60.

92. Longacre, *The Early Morning of War*, 422, 423, made a compelling case for a multipronged Confederate assault that drove the Thirteenth and Thirty-Eighth New York off Henry Hill into a retreat. He also affirmed that this assault drove the Sixty-Ninth New York into retreat but also that they panicked as well. If this scenario is correct, then White's narrative could still fit within its framework. The possibility of a different interpretation of the events that transpired on Henry Hill during the afternoon of July 21, 1861, does not necessarily threaten the viability of White's supernatural narrative.

93. White, *Testimonies for the Church*, 1:267.

94. Ibid.

95. Ibid.

96. Beauregard, "The First Battle of Bull Run," 217, 218.

97. White, *Testimonies for the Church*, 1:267.

98. Edward P. Alexander, *Military Memoirs of a Confederate: A Critical Narrative* (New York: Charles Scribner's Sons, 1907), 50.

99. White, *Testimonies for the Church*, 1:267.

100. Winfield Scott, quoted in *Official Records of the Union and Confederate Armies,* ser. 1, vol. 2 (Washington, DC: Government Printing Office, 1880), 752, 753 (emphasis added).

101. Louis Blenker, quoted in *Report of the Joint Committee*, pt. 2, 76.

102. Whitman, *Specimen Days and Collect*, 22, 23 (emphasis added).

103. Whitman was living in Brooklyn when he learned of the defeat at Bull Run from the New York newspapers. In 1863, he moved to Washington, "and it is likely that he spoke there with witnesses to the aftermath of the battle." See Simpson, Sears, and Sheehan-Dean, *The Civil War*, 500.

104. White, *Testimonies for the Church*, 1:267.

105. Ibid.

106. Beauregard, e.g., discounted what he called a "sentimental or ultra-dramatic explanation" of the retreat in "The First Battle of Bull Run," 216, 217.

107. White, *Testimonies for the Church*, 1:267.

CHAPTER 6

A FORECAST OF THE BATTLES:
FIRST MANASSAS TO STONES RIVER

Years after the Civil War ended, Confederate General P. G. T. Beauregard conjectured that the Battle of First Manassas, and all other battles afterward, were based on "the gradual result of the operation of many forces, both of opposing design and actual collision, modified more or less by the falls of chance."[1] He thus rejected the idea of any supernatural intervention as a valid explanation for the outcome of any one battle. Ellen White, however, claimed to have seen an angel intervene in First Manassas and dramatically influence its outcome. After describing the angel on the battlefield, she gave a supernatural explanation of the vision: "Then it was explained that God had this nation in His own hand, and would not suffer victories to be gained faster than He ordained, and would permit no more losses to the Northern men than in His wisdom He saw fit, to punish them for their sins."[2]

This explanation set forth a theological interpretation of the war—a nation in God's hands—and then announced divine intervention in the battles. While all wars involve battle patterns of victories and losses, the significance of this statement is its emphasis on the nature of God's involvement in this particular war. In one broad sweep, White forecast the pattern of Union victories and losses throughout the entire course of the forthcoming conflict and attributed it to God's punitive action.

The forecast

As she began the account of this vision, White set forth her view very clearly: "God is punishing this nation for the high crime of slavery." Her indictment included both sides in the war: "He will punish the South for the sin of slavery, and the North for so long suffering its overreaching and overbearing influence." Yet, "He has the destiny of the nation in His hands."[3] In the backdrop of the indictment, White set forth her vision of the battle of First Manassas in which she saw an angel descend and "waved his hand backward," causing instant confusion in the advancing Northern troops and "a precipitate retreat."[4] Immediately following the angel in the vision, she wrote the explanation given her as quoted above and then stated, "And had the Northern army at this time pushed the battle still further in their fainting, exhausted condition, the far greater struggle and destruction which awaited them would have caused great triumph in the South. God would not permit this, and sent an angel to interfere."[5] *This angelic intervention in the first major battle of the Civil War was the context in which White understood how God would involve Himself in the entire war.*

The angel on the battlefield was, therefore, an illustration of how God "had this nation in His own hand" and would guide the ultimate outcome—a Northern victory. This victory would not come quickly and easily, however. For God "would not *suffer* [allow] victories to be gained faster than He ordained, and would *permit* no more losses to the Northern men than in His wisdom He saw fit." This forecast, first published approximately a month after the First Battle of Bull Run, depicted a seesaw pattern of Union victories and losses in the forthcoming war. That is, there would be up periods of victories and down periods of losses in the Union battles. The up periods would involve those victories that came only when God "ordained" them, and the down periods would involve only enough losses as "in His wisdom He saw fit." This up-down pattern of the battles would be directly related to God's punishment of the North for compromising with the South in the sin of slavery.

This prediction should not be viewed in isolation from White's other statements about the war, particularly the following statement: "When our nation observes the fast which God has chosen, then will He accept their prayers as far as the war is concerned."[6] This "fast" to which she pointed was the emancipation of the slaves.[7]

Thus, the nature of this up-and-down pattern of the Union battles would be directly influenced by the progress of emancipation. The implication of these statements, when taken together, is that once God's purpose of punishment ran its course and emancipation of the slaves became a reality, the pattern of the battle outcomes would be decidedly in favor of the Union.

Because this brief but sweeping vision gave only the big picture without much detail, and White herself never referenced this statement in relation to the progress of the war, the interpreter is left to study the battles and determine where (or whether) the victory-loss pattern she described can be found in the course of the war. This chapter and the next two will therefore survey the rising and falling fortunes of the Union battles in relation to the story of emancipation. In a sense, these chapters will tell the story of the war with its drama but with the theological perspective of White's prophecy. Only the battles of significance are discussed, and they are placed generally in chronological order, rather than by theaters of the war. The personal interest story of Abraham Lincoln, emancipation, the generals, and Ellen White's family will be featured in the story as well.

It should be noted that these three chapters are the author's interpretation of the Civil War battles from the perspective of White's forecast. There are, of course, other ways of interpreting the events of the Civil War, each with its own merit.[8] This interpretation consists of a proposal where one could apply White's theological prognostication to the battles and political events of the war and therefore suggests only possibilities. That there is an inevitable subjective element in this way of interpreting the Civil War cannot be denied. The history of the war is available for all to study and compare with White's vision, which was first published in August 1861.

Series of losses in the autumn of 1861

Battle of First Manassas. The Union experienced a painful and humiliating loss at this first battle, as discussed in the previous chapter. The shock of defeat created in the North a grim determination to regroup and strike at the rebels again. Consequently, three-year volunteers flooded recruiting offices in the North, and President Lincoln appointed George B. McClellan to be commander of the newly named Army of the Potomac.

Battle of Wilson's Creek and Battle of Ball's Bluff. The Battle of Wilson's Creek on August 10 was another Union loss that sent waves of shock and disappointment throughout the North, although not as large as the shock of the Bull Run loss.[9] The Battle of Ball's Bluff on October 21 was a small battle in terms of numbers, but it was one of the worst defeats, proportionally, that either side suffered during the entire Civil War.[10] Thus, the first six months of the war were a difficult period of losses for the Union.

Series of union victories in the winter and spring of 1862

January 1862 was a month of gloom in Washington, especially for President Lincoln. The *Trent* affair, with the release of James Murray Mason and John Slidell, had produced a feeling of depression. The Northern banks and the U.S. Treasury were reneging on previous commitments to fund the war. News of war contract scandals dominated the front pages of the papers. And, most significantly, General McClellan's Army of the Potomac had done nothing for six months except send several regiments to disaster at Ball's Bluff, which included the death of a U.S. senator. To top this all off, McClellan had fallen ill with typhoid fever.[11] "What shall I do?" the president lamented to one of his generals, "The bottom is out of the tub."[12] Fortunately for Lincoln and the North, however, February would be the beginning of a string of stunning victories for the Union. If we look at this period from White's perspective, God "in His wisdom" permitted "no more losses to the Northern men."

Battles of Fort Henry and Fort Donelson. Forts Henry and Donelson, twelve miles apart on the Tennessee and Cumberland Rivers just south of the Kentucky-Tennessee border, were vital defenses on the Confederate line. Ulysses S. Grant, an obscure Union commander at the time, recognized the two forts as the gateways into the enemy's heartland and took them both in February 1862. After several days of bloody fighting at Fort Donelson, Grant called for "unconditional surrender," a phrase that made him famous throughout the North. Because his initials were U. S., he became known as "Unconditional Surrender" Grant.[13] Nashville, the hub of transportation, communications, and ammunition for the Confederacy, soon fell and was a devastating loss.

Grant wanted to forge ahead and take more of the Confederacy, but the Union high command held him back. Years later, he reflected on this experience: "My opinion was and still is that immediately after the fall of Fort Donelson the way was opened to the National forces all over the South-west without much resistance." Federal troops, he believed, "could have marched to Chattanooga, Corinth, Memphis and Vicksburg" and ended the war in the West, avoiding the carnage that followed later. But "providence ruled differently," Grant penned in his *Memoirs*. "Time was given the enemy to collect armies and fortify his new positions."[14] Thus, the war was prolonged when it could have been shorter. Grant's understanding of providence had a similar ring to Ellen White's understanding that God "would not suffer victories [for the North] to be gained faster than He ordained."

Battle of Pea Ridge. On March 7–8, Confederate Major General Earl Van Dorn led some twenty thousand troops in an attack on the Union army led by Brigadier General Samuel R. Curtis in northwestern Arkansas at the Battle of Pea Ridge, or Elkhorn Tavern. The Confederates were repulsed, and the Federals thus maintained control of Missouri and northwestern Arkansas. In the meantime, Grant moved his Union forces to Pittsburg Landing on the Tennessee River, twenty miles from Corinth, Mississippi, and waited for the troops of Brigadier General Don Carlos Buell to join him. With the Confederate army of about forty-five thousand troops and the Union army of about seventy-five thousand converging on the same area, the stage was set for the first great battle of the Civil War—the Battle of Shiloh.

Battle of Shiloh. Neither side anticipated the horror of what happened on April 6–7 in the customarily serene woods and fields of Shiloh, Tennessee. The dead, dying, and wounded lay everywhere, and the blood-soaked surgeons in the improvised hospitals created ghastly mounds of severed arms and legs from their cutting and sawing. With more than twenty-three thousand casualties on both sides combined, Shiloh dwarfed all previous battles, including the First Battle of Bull Run. Although the battle turned back a Confederate attempt to recapture Middle Tennessee, the Northern populace was shocked when reports of the horrific casualties filtered through the papers. The Union's unpreparedness for the battle also made the rounds and turned the public against Grant. Stories of his drinking resurfaced in the White House, and many friends and advisors urged Lincoln to remove Grant from command. After listening attentively one evening to those who wanted to sack Grant, "the president rose from his chair and spoke in an earnest tone that ended the conversation: 'I can't spare this man; he fights.' "[15]

Naval victories. In addition to the Federal victories in Tennessee, the North was thrilled to learn about the stunning naval victories of Flag Officer David G. Farragut, with his Gulf expeditionary force of twenty-four wooden warships carrying 245 guns, nineteen mortar boats, and fifteen thousand soldiers under the command of

Benjamin Butler. Controlling the Mississippi River was essential to winning the war and was the "key to the whole situation,"[16] according to President Lincoln. Winfield Scott's "Anaconda Plan" had called for the dividing of the Confederacy by seizing control of the Mississippi River, and it was Farragut who undertook this enterprise. Entering the mouth of the Mississippi, he bombarded and fought his way through Fort Jackson and Fort St. Philip and was essentially unopposed on the rest of the journey to New Orleans, in Louisiana.

The capture of New Orleans during April 25 to May 1 was Farragut's most significant naval achievement, followed by the surrender of Baton Rouge, the second state capital to fall, and then Natchez, Mississippi. Vicksburg, Mississippi, put up a fight with its big guns, and Farragut let it go for the time being. Thus, "from New Orleans to Vicksburg, the Mississippi was a 400-mile Union highway by the end of May." Up north, on June 6, the Union river fleet launched an attack on Memphis and captured most of its river fleet, resulting in the city's surrender.[17]

Later in June, the Union launched another assault against Vicksburg, with Farragut's fleet taking a leading role. But due to the low levels of the river and troops prostrated by malaria, dysentery, and typhoid, the Federals gave up the first Vicksburg Campaign by the end of July. "Despite the failure to capture Vicksburg in 1862," explained James McPherson, "the four months from the fall of Fort Henry on February 6 to the fall of Memphis were a period of remarkable Union success in the West."[18] During this time, the *New-York Daily Tribune* announced, "The rebels themselves are panic-stricken or despondent. It now requires no very far reaching prophet to predict the end of this struggle."[19]

One "far reaching prophet," however, had forecast at the beginning of the war that it would not be over as soon as everyone had hoped. This remarkable series of Union victories in the Western theater during the winter and spring of 1862 appeared to be the end of the Confederacy. But Vicksburg, the "Gibraltar on the Mississippi,"[20] remained defiant, and Thomas "Stonewall" Jackson was already engaging Union forces in what would become one of the most celebrated campaigns of the Civil War. If we view this period of the war from White's interpretation, God "would not suffer [Union] victories to be gained faster than He ordained."

Series of Union losses in the spring and summer of 1862

Jackson's Shenandoah Valley Campaign. In a series of brilliant maneuvers and battles in Virginia, Confederate General Stonewall Jackson outmaneuvered and outfought multiple Federal forces of about sixty-four thousand strong with roughly sixteen thousand troops. The deeply religious, eccentric, secretive, unpredictable, and gifted Jackson proved to be one of the best generals of the Civil War. From May 8 to June 9, Jackson marched his army of seventeen thousand men across 350 miles, fought and won four battles against three separate Union armies with combined numbers twice Jackson's own, inflicted twice as many casualties as Jackson's army suffered, and immobilized nearly sixty thousand enemy troops.[21] As a result of his conquests (McDowell, May 8; Front Royal, May 23; Winchester, May 25; Cross Keys, June 8; and Port Republic, June 9), Jackson established himself as a terror in parts of the North and the foremost hero in the Confederacy. His Shenandoah Valley Campaign gave the South a ray of hope in the midst of a dismal Confederate outlook.

Battle of Seven Pines. As Jackson was battling in the valley during May, General George B. McClellan had positioned his large army outside of Richmond, Virginia, with two wings divided north and south on the Chickahominy River. Arrayed against him to defend the Confederate capital was General Joseph E. Johnston's army. After a huge storm threatened to wipe out the bridges connecting the two halves of McClellan's army, Johnston seized the opportunity and threw part of his army against one of the Union corps south of the river on May 31 and June 1. The result was the Battle of Seven Pines, or Fair Oaks, in which the men fought up to their knees in swamp water, blinded by thick brush. It was the most brutal battle since Shiloh seven weeks earlier. The fighting ended in a tactical draw, with both sides claiming victory.

The significance of this battle was its profound impact on the commanders of both armies. On the Union side, McClellan had fought his first big battle and was unnerved by the carnage and loss of life as he surveyed the battlefield. Already reluctant to send his beloved troops into battle, this experience reinforced his propensity to lay siege rather than battle, which became one of Lincoln's great frustrations with him.[22] On the Confederate side, General Johnston had been wounded during the first day's fighting, and Jefferson Davis chose to replace him with an unassuming general who had already served his country for thirty years as an honorable soldier. McClellan believed that this new opponent was "*too* cautious & weak under grave responsibility" and was "likely to be timid & irresolute in action."[23] The irony behind these words was that McClellan actually described *himself* in battle.

But Robert E. Lee, the new general of the principal Confederate army, was about to change the course of the Civil War and prove himself to be one of the great field commanders in military history.

Seven Days Battles. In early June 1862, Confederate morale was in a terrible state. With the series of losses in the West along the Mississippi River and in Tennessee, they desperately needed victories. The Confederate capital of Richmond was especially filled with alarm as George McClellan's Federal army of more than one hundred thousand moved within five miles of the city, intending to take it. If McClellan played his cards right, he could take Richmond and the war would be over. But, typical of his style, he delayed, while Lee used June to build a formidable army in Richmond of about ninety thousand men, including Stonewall Jackson's army, to defend the city. Never being one to react to the enemy, Lee chose to take the initiative and strike McClellan first in what would become a series of significant engagements called the Seven Days Battles.

The Seven Days campaign actually consisted of five major battles that "introduced warfare on a massive scale to the Eastern Theater."[24] On June 26, the first engagement took place at Mechanicsville, Virginia, even though Jackson failed to arrive on time, upsetting Lee's plan. The next engagement was at Gaines's Mill on June 27, in which Lee launched fifty thousand men in the largest single attack of the war. Things didn't go as Lee had planned, but he persisted in striking McClellan at Savage Station on June 29, Glendale Farm on June 30, and finally at Malvern Hill on July 1. Lee's army sustained significant casualties of about twenty thousand, compared to sixteen thousand Union casualties. The assault on Malvern Hill was especially bloody, as Lee sent his troops against the Union artillery in a strong fortified position. The units of charging Confederate soldiers were literally pulverized by the bombardment. One Confederate division commander remarked that "it was not war—it was murder."[25]

Although the Federals had suffered only one tactical defeat at Gaines's Mills, their commander had led them in constant retreats over the last seven days, ultimately withdrawing to Harrison's Landing after Malvern Hill. Several of McClellan's generals felt that, instead of ordering a final retreat, he should have launched an immediate counterstrike to capture Richmond. "The idea of stealing away in the night from such a position, after such a victory," wrote Captain Biddle of McClellan's staff, "was simply galling." One general felt that the final order to retreat was "prompted by cowardice or treason."[26] Northern morale that had soared in the spring due to the victories in the Western theater now plummeted because of McClellan's failure in front of Richmond. The hope that the war would soon be over dissipated, and Northerners finally recognized that enormous sacrifice and loss would be necessary to win the war.

On the Confederate side, General Lee's assaults on the Federal army during the Seven Days campaign, although marred by tactical lapses, ended in ultimate victory, because he had driven the Federal army away from Richmond and had saved the Confederate capital. Lee had given the South their "first major victory in nearly a year, helping to erase some of the sting from losses in the Mississippi Valley, Middle Tennessee, and along the Atlantic coast." Southerners were elated, and Lee was propelled into the limelight, soon "to become the unchallenged military hero of the Confederacy."[27]

Viewing the Seven Days Battles from Ellen White's vision, one could say that God "in His wisdom" allowed this significant loss to the Union because He "had this nation in His own hand."[28] From this theological perspective, the events connected with the Seven Days Battles can be considered a part of God's divine intervention. If McClellan had taken Richmond and the war ended slavery would have been left largely in tact. Consequently, this down period in the Northern war effort would serve its purpose in bringing about ultimate victory and, most importantly, ultimate emancipation.

First draft of the Emancipation Proclamation. Impacted by the outcome of the Seven Days Battles, Lincoln stunned his cabinet on July 22 by reading the initial draft of a proclamation promising emancipation.[29] At the beginning of the war, his goal was only to save the Union. In his inaugural address and his special message to Congress on July 4, 1861, for example, the subject of slavery was essentially absent. "But now, sixteen months later, his developing ideas, the press of events, the military defeats, and his own sense of timing, coalesced into a determination to redefine the war's purpose."[30] He thus added emancipation as a second war goal in order to achieve the first—restoration of the Union. This document proposed emancipation as a "fit and necessary military measure" and declared that on January 1, 1863, "all persons held as slaves within any state or states, wherein the constitutional authority of the United States shall not then be practically recognized, ... shall then, thenceforward, and forever, be free."[31] The president made it clear to the cabinet that he "had resolved upon this step, and had not called them together to ask their advice, but to lay the subject-matter before them" and solicit their feedback.[32] Secretary Seward urged Lincoln to wait and issue the proclamation after military success on the battlefield, rather than immediately following the Peninsula disaster.[33] Lincoln later recalled, "The wisdom of the view of the Secretary of State struck me with very great force."[34] So the president put the proclamation away in his desk and waited for a victory on the battlefield—a victory that was painfully slow in coming.

Battle of Second Manassas. After the Seven Days Battles, Lee set his sights on striking the newly organized Federal Army of Virginia, commanded by John Pope, an antislavery commander who had experienced success in the West and whom Lincoln hoped would bring victory in Virginia. But this was not to be. Lee moved his forces northwest from Richmond to counter Pope's maneuvers, splitting his army between his two top generals, Stonewall Jackson and James Longstreet. On August 9, Jackson's twenty-four thousand Confederates clashed with part of Pope's army of about nine thousand, commanded by Nathaniel Banks, at Cedar Mountain, Virginia, and achieved a hard-fought victory. Jackson's famous "foot cavalry" then marched fifty-five miles around Pope's flank (August 25–26) in order to seize the Federal supply depot at Manassas Junction. Jackson eventually positioned his army in strong defensive lines on the field of the 1861 Bull Run, or Manassas, battlefield.

On August 29, the Battle of Second Manassas, or Bull Run, began when Pope launched a series of assaults on Jackson's lines with his force of sixty thousand troops. The Confederates repulsed the attacks; by the end of the day, both sides had experienced heavy casualties. In the meantime, the other half of Lee's army, commanded by Longstreet, arrived and took a position on Pope's left flank. The next day, August 30, Pope renewed his attacks on Jackson, apparently unaware of Longstreet's twenty-eight thousand men to his left. Late in the afternoon Longstreet launched a punishing assault on Pope, sending the Federal army in another retreat from the battlefield of Manassas.[35]

It was a humiliating defeat and a repetition of the first battle at Manassas on July 21, 1861. "I have heard of people being knocked into the middle of next week," Lincoln remarked on September 4, "but this is the first time I ever knew of their being knocked into the middle of last year."[36] The discouragement and frustration from another major military setback was compounded with the news that McClellan had failed to send Pope the military support he needed to win the battle. One general, Fitz John Porter, was eventually court-martialed for failing to support Pope on August 29.

Additionally, England viewed the defeat at Second Manassas as proof that the North was losing the war. The British government believed that Pope's army had received a "very complete smashing" at the Second Battle of Bull Run and that both Washington and Baltimore were soon to fall. They were poised to acknowledge the independence of the South with one more major Union loss. As such, these were very dark, dismal days for the North. As the news of the devastating loss spread throughout the Yankee newspapers in early September, the cry was one of despondency.[37] It is no small wonder that Lincoln was reported to be "very downcast" and full of "apprehension" during this period.[38] Nevertheless, the president had already declared earlier in June that he would "maintain this contest until successful, or till I die, or am conquered, or my term expires, or Congress or the country forsakes me."[39]

As the shattered Federal army made its way back to Washington after the battle on the night of August 30, 1862, the fate of the Union was at stake. Confederate forces were already at work to take the border state of Kentucky and invade western Tennessee. The war had changed dramatically by summer's end, and Confederate hopes were high as Lee's army splashed across the Potomac into Maryland on September 4, hoping to strike a powerful blow to Northern morale. "Never afterward was a final southern victory quite as close as it was in September 1862," wrote Bruce Catton. "The two halves of the war met here—the early formative half, when both the war and the change that would come from the war might still be limited and controlled, and the terrible latter half, which would grind on to its end without limits and without controls."[40]

Those Adventists who remembered Ellen White's message must have found courage during this discouraging down period in the war. Although the Seven Days and Second Manassas battles were significant losses to the Union, there was hope in the words that God "has the destiny of the nation in his hands" and would permit "no more losses to the Northern men than in his wisdom he saw fit."[41] President Lincoln also waited and hoped for a victory as his Emancipation Proclamation remained hidden from the public, tucked away in his desk.

Lee's Maryland Campaign and the lost orders

Once Lee's army arrived in Frederick, Maryland, he decided on his strategy for the campaign and articulated it in Special Order 191. He split his army into various pieces, sending three of those pieces under the command of Stonewall Jackson against Harpers Ferry, a critical point in Union hands. The other pieces he sent deeper into Maryland across the South Mountain range toward Hagerstown. Unfortunately, as all the Confederates marched away from Frederick, the campaign began to unravel. Part of the problem was that Lee's army was suffering from straggling and desertion. He estimated later that of the fifty-five thousand he started with on the campaign, one-third to one-half of the army fell out of the ranks due to exhaustion, poor diet, and inadequate clothing. Additionally, Marylanders did not join the Confederate ranks as Lee had anticipated. Worst of all, his Special Order 191 fell into Union hands.[42]

On September 7, McClellan, who had been demoted because of Second Manassas but later restored, marched his large army out of Washington northward into Maryland at a snail's pace in search of Lee. McClellan was cautious as usual and uncertain of the whereabouts of the Confederate army, fearful that it was much larger than his. Three days after Lee's army had left Frederick, the Union army marched into town on September 13, greeted by the cheers of citizens waving flags and hugging McClellan's horse. On that same day, an extraordinary event transpired outside of town in the ranks of the Twenty-Seventh Indiana, as told by James McPherson:

> Corporal Barton W. Mitchell flopped down in the shade of a tree along a fenceline to enjoy a welcome rest. As he relaxed, however, Mitchell noticed a bulky envelope lying in the grass. Curious, he picked it up and discovered inside a sheet of paper wrapped around three cigars. As a comrade went off to hunt for a match so they could smoke their lucky find, Mitchell noticed that the paper contained writing under the heading "Headquarters, Army of Northern Virginia, Special Orders, No. 191," and was dated September 9. Mitchell's eyes grew wider as he read through the orders studded with names that Northern soldiers knew all too well—Jackson, Longstreet, Stuart, Hill—and was signed "R.H. Chilton, Assist. Adj.-Gen. By command of Gen. R.E. Lee."[43]

The incredible find was passed up the lines and authenticated before it was given to McClellan in his headquarters. The surprised general studied the document carefully and then, throwing up his hands, exclaimed, "Now I know what to do!" At noon that day, he sent a telegram to the president: "I have all the plans of the Rebels and will catch them in their own trap if my men are equal to the emergency."[44] As Bruce Catton explained, "The fog of war which always limits the vision of an army commander suddenly dissolved and everything became clear. McClellan knew as much about Lee's plans as if he had personally attended Lee's last staff conference. The game was being handed to him on a silver platter." McClellan had become "the beneficiary of the greatest security leak in American military history."[45] According to Catton, "Lee's army of invasion had split into pieces like an exploding shell, and the Army of the Potomac, massed in and near Frederick, Maryland, was ideally situated to exploit this situation. No Civil War general was ever given so fair a chance to destroy the opposing army one piece at a time."[46]

If McClellan acted quickly and put his troops into immediate action, marching them toward the scattered divisions of Lee's army and forcing the South Mountain gaps, he could deliver a decisive blow to the Confederacy's principal army and possibly end the war. But this didn't happen. Hours passed before he issued the first orders to the commanders who were to march west and attack the divided enemy in the South Mountain gaps. His plan was good on paper, but its execution was slower than a turtle. Not until the next day did McClellan finally get his columns moving—eighteen hours after first reading Lee's lost orders! By the time the Federal army reached the South Mountain passes, Lee had received word of the movement and had plugged the gaps with his forces.[47] Had the situation been reversed, with Lee in McClellan's place, Lee would have sent his army marching within the hour of finding the lost orders.[48]

Battle of Antietam

McClellan had lost a once-in-a-lifetime opportunity to deal the Confederacy a mortal blow. The subsequent events prepared the way for the bloodiest one-day battle in American history at Antietam Creek. On the morning of September 17, McClellan had more than seventy thousand troops in place against the Confederate force of approximately thirty-six thousand, almost a two-to-one advantage. His plan was to put pressure on both of Lee's flanks, weaken the center, and punch through and cut the Confederates off from the Potomac River, which was a few miles away. Lee was taking a huge risk in backing his army against the Potomac with only one ford to cross. If things went wrong for him, the situation could be disastrous. The battle ended up being three separate battles as the day progressed. It started at the northern end of the field with heavy Union attacks that were resisted by the rebel side. It then shifted to the center field with heavy Union attacks and a breakthrough. The Federal commanders begged for reinforcements to exploit the break, but McClellan refused to commit his last reserves, and the fighting dissipated. In the afternoon, the battle shifted to the southern end of the field, where the Federals pushed the rebels back dangerously close to the river. As one Union private witnessed the carnage before him, he observed that "the whole landscape for an instant turned slightly red."[49] Just as the Confederates were on the brink of defeat, the last division from Harpers Ferry arrived from an all-day march and immediately deployed on the field, plowing into the Union left flank and stopping the final attacks. The battle soon sputtered to an end late in the afternoon, essentially a tactical draw.[50]

Aftermath of Antietam

According to James McPherson, "Night fell on a scene of horror beyond imagining—2,108 Union dead and estimates ranging from 1,546 to 2,700 Confederate dead on the battlefield; 9,549 Union wounded and estimates of 7,752 to 9,024 Confederate wounded. Of the wounded on both sides, at least two thousand would die of their wounds. The detritus of battle lay thickly on the field: smashed weapons and gun carriages, dead horses, scraps of bloody clothing, discarded knapsacks and blanket rolls, and the smell of rotting corpses, vomit, and excrement."[51] As the sun rose the next morning and illuminated the landscape, a Pennsylvania soldier wrote in his diary: "No tongue can tell, no mind can conceive, no pen portray the horrible sights I witnessed."[52] It had been the bloodiest day in American history.

Men on both sides expected the battle to resume on September 18, but nothing really happened, other than sporadic picket firing, as burial squads began their grisly task. McClellan received thirteen thousand reinforcements during the day that, combined with the twenty-thousand who had remained in reserve during the battle, gave him more fresh troops than Lee had men in his entire force. Because he still assumed that the enemy's forces outnumbered his own, however, McClellan decided not to renew the attack. In the meantime, Lee planned a retreat across the Potomac during the day, and his army made a clean escape that night. Although the battle was a tactical standoff as neither side drove the other from the field, Lee did ultimately retreat and thus gave a marginal victory to the Union.[53]

McClellan considered Antietam a great victory and decided not to pursue Lee across the river. Days went by, and the huge Army of the Potomac slumbered in the Sharpsburg Valley. Finally, in early October, the president went to visit McClellan in person and told the general that "he would be a ruined man if he did not move forward, move rapidly and effectually."[54] Most of October passed with no movement of the army until October 26, when McClellan finally sent troops splashing across the Potomac, a halfhearted advance at best. After the November elections, Lincoln relieved McClellan of command and replaced him with Ambrose Burnside.[55] "The President's patience is at last completely exhausted with McClellan's inaction and never-ending excuses," wrote John G. Nicolay.[56] Robert E. Lee, the nemesis of "Little Mac," however, was sorry to see McClellan go and remarked to James Longstreet that "we always understood each other so well. I fear they may continue to make these changes until they find someone I don't understand."[57]

The consequences of Antietam were enormous. On the diplomatic front, England had been moving toward some kind of intervention in the war. As the Battle of Antietam loomed on the horizon, key British leaders had said that if Lee won another major battle, they would then endeavor to mediate an end to the war. When they learned that Lee had retreated, they decided to wait and see what the Confederates would do in the next campaign. On the home front, the battle impacted the November midterm elections. Before Antietam, the prospect of Democratic control of the House was all but certain. Peace Democrats wanted to restore the Union without war, and War Democrats wanted the Union restored as it was, through military victory. Both positions were disastrous for the Republican cause. As a result of Lee's retreat at Antietam, the Republicans retained the House and gained five seats in the Senate.[58]

The president's vow: Emancipation Proclamation

The most important consequence of Antietam was that Lincoln now had the victory he needed to issue his Emancipation Proclamation. Although a marginal victory, it would suffice. Five days after the battle, he called a special meeting of the cabinet. Salmon Chase recorded the highlights of the discussion in his diary: "I have, as you are aware, thought a great deal about the relation of this war to Slavery," Lincoln told

First reading of the Emancipation Proclamation by Francis Bicknell Carpenter.

them. After mentioning the original draft of the Emancipation Proclamation he had proposed back in July, the president said, "Ever since then, my mind has been much occupied with this subject, and I have thought all along that the time for acting on it might very probably come. I think the time has come now. I wish it were a better time. I wish that we were in a better condition. The action of the army against the rebels has not been quite what I should have best liked. But they have been driven out of Maryland, and Pennsylvania is no longer in danger of invasion."[59]

In a most solemn tone, Lincoln shared what was in his heart: "When the rebel army was at Frederick, I determined, as soon as it should be driven out of Maryland, to issue a Proclamation of Emancipation such as I thought most likely to be useful. I said nothing to any one; but I made the promise to myself, and (hesitating a little)—to my Maker. The rebel army is now driven out, and I am going to fulfill that promise."[60] Gideon Welles recorded in his diary that in the course of the "long" and "earnest" discussion, the president used the terms *vow* and *covenant* to describe his promise to himself and to God. The victory at Antietam was thus "an indication of Divine Will" to the president that "it was his duty to move forward in the cause of emancipation." His mind was made up; "God had decided this question in favor of the slave," he declared.[61]

As the cabinet sat in silence, the president began to read the preliminary draft of the Emancipation Proclamation. It was preliminary in the sense that it would not go into effect until January 1. The document essentially declared that the Confederate slaveholders would have one hundred days to cease rebelling against the Union and lay down their arms. If they did, they could keep their slaves. But if they did not, then as of January 1, 1863, their slaves "shall be then, thenceforward, and forever free."[62] Lincoln didn't believe that the Southern states would stop fighting the war, "but this gesture was politically necessary to maintain his support in Congress and in the nation, and it included the carrot of compensation to loyal slave owners. Although promised in this executive order, such compensation never occurred."[63] After the cabinet suggested a few changes, the document was complete, and newspapers around the country published it, announcing that the president would sign it into law on January 1, 1863.

The reaction around the country was obviously mixed. Charles Sumner spoke for most abolitionists when he declared that "the skies are brighter and the air is purer, now that slavery has been handed over to judgment." Although concerned that the proclamation did not address the moral problems of slavery, Frederick Douglass still rejoiced that "we live to record this righteous decree." Horace Greeley, the editor of the *New-York Daily Tribune*, believed that the document was the "beginning of a new life for the nation," and "one of those stupendous facts in human history which marks not only an era in the progress of the nation, but an epoch in the history of the world."[64] On September 30, the *Review and Herald* published the entire proclamation.[65] Critics, however, attacked the proclamation from every angle, calling it "hollow" and "tyrannous."[66]

But none of what the critics said about the proclamation deterred Lincoln from his purpose. The nature of the war was different now. It was no longer a war to save the Union only; it was a war to destroy the Confederacy and end slavery. The Union would never be the same, and Lincoln knew it was a major risk, but it was one he was willing to take, no matter the consequences.[67]

Major turning point in the war

There was a new phase in the war. Antietam had changed everything. "Many soldiers who fought there would have agreed that Antietam was 'the event' that decided 'the fate of the American Civil War.' They believed that the destiny of their respective nations—the United States and the Confederate States—rested on the outcome of this battle." According to James McPherson: "Antietam was arguably, as Karl Marx and Walter Taylor believed, *the* event of the war."[68] If we interpret Antietam from Ellen White's August 1861 forecast, God had "ordained" the much-needed victory at Antietam. Its timing was delicate and precise, a moment in the war when so much hung in the balance. From this theological perspective, one could say that God's hand was in the outcome of this crucial battle.[69] The union triumph at Antietam initiated the process of emancipation yet prolonged ultimate victory.

Union victories in Kentucky and Mississippi

As the events surrounding Antietam were taking place, Confederate forces were attempting to take Kentucky, the Border State still in the Union. Two rebel armies marched into Kentucky during August and September. Braxton Bragg commanded the larger of the two forces, and Kirby Smith, the other smaller army. Their nemesis was Don Carlos Buell, who was ordered to take Chattanooga by the Union's general-in-chief, Henry Halleck. Buell's summer march across northern Alabama to reach Chattanooga was fraught with problems and was a slow crawl through the state. Bragg got to Chattanooga first with a concentration of thirty thousand troops, while Smith was in Knoxville with ten thousand troops. Jefferson Davis ordered Bragg and Smith to invade Kentucky and draw Buell out of Tennessee. With the two Confederate forces marching northward in Kentucky, Buell had to abandon his stalled campaign against Chattanooga and pursue the rebels to keep them from taking Louisville.

The armies finally clashed at the Battle of Perryville, Kentucky, on October 8, the largest and bloodiest battle in the state. With a marginal Union victory, the Confederates retreated back to Tennessee without further fighting, thus ending the Confederate campaign in Kentucky. The Bluegrass State would remain in the Union for the rest of the war, and the dream of a Confederate Kentucky was gone forever. Historian Christopher Kolakowski believed, "In many ways, both the fate of Kentucky and the fate of the United States rested on the outcome of the campaign and Battle of Perryville."[70]

Meanwhile, Federals dispatched by Ulysses S. Grant to Iuka, Mississippi, collided with Confederate troops under Major General Sterling Price, who were deployed near the Tennessee border to prevent Grant's forces from assaulting Bragg's rear in his Kentucky campaign. Defeated by the bluecoats at Iuka on September 19, Price fell back and joined forces with Major General Earl Van Dorn's troops at the important rail center of Corinth, which had been in Union hands since the withdrawal of General P. G. T. Beauregard's forces in May. On October 3, the combined forces of Price and Van Dorn assaulted the Federals at Corinth and drove them back two miles during the first day of fighting. The next morning fierce Federal resistance ripped the Confederates to pieces, and they made a narrow escape.

Although this was clearly an up period for the Union, the war was far from over. Because of General McClellan's hesitancy to destroy Lee's army after Antietam, the principal rebel army lived to fight again. Additionally, because General Buell failed to take Chattanooga, the gateway to the Confederacy remained closed to the Union. According to Grant, if Buell had advanced "as rapidly as he could march, leaving two or three divisions along the line of the railroad from Nashville forward, he could have arrived [in Chattanooga] with but little fighting, and would have saved much of the loss of life which was afterwards incurred."[71]

Historian Gerald J. Prokopowicz postulated that "if Buell managed to defeat a

Confederate army at Chattanooga in 1862, it would have put Union forces in position to launch a campaign for Atlanta in 1863 instead of 1864. July 1863 might then have been marked by three great Northern victories—at Gettysburg, Vicksburg, and Atlanta—instead of two, a combined blow that might have sealed the fate of the Confederacy twenty-one months early, without the costly summer campaigns of 1864."[72]

If we view Buell's failure to take Chattanooga in 1862 in light of White's prophecy that God "would not suffer victories to be gained faster than He ordained," until "in His wisdom He saw fit, to punish them for their sins,"[73] then this significant delay in the war could be interpreted as divine punishment on the North because they were not yet ready to terminate slavery in the South.

As winter began to chill the landscape, Grant launched a major overland campaign against Vicksburg, Mississippi, that, although it failed, taught him valuable lessons. Lincoln replaced McClellan with Ambrose Everett Burnside, and Buell with William Starke Rosecrans, and made it clear to both of them that he wanted victories before the end of the year. This was unusual, because most Civil War campaigns took place in the spring, summer, and fall, not in the winter. Lincoln believed it was important to have good news from the battlefield so that the Northern people could take heart and support the Union cause. But this was not to be during December and January 1862–1863.

Fredericksburg Campaign

McClellan's successor, Major General Ambrose E. Burnside (known for his whiskers running down the side of his face with his chin clean shaven, initially called the "Burnside cut" and later inverted to "sideburn"), quickly developed a plan in response to Lincoln's bidding to fight. He would rapidly move the largest army in the United States to Fredericksburg, Virginia, before Lee got there and then be in a position to take Richmond. Initially, things went well, and he got there by November 19, 1862, ahead of Lee, whose army was still spread out near Culpepper and the Shenandoah Valley. Unfortunately for Burnside, things didn't work out the way he planned, and Lee brought his army of seventy-five thousand to the Fredericksburg area and embedded the bulk of them in strong positions west of the Rappahannock River on a series of hills that paralleled the river. By the end of December 12, the bulk of Burnside's 120,000-man army was in place, and the stage was set for a huge battle on the next day.

On the morning of December 13, Burnside hoped to apply pressure to Lee's line and get around his right flank on the southern end. Lee's two top generals were commanding the flanks: Stonewall Jackson on the right, and James Longstreet on the left. The Federals began the battle with attacks on Jackson's flank and at one point broke through, only to be repelled. The battle then shifted to Longstreet's left flank at Marye's Heights, the highest ground held by the Confederates. Burnside sent his Federal brigades in huge lines up the gentle slopes, one after the other, only to have them mercilessly mowed down by Confederate fire. At the end of this bloody winter day, the Federals retreated, leaving piles of the dead and wounded on the field behind them. It was one of the most one-sided battles in the war, with the Federals suffering 12,600 casualties and the Confederates fewer than 5,000. Lee prepared for a renewal of the attacks the next morning, but no movement on the Union side occurred. By December 15, Burnside's army had escaped across the river. Lee had lost his opportunity to destroy the Union army.[74]

What momentum the Union had achieved since Antietam was shattered. The South breathed a sigh of relief, while the North reeled in despair. *Harper's Weekly* captured the state of the Northern public: "They have borne, silently and grimly, imbecility, treachery, failure, privation, loss of friends and means, almost every suffering which can afflict a brave people. But they can not be expected to suffer that such massacres as this at Fredericksburg shall be repeated."[75] When Lincoln learned of the disaster, he sank into despair. Burnside's debacle, the staggering Federal losses, and the battle's potential impact on Northern politics and morale sent him into deep depression. When he heard descriptions of the carnage at Fredericksburg, his face "darkened with pain," and he "moaned and groaned in anguish," walking "the floor, wringing his hands and uttering exclamations of grief." He declared to a friend: "If there is a worse place than hell I am in it."[76] The Union and its president were in a crisis. But for any of those Adventists who remembered White's words that God would "permit no more losses to the Northern men than in His wisdom He saw fit," there was hope.

Battle of Stones River

After the Battle of Perryville, General Buell took his troops to Nashville, Tennessee, where the Union high command replaced him with General William Starke Rosecrans, whom they instructed to engage the Confederate army soon. Following the same battle, General Bragg had marched his army back to Knoxville, Tennessee, and from there traveled by train to Chattanooga. Hoping to threaten Union troops, he moved his army to the vicinity of Murfreesboro, about thirty miles southeast of Nashville. In light of intelligence on Bragg's location, Rosecrans launched his winter campaign toward Murfreesboro the day after Christmas. On the evening of December 30, the two armies camped close to each other, less than a mile apart, awaiting battle the next morning.

It was during this evening that one of those unforgettable Civil War stories took place. Like an eerie prelude to battle, the military bands on both sides began to play their favorite tunes: "The music carried clearly on the cold, still air and each could hear the other's playing. 'Yankee Doodle' and 'Hail, Columbia' drifted into everyone's ears, answered by 'Dixie' and 'The Bonnie Blue Flag.' The exchange continued for a time and then one band struck up a tune known and loved by all soldiers, regardless of allegiance, 'Home Sweet Home.' Suddenly all bands on both sides joined in its playing, while thousands of voices, most betraying homesickness, joined in with the words."[77]

In a few short hours, however, these singing soldiers would be slaughtering each other in what would become, percentage-wise, the bloodiest battle of the Civil War.

Early on the morning of December 31, the armies of Bragg (thirty-seven thousand troops) and Rosecrans (forty-six thousand troops) clashed a mile north of Murfreesboro, astride the Nashville Turnpike and Stones River, a stream about thirty yards in width that ran generally parallel to the turnpike. The battle lasted three days, with the most intense fighting taking place on December 31 and January 2, and mostly resting and reorganizing on January 1. Tactically, the battle was a draw, but Bragg withdrew from the field and gave a strategic victory to the Union. In three days of fighting, the Federals lost 13,249 men—killed, wounded, missing, or captured—a 28 percent loss rate. The Confederate army lost 10,266 men, a 27 percent loss rate. More than one out of every four men on both sides who fought in the battle was a casualty, making the Battle of Stones River the Civil War's bloodiest battle by percentage of loss.[78]

"God has crowned our arms with victory," Rosecrans telegraphed to the War Department in Washington. The enemy was "badly beaten, and in full retreat."[79] Washington was elated, and Lincoln telegraphed back to the general: "God bless you, and all with you! Please tender to all, and accept for yourself, the nation's gratitude for yours and their skill, endurance, and dauntless courage."[80] This modest victory was a bright spot in the midst of the gloom over the Fredericksburg debacle and several other losses that had occurred.

A year later in December 1863, even after the significant Federal victories of that year, Lincoln still believed that the victory at Stones River was "one of the most if not the *most* important proofs of support the country has had since the war. If that battle had been lost," the president exclaimed, "it is difficult to see where our fortunes would have landed."[81] From the perspective of Ellen White's forecast, "God had this nation in His own hand, and would not suffer victories to be gained faster than He ordained, and would permit no more losses to the Northern men than in His wisdom He saw fit."[82]

Conclusion

The war touched the lives of James and Ellen White personally during 1862. Their older sons, Edson and Henry, developed a lively interest in the war and frequently traveled to the Battle Creek fairgrounds nearby to watch the recruits for the Union army march and prepare for battle. According to W. C. White, his older brothers "got hold of wartime songs and many a sunny afternoon sat on the fence and practiced, 'Tramp, Tramp, Tramp, the Boys Are Marching' and 'We are Coming, Father Abraham.'" They built their own drums and even supplied themselves with warlike weapons, such as bows and arrows, and shot "troublesome birds" as if in battle. The musically talented Henry was especially good at whistling and once went to the fairgrounds and marched along with the soldiers, "whistling in harmony with the fife [small flute]. The captain gave the signal to the fifers to be silent, and the company of soldiers made their one-mile march keeping step to music of the drum and Henry's whistle."[83]

Some of the noncombatant neighbors were offended at the White boys' warlike play, and they complained. As noncombatants themselves, James and Ellen grew concerned at their sons' interest in the war. They were especially concerned when Henry expressed the desire to join the army as a drummer. After plenty of discussion, Henry chose to abandon his "cherished thought of being in the Army," because he loved his mother and respected her wishes. In 1863, James and Ellen moved their children away from the war influence at Battle Creek.[84] The war touched the lives of

Henry White in 1862
(egwwritings.org)

Edson White in 1862
(egwwritings.org)

all Americans in various ways and would only get worse as more sons were killed in battle.

Chapter in a nutshell

After the vision of the angel on the Manassas battlefield, Ellen White set forth a theological interpretation of the war: "Then it was explained that God had this nation in His own hand, and would not suffer victories to be gained faster than He ordained, and would permit no more losses to the Northern men than in His wisdom He saw fit, to punish them for their sins."[85] Because God had this nation in His hand, He would intervene in the battles of the war. In one broad sweep, White predicted the pattern of Union victories and losses throughout the entire course of the forthcoming conflict and attributed it to God's punitive action. This forecast, first published approximately a month after the First Battle of Bull Run, depicted a seesaw pattern of Union victories and losses in the forthcoming war. That is, there would be up periods of victories and down periods of losses in the Union battles. The up periods would involve those victories that came only when God "ordained" them, and the down periods would involve only enough losses as "in His wisdom He saw fit." This up-down pattern of the Union battles would be directly related to God's punishment on the North for compromising with the South in the sin of slavery. Once God's punishment ran its course and emancipation became a reality, the pattern of battle outcomes would be decidedly in favor of the Union.

The rest of the chapter traces this up-down pattern in the following Union battles of First Manassas to Stones River:

1861 BATTLES	PATTERN
First Manassas	Loss
Wilson's Creek	Loss
Ball's Bluff	Loss
1862 BATTLES	**PATTERN**
Fort Henry	Victory

Fort Donelson	Victory
Pea Ridge	Victory
Shiloh	Victory
New Orleans	Victory
Baton Rouge	Victory
Natchez	Victory
Memphis	Victory
Vicksburg	Loss
Shenandoah Valley	Loss
Seven Pines	Draw
Seven Days	Loss
Second Manassas	Loss
Antietam	Victory
PRELIMINARY DRAFT OF EMANCIPATION PROCLAMATION	
Iuka	Victory
Perryville	Victory
Corinth	Victory
Chattanooga	Loss
Fredericksburg	Loss
Stones River	Victory

1. Beauregard, "The First Battle of Bull Run," in Underwood and Buel, *Battles and Leaders of the Civil War*, 1:217.

2. White, *Testimonies for the Church*, 1:267.

3. Ibid., 1:264.

4. Ibid., 1:267.

5. Ibid.

6. Ibid., 1:258.

7. See chapter 10 for the full discussion.

8. In his classic study *Battle Cry of Freedom*, e.g., preeminent Civil War historian James McPherson set forth an interpretation of the Civil War in the concept of "contingency." He described this as "the recognition that at numerous critical points during the war things might have gone altogether differently." That is, the outcomes of battles were contingent on previous events. "Northern victory and southern defeat in the war," McPherson explained, "cannot be understood apart from the contingency that hung over every campaign, every battle, every election, every decision during the war. This phenomenon of contingency can best be presented in a narrative format—a format this book has tried to provide." McPherson, *Battle Cry of Freedom*, 858.

9. On the Battle of Wilson's Creek, see William Garrett Piston and Richard W. Hatcher III, *Wilson's Creek: The Second Battle of the Civil War and the Men Who Fought It* (Chapel Hill, NC: University of North Carolina Press, 2000).

10. On the Battle of Ball's Bluff, see James A. Morgan III, *A Little Short of Boats: The Battles of Ball's Bluff & Edwards Ferry, October 21–22, 1861*, rev. and exp. ed. (New York: Savas Beatie, 2011).

11. This gloom is succinctly described in McPherson and Hogue, *Ordeal by Fire*, 243.

12. Abraham Lincoln, quoted in David Von Drehle, *Rise to Greatness: Abraham Lincoln and America's Most Perilous Year* (New York: Pricador, 2012), 44.

13. Jean Edward Smith, *Grant* (New York: Simon & Schuster Paperbacks, 2001), 162, 165, 166. For details of this battle, see also James R. Knight, *The Battle of Fort Donelson: No Terms but Unconditional Surrender* (Charleston, SC: History Press, 2011). The importance of the Fort Henry-Fort Donelson Campaign is often overlooked in Civil War history, and two studies provide penetrating analysis: Benjamin Franklin Cooling, *Forts Henry and Donelson: The Key to the Confederate Heartland* (Knoxville, TN: University of Tennessee Press, 1987); and Kendall D. Gott, *Where the South Lost the War: An Analysis of the Fort Henry–Fort Donelson Campaign, February 1862* (Mechanicsburg, PA: Stackpole Books, 2003).

14. Grant, *Memoirs and Selected Letters*, 214, 215.

15. Smith, *Grant*, 205.

16. Abraham Lincoln, quoted in William L. Shea and Terrence J. Winschel, *Vicksburg Is the Key: The Struggle for the Mississippi* (Lincoln, NE: University of Nebraska Press, 2003), 1.

17. See McPherson, *Ordeal by Fire*, 253, 254.

18. See ibid., 256.

19. *New-York Daily Tribune*, February 18, 1862, quoted in ibid.

20. See Shea and Terrence, *Vicksburg Is the Key*, 17, 18.

21. McPherson and Hogue, *Ordeal by Fire*, 264 ; see also Robert G. Tanner, *Stonewall in the Valley: Thomas J. "Stonewall" Jackson's Shenandoah Valley Campaign, Spring 1862* (Mechanicsberg, PA: Stackpole Books, 1996).

22. See T. Harry Williams, *Lincoln and His Generals* (New York: Vintage Civil War Library, 1980), 106, 107, 177, 178.

23. George McClellan to Abraham Lincoln, April 20, 1862, quoted in Stephen W. Sears, ed., *The Civil War Papers of George B. McClellan* (Cambridge, MA: Da Capra Press, 1992), 244, 245 (emphasis in the original).

24. Gary W. Gallagher, ed., *The Richmond Campaign of 1862: The Peninsula and the Seven Days* (Chapel Hill, NC: University of North Carolina Press, 2000), ix. See also McPherson, *Battle Cry of Freedom*, 471.

25. Daniel H. Hill, "McClellan's Change of Base and Malvern Hill," in Underwood and Buel, *Battles and Leaders*

of the Civil War, 2:394.

26. W. F. Biddle, quoted in Stephen W. Sears, To the Gates of Richmond: The Peninsula (New York: Houghton Mifflin, 1992), 337, 338.

27. Gary W. Gallagher, "A Civil War Watershed: The 1862 Richmond Campaign in Perspective," in Gallagher, The Richmond Campaign of 1862, 19, 22.

28. White, Testimonies for the Church, 1:267.

29. For the story of this fateful cabinet meeting, see Michael Burlingame, Abraham Lincoln: A Life (Baltimore, MD: Johns Hopkins University Press, 2008), 2:362–364.

30. Ronald C. White Jr., A. Lincoln: A Biography (New York: Random House, 2009), 495, 496.

31. Basler, The Collected Works of Abraham Lincoln, 5:336, 337.

32. Abraham Lincoln, quoted in Burlingame, Abraham Lincoln: A Life, 2:363.

33. Ibid., 2:363, 364.

34. Abraham Lincoln, quoted in Ronald C. White, A. Lincoln: A Biography, 496.

35. For details of this battle, see John Hennessy, Return to Bull Run: The Campaign and Battle of Second Manassas (New York: Simon & Schuster, 1993). For analysis of the battle in the larger framework of the Confederate counter-thrust in mid-1862, see Benjamin F. Cooling, Counter-Thrust: From the Peninsula to the Antietam (Lincoln, NE: University of Nebraska Press, 2007).

36. Abraham Lincoln, quoted in Burlingame, Abraham Lincoln: A Life, 2:375.

37. James McPherson, Crossroads of Freedom: Antietam (New York: Oxford University Press, 2002), 85, 86.

38. James Wadsworth, quoted in Burlingame, Abraham Lincoln: A Life, 2:375.

39. Basler, The Collected Works of Abraham Lincoln, 5:292.

40. Bruce Catton, This Hallowed Ground: A History of the Civil War (New York: Vintage Civil War Library, 2012), 159.

41. White, "Communication From Sister White," 100, 101.

42. Gary W. Gallagher, The American Civil War: Lectures 1–24, The Great Courses (Chantilly, VA: Teaching Co., 2000), 247, 248.

43. McPherson, Crossroads of Freedom, 107, 108.

44. George McClellan, quoted in Stephen W. Sears, Landscape Turned Red: The Battle of Antietam (New York: Houghton Mifflin, 1983), 113.

45. Bruce Catton, The Army of the Potomac: Mr. Lincoln's Army (Garden City, NY: Doubleday, 1962), 213, 215.

46. Bruce Catton, Terrible Swift Sword (Garden City, NY: Doubleday, 1963), 449.

47. McPherson, Crossroads of Freedom, 111.

48. Ibid., 109.

49. This oft-quoted statement about this battle, and the basis for the title of Sears's book, Landscape Turned Red, comes from Ninth New York Private David L. Thompson, "With Burnside at Antietam," in Underwood and Buel, Battles and Leaders of the Civil War, 2:662.

50. See Gallagher, The American Civil War: Lectures 25–48, 250; Sears, Landscape Turned Red, 180–297; and McPherson, Crossroads of Freedom, 116–129.

51. McPherson, Crossroads of Freedom, 129.

52. Quoted in ibid.

53. McPherson, Crossroads of Freedom, 129, 130.

54. Don Fehrenbacher and Virginia Fehrenbacher, eds., Recollected Words of Abraham Lincoln (Stanford, CA: Stanford University Press, 1996), 132.

55. McPherson, Crossroads of Freedom, 150–154.

56. John G. Nicolay to Therena Bates, November 9, 1862, in Michael Burlingame, ed., With Lincoln in the White House: Letters, Memoranda, and other Writings of John G. Nicolay, 1860-1865 (Carbondale and Edwardsville, IL: southern Illinois University press, 2000), 90.

57. James Longstreet, "The Battle of Fredericksburg," in Underwood and Buel, *Battles and Leaders of the Civil War*, 3:70.

58. See McPherson, *Crossroads of Freedom*, 153, 154.

59. David Herbert Donald, ed., *Inside Lincoln's Cabinet: The Civil War Diaries of Salmon P. Chase* (New York, NY: Longmans, Green, and Co., 1954), 149, 150.

60. Ibid, 150.

61. William E. Gienapp and Erica L. Gienapp, eds., *The Civil War Diary of Gideon Wells: Lincoln's Secretary of the Navy* (Urbana, IL: University of Illinois Press, 2014), 54.

62. "Preliminary Emancipation Proclamation, September 22, 1862," in Basler, *The Collected Works of Abraham Lincoln*, 5:434.

63. Thomas C. Mackey, *A Documentary History of the American Civil War Era*, vol. 2 (Knoxville, TN: University of Tennessee Press, 2013), 325.

64. Quotations from Burlingame, *Abraham Lincoln: A Life*, 2:411, 412.

65. "Proclamation by the President," *Review and Herald*, September 30, 1862, 139.

66. See Von Drehle, *Rise to Greatness*, 292.

67. See Harry S. Stout, *Upon the Altar of the Nation* (New York: Penguin Books, 2006), 168.

68. McPherson, *Crossroads of Freedom*, 8, 9 (emphasis in original); see also D. Scott Hartwig, *To Antietam Cree: The Maryland Campaign of September 1862* (Baltimore, MD: The John Hopkins University Press, 2012). Hartwig's work is the first installment of a two-volume study of the campaign and the climactic Antietam battle. Volume Two is forthcoming at the time of this writing.

69. White, *Testimonies for the Church*, 1:267.

70. Christopher L. Kolakowski, *The Civil War at Perryville: Battling for the Bluegrass* (Charleston, SC: History Press, 2009), 12.

71. Grant, *Memoirs and Selected Letters*, 257.

72. Gerald J. Prokopowicz, "Last Chance for a Short War: Don Carlos Buell and the Chattanooga Campaign of 1862," in Evan C. Jones and Wiley Sword, eds., *Gateway to the Confederacy: New Perspectives on the Chickamauga and Chattanooga Campaigns, 1862–1863* (Baton Rouge, LA: Louisiana State University Press, 2014), 45.

73. White, *Testimonies for the Church*, 1:267.

74. On the Fredericksburg battle, see George C. Rable, *Fredericksburg! Fredericksburg!* (Chapel Hill, NC: University of North Carolina Press, 2002); Francis Augustin O'Reilly, *The Fredericksburg Campaign: Winter on the Rappahannock* (Baton Rouge, LA: Louisiana State University Press, 2006); Gary W. Gallagher, ed., *The Fredericksburg Campaign: Decision on the Rappahannock* (Chapel Hill, NC: University of North Carolina Press, 1995); and Chris Mackowski and Kristopher D. White, *Simply Murder: The Battle of Fredericksburg, December 13, 1862* (El Dorado Hills, CA: Savas Beatie, 2012).

75. *Harper's Weekly*, December 27, 1862, 818.

76. Lincoln, quoted in Burlingame, *Abraham Lincoln: A Life*, 2:446.

77. Herman Hattaway and Archer Jones, *How the North Won: A Military History of the Civil War* (Chicago: University of Illinois Press, 1983), 320.

78. Christopher L. Kolakowski, *The Stones River and Tullahoma Campaigns* (Charleston, SC: History Press, 2011), 87; for detailed studies of the battle, see James Lee McDonough, *Stones River: Bloddy Winter in Tennessee* (Knoxville, TN: The University of Tennessee Press, 1980); and Larry J. Daniel, *Battle of Stones River: The Forgotten Conflict Between the Confederate Army of tennessee and the Union Army of the Cumberland* (Baton Rouge, LA: Louisiana State University press, 2012).

79. William Starke Rosecrans, quoted in *Official Records of the Union and Confederate Armies*, ser. 1, vol. 20 (Washington, DC: Government Printing Office, 1902), pt. 1, 185.

80. Basler, *The Collected Works of Abraham Lincoln*, 6:39.

81. Abraham Lincoln, quoted in Allan Nevins, *The Organized War, 1863–1864*, vol. 3 of *The War for the Union*

(New York: Konecky & Konecky, 1971), 203.

82. White, *Testimonies for the Church*, 1:267.

83. William C. White, quoted in Arthur White, *Ellen G. White*, vol. 2, *The Progressive Years, 1862–1876* (Washington, DC: Review and Herald', 1986), 59, 60.

84. Ibid., 2:60, 61.

85. White, *Testimonies for the Church*, 1:267.

CHAPTER 7

A FORECAST OF THE BATTLES: CHANCELLORSVILLE TO CHATTANOOGA

On January 1, 1863, Abraham Lincoln sat down to sign the most important document of his presidency—the final draft of the Emancipation Proclamation.[1] As his bony fingers grasped the pen and dipped it into the inkwell, his hand and forearm trembled. "I could not for a moment, control my arm," he later recalled, "and a superstitious feeling came over me which made me hesitate."[2]

Dropping the pen, he pondered the occasion for a moment.[3] "Was this all a mistake? Was the trembling a sign, yet another divine warning, this time that he had gone too far, had overreached himself, had taken a step which would end only in disaster?"[4] Then it occurred to the president that for hours he had been shaking hands with hundreds of visitors to the White House for the New Year's Day reception. The tremor was not because of any doubt or hesitation on his part about the proclamation.

Turning to the secretary of state by his side, William Seward, Lincoln said, "I have been shaking hands since nine o'clock this morning, and my right arm is almost paralyzed. If my name ever goes into history it will be for this act, and my whole soul is in it."[5] Seward's son, who was also present, heard the president say, "I never in my life felt more certain that I was doing right than I do in signing this paper."[6] But Lincoln worried, "If my hand trembles when I sign the Proclamation, all who examine the document hereafter will say, 'He hesitated.' "[7] Nevertheless, "It is going to be done," he declared[8] and picked up the pen and "slowly and carefully" signed the Proclamation into history. Looking at those around him with a smile, the president laughed at his earlier apprehension and then quietly remarked, "That will do."[9]

It did do. With this momentous act, Lincoln officially changed the nature of the war and the history of this nation. No longer was the war's only purpose to restore the Union. The newly revised purpose was to restore the Union *and* to emancipate the slaves. Hence, the new Union would be entirely different from the one before the war. Slavery would be gone, and the South's entire social fabric would be radically different. Technically, the proclamation didn't free the slaves immediately. In fact, it only theoretically freed slaves in rebel territory not controlled by U.S. troops. Those slaves in the Border States remained in bondage, because the president lacked the constitutional authority to free them. But he did have the constitutional authority to free rebel slaves as a "war measure." In this sense, then, the final draft of the Emancipation Proclamation signed on January 1, 1863, was a measure of "military necessity"[10] but, nevertheless, a powerful step in a process that ultimately led to the Thirteenth Amendment and the abolition of slavery in the United States.[11]

Although the Emancipation Proclamation addressed the freedom of the slaves, two issues needed to be resolved. First, Lincoln still wanted to compensate the slave owners for their financial loss and colonize the freed slaves in another country, but this was a plan that he would dispense with as the war progressed. Second, the South needed to be completely defeated, so more battles had to be fought and won before freedom became a reality in the nation. In the framework of Ellen White's Civil War interpretation, one could say that the war continued after the proclamation as a punishment on the North for its sin of so long compromising with the slave power in the South. Thus, more suffering and battle losses were in store for the Union, even after the Emancipation Proclamation.

On March 30, Lincoln released his second proclamation for a day of fasting and prayer to occur on April 30. He acknowledged "the deceitfulness" in the people's hearts and that the war "may be but a punishment, inflicted upon" them for their "presumptuous sins, to the needful end" of the "national reformation as a whole People." He called the nation to "humble" itself "before the offended Power," to confess its "national sins, and to pray for clemency and forgiveness."[12] Historian Nicholas Parrillo noted that this proclamation was in "stunning contrast" to Lincoln's August 12, 1861, proclamation for a day of national fasting and prayer. This "document burned with the conviction of sin," whereas the previous one was a "rhetorical flop."[13] On the appointed day of fasting, the nation prayed, but their prayers appeared to bounce off the heavens, for that very day was the beginning of a major disaster on the battlefield.

Battle of Chancellorsville

After the disaster at Fredericksburg, Burnside attempted to compensate by launching a winter offensive in January to outflank Lee. The weather was unseasonably warm, and the rain soaked the ground, causing the artillery and wagons to be swamped in the mud. This failed campaign was known derisively as Burnside's "Mud March."[14] Beside himself, Lincoln relieved Burnside and gave the command of the Army of the Potomac to Joseph Hooker, a brash and egotistical commander known for his fighting spirit, who claimed that he was the one to defeat Lee. Hooker reorganized the army and brought it back into prime fighting condition. As spring approached, Hooker planned to outflank Lee's strong position in Fredericksburg. But Lee left a covering force at Fredericksburg and marched the rest of his army to confront Hooker's Federals, who had concentrated at Chancellorsville, Virginia.

The climactic battle took place April 30–May 6 and ended up being one of the most dramatic engagements of the Civil War. Although outnumbered two to one, Lee took a major chance and divided his small army, sending Stonewall Jackson on a fourteen-mile march around the Union flank. Jackson's troops then charged the Federals with the rebel yell and destroyed an entire corps. The next day, May 3, Lee broke the Federal line and drove Hooker across the Rappahannock River. Chancellorsville was a stunning tactical victory for Lee and was considered to be his masterpiece battle of the war.[15]

Although Chancellorsville was a great victory for Lee, it also involved a great loss for the rebel army. Thomas "Stonewall" Jackson, the famed general of the Confederacy, was making a night reconnaissance during the evening of May 2 and was shot accidently by some of his own troops. He lost a good deal of blood, and his doctor removed his mangled left arm.[16] Upon hearing that Jackson's left arm had been amputated in order to save his life, Lee remarked, "He has lost his left arm, but

I have lost my right."[17] On May 10, Jackson died from his wound, complicated by pneumonia. Grief stricken, Lee wrote to his son, Custis, saying, "It is a terrible loss. I do not know how I will replace him."[18]

Chancellorsville was a devastating loss for the North. This was an exceptionally bad piece of news so soon after the defeat at Fredericksburg. When Lincoln received the dispatch of the defeat, according to those around him, he turned as pale as a ghost and paced the room with tears streaming down his face, exclaiming: "My God! My God! What will the country say! What will the country say!" He believed that Hooker was his "last card," and he was inconsolable. It was one of the lowest points in his presidency. "I am the loneliest man in America," he sadly confessed to Bishop Charles Gordon Ames.[19]

Organization of the General Conference of Seventh-day Adventists

Interestingly, as the nation was falling apart during the war, the Sabbatarian Adventists were coming together. They had struggled to organize themselves during the 1850s and into the war years. The debates on organization throughout the 1850s culminated in the fall of 1860, on the eve of secession, when the believers gathered in Battle Creek, Michigan, from September 28 to October 1, to discuss holding church property and choosing a name. This conference accomplished three main goals: First, it adopted a constitution for the legal incorporation of the publishing association. Second, it established a platform so that individual churches could organize in order to legally own their own property or buildings. Third, the conference chose the denominational name "Seventh-day Adventist."[20]

The next important organizational meeting took place early in the war, during October 4–6, 1861, so as to organize the first state conference. James White recommended that the members in each congregation formally organize themselves by signing a covenant that read, "We, the undersigned, hereby associate ourselves together, as a church, taking the name, Seventh-day Adventists, covenanting to keep the commandments of God, and the faith of Jesus Christ." Once the covenant was adopted, the business focused on the organization of the churches in the state of Michigan, which resulted in the first state conference, the "Michigan Conference of Seventh-day Adventists."[21] This became the model for other states to organize by, thus laying the foundation for an umbrella structure to unite the local conferences.[22]

This final step of church organization took place several weeks after the Battle of

Chancellorsville on May 20–23, 1863. At this important meeting, the delegates adopted a constitution and officially organized the General Conference of Seventh-day Adventists. They also elected officers, with John Byington as the first General Conference president. This first General Conference session was a momentous accomplishment that culminated years of vigorous discussion and debate.[23] Although a tiny minority among American Christians at the time (approximately thirty-five hundred members in 1863 were spread across the northern United States, from Maine to Minnesota and Missouri), Seventh-day Adventists would grow significantly after the war years, eventually becoming a global church by the turn of the century.

Shortly after the adjournment of the General Conference session on June 6 in Otsego, Michigan, a notable event transpired in Ellen White's visionary experience. She later explained, "The great subject of Health Reform was opened before me in vision."[24] "I saw that it was a sacred duty to attend to our health, and arouse others to their duty," she wrote. "We have a duty to speak, to come out against intemperance of every kind,—intemperance in working, in eating, in drinking, in drugging—and then point them [the public] to God's great medicine: water, pure soft water, for diseases, for health, for cleanliness." She emphasized that the church "should not be silent upon the subject of health but should wake up minds to the subject."[25] These counsels would become the impetus for the church's major emphasis on healthful living and medical ministry in the coming years.[26] In the meantime, the newly organized denomination faced the challenges of war, especially the issue of conscription.

Battle of Gettysburg

After the losses at Fredericksburg and Chancellorsville in the Eastern theater, the North was full of uncertainty and unrest. Nothing much was happening in the Western theater, due to the stalemate in Tennessee and failure along the Mississippi River. Politically, the antiwar sentiment was growing among civilians, and the antiwar Democrats were becoming more aggressive. Moreover, Lincoln had lost confidence in Hooker and had replaced him with Major General George G. Meade, the fourth commander of the Army of the Potomac in seven months. Lincoln had faced continual frustration with the previous generals of this army—McClellan, Burnside, and Hooker—and would feel the same about Meade in the end. At the time, though, Meade was the best he could find for the principal Union army in the East.

A NATION IN GOD'S HANDS

In the meantime, Lee resisted suggestions that he move into the West to relieve pressure on Vicksburg and Middle Tennessee. He was determined that another invasion into the North would have the most benefits for the Confederacy: the North's Army of the Potomac would have to follow him and he could live off the land, the presence of his army would strengthen the Peace Democrats, and there was the slight possibility that a successful campaign in the North might rekindle the chance that European powers would decide to help the Confederacy. Lee commenced his movement north in early June with seventy-five thousand troops, crossed the Potomac River, and eventually moved into Pennsylvania.

As Lee moved north, Hooker shadowed him until Lincoln replaced him with Meade. When Lee learned that Meade was in charge of the Army of the Potomac and in pursuit of him, he pulled his army that was spread out over Pennsylvania back together and selected the area between Gettysburg, Pennsylvania, and the South Mountain range, a few miles west of Gettysburg, in which to converge. The armies made first contact near Gettysburg on June 30, and the largest, bloodiest battle of the Civil War took place July 1–3, 1863.

On the first day of the battle, both armies had not fully arrived yet; nevertheless, the fighting was intense and resulted in a striking Confederate success. On the second day, Lee continued his tactical offensive and, despite poor execution, shook Meade's line. On the third day, Lee launched his last major tactical offensive in the well-known Pickett's Charge, in which approximately 12,500 men charged across an open field under heavy artillery and rifle fire by Meade's Federals entrenched on Cemetery Ridge. Lee's troops were repulsed, with more than 50 percent casualties. The three-day battle ended with Lee's retreat from the battlefield. The two sides together suffered more than fifty thousand casualties—the largest number reported for a single battle in the entire Civil War. At least a third of Lee's army had been shot down, and Meade's army of eight-five thousand lost about twenty-three thousand men.[27]

Although the Battle of Gettysburg was over, the campaign was not. On July 4, Lee began his extensive retreat back to Virginia in a rainstorm, one of the great feats of his generalship. Pulling together what was left of his army and supplies, in addition to the thousands of wounded soldiers, was a logistical nightmare. In the end, Lee and his generals constructed a wagon and ambulance train that was more than fifty-seven miles long, with tens of thousands of livestock accompanying his army.

Lincoln followed Lee's slow-moving army with great interest and urged Meade to attack.[28] Lincoln believed that if Meade would follow up on his victory at Gettysburg "by the literal or substantial destruction of Lee's army, the rebellion will be over."[29] Meade did make several attempts to attack Lee during the retreat but remained cautious of delivering a decisive blow.[30]

As the days passed and Lee's retreat continued, the president grew extremely frustrated and despondent. Telegrapher, Albert B. Chandler, recalled that as the telegrams came in from Meade, Lincoln traced the position of the two armies on the map and sometimes "walked up and down the floor, his face grave and anxious, wringing his hands and showing every sign of deep solicitude."[31] When Lee approached the Potomac, it was high from the recent rains and impossible to cross, so he fortified his lines and waited for Meade to attack. On July 12, Meade was in a position to attack Lee and called a council of war with his generals. Lincoln was anxious and hopeful for a decisive victory as he awaited the outcome. The council voted not to attack until reconnaissance of the enemy's strength could be ascertained. Meade agreed and began to probe the Confederate line for a weak spot. In the meantime, the river waters receded, and the rebels crossed on the night of July 13–14, safely escaping into Virginia and officially ending the Gettysburg Campaign.

"We had only to stretch forth our hands and they were ours," moaned the president, "and nothing I could say or do could make the Army move."[32] Gideon Welles recalled that he had rarely seen the president "so troubled, so dejected and discouraged."[33] Lincoln had feared a repeat of the McClellan days when Lee had escaped at Antietam and could hardly bear its happening again. Lincoln's worst fears were justified, as Lee's successful retreat continued the balance of power in the Eastern theater and ensured that Lee's Confederate army would fight again as an effective force.

Upon hearing of Lincoln's great dissatisfaction with his performance, Meade asked to be relieved of command immediately. In seeking to console the general, Lincoln penned an extraordinary letter in which he expressed gratitude for the "magnificent success" at the Battle of Gettysburg. But then he expressed his view of the retreat in some of the strongest words he ever wrote to a general: "I do not believe you appreciate the magnitude of the misfortune involved in Lee's escape. He was within your easy grasp, and to have closed upon him would, in connection with our other late successes [the capture of Vicksburg on July 4], have ended the war."[34]

Although historians debate whether or not Meade could have successfully defeated Lee during the retreat, Lincoln was right that the survival of Lee's army meant that the war would be "prolonged indefinitely."[35] Fortunately for Meade, Lincoln decided not to send the letter, and he filed it among his papers.[36]

If we interpret this situation from White's vision, then one might suggest that God was involved in the circumstances surrounding Meade's inability to destroy Lee's army, and He prolonged the war to punish the North.[37]

Vicksburg, Port Hudson, and the Tullahoma Campaign

The day after Meade's victory on the fields of Gettysburg, Grant achieved a major victory at Vicksburg on "the glorious old 4th," as Lincoln put it.[38] It was a victory that the Union had pursued, with numerous unsuccessful attempts, for more than a year. Early in the war, Lincoln identified Vicksburg as the key to the Confederacy. With his ranking civil and military leaders around him during a meeting on the strategy to win the war, the president pointed to the Mississippi Valley on a map before them and said, "The war can never be brought to a close until that key is in our pocket."[39] Thus, from Farragut's naval campaign against Vicksburg in the summer of 1862 (discussed in the previous chapter) to Grant's operations during the winter and the spring and summer of 1863, Vicksburg was a priority for the Union war effort.

Grant's campaign consisted of various naval operations, troop maneuvers, failed initiatives, and numerous distinct battles from December 1862 to July 4, 1863. After converging on Vicksburg and trapping Confederate General John Pemberton's force in May, Grant attempted two Federal assaults against the city on May 19 and 22. Both assaults failed, and he chose to lay siege to Vicksburg. After six weeks of starvation and constant bombardment, Pemberton surrendered the city and his army on July 4.[40] The "key" to the Confederacy was now in the pocket of the Union. Grant had accomplished one of the most significant objectives of Lincoln's strategy. Jefferson Davis's "nailhead that held the South's two halves together"[41] no longer existed, and the eastern and western parts of the Confederacy were rent asunder.

Grant later wrote that "the fate of the Confederacy was sealed when Vicksburg fell. Much hard fighting was to be done afterwards and many precious lives were to be sacrificed; but the *morale* was with the supporters of the Union ever after."[42] Grant was right. The momentum of the war was now on the Union side. The fall of Vicksburg and Lee's retreat from Gettysburg confirmed the receding tide of the

Confederacy.[43] But, as Grant remembered, bloody fighting was still ahead. The war was far from over. The timing of these two significant Union victories two years into the war seem to support Ellen White's perspective, that God "would not suffer victories to be gained faster than He ordained, and would permit no more losses to the Northern men than in His wisdom He saw fit, to punish them for their sins."[44]

After the fall of Vicksburg, the only obstacle that kept the Union from full control of the Mississippi River was Port Hudson, Louisiana, the next defensive Confederate garrison on the river, more than one hundred miles south of Vicksburg. General Nathaniel P. Banks moved against Port Hudson in late May and laid siege to it. When the Confederate commander learned of the surrender of Vicksburg, he decided not to continue his resistance and surrendered the garrison on July 9, 1863. Now the entire length of the Mississippi, the most important river in the country, belonged to the Union. It was a catastrophic loss to the Confederacy.

Since the Battle of Stones River in Tennessee, the Union and Confederate armies had been keeping an eye on each other, with nothing happening. Lincoln had encouraged Rosecrans to move, but he stayed put until he felt his army was ready. On June 24, however, he moved his sixty-three thousand men against Braxton Bragg's army of forty-five thousand in a series of flanking maneuvers that befuddled the Confederate commander. Within two weeks, Rosecrans pushed the rebel army all the way back to Chattanooga, Tennessee, with fewer than six hundred casualties—a remarkable feat. Rosecrans's successful maneuvers in Tennessee, known as the Tullahoma Campaign, coupled with the fall of Vicksburg and Port Hudson, provided the North with a splendid boost in national morale and a significant strategic advantage over the Confederates.[45]

Lincoln and his war leaders endeavored to capitalize on this situation and deliver decisive blows in Virginia and the West. But their plans to bring an end to the war were thwarted by two obstacles: First, Lincoln still could not get Meade to move against Lee in a decisive attack. Throughout the autumn, the two went back and forth on the pros and cons of bringing Lee to battle. By December, Meade's army had settled into winter quarters, with nothing of significance accomplished in the Eastern theater. Second, the Union suffered a major defeat in the Western theater at a place across a small stream bearing the Native American name of "Chickamauga."[46] The up period for the Union in the summer of 1863 took a sudden plunge in the early fall.

Battle of Chickamauga

During midsummer, General Rosecrans's Army of the Cumberland, the major Federal army in Tennessee, was just outside of Chattanooga, resting after the Tullahoma Campaign.[47] The Lincoln administration urged immediate action, but the careful Union general would not move until he was ready. In the meantime, the Confederate government sensed the importance of the situation at Chattanooga and began sending reinforcements to General Bragg. On August 16, Rosecrans launched his campaign for Chattanooga and, once again, outmaneuvered Bragg, resulting in the Confederate abandonment of the strategic city on September 9.

Chattanooga was extremely important to the Union objectives of winning the war. Located in southeastern Tennessee, close to northern Georgia, with the Blue Ridge Mountains and Appalachian Plateau to the east and the mountains of the Cumberland Plateau to the west, the city was a convergence of roads, major railroads, and the Tennessee River. It has been called the "gateway to the Confederacy" because of its major east-west railroads and its major railroad south to the important city of Atlanta.[48] It was vital to the Confederacy's ability to transport troops and supplies to its armies and was thus "the most important strategic point in the Confederacy."[49] Union control of Chattanooga would split the Confederacy again and open the gate to strike at its heartland. When Rosecrans telegraphed to Washington that "Chattanooga is ours without a struggle, and East Tennessee is free,"[50] the administration was delighted.

But Rosecrans and his army did not stay in Chattanooga. They pushed on with the belief that Bragg's retreating army was demoralized and panicked. Rosecrans believed that he had an opportunity to destroy the Confederate Army of Tennessee and pressed on, dividing his army into separated columns in order to envelop the fragmented parts of the fleeing enemy. But, unbeknown to Rosecrans, Bragg had actually lured him out of Chattanooga and was planning to pounce on the separated Federal columns individually in the valley south of the city. Several times during the period of time from September 10 to 13, Bragg ordered his divisions to attack the fragments of the enemy, only to experience frustration by the failure of his generals to obey orders.

Rosecrans eventually realized that his army was in danger, and he pulled it back together. By September 17, he had concentrated his approximately fifty-eight thousand men in a position several miles south of Chattanooga in the valley of Chickamauga Creek. On the morning of September 19, Bragg had his approximately seventy thousand Confederates on the west side of Chickamauga Creek facing the Federals. This was one of the few times in the Civil War when a Confederate army outnumbered the Federal army. The rebels struck first, and the battle raged throughout the day. Bragg's goal was to envelop the Federal's left flank to the north, thereby cutting off Rosecrans's line of communication and retreat to Chattanooga. But due to uncoordinated assaults, the previous tactical gains were lost. Rosecrans sent a message to Washington that his army had "just concluded a terrific day's fighting, and have another prospect for to-morrow." The enemy, he explained, "attempted to turn our left," but the design was rendered "abortive." Tomorrow, "by the blessing of Providence, the defeat of the enemy will be total."[51]

The morning of September 20, the second day of fighting, began with silence. Bragg had ordered a series of assaults on the Federal battle line beginning at dawn but heard no thunder of artillery or crackling of musketry fire. In distress, he dispatched a staff officer to ascertain the reason for the delay. Eventually, Bragg himself rode to the line and found his army unprepared to launch an immediate attack. As the minutes turned into hours, Rosecrans used the time to personally tour his lines and get the unprepared troops ready for battle. Finally, by midmorning, when the Confederates launched their attack, the Federals were barricaded behind breastworks.

The battle raged, taking its toll of blood and death on both sides. About eleven o'clock, as Rosecrans was shifting reinforcements to his battered left flank, a staff officer reported what he thought was a gap in the Federal line. Rosecrans ordered another division to fill the gap and inadvertently created a real gap in the center of his line, which the troops of Confederate General Longstreet took full advantage of. The gray soldiers surged into the gap and destroyed everything in their path. The right flank was literally swept from the field, taking its commander with it. Rosecrans tried to rally the scattered units on a ridge, but they were driven back.[52] The shattered right of the Army of the Cumberland streamed northward toward Chattanooga some eight miles away.

But all was not lost. General George H. Thomas, Rosecrans's right-hand man, pulled together the fragments of the Union army that had not been driven from the field and held the left flank, providing a guard for the retreating troops moving toward Chattanooga. He gathered these remaining troops into a defensive line on Snodgrass Hill and stood firm, fighting back the Confederate assaults for the rest of the day. After holding together what was left of the Federal army, Thomas and his men withdrew in good order back to Chattanooga, earning him the nickname "Rock of Chickamauga."

As the Confederate troops sensed a great victory, the rebel yell thundered from one end of the line to the other. Their commander, General Bragg, wasn't so sure that it was a victory. But he would soon discover that it was the Confederacy's most significant tactical victory in the West, which gave a temporary boost to Southern morale. It was also their last major battlefield victory of the entire war. Rosecrans telegraphed Washington, "We have met with a serious disaster."[53] Anticipating an attack on his forces in Chattanooga, the Union general did his best to organize the army and prepare it for another battle.

As the "most complete Confederate victory and worst Union defeat in the western theater," the casualties from the 125,000 participants were staggering: a total of "34,805 killed, wounded, and missing," second only to Gettysburg for the largest number of casualties in the entire war. This amounted to a 28 percent loss to both armies.[54] One Confederate soldier observed, after the first day of battle, that "the dead of both sides were lying thick over the ground." In fact, fallen men and horses covered the ground so that "one could hardly walk for them."[55] Bragg was so dismayed by the heavy losses in his army that he waited until September 23 to occupy the heights overlooking Chattanooga, and he chose to besiege the town rather than assault it.[56]

Several interesting features of the Chickamauga battle illustrate how events in the Civil War often turned on a dime and changed everything. One is that several Union generals, including Burnside (who had recently taken Knoxville, north of Chattanooga) and Grant (who was operating in the Vicksburg area after his victory), were ordered to come and assist Rosecrans at Chattanooga. None of them, however, obeyed the order. If they had, Rosecrans would not have been so outnumbered, and the outcome of the Chickamauga battle might have been a Union victory.[57] Another is that Bragg's plan to launch a series of attacks at dawn on September 20 was not carried out as he had ordered. If those attacks had launched early in the morning when the Union line was still unprepared, the Confederate victory would have been complete, destroying Rosecrans's army and retaking Chattanooga.[58] Finally, on the day after the battle, several of Bragg's generals, particularly James Longstreet and Nathan Bedford Forrest, wanted him to pursue and destroy the fleeing Federal army before it reorganized at Chattanooga. But Bragg was overwhelmed by his losses, refused to pursue Rosecrans's army, and chose a siege instead. If Bragg had pursued Rosecrans and dispersed his army, the success at Chickamauga would have been a significant strategic victory for the Confederacy. Instead, it was only a hollow victory, with Chattanooga still in Union hands.[59]

Once again, if we view these possible outcomes of Chickamauga in light of Ellen White's assertions of divine involvement in the war, then what happened could be interpreted as "divine providence" or "supernatural elements" working in and through human choices and the turn of events. The Battle of Chickamauga could have been a total disaster for the Union rather than what it was—a punishing defeat that set the Union back but did not destroy its momentum in the war. Such was the delicate balance of events throughout the war, which were projected in White's sweeping forecast that God was in control of the battles.

Battles of Chattanooga

After the Battle of Chickamauga, Chattanooga became the central focus of both the Union and the Confederate war efforts. The city was strategically located and was the transportation nexus of the Confederacy. Its occupation was vital for the Confederates' survival in the war. Since the middle of 1862, the Union had endeavored to take Chattanooga, and now the Lincoln administration was determined to hold the city. As Bragg settled his troops on the mountain heights at Missionary Ridge to the east and Lookout Mountain to the south, he hoped that the siege would starve the Federals out of the city, so he could retake it without a fight. Rosecrans was determined to hold Chattanooga, and he bunkered his troops down for the siege.

Both sides, however, were experiencing internal problems with command. On the Confederate side, Bragg's subordinate generals were upset with the way he had handled the Chickamauga battle and his failure to follow up on the victory by pursuing the Federal army. The internal bickering resulted in a call for Bragg's removal. The conflict was so bad that President Jefferson Davis made a personal visit to the Army of Tennessee in order to resolve the situation. In the end, Davis decided to keep Bragg in command—a decision that he would later regret.[60]

On the Union side, Rosecrans was doing the best he could as the days of the siege

Grant views the charge up Missionary Ridge through a field glass on Orchard Knob

passed. According to the later testimonies of his subordinate generals and soldiers, he was doing a good job of organizing the defenses and creating a supply line for food. But negative reports were sent to Washington, and the Lincoln administration lost faith in Rosecrans. He was depicted as confused, disoriented, and "completely broken down." Based on these reports, Lincoln believed that after Chickamauga, Rosecrans was "confused and stunned like a duck hit on the head."[61] Since Stones River, Lincoln greatly valued Rosecrans as a general; but, he reasoned, Chattanooga must be saved at all costs. So the president decided to reorganize the western command system and placed Ulysses S. Grant in charge of all the Federal forces between the Appalachian Mountains and the Mississippi River. This move was consistent with a statement that Lincoln had made shortly before he received the news of Grant's victory at Vicksburg. If Grant took Vicksburg, Lincoln said, "Why, Grant is my man and I am his the rest of the war."[62]

One of Grant's first decisions was to remove Rosecrans from command of the Army of the Cumberland and then go to Chattanooga himself.[63] Once there, he opened a supply line that Rosecrans had been constructing and laid out a plan to end the siege and place Chattanooga in Union control permanently. Pulling together reinforcements sent there to bolster Rosecrans and the Army of the Cumberland, Grant laid out his plan to the generals under his command: Joseph Hooker's troops would cause a "demonstration" on Lookout Mountain to distract the Confederates on Missionary Ridge; William T. Sherman's soldiers would flank Bragg's right end at the northern end of Missionary Ridge and move along the crest of the ridge, rolling up the Confederate line as he advanced; and George H. Thomas, now in command of the Army of the Cumberland, would assault the center of Missionary Ridge to distract the Confederates from what would happen on their right. All of this was to take place simultaneously as a coordinated attack. But things didn't go perfectly according to plan.

The battle commenced on the cold and rainy morning of November 24.[64] Hooker's troops charged up the rocky slopes of Lookout Mountain and clashed with the embedded Confederates. Fog and low clouds enveloped the mountain, obscuring the vision of soldiers on both sides. As the morning hours passed into the afternoon, the Union forces in the valley below listened carefully to the sounds of musket fire and artillery explosions on the mountain. When they anxiously peered at the heights, all they could see was fog and smoke drifting up the slopes.

By early afternoon, Hooker's effort became more than just a "demonstration"—the Confederate defense line began to give away. As it did, an unexpected and welcome event transpired, one of those Civil War miracles. The clouds and fog and smoke suddenly lifted for a moment, and the sun shone brightly across the entire mountain.

> The men of the Army of the Cumberland could see everything, the Confederates were in full retreat, and around the curving slope came rank after rank of Hooker's men, flags flying, rifle barrels shining in the sunlight, victory achieved in plain view of everybody—and Thomas's soldiers jumped up and yelled and tossed their caps in the air, regimental bands spontaneously began to play from one end of the line to the other, the artillery fired wild salutes aimed haphazardly at Missionary Ridge, and the noise of the fighting was drowned in the noise of a general jubilee.[65]

"Then," as Bruce Catton aptly puts it, "just as if a stage manager knew when to close a brilliant scene, the clouds hid the sun again, the drifting fog came back, the Lookout Mountain battle lines vanished from sight."[66] By nightfall, the Confederates had abandoned Lookout Mountain, and Hooker's troops planted the Stars and Stripes on the summit. Although the battle was later called the "Battle Above the Clouds," it was actually the battle "*in* the clouds."[67]

As Hooker assaulted Lookout Mountain on November 24, Sherman crossed the river northeast of Chattanooga and ascended the heights around Missionary Ridge, intending to flank Bragg's right, which was the main thrust of Grant's plan. The terrain was confusing, and the troops were delayed, finally digging in for the night. The next day, on November 25, Sherman continued to struggle with the rugged terrain and clashed with the best division in Bragg's army, commanded by Patrick R. Cleburne. Overall, Sherman was not having much success on the second day of the Chattanooga battles.[68]

By midafternoon, Grant realized that his plan was not working out. He had originally meant for Thomas's Army of the Cumberland to take the rifle pits in the center of Missionary Ridge simultaneously as Sherman advanced along the ridge. But because Sherman was stalled, Grant began to improvise, one of his great strengths during the shifting nature of battle. He ordered Thomas to send his army up the ridge and take the rifle pits at the foot of Missionary Ridge, "and when carried to reform his lines on the rifle-pits with a view to carrying the top of the ridge."[69] About 3:40 P.M., approximately twenty-three thousand men in four divisions surged forward over the cleared plain and up to the heights, where a line of approximately nine thousand Confederates nervously waited. Although the Federals outnumbered the Confederate line, the Confederates had the high ground, which give them a distinctive advantage. "It looked like a reprise of Pickett's charge at Gettysburg, with blue and gray having switched roles. And this assault seemed even more hopeless than Pickett's, for the rebels had had two months to dig in and Missionary Ridge was much higher and more rugged than Cemetery Ridge."[70]

Nevertheless, Thomas's Cumberlanders forged ahead in a rain of enemy fire and quickly seized the rifle pits, inducing the rebel riflemen to flee "like bees from a hive."[71] Since Grant's orders were not absolutely clear on what to do after taking the rifle pits, there was confusion as to whether or not they should continue up to the crest of the ridge and engage the Confederate line. One thing was certain— because of the heavy fire raining down from the top of the ridge, the rifle pits were not a safe place for the Cumberland troops. Some men began the ascent, while others waited for a word from their officers. "One way and another, on somebody's orders or no one's at all, the various units of the four assaulting divisions all began their climb up the six-hundred-foot slope of Missionary Ridge."[72] Some of these men were seeking revenge for Chickamauga and pressed forward, shouting "Chickamauga! Chickamauga!"[73] When the divisions reached the enemies' position, it was pandemonium, with point-blank shooting and fierce hand-to-hand combat. Within minutes, though, the Confederate line broke, and those rebels who did not surrender fled down the back slope. It was a stunning Union victory, perhaps the most dramatic victory of the entire war—later called by some the "miracle at Missionary Ridge."[74]

One eyewitness, Charles A. Dana, recalled that "the storming of the ridge by our troops was one of the greatest miracles in military history. No man who climbs the ascent by any of the roads that wind along its front can believe that 18,000 men were moved up its broken and crumbling face unless it was his fortune to witness the deed." He then exclaimed, "It seems as awful as a visible interposition of God."[75] Even General Grant was amazed that the advancing troops survived such a "fearful volley of grape and canister." He noted that "their progress was steadily onward until the summit was in their possession," and "the casualties were remarkably few for the fire encountered."[76]

What kept it from being a slaughter like Pickett's Charge at Gettysburg or the Union charges at Fredericksburg? The general struggled to find an adequate answer: "I can account for this only on the theory that the enemy's surprise at the audacity of such a charge caused confusion and purposeless aiming of their pieces."[77] It was difficult to explain such a sudden reversal in military fortunes—from a position of being trapped in the rifle pits to charging up the steepest part of the ridge under heavy fire to full possession of the summit—all within an hour's time. There are other natural reasons that have been attributed to the "miracle on Missionary Ridge," such as the problematic Confederate position on the ridge and so forth.

But Dana's statement that the charge to the summit was "a visible interposition of God" deserves attention in light of Ellen White's sweeping prophecy of the Union battles. If, as she said, "God has this nation in His own hand" and would oversee the wins and losses of the Union battles, as suggested throughout this chapter and the previous one, then, from that perspective, it seems that God was involved in the decisive battle on Missionary Ridge that gave Chattanooga permanently into Union hands. Whatever moved those divisions at the rifle pits to begin ascending the steep slopes—whether it was a calculated order by officers, the impulse of the soldiers, a combination of both, or some supernatural influence—many believers of that era would say it was an act of divine providence.[78]

In the larger scheme of the war, Chattanooga was a significant strategic victory that set the Union on a final course for ultimate victory over the Confederacy. Once loose ends were tied up in East Tennessee and Knoxville was safely in Union hands, all of Tennessee as well as Kentucky belonged to the Federals. Additionally, the entire Mississippi River was in Union control, due to the victories at Memphis, Vicksburg, Port Hudson, and New Orleans. What Grant began in taking Fort Henry and Fort Donelson in the beginning of 1862, he now finished in Chattanooga at the end of 1863. The West belonged to the Union, and the Confederacy's days were numbered. Their golden opportunity to crush a Union army after the victory at Chickamauga was gone.

The death of Henry White

As the North was in high spirits during December 1863, James and Ellen White were weighed down with sadness. Their eldest son, Henry, who had wanted to join the army as a drummer, was gravely ill with pneumonia. Sensing that he was dying, Henry drew near to God and embraced his family with love and affection.[79] He told his father that if he died, at least he would "escape being drafted" into the army.[80] To his mother, he said, "I shall meet you in heaven in the morning of the resurrection, for I know you will be there."[81] He also requested to be buried by the side of his little brother, John Herbert, who had died on the eve of the war, so they could "come up together in the morning of the resurrection."[82] Henry died on December 8 and was put to rest beside his little brother at Oak Hill Cemetery in Battle Creek, Michigan. Of the four White sons, the youngest and oldest had been taken by disease during the Civil War era. "We feel the loss of our dear Henry very much," Ellen wrote after the funeral. "The youngest and oldest branches of the family tree have been broken off."[83]

Years later, when the medical field understood germ theory, Ellen remarked to her granddaughter as she wrung her hands, "If we had only known then what we know now, we could have saved Henry."[84] This statement is significant, for it illustrates the state of medical practice during the Civil War era. William A. Hammond, the Union's surgeon general, later recalled that the war was fought at the "end of the medical middle ages."[85] "Neither the germ theory nor the nature and necessity for antisepsis was yet understood. A wave of epidemic diseases—measles, mumps, and smallpox—swept through" the camps of both the Union and Confederate armies, along with dysentery, typhoid, malaria, and pneumonia. According to one scholar, "twice as many Civil War soldiers died of disease as of battle wounds."[86] America was, indeed, a "Republic of suffering."[87]

Conclusion

November 26, the day after the Battle of Missionary Ridge, was America's first official and national Thanksgiving Day, proclaimed by Abraham Lincoln on October 3. He called for the nation to set the day aside and give thanks to God for the work done by the "advancing armies and navies of the Union." The president's proclamation recounted the nation's material and military blessings over the last year and then stated: "No human counsel hath devised nor hath any mortal hand worked out these great things. They are the gracious gifts of the Most High God, who, while dealing with us in anger for our sins, has nevertheless remembered mercy."[88] Interestingly, these words fit the theological framework of Ellen White's forecast of the Union's victory-loss pattern of battles.

As the news of the Chattanooga victory spread across the North, there was good reason to be thankful. On top of the other victories that year, Chattanooga was a great gift. November 26 was no day of thanksgiving for the Confederacy, however. As Bragg's army sadly retreated southward after the defeat at Missionary Ridge, a junior officer said to his company commander, "Captain, this is the death knell of the Confederacy. If we cannot cope with those fellows with the advantages we had on this line, there is not a line between here and the Atlantic Ocean where we can stop them."[89] The junior officer was right that Chattanooga was the beginning of the end for the Confederacy. But the rebels would not give up easily. The war would go on for another year and a half, with some of the most violent and bloody fighting yet ahead.

Chapter in a Nutshell

This chapter traced the up-down pattern of the following Union battles from Chancellorsville to Chattanooga:

BATTLES 1863	PATTERN
FINAL DRAFT OF EMANCIPATION PROCLAMATION SIGNED	
Chancellorsville	Loss
Gettysburg	Victory
Vicksburg	Victory
Port Hudson	Victory
Tullahoma	Victory
Chickamauga	Loss
Chattanooga	Victory

1. For sources that provide engaging narratives of the signing of the Emancipation Proclamation, see Allen C. Guelzo, *Lincoln's Emancipation Proclamation: The End of American Slavery in America* (New York: Simon & Schuster, 2004), 206, 207; Von Drehle, *Rise to Greatness*, 374, 375; Louis P. Masur, *Lincoln's Hundred Days: The Emancipation Proclamation and the War for the Union* (Cambridge, MA: Belknap Press, 2012), 206; and Burlingame, *Abraham Lincoln: A Life*, 2:468-469.

2. Burlingame, *Abraham Lincoln: A Life*, 2:469.

3. Francis B. Carpenter, *The Inner Life of Abraham Lincoln: Six Months at the White House* (New York: Hurd and Houghton, 1868), 269.

4. Guelzo, *Lincoln's Emancipation Proclamation*, 206.

5. Carpenter, *The Inner Life of Abraham Lincoln*, 269.

6. Fehrenbacher and Fehrenbacher, *Recollected Words of Abraham Lincoln*, 397.

7. Carpenter, *The Inner Life of Abraham Lincoln*, 269.

8. Fehrenbacher and Fehrenbacher, *Recollected Words of Abraham Lincoln*, 397.

9. Burlingame, *Abraham Lincoln: A Life*, 2:469. See also Carpenter, *The Inner Life of Abraham Lincoln*, 270; and Guelzo, *Lincoln's Emancipation Proclamation*, 207.

10. Basler, *The Collected Works of Abraham Lincoln*, 6:29, 30.

11. For helpful studies on the Emancipation Proclamation, see John Hope Franklin, *The Emancipation Proclamation* (Wheeling, IL: Harlan Davidson, 1995); Guelzo, *Lincoln's Emancipation Proclamation*; Burrus M. Carnahan, *Act of Justice: Lincoln's Emancipation Proclamation and the Law of War* (Lexington, KY: University Press of Kentucky, 2007); and Michael Vorenberg, *The Emancipation Proclamation: A Brief History With Documents* (New York: Bedford / St. Martin's, 2010). On the Thirteenth Amendment, see Michael Vorenberg, *Final Freedom: The Civil War, the Abolition of Slavery, and the Thirteenth Amendment* (New York: Cambridge University Press, 2001).

12. Basler, *The Collected Works of Abraham Lincoln*, 6:156.

13. Nicholas Parrillo, "Lincoln's Calvinist Transformation: Emancipation and War," *Civil War History* 46, no. 3 (September 2000): 246.

14. For a detailed discussion on the aftermath of Fredericksburg, see A. Wilson Greene, "Morale, Maneuver, and Mud: The Army of the Potomac, December 16, 1862–January 26, 1863," in Gary W. Gallagher, ed., *The Fredericksburg Campaign* (Chapel Hill, NC: University of North Carolina Press, 1995), 171–227.

15. For a definitive account of the battle, see Stephen W. Sears, *Chancellorsville* (New York: Houghton Mifflin, 1996).

16. For the most helpful narrative on the story of the accidental shooting of Jackson, see Samuel C. Gwynne, *Rebel Yell: The Violence, Passion, and Redemption of Stonewall Jackson* (New York: Scribner, 2014), 540–543.

17. Robert E. Lee, quoted in Douglas Southall Freeman, *R. E. Lee: A Biography*, vol. 2 (New York: Charles Scribner's Sons, 1934), 560.

18. Lee, quoted in Douglas Southall Freeman, *R. E. Lee: A Biography*, vol. 3 (New York: Charles Scribner's Sons, 1935), 1. See also Edwin C Bearss and Parker Hills, *Receding Tide: Vicksburg and Gettysburg: The Campaigns That Changed the Civil War* (Washington, DC: National Geographic, 2010), 161.

19. Lincoln, quoted in Burlingame, *Abraham Lincoln: A Life*, 2:498.

20. For more details, see George R. Knight, *Organizing for Mission and Growth: The Development of Adventist Church Structure* (Hagerstown, MD: Review and Herald®, 2006), 48–52.

21. "Doings of the Battle Creek Conference, Oct. 5 & 6, 1861," *Review and Herald*, October 8, 1861, 148.

22. See Knight, *Organizing for Mission and Growth*, 52–57.

23. See ibid., 57–61. See also the following studies on church organization: Schwarz and Greenleaf, *Light Bearers*, 83–99, who put their discussion in the context of the Civil War; Andrew G. Mustard, *James White and SDA Organization: Historical Development, 1844–1881*, Andrews University Seminary Doctoral Dissertation Series (Berrien Springs, MI: Andrews University Press, 1987); and Anderson, "Sectarianism and Organization, 1846–1864," 29–52.

24. Ellen G. White, *Selected Messages*, vol. 3 (Washington, DC: Review and Herald®, 1980), 276.

25. Ibid., 3:280.

26. For the story of the Adventist health message, see Dores E. Robinson, *The Story of Our Health Message: The Origin, Character, and Development of Health Education in the Seventh-day Adventist Church*, 3rd ed. (Nashville, TN: Southern Publishing Association, 1965). For more recent developments, see Schwarz and Greenleaf, *Light Bearers*, 478-498.

27. For two definitive accounts of the Battle of Gettysburg, see Stephen W. Sears, *Gettysburg* (New York: Houghton Mifflin, 2003); and Allen C. Guelzo, *Gettysburg: The Last Invasion* (New York: Vintage Books, 2013). See also Edwin B. Coddington, *The Gettysburg Campaign: A Study in Command* (New York: Simon & Schuster, 1997). For a concise overview of the battle, see Gallagher, *The American Civil War: Lectures 1–24*, 350–366.

28. For discussion on Lincoln's interaction with Meade during Lee's retreat, see T. Harry Williams, *Lincoln and His Generals* (New York: Vintage Books, 1980), 264–271. For an insightful, sympathetic study of Meade, see Tom Huntington, *Search for George Gordon Meade: The Forgotten Victor of Gettysburg* (Mechanicsburg, PA: Stackpole Books, 2013).

29. Lincoln to Halleck, July 7, 1863, in Basler, *The Collected Works of Abraham Lincoln*, 6:319.

30. For two definitive accounts of Lee's retreat after Gettysburg and Meade's pursuit, see Kent Masterson Brown, *Retreat From Gettysburg: Lee, Logistics, and the Pennsylvania Campaign* (Chapel Hill, NC: University of North Carolina Press, 2005); and Eric J. Wittenberg, J. David Petruzzi, and Michael Nugent, *One Continuous Fight: The Retreat From Gettysburg and the Pursuit of Lee's Army of Northern Virginia, July 4–14, 1863* (New York: Savas Beatie, 2008).

31. Albert B. Chandler, quoted in Burlingame, *Abraham Lincoln: A Life*, 2:512.

32. Michael Burlingame and John R. Turner Ettlinger, eds. *Inside Lincoln's White House: The Complete Civil War Diary of John Hay* (Carbondale, Ill.: Southern Illinois University Press, 1997) 62.

33. Gideon Welles, diary entry for July 14, 1863, in William E. Gienapp and Erica L. Gienapp, eds. *The Civil War Diary of Gideon Wells: Lincoln's Secretary of the Navy* (Urbana, IL: University of Illinois Press, 2014), 248.

34. Roland, *An American Iliad*, 145.

35. Basler, *The Collected Works of Abraham Lincoln*, 6:327, 328.

36. Ibid., 6:328n1.

37. White, *Testimonies for the Church*, 1:267.

38. Basler, *The Collected Works of Abraham Lincoln*, 6:321.

39. Admiral David Dixon Porter, who was at this meeting, recalled the president's words in his *Incidents and Anecdotes of the Civil War* (New York: D. Appleton, 1885), 95, 96.

40. For the definitive study on the Vicksburg Campaign, see Edwin C. Bearss, *The Campaign for Vicksburg*, 3 vols. (Dayton, OH: Morningside, 1991).

41. Jefferson Davis, quoted in Terrence J. Winschel, *Triumph & Defeat: The Vicksburg Campaign* (New York: Savas Beatie, 2004), 2.

42. Grant, *Memoirs and Selected Letters*, 381 (emphasis in the original).

43. See Bearss and Hills, *Receding Tide*.

44. White, *Testimonies for the Church*, 1:267.

45. On the significance of the Tullahoma Campaign, see Michael R. Bradley, *Tullahoma: The 1863 Campaign for the Control of Middle Tennessee* (Shippensburg, PA: White Mane Publishing, 1999); Kolakowski, *The Stones River and Tullahoma Campaigns*; and David Powell, *The Chickamauga Campaign: A Mad Irregular Battle: From the Crossing of the Tennessee River Through the Second Day, August 22–September 19, 1863* (El Dorado Hills, CA: Savas Beatie, 2014), xii–xix.

46. See Gallagher, *The American Civil War*, 387–388, 395; and Williams, *Lincoln and His Generals*, 285–289.

47. For a helpful overview of the Chickamauga Campaign used in this book, see Jack H. Lepa, *The Civil War in Tennessee, 1862–1863* (Jefferson, N.: McFarland, 2007), 125–151; Gallagher, *The American Civil War*, 383–399; and Steven E. Woodworth, *Six Armies in Tennessee: The Chickamauga and Chattanooga Campaigns* (Lincoln, NE:

University of Nebraska Press, 1998). For more in-depth studies, see Peter Cozzens, *This Terrible Sound: The Battle of Chickamauga* (Chicago: University of Illinois Press, 1992); Steven E. Woodworth, ed., *The Chickamauga Campaign* (Carbondale, IL: Southern Illinois University Press, 2010); and Powell, *The Chickamauga Campaign*, part of a three-volume series, published by Savas Beatie, El Dorado Hills, California.

48. See Jones and Sword, *Gateway to the Confederacy*, 1, 2.

49. James J. Andrews, quoted in introduction to *Gateway to the Confederacy*, eds. Jones and Sword, 1.

50. Rosecrans to H. W. Halleck, quoted in *Official Records of the Union and Confederate Armies,* ser. 1, vol. 30 (Washington, DC: Government Printing Office, 1890), pt. 3, 479.

51. *Official Records of the Union and Confederate Armies*, ser. 1, vol. 30, pt. 1, 136.

52. See Frank P. Varney, *General Grant and the Rewriting of History: How the Destruction of General William S. Rosecrans Influenced Our Understanding of the Civil War* (El Dorado Hills, CA: Savas Beatie, 2013), 171–206.

53. See *Official Records of the Union and Confederate Armies*, ser. 1, vol. 30, pt. 1, 142, 143.

54. Jones and Sword, *Gateway to the Confederacy*, 4.

55. John S. Jackman, diary entry for September 20, 1863, quoted in Brooks D. Simpson, ed., *The Civil War: The Third Year Told by Those Who Lived It* (New York: Library of America, 2013), 532.

56. Ibid., 531.

57. Varney, *General Grant and the Rewriting of History*, 182–190.

58. See John R. Lundberg, "A Minute Now Is Worth an Hour Later," in Woodworth, *The Chickamauga Campaign*, 112, 113; and Steven E. Woodworth, *Six Armies in Tennessee*, 106, 107.

59. Lepa, *The Civil War in Tennessee,* 153, 154.

60. For details, see Craig L. Symonds, "War and Politics: Jefferson Davis Visits the Army of Tennessee," in Jones and Sword, *Gateway to the Confederacy*, 159–171.

61. It was Charles A. Dana, the assistant secretary of war, who sent the negative reports to the Lincoln administration that Rosecrans was "broken down" and who most likely skewed Lincoln's view of how Rosecrans was mishandling Chattanooga. Both Lincoln's and Dana's statements are found in Michael Burlingame and John R. Turner Ettlinger, eds., *Inside Lincoln's White House: The Complete Civil War Diary of John Hay* (Carbondale, IL: Southern Illinois University Press, 1999), 98, 99. Frank Varney provided compelling evidence that refutes the traditional view of Rosecrans being "stunned like a duck hit on the head." See Varney, *General Grant and the Rewriting of History*, 207–239.

62. Quoted in Williams, *Lincoln and His Generals*, 272.

63. For discussion on Grant's attempt to discredit Rosecrans at Chattanooga and for the rest of the war, see Varney, *General Grant and the Rewriting of History,* 207–239; and Evan C. Jones, "A 'Malignant Vindictiveness': The Two-Decade Rivalry Between Ulysses S. Grant and William S. Rosecrans," in Jones and Sword, *Gateway to the Confederacy*, 172–226.

64. For helpful and well-informed narratives of what happened on November 24–25, 1863, see Lepa, *The Civil War in Tennessee*, 180–203; and Woodworth, *Six Armies in Tennessee*, 180–205. For classic treatments on the battles of Chattanooga, see James Lee McDonough, *Chattanooga: A Death Grip On the Confederacy* (Knoxville, TN: University of Tennessee Press, 1984); Peter Cozzens, *The Shipwreck of Their Hopes: The Battles for Chattanooga* (Chicago: University of Illinois Press, 1994); and Wiley Sword, *Mountains Touched With Fire: Chattanooga Besieged, 1863* (New York: St. Martin's Press, 1995).

65. Bruce Catton, *Grant Takes Command, 1863–1865* (Boston: Little, Brown and Co., 1969), 74.

66. Ibid.

67. The phrase "above the clouds" was first used by General Montgomery C. Meigs in *Official Records of the Union and Confederate Armies*, ser. 1, vol. 31 (Washington, DC: Government Printing Office, 1890), pt. 2, 78, and was later widely publicized, eventually becoming legend. A veteran infantryman present at the battle, however, said that the part about being "above the clouds" was pure fiction. Rather, he said, it was a battle "in the clouds," which was technically correct. Sword, *Mountains Touched With Fire*, 229, 230.

68. For details, see Steven E. Woodworth, " 'The Very Ground Seemed Alive': Sherman's Assault on the North End of Missionary Ridge," and John R. Lundberg, "Baptizing the Hills and Valleys: Cleburne's Defense of Tunnel Hill," in Steven E. Woodworth and Charles D. Grear, eds., *The Chattanooga Campaign* (Carbondale, IL: Southern Illinois University Press, 2012), 53–83.

69. Ulysses S. Grant, quoted in *Official Records of the Union and Confederate Armies*, ser. 1, vol. 31, pt. 2, 34.

70. McPherson, *Battle Cry of Freedom*, 678.

71. According to Grant, who observed from Orchard Knob, *Official Records of the Union and Confederate Armies*, ser. 1, vol. 31, pt. 2, 34.

72. Woodworth, *Six Armies in Tennessee*, 198. Pulling from all of the historical analysis of this charge, Woodworth's depiction is the most accurate. We may never know exactly what brought on the simultaneous charge on Missionary Ridge. For analysis of all the differing reports on ordering the assault on Missionary Ridge, see Brooks D. Simpson, "What Happened on Orchard Knob? Ordering the Attack on Missionary Ridge," in Woodworth and Grear, *The Chattanooga Campaign*, 84–105. Simpson concludes that there was "mass confusion among Thomas's subordinates as to what they were to do." Ibid., 101.

73. James A. Connolly, *Three Years in the Army of the Cumberland*, ed. Paul M. Angle (Bloomington, IN: Indiana University Press, 1959), 158.

74. McPherson, *Battle Cry of Freedom*, 680.

75. C. A. Dana to E. M. Stanton, in *Official Records of the Union and Confederate Armies*, ser. 1, vol. 31, pt. 2, 69.

76. *Official Records of the Union and Confederate Armies*, ser. 1, vol. 31, pt. 2, 35.

77. Ibid.

78. See Rable, *God's Almost Chosen Peoples*, 301.

79. Uriah Smith, *An Appeal to the Youth: Funeral Address of Henry N. White, at Battle Creek, Mich., Dec. 21, 1863* (Battle Creek, MI: Steam Press, 1864), 26.

80. Henry White, quoted in ibid., 29.

81. Henry White, quoted in ibid., 31.

82. Henry White, quoted in ibid., 26.

83. Ellen G. White, "The Death of Henry White," MS 13, 1863, December 1863, in Ellen G. Writings, accessed November 21, 2016, https://m.egwwritings.org/en/book/3016.2000001.

84. Kathy Lewis, "White, Henry Nichols," in Fortin and Moon, *The Ellen G. White Encyclopedia*, 554; and James R. Nix, "Ellen White's Dedicated Hands," in Alberto R. Timm and Dwain N. Esmond, eds., *The Gift of Prophecy in Scripture and History* (Silver Spring, MD: Review and Herald®, 2015), 356.

85. William A. Hammond, quoted in Drew Gilpin Faust, *This Republic of Suffering: Death and the American Civil War* (New York: Vintage Civil War Library, 2008), 4.

86. Faust, *This Republic of Suffering*, 4.

87. Ibid.

88. Basler, *The Collected Works of Abraham Lincoln*, 6:496, 497. See also Rable, *God's Almost Chosen Peoples*, 267–270, 301.

89. Quoted in Shelby Foote, *The Civil War: A Narrative*, vol. 2, *Fredericksburg to Meridian* (New York: Random House, 2011), 859.

CHAPTER 8

A FORECAST OF THE BATTLES:
THE WILDERNESS TO APPOMATTOX

There were moments in the Civil War when, according to historian Allen Guelzo, "the entire Republic was at stake, when everything could have changed, when everything could have turned on a dime."[1] Never was this truer than in 1864, the last full year of the war. In March, Lincoln appointed Ulysses S. Grant as lieutenant general of all the Union armies, a revived position held earlier only by George Washington. Grant immediately set forth a master plan that involved simultaneous advances, the most notable being his advance of 120,000 men against Lee's 64,000 men of the Army of Northern Virginia and William T. Sherman's advance of 100,000 men from Chattanooga to take Atlanta. The future of the Republic was in the outcome of these campaigns, and events of epic importance took place. Once again, we will interpret these events in light of Ellen White's vision at the beginning of the war and note the outcome at the end.

Grant's Overland Campaign: May–June

Grant's advance against Lee, known as the Virginia Overland Campaign, lasted from May 4 to June 12, 1864, and involved some of the most violent and bloody fighting of

Generals Ulysses S. Grant and Robert E. Lee 1864–1865
(U.S. Archives Civil War Photos)

the entire war.[2] Grant's goal with the Army of the Potomac was to defeat Lee's Army of Northern Virginia and then take the Confederate capital of Richmond. Lee's goal was to hold back the Federals and punish them enough to influence Northern morale and elections.[3]

The Wilderness. The first major battle of the campaign was the Battle of the Wilderness, which was fought on May 5–7, 1864. "More desperate fighting has not been witnessed on this continent than that of the 5th and 6th of May," Grant recalled.[4] "No one could see the fight fifty feet from him," wrote a Union private, "the roll and crackle of the musketry was something terrible, even to the veterans of many battles. The lines were very near each other, and from the dense underbrush and tops of trees came puffs of smoke, the '*ping!*' of the bullets, and the yell of the enemy. It was a blind and bloody hunt to the death, in bewildering thickets, rather than a battle."[5]

At the end of the second day, the scene at night was horrible. The woods began to burn from the intense musketry fire, and many of the wounded lying on the ground were unable to crawl away. Soldiers sitting in the lines on both sides grimaced as they listened helplessly to the terrible screams of their comrades burning in the flames.[6] In the end, there was no real winner in the Battle of the Wilderness, and the losses were heavy: Grant had lost about seventeen thousand men, and Lee lost about eleven thousand.[7]

Spotsylvania Court House. After the Wilderness, the armies clashed again in the Battles of Spotsylvania Court House from May 8 to 21. The most memorable of these was a major Union attack on a system of Confederate defensive earthworks shaped like a mule shoe, which were more than one-fourth of a mile wide, not far from the Spotsylvania Court House. On the wet, rainy morning of May 12, as Grant threw his forces at this mule shoe and Lee responded with fresh reinforcements, the battle concentrated on the west angle of the earthworks—"Bloody Angle," the soldiers later dubbed it.

According to historian Gordon Rhea, "The Civil War had seen its share of horrors. The Bloody Lane at Antietam, the stone wall at Fredericksburg, and the Wheatfield at Gettysburg were synonymous with carnage. They paled . . . when measured against the slaughter along the short stretch of earthworks where the salient's [mule shoe's] western tip bent south."[8] According to a New Jersey officer, "It was the concentration of each party in one of the grandest struggles of the war. . . . At every assault and every repulse new bodies fell on the heaps of the slain, and over the filled ditches the living fought on the corpses of the fallen. The wounded were covered by the killed, and expired under piles of their comrades' bodies."[9] At the end of the day, the fight was a draw, with staggering losses on both sides.[10]

North Anna River. After the Spotsylvania battles, the armies moved again: "Lee seeking to elude or destroy his dogged pursuer, Grant skirting south and east to get around him, the two armies locked in a brutal, clumsy lockstep as the battle lines lurched toward Richmond."[11] Lee eventually chose to make a stand twenty-five miles south of Spotsylvania at the North Anna River. He set a trap for Grant by anchoring his line at a particularly strong point on the river and forming his flanks into the shape of an inverted V. Grant pursued Lee, splitting his army on each side of the V, and fell into the snare. But Lee was prostrated with an illness and couldn't coordinate an attack on the divided Union army. Grant realized his peril at the last minute and quickly maneuvered his army out of the trap.[12]

Cold Harbor. From the North Anna River, both armies raced for the crossroads of Cold Harbor near the Chickahominy River during May 27–June 1. Lee arrived first and had his men dig in and ready themselves for an assault from Grant's army, which took place on June 1 and 2 along the lines at Cold Harbor, Virginia. Grant had his mind set on a large head-on assault and lost an opportunity of turning Lee's flank on June 2, which could have given him victory in the campaign.[13] The Republican Party's convention was a week away, and Grant hoped that a decisive victory at Cold Harbor would clinch Lincoln's nomination to the presidency.

At four thirty in the morning on June 3, the large Federal assault began with the signal of a single cannon boom.[14] The nervous but well-entrenched Confederates along the six-mile line aimed their muskets and artillery toward the enemy, waiting for the right moment to fire. Contrary to Grant's plan, the Federals surged toward the enemy in piecemeal fashion. Once the bluecoats were in the line of fire, the Confederates unleashed their deadly firepower. In some places, the men went down in rows and "seemed to melt away like snow falling on moist ground," according to a Massachusetts man.[15] One Alabamian recalled the gruesome image of "heads, arms, legs, and muskets . . . flying through the air at every discharge."[16] Another participant wrote: "Conceive the fierce onslaught, midst deafening volleys of musketry, thunderings of artillery, and the wild, mad yell of battle. See the ranks mowed down as they contend for every inch they advance, until the lines crumble and break before the iron tempest."[17]

In some areas of the charge, Federal units made it to the rebel earthworks, and a brutal hand-to-hand fight ensued, with sword and bayonet thrusts piercing deep into tender flesh and organs.[18] Remembering the charge as a whole, one Confederate general stated, "I had seen the dreadful carnage in front of Marye's Hill at Fredericksburg, and on the 'old railroad cut' which Jackson's men held at the Second Manassas; but I had seen nothing to exceed this. It was not war; it was murder."[19] By the end of the day about four thousand men fell.[20] "I have always regretted that the last assault at Cold Harbor was ever made," Grant later wrote. "No advantage whatever was gained to compensate for the heavy loss we sustained."[21]

Petersburg. Nevertheless, for Grant, Cold Harbor was only a major setback, and he planned his next move carefully. "As he sat at his desk writing dispatches and chewing on a cigar, Grant may very well have noticed a map of Virginia. Tracing his index finger from his current position to the southwest brought his eyes to the city of Petersburg, Virginia." It was time to revert to the "strategy now being executed by Sherman." The Union general "decided to shift his focus from Lee to Lee's logistics. If Grant could carry Petersburg, Richmond and Lee's army would be at his mercy."[22] Shortly thereafter, the Army of the Potomac was on its way to cross the James River and take Petersburg.

Once there, Grant launched several assaults throughout the summer, but his army failed to break through each time.[23] According to historians Edwin C. Bearss and Bryce A. Suderow, the assault from June 15 through June 18, in particular, "was one of the few opportunities that would have changed the course of the war" if it had been successful. "The failed attacks and orders to dig in marked the beginning of ten months of long, grueling, and bloody siege warfare."[24] Additionally, the bloody assault at the Crater on July 30 was, in Grant's words, "a stupendous failure."[25] Like Lincoln, Grant must have wondered more than once about the grinding wheels of providence.

Grant the Butcher. Although Grant's Virginia Overland Campaign maneuvered Lee's army into a siege at Petersburg, the shocking losses (about fifty-five thousand) diminished its significance at the time. The Northern public had become disenchanted with Grant because of his extremely bloody encounters in the battles. In fact, the Democratic newspapers in the North questioned his persistent attacking strategy and labeled him "Grant the Butcher."[26] The public had expected decisive victories but saw only the staggering losses at the Wilderness, Spotsylvania, and

Cold Harbor. While considered a major part of Grant's overall strategy for defeating the Confederacy, the Overland Campaign was clearly a disappointing period in the Union battles.

From Grant's perspective, he was simply executing his military philosophy (which ultimately defeated Lee): "Find out where your enemy is. Get at him as soon as you can. Strike at him as hard as you can and as often as you can, and keep moving on."[27] From the religious perspective of White's prophecy, the loss and disappointment for the North during the Overland Campaign seemed to be part of God's wisdom, punishing them for the sins of slavery. The same could be said about the bloody stalemate during the summer phase of the Petersburg Campaign.

Sherman's Atlanta Campaign: May–August

Meanwhile, William T. Sherman launched his campaign for Atlanta, Georgia, on May 5 with more than one hundred thousand troops, divided into three separate armies. His objective was to destroy the army of his opponent, Joseph E. Johnston, who had replaced Bragg after the Chattanooga battles; push the approximately 120 miles from Chattanooga to Atlanta; take that major Confederate city; and then pierce the rebel heartland in Georgia. Whereas Grant employed the tactic of frontal assault on Lee's defensive positions, Sherman chose to engage Johnston in a war of maneuver. "Rather than assault the Confederates' strong defensive positions, Sherman executed a series of flanking movements that forced Johnston repeatedly to fall back to protect his communications."[28] Nevertheless, the wily Johnston, with his smaller army of sixty-five thousand, countered the Union flanking maneuvers and survived battle after battle to vex and annoy Sherman, until Johnston was replaced by John B. Hood. The battles of the campaign can be divided into two phases: first, Sherman versus Johnston on the way to Atlanta (May 7–July 5); and second, Sherman versus Hood in the Atlanta vicinity (July 17–September 2).[29]

Sherman versus Johnston. The key to Sherman's plan was to force Johnston to fight early in the campaign, defeat his army, and travel unhindered to Atlanta. But this plan was foiled at the outset. At a crucial moment during the early maneuvers on the city of Resaca, Georgia, Major General James B. McPherson, who commanded the right-flanking Army of the Tennessee (about twenty-five thousand troops), uncharacteristically hesitated. As the army was in sight of the railroad it was supposed to capture outside of Resaca, McPherson suddenly pulled his troops back, retreated to the end of Snake Creek Gap, and dug in for the night. Although McPherson believed his flank was at great risk, Sherman was keenly disappointed when the operation failed. If McPherson had continued and taken the railroad and Resaca, the general believed, he could have dislodged Johnston from his entrenched position at Dalton, Georgia, drawn him into battle, and doomed his army to destruction.[30] An "opportunity" such as this, Sherman wrote, "does not occur twice in a single life." McPherson was "a little cautious" at "the critical moment."[31]

This series of events led to the Battle of Resaca, the first major battle in the Atlanta Campaign. Once Johnston learned that Sherman's massive army was moving towards him through the deep valleys and heavy forests, he immediately evacuated Dalton to concentrate in front of the Yankees at Resaca. By May 13, both armies were consolidating around Resaca. The Confederate position was a strong one and posed a major obstacle to Sherman. As the battle began on May 14, Sherman ordered his armies to press Resaca on all sides. The Confederates made a determined effort to hold the city; but in the end, Sherman threatened their line of retreat, and they were forced to move back toward Atlanta. During the night of May 15, Johnston abandoned the town.[32]

Although Sherman dislodged Johnston from Dalton and drove him out of Resaca, the opportunity of destroying the rebel army was lost. "In a very real sense," wrote Philip L. Secrist, "the escape of the Confederate army from the trap at Resaca was a major strategic defeat for Sherman."[33] The events surrounding the Resaca battle "would serve to remind the northern commander of his own deficiencies, and of the limitations of key subordinates." Combined, these "mistakes would produce a parade of missed opportunities," explained Secrist, "that would force William Tecumseh Sherman to revise his plan for the months ahead. It would be a long road to Atlanta."[34]

Thus began the downward spiral of defeats in the Atlanta Campaign that, in light of White's statement, could be interpreted as God's wisdom to "punish them for their sins."[35] If things had gone according to plan and McPherson had pursued the railroad and taken Resaca, or if Sherman had destroyed Johnston's army at the Battle of Resaca, the campaign would have been over much sooner.

The peak of Sherman's disappointing experience with Johnston was the disastrous Battle of Kennesaw Mountain. Kennesaw Mountain, with its twin peaks near Marietta, Georgia, was the ninth fortified defensive position that Johnston had created to stop Sherman, and it proved to be the most difficult to bypass. During late June, Sherman had tried to turn Johnston's left flank but to no avail. Both armies were exhausted from constant artillery duels, sniping, and a fierce battle or two. "As the two sides tested each other, heavy rains descended, and the dirt roads of Georgia became quagmires." Frustrated with the delay, Sherman departed from his normal mode of operations and "threw eight brigades of veteran troops, some fifteen thousand men, at three locations along the heavily fortified Confederate line on June 27."[36]

The result was a disaster, as three thousand men fell, with no dent in the rebel defenses. Those Federals who survived remembered the attack for the rest of their lives. It took over a week for Sherman to regroup and continue his flanking maneuvers against Johnston.[37] The rain continued to descend in torrents, causing suffering for the soldiers and frustration for the commanders, but Sherman maintained his advance toward Atlanta.[38]

Sherman versus Hood. Confederate president Jefferson Davis was concerned that Johnston would not defend Atlanta; on July 17, he replaced him with his subordinate John B. Hood. Known for his aggressive fighting, Hood wasted no time. Sherman's army was now in the vicinity of Atlanta, and on July 20, Hood attacked him in what is known as the Battle of Peachtree Creek.[39] Hood's army was repulsed, and Sherman experienced his first decisive victory of the campaign. By evening, the Confederates had lost twenty-five hundred troops, while the Union had lost about nineteen hundred.[40] Hood retreated back into the fortifications of Atlanta, only to emerge on July 22 in another attack known as the Battle of Atlanta. Hood's forces tore into Sherman's Federals with relentless fury that day, scoring a critical blow in the death of General McPherson. Nevertheless, Sherman's men held the lines in what was the costliest battle of the campaign, with a loss of 5,500 Confederate men and 3,722 Union casualties.[41]

On July 28, as Sherman's advancing armies endeavored to cut the last Confederate supply line into Atlanta, Hood again threw his troops against the Federals near a chapel in the Battle of Ezra Church. After five hours of hard fighting, 5,000 Confederates lay dead and wounded, with only 632 Union casualties.[42] Although Sherman was another step closer in his long effort to take Atlanta, Hood had salvaged his lifeline and remained entrenched in Atlanta. So the Union army dug in and bombarded the city's defenses as the general contemplated his next move. The great Confederate city would be under siege for the time being.

When taken as a whole, the Atlanta Campaign seems to reflect the tension in White's statement between the victories and losses. Even though Sherman never completed his original objective of destroying Johnston's army and experienced significant losses along the way, he was still able to push toward Atlanta, getting closer with each flanking movement and resulting battle. Once in the vicinity of Atlanta and facing Hood, Sherman's armies achieved victories but could not take the city. Interpreting the situation with the light of White's forecast, one could propose that God in "His wisdom" would not give Atlanta to the Union armies until He "ordained" it so.

Shenandoah Valley Campaign: May–June

The fertile Shenandoah Valley of Virginia, nestled between the Allegheny Mountains to the west and the Blue Ridge Mountains to the east, served as the source of food and other necessities for Robert E. Lee's army. It also formed a sheltered highway for the Confederate forces as they traveled north during their invasion of Maryland in 1862 and Pennsylvania in 1863. It was the place of Thomas "Stonewall" Jackson's famous valley campaign in the summer of 1862. Now, in the summer of 1864, its strategic importance loomed larger than ever as Grant engaged Lee's army around Richmond, Virginia. If the valley could be brought under Union control, then Lee's army could be starved into submission.[43]

Grant wasn't excited about sending Franz Sigel to the valley, as Sigel was a political general who got his position because of connections.[44] But he hoped for the best and sent Sigel on his way with some ten thousand men to clear the valley and threaten Lee's left flank. Sigel's opponent was Major General John C. Breckinridge, a former U.S. vice president, who had assembled a tiny army of forty-five hundred men, including cadets from the Virginia Military Institute. The two armies clashed on May 15 at the Battle of New Market during a drenching rainstorm. At the peak of the battle, Breckinridge inserted the young cadets into the battle, whose charge on the Federals would be remembered most. It was a humiliating defeat for Sigel[45] and the beginning of a seesaw pattern of Union losses and victories in the valley.

Grant soon replaced Sigel with the more capable Major General David Hunter, who led a raid through the valley, destroying railroads and facilities supporting the Confederate war effort. Hunter won the Battle of Piedmont on June 5, took Staunton,

Virginia, the next day,[46] then proceeded south to Lexington and burned the Virginia Military Institute, among other structures, probably in retaliation for the cadet charge at New Market.[47] While Hunter's army lingered in Lexington, Confederate General Jubal A. Early brought his forces to reinforce Lynchburg, and a battle ensued on June 16–18. Although Hunter still held the advantage in manpower, he was bluffed by Early at the Battle of Lynchburg into thinking that his army was outnumbered. Consequently, Hunter withdrew into the mountains of West Virginia and left the Shenandoah Valley in Confederate control.[48] Once again, one could infer in this early phase of the Shenandoah Valley Campaign the seesaw pattern of Union battles as predicted by White.

Confederate raid on the gates of Washington: July

One of the most dramatic events in the Civil War was Jubal A. Early's raid on Washington. Early was a capable veteran officer who had led men into battle at First and Second Manassas, Antietam, Fredericksburg, Chancellorsville, and Gettysburg. General Lee had given "Old Jube," as he was called, the assignment of advancing on the Federal capital in hopes of drawing forces away from Grant at Petersburg and inflicting, at the very least, an emotional wound on those in the capital as well as the North in general.[49]

With the Shenandoah Valley clear of Union troops, Early launched his army of fourteen thousand men toward Washington in late June, and after traveling northeast for over a week, they arrived in the vicinity of Frederick, Maryland, northwest of Washington, on July 8. When news of Early's advance reached Grant, he immediately dispatched General Lew Wallace, commander of the Middle Department of Atlantic states, to confront Early's forces and turn them back. Unfortunately, Wallace was not an experienced commander, and the troops he commanded were green. Grant also dispatched seventeen thousand men to aid Wallace, but they were en route from the Richmond area and would not make it in time.

On July 9, Early's battle-hardened forces encountered the inexperienced, smaller army of Wallace at the Monocacy River, and the result was predictable. By late afternoon, the Federals were in full retreat, with thirteen hundred casualties, and Early, who suffered eight hundred losses, had won the northernmost Confederate battle of the war during the Battle of Monocacy. Now the path to Washington was open for the rebels' advance. What made matters worse was that the massive fortifications around Washington were pitifully undermanned as the army was with Grant in his Overland Campaign. As the Confederates pressed toward the city on July 10, only reservists—clerks, office workers, and frightened militia—were thrown into service to defend the forts. Aware of this situation, Early planned to exploit it fully.

When the Confederate forces arrived in front of Washington on July 11, they were exhausted from fighting at Monocacy and the long march in the heat. It had been exceptionally hot during this time, and Early refrained from launching an attack. Instead, he chose to employ artillery fire and skirmishing. On the morning of July 12, he decided to attack but held back when he discovered that Grant's forces were arriving.

Meanwhile, Washington was full of fear and confusion. "Refugees were everywhere, with their tales of death and destruction, few people in the administration had any accurate information as to what was going on and the military authorities were rushing anyone in a uniform out to the forts. About all anyone knew for sure was that no one knew anything for sure." Suddenly, in the midst of all the fear and chaos in the city, the sound of cheering erupted. Now "strong, tanned men in faded blue uniforms were flooding out of the transports and forming their ranks in the streets: the Sixth Corps had arrived." An hour before, Washington "was in a panic," according to one soldier, but "now as the people saw the veterans wearing the badge of the Greek cross marching through their streets, the excitement subsided and confidence prevailed."[50] Grant's veteran soldiers defended Washington's forts, and Early retreated back to the valley. "Early should have attacked early in the morning." Elisha Hunt Rhodes mockingly penned in his diary: "Early was late."[51]

The most interesting aspect of Early's raid on Washington was the outcome of the Battle of Monocacy. This battle, although a loss to the Union, ended up delaying Early by a day in his advance on Washington. According to Grant, "If Early had been but one day earlier he might have entered the capital before the arrival of the reinforcements I had sent. Whether the delay caused by the battle amounted to a day or not, General Wallace contributed on this occasion, by the defeat of the troops under him a greater benefit to the cause than often falls to the lot of a commander of an equal force to render by means of a victory."[52]

According to historian Gary Gallagher, "It can be said with confidence that Wallace's troops spared the Lincoln government a potential disaster, and for that reason the battle of the Monocacy must be considered one of the more significant actions of the Civil War."[53] Not surprisingly, Monocacy has been called "the battle that saved Washington."[54]

This battle is clearly one of those interesting events in the war when the fortunes of the nation could have turned on a dime. The fall of Washington during this crucial phase in the war would have been devastating to the Union cause. From the perspective of White's forecast, however, one might conclude that it was the activity of God that saved Washington and thus permitted "no more losses to the Northern men than in His wisdom He saw fit."[55]

President Lincoln was almost shot

During Early's demonstration in front of Fort Stevens, near Washington, President Lincoln paid a visit to the front lines, an event that many would long remember. To get a better look at the action, Lincoln climbed up on the masonry terraces running around the fort. According to witnesses, as he stood fully exposed, at six feet four inches tall and more than seven feet tall with his stovepipe hat, he was an easy target. Bullets whizzed past him as Confederate sharpshooters fired at his tall, recognizable form.

One Union officer, evidently not recognizing who the tall figure was, shouted, "Get down, you fool!" The president quickly got down from the line of fire. For the first time in American history, a president of the United States came under enemy fire while in office. The second time Lincoln stood on the masonry terraces to view the action, a sniper bullet hit an officer close to him. Scrambling down, he still continued to bob his head up and down, peering over the ramparts at the action unfolding in front of the fort and making everybody nervous.[56]

That President Lincoln, the capable and cautious leader of the nation, would subject himself to such danger is puzzling, especially when compared with the high standards of the U.S. Secret Service today. Whatever Lincoln's reasoning was in exposing himself to enemy fire, if he had been shot and killed at this juncture in the war, the Union cause would have been over, much as if Early had taken the city. It was a great risk on Lincoln's part, but he survived without a scratch. Perhaps he knew in his heart that his work was not yet over, and it was worth the risk to show the enemy that he was in charge. Gabor S. Boritt pondered this odd Lincoln occurrence and wrote, "I see a man standing there looking not at the Confederates, but [at] God, saying silently: if I am wrong, God, strike me down."[57]

From White's theological perspective, it seems that God in His wisdom spared the president during this crucial time of the war.

The summer stalemate and the presidential election

By August of 1864, the morale of the Northern people had reached its lowest point in the war. Their high expectations of the hostilities ending during the summer were devastated. One discouraging event after the other—the slaughter at the Wilderness, Spotsylvania, and Cold Harbor; Grant's stalemate in front of Petersburg after several unsuccessful bloody attempts to break through; Sherman's repulse at Kennesaw Mountain in June, and his bloody battles outside of Atlanta without taking the city; the notorious raids of Jubal E. Early, especially his near miss at taking the city of Washington; and Early's most recent actions in the Shenandoah Valley—all combined to create a foreboding of worse to come.

Lincoln had been renominated for president at the Republican national convention back in early June and was keenly aware of the nation's mood. During July, Lincoln had called for a day of prayer on August 4, asking the nation to "confess and to repent of their manifold sins; to implore the compassion and forgiveness of the Almighty," and to beg Him "not to destroy us as a people, nor suffer us to be destroyed by the hostility or connivance of other Nations, or by obstinate adhesion to our own counsels, which may be in conflict with His eternal purposes, and to implore Him to enlighten the mind of the Nation to know and do His will."[58] There was a deep sense of repentance for national sin in this post–Emancipation Proclamation day of prayer that was not in the September 26, 1861, fast proclamation. The North prayed for military success on August 4, but no answer came. The national morale plunged to its deepest level yet.

In mid August, Lincoln told Francis Pierpont, the governor of loyal West Virginia, that "the people seem despondent, and our opponents are pressing the howl that the war is a failure and it has had its effect in the army and among the people. We must have military success."[59] But no such success was in sight. The Democrats capitalized upon this situation and declared that the war was a total failure and only a peace agreement would save the nation. Already word was out that the new Democratic candidate would be none other than George B. McClellan. The Confederates were especially interested in the upcoming election because they knew that if Lincoln lost, they would have a good chance of obtaining their national independence.

The president was adamant that "he would never consent to an armistice, or to peace, on any other terms but the explicit abolition of slavery in all the Southern States."[60] But without military victories, the tide was against him. The atmosphere became more anti-Lincoln as the hot August days ticked by. Even the president's advisors were unanimously pessimistic about his reelection. Finally, on August 23, Lincoln himself acknowledged that he would not win the election and penned in a memorandum that "it seems exceedingly probable that this Administration will not be re-elected."[61] He sealed the document and asked his cabinet to sign it with no knowledge of its contents. Perhaps "Lincoln may have feared that its contents would be leaked to the press if the cabinet had been allowed to read it."[62]

As predicted, George McClellan was nominated as the Democratic candidate for the presidency at the National Democratic Convention in Chicago on August 31. If McClellan won the 1864 election, the republic would have changed dramatically. The general had already laid out his view of things back in July 1862 when, at Harrison's Landing, he presented Lincoln with a letter outlining his "soft war" policy. It is almost a given that he would have sat down at the negotiating table with Confederate leaders and come up with a peace plan to end the war with the institution of slavery still intact.

Unless Lincoln won the election, everything he had tried to accomplish since the war began would be completely reversed. The Emancipation Proclamation, which McClellan had criticized from the beginning, would surely have been abolished. "I'm going to be beaten," Lincoln told a friend, "and unless some great change takes place *badly beaten*."[63]

Seven words that changed everything

Sherman decided to make his move on August 25 in a wide-flanking maneuver that would cut off the Confederate armies' last railroad connections. Hood thought that a previous cavalry raid had routed the Federals, and he telegraphed the news of his "great victory" to Richmond and "planned a civic celebration in Atlanta."[64] It wasn't until August 30 that Hood realized what Sherman was doing some twenty miles south of the city in Jonesborough, Georgia. He sent two corps south to protect the railroad, which commenced the Battle of Jonesborough on August 31, the final battle for Atlanta.[65] The next day, September 1, the Federals drove Hood's Confederates away. In fear of being surrounded, Hood evacuated the rest of his army from Atlanta on the night of September 1–2, while burning everything of military value in the city.[66] The next day the Federals marched into the city of Atlanta.

Sherman telegraphed Washington: "So Atlanta is ours, and fairly won."[67] These seven words sent shockwaves of joy throughout the North. "Glorious news this morning—*Atlanta taken at last!!!*" penned New York lawyer George Templeton Strong in his diary.[68] Boys skipped through cities and towns waving the newspapers, shouting to the crowds: "Sherman's taken Atlanta! Atlanta's fallen!" Men stopped what they were doing and waved their hats. "On porches women listened to the shouting neighbor boys, then threw their aprons over their heads and ran into the house sobbing in joy."[69] Delighted with the news, Lincoln wrote Sherman and rendered him "national thanks" for "the distinguished ability, courage, and perseverance displayed in the campaign in Georgia, which, under Divine favor, has resulted in the capture of the City of Atlanta." Lincoln described Sherman's operations as "famous in the annals of war."[70]

The significance and timing of Atlanta's fall cannot be overestimated. "Everybody realized that General Sherman had done more than just win an important battle," explained David Alan Johnson. "By taking Atlanta, he had permanently damaged the Confederacy's very ability to wage war, and he probably dealt a fatal injury to the Confederacy itself. After Atlanta, there was no longer any doubt in anyone's mind that the North was going to win the war. Though it might take a while yet, the outcome of the war was now inevitable—the Union would win!"[71] No small wonder that Strong called it "the greatest event of the war."[72]

As for Lincoln, his political fortunes changed dramatically. Sherman's seven-word message "was the best and most effective political endorsement Lincoln ever could have hoped for." Johnson explained,

Just a few weeks before, Lincoln's political prospects appeared to be a dead issue. But now all that had changed, suddenly and dramatically. With the fall of Atlanta, his fortunes had taken a 180-degree turn for the better. After the first week of September, it began to look as though nothing could derail Lincoln's drive to the White House. Sherman had certainly taken the steam out of the Democrat's peace platform. Nobody could claim that the war was an undiluted failure anymore, not with the Confederacy's second most important city in Union hands. Only the capture of Richmond could have made more of an impact.[73]

Adding to Sherman's accomplishment was Admiral Farragut's victory in Mobile, Alabama, achieved on August 5. His Union fleet charged into Mobile Bay and engaged the forts "in a spectacular duel of heavy guns,"[74] eventually forcing them to surrender and securing the bay for the Union. This victory, although somewhat eclipsed by the general gloom in August, now took on vast significance when combined with Sherman's victory in Atlanta. Appropriately, on September 3, the same day he congratulated Sherman, the president tendered official thanks to Farragut and his commanders for "their energy and courage, which, under the blessing of Providence, have been crowned with brilliant success."[75]

The victory of Atlanta is one of those moments in the war when things suddenly changed or turned on a dime for the good of the Union. The victory came just in the nick of time. Looking back on the Atlanta victory from the perspective of White's forecast, one could say the period of "losses to the Northern men" was over. God "in His wisdom" gave them the Mobile Bay and Atlanta victories when they needed them most and distinctly changed the momentum in favor of the Union.

Lincoln recognized God's involvement when, after attributing Sherman's and Farragut's victories to "Divine Providence," he called for a national day of "Thanksgiving and Prayer." Because of the "glorious achievements of the Army," the president entreated the nation to "call for devout acknowledgement to the Supreme Being in whose hands are the destinies of nations."[76] This appeal from the nation's president must have resonated with Ellen White and all others in the North who were looking for God's hand in the war.

Shenandoah Valley Campaign and the November election

To address the problems in the Shenandoah Valley caused by Early's July raids,[77] Grant and the president had jointly decided to send into the valley General Philip Sheridan, the short Irishman (five feet five inches) who was an aggressive warrior and never known to back down from a fight. Sheridan's instructions from Grant were clear and specific: destroy Early's army and lay waste to the valley so that the Confederate's breadbasket could no longer feed its armies. Sheridan launched his campaign; throughout August, the two opposing armies sparred and skirmished, neither really scoring a knockout blow. Grant applied pressure to Lee at Petersburg by attacking both his flanks and forced him to recall a division from Early, which gave Sheridan a sizable numerical advantage.

Consequently, Sheridan's "terrible swift sword"[78] conquered Early at Winchester, Virginia, on September 19, and again, three days later, he drove Early back at the Battle of Fisher's Hill. These victories added significant momentum to the upcoming election for Lincoln. On September 23, James A. Garfield, a former general and congressman, wrote to his wife that "Phil Sheridan had made a speech in the Shenandoah Valley more powerful and valuable to the Union cause than all the stumpers in the Republic can make—our prospects are everywhere heightening."[79] Sheridan then implemented the second part of his assignment during early October, the "hard war" directive from Grant, and burned the farms in the Shenandoah Valley, destroying the Confederates' source of food and other provisions.

By the end of September, Sheridan was convinced that his Shenandoah Valley Campaign was over, and this idea spread throughout the entire chain of command in his army. In mid-October, Sheridan went northward and prepared to return his army to Grant so that he could finish Lee at Petersburg. On October 18–19, however, Old Jube launched a surprise attack on the complacent bluecoats at Cedar Creek, and they fell apart. Early on the morning of the nineteenth while in Winchester, Sheridan heard the roar of the artillery fire some twenty miles southward. He quickly mounted his horse and raced toward the battle. At the last minute, Sheridan saved the day by rallying his retreating troops to go back to the fight. Once there, he organized them for a counterattack and defeated the Confederates, practically eliminating Early's army as a fighting force. A Confederate victory at Cedar Creek could have altered the entire Shenandoah Valley Campaign, but Sheridan's remarkable ability to rally and reorganize his troops concluded the campaign with the entire valley in Union hands.[80]

It is not surprising that Lincoln called for another proclamation of thanksgiving on October 20 for the "many and signal victories," setting the last Thursday in November as the day of "Thanksgiving and Praise to Almighty God the beneficent Creator and Ruler of the Universe." The president urged his "fellow-citizens" to "humble themselves in the dust and from thence offer up penitent and fervent prayers and supplications to the Great Disposer of events for a return of the inestimable blessings of Peace, Union and Harmony throughout the land."[81]

"Sherman and Sheridan had given the Confederacy a one-two punch," wrote McPherson. "Now Grant hoped to follow up with a knockout blow." Grant believed his final victory with the fall of Petersburg and Richmond would affirm Lincoln's reelection. At the end of October, he struck both of Lee's flanks at Petersburg, but in the end failed "to strike his knockout blow."[82] Nevertheless, Sheridan's victory at Cedar Creek solidified Abraham Lincoln's reelection and guaranteed that the war would end on his terms. "The capture and destruction of the Shenandoah Valley showed a weary populace that Union fortunes were indeed turning."[83] Additionally, "the legendlike details of what Sheridan achieved made the candidacy of McClellan appear almost pitiful in late October."[84]

The election

"The 1864 election," explained McPherson, "was a referendum on the war and emancipation. No one could be entirely sure what the consequences of a Democratic victory would be: Confederate independence, restoration of the Union with slavery, or something else. But the consequences of a Republican victory were certain: the doom of slavery and the continuation of war until the South surrendered."[85] With this understanding in mind, voters in the North, as well as Union soldiers, went to the polls on November 8 and reelected Lincoln by a majority vote. "The overwhelming majority received by Mr. Lincoln and the quiet with which the election went off," Grant wrote to a friend, "will prove a terrible damper to the Rebels. It will be worth more than a victory in the field both in its effect on the Rebels and in its influence abroad."[86]

Indeed, Grant was right that Lincoln's election was "worth more than a victory in the field." It was, without question, a major turning point in the war.[87] It meant that Lincoln could pursue the war effort until the rebels surrendered and continue on the path of emancipation for the slaves. More specifically, it was an affirmative vote by the North against the continuance of slavery. One item now remained to address: an amendment to the Constitution on the issue of slavery. As things progressed on the battlefield, the newly reelected president would advance his agenda to officially rid slavery from the land.[88] In light of White's forecast, Lincoln's reelection could be interpreted as one of those war events ordained of God.

Sherman's March to the Sea and Hood's campaign in Tennessee

After the election, Sherman made a daring proposal to divide his forces, leave Atlanta, and march through the Georgia heartland to destroy Confederate resources and morale. Grant and Lincoln were reluctant to embrace the proposal at first; but upon Sherman's insistence that it would work, they approved the "March to the Sea."

Part of the plan sent General Thomas with his army into Tennessee to deal with Hood's army. Predictably, the Confederate general invaded Tennessee with hopes that he could draw Sherman away from Georgia. On November 15, Sherman burned everything of military value in Atlanta and left for the sea. The flames, however, spread out of control and consumed one-third of the city, leveling it to the ground. "The 62,000 bluecoats moved at a leisurely pace of ten miles a day, giving them plenty of time to cut a swath of destruction fifty miles wide through the heart of the Confederacy."[89]

Meanwhile, Hood advanced through Tennessee with his thirty-nine thousand men, who were really ill equipped for a major campaign such as this. (Thousands of the soldiers were barefoot due to their poor-quality shoes falling apart early in the march.)[90] After several flanking encounters with the Federals, Hood pursued them to Franklin, Tennessee, where they were entrenched and ready to fight. On November 30, the desperate general ordered an ill-advised frontal assault that ended hours later in utter devastation, with sixty-three hundred Confederate casualties, nearly three times that of the Federal loss.[91]

Among the casualties—killed, wounded, or captured—at Franklin were twelve generals and fifty-four regimental commanders.[92] Veteran Sam Watkins, who had fought in all of the major battles of the Army of Tennessee, never forgot Franklin: "I shrink from butchery. Would to God I could tear the page from these memoirs and from my own memory. . . . It was the finishing stroke to the Independence of the Southern Confederacy. I was there. I saw it. My flesh trembles, and creeps, and crawls when I think of it today."[93] But the slaughter wasn't over.

Instead of retreating with his crippled army, "the sensible thing to do," Hood chose to pursue the Federals as they retreated to join General Thomas's army at Nashville. Once his rebel army was entrenched on the hills south of the city, Hood wasn't sure what to do. "His forces were too weak to attack the Nashville defenses; it was logistically impossible for them to continue north, and Hood believed that a retreat would demoralize his army." In fact, the "army was already demoralized as it awaited the inevitable attack."[94] On December 15, Thomas launched his assault and pounded the weakened Confederate army, routing them the next day, on December 16. According to McPherson, "The battle of Nashville was one of the most crushing Union victories of the war."[95] The Confederate army was essentially decimated as its remnant fled from Nashville towards Mississippi. Hood resigned in January.[96]

The Thirteenth Amendment

After Abraham Lincoln's overwhelming victory in the election, he "found his pockets full of political capital." As his armies achieved victories over the enemy—namely, Thomas's victory over Hood at Nashville and Sherman's successful march—he used this capital to make sure "that the constitutional amendment abolishing slavery was enacted as quickly as possible."[97] His administration "lobbied earnestly to persuade a dozen or more Democrats to change their previous negative votes."[98] According to historian Michael Vorenberg, "No piece of legislation during Lincoln's presidency received more of his attention than the Thirteenth Amendment."[99] The final vote took place on January 31, 1865.

As the House of Representatives assembled on this memorable day for the final vote, the floor was densely packed with all the political "who's who" in the government: the chief justice, four associate justices, various senators, the secretary of the treasury, and the secretary of state. The galleries were also overflowing with people, including African Americans "whose presence already had occasioned some remarks by congressmen. Particularly attentive among the black observers was Frederick Douglass's son Charles, a former Union soldier now working at the Freedman's Hospital in Washington." Vorenberg captures the significance of this moment: "A collective excitement swelled among the hundreds of men and women as the realization dawned on them that they were taking part in one of the most significant moments in American history."[100]

The votes were tallied, and two-thirds of the House voted in the affirmative—Congress had adopted the Thirteenth Amendment! After a moment of silent awe, the House erupted with cheers. "Members threw their hats to the roof, caught them, and smashed them against their desks." The audience roared with approval, embracing one another and wiping tears from their eyes. "Blacks in the audience were equally moved, not only by the meaning of the event but by the reaction of the whites around them."[101] Charles Douglass wrote to his well-known abolitionist father: "I wish that you could have been here, . . . such rejoicing I never before witnessed . . . (white people I mean)."[102]

It was a crowning moment for most Republican congressmen. "We have wiped away the black spot from our bright shield and surely God will bless us for it," wrote Martin Russell Thayer of Pennsylvania. "He [God] seemed to smile from Heaven

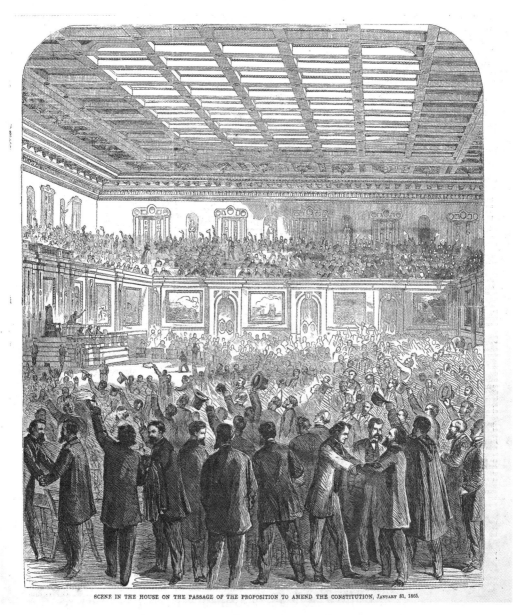

SCENE IN THE HOUSE ON THE PASSAGE OF THE PROPOSITION TO AMEND THE CONSTITUTION, January 31, 1865.

Cartoon depicting celebration in the House of Representatives
after adoption of the Thirteenth Amendment, *Harpers Weekly,* Feb. 18, 1865.

upon a regenerated people for as the great throng poured out of the House immediately afterwards the Sun broke through the clouds which had all day concealed him and lit up everything with his effulgence."[103] The day after the vote, the news was all over the country.

In February, William Lloyd Garrison stated the following in a speech delivered at a grand jubilee meeting celebrating the Thirteenth Amendment: "The event we are here to celebrate is one of these—grand, inspiring, glorious, beyond all power of utterance, and far-reaching beyond all finite computation. At last, . . . the nation, rising in the majesty of its moral power and political sovereignty, has decreed that LIBERTY shall be 'PROCLAIMED THROUGHOUT ALL THE LAND, TO ALL THE INHABITANTS THEREOF,' and that henceforth no such anomalous being as slaveholder or slave shall exist beneath the 'stars and stripes,' within the domain of the republic." At these words, the audience burst into cheers.[104]

Garrison spoke for all abolitionists in these words, including the Adventists. Although the amendment wouldn't be ratified until December 6, 1865, the nation had nevertheless accepted what Ellen White called "the fast which God has chosen," employing imagery from Isaiah 58:5–7, which abolitionists used as a call for the nation to set the captives free. Slavery would finally be eradicated from the Constitution itself. Now, according to White, God would "accept" the prayers of the nation "as far as the war is concerned."[105] On November 24, 1864, the last Thursday of the month, the nation had prayed, as its president had asked, and offered "up penitent and fervent prayers and supplications to the Great Disposer of events for a return of the inestimable blessings of Peace, Union and Harmony throughout the land."[106] With the passing of the Thirteenth Amendment, God apparently heard these prayers, and the end of the war came swiftly.

The end of the war

As the cold winter weather set in, the armies hunkered down until they could move again. Sherman, however, moved out in spite of the weather. This time the target of his march was the Carolinas. In February 1865, he unleashed his "60,000 avengers" on the countryside of South Carolina in a formation similar to his march through Georgia but which was even more destructive. The plan was to destroy all Confederate resources in his path and move up on Lee's rear "to catch the Army of Northern Virginia in a vise between his army and Grant's." In spite of relentless rain, Sherman's men forged ahead, successfully managing the logistical nightmare of crossing swollen rivers and swamps and fighting off Confederate attackers.[107]

The two wings of the army split, one taking Augusta, Georgia, and the other Charleston, South Carolina—the "Queen city of the South" and the "taproot of secession"—whose fall "was the most dramatic sign of the Confederacy's collapse."[108] The worst destructive power of the "blue bulldozer" was in Columbia, the capital of South Carolina. Much of it was burned to the ground, which is a source of controversy to this day.[109] After moving through North Carolina and completing their seven-week march, "Sherman's troops left 425 miles of desolation that would never again support a Rebel army."[110]

Early in March, Sheridan's forces destroyed the remnant of Early's army at the Battle of Waynesboro, Virginia, thus eliminating all Confederate threats in the Shenandoah Valley. Sheridan then took his army over the Blue Ridge Mountains and eventually joined with Grant's army at Petersburg, Virginia. In the meantime, Confederate General Johnston had assembled a force of twenty-two thousand to counter Sherman's marching army. Lee had hoped to escape from Petersburg and join with Johnston to beat Sherman and then return to fight Grant again.

But it was not to be. Lee attempted his breakout on March 25 by attacking Fort Stedman, an earthwork in the Union line around Petersburg. His forces initially broke through the line and penetrated the Union defenses, only to be driven back by a Federal counterattack. Grant sent the newly returned Sheridan from the valley with his cavalry and two infantry corps to destroy the last open railroad into Petersburg and to intercept Lee's escape route to the southwest. These maneuvers culminated in the Battle of Five Forks on April 1, in which Sheridan's forces flanked and routed ten thousand Confederates. Once Grant learned of the rout at Five Forks, he ordered an assault on all the Petersburg lines before sunrise the next day. It was a long and bloody fight, in which the remaining Confederates were driven back from one line of trenches to the next. But in the end, Grant achieved a breakthrough and took Petersburg. President Jefferson Davis was in his church at Richmond when he received the news that Petersburg had fallen, and he was told to leave the city. On April 3, the Confederates abandoned Richmond and burned much of its resources, leaving it a blazing inferno.[111]

Before Grant could trap the Confederates after the assault on Petersburg, Lee had escaped with what was left of his army across the Appomattox River and had fled

Lee surrenders to Grant in the McLean house parlor
(Library of Congress)

westward. With Federal forces to his left and rear, he advanced as far as he could until Sheridan trapped him on the morning of April 8. After a final attempt to break through the encircling Union lines on April 9, Lee realized that it was over. Later that day he met with Grant at a personal residence in the village of Appomattox Court House to surrender. Grant offered generous terms to Lee and his army, which Lee gladly accepted. With the principal Confederate army surrendered, the war was essentially over.[112]

As the news of Lee's surrender spread throughout the Union camps, officers and soldiers celebrated. Even General Meade joined the jubilation, racing on his horse, followed by a wild group of mounted men and two squadrons of cavalry, "everybody yelling and waving swords and riding like mad. Meade was bareheaded, both arms in the air shouting: 'It's all over, boys! Lee's surrendered! It's all over!' "[113] One soldier wrote down what he saw:

> The air is black with hats and boots, coats, knapsacks, shirts, and cartridge boxes, blankets and shelter tents, canteens and haversacks. They fall on each others' necks and laugh and cry by turns. Huge, lumbering, bearded men embrace and kiss like school-girls, then dance and sing and shout, stand on their heads and play at leapfrog with each other. . . . All the time, from the hills around, the deep-mouthed cannon give their harmless thunders, and at each hollow boom the vast concourse rings out of its joy anew that murderous shot and shell no longer follow close the accustomed sound.[114]

Elisha Hunt Rhodes, who cried and laughed with his fellow soldiers, recorded his thoughts on April 9, the day of Lee's surrender: "Well I have seen the end of the Rebellion. I was in the first battle fought by the dear old Army of the Potomac, and I was in the last. I thank God for all his blessings to me and that my life has been spared to see this glorious day. Hurrah, Hurrah, Hurrah!"[115]

Events followed in quick succession: Johnston surrendered his army to Sherman on April 26; Jefferson Davis was captured on May 10; two days later Federal and Confederate forces clashed for the final time on May 12–13 at Palmito Ranch, Texas; and the last substantial Confederate army surrendered on May 26.[116] The long, bloody conflict was over. With slavery soon to be abolished by the ratification of the Thirteenth Amendment, the land was finally at rest.

Conclusion

When the two great armies of the North and the South converged on the farm of Wilmer McLean and a shell tore through his kitchen window during the First Battle of Bull Run in Manassas, Virginia, on July 21, 1861, he decided to move his family far away from the dangers of war. He chose a place to the south and west of Richmond—a little crossroads town called Appomattox Court House. There, free from harm's way, McLean hoped his family could wait out the terrible War Between the States in their neat brick house that stood across from the courthouse.

Three and a half years later, on the afternoon of April 9, 1865, McLean encountered Confederate Colonel Charles Marshall, who was accompanied by an orderly, Private Joshua O. Johns, as they were looking for a place that the two generals, Lee and Grant, could meet to discuss the terms of surrender. It was Sunday and difficult to find a suitable place, so McLean reluctantly offered the parlor of his own home, and the historic meeting took place there.[117] At the end of the day, Wilmer McLean could say, "The war began in my front yard and ended in my front parlor."[118]

Between the beginning and ending of the Civil War in the McLean home, Ellen White's forecast had apparently comprehended the nature of the battles. While the McLeans decided to escape the war after the First Battle of Bull Run, only to find it again at Appomattox, Ellen White interestingly predicted the outcome of the war at the First Battle of Bull Run, only to find it fulfilled at Appomattox. In this chapter and the previous two, we have noted the consistency in which this short, sweeping forecast was apparently fulfilled in the battles and political events of the war: "God had this nation in His own hand, and would not suffer victories to be gained faster than He ordained, and would permit no more losses to the Northern men than in His wisdom He saw fit, to punish them for their sins."[119] Once events favored ending slavery and divine punishment ran its course, the battle outcomes were decidedly in favor of the Union.

If one takes White's statement as a genuine prophetic utterance, like her Parkville vision, then it can only be described as uniformly fulfilled in the events of the war. Interpreting it as such, this forecast, first published in August 1861 during the beginning of the war, clearly comprehended the big picture of what played out in the battles and how God accomplished His purpose of punishing the North and exterminating slavery. Rather than the battle patterns of victories and losses being totally dependent on the decisions of generals and commanders, the strengths or

The McLean house in Appomattox about 1865
(Library of Congress)

weaknesses of the armies, or the "fall of chance," God, according to White, had the final word in the battles of the Civil War. Viewed this way, the events of the war reinforced the theological truth of her statements that this nation is in God's own hand and "God alone can wrench the slave from the hand of his desperate, relentless oppressor."[120] In this interpretation, the entire war was God's agent to free the slaves.

Now that we have seen how the entire war played out, the next three chapters will take us back to the winter of 1862, before the big battles of the war took place, when White provided her readers with some interesting and provocative insights on the state of the war during that time.

Chapter in a nutshell

This chapter traced the up-down pattern of the following Union battles from the Wilderness to Lee's surrender at Appomattox and the end of the war:

BATTLES 1864	PATTERN
GRANT'S OVERLAND CAMPAIGN	
The Wilderness	Draw
Spotsylvania	Draw
North Anna River	Draw
Cold Harbor	Loss
Petersburg	Siege
SHERMAN'S ATLANTA CAMPAIGN	
Resaca	Loss
Kennesaw Mountain	Loss
Peachtree Creek	Victory (Tactical)
Atlanta	Victory (Tactical)
Ezra Church	Victory (Tactical)
Atlanta	Siege
SHENANDOAH VALLEY SUMMER CAMPAIGN	

New Market	Loss
Piedmont	Victory
Lynchburg	Loss
WASHINGTON, DC	
Monocacy	Loss/Victory
LINCOLN RENOMINATED — REPUBLICAN	
MCCLELLAN NOMINATED — DEMOCRAT	
Mobile	Victory
Atlanta	Victory
Winchester	Victory
Fisher's Hill	Victory
Cedar Creek	Victory
LINCOLN REELECTED PRESIDENT	
Sherman's March	Victory
Franklin	Victory
Nashville	Victory
THIRTEENTH AMENDMENT	
BATTLES 1865	**PATTERN**
Sherman's March Carolinas	Victory
Waynesboro	Victory
Five Forks	Victory
Petersburg	Victory
Richmond	Victory
Appomattox	Confederate Surrender
END OF WAR: UNION VICTORY	
SLAVES EMANCIPATED	

A NATION IN GOD'S HANDS

1. Interview with Allen Guelzo, "Death Knell of the Confederacy," in *Civil War: The Untold Story* (Silver Spring, MD: Athena, 2014), DVD.

2. For helpful one-volume treatments of the campaign, see Noah Andre Trudeau's classic, *Bloody Roads South: The Wilderness to Cold Harbor, May–June 1864* (Boston: Little, Brown and Co., 1989); the more recent but superior Joseph Wheelan, *Bloody Spring: Forty Days That Sealed the Confederacy's Fate* (Philadelphia: Da Capo Press, 2014); and Mark Grimsley, *And Keep Moving On: The Virginia Campaign, May–June 1864* (Lincoln, NE: University of Nebraska Press, 2002). Then there are, of course, the excellent, gripping narratives of Bruce Catton and Shelby Foote (referenced in the appendix). The most important are the well-researched and readable volumes by Gordon C. Rhea, *The Battle of the Wilderness, May 5–6, 1864* (Baton Rouge, LA: Louisiana State University Press, 1994); Gordon C. Rhea, *The Battles for Spotsylvania Court House and the Road to Yellow Tavern, May 7–12, 1864* (Baton Rouge, LA: Louisiana State University Press, 1997); Gordon C. Rhea, *To the North Anna River: Grant and Lee, May 13–25, 1864* (Baton Rouge, LA: Louisiana State University Press, 2000); Gordon C. Rhea, *Cold Harbor: Grant and Lee, May 26–June 3, 1864* (Baton Rouge, LA: Louisiana State University Press, 2002). Other volumes dealing with aspects of the campaign are Gary W. Gallagher, ed., *The Wilderness Campaign* (Chapel Hill, NC: University of North Carolina Press, 1997); and Gary W. Gallagher, ed., *The Spotsylvania Campaign* (Chapel Hill, NC: University of North Carolina Press, 1998).

3. Gary W. Gallagher, *The American Civil War: Lectures 25–48, Transcript Book* (Chantilly, VA: The Teaching Company, 2000), 187, 188.

4. Grant, *Memoirs and Selected Letters*, 534.

5. Warren Goss, *Recollections of a Private* (New York: T. Y. Crowell, 1890), quoted in Commager, *The Blue and the Gray*, 979 (emphasis in the original).

6. Gallagher, *The American Civil War: Lectures 25–48*, 199.

7. See Rhea, *The Battle of the Wilderness*, 435, 436, 440.

8. Rhea, *The Battles for Spotsylvania Court House*, 291, 292.

9. Quoted in ibid., 292.

10. Rhea estimates a total of seventeen thousand were killed, wounded, and captured on May 12. *The Battles for Spotsylvania Court House*, 311, 312.

11. Geoffrey Ward, Ric Burns, and Ken Burns, *The Civil War* (New York: Vintage Civil War Library, 1990), 252, 253.

12. For a detailed discussion of Lee's trap and Grant's response, see Rhea, *To the North Anna River*, 325–354. For a concise summary, see Daniel T. Davis and Phillip S. Greenwalt, *Hurricane From the Heavens: The Battle of Cold Harbor, May 26–June 5, 1864*, Emerging Civil War Series (El Dorado Hills, CA: Savas Beatie, 2014), 135–141.

13. For details, see Rhea, *Cold Harbor*, 279–317, 392.

14. The most vivid and well-researched account is ibid., 318–358. For another vivid, well-written account, not only on the June 3 charge but the entire Cold Harbor experience, see Ernest B. Furgurson, *Not War but Murder: Cold Harbor 1864* (New York: Vintage Books, 2000).

15. Quoted in Grimsley, *And Keep Moving On*, 215.

16. Quoted in ibid., 219.

17. Rhea, *Cold Harbor*, 356.

18. Ibid., 322, 323.

19. E. M. Law, quoted in ibid., 357.

20. See Rhea, *Cold Harbor*, 359; and Davis and Greenwalt, *Hurricane From the Heavens*, 97.

21. Grant, *Memoirs and Selected Letters*, 588.

22. Davis and Greenwalt, *Hurricane From the Heavens*, 109.

23. A good place to begin studying the Petersburg Campaign is Edwin C. Bearss and Bryce A. Suderow, *The Petersburg Campaign*, vol. 1, *The Eastern Front Battles, June–August 1864* (El Dorado Hills, CA: Savas Beatie, 2012); Edwin C. Bearss and Bryce A. Suderow, *The Petersburg Campaign*, vol. 2, *The Western Front Battles, September 1864–April 1865* (El Dorado Hills, CA: Savas Beatie, 2014); and Noah Andre Trudeau, *The Last Citadel: Petersburg, June 1864–April 1865*, rev. and exp. ed. (El Dorado Hills, CA: Savas Beatie, 2014).

24. Bearss and Suderow, *The Petersburg Campaign,* 1:130. For a detailed study of this battle, see Sean Michael Chick, *The Battle of Petersburg, June 15–18, 1864* (Lincoln, NE: Potomac Books, 2015).

25. Bearss and Suderow, *The Petersburg Campaign,* 1:237. A good starting place for reading on this famous battle is Earl J. Hess, *Into the Crater: The Mine Attack at Petersburg* (Columbia, SC: University of South Carolina, 2010).

26. Gallagher, *The American Civil War,* 214.

27. Ulysses S. Grant, quoted in Grimsley, *And Keep Moving* On, xiii.

28. McPherson, *Ordeal by Fire,* 463.

29. The following are several helpful studies of Sherman's Atlanta Campaign: Richard M. McMurry, *Atlanta 1864: Last Chance for the Confederacy* (Lincoln, NE: University of Nebraska Press, 2000); Albert Castel, *Decision in the West: The Atlanta Campaign of 1864* (Lawrence, KS: University Press of Kansas, 1992); and Philip L. Secrist, *Sherman's 1864 Trail of Battle to Atlanta* (Macon, GA: Mercer University Press, 2006). For studies focusing on Atlanta, see Russell S. Bonds, *War Like the Thunderbolt: The Battle and Burning of Atlanta* (Yardley, PA: Westholme, 2009); and Marc Wortman, *The Bonfire: The Seige and Burning of Atlanta* (New York: Public Affairs, 2009).

30. On Sherman's failure to provide McPherson with the cavalry support he needed, see McMurry, *Atlanta,* 65.

31. Sherman, *Memoirs of General W. T. Sherman,* 500.

32. For a detailed discussion on this battle, see Philip L. Secrist, *The Battle of Resaca: Atlanta Campaign, 1864* (Macon, GA: Mercer University Press, 2010).

33. Ibid., 64.

34. Ibid., 7.

35. White, *Testimonies for the Church,* 1:267.

36. Earl J. Hess, *Kennesaw Mountain: Sherman, Johnston, and the Atlanta Campaign* (Chapel Hill, NC: University of North Carolina Press, 2013), xiii.

37. This concise overview of the battle has been drawn heavily from Hess, *Kennesaw Mountain.*

38. For more detail, see Hess, *Kennesaw Mountain*; and Daniel J. Vermilya, *The Battle of Kennesaw Mountain* (Charleston, SC: The History Press, 2014).

39. For coverage of the events between Kennesaw Mountain and Peachtree Creek, see Robert D. Jenkins Sr., *To the Gates of Atlanta: From Kennesaw Mountain to Peach Tree Creek* (Macon, GA: Mercer University Press, 2015).

40. The figures are from Earl J. Hess, *The Battle of Ezra Church and the Struggle for Atlanta* (Chapel Hill, NC: University of North Carolina Press, 2015), 6.

41. The numbers are from ibid., 8. For a detailed narrative and coverage of this significant battle, see Kenneth A. Griffiths, *Seven Days in July: A Historic Account of the Battle of Atlanta* (Pensacola, FL: Indigo River Publishing, 2014); and Gary Ecelbarger, *The Day Dixie Died: The Battle of Atlanta* (New York: Thomas Dunne Books, 2010).

42. See Hess, *The Battle of Ezra Church,* for full coverage of the battle.

43. See Joseph Adamczyk, "Shenandoah Valley," in Spencer C. Tucker, ed., *American Civil War: The Definitive Encyclopedia and Document Collection* (Santa Barbara, CA: ABC-Clio, 2013), 4:1759, 1760. For a helpful description and history of the valley, see Scott C. Patchan, *The Battle of Piedmont and Hunter's Raid on Staunton: The 1864 Shenandoah Campaign* (Charleston, SC: History Press, 2011), 9, 10.

44. Neil M. Heyman and Paul G. Pierpaoli Jr., "Franz Sigel," in Tucker, *American Civil War: The Definitive Encyclopedia and Document Collection,* 4:1787, 1788.

45. On the battle, see Charles R. Knight, *Valley Thunder: The Battle of New Market and the Opening of the Shenandoah Valley Campaign, May 1864* (New York: Savas Beatie, 2010); and the classic study by William C. Davis, *The Battle of New Market* (Baton Rouge, LA: Louisiana State University Press, 1975).

46. For detailed coverage, see Patchan, *The Battle of Piedmont.*

47. See Richard G. Williams Jr., *Lexington, Virginia and the Civil War* (Charleston, SC: History Press, 2013), 77–102.

48. Kanisorn Wongsrichanalai, "David Hunter," in Tucker, *American Civil War: The Definitive Encyclopedia and Document Collection,* 2:956–958.

49. For a detailed account of Early's raid, see Benjamin Franklin Cooling, *Jubal Early's Raid on Washington* (Tuscaloosa, AL: University of Alabama Press, 1989); and Steven Bernstein, *The Confederacy's Last Northern Offensive: Jubal Early, the Army of the Valley and the Raid on Washington* (Jefferson, NC: McFarland, 2011).

50. Jack H. Lepa, *The Shenandoah Valley Campaign of 1864* (Jefferson, NC: McFarland, 2003), 110.

51. Rhodes, diary entry for July 12, 1864, in Rhodes, *All for the Union*, 163.

52. Grant, *Memoirs and Selected Letters*, 606, 607.

53. Gary Gallagher, quoted in Marc Leepson, *Desperate Engagement: How a Little-Known Civil War Battle Saved Washington, D.C., and Changed American History* (New York: Thomas Dunne Books, 2007), 222.

54. See Benjamin Franklin Cooling, *Monocacy: The Battle That Saved Washington* (Shippensburg, PA: White Mane Publishing, 2000).

55. White, *Testimonies for the Church*, 1:267.

56. See John C. Waugh, *Reelecting Lincoln: The Battle for the 1864 Presidency* (Cambridge, MA: Da Capo Press, 1997), 241, 242. For a detailed study of this event with analysis of the various reports, see Benjamin Franklin Cooling III, *The Day Lincoln Was Almost Shot: The Fort Stevens Story* (Lanham, MD: Rowman & Littlefield, 2013).

57. Gabor S. Boritt, quoted in Richard Striner, *Father Abraham: Lincoln's Relentless Struggle to End Slavery* (New York: Oxford University Press, 2006), 231.

58. Basler, *The Collected Works of Abraham Lincoln*, 7:431.

59. Lincoln, quoted in Burlingame, *Abraham Lincoln: A Life*, 2:668.

60. Burlingame, *Abraham Lincoln: A Life*, 2:672.

61. Basler, *The Collected Works of Abraham Lincoln*, 7:514.

62. Burlingame, *Abraham Lincoln: A Life*, 2:675.

63. Abraham Lincoln, quoted in David Herbert Donald, *Lincoln* (New York: Simon & Schuster, 1995), 529 (emphasis in the original).

64. Lloyd Lewis, *Sherman: Fighting Prophet* (Lincoln, NE: University of Nebraska Press, 1960), 406.

65. On the battle of Jonesborough, see Castel, *Decision in the West*, 480–547; and Bonds, *War Like the Thunderbolt*, 239–276.

66. McPherson and Hogue, *Ordeal by Fire*, 478.

67. *Official Records of the Union and Confederate Armies*, ser. 1, vol. 38 (Washington, DC: Government Printing Office, 1891), pt. 5, 777. Also quoted in ibid., 409.

68. Allan Nevins and Milton H. Thomas, eds., *The Diary of George Templeton Strong* (New York: Macmillan, 1952), 3:480.

69. Lewis, *Sherman: Fighting Prophet*, 409.

70. Basler, *The Collected Works of Abraham Lincoln*, 7:533.

71. David Alan Johnson, *Decided on the Battlefield: Grant, Sherman, Lincoln and the Election of 1864* (New York: Prometheus Books, 2012), 191.

72. Nevins and Thomas, *The Diary of George Templeton Strong*, 3:481.

73. Johnson, *Decided on the Battlefield*, 193.

74. McPherson and Hogue, *Ordeal by Fire*, 477.

75. Basler, *The Collected Works of Abraham Lincoln*, 7:532, 533.

76. Ibid., 7:533.

77. During the latter part of July, Early engaged in a series of battles that hurt the Union war effort, culminating in a Federal defeat at Kernstown, Virginia, on July 24 and the burning of Chambersburg, Pennsylvania, over a week later. Old Jube was happy to help create the worst down period of the entire Union war effort. For a helpful study of Early's activity during July 1864, see Scott C. Patchan, *Shenandoah Summer: The 1864 Valley Campaign* (Lincoln, NE: University of Nebraska Press, 2007).

78. See Joseph Wheelan's biography of Sheridan, *Terrible Swift Sword: The Life of General Philip H. Sheridan* (Cambridge, MA: Da Capo Press, 2012).

79. James A. Garfield, quoted in Bruce Catton, *Never Call Retreat* (Garden City, NY: Doubleday, 1965), 388.

80. On the autumn Shenandoah Valley Campaign of 1864, see Jeffry D. Wert, *From Winchester to Cedar Creek: The Shenandoah Campaign of 1864* (Carbondale, IL: Southern Illinois University Press, 2010); Lepa, *The Shenandoah Valley Campaign of 1864*, 135–220; Daniel T. Davis and Phillip S. Greenwalt, *Bloody Autumn: The Shenandoah Valley Campaign of 1864*, Emerging Civil War Series (El Dorado Hills, CA: Savas Beatie, 2013); and Gary W. Gallagher, ed., *The Shenandoah Valley of 1864* (Chapel Hill, NC: University of North Carolina Press, 2006). Other studies are available on the various individual battles in the campaign but are too numerous to mention.

81. Basler, *The Collected Works of Abraham Lincoln*, 8:55, 56.

82. McPherson and Hogue, *Ordeal by Fire*, 480.

83. Davis and Greenwalt, *Bloody Autumn*, 84.

84. Striner, *Father Abraham*, 244.

85. McPherson and Hogue, *Ordeal by Fire*, 492.

86. Ulysses S. Grant, quoted in Catton, *Grant Takes Command, 1863–1865*, 384.

87. Antietam is generally considered the first major turning point in the war; Gettysburg, Vicksburg, and Chattanooga, the second major turning point; and Atlanta and Lincoln's election, the third major turning point.

88. On the significance of Lincoln's reelection, the following studies are noteworthy: Johnson, *Decided on the Battlefield*; Charles Bracelen Flood, *1864: Lincoln at the Gates of History* (New York: Simon & Schuster, 2009); Waugh, *Reelecting Lincoln*; David E. Long, *The Jewel of Liberty: Abraham Lincoln's Re-election and the End of Slavery* (Mechanicsburg, PA: Stackpole Books, 1994).

89. McPherson and Hogue, *Ordeal by Fire*, 498. I have followed closely McPherson's and Hogue's concise narrative of these events. For studies and narratives of Sherman's march to the sea, see Burke Davis, *Sherman's March* (New York: Vintage Books, 1980); Joseph T. Glatthaar, *The March to the Sea and Beyond: Sherman's Troops in the Savannah and Carolinas Campaigns* (Baton Rouge, LA: Louisiana State University Press, 1985); Lee Kennett, *Marching Through Georgia: The Story of Soldiers & Civilians During Sherman's Campaign* (New York: Harper Perennial, 1995); Noah Andre Trudeau, *Southern Storm: Sherman's March to the Sea* (New York: Harper Perennial, 2008).

90. On Hood's Tennessee Campaign, see James R. Knight, *Hood's Tennessee Campaign: The Desperate Venture of a Desperate Man* (Charleston, SC: History Press, 2014); Michael Thomas Smith, *The 1864 Franklin-Nashville Campaign: The Finishing Stroke* (Santa Barbara, CA: Praeger, 2014); Winston Groom, *Shrouds of Glory: From Atlanta to Nashville: The Last Great Campaign of the Civil War* (New York: Atlantic Monthly Press, 1995); Wiley Sword, *The Confederacy's Last Hurrah: Spring Hill, Franklin, and Nashville* (New York: HarperCollins, 1992).

91. McPherson and Hogue, *Ordeal by Fire*, 500, 501. For studies on the battle, see James R. Knight, *The Battle of Franklin: When the Devil Had Full Possession of the Earth* (Charleston, SC: History Press, 2009); and James Lee McDonough and Thomas L. Connelly, *Five Tragic Hours: The Battle of Franklin* (Knoxville, TN: University of Tennessee, 1983).

92. McPherson and Hogue, *Ordeal by Fire*, 501.

93. Sam Watkins, *"Co. Aytch": A Side Show of the Big Show* (New York: Macmillan, 1962), quoted in Smith, *The 1864 Franklin-Nashville Campaign*, 61.

94. McPherson and Hogue, *Ordeal by Fire*, 502.

95. Ibid., 503.

96. On the Battle of Nashville, see James Lee McDonough, *Nashville: The Western Confederacy's Final Gamble* (Knoxville, TN: University of Tennessee Press, 2004); and Stanley F. Horn, *The Decisive Battle of Nashville* (Baton Rouge, LA: Louisiana State University Press, 1984).

97. Michael Vorenberg, "The Thirteenth Amendment Enacted," in Harold Holzer and Sara Vaughn Gabbard, eds., *Lincoln and Freedom: Slavery, Emancipation, and the Thirteenth Amendment* (Carbondale, IL: Southern Illinois University Press, 2007), 180.

98. McPherson and Hogue, *Ordeal by Fire*, 503.

99. Vorenberg, *Final Freedom*, 180.

100. Ibid., 205.

101. Ibid., 207.

102. Charles Douglass, quoted in ibid.

103. Martin Russell Thayer, quoted in Vorenberg, *Final Freedom*, 208.

104. William Lloyd Garrison, "The Death of Slavery," in William E. Cain, ed., *William Lloyd Garrison and the Fight Against Slavery: Selections From* The Liberator (Boston: Bedford / St. Martins, 1995), 176, 177.

105. White, *Testimonies for the Church*, 1:258.

106. Basler, *The Collected Works of Abraham Lincoln*, 8:55, 56.

107. McPherson and Hogue, *Ordeal by Fire*, 508.

108. Ibid.

109. See Marion B. Lucas, *Sherman and the Burning of Columbia* (Columbia, SC: University of South Carolina Press, 2000); and Patricia G. McNeely, *Sherman's Flame and Blame Campaign Through Georgia and the Carolinas . . . and the Burning of Columbia* (Columbia, SC: Patricia G. McNeely, 2014).

110. McPherson and Hogue, *Ordeal by Fire*, 509, 512. For a detailed discussion, see Glatthaar, *The March to the Sea and Beyond*; and John G. Barrett, *Sherman's March Through the Carolinas* (Chapel Hill, NC: University of North Carolina Press, 1956).

111. See Nelson Lankford, *Richmond Burning: The Last Days of the Confederate Capital* (New York: Penguin Books, 2003); and David D. Ryan, *Four Days in 1865: The Fall of Richmond* (Richmond, VA: Cadmus Communications, 1993).

112. This section is drawn from McPherson's and Hogue's concise narrative in *Ordeal by Fire*, 508–513, 515–520. For detailed studies on the last days of the war, which are helpful, see Joseph Wheelan, *Their Last Full Measure: The Final Days of the Civil War* (Boston: Da Capo Press, 2015); Perry D. Jamieson, *Spring 1865: The Closing Campaigns of the Civil War* (Lincoln, NE: University of Nebraska Press, 2015). On the final battles and breakthrough at Petersburg, see Bearss and Suderow, *The Petersburg Campaign*, vol. 2; A. Wilson Greene, *The Final Battles of the Petersburg Campaign: Breaking the Backbone of the Rebellion*, 2nd ed. (Knoxville, TN: University of Tennessee Press, 2008); and Edward S. Alexander, *Dawn of Victory: Breakthrough at Petersburg, March 25–April 2, 1865*, Emerging Civil War Series (El Dorado Hills, CA: Savas Beatie, 2015). On Appomattox, see Burke Davis, *To Appomattox: Nine April Days, 1865* (Short Hills, NJ: Burford Books, 1959); William Marvel, *Lee's Last Retreat: The Flight to Appomattox* (Chapel Hill, NC: University of North Carolina Press, 2002); Elizabeth R. Varon, *Appomattox: Victory, Defeat, and Freedom at the End of the Civil War* (New York: Oxford University Press, 2014); Michael E. Haskew, *Appomattox: The Last Days of Robert E. Lee's Army of Northern Virginia* (Minneapolis: Zenith Press, 2015).

113. Catton, *Grant Takes Command, 1863–1865*, 469.

114. Quoted in ibid.

115. Rhodes, diary entry for April 9, 1865, in *All for the Union*, 222.

116. For a helpful discussion of the final surrenders in the Civil War, see Robert M. Dunkerly, *To the Bitter End: Appomattox, Bennett Place, and the Surrenders of the Confederacy*, Emerging Civil War Series (El Dorado Hills, CA: Savas Beatie, 2015).

117. For a thorough discussion of McLean's home during the First Battle of Bull Run and Lee's surrender to Grant, see William Marvel, *A Place Called Appomattox* (Carbondale, IL: Southern Illinois University Press, 2008); see also Haskew, *Appomattox*, 229, 230.

118. Ward, Burns, and Burns, *The Civil War*, xii. See also Haskew, *Appomattox*, 229. The other side of the story is often not told. Immediately after the surrender, soldiers rummaged through the house and took souvenirs of the historic occasion, and the farm was devastated by the presence of so many soldiers and artillery. The war essentially ruined McLean financially. Haskew, *Appomattox*, 229, 230.

119. White, *Testimonies for the Church*, 1:267.

120. Ibid., 1:266.

PART IV

BATTLE CREEK VISION (JANUARY 1862):
"SOME THINGS IN REGARD TO OUR NATION"

CHAPTER 9

A MOST SINGULAR
AND UNCERTAIN WAR

Ellen White wrote that on "January 4, 1862, I was shown some things in regard to our nation."[1] Much had happened in the war during the previous five months since her last communication in August 1861.[2] The Union had lost the Battle of Wilson's Creek and the Battle of Ball's Bluff but had renewed its determination under the leadership of General George B. McClellan as he rebuilt a massive army outside of Washington, D.C. When the Adventist audience first read these words in February 1862, the North was impatiently waiting for McClellan to move his great Army of the Potomac and strike the enemy.

As noted previously, White first published *Testimony for the Church, No. 7* as a pamphlet in February 1862 and later in volume 1 of *Testimonies for the Church*. Of the nine sections in the *Testimony*, the first four dealt with the war. The first section, "The North and the South," addressed the misguided focus and uncertainty of the war, condemned the national fasts, and analyzed the tension between the United States and England.[3] The second section, "Great Distress Coming,"[4] foretold the "greater distress" coming in the war by apparently recasting the Parkville vision and then admonished the believers on how to live in "the perils of the last days."[5] The third section, "Slavery and the War," addressed the sin of slavery in the South and provided a supernatural interpretation of the First Battle of Bull Run at Manassas, Virginia, on July 21, 1861.[6] The fourth and final section on the war, "Perilous Times," again provided practical counsel for living in the last days during the war.[7]

This chapter will concentrate on White's comments about the singular and uncertain nature of the war, and the next two chapters will address her statements about the national fasts and war with England. These three chapters provide a snapshot into White's understanding at the beginning of 1862, before the heavy fighting began at Shiloh, and do not reflect the dramatic changes with regard to emancipation, which took place during the latter half of the war. At the time she wrote, the war was, in her mind, "singular and uncertain."[8]

Secession and quick formation of the Confederacy

In this vision, White's "attention was called to the Southern rebellion."[9] As a Yankee and as a Radical Republican in principle,[10] she considered Southern secession and the Confederacy a rebellion against the freedom of the Union. Later, in *Testimony for the Church, No. 9*, she would liken the South's rebellion to the cosmic rebellion of Satan and his angels against the government of God.[11] "The South had prepared themselves for a fierce conflict," she explained, "while the North were asleep as to their true feelings."[12]

The North was caught off guard by the secession and by the quick formation of the Confederacy. "Before President Lincoln's administration commenced," White explained, "great advantage was taken by the South. The former administration planned and managed for the South to rob the North of their implements of war."[13] She was, of course, referring to the fifteenth president of the United States, James Buchanan, whose administration was in its lame-duck stage during the five months between Lincoln's election and inauguration. Buchanan was a classic *doughface*—a term Northerners used to describe a Northern politician who sympathized with the South and its principles.[14] Because of his Southern loyalties and connections, he was one of the few in the North who really understood the determination of the South in its secession.

In his speech to Congress on December 3, 1860, shortly before South Carolina seceded from the Union, Buchanan blamed the crisis on Northern people for constantly interfering with the institution of slavery, which, he bemoaned, had produced a feeling of insecurity in the South about the future of their institution. Yet, in the end, he stood for the Union and could not support its breakup by secession. Needless to say, this troubled president, who hoped to finish his term peacefully before any major crisis, was attacked from both sides in the North and the South.

The major issue that plagued his outgoing administration was the federal territory in South Carolina after it seceded. His handling of the situation alienated the South and was perceived by the North as a failure in dealing with the secession crisis. According to historian Kenneth M. Stampp, Buchanan "had issued no call for volunteers to enforce the laws and defend the Union; had made no attempt to recover Federal property which fell into Confederate hands; had never sent warships to southern ports to force the continued collection of government revenues. The mere refusal to surrender Sumter or recognize secession was not enough; these other shortcomings destined him to appear weak and vacillating to northern nationalists."[15]

These issues are probably what White had in mind when she wrote that the "former administration planned and managed for the South to rob the North of their implements of war."[16] Two paragraphs later, she expressed the view that if "prompt and thorough measures" had "been carried out by our Government at an early period of the rebellion," then the Southern Confederacy would not have had so many converts to its cause.[17] The South took "great advantage" of this period "before President Lincoln's administration commenced."[18] Thus, between the election of Abraham Lincoln in November 1860 and his inauguration in March 1861, seven states seceded from the Union while under the administration of the vacillating Buchanan and formed the Confederate States of America.

In seizing the opportunity, the South had "two objects" in mind, according to Ellen White's interpretation. First, she said, "they were contemplating a determined rebellion, and must prepare for it."[19] Emory M. Thomas, a specialist on the Confederacy, has shown that secession was not just something that sprang up in 1861 but "was the culmination of years of radical tactics and revolutionary propaganda." For years, the "fire-eaters," those who agitated for the South to secede and become a separate nation, had pushed their radical agenda on the South. "By 1861, major institutions of Southern society—press, pulpit, and school—were repeating the Southern line."[20] The contemplation and planning of "a determined rebellion," therefore, began long before 1860.[21]

The second object of the South was to catch the North off guard. "When they should rebel, the North would be wholly unprepared."[22] Although the formation of the Confederacy was a careful, methodical process, once the new government was formed, it moved quickly. South Carolina wanted Fort Sumter captured before Abraham Lincoln became president and before the new Confederate president, Jefferson Davis, took negotiations for the fort's surrender into his own hands. Through this process, Ellen White said, "they would thus gain time, and by their violent threats and ruthless course they thought they could so intimidate the North that they would be obliged to yield to them and let them have everything their own way."[23]

While there are a number of events that Ellen White probably had in mind regarding this statement, Alexander Stephens's and Jefferson Davis's speeches may have drawn forth the harsh terms "violent threats" and "ruthless course." When the president-elect of the Confederacy first arrived in Montgomery, Alabama, for example, Jefferson Davis declared to his greeters: "The time for compromise has now passed, and the South is determined to maintain her position, and make all who oppose her smell Southern powder and feel Southern steel if coercion is persisted in."[24] There will be "no compromise; nor reconstruction can be now entertained." (He received "tremendous applause" after this statement.)[25] In his well-publicized Cornerstone speech, Alexander Stephens said that, although he hoped for peace, Southerners should still keep their "armor bright" and "powder dry." (He received "enthusiastic applause" from the audience at this point.)[26]

The South's hatred of the North

A major point that Ellen White wanted her readers to know was that the "North did not understand the bitter, dreadful hatred of the South toward them."[27] In an address to the Southern slaveholding states, for example, the South Carolina Convention stated emphatically, after recounting its history with the North: "All fraternity of feeling between the North and the South is lost, or has been converted into hate, and we, of the South, are at last driven together, by the stern destiny which controls the existence of nations."[28] In explaining why the North and the South were separate, Southerner Mary Boykin Chesnut exclaimed in her diary: "We separated because of incompatibility of temper; we are divorced, North from South, because we have hated each other so."[29]

Early in the crisis, Abraham Lincoln hadn't fully comprehended the intensity of the South's hatred for the North. As the various Deep South states seceded from the Union during the winter of 1861, the president-elect repeatedly referred to the situation as an "artificial one." In his speech at Pittsburgh, Pennsylvania, on February 15, 1861, for example, he stated, "Notwithstanding the troubles across the river, [the speaker pointing southwardly, and smiling] there is really no crisis, springing from anything in the government itself. In plain words, there is really no crisis except an *artificial one*!"[30] Not everyone in the South was a fire-eater secessionist, and Lincoln had hoped for a backlash against the radicals by the more moderate cooperationists in the South.[31] Historian Emory Thomas believed that the president-elect had "settled into a rhetoric of denial."[32]

Black abolitionist Frederick Douglass had no reservations about the South's hatred for the North. In August 1861, he wrote, "The slaveholders have no scruples; they wage this war with unrelenting and desperate earnestness, sustained and fed by immeasurable malice, unmixed, and as deadly as the poison from the fang of a rattlesnake. Herein is the secret of their success. It is not their numbers, not their wealth, not the goodness of their cause, not their skill, but the quenchless fire of a deadly hate, which spurns all restraints of law and humanity, and walks to its purpose with a single eye and a determined hand."[33]

The South's deep-laid plots to protect slavery

The North not only underestimated the South's hatred but was also "unprepared for their deep-laid plots."[34] "The North had boasted of their strength and ridiculed the idea of the South leaving the Union. They considered it like the threats of a willful, stubborn child" that "would with humble apologies return to their allegiance."[35] As noted earlier, Horace Greeley's *New-York Daily Tribune* initially made fun of South Carolina's secession. But the South showed its determination through carefully planned arguments for secession and the formation of a well-organized Confederate government by the spring of 1861.[36]

In Ellen White's mind, what the North had failed to really understand was "the strength of the accursed system of slavery." In no uncertain terms, she declared, "It is this, and this alone, which lies at the foundation of the war."[37] Her use of the term *foundation* indicated that while there were other issues that contributed to the war, she understood slavery to be the foundation and thus the driving force behind the Southern rebellion. A contemporary of White, abolitionist Frederick Douglass, made the same case with vivid language: "The very stomach of this rebellion is the Negro in the condition of a slave. Arrest that hoe in the hands of the Negro, and you smite rebellion in the very seat of its life.—Change the status of the slave from bondage to freedom, and you change the rebels into loyal citizens. The Negro is the key to the situation—the pivot upon which the whole rebellion turns."[38]

By saying that slavery was the "foundation of the war," she addressed the issue of causality. What caused the Civil War? Was it slavery, state's rights, or other political/economical issues? These questions have been a subject of much controversy over the years.[39] Three basic positions can be identified in the discussion among historians:[40] first, the fundamentalists, who argue that slavery was front and center;[41] second, the revisionists, who argue that slavery was buried beneath layers of white ideology and politics;[42] and third, the catalysts, who argue that both fundamentalists and revisionists have a point and that slavery was thus the "key catalytic agent" in the complexity of antebellum life and politics.[43] The arguments of the fundamentalists and catalysts make the strongest case.

From the southern secession documents[44] to the northern unwillingness to expand slavery in the west,[45] the primary sources support the assertion that slavery lay at the "foundation of the war."[46] One illustration will suffice. On the eve of secession, Benjamin Morgan Palmer, the most prominent Presbyterian clergyman in the antebellum South and representative of Southern-clergy ideology on slavery, preached a powerful pro-slavery sermon that supported secession and ignited much of the Deep South. Preached to a large audience of more than two thousand on November 29, 1860, the sermon, "Slavery a Divine Trust: Duty of the South to Preserve and Perpetuate It," employed every major secession argument and set forth in concise form more than two decades of southern nationalist thought. The divine "providential trust" committed to southern people by God, Palmer declared, "is to conserve and perpetuate the institution of slavery as now existing." This system "is interwoven with our entire social fabric" and southerners are "the constituted guardians of the slaves themselves." We "defend the cause of God and religion, he argued, because the "Abolition spirit is undeniably atheistic." Thus, at the heart of the sermon was the issue of perpetuating slavery. The South's "present trust," he proclaimed, is "to preserve and transmit our existing system of domestic servitude, with the right unchanged by man, to go and root itself wherever Providence and nature may carry it."

This "right" and "trust," however, was under fire by the North, who had "cast their ballot for a candidate who is sectional, who represents a party that is sectional, and the ground of that sectionalism, prejudiced against the established and constitutional rights and immunities and institutions of the South." This new government, Palmer believed, threatens to "be employed in demolishing the guaranteed institutions of the South."[47] In the heart of the sermon's appeal, Palmer again placed slavery, the "great trust," at the center:

> As it appears to me, the course to be pursued in this emergency is that which has already been inaugurated. Let the people in all the Southern States, in solemn counsel assembled, reclaim the powers they have delegated. Let those conventions be composed of men whose fidelity has been approved—men who bring the wisdom, experience and firmness of age to support and announce principles which have long been matured. Let these conventions decide firmly and solemnly what they will do with this great trust committed to their hands [slavery]. Let them pledge each other, in sacred covenant, to uphold and perpetuate what they cannot resign without dishonor and palpable ruin. Let them, further, take all the necessary steps looking to separate an independent existence, and initiate measures for framing a new and homogeneous confederacy. Thus, prepared for every contingency, let the crisis come.[48]

According to one listener of the sermon, the audience was "in solemn silence, no man speaking to his neighbor, the great congregation of serious and thoughtful men and women dispersed; but afterwards the drums beat and the bugles sounded; for New Orleans was shouting secession." The sermon was published, and thousands of copies spread across the South, creating a "great sensation." One southerner recalled that Palmer had done more than "any other non-combatant in the South to promote rebellion." It's no small wonder that when Union General Benjamin F. Butler's troops occupied New Orleans in 1862, he put a bounty on Palmer's head.[49]

The slave power

In the rest of that paragraph, Mrs. White described what was known in her day as the "slave power."[50] She clearly understood the nature of this power, as other Northerners did, and later in this *Testimony* identified it by name: "God's scourge is now upon the North, because they have so long submitted to the advances of the slave power."[51] The slave power was the vast social, economic, and political influence that the slaveholders exerted in the South and on the Federal government during the antebellum years. They were entrenched in the legislative, executive, and judicial branches of government and had significant voting power.[52] The "animating principle" of the slave power, according to the radical Charles Sumner, was "the perpetuation and extension of Slavery and the advancement of Slaveholders."[53]

The Republicans, the enemies of these slaveholders, pointed out that "a large majority of the Presidents, Secretaries of State, Chief Justices, and Congressional committee chairmen since 1789 had been southerners." In 1855, Salmon P. Chase stated that "no one in Washington could 'fail to observe the immense, not to say overpowering influence, which slavery exerts over almost every act of the Government.'" In 1859, one Republican congressman from Maine repeated Chase's thoughts: "The national Government, and every branch of the national Government, is as fully under the control of these few extreme men of the South, as are the slaves on their plantations."[54] Historian Leonard L. Richards noted that between 1820 and 1860, 320 Northern congressmen were "doughfaces."[55] In light of this background, it is no small wonder that the North made so many compromises with the South on the issue of slavery.

Historian Eric Foner pointed out that in 1854, the newly formed Republican Party "believed in the existence of a conspiratorial 'Slave Power' which had seized control of the federal government and was attempting to pervert the Constitution for its own purposes."[56] At the heart of the conspiracy was the idea that the South was working to spread slavery all over the country. Abraham Lincoln believed in "the existence of a conspiracy to nationalize slavery"[57] and referred to it in his famous House Divided speech in Springfield, Illinois, on June 16, 1858. "I believe this government cannot endure, permanently half *slave* and half *free*," he declared. "It will become *all* one thing, or *all* the other. Either the *opponents* of slavery, will arrest the further spread of it, and place it where the public mind shall rest in the belief that it is in course of ultimate extinction; or its *advocates* will push it forward, till it shall become alike lawful in *all* the States, *old* as well as *new—North* as well as *South*."[58] Today not all historians today support the notion of a slave power conspiracy during the antebellum years, but the Republicans and abolitionists nevertheless capitalized on it as fundamental to the country's problems.[59]

During the antebellum years, the average person probably did not think of "a conscious conspiracy with secret goals and instruments" when they referred to the slave power. Rather, "they were talking about the slave *interest*, and the way that powerful interest prompted people to defensive measures, whether short-term or long-range." They thus viewed the slave power simply as "the political efforts exerted to protect and extend slavery."[60] This understanding is, most likely, what Ellen White meant when she used the phrase "slave power."[61] In simple language, she captured the essence of the slaveholder's power: "The South have been more and more exacting. They consider it perfectly right to engage in human traffic, to deal in slaves and the souls of men. They are annoyed and become perfectly exasperated if they cannot claim all the territory they desire. They would tear down the boundaries and bring their slaves to any spot they please, and curse the soil with slave labor. The language of the South has been imperious, and the North have not taken suitable measures to silence it."[62]

Soldiers and slavery

Continuing her previous thought about slave power, White described it as a "rebellion" that "was handled so carefully, so slowly, that many who at first started with horror at the thought of rebellion were influenced by rebels to look upon it as right and just, and thousands joined the Southern Confederacy who would not had prompt and thorough measures been carried out by our Government at an early period of the rebellion, even as ill-prepared as it then was for war."[63] This is probably a reference to those in the Upper South states who were not initially supportive of secession but who eventually embraced it due to the influence of the fire-eaters. Since the formation of the Confederacy and the shelling of Fort Sumter, the North has "been preparing for war ever since, but the rebellion has been steadily increasing, and there is now [January 1862] no better prospect of its being subdued than there was months ago."[64]

Pointing out the loss of life and the suffering over the first six months of the war, Ellen White then moved to the subject of enlistment:

Thousands have been induced to enlist with the understanding that this war was to exterminate slavery; but now that they are fixed, they find that they have been deceived, that the object of this war is not to abolish slavery, but to preserve it as it is.

Those who have ventured to leave their homes and sacrifice their lives to exterminate slavery are dissatisfied. They see no good results from the war, only the preservation of the Union, and for this thousands of lives must be sacrificed and homes made desolate.[65]

In view of all the suffering and death, these soldiers inquire, "If we succeed in quelling this rebellion, what has been gained? They can only answer discouragingly: Nothing."[66] Later she asserted, "A great share of the volunteers enlisted fully believing that the result of the war would be to abolish slavery. Others enlisted intending to be very careful to keep slavery just as it is, but to put down the rebellion and preserve the Union."[67]

The subject of why Civil War soldiers fought in the war has received significant attention by scholars in recent years.[68] It has become clear that soldiers on both sides of the Mason-Dixon Line had ideological motivation for fighting in the war. In *The Life of Billy Yank*, the classic study of Union soldiers, Bell I. Wiley provided examples of letters from soldiers who entered the war to destroy slavery and who were disappointed in the government for not supporting emancipation.[69] For example, in January 1863, Chauncey H. Cooke of the Twenty-Fifth Wisconsin wrote, "I have no heart in this war if the slaves cannot be free. . . . I am disappointed in Lincoln." Private Urich N. Parmelee of Connecticut enlisted "to free the slave" but felt enormous frustration at the government for not making emancipation the object of the war. He complained bitterly to his mother in a letter: "You cannot expect me . . . much longer to remain with this army as it is. If it does not change *soon*, either in its principles or its actions I trust in God that I shall have the moral courage to desert it."[70]

Wiley points out, however, that those Northern men who enlisted to end slavery were in the minority. "A polling of the rank and file through their letters and diaries indicates that those whose primary object was the liberation of the Negroes comprised only a small part of the fighting forces. It seems doubtful that one soldier in ten at any time during the conflict had any real interest in emancipation per se."[71] This might cause one to pause over Ellen White's "thousands" or "great share of the volunteers" who entered the war to exterminate slavery. But even if only one in a hundred had interest in emancipation of the slaves during the first year of the war, then White's approximation is still a conservative figure in proportion to the more than seven hundred thousand men who enlisted in the Union army during 1861.[72]

Interestingly, historian James McPherson analyzed Wiley's estimate that "one in ten Union soldiers 'had any real interest in emancipation per se' " and explained that "if by 'per se' Wiley meant 'in and of itself alone' [in emancipation only], one in ten may be an exaggeration." But "if 'emancipation per se' meant a perception that the abolition of slavery was inseparably linked to the goal of preserving the Union, then three in ten Union soldiers," he calculated (based on the letters and diaries he studied), "took that position during the first eighteen months of the war."[73] If Mrs. White's "great share" of volunteers who "enlisted fully believing that the result of the war would be to abolish slavery" also wanted to save the Union, then her approximation of a "great share" is no exaggeration. She contrasted this group with the others who "enlisted intending to be very careful to keep slavery just as it is, but to put down the rebellion and preserve the Union."[74] In the end, scholars have concluded that the majority of Northern men who enlisted in the Civil War did so for reasons other than slavery. But the minority who did have abolishing slavery on their minds was more than a few in proportion to the total number of those who enlisted during the first year.[75]

One other noteworthy study on this subject is Chandra Manning's book *What This Cruel War Was Over: Soldiers, Slavery, and the Civil War.*[76] She explores and amply demonstrates how both Union and Confederate soldiers identified slavery as the central issue of the war. While earlier studies on soldiers, like those of Wiley and McPherson, address the issue of slavery in the context of a much larger picture of soldiers' lives and motivations, Manning focuses on what both Union and Confederate soldiers thought about slavery, including when, how, and why their ideas changed. This study and the others affirm that Ellen White's comments on Northern soldiers, enlistment, and slavery are insightful and worthy of serious consideration.

Civil War hospitals and prisons

Following her thought of soldiers who enlisted to end slavery, White explained that these soldiers "see no good results from the war, only the preservation of the Union, and for this thousands of lives must be sacrificed and homes made desolate." Of these thousands, she further explained, "Great numbers have wasted away and expired in hospitals."[77] Civil War hospitals were mostly the requisitioned homes, barns, and any other serviceable buildings on or near the fields of battle. On rural battlefields, tents were used, and often the wounded lay in open spaces. Walt Whitman reflected on a visit to one such place:

> O heavens, what scene is this?—is this indeed *humanity*—these butchers' shambles? There are several of them. There they lie, in the largest, in an open space in the woods, from 200 to 300 poor fellows—the groans and screams— the odor of blood, mixed with the fresh scent of the night, the grass, the trees—that slaughter-house! O well is it their mothers, their sisters cannot see them—cannot conceive, and never conceiv'd, these things. One man is shot by a shell, both in the arm and leg—both are amputated—there lie the re- jected members. Some have their legs blown off—some bullets through the breast—some indescribably horrid wounds in the face or head, all mutilated, sickening, torn, gouged out—some in the abdomen—some mere boys—many rebels, badly hurt—they take their regular turns with the rest, just the same as any—the surgeons use them just the same. Such is the camp of the wounded— such a fragment, a reflection afar off of the bloody scene—while over all the clear, large moon comes out at times softly, quietly shining.[78]

"Others," White continued, "have been taken prisoners by the rebels, a fate more to be dreaded than death."[79] In early 1862, the full-blown horror of Civil War pris- ons had not really registered yet during this stage of the war. Nevertheless, some of the prisons already in existence were "makeshift" prisons, as Lonnie R. Speer called them in his appropriately titled study *Portals to Hell: Military Prisons of the Civil War*.[80] These early prisons were "created haphazardly and were ill-planned and ill-conceived from the start."[81] Some were created in Richmond, Virginia, and by October 1861, the city contained a total of 2,685 Federal prisoners, many of whom were captured at the battles of First Bull Run and Ball's Bluff.[82] One such prison was a tobacco factory building with the tobacco presses still in it. The men were crammed into the rooms, with inadequate bathroom facilities, and they slept on the floor without blankets.

Although White had already seen the horrors of Civil War prisons in her Parkville vision, it is probable that she had also read in the papers about Confederate prisons when she described them as "a fate more to be dreaded than death."[83] Northern papers had been printing stories of suffering and mistreatment in the rebel prisons.

Interestingly, one of the stories printed in the *New York Times* was about Confederate prison guard Lieutenant David H. Todd, brother of Mary Todd Lincoln, who reportedly wanted "no better amusement than to come into the prison on a forenoon and kick the helpless, crippled and wounded soldiers."[84] As the war progressed, the conditions of Civil War prisons in both the North and the South got worse and were best depicted as "portals to hell" and "a fate more to be dreaded than death."

But White's concern at this point in the war was that the cause of the "rebellion is not removed," and those soldiers who fought to end slavery "are bitter" and "suffer the greatest privations." They would willingly endure this suffering but "find they have been deceived, and they are dispirited."[85]

A most singular war: Preserve the Union with slavery

At the heart of the essay "The North and the South," White stated, "As this war was shown to me, it looked like the most singular and uncertain that has ever occurred." By "singular," she meant the single aim to preserve the Union only, and by "uncertain," she meant the "perplexing and uncertain" issue of "officers in command" who were "strong proslavery men whose sympathies" were "all with the South."[86]

At the outbreak of the war, the focus of the Lincoln administration was to restore the Union, not to end slavery. Because he was bound by the Constitution that protected slavery in the states, Lincoln's purpose during the first year of the war was to preserve the Constitution and restore the Union as it had existed before 1861. This meant leaving slavery alone in the Southern states. Lincoln had insisted from the beginning of his political career that this was his purpose.

Once the Southern states seceded and formed the Confederacy, Lincoln's theory of the war interpreted secession as illegal. Technically, then, the Confederate states were still in the Union legally but were temporarily under the control of insurrectionists. The purpose of the government, then, was to suppress the insurrection and gain control of the Southern states, thus preserving the Union. "The conflict was therefore," explained James McPherson, "a limited war with the limited goal of restoring the status quo ante bellum, not an unlimited war to destroy an enemy nation and reshape its society. And since, in theory, the southern states were still in the Union, they continued to enjoy all their constitutional rights, including slavery."[87]

One of Lincoln's great concerns was the Border States of Missouri, Kentucky, Maryland, and Delaware. Although still in the Union, three of these states contained a strong pro-Confederate presence, and any hasty action on the part of the government against slavery might drive them into the Confederacy. For this reason, Lincoln refused to endorse the efforts of two generals, John C. Frémont and David Hunter, to free slaves in the sectors under their command. This was an act that upset many abolitionists.[88] Ellen White seemed to have grasped this situation when she wrote,

> Our leading men are perplexed, their hearts are failing them for fear. They fear to proclaim freedom to the slaves of the rebels, for by so doing they will exasperate that portion of the South who have not joined the rebellion but are strong slavery men. And again they have feared the influence of those strong antislavery men who were in command, holding responsible stations. They have feared the effects of a bold, decided tone, for it fanned to a flame the strong desire of thousands to wipe out the cause of this terrible rebellion, by letting the oppressed go free and breaking every yoke.[89]

It's no small wonder that as Ellen White pondered the North's singular focus on preserving the Union rather than ending slavery, she exclaimed, "It looked to me like an impossibility now for slavery to be done away." Things would change, but at the time, the outlook was discouraging. "God alone," she exclaimed, "can wrench the slave from the hand of his desperate, relentless oppressor."[90]

A most uncertain war: Proslavery men in the Northern armies

According to White, the war was uncertain because of Union officers in the army who, although "opposed to a separate government," are still "strong proslavery men whose sympathies are all with the South."[91] She depicted this uncertainty in the Union command thus:

> Many of those who are placed high in command to fill responsible stations have but little conscience or nobility of soul; they can exercise their power, even to the destruction of those under them, and it is winked at. These commanders could abuse the power given them and cause those subject to them to occupy dangerous positions where they would be exposed to terrible encounters with the rebels without the least hope of conquering them. In this way they could

dispose of daring, thoroughgoing men, as David disposed of Uriah. 2 Samuel 11:14, 15.

Valuable men have thus been sacrificed to get rid of their strong antislavery influence. Some of the very men whom the North most need in this critical time, whose services would be of the highest value, *are not*. They have been wantonly sacrificed. The prospects before our nation are discouraging, for there are those filling responsible stations who are rebels at heart. There are commanding officers who are in sympathy with the rebels. While they are desirous of having the Union preserved, they despise those who are antislavery. Some of the armies also are composed largely of such material; they are so opposed to one another that no real union exists among many regiments.[92]

The strong language—"little conscience or nobility of soul"—revealed not only White's strong personal feelings about those who sympathized with the South but also her partisan orientation towards the Radical Republican and abolitionist position on the war. The radicals had little patience with proslavery sympathizers and often used strong language in expressing their views. In Ellen White's mind, there were no shades of gray with the Southern cause and its "accursed" institution of slavery. Those civilians or military commanders who supported the South and its cause in any way were "rebels at heart."

Adventist historian Eric Anderson believed that Ellen White had in mind the recent Union defeat at the Battle of Ball's Bluff on October 21, 1861.[93] Certainly, her readers would have recognized that well-known disaster in her depiction. Colonel Edward D. Baker, a U.S. senator and close friend of Lincoln, was ordered to take his men into the battle and, due to his tactically inept operation, got his command ambushed. The twelve hours of fighting that followed ended in one of the worst defeats (proportionally speaking) either side suffered during the entire Civil War.[94] Baker was killed, and the disaster rocked the Northern public, who were still reeling from the recent defeats of Bull Run and Wilson's Creek. Baker's commanding officer, General Charles P. Stone, was accused of being a Southern sympathizer and was blamed for sending Baker to his death.[95] Adam Gurowski's diary reflected the public sentiment: "The massacre at Ball's Bluff . . . is the work of either treason, or of stupidity, or of cowardice, or most probably of all three united." One journalist wondered who was responsible for sending Baker into the "jaws of death." There is no "parallel to such insanity," he wrote. "The ignorance or incompetence which directed the attempt is without excuse."[96]

Ellen White most likely had in mind the Stone-Baker affair when she wrote about "commanders" who "abuse the power given them and cause those subject to them to occupy dangerous positions where they would be exposed to terrible encounters with the rebels without the least hope of conquering them." Baker must have come to the minds of some readers when she employed the biblical story of David and Uriah as an analogy: "Valuable men have thus been sacrificed to get rid of their strong antislavery influence. Some of the very men whom the North most need in this critical time, whose services would be of the highest value, *are not*." The fact that her language is in the plural—"commanders" and "valuable men"—indicated she was possibly thinking on a larger scale than the Ball's Bluff affair. Apparently, she believed that on numerous occasions, the Northern armies had been "repulsed and unmercifully slaughtered on account of the management of these proslavery men."[97] Perhaps she had in mind the future of the war as well.

A small battle by Civil War standards, Ball's Bluff had ramifications beyond its size. The humiliating defeat moved Congress to create the Joint Committee on the Conduct of the War in early December 1861. The committee was given "broad discretion to investigate any aspect of Northern military affairs." Republicans dominated the committee by a margin of five to two and were hard on those suspected of being soft on the Confederates and not destroying slavery.[98] Although the committee was far from perfect in achieving its objectives, it required accountability from officers that didn't exist in the first eight months of the war.[99] Thus, crimes were not as easily "winked at" later in the war.

In the second paragraph of the *Testimony* cited above, White mentioned "commanding officers" who were "in sympathy with the rebels."[100] It is possible that she had in mind military commanders like General George B. McClellan, whom Lincoln had appointed to command his armies after Irving McDowell was defeated at Bull Run in July 1861. McClellan had made it clear from the start that, as a conservative Democrat, he fought for restoration of the Union but not for the abolition of slavery. He believed in a limited war that in the end would leave slavery alone in the South, as long as there was a peaceful Union. Republicans in general believed that the army's leadership was sympathetic to the South, and they accused Democrats of being "willing accomplices in expanding the institution of slavery."[101]

Moreover, there were concerns that Democratic generals participated in disloyal secret societies such as the Knights of the Golden Circle, a society that was allegedly created to extend slavery into the southwestern part of the country. "Already in fall 1861," according to historian Bruce Tap, "there were rumors that linked the Democratic party in the North to the Knights. Hence, in a capital already suffering from impatience and frustration, talk of disloyalty and suspicion of treason increasingly permeated the atmosphere."[102]

One clear example of a commander with Southern sympathies was Major John J. Key, a staff officer who worked in the office of General-in-Chief Henry W. Halleck and who was the brother of Thomas Key, a colonel on McClellan's staff. Shortly after the Battle of Antietam, Key expressed his opinion as to why the rebel army was not completely destroyed: "That is not the game," he said. "The object is that neither army shall get much advantage of the other; that both shall be kept in the field till they are exhausted, when we will make a compromise and save slavery."[103]

Lincoln heard about this remark and, after interviewing Major Key, dismissed him from the military service of the United States. Later, Lincoln wrote Key to clarify his reasons for the dismissal:

I did not charge, or intend to charge you with disloyalty. I had been brought to fear that there was a class of officers in the army, not very inconsiderable in numbers, who were playing a game to not beat the enemy when they could, on some peculiar notion as to the proper way of saving the Union; and when you were proved to me, in your own presence, to have avowed yourself in favor of that "game," and did not attempt to controvert the proof, I dismissed you as an example and warning to that supposed class.[104]

Key's case, while occurring after Ellen White wrote these words, nevertheless illustrates that officers with Southern sympathies existed in Lincoln's army.

When McClellan refused to pursue Lee and destroy his army after Antietam, Lincoln suspected that McClellan "did not want to hurt the enemy," and he said to his secretary, John Hay, that he also "dismissed Major Key for his silly, treasonable talk because I feared it was staff talk, and I wanted an example."[105] On other occasions, Lincoln expressed concern about the Southern leanings in his army before he released the Emancipation Proclamation. In September 1861, the president said to a clergyman: "We didn't go into the war to put down slavery, but to put the flag back, and to act differently at this moment, would, I have no doubt, not only weaken our cause but smack of bad faith; for I never should have had votes enough to send me here if the people had supposed I should try to use my power to upset slavery. Why, the first thing you'd see, would be a mutiny in the army."[106]

On July 4, 1862, Charles Sumner urged Lincoln to issue an emancipation proclamation in celebration of the day, to which he replied: "I would do it if I were not afraid that half the officers would fling down their arms."[107] Thus, Ellen White's comments on the Southern sympathizers in the Union army, although harsh, were evidently on the mark.

As she reflected on the state of the war in early 1862, White exclaimed to her readers: "It seems impossible to have the war conducted successfully, for many in our own ranks are continually working to favor the South, and our armies have been repulsed and unmercifully slaughtered on account of the management of these proslavery men. Some of our leading men in Congress also are constantly working to favor the South."[108] She probably had in mind the "doughfaces" still in Congress who favored the South—Democratic Copperheads, as they were called, because they attacked the Lincoln administration like the venomous snake in the South—and possibly some prominent Democratic political figures that were connected to the secret societies that allegedly aided the Confederacy.[109] Whatever Ellen White meant specifically, the main issue was the various forms of Southern sympathizers in the government and the military who were the root cause of the uncertain nature of the war.

Conclusion

Up to this point in *Testimony for the Church, No. 7*, Ellen White had offered no solution for the problem facing the North in the war effort. Until the North confronted the crime of slavery head on, it would continue to wander aimlessly through the war. Her vision of a war that was "most singular and uncertain" was true to the actual situation in early 1862. In this setting, she called the Adventist people to "be closely united in the bonds of Christian fellowship and love." Only God, she told them, "can be our shield and strength in this time of our national calamities." Already, "distress and perplexity and famine" were in the land. But it would get worse: "Greater perils are before us, and yet we are not awake."[110] "What shall I say to arouse the remnant people of God?" In light of what she had seen in vision about the war, she wrote, "Dreadful scenes are before us; Satan and his angels are bringing all their powers to bear upon God's people."[111] Thus, her ultimate purpose came through in her writing—to prepare a people for the Second Coming. All of her Civil War statements were colored with that influence and are best understood in that framework.

This first part of "The North and the South" left readers with no solution for the "singular and uncertain nature of the war." But in the next section, in which she condemned the national fasts, there was an allusion to emancipation as the key to success in the North's war with the South. It is to this subject that we now turn.

Chapter in a nutshell

In February 1862, when Mrs. White published *Testimony for the Church, No. 7*, she believed that the war was singular and uncertain. The North was caught off guard by the Southern rebellion and failed to understand the accursed system of slavery and the depth of the Southern hatred for the North, she explained to the Adventist audience. The slave power (the vast social, economic, and political influence that the slaveholders exerted in the South and on the Federal government during the antebellum years) had become more and more demanding in its effort to spread slavery across the country. Thousands of Northern soldiers enlisted with the understanding that the war's purpose was to end slavery but were to be disappointed. The singular nature of the Northern war effort was to restore the Union as it was, with Southern slavery left alone. The war was uncertain because of the proslavery men in the Northern army. To White, it seemed impossible for the war to be conducted successfully because of these proslavery influences. Her analysis accurately captured the historical situation with the "doughfaces" and Democratic Copperheads in the different levels of the Northern government and military. At this point, she exclaimed, "It looked to me like an impossibility now for slavery to be done away." It is "God alone," she exclaimed, who can free the slaves. Such was the grim situation at this stage in the war.

1. White, *Testimonies for the Church*, 1:253.

2. See ibid., 1:264–268.

3. Ibid., 1:253–260.

4. Ibid., 1:260–264.

5. Ibid., 1:260.

6. Ibid., 1:264–268.

7. Ibid., 1:268–270.

8. Ibid., 1:256.

9. Ibid., 1:253.

10. Within the Republican Party during the 1850s and 1860s, one could find three basic orientations towards the slavery issue: conservative, moderate, and radical. The conservatives wanted to restrict slavery to the South, where it already existed, and compromise with slaveholders. The moderates took a middle-of-the-road position and disavowed the idea of slavery but objected to extreme methods, such as immediate emancipation. The radicals were nonextensionists of slavery in the Western territories like the conservatives and moderates, but they were much more extreme in their attitude against slavery, which made them relevant to the Adventists. While they did not think alike on all matters, what they did have in common was a strong opposition to slavery as being morally wrong. Influenced by abolitionist writings, they viewed slavery as a sin against God. Because the Bible was the supreme authority on every moral question, they argued, its injunctions against slavery should be heeded. Thus, they refused to compromise on the issue of nonextension of slavery before the war and pushed for immediate emancipation and civil rights during the war and reconstruction. Ellen White and the Adventists harmonized with the Radical Republicans in their strong opposition to slavery. Reading through the *Review and Herald* in the 1850s and 1860s, e.g., one can find printed excerpts from articles and speeches by the Radical Republicans, such as William H. Seward and Thaddeus Stevens. But the way they used these writings reflected their theological convictions about slavery and their unique, radical apocalyptic view of the American republic. Adventist historian Douglas Morgan summarized the Sabbatarian Adventist position before and during the Civil War: "In accordance with their radical, apocalyptic view of the Republic, the Sabbatarian Adventists of the 1850s and 1860s spoke out on political issues with a vigor unparalleled in the subsequent history of the church. They utilized a Radical Republican critique of the government to support their contention that America was forsaking its highest principles as Revelation 13 indicated it would. But they did not work to change the American system. The nation's doom was foreordained." Only the second coming of Christ would free the slaves. "Yet," Morgan argued, "the Sabbatarian Adventists would not fight their war with bullets or at this time even with ballots. Their tactic was to deliver their warning message and stand fast, waiting for divine deliverance." Thus, Sabbatarian Adventists used the Radical Republican rhetoric "to support their two-horned-beast prophecy that the nation was in grave peril." Morgan, *Adventism and the American Republic*, 70. See also Butler, "Adventism and the American Experience," 186.

11. White, *Testimonies for the Church*, 1:359.

12. Ibid., 1:253.

13. Ibid.

14. On the meaning and origin of the term *doughface*, see Leonard L. Richards, *The Slave Power: The Free North and Southern Domination, 1789–1860* (Baton Rouge, LA: Louisiana State University Press, 2000), 85, 86.

15. Stampp, *And the War Came*, 103. For details on Buchanan's handling of the secession crisis, see ibid., 46–109. For a more recent discussion of the secession crisis from a broader perspective, see William J. Cooper Jr., *We Have the War Upon Us: The Onset of the Civil War, November 1860–April 1861* (New York: Alfred A. Knopf, 2012).

16. White, *Testimonies for the Church*, 1:253.

17. Ibid., 1:254.

18. Ibid., 1:253.

19. Ibid.

20. Thomas, *The Confederate Nation, 1861–1865*, 37, 38.

21. For an insightful discussion on the history of the South's emphasis on secession and Southern independence long before 1860, see Emory M. Thomas, *The Confederacy as a Revolutionary Experience* (Columbia, SC: University of South Carolina Press, 1991), 23–38.

22. White, *Testimonies for the Church*, 1:253.

23. Ibid.

24. Jefferson Davis, quoted in Long, *The Civil War Day by Day*, 37.

25. Jefferson Davis, quoted in William J. Cooper Jr., *Jefferson Davis: The Essential Writings* (New York: Modern Library, 2004), 196, 197.

26. Alexander Stephens, "Speech of A. H. Stephens," in Moore, *The Rebellion Record*, 1:48.

27. White, *Testimonies for the Church*, 1:253.

28. Edward McPherson, ed., *The Political History of the United States, During the Great Rebellion* (Washington, DC: J. J. Chapman, 1876), 15.

29. Mary Boykin Chesnut, quoted in Potter, *The Impending Crisis*, 471n49.

30. Basler, *The Collected Works of Abraham Lincoln*, 4:211 (interpolation and emphasis in the original).

31. Gallagher, *The American Civil War: Lectures 1–24*, 48, 49. Gallagher set forth three camps in the slaveholding South in relationship to secession: "immediate secessionists," who wanted each state to take immediate action and secede; "cooperationists," who favored waiting until the South could act as a whole; and "unconditional Unionists," those who opposed secession.

32. Emory M. Thomas, *The Dogs of War: 1861* (New York: Oxford University Press, 2011), 41. For a discussion on Lincoln and his administration's failure to understand the gravity of the situation with the South during this time, see pages 38–45.

33. Frederick Douglass, "The Rebels, the Government, and the Difference Between Them," *Douglass' Monthly*, August, 1861, quoted in *Frederick Douglass: Selected Speeches and Writings*, eds. Philip S. Foner and Yuval Taylor (Chicago: Lawrence Hill Books, 1999), 469.

34. White, *Testimonies for the Church*, 1:253.

35. Ibid., 1:253, 254.

36. For discussion on the five main arguments used for state sovereignty and the right of secession by political theorists in the South, see Potter, *The Impending Crisis*, 479–482.

37. White, *Testimonies for the Church*, 1:254.

38. Douglass, *Douglass' Monthly*, July 1861, quoted in Foner and Taylor, *Frederick Douglass*, 455.

39. See Thomas J. Pressly, *Americans Interpret Their War* (New York: The Free Press, 1962); Kenneth M. Stampp, ed., *The Causes of the Civil War* (New York: Simon & Schuster, 1991); Gabor S. Boritt, ed., *Why the Civil War Came* (New York: Oxford University Press, 1996); Hugh Tulloch, *The Debate on the American Civil War Era* (New York: Manchester University Press, 1999), 104–153; Paul Calore, *The Causes of the Civil War: The Political, Cultural, Economic and Territorial Disputes Between the North and South* (Jefferson, NC: McFarland & Company, 2008).

40. For a helpful discussion on the three positions, see Edward L. Ayers, *What Caused the Civil War? Reflections on the South and Southern History* (New York: W. W. Norton, 2005, 131–144; and Varon, *Disunion!*, 3, 4.

41. James McPherson is an example of this position; see McPherson, *This Mighty Scourge: Perspectives on the Civil War* (New York: Oxford University Press, 2007), 3–19.

42. Avery O. Craven is an example of this position; see Craven, *The Coming of the Civil War*, 2nd ed. (Chicago, IL: University Chicago Press, 1957).

43. Ayers, *What Caused the Civil War?*, 142, best articulated this view.

44. For primary sources, such as the secession documents of the Southern states, see *Encyclopedia of the Civil War*, eds. Davis S. Heidler and Jeanne T. Heidler (New York: W. W. Norton, 2000), 2240–2252; and Jon L. Wakelyn, ed., *Southern Pamphlets on Secession, November 1860–April 1861* (Chapel Hill, NC: University of North Carolina Press, 1996); on secession commissioners, see especially Charles B. Dew, *Apostles of Disunion: Southern Secession Commissioners and the Causes of the Civil War* (Charlottesville, VA: University of Virginia Press, 2001).

45. McPherson, *This Mighty Scourge*, 13–18.

46. For evidence that both slave owners and Confederate leaders viewed the Civil War as a war for slavery, see James L. Roark, *Masters Without Slaves: Southern Planters in the Civil War and Reconstruction* (New York: W. W. Norton, 1977), 1–32, 68–108; and Drew Gilpin Faust, *The Creation of Confederate Nationalism: Ideology and Identity in the Civil War South* (Baton Rouge, LA: Louisiana State University Press, 1988), 58–63.

47. Benjamin M. Palmer, "Slavery a Divine Trust: Duty of the South to Preserve and Perpetuate It," in *Fast Day Sermons: Or, the Pulpit on the State of the Country* (New York: Rudd & Carleton, 1861), 62, 64, 65, 68, 71, 72; also published as *The South: Her Peril and Her Duty: A Discourse Delivered in the First Presbyterian Church, New Orleans* (New Orleans, LA: Office of the True Witness and Sentinel, 1860); for the sermon, see also Wakelyn, ed., *Southern Pamphlets on Secession*, 63–77.

48. Palmer, "Slavery a Divine Trust," 77.

49. Quotes from Mitchell Snay, *Gospel of Disunion: Religion and Separatism in the Antebellum South* (Chapel Hill, NC: The University of North Carolina Press, 1993), 179; for analysis of Palmer's sermon, see ibid., 175–180.

50. For the definitive study, see Richards, *The Slave Power*.

51. White, *Testimonies for the Church*, 1:264.

52. This is because of the three-fifths clause in the Constitution, in which five slaves counted as three whites in determining how many seats a state would have in the House of Representatives. See Richards, *The Slave Power*, 32ff.; and Garry Wills, *"Negro President": Jefferson and the Slave Power* (New York: Houghton Mifflin, 2003), 1–13.

53. Charles Sumner, quoted in Eric Foner, *Free Soil, Free Labor, Free Men: The Ideology of the Republican Party Before the Civil War* (New York: Oxford University Press, 1995), 88.

54. Quoted in Foner, *Free Soil*, 88.

55. Richards, *The Slave Power*, 109.

56. Foner, *Free Soil*, 9.

57. Basler, *The Collected Works of Abraham Lincoln*, 2:548, 549. This is from notes Lincoln made for his debate with Douglas, where he expressed his concerns about the conspiracy.

58. Ibid., 2:461, 462 (emphasis in the original).

59. For the debate among historians on the slave power thesis, see Richards, *The Slave Power*, 18; Avery Craven, "Coming of the War Between the States: An Interpretation," *The Journal of Southern History* 2, no. 3 (1936): 303–322; and Russel B. Nye, "The Slave Power Conspiracy: 1830–1860," Science & Society 10, no. 3 (1946): 262–274.

60. Wills, *"Negro President,"* 11 (emphasis in original).

61. White, *Testimonies for the Church*, 1:264.

62. Ibid., 1:254.

63. Ibid.

64. Ibid.

65. Ibid.

66. Ibid., 1:255.

67. Ibid., 1:256.

68. See the classic studies of Bell I. Wiley, *The Life of Johnny Reb* (Indianapolis: Bobbs-Merrill, 1943); *The Life of Billy Yank* (Indianapolis: Bobbs-Merrill, 1952). James McPherson's works in this area are indispensable: *What They Fought For: 1861–1865* (New York: Anchor Books, 1995); *For Cause and Comrades: Why Men Fought in the Civil War* (New York: Oxford University Press, 1997); *The Negro's Civil War: How American Blacks Felt and Acted During the War for the Union* (New York: Vintage Books, 1993). Reid Mitchell addresses soldiering life in general but touches on the slavery issue in *Civil War Soldiers* (New York: Penguin Books, 1988); *The Vacant Chair: The Northern Soldier Leaves Home* (New York: Oxford University Press, 1993). Chandra Manning specifically addresses soldiers and the issue of slavery in her book *What This Cruel War Was Over: Soldiers, Slavery, and the Civil War* (New York: Vintage Books, 2007).

69. Wiley, *The Life of Billy Yank*, 40–42.

70. Chauncey H. Cooke and Urich N. Parmelee, quoted in ibid., 40, 41 (emphasis in the original). For several quotations from soldiers in 1861 who believed the war should be to free the slaves, see McPherson, *What They Fought For*, 57, 58.

71. Wiley, *The Life of Billy Yank*, 40.

72. McPherson and Hogue, *Ordeal by Fire*, 181.

73. McPherson, *For Cause and Comrades*, 117, 118.

74. White, *Testimonies for the Church*, 1:256.

75. McPherson demonstrates effectively through the writings of Union soldiers that more and more of them converted over the course of the war to the idea of saving the Union and liberating the slaves, especially after the Emancipation Proclamation went into effect in January 1863. McPherson, *For Cause and Comrades*, 117–130.

76. Manning, *What This Cruel War Was Over*.

77. White, *Testimonies for the Church*, 1:254, 255.

78. Whitman, *Specimen Days and Collect*, 35. The scene is part of the aftermath at the Battle of Chancellorsville, which took place more than a year after White penned her January 1862 vision.

79. White, *Testimonies for the Church*, 1:255.

80. Speer, *Portals to Hell*, 19.

81. Ibid.

82. Ibid., 20, 21.

83. White, *Testimonies for the Church*, 1:255.

84. *New York Times*, quoted in Speer, *Portals to Hell*, 21.

85. White, *Testimonies for the Church*, 1:255.

86. Ibid., 1:256.

87. James McPherson, *Abraham Lincoln and the Second American Revolution* (New York: Oxford University Press, 1991), 31.

88. For further discussion of the Frémont proclamation, see the next chapter.

89. White, *Testimonies for the Church*, 1:255.

90. Ibid., 1:266. At the time White wrote this statement, the constitution was, as originally proposed and adapted, pro-slavery with its Fugitive Slave Clause, Three-Fifths Clause, and Slave Importation Clause. "If slavery was our nation's original sin," explains Michael Stokes Paulsen and Luke Paulsen, "the Constitution was the nation's deal with the devil. And repentance, redemption, and restoration did not come easily." Michael Stokes Paulsen and Luke Paulsen, *The Constitution: An Introduction* (New York: Basic Books, 2015), 74; see pages 73–89 for discussion of the original constitution as pro-slavery.

91. Ibid., 1:256.

92. Ibid., 1:255, 256 (emphasis in the original).

93. Eric Anderson, "War, Slavery, and Race," in Aamodt, Land, and Numbers, *Ellen Harmon White: American Prophet*, 267.

94. For the definitive study of the Battle of Ball's Bluff, see Morgan, *A Little Short of Boats*.

95. See Tim J. Watts, "Battle of Ball's Bluff," in Heidler and Heidler, *Encyclopedia of the American Civil War*, 167–169.

96. Quoted in Bruce Tap, *Over Lincoln's Shoulder: The Committee on the Conduct of the War* (Lawrence, KS: University of Kansas, 1998), 18.

97. White, *Testimonies for the Church*, 1:256.

98. Bruce Tap, "Joint Committee on the Conduct of the War," in Heidler and Heidler, *Encyclopedia of the American Civil War*, 1086, 1087.

99. The definitive study on the committee is Tap, *Over Lincoln's Shoulder*.

100. White, *Testimonies for the Church*, 1:256.

101. Tap, *Over Lincoln's Shoulder*, 21.

102. Ibid. See also David C. Keehn, *Knights of the Golden Circle: Secret Empire, Southern Secession, Civil War* (Baton Rouge, LA: Louisiana State University Press, 2013); Frank L. Klement, *Dark Lanterns: Secret Political Societies, Conspiracies, and Treason Trials in the Civil War* (Baton Rouge, LA: Louisiana State University Press, 1984); Mark A. Lause, *A Secret Society History of the Civil War* (Chicago: University of Illinois Press, 2011); and William A. Blair, *With Malice Toward Some: Treason and Loyalty in the Civil War Era* (Chapel Hill, NC: University of North Carolina Press, 2014).

103. John J. Key, quoted in Basler, *The Collected Works of Abraham Lincoln*, 5:442.

104. Basler, *The Collected Works of Abraham Lincoln*, 5:508.

105. Fehrenbacher and Fahrenbacher, *Recollected Words of Abraham Lincoln*, 231.

106. Ibid., 295.

107. Ibid., 434.

108. White, *Testimonies for the Church*, 1:256.

109. See Bruce Tap, "Copperheads," in Heidler and Heidler, *Encyclopedia of the American Civil War*, 498; Jennifer L. Weber, *Copperheads: The Rise and Fall of Lincoln's Opponents in the North* (New York: Oxford University Press, 2006); and the sources in note 102.

110. White, *Testimonies for the Church*, 1:260.

111. Ibid., 1:263.

CHAPTER 10

NATIONAL FASTS:
AN INSULT TO JEHOVAH

I saw that these national fasts were an insult to Jehovah," declared Ellen White as she wrote out her third war vision in January 1862.[1] "He accepts of no such fasts."[2] These words were a harsh pronouncement on the North's effort to seek God at a time of great peril in its history. Why would she speak such strong words against Abraham Lincoln's leadership in a day of national humiliation and prayer before God? Some have felt that her words were nothing more than "a bitter denunciation of Lincoln's administration and his management of the war."[3] This chapter will examine the historical and literary context of this jeremiad against the Union's national fasts.

During the Civil War, Abraham Lincoln proclaimed three days of national humiliation, prayer, and fasting, and four days of national thanksgiving in the Union;[4] and Jefferson Davis proclaimed eight days of national prayer and fasting, one day of national prayer and worship, and one day of national thanksgiving in the Confederacy.[5] The days of thanksgiving usually followed battle victories, whereas the days of fasting followed battle losses. This practice found its roots in the idea that the people of the United States stood in a covenantal relationship with God. "For most of them, a vocabulary of corporate repentance and renewal, handed down from the

Puritans, remained an appropriate vocabulary for addressing the American public about its privileges and duties before God."[6] The enduring power of this covenantal relationship found expression in the public acceptance of the numerous fast-day proclamations. "For both North and South," explained historian Mark Noll, "the template for these national religious observances was the time-honored pattern of covenant, as taken over from a reading of the Old Testament: repent and God may reverse evil days; give thanks and He may allow the propitious times to continue."[7]

Buchanan's fast proclamation for January 4, 1861

Since James Madison had proclaimed the last national day of prayer for 1813, the turbulent antebellum years saw no such event until December 14, 1860, when a desperate James Buchanan proclaimed a day of humiliation, fasting, and prayer.[8] His proclamation set aside January 4, 1861, as the day for seeking the "Most High" with "deep contrition and penitent sorrow." In an allusion to the imminent breakup of the Union through Southern secession, he stated, "The Union of the States is at the present moment threatened with alarming and immediate danger; panic and distress of a fearful character prevails throughout the land." The president then appealed to "every individual" in the nation to earnestly pray for God "to restore the friendship and good will which prevailed in former days among the people of the several States; and, above all, to save us from the horrors of civil war and 'blood-guiltiness.' "[9] Abolitionists, however, believed that the call for national repentance by a known "doughface" was hypocritical, to say the least. Within a week of the proclamation, South Carolina seceded from the Union, and by the time the day of fasting came, the nation was well on its inevitable march toward war.

Lincoln's fast proclamation for September 26, 1861

About three weeks after the humiliating defeat at the Battle of First Manassas on July 21, 1861, the North suffered another disaster in the bloody Battle of Wilson's Creek, Missouri, on August 10. In response to these consecutive defeats, a joint committee of both houses of Congress requested President Lincoln to call for a day of national prayer and fasting in September.[10] In his proclamation published on August 12, Lincoln set aside Thursday, September 26, as "a day of humiliation, prayer and fasting for all the people of the nation." In the heart of the proclamation, he stated:

And whereas, when our own beloved Country, once, by the blessing of God, united, prosperous and happy, is now afflicted with faction and civil war, it is peculiarly fit for us to recognize the hand of God in this terrible visitation, and in sorrowful remembrance of our own faults and crimes as a nation and as individuals, to humble ourselves before Him, and to pray for His mercy,—to pray that we may be spared further punishment, though most justly deserved; that our arms may be blessed and made effectual for the re-establishment of law, order and peace, throughout the wide extent of our country; and that the inestimable boon of civil and religious liberty, earned under His guidance and blessing, by the labors and sufferings of our fathers, may be restored in all its original excellence.[11]

It is noteworthy that although Lincoln recognized "the hand of God in this terrible visitation [the war]" and the "faults and crimes" of the nation, he did not specify the nature of these offenses. According to one historian, "his words do not reflect the reality or seriousness of sin."[12] Lincoln's view of slavery and emancipation was slowly evolving at this point in the war, and he still believed that emancipation should be slow and gradual.[13] The proclamation admitted no remorse for the sin of slavery and showed no motivation to end it.[14]

The abolitionist concern over Lincoln's Republican administration

This mind-set of gradual emancipation was typical of Lincoln's Republican Party in general. Although nominally antislavery and officially opposed to the extension of slavery into the new territories, the party refused to take any action against slavery where it already existed in the South. Horace Greeley, the editor of the *New-York Daily Tribune*, clarified this position when he wrote on September 7, 1860, that "never on earth did the Republican party propose . . . to abolish Slavery. . . . Its object with respect to Slavery is simply, nakedly, avowedly, its restriction to the existing Slave States."[15] Greeley's statement reflected the general understanding of most Republicans, with the most significant voice being that of Abraham Lincoln, who, according to historian James McPherson, "had a deep-rooted moral abhorrence of slavery" but "favored no stronger measures against the institution than its exclusion from the territories."[16]

This position was not acceptable to Radical Republicans, abolitionists, and free black men in the North. The *Weekly Anglo-African*, a weekly newspaper founded in 1859 by Thomas Hamilton that spoke for African Americans in New York City, captured the abolitionist protest against both the Democratic and Republican Parties in the North when it declared,

> The two great political parties separate at an angle of two roads, that they may meet eventually at the same goals. They both entertain the same ideas, and both carry the same burdens. They differ only in regard to the way they shall go, and the method of procedure. . . .
>
> The Democratic party would make the white man the master and the black man the slave, and have them thus together occupy every foot of the American soil. . . .
>
> The Republican party . . . though with larger professions for humanity, is by far its more dangerous enemy. Under the guise of humanity, they do and say many things—as, for example, they oppose the re-opening of the slave-trade. . . . They oppose the progress of slavery in the territories, and would cry humanity to the world. . . . Their opposition to slavery means opposition to the black man—nothing else. Where it is clearly in their power to do anything for the oppressed colored man, why then they are too nice, too conservative, to do it. . . .
>
> . . . We have no hope from either as political parties. We must rely on ourselves, the righteousness of our cause, and the advance of just sentiments among the great masses of the . . . people.[17]

Such was the abolitionist mind-set that fueled Ellen White's protest against the national fasts.

Response of the clergy to Lincoln's proclamation

Northern clergy and the religious press "saw, in the ritual of the fast, the equivalent of a constitutional invocation of God," explained Harry S. Stout. In their understanding, "when Lincoln proclaimed a fast day 'to be observed by the people of the United States with religious solemnities and the offering of fervent supplications to Almighty God,' he was saying, in effect, that the United States was a Christian nation as much as if it had been written in the Constitution."[18] Many of the published sermons delivered on the day of the fast show a "widespread acceptance of the war as a just and moral cause worthy of the support of all loyal citizens." The typical fast sermon addressed the standard theme of America's providential destiny and cataloged various national sins the nation needed to overcome to regain God's favor, such as "national pride, greed, governmental corruption, and Sabbath-breaking."[19]

A few fast sermons, however, insisted that "slavery was the chief cause of contention that ultimately had provoked war." Four pastors—"J. B. Bittinger of Cleveland's Euclid Street Presbyterian Church, Cincinnati Presbyterian M. L. P. Thompson, William W. Patton of Chicago's First Congregational Church, and Indianapolis minister James Simmons of First Baptist Church"—preached that slavery was the national sin the war should eradicate.[20] Simmons preached from Isaiah 58:6 on God's chosen fast (the same text Ellen White used in condemning this fast) and concluded that Americans should repent and embrace "the work of emancipation or suffer the destruction of the Republic."[21]

The Sabbatarian Adventist response to the fast

Since 1855, the Sabbatarian Adventists had been discussing the topic of prayer and fasting and had concluded that it was important for the church to practice.[22] In 1861, the Adventist church set August 3 aside for a day of "humiliation, fasting, and prayer." The day was greatly anticipated as a day to plead for God's blessing and to look for the "end of all things," particularly in view of the recent Union defeat at Bull Run on July 21.[23] Interestingly, it was during that day that Ellen White had one of her Civil War visions: "At the Conference at Roosevelt, New York, August 3, 1861, when the brethren and sisters were assembled on the day set apart for humiliation, fasting, and prayer, the Spirit of the Lord rested upon us, and I was taken off in vision and shown the sin of slavery, which has so long been a curse to this nation."[24] Clearly, Ellen White and the Adventists were in favor of the practice of a day of fasting and prayer. Because they believed that America was committing a "national sin" in supporting slavery and that the purpose of the war was to save the Union rather than to end slavery, however, Adventists did not support the national fast day on September 26, 1861.[25]

About three weeks after the national fast day, J. M. Aldrich[26] of Somerset, New York, published an article about the national fast in the *Review and Herald* on October 15:

Among the important events of the day is our country's "national fast." And truly such a fast as has been proclaimed by the highest authority of our great nation, and which has been celebrated so generally throughout our land, may in fact be considered a noteworthy event. A secular paper says of it thus:

"A solemn, sudden pause of a mighty but distracted nation. An apparent calm amid the pelting of an awful storm. From St. Louis to Boston, from Washington to the Northern Lakes, in every city and hamlet, around thousands of church altars, and by a million firesides, the awful pause is felt. It may be said with considerable truth, that yesterday a nation was at prayer. Yesterday a nation was upon its knees before the King of kings."[27]

Then Aldrich launched into his jeremiad on the fast day: "Indeed, if such were the case, what an imposing spectacle! 'A nation at prayer!' 'A nation upon its knees before the King of kings!' Surely if there be no response to *such* a prayer, it must be because *sin* lieth at the door. But how is it with our nation? Has she put away her sins? Has she put away the *great* sin whereof she has been so long guilty? Has she considered the *real cause* of her present peril, and removed the same forever?"[28]

That great sin, of course, was slavery. "Does the blood of *four million slaves* still cry to God for vengeance?" Aldrich asked rhetorically. The main theme running through this condemnation of the fast day was the hypocrisy of the nation in fasting and calling on God when the great sin of slavery still lingered in its midst. Aldrich cited Isaiah 58:6, a text used often by abolitionists since the 1830s, as the heart of his jeremiad. The only national fast that God will accept, he argued, is the fast that will "undo the heavy burdens" and "let the oppressed go free"—the emancipation of the slaves. That is the only kind of prayer that God will answer with an affirmative response.[29] This article was in keeping with the abolitionist theme that had been articulated in the *Review and Herald* since its beginning in 1850 and which formed the framework for Ellen White's comments on the national fasts.

Ellen White's jeremiad on the national fast

Ellen White's response was forceful. In her second essay on the war, published in February 1862, she declared, "I saw that these national fasts were an insult to Jehovah. He accepts no such fasts." Twice in her jeremiad, she declared that the national fasts were "an insult to Jehovah."[30] Such strong words are easily misunderstood when read outside their context.

As we saw in the previous chapter, which forms the immediate context for this jeremiad on national fasts, White had set forth the problems in the Union war effort: the Buchanan administration's accommodation of the South, the Lincoln administration's purpose to preserve the Union and leave slavery in the South alone, and the proslavery influences in the Northern army and in Congress. "As this war was shown to me, it looked like the most singular and uncertain that has ever occurred," she explained. "It seems impossible to have the war conducted successfully, for many in our own ranks are continually working to favor the South. . . . Some of our leading men in Congress also are constantly working to favor the South," she exclaimed.[31]

White declared, "In this state of things, proclamations are issued for national fasts, for prayer that God will bring this war to a speedy and favorable termination."[32] The transitional phrase "in this state of things" encompassed everything she had said about the issue of slavery and the Union's mismanagement of the war. The plural "national fasts" referred to the two Union fast days issued by the outgoing Buchanan administration for January 4, 1861, and the more recent fast issued by Lincoln for September 26. Although it is possible she might also have had in mind the two Confederate fasts called for by Jefferson Davis during the summer and fall of 1861,[33] the context points to the two Union fasts, particularly the one called by Lincoln on September 26.

"I was then directed," White explained, "to Isaiah 58:5–7," which she quoted in full from the King James Version:

"Is it such a fast that I have chosen? a day for a man to afflict his soul? is it to bow down his head as a bulrush, and to spread sackcloth and ashes under him? wilt thou call this a fast, and an acceptable day to the Lord? Is not this the fast that I have chosen? to loose the bands of wickedness, to undo the heavy burdens, and to let the oppressed go free, and that ye break every yoke? Is it not to deal thy bread to the hungry, and that thou bring the poor that are cast out to thy house? when thou seest the naked, that thou cover him; and that thou hide not thyself from thine own flesh?"[34]

As noted above, this is a classic abolitionist text, often quoted and alluded to by

William Lloyd Garrison and Frederick Douglass in their speeches and writings.[35] In the context of Isaiah 58, the previous verses (2–4) set forth God's rejection of His people's fast. It was a selfish fast directed at the Lord, "a day of self-pleasing to the disadvantage of others . . . and provocative of the worst elements in the human spirit." Because of its formalism, it brought no spiritual result and consequently had "no currency in heaven." The objectives of a true fast, according to the text, are to obtain a just and fair society and meet the needs of suffering individuals.[36] Isaiah specialist Alec Motyer explained verse 6, in which all the main verbs relate directly to liberation:

> To *loose the chains of injustice* [bands of wickedness] . . . points to the need to labour for the abolition of every way in which wrong social structures, or wrongdoers in society, destroy or diminish the due liberty of others. To *untie the cords of the yoke* [break every yoke] refers to the need to eliminate every way in which people are treated like animals. The *oppressed* are those "broken" by life. It is not enough to work for amelioration; the objective is also to secure the positive values that have been lost. Instead of bondage and brokenness there should be freedom—not only the loosing of the yoke's harness but also the breaking of the yoke itself, whether of injustice (6b), inhumanity (6c) or inequality (6d).[37]

Ellen White thus stood in the tradition of abolitionists when she applied the original meaning of this text to chattel slavery in the American republic. Like James Simmons and J. M. Aldrich above, she applied this passage to the hypocrisy of the national fasts called for by Buchanan and Lincoln. The difference was that she claimed prophetic authority for her jeremiad and spoke specifically to the issue of the slaves fleeing to the Northern army and being repulsed. White made her case with the strongest language possible when she called the fasts an "insult to Jehovah."

The Union fasts were no different from the condemned ancient fasts, White explained: "The recording angel writes in regard to them: 'Ye fast for strife and debate, and to smite with the fist of wickedness.' "[38] The original meaning of this verse, Isaiah 58:4, is somewhat uncertain. John N. Oswalt, another Isaiah specialist, suggested that Isaiah is "speaking hyperbolically." Most likely, the point is "that since these people saw no connection between their mistreatment of the poor and the lowly and their religion, that mistreatment cancelled out all their religious acts."[39] This seems to be the application White gave to the text. The way the Union army mistreated the fleeing "poor slaves" canceled out any true spiritual meaning in their national fasts.

Mistreatment of escaping slaves to Union lines

"I was shown how our leading men have treated the poor slaves who have come to them for protection," White stated. "Angels have recorded it." The rest of the lengthy paragraph unpacked the lead sentence. "Love of liberty" led many of the slaves to "leave their masters and risk their lives to obtain liberty." They "endured untold hardships and dangers to obtain their freedom, and as their last hope, with the love of liberty burning in their breasts, they apply to our Government for protection; but their confidence has been treated with the utmost contempt." Union men, "professing to have human hearts, have seen the slaves almost naked and starving, and have abused them, and sent them back to their cruel masters and hopeless bondage, to suffer inhuman cruelty for daring to seek their liberty." Consequently, they are deprived "of the liberty and free air which heaven has never denied them," and then they are left "to suffer for food and clothing."[40]

Several observations about this paragraph are in order. First, from the beginning of the war, many slaves viewed "the conflict as heralding the long-awaited destruction of slavery." Blacks in both the North and the South called the conflict a "freedom war." "Even before the firing on Fort Sumter, eight slaves sought refuge at Fort Pickens," a Union outpost in Pensacola, Florida, "entertaining the idea," according to the commander, that federal forces "were placed here to protect them and grant them their freedom." Slaves thus understood that the presence of Union troops fundamentally changed the balance of power in the South between black and white, slave and master. As the Federal army occupied territory on the edges of the Confederacy, slaves by the thousands, including large numbers of women, children, and elderly men, abandoned plantations at great peril to their lives in the pursuit of freedom.[41] By the end of the war, approximately five hundred thousand slaves had gone within Union lines.[42]

Second, White's recognition of the slave's "love of liberty," which led many of them to escape the bondage of their masters, speaks to the contemporary debate

A Ride for Liberty 1863, by Eastman Johnson, Brooklyn Museum

over the part the slaves themselves played in their emancipation. The debate centers around this issue: Was emancipation primarily the product of the slaves' struggle to free themselves, or was it the work of Abraham Lincoln, the Great Emancipator; and the Union armies? The historians James McPherson and Ira Berlin have addressed this issue and provided significant insights on both sides of the debate. McPherson emphasized the central role of President Lincoln as the prime mover in the Emancipation Proclamation and the Thirteenth Amendment and as commander of the Union armies. Berlin emphasized the central role of the slaves as prime movers who, by emancipating themselves, made it possible for legislators, military officers, and the president to act.[43] Although the debate continues about the prime mover in emancipation, all sides would agree that both the slaves themselves and Lincoln and his armies contributed to emancipation. In this passage, White emphasized the role the slaves themselves played in their own emancipation and capitalized on the difficulties they encountered and their desire for liberty, adding the theological dimension "which heaven has never denied them."

Third, there were military commanders who upheld the Fugitive Slave Law by returning runaway slaves to their masters and those who accepted the slaves into their lines. The most well-known example of the latter was General Benjamin Butler, a former proslavery Democrat who eventually converted to the Republican side. Assigned to Fort Monroe, the Union toehold on the southern Virginia coastline, Butler refused to return slaves who had escaped from their masters and crossed into his lines. "An astute lawyer, he declared them contraband of war—enemy property subject to seizure."[44] The term *contraband* usually applied to weapons and supplies, but "Butler and other military personnel invoked the insidious doctrine that slaves were property, not humans. With the will and calculation of humans, slaves had run from their masters to Union lines, but it was only as property that Union armies granted them asylum."[45] Northern newspapers picked up the term, "and it was used thereafter to describe all slaves who came under Union control." Word quickly spread among slaves on the Virginia Peninsula, and scores of them escaped to Butler's lines. The Lincoln administration sanctioned the contraband policy, and on August 6, Congress ratified it by enacting "a Confiscation Act that authorized the seizure of all property used in military aid of the rebellion—including slaves." This law "did not specify the permanent future status of the contrabands, but few expected they would ever be returned to slavery."[46]

Union commanders in the former group, however, held fast to Lincoln's promise that the army would respect the property rights of slaveholders and return runaway slaves.[47] William S. Harney, for example, the commander in St. Louis, Missouri, confirmed in a letter written on May 14, 1861, that "since the commencement of these unhappy disturbances, slaves have escaped from their owners, and have sought refuge in the camps of the United States troops from Northern states and commanders by a Northern General. They were carefully sent back to their owners."[48] On May 26, Major General George McClellan instructed a field commander in western Virginia to "see that the property [including slaves] and rights of the inhabitants are in every respect carefully protected, and use every effort to conciliate the people and strengthen the Union feeling."[49] In July 1861, a Union colonel who had asked for counsel on what to do with runaway slaves, was instructed by his commanding officer to "respect private property, and to send back to the farm the negroes his troops brought away."[50] On October 15, 1861, Brigadier General William T. Sherman reminded one of his colonels that "the laws of the United States and of Kentucky all of which are binding on us compel us to surrender a runaway negro on application of [the] negro's owner or agent. I believe you have not been instrumental in this but my orders are that all negroes shall be delivered up on the claim of the owner or agent. Better keep the negroes out of your camp altogether unless you brought them along with the regiment."[51] Justin Dimmick and A. J. Slemmer were other Union officers who sent back the fugitives that sought protection from them. "They refuse to let the white men sell the Southerners food," complained J. Sella Martin, a former slave who had escaped to the North, "and yet they return slaves to work on the plantation to raise all the food that the Southerners want."[52]

One Tennessee fugitive en route to Canada reported abuse of escaping slaves to a sympathetic Michigan Quaker named Willis, who communicated this disturbing news to Secretary of War Simon Cameron. The Quaker explained that the fugitive said, "5 Slaves that was Sent over from Kentucky by our Federal Troops Say that they were badly treated by our officers altho the[y] offered to work or Fight for the Government, but w[e]re told to Clear out that the officers wanted no D____d N_____s about them," and they were "actually driven to their old Homes." Willis added, "If the Administration Dont put a Stop to the Ill Treatment of the Slaves by our Army I greatly fear that we will be the Losers thereby."[53]

It was this group of officers that refused the slaves "the liberty and free air which heaven has never denied them," which Ellen White condemned in her protest against the national fast. General Butler's actions at Fort Monroe were evidently beyond her purview as she wrote. White focused only on the cruelty and abuse of those Union commanders who sent "naked and starving" human beings back to "hopeless bondage." Although there were hints that emancipation might be a future possibility (the first Confiscation Act, passed on August 6, 1861, was an early portent), there was no promise in these early months of the war that it would ever be a reality.

A national fast at a time when slaves were seeking refuge behind Union lines and then were returned to their masters was, to White, a hypocrisy: "In view of all this, a national fast is proclaimed! Oh, what an insult to Jehovah!" She ended this paragraph as she began it by using the words "insult to Jehovah," which emphasized that the national fast (in the singular this time—a reference to the September 26 fast) was offensive to God. To buttress this point, she employed another quotation from the prophet Isaiah: "The Lord saith by the mouth of Isaiah: 'Yet they seek Me daily, and delight to know My ways, as a nation that did righteousness, and forsook not the ordinance of their God' [Isaiah 58:2]."[54] The federal government had, like ancient Judah, professed to be a righteous nation and to seek God in its national fasts but was in rebellion against God because it harbored an oppressive bondage in its midst.

White's next paragraph continued the thought on the North's treatment of runaway slaves but added the aspect of what the Southern masters told their slaves about the North:

> The escaped slaves have been told by their masters that the Northern men wanted to get possession of them that they might cruelly misuse them; that the abolitionists would treat them worse than they had been treated while in slavery. All manner of horrible stories have been repeated in their ears to make them detest the North, and yet they have had a confused idea that some hearts in the North felt for their grievances and would yet make an effort to help them. This has been the only star which has shed its glimmering light upon their distressed and gloomy bondage.[55]

The larger background to this statement is the earnest attention that black Southerners gave to the events happening around them. From secession to the outbreak of the war, they tried to "ascertain exactly what it all meant for them and how best to make use of the novel and rapidly evolving situation."[56] George E. Stephens, a free black Northerner who was the cook for the Twenty-Sixth Pennsylvania Regiment, observed firsthand, as he traveled with the regiment through the Chesapeake region during December 1861, that the slaves "are watching the events of the hour, and . . . hope lights up in their hearts; bright and all-absorbing visions of liberty and freedom crowd upon their mind."[57]

Southern masters observed this attitude and "did what they could to mislead their slaves about the events unfolding around them. The most common tactic was to paint terrifying word pictures of how northerners would deal with black people," explained Bruce Levine.[58] "Harry, a slave foreman on one plantation, remembered his master telling him 'dat de Yankees would shoot we, when dey come.' But Harry 'knowed he wasn't tellin' de truth all de time.' He and most others had heard that 'de Yankees was our friends, an' dat we'd be free when dey come, an' 'pears like we believe dat.' "[59] Those slaves who, with hope in their hearts, escaped to Northern lines like Fort Monroe found refuge and, although labeled as "contraband of war," were not sent back to their masters in the South.

Other slaves, however, received no such reward for their faith in the Yankees and were returned to their former bondage. In his letter to the secretary of war, quoted above, Quaker Willis explained that the fugitive told him "that Tens of Thousands of Slaves are in the greatest Alarm" from the stories their masters have told them and that the abusive treatment they have received from the Yankees "almost Sett them Cra[z]y" because they "expected Friends of us in Stead of Enemys."[60] Thus, White lamented, "The manner in which the poor slaves have been treated has led them to believe that their masters have told them the truth in these things." The incongruity of a day for national fasting and prayer for God's blessing, when fleeing slaves were mistreated and repulsed, drew another lament from White's abolitionist heart: "And yet a national fast is proclaimed!"[61]

God's chosen fast: Emancipation

At the core of this jeremiad on the national fasts was a message of hope if the Union changed its posture toward slavery. After citing Isaiah 58:6 again, White stated, "When our nation observes the fast which God has chosen, then will He accept their prayers as far as the war is concerned; but now they enter not into His ear."[62] This important statement deserves a detailed analysis.

The fast that "God has chosen," as White defined by Isaiah 58:6, was "to loose the bands of wickedness, to undo the heavy burdens, and to let the oppressed go free," and to "break every yoke"—in short, emancipation from slavery and the extermination of bondage in the land. The phrase "accept their prayers as far as the war is concerned" referred to the North's prayers for victory in the war as specified in Lincoln's proclamation when he called on Americans to petition God "for a blessing upon their present and prospective action" and "that our arms may be blessed and made effectual for the re-establishment of law, order and peace, throughout the wide extent of our country."[63] White's meaning was thus clear to her audience: "When," or *if*,[64] the nation turns the war into an effort to free the slaves, then—and only then—will God honor its national fasts and answer its prayers for military victory.

When this statement is coupled with two other remarks White made, the larger picture in her mind becomes clear. Shortly after the First Battle of Bull Run, she wrote that "God had this nation in His own hand, and would not suffer victories to be gained faster than He ordained, and would permit no more losses to the Northern men than in His wisdom He saw fit."[65] Although this statement described a kind of seesaw pattern of victories and losses, the United States would ultimately prevail. Later in the war, she affirmed what she had intimated so early following the First Battle of Bull Run: "I saw that God would not give the Northern army wholly into the hands of a rebellious people, to be utterly destroyed by their enemies."[66] Again, she indicated a severe struggle in the North's efforts to win the war but with ultimate victory in the end.

These two statements in connection with the comments on the fasts show that the larger picture in White's mind was that the North would ultimately prevail in the intense war with the South and that the struggle would end with the emancipation of the slaves. "She was convinced," wrote Lee Ellsworth Eusey, "that Heaven, whenever necessary, would work 'strangely' in military and political matters (as in the First Bull Run engagement) to accomplish its purposes, one of which was clearly the end of bondage in the land."[67]

But the way things looked to White early in the war, she could only say that "it looked . . . like an impossibility now for slavery to be done away. God alone can wrench the slave from the hand of his desperate, relentless oppressor."[68] A radical change had to take place in the war's aims and the Constitution. God would be the key agent in that change.

Proslavery actions of the government

In the meantime, the prayers for military victory on the September 26, 1861, national fast day were, in the seer's mind, canceled by the North's support of the institution of slavery: "Now they enter not into His ear." The word *now* in this phrase referred to the early months of the war in 1861 up to the time of the publishing of the vision in February 1862, when the actions of the federal government were focused on protecting the "peculiar" institution of slavery in the South.[69] In his first inaugural address on March 4, 1861, for example, President Lincoln had stated his administration's policy with regard to slavery: "I have no purpose, directly or indirectly, to interfere with the institution of slavery in the States where it exists. I believe I have no lawful right to do so, and I have no inclination to do so."[70]

Lincoln reinforced this statement with a nod to the March 2 action of Congress—passing the Corwin Amendment, or proposed Thirteenth Amendment—which, if ratified, would protect slavery where it existed forever.[71] Of this proposed amendment, he said, "I have no objection to its being made express, and irrevocable."[72] A disappointed Frederick Douglass wrote that the new president declared "his complete loyalty to slavery" and even denied "having the least '*inclination*' to interfere with slavery in the States."[73] "Thus Lincoln began his presidency with an offer to guarantee permanently the status of slavery in every state where it already existed," explained historian Paul D. Escott. "The existing institution, which he believed was '*wrong*, and ought to be restricted' from new territory, thus would have gained security for all time from federal interference."[74]

Another action of the government was the Crittenden-Johnson Resolutions passed by the Thirty-Seventh Congress two days after the Federal army's disaster at First Bull Run on July 21, 1861. These resolutions, fully in line with the Lincoln administration's stated position, emphasized that preservation of the Union was the main war goal and not the destruction of slavery.[75] Additionally, the Lincoln administration respected the property rights of slaveholders, which, as we have already seen, meant it upheld the Fugitive Slave Law.[76] Such were the federal government's policies and actions early in the war upheld by the president. In this state of things, declared White, God would not hear the nation's prayers. In fact, "He turns from them, they are disgusting to Him."[77] These are harsh words. But in White's understanding, the government was compromising with the slaveholders, and God could not and would not bless the nation as long as this was the case. All of the religious proclamations and actions were consequently meaningless in His sight.

It is important to note at this juncture that, although the Lincoln administration was concerned with preserving the Union rather than abolishing slavery, the Northern public was undergoing a change of mind since the disaster at First Bull Run. They were beginning to view the destruction of slavery as the way to end the war. "Public sentiment is undergoing a change," observed a *New York Times* correspondent at the end of August. "The same change of sentiment occurred rapidly in the army."[78] "Between August and December of 1861," concludes Chandra Manning, "soldier after soldier began to insist that since slavery had caused the war, only the destruction of slavery could end it."[79]

Abolitionists had declared this sentiment from the beginning of the war, especially Frederick Douglass: "The simple way, then, to put an end to the savage and desolating war now waged by the slaveholders, is to strike down slavery itself, the primal cause of that war." Although the government in Washington and the American people "may refuse to recognize it for a time," he declared, "the 'inexorable logic of events' will force it upon them in the end; that the war now being waged in this land is a war for and against slavery; and that it can never be effectually put down till one or the other of these vital forces is completely destroyed."[80] If our seer was correctly declaring God's will, then abolitionists, some Union soldiers and Northern citizens, were ahead of the government in beginning to understand what God wanted to do with the war and where the "inexorable logic of events" was headed.

John C. Frémont and emancipation

White ended her jeremiad on the national fast with a reference to another proslavery action of the government: "It is so managed that those who would undo the heavy burdens and break every yoke are placed under censure, or removed from responsible stations, or their lives are planned away by those who 'fast for strife and debate, and to smite with the fist of wickedness.' "[81] This statement most likely included the well-known incident involving John C. Frémont. Frémont had been the presidential candidate of the Republican Party in 1856, but now he was a Union general of the "Western Department." He issued a military proclamation on August 30, 1861, that declared all the slaves of the rebels in Missouri were emancipated by martial law. Lincoln, concerned that the proclamation would cause the Border

States still in the Union to join the Confederacy, urged Frémont to modify the order. Frémont refused. Consequently, Lincoln rescinded the order and then, due to his concerns about the soundness of the general's judgment, removed Frémont from command two months later.[82]

Abolitionists had applauded Frémont's proclamation but were appalled when Lincoln revoked it. William Lloyd Garrison called the president's decision a "serious dereliction of duty" and stormed in private that "even if Lincoln was 'six feet four inches high, he is only a dwarf in mind.'" Edmund Quincy said the reversal of the order "was one of those blunders which are worse than crimes."[83] Frederick Douglass believed that "Frémont was removed from his post when in the act of striking the foe."[84] White could have had other events in mind, but the Frémont case was the most well-known and publicized event of this nature.[85] As such, she stated her complaints about the federal government in the same spirit as that of the well-known abolitionists.

In one of President Lincoln's efforts to defend his decision about Frémont, he answered a critical letter from his friend Orville Browning and set forth his strategy for the war at that stage. He believed that Frémont's proclamation would lose Kentucky to the Confederacy. "Kentucky gone, we can not hold Missouri, nor, as I think, Maryland," he explained. Lincoln also stated his constitutional objection to Frémont's edict: "Can it be pretended that it is any longer the government of the U.S.—any government of Constitution and laws,—wherein a General, or a President, may make permanent rules of property by proclamation?"[86]

"The date of this letter to Browning," wrote James McPherson, "is ironic: September 22, 1861, one year to the day before Lincoln did precisely what he said a general or a president could not do—proclaim slaves in rebellious states 'forever free' unless those states returned to the Union within one hundred days. But the war intensified and took on a new character between those two Septembers that changed policies—and constitutional interpretations."[87] September 22, 1862, the day that Lincoln released the first draft of the Emancipation Proclamation, did indeed represent a major change in government policy with regard to the institution of slavery.

But it was only the beginning of a lengthy process—a process that included two and a half more years of war, with its battle victories and losses; the final draft of the Emancipation Proclamation being signed on January 1, 1863; the president's growth in understanding the war goals and slavery; the involvement of black soldiers in the

Northern war effort; the transition from a partial war to hard war, with its destruction of the Confederacy; constitutional debate; and, ultimately, the passing of the Thirteenth Amendment that abolished slavery.[88]

Once this process of emancipation was moving forward, it seems, according to White's visions, that the nation's relationship with God was moving forward, and Lincoln's proclamations for prayer and fasting that took place on April 30, 1863, and August 4, 1864, were evidently heard in heaven.

God's answers came slowly, though. Immediately after the national day of fasting and prayer on April 30, 1863, the North suffered a major loss at the Battle of Chancellorsville on May 1–3. But later that summer two major Northern victories—Gettysburg on July 1–3 and Vicksburg on July 4—could be considered answers to the national prayers. The third and last day of national fasting and prayer on August 4, 1864, occurred during a very difficult period in the war for the Union. Grant's army had suffered major losses during the summer months of fighting Lee's army and was stuck in a siege around Petersburg. Sherman was also stalled outside of Atlanta. No victories appeared to be in sight, and Northern morale was at its lowest point in the war. Within a month of the national fast day, however, Sherman took Atlanta on September 2, and the heart of Dixie fell. The fall of Atlanta was a major turning point in the war and set the North on the trajectory to ultimate victory.

Conclusion

The Civil War is full of ironies. As noted above, one of those ironies was the change in Lincoln's constitutional understanding between his September 22, 1861, letter to his friend Browning and the release of the first draft of his Emancipation Proclamation exactly one year later on September 22, 1862. Another irony was the direct contrast between the two Thirteenth Amendments. The first Thirteenth Amendment, also known as the Corwin Amendment, was passed by Congress on March 2, 1861, as a last-ditch effort to placate the South and contain secessionist sentiment. It proposed to prohibit Congress from interfering with "domestic institutions," the common euphemism for slavery, within the states. If ratified, it would have protected the South's institution of slavery forever.[89] But this proposed Thirteenth Amendment at the beginning of the war was rendered meaningless by the ratification of the second Thirteenth Amendment at the end of the war on December 6, 1865, which prohibited slavery in the United States of America.[90] In short, the irony is that the first

Thirteenth Amendment perpetuated slavery; the second one abolished it.

The turning point between these two amendments was Lincoln's Emancipation Proclamation, which was released on January 1, 1863. This significant event changed the war from a war for union only to a war for union and emancipation. Although the proclamation did not immediately free the slaves, it was the first crucial step that led to many other steps that ultimately destroyed slavery.[91] Declared by Lincoln to be "warranted by the Constitution upon military necessity," it was, nevertheless, "an act of justice" that invoked "the considerate judgment of mankind, and the gracious favor of Almighty God."[92] By invoking the favor of God, Lincoln "gave the war a noble, even a holy, purpose."[93]

Ellen White's jeremiad against the national fasts in 1861 was relevant to that early phase in the war when the federal government was focused only on saving the Union with no intention of freeing the slaves. But once the "inexorable logic of events" forced the government to change its policies about the war and make emancipation a war aim, or "necessity," then the nation began moving toward the "fast which God has chosen"—the fast that would "loose the bands of wickedness, . . . undo the heavy burdens, . . . let the oppressed go free, and . . . break every yoke" (Isaiah 58:6)—the emancipation of the slaves. As the nation began seriously moving in this direction, then "their prayers as far as the war is concerned" entered into God's ear, and He answered them.[94]

According to Arthur White, the grandson of James and Ellen White, "When a national fast was appointed for April 30, 1863, Seventh-day Adventists felt they could join in its observance, for the government was lining up more in harmony with the testimony of Isaiah 58."[95] This may have been true for many Adventists, but no evidence has been found that the church gave its official support to the national fast day. No part of the proclamation was published in the *Review and Herald*, and nothing was said, positively or negatively, about the fast day. Neither did Ellen White comment, one way or the other. The same is true of the August 4, 1864, day of national prayer. Evidently, the Adventists were following their own appointed days of prayer and fasting.[96] Nevertheless, they united their prayers with the rest of the North for a speedy end to the war and prayed specifically for deliverance of the slaves.

Significantly, Seventh-day Adventists gave their support to President Lincoln's proclamation for a day of thanksgiving on the last Thursday in November 1864 by printing it in the *Review and Herald*.[97] Moreover, after the war ended in May 1865, when the Northern armies had defeated the Confederacy and the Thirteenth Amendment had passed Congress (waiting to be ratified), the third annual session of the General Conference voted officially to "recognize civil government as ordained of God" and "acknowledge the justice of rendering tribute, custom, honor, and reverence to the civil power." In this action, they declared their loyalty as Seventh-day Adventists to the U.S. government.[98]

Chapter in a nutshell

James Buchanan declared a national fast on January 4, 1861, and Abraham Lincoln declared one on September 26, 1861, and asked the country to pray that God would bless their arms in the war with the South. Ellen White condemned these fasts and called them "an insult to Jehovah." At the time she published this statement in February 1862, the focus of the Northern government was to restore the Union and leave slavery alone in the South. Furthermore, as many slaves escaped from the South and ran to the Northern armies, many officers sent them back to slavery. A national fast at a time when slaves were seeking refuge behind Union lines but were being returned to their masters was, to White, hypocrisy. Other proslavery actions of the government troubled her as well. At the heart of this jeremiad, she stated, "When our nation observes the fast which God has chosen, then will He accept their prayers as far as the war is concerned; but now they enter not into His ear." The "fast which God has chosen" was that found in Isaiah 58:5–7, a reference to freeing the captives. Thus, God's fast was emancipation of the slaves. Not until this became the Union's purpose in the war would the prayers for military victory be heard. When emancipation did become the Union's war aim, the nation's relationship with God changed, and Lincoln's proclamations for prayer and fasting that took place on April 30, 1863, and August 4, 1864, were apparently heard in heaven.

A NATION IN GOD'S HANDS

1. This chapter was first presented as a session paper at the American Society of Church History: "Contact and Exchange Among SDAs During the American Civil War" (American Society of Church History, Minneapolis, Minnesota, April 16, 2015).

2. White, *Testimonies for the Church*, 1:257.

3. D. M. Canright, *Life of Mrs. E. G. White, Seventh-day Adventist Prophet: Her False Claims Refuted* (Salt Lake City, UT: Grant Shurtliff, 1998), 145.

4. Lincoln proclaimed prayer and fast days for September 26, 1861; April 30, 1863; and August 4, 1864 (prayer only); and set apart thanksgiving days on April 10, 1862 (this proclamation, issued on April 10, specified thanksgiving should occur during the nation's "next weekly assemblages" for "public worship," which would have been the following Sunday); August 6, 1863; November 26, 1863; and November 24, 1864. For the proclamations, see Basler, *The Collected Works of Abraham Lincoln*, 4:482, 483, 5:185, 186, 6:155, 156, 332, 333, 496, 497, 7:431, 432, 8:55, 56; and H. S. J. Sickel, *Thanksgiving: Its Source, Philosophy, and History with All National Proclamations and Analytical Study Thereof* (Philadelphia, PA: International Printing Company, 1940), 145–149, 162–166.

5. Davis proclaimed prayer and fast days for June 13, 1861; November 15, 1861; February 28, 1862; May 16, 1862 (prayer only); March 27, 1863; August 21, 1863; April 8, 1864; November 16, 1864 (prayer and worship only, and the event actually occurred on December 16); and March 10, 1865. He proclaimed a day of thanksgiving on September 18, 1862. For the proclamations, see James D. Richardson, *A Compilation of the Messages and Papers of the Confederacy Including the Diplomatic Correspondence* (Nashville, TN: United States Publishing Company, 1906), 103, 104, 135, 217, 218, 227, 228, 268, 269, 324, 325, 328, 412–414, 563–565, 567, 568.

6. Mark Noll, *The Civil War as a Theological Crisis* (Chapel Hill, NC: University of North Carolina Press, 2006), 18.

7. Ibid.

8. Sickel, *Thanksgiving*, 30.

9. For the proclamation, see ibid., 144.

10. Ibid., 32.

11. Basler, *The Collected Works of Abraham Lincoln*, 4:482.

12. Parrillo, "Lincoln's Calvinist Transformation," 240.

13. For discussion on Lincoln's evolving strategy for addressing the slavery issue, see Striner, *Father Abraham*, 117–150.

14. According to Harry S. Stout, Secretary of State William Seward most likely wrote the proclamation, but Lincoln was, nevertheless, intimately involved in the process. Stout, *Upon the Altar of the Nation*, 479n9. For a helpful analysis of the proclamation, see Lucas E. Morel, *Lincoln's Sacred Effort: Defining Religion's Role in American Self-Government* (Lanham, MD: Rowman & Littlefield, 2000), 108–110.

15. Horace Greeley, "Last Words to Hiram Ketchum," *New-York Daily Tribune*, September 7, 1860, 4.

16. McPherson, *The Negro's Civil War*, 4.

17. "The Two Great Political Parties," *Weekly Anglo-African*, March 17, 1860, 2.

18. Stout, *Upon the Altar of the Nation*, 77.

19. Sean A. Scott, *A Visitation of God: Northern Civilians Interpret the Civil War* (New York: Oxford University Press, 2011), 40.

20. Ibid., 40, 41.

21. James Simmons, quoted in ibid., 41. For a discussion on these four preachers and their sermons on the fasts, see ibid.

22. See Connell Bruce Bowen, "Fasting and Prayer: The Practice and Belief, 1855–1864" (term paper, Andrews University, 1975).

23. A. W. Spalding, *Origin and History of Seventh-day Adventists*, vol. 1 (Washington, DC: Review and Herald®, 1961), 327, 329.

24. White, *Testimonies for the Church*, 1:264.

25. See Uriah Smith, "The National Sin," *Review and Herald*, August 20, 1861, 94.

26. On Jotham Aldrich, see Michael Campbell, "Aldrich, Jotham M. and Jerusha B.," in Fortin and Moon, *The Ellen G. White Encyclopedia*, 290, 291; and Kevin M. Burton, "An Adventist Gentleman in Battle Creek: The Leadership of Jotham M. Aldrich, 1866–1868," *Journal of Asia Adventist Seminary* 16, no. 2 (2013): 127–152.

27. J. M. Aldrich, "The National Fast," *Review and Herald*, October 15, 1861, 157.

28. Ibid.

29. Ibid.

30. White, *Testimonies for the Church*, 1:257.

31. Ibid., 1:256.

32. Ibid.

33. See note 5 for the dates of the Confederate fasts.

34. White, *Testimonies for the Church*, 1:256, 257.

35. See, e.g., "Declaration of the National Anti-Slavery Convention," *The Liberator*, December 1833, quoted in Cain, *William Lloyd Garrison*, 91; and Foner and Taylor, *Frederick Douglass*, 450.

36. J. Alec Motyer, *The Prophecy of Isaiah: An Introduction and Commentary* (Downers Grove, IL: InterVarsity Press, 1993), 480.

37. Ibid., 481 (emphasis in the original).

38. White, *Testimonies for the Church*, 1:257.

39. John N. Oswalt, *The Book of Isaiah: Chapters 40–66*, New International Commentary on the Old Testament (Grand Rapids, MI: Eerdmans, 1998), 498.

40. White, *Testimonies for the Church*, 1:257.

41. Eric Foner, *Forever Free: The Story of Emancipation and Reconstruction* (New York: Vintage Books, 2005), 42, 43. For the background of African Americans and the coming of the war, see David Blight, "They Knew What Time It Was: African-Americans," in Gabor S. Boritt, ed., *Why the Civil War Came* (New York: Oxford University Press, 1996), 51–77.

42. McPherson, *The Negro's Civil War*, xvii.

43. See McPherson, "Who Freed the Slaves?" in *Drawn With the Sword*, 192–207; Ira Berlin, "Who Freed the Slaves? Emancipation and Its Meaning," in *Union and Emancipation: Essays on Politics and Race in the Civil War Era*, eds. David W. Blight and Brooks D. Simpson (Kent, OH: State University Press, 1997), 107–121. Both documents can be found in Vorenberg, *The Emancipation Proclamation*, 128–151.

44. James McPherson, *Tried by War: Abraham Lincoln as Commander in Chief* (New York: Penguin, Books, 2008), 58.

45. Vorenberg, *The Emancipation Proclamation*, 11.

46. McPherson, *Tried by War*, 58, 59. For the Confiscation Act document with a concise introduction, see "The First Confiscation Act, August 6, 1861," in Thomas C. Mackey, *A Documentary History of the American Civil War Era*, vol. 1 (Knoxville, TN: University of Tennessee Press, 2012), 47, 48.

47. See Lieutenant Colonel Schuyler Hamilton to Brigadier General McDowell, July 16, 1861: "The general-in-chief desires me to communicate to you that he has received from the President of the United States a second note dated to-day on the subject of fugitive slaves in which he asks: 'Would it not be well to allow owners to bring back those which have crossed the Potomac with our troops?' The general earnestly invites your attention to this subject knowing that you with himself enter fully into His Excellency's desire to carry out to the fullest all constitutional obligations." *Official Records of the Union and Confederate Armies*, ser. 2, vol. 1 (Washington, DC: Government Printing Office, 1894), 760. The constitutional obligations included obeying the Fugitive Slave Law.

48. General William S. Harney to Thomas T. Gantt, May 14, 1861, quoted in *Free at Last: A Documentary History of Slavery, Freedom, and the Civil War*, eds. Ira Berlin et al. (New York: New Press, 1992), 7, 8.

49. Major General George B. McClellan to Colonel B. F. Kelly, May 26, 1861, in *Official Records of the Union and Confederate Armies*, ser. 1, vol. 2, 46.

50. Endorsement from Colonel D. S. Miles, July 14, 1861, in *Official Records of the Union and Confederate Armies*, ser. 1, vol. 2, 299, 300.

51. Brigadier General William T. Sherman to Colonel Turchin, October 15, 1861, in *Official Records of the Union and Confederate Armies*, ser. 2, vol. 1, 774.

52. J. Sella Martin, quoted in McPherson, *The Negro's Civil War*, 23. For further documentation on the return of runaway slaves and the exclusion of them from Union lines, see Ira Berlin et al., *The Destruction of Slavery*, Freedom: A Documentary History of Emancipation, 1861–1867 1 (New York: Cambridge University Press, 1985), 417, 522, 523.

53. Berlin, *The Destruction of Slavery*, 269.

54. White, *Testimonies for the Church*, 1:257.

55. Ibid., 1:258.

56. Bruce Levine, *The Fall of the House of Dixie: The Civil War and the Social Revolution That Transformed the South* (New York: Random House, 2013), 93.

57. George E. Stephens, quoted in ibid.

58. Levine, *The Fall of the House of Dixie*, 93, 94.

59. Quoted in ibid., 94.

60. Berlin, *The Destruction of Slavery*, 269.

61. White, *Testimonies for the Church*, 1:257.

62. Ibid., 1:258.

63. Basler, *The Collected Works of Abraham Lincoln*, 4:482.

64. "When" functions as a conditional "if" in the grammar of the sentence.

65. White, *Testimonies for the Church*, 1:267.

66. Ibid., 1:365.

67. Eusey, "The American Civil War," 66.

68. White, *Testimonies for the Church*, 1:266.

69. This was actually the case until the autumn of 1862.

70. Basler, *The Collected Works of Abraham Lincoln*, 4:263. Although Lincoln personally opposed slavery, he understood the Constitution as legally protecting the institution, and thus he would not interfere with it in the Southern states. But the Constitution did not require slavery's expansion and here the president drew the line. See Paulsen and Paulsen, *The Constitution*, 159–161, for discussion.

71. See "Proposed Thirteenth Amendment, 1860," in Mackey, *A Documentary History of the American Civil War Era*, 1:33.

72. Basler, *The Collected Works of Abraham Lincoln*, 4:270.

73. Douglass, *Douglass' Monthly*, April 1861, quoted in Foner and Taylor, *Frederick Douglass*, 433 (emphasis in the original).

74. Paul D. Escott, *"What Shall We Do With the Negro?": Lincoln, White Racism, and Civil War America* (Charlottesville, VA: University of Virginia Press, 2009), 20, 21 (emphasis in the original).

75. For the resolution, see "The Crittenden-Johnson Resolutions on the Objects of the War, July 22, 1861," in Mackey, *A Documentary History of the American Civil War Era*, 1:45, 46. The resolutions were weakened, however, by the passing of the first Confiscation Act on August 6, 1861.

76. Basler, *The Collected Works of Abraham Lincoln*, 4:264, 269.

77. White, *Testimonies for the Church*, 1:258.

78. Quoted in Escott, *"What Shall We Do With the Negro?"* 31.

79. Manning, *What This Cruel War Was Over*, 45.

80. Douglass, *Douglass' Monthly*, May 1861, quoted in Foner and Taylor, *Frederick Douglass*, 448, 451.

81. White, *Testimonies for the Church*, 1:258.

82. For a comprehensive yet concise discussion of the Frémont affair, see James A. Rawley, *A Lincoln Dialogue*

(Lincoln, NE: University of Nebraska Press, 2014), 152–165.

83. Quotations in McPherson, *The Struggle for Equality*, 73.

84. Douglass, *Douglass' Monthly*, April 1862, quoted in Foner and Taylor, *Frederick Douglass*, 491.

85. See McPherson, *The Struggle for Equality*, 73, 74.

86. Basler, *The Collected Works of Abraham Lincoln*, 4:532. For an analysis of Lincoln's letter to Browning, see McPherson, *Tried by War*, 60.

87. McPherson, *Tried by War*, 60, 61.

88. For a thorough study of emancipation after the proclamation and the Thirteenth Amendment, see Vorenberg, *Final Freedom*.

89. See "Proposed Thirteenth Amendment, 1860," in Mackey, *A Documentary History of the American Civil War Era*, 1:33.

90. See "Thirteenth Amendment, Passed by Congress January 31, 1865, and Ratified December 6, 1865," in ibid., 1:149.

91. See Vorenberg, *Final Freedom*.

92. Basler, *The Collected Works of Abraham Lincoln*, 6:30. See also "President Abraham Lincoln, the Emancipation Proclamation, January 1, 1863," in Mackey, *A Documentary History of the American Civil War Era*, 2:329–332.

93. Vorenberg, *The Emancipation Proclamation*, 18.

94. White, *Testimonies for the Church*, 1:258.

95. Arthur White, *Ellen G. White*, 2:52.

96. Bowen, "Fasting and Prayer," 5–16.

97. "National Thanksgiving, the President's Proclamation," *Review and Herald*, November 8, 1864, 191. See also Basler, *The Collected Works of Abraham Lincoln*, 8:55, 56.

98. Uriah Smith, "Report of the Third Annual Session of the General Conference of S. D. Adventists," *Review and Herald*, May 23, 1865, 197.

CHAPTER 11

WHEN ENGLAND DOES DECLARE WAR

One of Ellen White's most controversial Civil War statements was made in the context of two sweeping paragraphs about foreign diplomatic relations between the United States and England.[1] Although a complex subject, she comprehended the essence of the situation and articulated it for readers in her February 1862 essay "The North and the South."[2] In the immediate context, she shifted from the subject of the national fasts to the relationship of England and the United States.[3] At the heart of her discussion is the following statement: "When England does declare war, all nations will have an interest of their own to serve, and there will be general war."[4] Because England never officially declared war on the United States during the Civil War, some readers have understood this sentence as a prediction that failed.[5]

Many others readers of this statement, however, have understood it as a possibility rather than a prediction. White's purpose was not so much to present new information or make a prediction about the war but to exhort the Adventist people to greater faithfulness in the "perils of the last days."[6] The larger context of the *Testimony* is about spiritual alertness during this time of calamity in the nation. The section "Great Distress Coming" immediately follows the comments on national fasts and England. Here she encouraged her readers that "God alone can be our shield and strength in this time of our national calamities." Her main burden was to prepare her readers for the return of Christ. "All heaven is astir," she declared. "The scenes of earth's history are fast closing. We are amid the perils of the last days. Greater perils are before us, and yet we are not awake."[7]

White's focus, therefore, was to "arouse the remnant people of God."[8] In light of the strife within the nation and the potential of war with England and the rest of Europe, she stated emphatically, "There is no help for us but in God; in this state of earth's confusion we can be composed, strong, or safe, only in the strength of living faith; nor can we be at peace, only as we rest in God and wait for His salvation."[9] This understanding was the driving force behind her comments on the possibility of a war with England and other nations, which could potentially cause "general war, general confusion" in the world.[10] The following analysis will show the sensibleness and conditional nature of White's comments about war with England.

Great Britain and the United States

Since the conclusion of the War of 1812, relations between Great Britain and the United States had been uneasy but were nevertheless maintained by economic interests.[11] By the mid-nineteenth century, the North American economy was central to Atlantic Ocean trade. Northern grain and Southern cotton established this Atlantic economy and created a unique relationship between the United States and England (and to a lesser degree, France and other European countries). The outbreak of the American Civil War disrupted this relationship and caused great distress in England and the rest of Europe.

From the beginning of its existence in February 1861, the Confederacy's chief objective was to secure diplomatic recognition from England first and then from other European powers. The South sent three commissioners abroad to Great Britain, France, Russia, and Belgium, with England as their priority. Once England recognized the Confederacy, Southern leaders hoped that France and other nations would follow suit. Official recognition would give the South a morale boost, financial loans from abroad, military and economic assistance, and possibly a military alliance that would foster permanent disunion and ultimate independence. This was a situation that the North could not and would not tolerate.

Because the American war caused great economic hardships in England, its own self-interest moved it to find a way to end the fighting as quickly as possible. Because it did not want to get entangled in the American war, on May 13, 1861, about a month into the hostilities, England decided on a declaration of neutrality that conferred legitimacy on the South as a belligerent (a nation at war). France followed England in June and declared neutrality as well.

The Lincoln administration was outraged over this situation. Conferring legitimacy on the South as a belligerent was one step toward diplomatic recognition of the Confederacy as a nation. Lincoln considered the Confederacy a rebellious faction within the United States rather than a separate nation warring against the United States. Recognition of the Confederacy would be a devastating blow to the Union that would justify secession and compromise the Constitution. Consequently, the Lincoln administration sought to block foreign intervention in various ways—one of which was to threaten England with war. On July 4, 1861, William H. Seward, Lincoln's secretary of state, delivered an ominous warning to a British news correspondent: "If any European Power provokes a war, we shall not shrink from it. A contest between Great Britain and the United States would wrap the world in fire."[12]

Lord Palmerston, Britain's prime minister, was in full control of British foreign policy at the start of the American Civil War and did not want a war with the United States. He counseled his foreign minister, Lord Russell, that Britain's "best and true policy seems to be to go on as we have begun, and to keep quite clear of the conflict between North and South."[13] No friend of the U.S. government, Palmerston believed that the South's separation from the North was an accomplished fact and that the North would not succeed in subduing the Southern rebellion. Most observers from England, France, and other countries also believed that the aggregate of eleven states, composed primarily of Anglicized people earnestly fighting for independence, could not be subjugated by the North. The Russian ambassador to England reported that "The English Government, at the bottom of its heart, desires the separation of North America into two republics, which will watch each other jealously and counterbalance one the other. Then England, on terms of peace and commerce with both, would have nothing to fear from either; for she would dominate them, restraining them by their rival ambitions."[14]

After the Union defeat at the First Battle of Bull Run, England and other foreign powers were more assured that the Confederacy would prevail and should be recognized as a separate nation. Before Bull Run, Lincoln had hoped to demonstrate to

Europe that he could subdue the rebellion. If his army could show their strength, the president believed, European powers would be less likely to side with the Confederacy. But the disaster at Bull Run shattered this hope. The Minister to Spain, Carl Schurz, reported to Lincoln from Spain that the "public press all over Europe is treating us with sneering contempt or granting us the small boon of a little pitiful sympathy." "Our prestige in Europe [is] gone," the diplomat told Lincoln, and the defeat at Bull Run was "bitter and humiliating in the extreme." Schurz then stated to Lincoln something he would not forget: "Nowhere can this disgrace be washed off but on the battlefields of America."[15]

Lincoln showed the Union's resiliency when he put General George McClellan in charge of building a great army to defeat the South during the fall of 1861. The Lincoln administration's commitment to the concept of the Union was something that the British failed to understand, even several years into the war. The United States would never allow the rebels in the South to split the Union, and they categorically rejected any interference from European powers. Thus, when England considered mediating in the war and recognizing the Confederacy in late August 1862, the Lincoln administration repeated its threat that to do so would be an act of war.

The *Trent* affair

The one time during the Civil War when England came very close to actually declaring war on the United States was during the *Trent* affair in the fall of 1861. Two Confederate commissioners, James Mason to England and John Slidell to France, were aboard the British ship *Trent*, cruising about 250 miles east of Havana, Cuba, when it was intercepted on November 8, 1861, by the U.S. warship *San Jacinto*. The *San Jacinto* commander, Captain Charles Wilkes, went against legal advice and took the two Confederate diplomats off the *Trent* and carried them to a Northern prison in Boston. In light of the recent Union losses at Bull Run and Ball's Bluff, the North needed good news and saw it in Wilkes's action on the high seas. He was hailed as a hero.

But the British saw this event as a violation of international law and an insult to their flag. Lord Palmerston declared in cabinet that he would not stand for this kind of treatment from America. Consequently, the British government ordered its warships to prepare for war and dispatched eight thousand troops to Canada, which was vulnerable to a United States invasion. The British cabinet then sent an official

THE "SAN JACINTO" STOPPING THE "TRENT."

The USS warship *San Jacinto* intercepting the British *Trent*.

demand to Washington that stated the United States must release the two prisoners and offer an apology for violating British neutrality. The United States and England were thus on the verge of war. In the end, though, both sides realized that a war was not in their best interests. Lincoln knew that the United States could only fight "one war at a time"[16] and searched for a way to back down without losing national honor. Fortunately, the British cooled down and dropped the demand for an apology, on the notification that Wilkes acted without authority from the U.S. government. Lincoln gave them this assurance and released the Confederate diplomats. Although this crisis was over, the United States and England would clash again over diplomatic recognition of the Confederacy.[17]

The object of the war and England

The *Trent* affair was the immediate historical context for Ellen White's discussion on England's contemplation of war on the United States. But her words also foreshadowed the conflict between England and the United States over recognition in late 1862. "I was shown," she penned, "that if the object of this war had been to exterminate slavery, then, if desired, England would have helped the North."[18] Because England had outlawed slavery within its empire in 1833 and had hosted world antislavery conventions in London during the early 1840s, it would have been a matter of conscience for it to aid the Union in an effort to rid slavery from the land, if requested. But this scenario never had a chance early in the war, because Lincoln had made it clear not only to the North and the South but to the whole world in his March 4, 1861, inaugural address that, as president, he had "no purpose, directly or indirectly, to interfere with the institution of slavery in the States where it exists."[19] His purpose, rather, was to save the Union. According to historian Howard Jones, "By bowing to domestic pressure and steering around the slavery issue, Lincoln relieved the British from having to make a decision between their moral commitment to antislavery and their economic interests in Southern cotton. With moral questions cast aside, economic considerations became paramount."[20]

It is important to note that Ellen White intended this vision not so much as new information for her readers but as part of the mounting evidence that the Union was divided over the issue of slavery, and England's lack of support was a consequence of this division. "England fully understands the existing feelings in the Government," she explained, "and that the war is not to do away [with] slavery, but merely to preserve the Union; and it is not for her interest to have it preserved."[21] As noted above by the Russian ambassador to England, the English government would have preferred for the Union to be split into the North and the South and to counterbalance each other, "for she would dominate them, restraining them by their rival ambitions."[22]

In order to gain recognition by England, the Confederacy argued that the sectional struggle was not about slavery but about its quest for independence against the oppressive Northern government. Additionally, it focused on the British economic need for cotton as a uniting factor between it and its Atlantic cousin. Senator Louis T. Wigfall of Texas had declared in a famous speech "that cotton is King, and that he waves his scepter not only over these thirty-three States, but over the island of Great Britain and over continental Europe." In the long run, the Confederacy had overestimated the power of cotton, but the British nevertheless saw it as an economic factor and turned a blind eye to the American issue of slavery.[23] Howard Jones perceptively noted that "slavery was the great issue standing before the three principals—Union, Confederacy, and England—and yet no one seemed willing to address it. Although slavery was integrally connected to almost every issue leading to the Civil War, many Americans from both North and South sidestepped the peculiar institution and insisted that other matters were more decisive."[24]

Hypocrisy of the United States

In light of this situation, Ellen White castigated the hypocrisy of the nation:

> Our Government has been very proud and independent. The people of this nation have exalted themselves to heaven, and have looked down upon monarchical governments, and triumphed in their boasted liberty, while the institution of slavery, that was a thousand times worse than the tyranny exercised by monarchial governments, was suffered to exist and was cherished. In this land of light a system is cherished which allows one portion of the human family to enslave another portion, degrading millions of human beings to the level of the brute creation. The equal of this sin is not to be found in heathen lands.[25]

In this sweeping jeremiad, our seer captured the contradiction of slavery with America's political ideals. In contrast to monarchial governments, America's

Declaration of Independence declared that "all men are created equal, that they are endowed by their Creator with certain unalienable Rights, that among these are Life, Liberty and the pursuit of Happiness."[26] But all men were actually not free to pursue these lofty American ideals; the black race was in bondage to the American slave master.[27] The slavery issue was thus a deadly snake coiled up under the table upon which the Declaration of Independence was signed.[28] That chattel slavery "was suffered to exist and was cherished" in this "land of light" was the height of hypocrisy in White's mind—not only to the world but before Heaven.

In the context of America's lofty view of freedom and equality of all men, White declared "the equal of this sin is not to be found in heathen lands." Although slavery had existed in other countries, it had a unique flavor of its own in the American South. In Haiti, Brazil, and many of the Spanish colonies, for example, slavery was not entirely defined by race.[29] But in the American South, "white skin was the distinguishing badge of mind and intellect. Black skin was the sign that a given people had been providentially designed to serve as menial laborers."[30] Additionally, treatment of American slaves differed from other countries. According to David Brion Davis, a specialist in the history of slavery, "if an African slave had been given an informed choice of location, he or she might well have preferred Jamaica to most parts of North America. In Jamaica such a slave would be surrounded by his or her own people, would share in their developing culture, and might even have an opportunity to escape to a protected maroon [an independent African settlement] community. In North America the same African would be outnumbered by whites and placed under their constant supervision, care, and control."[31] Southern proslavery ideology also took on its own distinctive argumentation politically, economically, legally, theologically, and sociologically.[32] Slavery was America's "peculiar institution," and its equal was not to be found in the slavery of other countries during the nineteenth century.[33]

The next paragraph of Ellen White's discussion contained three of her most controversial statements about the Civil War. First, "This nation will yet be humbled into the dust" is often interpreted as the destruction of the United States, which didn't happen. Second, "When England does declare war" is interpreted as a prediction that England would declare war on the United States, which didn't happen. And third, "Had our nation remained united it would have had strength, but divided it must fall" is interpreted as though our nation would remain divided and fall in the

Civil War, which didn't happen.[34] But each of these interpretations fails to take into consideration the literary and historical context of the paragraph.

"Humbled into the dust"

Continuing the thought from the previous paragraph in which White penned a concise jeremiad on the hypocrisy of the United States in harboring slavery, she began this controversial paragraph thus: "Said the angel: 'Hear, O heavens, the cry of the oppressed, and reward the oppressors double according to their deeds.' "[35] This cryptic statement of judgment indicated that the "cry of the oppressed"—the slaves—had been heard and that God would "reward the oppressors [the U.S. government] double according to their deeds." The double punishment probably referred to punishment on the "North for so long suffering its [slavery's] overreaching and overbearing influence," and "the South for the sin of slavery."[36] It also referred to the intensity of national suffering and massive loss of life during the war.

The next sentence addressed the North: "This nation will yet be humbled into the dust." This statement took on a predictive form at the outset of the paragraph. The phrase "humbled into the dust" (only used here), when compared with similar phrases in White's writings—"humbled in the dust" and "humbled in the very dust"—never indicated total destruction of a person or nation. Rather, these phrases referred to the destruction of pride and ambition, a humbling and often humiliating experience.[37] Humiliation best fits the context here, because the previous paragraph noted that "our government has been very proud and independent," and the people "have exalted themselves to heaven."[38] The Union had already experienced great humiliation at the First Battle of Bull Run on July 21, 1861, and, according to this statement, would "yet" face another humiliating experience.

Just *how* the nation would be "humbled into the dust" or humiliated was not specified, but it evidently had something to do with England and other nations, as the following sentences pointed out: "England is studying whether it is best to take advantage of the present weak condition of our nation, and venture to make war upon her. She is weighing the matter, and trying to sound other nations."[39] This statement accurately comprehended how forthcoming events in the war would humble America "in the dust" before other nations.

America's "present weak condition" that England wanted to exploit was obviously the Civil War—the South's rebellion against the North. The nation as a whole was divided and was weakened by the war within itself. But even worse, the North itself was divided. Ellen White addressed this issue earlier in this *Testimony* when she wrote about the proslavery elements in the Union: "It seems impossible to have the war conducted successfully, for many in our own ranks are continually working to favor the South."[40] England was very aware of this situation within the Union, as White explained later: "England is acquainted with the diversity of feeling among those who are seeking to quell the rebellion. She well knows the perplexed condition of our Government; she has looked with astonishment at the prosecution of this war—the slow, inefficient moves, the inactivity of our armies, and the ruinous expenses of our nation."[41]

As England studied and weighed the matter of exploiting the weakness of the United States, it did so with a different posture than before the *Trent* affair. Historian D. P. Crook made the astute observation that after the *Trent* crisis, "The British now had a ready-made blueprint for war with America; and this placed them in an insuperably stronger military and diplomatic position *vis-à-vis* the United States than at any time prior to the *Trent* affair. A case could be put that the outcome of the settlement—far from smoothing Anglo-American relations and reinforcing a policy of British neutrality—encouraged a more truculent British disposition in 1862 toward joining in projects for mediation of the war or recognition of the South than would have been the case if the *Trent* affair had not occurred."[42]

Consequently, the British adopted a wait-and-see attitude on the battlefield. If the Confederacy achieved enough victories and showed that the Union could not defeat it, then England decided it would intervene and provide diplomatic recognition.

America humbled before the nations at Second Bull Run

Between June and September 1862, military events in the Eastern theater favored the Confederacy. During the Seven Days Battles of June 25–July 1, 1862, Lee drove McClellan's forces back from Richmond, which was a major defeat for the Union. Then Lee smashed Pope's troops at Second Bull Run (Manassas) in late August (August 28–30). Both the British and French remembered the Union's humiliating defeat at First Bull Run a year earlier in July 1861. To them, it was evidence that the Union could not defeat the Confederacy. According to Howard Jones, "British intervention appeared certain after the Union's second defeat at Bull Run in the autumn of 1862. Its attempt to defeat the Confederacy had again proved impossible, a truth that seemed obvious to contemporaries three thousand miles across the Atlantic. Surely the Lincoln administration would recognize the futility of continuing a war that could destroy both antagonists. Southern separation posed the only viable alternative to mounting atrocities."[43] Lord Palmerston noted the following to his foreign secretary, Lord Russell, about Second Bull Run: "The Federals got a very complete smashing, and it seems not altogether unlikely that still greater disasters await them, and that even Washington or Baltimore may fall into the hands of the Confederates. If this should happen, would it not be time for us to consider whether . . . England and France might not address the contending parties and recommend an arrangement upon the basis of separation?"

"If either or both antagonists rejected mediation, the prime minister added, the two European governments should 'acknowledge the independence of the South as an established fact.' "[44] Thus, according to Jones, "Second Bull Run encouraged the Palmerston ministry to consider southern separation as the key to stopping a war that the Union must accept as over. In light of their growing desperation, the prime minister and his foreign secretary refused to believe that Washington had any resiliency left. Palmerston and Russell thus linked either approval or rejection of mediation by the Union with an admission to independence that, by definition, pointed to ultimate recognition of a Confederate nation.[45]

Eduard Thouvenel, the French foreign minister, believed that there was "not a reasonable statesman in Europe" who thought that the North could win the American war. "A joint offer [of mediation] by several powers"—Britain, France, Russia, and possibly Austria and Prussia—was also under discussion as news of Confederate victories filtered across the Atlantic. Henry Adams and Thomas Dudley, the American diplomats in England, both reported that all Europe was against the United States.[46]

This humiliating situation for the Union certainly fit Ellen White's understanding that America would be "humbled into the dust" before England and the rest of Europe. Humiliation would come again on the battlefield with the following Federal defeats: Fredericksburg on December 13, 1862; Chancellorsville on May 1–4, 1863; and the battle losses during the summer of 1864 (Cold Harbor, Kennesaw Mountain, and the Crater, for example), which was the point of lowest Union morale in the entire war.

The intervention crisis after Antietam

The British and other European powers had underestimated the determination of the Lincoln administration, however. "Its remarkable resiliency refueled its determination to stave off intervention while resuming its efforts to win the war."[47] Palmerston thus felt uneasy about pushing mediation through, in light of the Union's stubborn insistence to stay in the fight. Seward's warnings about intervention as an act of war also vexed his mind. Jones again best articulated the situation in September 1862: "Thus the mediation effort came to a temporary standstill as Palmerston opted to await word of additional southern conquests on the battlefield. The Union would finally realize what most contemporaries already knew—that the Confederacy had demonstrated its separate status at First Bull Run and had now reaffirmed that truth by holding Richmond after the setbacks at Forts Henry and Donelson. Second Bull Run had driven home this point, and the two armies under Lee and McClellan would shortly engage each other again. What harm could come from postponing mediation a few days?"[48] And wait they did until news from the Battle of Antietam arrived.

On September 17, the huge armies of Lee and McClellan clashed in the Battle of Antietam, which would go down in military history as the bloodiest single day in the Civil War. It was a marginal victory for the Union and helped restore their morale, which had been badly shaken at the Second Battle of Bull Run. Several days later, on September 22, Lincoln released the first draft of his Emancipation Proclamation. Consequently, the British decided to wait before making any diplomatic move. Although mediation was on hold for the time being, it was still on the table as a possibility. "Contrary to the traditional story," explained Jones, "the battle of Antietam and the Emancipation Proclamation did not stop the British movement toward intervention; rather, they only slowed down a process that once again had gotten under way." Lord Palmerston preferred waiting, but his foreign secretary, Lord Russell, "sought an immediate mediation leading to an armistice that culminated in recognition."[49]

Chancellor of the Exchequer William E. Gladstone agreed with Russell and declared in a famous but controversial speech on October 7, 1862, "We may have our own opinions about slavery, we may be for or against the South; but there is no doubt that Jefferson Davis and other leaders of the South have made an army; they are making, it appears, a navy; and they have made what is more than either—they have made a nation." Thus, he dramatically concluded, "We may anticipate with certainty the success of the Southern States as far as regards their separation from the North."[50] This speech "crystallized the interventionist issue, causing a political firestorm in which the ministry's opponents accused the chancellor of meddling in other countries' domestic affairs and risking England's involvement in the America war."[51]

England's fear if it commenced war abroad

The second Earl of Granville, a liberal British statesman who opposed British intervention in the American Civil War, warned that any form of intervention would cause England to drift into war with the United States. "The North will become desperate," he warned, "and even against their intentions will give us innumerable *casus belli* [cause or reason for war]." Granville also warned that a war, "whether the French went with us or not," would adversely impact British-French relations.[52] "Granville's point was unassailable," according to D. P. Crook. "An Anglo-American war would not necessarily be a localized affair. It could throw the whole of Europe into the melting pot."[53] Granville expressed the concern of many in England regarding other nations. If England got into a war with the United States, it would be at risk in regard to its European neighbors, particularly France and Russia, who, although they agreed to work with Britain on intervention in the Civil War, were no friends of Britain, and some of them would exploit any opportunity to see it weakened on the international scene.[54]

The real crisis point of European intervention in the American Civil War came in early November 1862, when Napoleon III of France proposed that Britain, France, and Russia come together on an armistice plan. British Secretary of State for War George Cornewall Lewis criticized the plan and argued persuasively that intervention was fraught with many perils—namely, war with England. With numerous powers involved in the intervention, disagreement on how the process should unfold would occur, and then sides would be taken. England might stand alone, he argued. Thus, the "Englishmen debated the prospects of war with the north at length," and eventually concluded that it would not be in their best interest to risk a difficult, expensive, and unpopular war.[55] The greatest threat of England's involvement in the American Civil War, with its inevitable outcome of war, diminished after this time. Although there would be a few more diplomatic crises between Britain and the United States, the worst crisis in late 1862 had passed.[56]

In light of the scenario presented above, Ellen White's words that England was "studying whether it is best to take advantage of the present weak condition of our nation, and venture to make war upon her," and that "she is weighing the matter, and trying to sound other nations" most accurately described in lay terms the situation that developed in the latter part of 1862. Although her comments were brief and sweeping, they comprehended the complexity of Civil War diplomacy between the United States, England, and other nations. England did indeed fear that "if she should commence war abroad, that she would be weak at home, and that other nations would take advantage of her weakness."[57]

White also grasped the larger international scene: "Other nations are making quiet yet active preparations for war, and are hoping that England will make war with our nation, for then they would improve the opportunity to be revenged on her for the advantage she has taken of them in the past and the injustice done them."[58] Although it is another broad, sweeping statement, it did accurately set forth the feelings of France and, especially, Russia at the time. Jones again provided a helpful analysis of the situation:

> In actuality, European politics argued against British involvement in the American Civil War. The London ministry's endemic distrust of the French—in particular, the unpredictable and opportunistic Napoleon III—raised fear that its involvement in America or elsewhere would free him to engage in nefarious schemes wherever possible. Napoleon's interest in reestablishing French holdings on the Continent was legend; his ancestral loyalty drove him to restore a French Empire in the New World that would have the residual effect of enhancing his stature in the Old; his push for building a larger navy and broadening his involvement in the Mediterranean provided ample warning of an emerging challenge to maritime matters that England had long considered its special province. Then came reports in early 1861 of some form of private agreement between France and Russia that threatened to change the balance of power in Europe by healing the wounds of the Crimean War [Russia was defeated by France and Britain]. British involvement in the American crisis could take place only at heavy risk to the empire.[59]

Thus, Britain had good reason for fears that involvement in the American war would weaken its status on the world stage.[60]

Prediction that England would declare war on the United States

After describing England's diplomatic problems with other nations, White made a brief reference to Her Majesty's internal factions: "A portion of the queen's subjects are waiting a favorable opportunity to break their yoke." Ellen White then contrasted this with a major conditional statement: "But if England thinks it will pay, she will not hesitate a moment to improve her opportunities to exercise her power and humble our nation."[61] As we have seen above, England considered the risk of war with the United States greater than the benefits gained from supporting the Confederacy. Although it came close to intervening in the war during late 1862, Britain backed off when the Confederacy lost at Antietam and decided ultimately that it would not pay. Would England have intervened and exercised its power by diplomatically recognizing the Confederacy if Britain had thought it would pay, as White had proposed?

Interestingly, recognized Civil War historian James McPherson contributed a chapter to the provocative book *What If? The World's Foremost Military Historians Imagine What Might Have Been*, in which he imagined with expert analysis the scenario if the Union had lost another major battle after the Second Bull Run disaster. He set forth an imaginary situation in which the United States was essentially defeated and Britain saw no risk in recognizing the Confederacy. McPherson depicted the following conversation:

> The British minister to the United States, Lord Lyons, presented Secretary of State Seward with an offer signed by the governments of Great Britain, France, Russia, and Austria-Hungary to mediate an end to the war on the basis of separation. "We will not admit the division of the Union at any price," Seward responded. "There is no possible compromise." Very well, responded Lyons. In that case Her Majesty's Government will recognize the independence of the Confederate States of America. Other European governments will do the same. "This is not a matter of principle or preferences," Lyons told Seward, "but of fact."[62]

Thus, in this imaginary event, England exercised her power in recognizing the Confederacy, because it would be risk free and would permanently sever the United States.

This interesting scenario didn't happen, of course. But it wasn't out of the realm of possibility. In the wording of White's statement, the conditional *if* set the context for the next, often-misunderstood sentence: "When England does declare war, all nations will have an interest of their own to serve, and there will be general war, general confusion."[63] The immediate context of this sentence was cast in a conditional framework. Notice the conditional character of the preceding sentences: "She fears, *if* she should commence war abroad, that she would be weak at home," and "but *if* England thinks it will pay." These statements are then followed by the main sentence: "When England does declare war . . ."

Francis D. Nichol effectively explained the grammar at work here:

It is evident that Mrs. White is here using the word "when" as a synonym for "if," which is good English. In fact, if we do not thus understand the word "when" in this connection, we have an unusual situation—a series of problematical "ifs" is followed by a simple statement that England is going to declare war. Thus Mrs. White's last sentence would make pointless her preceding sentences.

A similar use of the word "when" is found on the preceding page in her work: "When our nation observes the fast which God has chosen, then will he accept their prayers as far as the war is concerned." No one, least of all the critic, will argue that the word "when" in this connection introduces a simple statement concerning a future fact that will undebatably happen.[64]

Thus, Nichol explained, "With the clause 'when England does declare war,' understood as synonymous with 'if England does declare war,' the statement changes from a prediction to a statement of mere possibility, but a possibility, however, whose full potentialities many might not realize."[65]

A careful analysis of the sentence in its entirety reveals that the main point is not so much *if* England declared war on the United States, but what would be the *result* if England declared war on the United States. In the event that England did declare war, "all nations will have an interest of their own to serve, and there will be general war, general confusion."[66] In other words, a war between England and the United States during the Civil War era would have been disastrous on the world stage. White's contemporaries agreed. Britain's *The Economist*, for example, warned that "a war between England and the *Northern* states of America would be the most affecting misfortune which could happen to civilization."[67] Seward's words, quoted earlier, also cast a similar tone: "A contest between Great Britain and the United States would wrap the world in fire."[68]

Howard Jones believes that British intervention in the American Civil War "would almost certainly have led to a third war between the Atlantic nations with repercussions reaching well into the twentieth century."[69] Allan Nevins prognosticated in his *War for the Union* what the implications would be for the world if England and the United States had gone to war:

Consequences of the greatest magnitude hung upon the deepening tension of European-American and especially Anglo-American relations in the late summer of 1862. It is hardly too much to say that the future of the world as we know it was at stake.

A conflict between Great Britain and America would have crushed all hope of the mutual understanding and growing collaboration which led up to the practical alliance of 1917–18, and the outright alliance which began in 1941. It would have made vastly more difficult if not impossible the coalition which defeated the Central Powers in the First World War, struck down Nazi tyranny in the Second World War, and established the unbreakable front of Western freedom against Communism. Anglo-French intervention in the American conflict would probably have confirmed the splitting and consequent weakening of the United States; might have given French power in Mexico a long lease, with the ruin of the Monroe Doctrine; and would perhaps have led to the Northern conquest of Canada. The forces of political liberalism in the modern world would have received a disastrous setback. No battle, not Gettysburg, not the Wilderness, was more important than the contest waged in the diplomatic arena and the forum of public opinion.[70]

When Ellen White's sentence "When England does declare war" is correctly understood as what could have happened if England and the United States went to war, then it is sensible as well as sobering. When she wrote, the North had just passed through the crisis of the *Trent* affair with England, and the explosive issue of Confederate recognition was looming on the horizon. Thus, the situation facing the U.S. government and all Northern citizens in 1862 was grave. There is no prediction here about England—only dangerous and disastrous possibilities *if* things went wrong and the War Between the States broke out into a war with the world. Fortunately, this never happened.

"Divided it must fall"

"England," White continued, "is acquainted with the diversity of feeling" and the "perplexed condition" in the U.S. government. "She has looked with astonishment at the prosecution of this war—the slow, inefficient moves, the inactivity of our armies, and the ruinous expenses of our nation."[71] This statement clearly reflected the problems that the Northern government had faced during the autumn of 1861 and continued to face into the next year: General McClellan's massive Army of the Potomac was well organized, but he refused to engage it in battle; the threat of Western secession cast its shadow over the North; President Lincoln had to deal with allegations of treason in the government; the nation's financial troubles mounted with the effort to equip the army and navy; and the Southern-sympathizing Copperheads were on the rise and sought to peacefully stop the war with slavery still intact.[72] These problems were open for other nations to ponder.

In this context, White explained, "The weakness of our Government is fully open before other nations, and they now conclude that it is because it was not a monarchial government, and they admire their own government, and look down, some with pity, others with contempt, upon our nation, which they have regarded as the most powerful upon the globe."[73] The American republic had risen to great power in the world, and monarchial European nations could not ignore the power of its democracy—until the Civil War began. "I believe that the dissolution of the Union is inevitable," exclaimed the Earl of Shrewsbury, "and that men before me will live to see an aristocracy established in America." A South African English-language newspaper declared in June 1861 that American's "boasted republic" had "fallen asunder at the first touch." A year later, a Spanish journal claimed that the "flaming theories of democracy" had failed now that Americans were "butchering each other." The Parisian newspaper *La patrie* in August 1861 savored that "the work of

George Washington has come to an end." Such were the sentiments of other nations around the time White penned these words.[74]

Ellen White's final sentence completes the thought of the entire paragraph by continuing the conditional element: "Had our nation remained united it would have had strength, but divided it must fall."[75] The first clause is clearly conditional with its use of the word *had* as an equivalent to *if,* which makes the "if" clause the past perfect tense. The phrase "would have had strength" is the conditional perfect in the "then" clause.[76] It could thus read, "If our nation remained united [then] it would have had strength." In light of the previous sentence, the meaning broadens from England to include the world stage. If our nation had remained united, White contended, then it would have remained strong before the other nations.

The word *but* indicates that the second part of the sentence is a contrasting clause: "but divided it must fall." The word *divided,* used as a past-participial adjective here, is parallel to the past perfect tense of "had our nation remained united" in the first clause; and the present tense "it must fall" is parallel to the conditional perfect "it would have had strength." Visually, the sentence looks like this:

> Had our nation remained united it would have had strength,
> **but** divided it must fall

The parallelism indicates that "divided" can be understood to mean "in its divided state," or "if it remains divided"; "it must fall" is a statement of certainty that in this divided state, the nation will inevitably fall and lose its strength before the nations. The shift to the present tense in the contrasting clause indicates that White was making a factual statement of the situation as she understood it at that time. She thus completed the conditional thought in the earlier sentences about England. If our nation went to war with England in the Union's divided state, its fall would be part of the disastrous result. No one knows the extent to which the nation would have fallen. But it was a possibility in the winter of 1862.

So here we have a conditional statement in the first clause that is followed by a statement of fact: in its divided state, the nation must fall. It's simple common sense, really. In its state of civil war—the North against the South, and even the North against itself—the nation was weak and could not remain standing as a world power. England and other nations would take advantage of a permanently divided America, as noted earlier. Remaining in this fragmented state, it would inevitably fall from its status as the greatest nation on the globe. Thus, the latter clause is not a prediction (the nation *will* fall) but rather a statement of fact or certainty: if the nation continues in its divided state, it must fall (or it certainly should fall). Put another way, White was saying that, divided as it is, this nation cannot remain standing on the world stage—it *must* fall.

The allusion to Abraham Lincoln's "House Divided" speech must have been noted by White's readers. On June 16, 1858, during the Republican state convention in Springfield, Illinois, when Lincoln was nominated as a candidate for the U.S. Senate, he gave his "A House Divided" speech. It was during this speech that Lincoln stated some of his most famous, oft-quoted lines: "A house divided against itself cannot stand," he declared. "I believe this government cannot endure, permanently half *slave* and half *free*. I do not expect the Union to be *dissolved*—I do not expect the house to *fall*—but I *do* expect it will cease to be divided. It will become *all* one thing or *all* another."[77] White's audience would have been familiar with this speech, as most of it was published in the *Review and Herald*.[78] But even if they somehow missed this connection, they certainly would have noted the allusion to Jesus' words (cf. Matt. 12:25; Mark 3:25).

No one understood Lincoln's speech as a prediction that the nation would fall. He simply declared that when a nation is divided against itself, it cannot stand. White said the same thing in different words—"divided it must fall." Like Lincoln, White believed the nation would survive this crisis, but she didn't know how at the time. A year earlier, in her August 1861 essay on the war, for example, she stated clearly that "God had this nation in His own hand, and would not suffer . . . more losses to the Northern men than in His wisdom He saw fit, to punish them for their sin [of tolerating slavery]."[79] A year after her January 1862 vision, she declared in the context of the Fredericksburg disaster, "God would not give the Northern army wholly into the hands of a rebellious people, to be utterly destroyed by their enemies."[80] Moreover, in the context of *Testimonies for the Church*, volume 1, both of these statements occur *after* the paragraph ending with "divided it must fall."[81] Clearly, then, White did not believe or predict that the Union would ultimately fall. She only presented this as a disastrous *possibility* if the situation remained unchanged.

But the situation did change. The North eventually united in its effort to defeat the South, and Congress passed the Thirteenth Amendment to abolish slavery in the land. England and the other nations backed off and never intervened. Once the war ended and the South reentered the Union, the unity of the United States was secure and strong. No one really knows what would have happened if the nation had remained divided as it was during the Civil War. But many would agree with White that if America stayed that way, it would inevitably have fallen from the global status it had before the war, and its relationship with other world powers would have been forever changed.

Conclusion

In addition to her "revelations" about the United States and England, Ellen White must have read the papers about the war and discussed them with her husband and other associates. This combined information evidently formed the basis for her writings about the war. As noted at the beginning of this chapter, her purpose was not to present new information or make predictions but to present a spiritual perspective on the present state of the war. In her understanding, the U.S. government's internal division on the issue of slavery would result in national humiliation ("humbled into the dust") and a potential fall in its international status ("divided it must fall"). This chapter has shown how this interpretation of the war fits the historical events that occurred in regard to the diplomatic relations between the United States and England.

Critics have exploited several of White's statements about England and the United States without reference to the literary and historical context of these statements. The fact that these statements were published openly in the *Testimony* series, during and after the war, indicated that the Adventist pioneers did not understand these statements as wild predictions that were never fulfilled. On the contrary, at the time Ellen White published her third Civil War vision in February 1862, these statements carried a special relevance for those who lived through the events. Years after the war ended, those Adventists who had experienced the events could see the veracity of the statements from the hindsight of history. They viewed these comments about England as neither ridiculous nor naive but as earnest, frank, and historically verified.[82]

A year later in January 1863, Ellen White published her final essay on the war. Several things had taken place during the war in 1862 that affected the Adventists, and White addressed them in *Testimony for the Church, No. 9.*

Chapter in a nutshell

After her statements about the national fasts, Ellen White turned to the subject of the relationship between England and the United States. In two sweeping paragraphs, she captured the essence of the foreign diplomatic relations between these two countries. In this context, she made three often-misunderstood statements. First, she declared that "this nation will yet be humbled into the dust." Second, "When England does declare war, all nations will have an interest of their own to serve, and there will be general war, general confusion." Third, "Had our nation remained united it would have had strength, but divided it must fall." These statements must be understood in the context of the tensions between England and the United States during the Civil War. England had pondered intervening in the conflict by recognizing the Confederacy as a separate nation, but the Lincoln administration had made it clear that to do so would be taken as an act of war. England would have preferred that America remain divided so it could have more control over the nation.

The first statement is best applied to the Union's loss to the Confederacy at the Battle of Second Manassas, where the North was "humbled into the dust." With regard to the second statement, England never officially recognized the Confederacy but came close. White's statement about war with England is more a possibility than a prediction. The grammar presents a condition: "If" England and the United States went to war, then the consequences would be profound for the Civil War era and thereafter. White only presents the possibility of that scenario: "general war, general confusion" all over the world. Fortunately, this never happened because England ultimately chose not to recognize the Confederacy and remain neutral. The third statement, "divided it must fall," is best viewed as a statement of certainty that reflected White's understanding at the time: if the nation continued in its divided state of North against South and North against North, it *must* fall. But the North united in its effort and defeated the South with its slavery, and the nation stood strong. Thus, when understood in their historical contexts, these statements are sensible as well as sobering.

1. This chapter was first presented as a paper at the Eleventh South American Biblical-Theological Symposium, in UNASP, São Paulo, Brazil, on May 1, 2015.

2. White, *Testimonies for the Church*, 1:253–260.

3. Ibid., 1:258–260.

4. Ibid., 1:259.

5. See, e.g., Canright, *Life of Mrs. E. G. White,* 144–149.

6. White, *Testimonies for the Church*, 1:260.

7. Ibid.

8. Ibid., 1:263.

9. Ibid., 1:262.

10. Ibid., 1:259.

11. The following section, and throughout the rest of the chapter, has been drawn from the following two sources: Howard Jones, *Union in Peril: The Crisis Over British Intervention in the Civil War* (Chapel Hill, NC: University of North Carolina Press, 1992), 1–36; and Howard Jones, *Blue and Gray Diplomacy: A History of Union and Confederate Foreign Relations* (Chapel Hill, NC: University of North Carolina, 2010), 1–45.

12. William H. Seward to William H. Russell, quoted in Jones, *Blue and Gray Diplomacy*, 58.

13. Lord Palmerston, quoted in Kevin Peraino, *Lincoln in the World: The Making of a Statesman and the Dawn of American Power* (New York: Crown Publishers, 2013), 136.

14. Baron de Brunow to Prince Gortchakov, January 1, 1861, quoted in B. B. Sideman and Lillian Friedman, eds., *Europe Looks at the Civil War* (New York: Orion Press, 1969), 20.

15. Carl Schurz, quoted in Peraino, *Lincoln in the World*, 121.

16. See Dean B. Mahin, *One War at a Time: The International Dimensions of the American Civil War* (Washington, DC: Brassey's, 1999), who based the book on this phrase that "was widely regarded during and after the war as Lincoln's maxim for U.S. diplomacy." Ibid., ix.

17. This section is drawn from Hubert F. Dubrulle, "Trent Affair," in Heidler and Heidler, *Encyclopedia of the American Civil War*, 1972–1974; and Mahin, *One War at a Time*, 58–82.

18. White, *Testimonies for the Church*, 1:258.

19. Basler, *The Collected Works of Abraham Lincoln*, 4:263.

20. Jones, *Union in Peril*, 16.

21. White, *Testimonies for the Church*, 1:258.

22. Baron de Brunow, quoted in Sideman and Friedman, *Europe Looks at the Civil War*, 20.

23. Louis T. Wigfall, quoted in Jones, *Blue and Gray Diplomacy*, 12. For an extended discussion on the Confederacy's attempt to appeal to British interest and avoid the issue of slavery, see ibid., 11–20.

24. Jones, *Union in Peril*, 17.

25. White, *Testimonies for the Church*, 1:258, 259.

26. For a discussion of the Declaration of Independence in the context of slavery, see John Saillant, "Declaration of Independence (1776)," in Hinks and McKivigan, *Encyclopedia of Antislavery and Abolition*, 1:210–212.

27. See David Brion Davis, *The Problem of Slavery in the Age of Revolution, 1770–1823* (New York: Oxford University Press, 1999).

28. This metaphor is borrowed from John Jay Chapman in his *William Lloyd Garrison* (New York: Moffat, Yard and Co., 1913), 9, who used it in reference to the issue of slavery under the table during the deliberations of the Constitutional Convention in 1787.

29. See Finkelman, *Defending Slavery*, 9.

30. David Brion Davis, *Inhuman Bondage: The Rise and Fall of Slavery in the New World* (New York: Oxford University Press, 2006), 189.

31. Ibid., 123.

32. For these arguments from primary sources, see Finkelman, *Defending Slavery*. See also Faust, *The Ideology of*

Slavery; and two primary sources: William Harper, Thomas Roderick Dew, James Henry Hammond, and William Gilmore Simms, *The Pro-slavery Argument, as Maintained by the Most Distinguished Writers of the Southern States* (Philadelphia: Lippincott, Grambo, & Co., 1853); and Elliott, *Cotton Is King*. Both books are available at Google Books.

33. For discussion on the unique nature of slavery in the American South, see Stampp, *The Peculiar Institution*; Kolchin, *American Slavery*; and Lacy K. Ford, *Deliver Us From Evil: The Slavery Question in the Old South* (New York: Oxford University Press, 2009).

34. White, *Testimonies for the Church*, 1:259, 260.

35. Ibid., 1:259.

36. Ibid., 1:264.

37. See these phrases on the White Estate Web site, http://www.whiteestate.org/.

38. White, *Testimonies for the Church*, 1:258.

39. Ibid., 1:259.

40. Ibid., 1:256.

41. Ibid., 1:259.

42. D. P. Crook, *The North, the South, and the Powers, 1861–1865* (New York: John Wiley & Sons, 1974), 169.

43. Jones, *Blue and Gray Diplomacy*, 215.

44. Lord Palmerston, quoted in ibid., 215, 216.

45. Jones, *Blue and Gray Diplomacy*, 216.

46. McPherson, *Battle Cry of Freedom*, 554, 555.

47. Jones, *Blue and Gray Diplomacy*, 212.

48. Ibid., 217.

49. Ibid., 235. See also Howard Jones' *Abraham Lincoln and a New Birth of Freedom: The Union and Slavery in the Diplomacy of the Civil War* (Lincoln, NE: University of Nebraska Press, 1999), where he explained this important nuance: "Although in the short run Antietam and emancipation had given added momentum to the interventionist crisis, in the long run these two epoch-making events forced British leaders to shy away from such a dangerous move." Jones, *Abraham Lincoln and a New Birth of Freedom*, 156.

50. William E. Gladstone, quoted in Jones, *Blue and Gray Diplomacy*, 236. For a discussion on the implications of Gladstone's speech, see also Crook, *The North, the South, and the Powers*, 227ff.

51. Jones, *Blue and Gray Diplomacy*, 238.

52. Granville, quoted in Crook, *The North, the South, and the Powers*, 225.

53. Crook, *The North, the South, and the Powers*, 225.

54. For England's concern regarding other nations, see ibid., 225ff., 268ff., 371, 372. Mahin, *One War at a Time*, 197–207, provides a helpful discussion of all the major European nations and their reaction to the American Civil War.

55. Crook, *The North, the South, and the Powers*, 373.

56. During the summer of 1863, a less serious crisis occurred regarding British construction of steam raiders and rams for the Confederacy. Also in 1863, French intervention in Mexico strained relations with the United States.

57. White, *Testimonies for the Church*, 1:259.

58. Ibid.

59. Jones, *Blue and Gray Diplomacy*, 24, 25; see also 96, 100.

60. Another factor that heightened Britain's fear of internal weakness from a war with the Union was that Britain's industrial workers were overwhelmingly on the side of the Union, not the Confederacy.

61. White, *Testimonies for the Church*, 1:259.

62. James McPherson, "If the Lost Order Hadn't Been Lost," in Robert Cowley, ed., *What If? The World's Foremost Military Historians Imagine What Might Have Been* (New York: Berkley Books, 2000), 237.

63. White, *Testimonies for the Church*, 1:259.

64. Francis D. Nichol, *Ellen White and Her Critics* (Washington, DC: Review and Herald®, 1951), 122.

65. Ibid., 123.

66. White, *Testimonies for the Church*, 1:259.

67. "How to Keep Out of It," *The Economist*, June 1 1861, quoted in Jones, *Blue and Gray Diplomacy*, 62.

68. William H. Seward, quoted in Jones, *Blue and Gray Diplomacy*, 58.

69. Jones, *Union in Peril*, 230.

70. Allan Nevins, *War Becomes Revolution, 1862–1863*, vol. 2 of *The War for the Union* (New York: Konecky & Konecky, 1960), 242.

71. White, *Testimonies for the Church*, 1:259.

72. For a discussion on the Northern government's problems during this time, see the excellent study by Weber, *Copperheads*, 34–37. For an overview of the Copperheads, see pages 1–12 of that work.

73. White, *Testimonies for the Church*, 1:259, 260.

74. Quoted in James McPherson, " 'The Whole Family of Man': Lincoln and the Last Best Hope Abroad," in Robert E. May, ed., *The Union, the Confederacy, and the Atlantic Rim* (West Lafayette, IN: Purdue University Press, 1995), 137–139.

75. White, *Testimonies for the Church*, 1:260.

76. See "If I Would Have Vs. If I Had," *GrammarBook.com* (blog), accessed December 1, 2016, http://data .grammarbook.com/blog/verbs/if-i-would-have-vs-if-i-had.

77. Basler, *The Collected Works of Abraham Lincoln*, 2:461 (emphasis in the original).

78. See Abraham Lincoln, "Republican Principles," *Review and Herald*, September 2, 1858, 126, 127; cf. Basler, *The Collected Works of Abraham Lincoln*, 2:461–468.

79. White, *Testimonies for the Church*, 1:267.

80. Ibid., 1:365.

81. See ibid., 1:260, 267, 365.

82. Eusey, "The American Civil War," 120.

PART V

BATTLE CREEK VISION (NOVEMBER 1862):
"THE WAR AND OUR DUTY IN RELATION TO IT"

CHAPTER 12

THE MILITARY DRAFT

A s the nation entered its third year of war in January 1863, the Union was still reeling from the disastrous loss at Fredericksburg on December 13, 1862, and a major battle was still raging at Stones River in Tennessee. On January 1, 1863, President Lincoln signed the final draft of the Emancipation Proclamation, and many Americans wondered what it meant for the nation. The militia drafting of 1862 had not been successful, and the Lincoln administration was seriously considering a national draft to furnish the necessary troops in order to continue the war. The prospects for the new year promised more battles, with their inevitable suffering and death.

In this conflicted atmosphere, Ellen White released her final counsel for the war in *Testimony for the Church, No. 9*. The January 6 edition of the *Review and Herald* stated that the testimony was about "the war, and our duty in relation to it" and that it would be ready in a few days.[1] White does not say when the vision for this counsel occurred, but apparently it took place on November 5, 1862,[2] and she chose to publish it in January 1863. Four themes stood out in the *Testimony* titled "The Rebellion": (1) how to address the military draft; (2) the lack of unity in the Northern army; (3) officers seeking guidance from spirit mediums; and (4) judgment on the nation. This chapter will discuss the first two themes: how the Adventists addressed the military draft and achieved recognition as noncombatants, and the lack of unity in the Northern army. Subsequent chapters will address the latter two themes.

As Adventists opened the first page of this *Testimony*, they read pointed words: "The dreadful state of our nation calls for deep humility on the part of God's people. The one all-important inquiry which should now engross the mind of everyone is: Am I prepared for the day of God? Can I stand the trying test before me?" Like her earlier two essays on the Civil War, Ellen White's paramount concern was in preparing people for the second coming of Christ—the culmination of the great controversy on earth. While she dealt with immediate issues related to the war, her main concern was the spiritual growth of Adventists. She thus began her testimony with appeals for faith and endurance. "I saw that God is purifying and proving His people," she penned. "God's people will be brought into most trying positions, and all must be settled, rooted, and grounded in the truth, or their steps will surely slide."[3]

White then turned to the theme of God's judgment on the nation for the sin of slavery. "The people of this nation have forsaken and forgotten God," she declared. "They have chosen other Gods and followed their own corrupt ways until God has turned from them."[4] These words seemed rather harsh in light of the recent release of Lincoln's Emancipation Proclamation. But from the perspective of that moment, the proclamation was only the first step in a lengthy process to free the slaves. With all the proslavery influences in the Northern government, such as the Peace Democrats who wanted to restore the "old Union" as it was before the war, many battles had to be fought, politically as well as militarily, to end the curse of slavery. At that moment, in White's mind, the nation still had not fully embraced the "fast which God has chosen" and changed its policies toward slavery (see chapter 10).[5]

Military draft

A major issue on Ellen White's mind was the potential military draft, which had stirred up quite a bit of heat recently in Adventist circles: "I was shown the excitement created among our people by the article in the *Review* headed, 'The Nation.' " On August 12, 1862, James White had published an article on the draft issue that caused a firestorm of responses; some of which were published in the *Review*. "Some understood it one way, and some another," she explained. "The plain statements were distorted, and made to mean what the writer did not intend. He gave the best light that he then had. It was necessary that something be said." The heart of her concern came in the next few sentences: "The attention of many was turned to Sabbath-keepers because they manifested no greater interest in the war and did not volunteer. In some places they were looked upon as sympathizing with the Rebellion. The time had come for our true sentiments in relation to slavery and the Rebellion to be made known. There was need of moving with wisdom to turn away the suspicions excited against Sabbathkeepers. We should act with great caution."[6]

To fully appreciate these comments, it will be necessary to first look at the historical context of conscription during the Civil War, then analyze James White's article and the responses, and finally note how Adventists responded to the national draft.

From volunteerism to conscription

After the shelling of Fort Sumter, the official beginning of the war, patriotism burned in the hearts of Americans. A shocked and angered people answered in unison President Lincoln's calls for troops: "We are coming, Father Abraham."[7] This surge of volunteers into the field had, by the end of 1861, placed more than a half million men into the Union army. In fact, "throughout the first year of the war the chief problem of the War Department was not to obtain enough volunteers, but rather to check the enthusiastic response to the call for troops, since it was unprepared to handle the numbers who offered their services."[8] The president had reported to Congress on July 4 that "one of the greatest perplexities of the government, is to avoid receiving troops faster than it can provide for them."[9]

At the beginning of 1862, Union military officials were optimistic about the war. With Grant's successes in the West, coupled with McClellan's Peninsular Campaign that was ready to pierce the Confederate heart in Richmond, it appeared that the war would be over soon. Edwin McMasters Stanton, the newly appointed secretary of war, was so optimistic that on April 3 he issued General Order 33 that discontinued the recruiting service. "Officers and men recruiting for old regiments were ordered back to their units, and the superintendents were instructed to auction off the public property and close the depots."[10] The public breathed a sigh of relief that the war would soon be over.

But this was a big mistake. Three days later the Union lost thirteen thousand men at the terrible Battle of Shiloh. Then during May and June, Jackson's Shenandoah

Valley Campaign, the Battle of Seven Pines, and McClellan's failure to take Richmond during the Seven Days Battles had disastrous impacts on the Union army as its ranks were depleted by discharge, death, and desertion. "The bubble of confidence which had buoyed Stanton's hopes in April burst in June. The army needed men." Consequently, on June 6, 1862, Stanton rescinded his General Order 33 in an attempt to renew recruiting. But despite his and Lincoln's efforts, the volunteer system never ran smoothly again.[11] Moreover, the patriotism manifested in the early part of the war waned as men carefully weighed their personal sacrifices in light of the death toll from the battles of the summer and fall. Also, wartime industries were attracting "many workers with wages substantially higher than soldier's meager pay," and "there was a growing agitation against the war throughout the country, led by the Peace Democrats and other anti-administration forces. All of these forces combined greatly discouraged volunteering during the summer and fall of 1862."[12]

In July 1862, Congress and various federal officials instituted two programs that they hoped would mobilize manpower for the Northern army. The first was a modification of the bounty system that had originated in the colonial period and was reinstituted shortly after the shelling on Fort Sumter. Bounties were monetary enticements used to encourage men to enlist in the militia or army. In May 1861, Congress authorized a hundred-dollar bounty for volunteers, a substantial sum, considering that a Union private received only eleven dollars per month as base pay. Generally, it was the local communities that supplemented the bounty with programs of their own to encourage enlistment. The system worked reasonably well until July 1862, when Congress and federal officials modified it due to various abuses.[13] Nevertheless, the bounty system continued throughout the war and, as we will see shortly, was an asset to noncombatant groups like the Seventh-day Adventists.[14]

The second program began with the Militia Act of 1862 signed by Lincoln on July 17, 1862. Although the Confederate Congress passed a conscription act on April 16, 1862,[15] the Militia Act is considered to be the first conscription act in the United States and "was by no means a comprehensive draft law."[16] Its focus was on the states, which were given quotas to fill and which carried the responsibility to raise their state militias. If a governor failed to fulfill the quota for his state through volunteerism, then the president was empowered to draft citizens into the state militia. The states generally met their quota through financially induced volunteering and sometimes through local drafts. As a step toward national conscription, the

Militia Act was fraught with problems and never really succeeded.[17]

Nevertheless, it brought the issue of conscription to the attention of the Northern population. During July and August 1862, major newspapers united in endorsing conscription as the necessary means of defeating the South. The *New York Times*, for example, had criticized the slowness of volunteering and had stressed that "if this war is to go on with any hope of success, the country must resort to a draft of militia, and that immediately."[18] On August 4, 1862, Stanton ordered a draft for three hundred thousand militiamen; and on August 9, his office issued detailed instructions on how each state should implement the draft. One citizen expressed the sentiment of many when he wrote on August 12 that "everybody is afraid of the draft."[19] Consequently, draft evasion became a widespread phenomenon, as numbers fled the country to Europe and especially Canada.[20] Such was the context for the Sabbatarian Adventists' concerns about the draft issue.

James White's response to the issue of conscription

As they watched events unfold before them during the summer of 1862, Adventists saw in the Militia Act of July 17 "the first tentative threat of a federal draft."[21] It was the "hand writing on the wall"[22] that caused many to tremble "over the prospect of a draft."[23] These circumstances in July and early August of 1862 brought forth a two-fold reaction from James White. First, he and other leading Adventists participated in meetings at Battle Creek (as they had already been doing since the beginning of the war) to raise funds for liberal bounties to be paid to volunteers. Their intention was to help reach the required quota of volunteers for their county as stipulated in the instructions for the state draft.[24] The Battle Creek bounties started at twenty-five dollars, then rose to one hundred dollars, and then to two hundred dollars by October 1862.[25]

James White and his colleagues were "particularly anxious to avoid the threatened draft which would involve Sabbathkeepers." The majority were conscientiously noncombatant, but "they felt it to be their duty to join heartily in raising money for the payment of the bonus offered to volunteers who had no religious scruples against army service."[26] Later in the war, some Adventists questioned White "as to whether it was right to contribute to raise local bounties for the purpose of encouraging enlistments."[27] The response in the *Review and Herald* stated, "We think it is, and have done so in Battle Creek."[28]

James and Ellen White about 1864
(egwwritings.org)

Second, James White responded to the issue of the draft in his article "The Nation," published in the August 12, 1862, issue of the *Review and Herald*.[29] The Militia Act of July 17, with its corresponding draft on August 4 and the discussion of the draft in the news, certainly aroused the attention of Adventists. The question on everyone's mind was, *What shall we do if there is a mandatory national draft with no reprieve?* Additionally, in some places such as Iowa, Adventists "were looked upon as sympathizing with the Rebellion" because they refused the draft.[30] These "rash spirits" were "overvaliant in proclaiming their noncombatancy, some of them declaring publicly that they would die before they would serve."[31] In response to these concerns, James White penned "The Nation."

Summary of James White's article "The Nation." At the outset of the article, James White was concerned that all understand that Seventh-day Adventists were anti-slavery. He set forth his argument in several points: First, "for the past ten years the Review has taught that the United States of America were a subject of prophecy, and that slavery is pointed out in the prophetic word as the darkest and most damning sin upon this nation." Second, God will punish this nation for "the sin of slavery." Third, "the anti-slavery teachings of several of our publications based upon certain prophecies have been such that their circulation has been positively forbidden in the slave States." Fourth, "those of our people who voted at all at the last Presidential election [fall 1861], to a man voted for Abraham Lincoln." And fifth, "we know of not one man among Seventh-day Adventists who has the least sympathy for secession."[32]

With the strong antislavery position of Seventh-day Adventists established, White then addressed the apparent contradiction between their antislavery position and the fact that they do not participate in the war. According to texts such as Revelation 6:12–17, slavery will be around until the end of time, he argued, and this must be the present time. Seventh-day Adventists were looking beyond this world to the second coming of Christ, which will bring down punishment on slaveholders. Moreover, the "requirements of war" would conflict with the fourth commandment ("Remember the sabbath day") and the sixth commandment ("Thou shalt not kill"). Up to this point, all of his Adventist audience universally agreed with him.[33]

Then he dropped a bomb: "But in the case of drafting, the government assumes the responsibility of the violation of the law of God, and it would be madness to resist. He who would resist until, in the administration of military law, he was shot down, goes too far, we think, in taking the responsibility of suicide."[34] Behind this statement was White's concern over the extremists who were recklessly proclaiming that they would rather die than face the draft, which led some to believe that Seventh-day Adventists were not supportive of the Northern effort to defeat the South.

Even though the "requirements of war" were not in harmony with the law of God, White added, the Adventist people are "enjoying the protection of our civil and religious rights, by the best government under heaven." Other than "the exception of those enactments pressed upon it by the slave power, its laws are good." Although people may "question the policy of the present administration" in the way it is handling the "precious blacks" and may say various things about the "amiable president, his cabinet, or of military officers, it is Christ-like to honor every good law of our land." After quoting Jesus' words, "Render therefore unto Caesar the things which are Caesar's; and unto God the things that are God's" (Matthew 22:21), White clinched his support of government: "Those who despise civil law, should at once pack up and be off for some spot on God's foot-stool where there is no civil law."[35]

White then brought his argument to its conclusion: "When it shall come to this, that civil enactments shall be passed and enforced to drive us from obedience to the law of God, to join those who are living in rebellion against the government of Heaven, see Rev. xiii, 15–17, then it will be time to stand our chances of martyrdom." But until that time comes, "for us to attempt to resist the laws of the best government under heaven, which is now struggling to put down the most hellish rebellion since that of Satan and his angels, we repeat it, would be madness." Consequently, "those who are loyal to the government of Heaven, true to the constitution and laws of the Ruler of the universe, are the last men to 'sneak' off to Canada, or to Europe, or to stand trembling in their shoes for fear of a military draft." God "has the nation in his hand, and will order events for his glory, and the best good of his loyal people."[36] His use of the phrase "[God] has the nation in his hand" most likely originated with his wife in her vision about the First Battle of Bull Run.[37]

Several points are worth noting in this groundbreaking article. First, Seventh-day Adventists were strongly antislavery and supportive of the Northern government's effort to defeat the rebellion in the South. This was a fundamental point that James White wanted to underscore throughout the article to ward off the impression that Adventists were in any way sympathetic to the Southern rebellion. Second, the Adventists respected the American government and appreciated its protection of civil and religious rights, even though they worried about its future role in the end-time crisis. If, however, the laws of men conflict with the law of God, Adventists should obey the latter—no matter the cost. This was the theological heart of the argument, and it would become vitally important to Adventism's future stance on the relationship between the laws of men and the laws of God. Third, most Adventists avoided participating in the war because it was not in harmony with their principles of Sabbath keeping and noncombatancy. White wanted readers to know that this is a major reason why Adventists had not generally involved themselves in the war.

Fourth, in the case of the draft, "the government assumes the responsibility of the violation of the law of God," and, therefore, Adventists should obey the draft law if it affects them personally. To resist the draft would "be madness," because one could be executed, and Christians should support the government, which was "now struggling to put down the most hellish rebellion since that of Satan and his angels." This reflected White's reasoning at the time and was his first tentative response to the draft. His major concern was to distance the movement from the fanatical attitudes among some Adventists and their extreme noncombatant position. Hence, those who resist the "administration of military law" to the point of death go too far and take upon themselves "the responsibility of suicide."

Fifth, those Adventists who were loyal to God's government would not try to escape the draft and flee to another country. The draft was highly controversial, and several thousand chose to flee to Canada and Europe instead of serving their country. This point would become increasingly important as resistance to the draft escalated into rioting during the summer of 1863 and the bounty system grew corrupt. White wanted a legitimate solution to the draft issue for his people, not one of violent protest or unethical behavior.

Ultimately, the purpose of the article at this stage was primarily to check the extreme views against the draft position that had been growing among the Adventist community. White's position represented an attempt to stay loyal to God and His commandments, while at the same time remaining loyal to the country in its effort to put down the rebellion. The problem at the moment was that the government made no provision for noncombatant service and would not do so until 1864.

Controversy about the article. As careful and nuanced as this article was, it created a firestorm of controversy. Two weeks later, on August 26, James White addressed the controversy in the *Review*:

Several brethren refer to our remarks . . . two weeks since, in rather a feverish style. . . . This is no time for Christian gentlemen to give way to feelings of prejudice, and virtually charge us with teaching Sabbath-breaking and murder. You had better all go to God with this matter, and secure to yourselves a humble, teachable spirit; then if any of you are drafted, and choose to have a clinch with Uncle Sam rather than to obey, you can try it. We shall not contend with you, lest some of you non-resistants get up a little war before you are called upon to fight for your country.[38]

White urged the "brethren" to "read the article again, and be sure they understand our position before opposing it." In light of this tentative position, he requested, "Any well-written articles, calculated to shed light upon our duty as a people in reference to the present war, will receive prompt attention."[39] Over the next several months, from August to October, numerous articles were published that represented a wide range across a spectrum of possible options. At one end of this spectrum were the "total pacifists, who believed that Christians should avoid military service altogether."[40] As Adventist historian George R. Knight pointed out, "It was probably such an orientation of members in Iowa whose aggressive pacifist agitation had triggered charges that Adventism was not patriotic that brought about the publication of White's initial thoughts on the topic."[41]

On the other end of the spectrum were those who argued that to take up arms for a just cause is right for the Christian. One writer believed that he was in harmony with White and asserted: "Is it murder to hang or shoot a traitor? No! no! When men rebel against just and good laws, death is their just due, and the executioner is clear." He stated that he liked "Bro. White's remarks on this point" and encouraged his fellow Adventists not to "shame the memory of Washington and other heroes whom God blessed upon the field of battle."[42] And so both ends of the spectrum, and those in between, battled on the issue in the pages of the *Review* as well as in unpublished correspondence. At one point, R. F. Cottrell exclaimed that "there is no necessity for brethren to go to war with each other on *peace principles.*"[43]

In October, as the debate was winding down, James White summarized the arguments and, distancing himself from those who read into his article total participation in the war, concluded that "true Seventh-day Adventists would make poor work at using carnal weapons." His purpose in the original article, he said, was to "check that spirit of fanaticism which would recklessly proclaim abroad that we should resist a military draft." He recalled the many letters received and noted how "many of our brethren were greatly excited, and trembled over the prospect of a draft." The way forward was still not clear at that time, and God's people should "leave the matter in the hands of God, without resistance, in case of draft." White now believed there was still no better course of action. "God designs the present state of things to bring us near to him. The nation is in his hands; and we cannot see how God can be glorified by his loyal people taking up arms."[44] After one more set of articles in the following week's *Review*, White ended the debate: "We have advised no man to go to war. We have struck at that fanaticism which grows out of extreme non-resistance, and have labored to lead our people to seek the Lord and trust in him for deliverance. How this can and will come, we have no light at present."[45]

Ellen White's counsel on the issue of the draft

Ellen White had remained silent during the debate, and many were waiting for her to speak. After the discussion in the *Review and Herald* had ended, but before conscription had seriously affected the brethren, she spoke in *Testimony for the Church, No. 9*, which was released in late January 1863. Her comments were right on the mark about her husband's article: "Some understood it one way, and some another. . . . He gave the best light that he then had."[46]

"I was shown," she continued, "that some moved very indiscreetly in regard to the article mentioned." James White's views "did not in all respects accord with their views, and instead of calmly weighing the matter, and viewing it in all its bearings, they became agitated, excited, and some seized the pen and jumped hastily at conclusions which would not bear investigation." Consequently, "they did that which Satan is ever hurrying them to do, namely, acted out their own rebellious feelings."[47]

White then addressed the situation that had developed in Iowa and had moved James White to write the article in the first place. "In Iowa they carried things to quite a length, and ran into fanaticism" and "were ready to become martyrs for their faith," she explained. Did this lead them to "greater humility" before God and to "trust in His power to deliver them from the trying position into which they might be brought?" No, this attitude did not, she exclaimed. "Instead of making their petitions to the God of heaven and relying solely upon His power, they petitioned the legislature and were refused."[48] B. F. Snook, the Iowa Conference president, who had led out in this petition movement, later acknowledged that it was a mistake and regretted "making any such move."[49] But the damage had already been done: "All this only served to bring that peculiar class, Sabbathkeepers, into special notice, and expose them to be crowded into difficult places by those who have no sympathy for them."[50]

White asserted that she "saw that those who have been forward to talk so decidedly about refusing to obey a draft do not understand what they are talking about." If they were really "drafted and, refusing to obey, be threatened with imprisonment, torture, or death, they would shrink and then find that they had not prepared themselves for such an emergency. They would not endure the trial of their faith. What they thought to be faith was only fanatical presumption."[51] Interestingly, before the exemption for conscientious objectors came in February 1864, those religious groups, such as the Mennonites and Quakers, who refused to bear arms often suffered serious abuse from both the Northern and Southern armies, yet they remained steadfast to their pacifist convictions.[52] In contrast, White claimed that this extreme group of Adventists would not survive the test of persecution.

Ultimately, she admonished her readers that "those who would be best prepared to sacrifice even life, if required, rather than place themselves in a position where they could not obey God, would have the least to say" and would make "no boast." Then came the practical counsel that would guide the Adventist people through this trying time: "Those who feel that in the fear of God they cannot conscientiously engage in this war will be very quiet, and when interrogated will simply state what they are obliged to say in order to answer the inquirer, and then let it be understood that they have no sympathy with the Rebellion."[53]

This practical advice resulted in a careful "middle-of-the road" approach to the draft concern for Adventists.[54] First, keep a low profile, and don't publicly protest against or resist the draft. Second, when interrogated by the draft marshals, simply state your reasons for not engaging in the war, and make absolutely clear your abhorrence for the rebellion. In White's view, the fanatical, boasting claims of the extremists should not be found anywhere among true Seventh-day Adventists.

Sabbath keepers who sympathized with slaveholders

White then moved on to an issue that caused concern among the leaders of the Seventh-day Adventists. "There are a few in the ranks of Sabbathkeepers who sympathize with the slaveholder. When they embraced the truth, they did not leave behind them all the errors they should have left." These individuals "have brought along with them their old political prejudices, which are not in harmony with the principles of truth." After a lengthy discussion of the equality of all human beings before God and a denouncement of the evils of slavery, White addressed the issue of influence: "Some have been so indiscreet as to talk out their pro-slavery principles—principles which are not heaven-born, but proceed from the dominion of Satan. These restless spirits talk and act in a manner to bring a reproach upon the cause of God."[55]

To illustrate this point, Ellen White provided an excerpt from a letter she wrote to one of these proslavery sympathizers, referred to as "Brother A," who was actually Alexander Ross, a member of the Roosevelt, New York, Seventh-day Adventist Church. Ross, a known Seventh-day Adventist, had been speaking out on his political views in favor of the South and slavery.[56] White told him that God had shown her his case in vision and that his influence was going against the truth. "You have given occasion for the enemies of our faith to blaspheme, and to reproach Sabbathkeepers. By your indiscreet course, you have closed the ears of some who would have listened to the truth." His "political principles" had, she told him, destroyed "your judgment and your love for the truth." He had "never looked upon slavery in the right light," and his views threw him "on the side of the Rebellion, which was stirred up by Satan and his host." She further admonished Ross that his "views of slavery cannot harmonize with the sacred, important truths for this time" and that he must yield his "views or the truth. Both cannot be cherished in the same heart, for they are at war with each other."[57]

White cast her remarks to Ross in the framework of the great controversy between Christ and Satan, as is mentioned in Revelation 12:7, 8: "Satan was the first great leader in rebellion. God is punishing the North, that they have so long suffered the accursed sin of slavery to exist; for in the sight of heaven it is a sin of the darkest dye. God is not with the South, and He will punish them dreadfully in the end. Satan is the instigator of all rebellion."[58]

With the rebellion of Satan as the bookends to the thought, White put at the center that slavery "in the sight of heaven . . . is a sin of the darkest dye." The punishment on both the North and the South resulted from the sin of slavery. Significantly, in this statement to Ross was a ray of hope. Although the outlook looked bleak for the North ("God is punishing the North"), neither was God with the South. Her statement that "He [God] will punish them [the South] dreadfully in the end" indicated the destruction of the Confederacy. So, in showing Ross the futile outcome of his hopes for the South, she provided hope for the North in its war on the rebellion.

Because Ross had given "publicity" to his sentiments, White gave him an ultimatum about his future relationship with the church: "Unless you undo what you have done, it will be the duty of God's people to publicly withdraw their sympathy and fellowship from you, in order to save the impression which must go out in regard to us as a people. We must let it be known that we have no such ones in our fellowship, that we will not walk with them in church capacity."[59]

To bring the point home with one last warning appeal to Ross and all other readers of this *Testimony*, she declared, "I was shown that as a people we cannot be too careful what influence we exert; we should watch every word. When we by word or act place ourselves upon the enemy's battle ground, we drive holy angels from us, and encourage and attract evil angels in crowds around us. This you have done, Brother A, and by your unguarded, willful course have caused unbelievers to look upon Sabbathkeepers all around you with suspicion."[60]

Here again we find the importance of influence—a key theme in this essay and in James White's concerns about how the extremists were addressing the threat of a national draft. Ross accepted the rebuke and eventually renounced his proslavery views.[61]

The Adventists' duty in relation to the war

About a week after James White published his appeal for "any well-written articles" on the issue of the draft, on August 19, Ellen White answered a letter from Mrs. Myrta Steward, who asked her about the duty of Adventists and the war. "I am not fully settled in regard to taking up arms, but this looks consistent to me," Ellen White replied. "I think it would please the enemy for us to obstinately refuse to obey the law of our country (when this law is not against our religious faith) and sacrifice our lives." At the time of this letter, White acknowledged that she had no more light on the matter than her husband did.[62] After the next vision, however, she could express with certainty the stand that her Adventist community should collectively take in response to the military draft whenever or however it should come:[63] "I was shown that God's people, who are His peculiar treasure, cannot engage in this perplexing war, for it is opposed to every principle of their faith. In the army they cannot obey the truth and at the same time obey the requirements of their officers. There would be a continual violation of conscience."[64]

At the time this statement was published in January 1863, there was no provision for noncombatants in the state drafts, and national conscription was imminent. If the draft was inescapable, then Seventh-day Adventists should find a legitimate way of avoiding military service. The reasons, White stated, are clear:

> Worldly men are governed by worldly principles. . . . But God's people cannot be governed by these motives. The words and commands of God, written in the soul, are spirit and life, and there is power in them to bring into subjection and enforce obedience. The ten precepts of Jehovah are the foundation of all righteous and good laws. Those who love God's commandments will conform to every good law of the land. But if the requirements of the rulers are such as conflict with the laws of God, the only question to be settled is: Shall we obey God, or man?[65]

Here Ellen White used the higher-law argument employed by abolitionists against the Fugitive Slave Law during the 1850s.[66] In the previous paragraph, she articulated this reasoning with clarity: "I saw that it is our duty in every case to obey the laws of our land, unless they conflict with the higher law which God spoke with an audible voice from Sinai, and afterward engraved on stone with His own finger. . . . He who has God's law written in the heart will obey God rather than men, and will sooner disobey all men than deviate in the least from the commandment of God."[67]

Her argument can be summarized thus: Adventists should avoid engagement in this war as it is presently being conducted. They should obey the good laws of the land as long as they are in harmony with the higher law of God. When there is a conflict between the two, they should obey God rather than men. Adherence to these principles would guide her people through the duration of the war.[68]

The Federal Conscription Act and Seventh-day Adventists

Three months after these counsels were published, Congress passed the Conscription Act on March 3, 1863: "All able-bodied male citizens of the United States," who were "between the ages of twenty and forty-five years" were "liable to perform military duty in the service of the United States when called out by the President for that purpose."[69] Although the Conscription Act made no provision for noncombatant service, it did allow the draftee to hire a substitute to take his place or, if he had enough money, to pay the federal government a three hundred dollar commutation fee and be exempted from the draft. These provisions were welcomed by Seventh-day Adventists as a "providential means of avoiding combatant service and conflicts over Sabbath observance."[70]

Unfortunately, the bounty system was corrupted by bounty jumpers—men who took the enlistment money, joined, deserted, assumed a different name, and then traveled to another town to repeat the procedure, often getting rich in the process.[71] The draft system in general provided huge opportunities for corruption, fraud, and error.[72] Furthermore, the commutation fee of three hundred dollars "represented more than half a year's wages for an unskilled workingman, and the cry arose that this practice made it a rich man's war and a poor man's fight."[73] Consequently, protests occurred throughout various Northern states, often erupting in violent riots, with the most notorious being the New York City draft riots July 13–16, 1863; these riots were the largest civil insurrection in American history.[74]

Seventh-day Adventists, however, aided each other in raising the three hundred dollar fee to be exempted legitimately from the draft. They also followed Ellen White's counsels in general and thus avoided the unethical draft practices taking place around them and stayed clear of riots.[75] It should be noted that prior to the date of this *Testimony,* a considerable number of Adventists had already enlisted and were serving in the Northern army. After this time, however, significantly fewer Adventists joined the military to fight for the North, while others, who were unable to pay the commutation fee, were drafted.[76]

Seventh-day Adventists were not alone in their struggle with the draft. Other groups, such as the Quakers, Mennonites, Dunkers, and Shakers, wrestled with the same problems and addressed them in different ways.[77] Although not all noncombatants realized it, President Lincoln and Secretary of War Stanton were friendly toward them.[78] Lincoln was well acquainted with the Quakers, the most well-known pacifist group, and had personal relationships with members, such as Eliza P. Gurney, who visited with him in the White House.[79] On several occasions, he heard and answered their requests "with the greatest patience and respect, and intervened with his prerogative on occasions of peculiar hardship," according to his secretaries, John Nicolay and John Hay. But "he could not legally relieve them from their liabilities" or recommend measures to Congress for their relief.[80]

The Quakers made repeated appeals to legislators,[81] though, and Congress finally amended the Conscription Act in February 1864, which made provision for "religious denominations" that were "conscientiously opposed to the bearing of arms." The amendment considered these groups to be "noncombatants" who would "be assigned by the Secretary of War to duty in the hospitals, or to the care of freed man," or would "pay the sum of three hundred dollars to such person as the Secretary of War" would "designate to receive it."[82] "While Seventh-day Adventists welcomed this new development, most of them continued to take advantage of the commutation provision."[83] In July 1864, however, Congress terminated commutation except for those conscientious objectors who were officially recognized.[84] "Would Seventh-day Adventists, an infant church actually organized during the war years [May 1863], be so recognized?"[85]

According to Adventist historian George R. Knight, "At that point the recently established General Conference of Seventh-day Adventists went on record as being a noncombatant denomination."[86] Knight aptly summarizes the events:

On August 3 the state of Michigan granted the new denomination noncombatant status. Other states soon followed. Then the church sent J. N. Andrews with letters from the various state governors to apply for noncombatant status from the federal government in Washington, D.C. Thus it was that in September 1864 the United States government recognized Adventism as a noncombatant church.

Theoretically that meant that if its members did get drafted they would not have to bear arms or kill enemies. But in practice noncombatant draftees often met with opposition and threats. On a more positive note, by the end of the war noncombatants could serve as medics both on the battlefront and in hospitals.

Adventists were happy with that arrangement, since it freed them from taking the lives of others and it was lawful to do good to others on the Sabbath.[87]

Ellen White's counsel on the draft issue provided principles that guided the church through the difficult war years. She reinforced the delicate tension between obedience to God and obedience to the civil laws of the government and provided spiritual insights on how to do this in such a way that God was honored and His people vindicated. As a religious group who did not interact with the government, the Adventists waited on God in faith for full resolution of the draft issue. Interestingly, it appears that during the Civil War, God used the Quakers to pave the way for all noncombatant groups, such as the Seventh-day Adventists, to obtain exemption from fighting on the battlefield and maintain their convictions on the higher law of God. In this way, many Adventists were able both to adhere to their noncombatant principles and to honor their country in its war against the rebellion. Thus, Ellen White's and her husband's advice to wait for God to work and not to take matters into one's own hand was the needed counsel during 1862 and early 1863.

Lack of unity in the Northern army

The rest of the section in the *Testimony* dealt with the problems in the Union army and echoed the themes from White's *Testimony for the Church, No. 7*, which were discussed in a previous chapter. Matters had grown worse. "Many were . . . grossly deceived in the last election" of October and November 1862, Ellen White explained. "Their influence was used to place in authority men . . . who are Southern sympathizers, and would preserve slavery as it is."[88] The Democrats, who sympathized with the South and rejected Lincoln's Emancipation Proclamation and policies of the war, had gained "thirty-two seats in the House" in the November election, along with the "governorships of New York and New Jersey." They had also "gained control of legislatures in New Jersey, Illinois, and Indiana." Although these "Democratic gains occurred in regions of the party's traditional strength" and the Republicans fared well overall in the election,[89] White still saw the results as a reason for concern.

Northern Democrats and Copperheads. The background of White's concern is found in the nature of the Northern Democrats at the time. The party had divided into two wings: "war" and "peace." The War Democrats generally supported President Lincoln's efforts to subdue the rebellion by military effort; General George B. McClellan being a classic example. In fact, some of them became Republicans during the war, such as General Benjamin Butler and Secretary of War Edwin M. Stanton, who both became Radical Republicans. The other wing was the Peace Democrats, who universally supported slavery and demanded an immediate peace settlement that would restore the Union with slavery still intact in the South.[90]

Republicans branded the Peace Democrats with the name *Copperheads* early in the war, and the name stuck. Like the poisonous snakes in the South, these antiwar Democrats were considered dangerous to the war effort. They operated under the slogan "The Union as it was, the Constitution as it is," and relentlessly attacked all of the Lincoln administration's war policies. Their opposition to the administration even "damaged the army's ability to prosecute the conflict efficiently."[91] Clement L. Vallandigham, a congressman from Ohio and the foremost Copperhead, expressed the desire of all of this wing when he said, "It is the desire of my heart to restore the Union, the Federal Union as it was forty years ago."[92] Although Ellen White never used the term *Copperheads*, they must have been on her mind while she wrote. As sympathizers with the Radical Republican wing, White and her readers were familiar with this political group and had no use for them.[93]

Southern sympathizers in the army. What made matters worse was the presence of Southern sympathizers in the military. "Many professed Union men, holding important positions," White wrote, "are disloyal at heart. Their only object in taking up arms was to preserve the Union as it was, and slavery with it."[94] Even the "rebels know they have sympathizers all through the Northern army. . . . Loyal men, who have had no sympathy with the Rebellion, or with slavery which has caused it, have been imposed upon."[95] Interestingly, on February 3, 1863, the *Review and Herald* printed an extract from the *New-York Daily Tribune*, titled "Traitors in Our Army," which described rebel sympathizers among the officers and men in the military.[96]

It is of no small importance that Ellen White wrote, "I saw that the Rebellion had been steadily increasing and that it had never been more determined than at the present moment."[97] At the time this was published, in January 1863, the shadow of the Fredericksburg disaster darkened Northern hope, and Lincoln's Emancipation Proclamation was in the storm of controversy. Copperheads capitalized on Fredericksburg as an example of the terrible way the Union was handling the war, and they vigorously opposed emancipating the slaves.

Additionally, talk was spreading across both the North and the South of a further split in the Union, a "Northwest Confederacy" that would make peace with the South and reconstruct the old Union with the New England abolitionists left out.[98] "I fear our country is on the verge of anarchy and despotism," wrote a Northern general. "God save us individually and, our country from the treason which surrounds us on every hand."[99] The desperation of the moment was captured vividly by a Boston lawyer who wrote, "My confidence is terribly shaken. So is everybody's. Things have never looked to me so black as at this moment."[100] Clearly, this was one of the lowest moments in the war at that point.

Lack of unity. According to a growing number of soldiers and officers, the heart of the problem was a lack of unity: "If the North would present to the rebbels [*sic*] a bold and united front and give them to understand that they could expect no other conditions than an unconditional submission to the laws and Constitution of the United States," stated an Indiana sergeant, "this war would not last two months." One soldier captured the situation in a comment that would often be repeated for the rest of the war: "One enemy in the rear is to be feared more than ten before us."[101] A member of the Twelfth Michigan wrote to his local paper in February: "I have heard a great many soldiers say that they would fight willingly as long as the North is united, . . . but when it is divided they say they will throw down their arms and fight no more. They say they did not enlist to fight both North and South."[102] Democrat General John White Geary suspected that his Democratic superior officers were disloyal to the Union: "Were it not for treason in our own army," he vented to his wife, "this wicked rebellion would have been, doubtlessly, long ago crushed."[103]

Reflecting these sentiments, Ellen White wrote, "If there were union in the Northern army, this Rebellion would soon cease."[104] She noted that "there are generals in the army who are wholly devoted and seek to do all they can to stop this dreadful Rebellion and unnatural war" and who are "true, whole-hearted soldiers" and "nobly perform their part when in an engagement with the enemy." But "most of the officers and leading men have a selfish purpose of their own to serve" and mistreat the soldiers under them. Those soldiers "are becoming fainthearted and discouraged."[105] Sadly, she wrote that these officers "in positions of trust" are "rebels at heart, who value the life of a soldier no more than they would the life of a dog. They can see them torn, and mangled, and dying, by thousands, unmoved." Moreover, Union intelligence was repeatedly leaked to the Southern army, and worst of all, "correct information" had "been given to Northern officers in regard to the movements and approach of rebels," but had "been disregarded and despised because the informer was black."[106] Consequently, the results on the battlefield were disastrous.

Second Manassas (Bull Run). "In some cases when generals have been in most terrible conflict," White explained, "where their men have fallen like rain, a reinforcement at the right time would have given them a victory."[107] She probably had in mind the Battle of Second Manassas from August 1862, when General Pope's army was defeated and driven from the field. General George McClellan could have helped Pope by sending him two sets of troops, but instead he remained passive before and during the conflict. Furthermore, Union commander Fitz John Porter was in a position to flank the enemy during a crucial point of the battle but also failed to execute.[108] Both McClellan and Porter had criticized Pope before the battle, McClellan even suggesting that Pope ought to be whipped in the battle.[109]

As the battle raged on August 29, McClellan suggested two options to Lincoln: either "concentrate all our available forces" toward Pope, or "leave Pope to get out of his scrape & at once use all our means to make the Capital perfectly safe."[110] Historian Bruce Tap observed that "for a general who claimed to have such affection for the men of the Army of the Potomac, he [McClellan] displayed a particularly callous attitude toward their plight, since some of these same soldiers were fighting under Pope."[111]

Stephen Sears, McClellan's biographer, was more generous in his assessment: "It is too much to say (as detractors later said) that George McClellan was deliberately conspiring to have the Army of Virginia beaten at Bull Run, if for no other reason than his strong feeling for the men of his own army fighting on that field." Having said that, Sears acknowledges that the general's "bruised sensibilities and his unreasoning contempt for Pope convinced him that general would be—and deserved to be—defeated." If Fitz John Porter, one of McClellan's favorites, had commanded the Army of Virginia instead of Pope, Sears believed that McClellan would have "acted far more vigorously." In the end, "the captive of his delusions, he put his own interests and his messianic vision ahead of doing everything possible to push reinforcements to the battlefield."[112]

Attorney General Bates described the situation as "a criminal tardiness, a fatuous apathy, a captious, bickering rivalry, among our commanders who seem so taken up with their quick made dignity, that they overlook the lives of their people & the necessities of their country."[113] Ellen White interpreted the situation similarly but more harshly. These "generals cared nothing how many lives were lost, and rather than come to the help of those in an engagement, as though their interests were one, they withheld the necessary aid, fearing that their brother general would receive the honor of successfully repulsing the enemy."[114]

Interestingly, John Hay, Lincoln's secretary, noted that McClellan's conduct at Second Manassas was best explained as "envy jealousy and spite."[115] White noted the same attitude with the consequent ramifications: "Through envy and jealousy they have even exulted to see the enemy gain the victory and repulse Union men. Southern men possess a hellish spirit in this Rebellion, but Northern men are not clear. Many of them possess a selfish jealousy, fearing that others will obtain honors and be exalted above themselves. Oh, how many thousands of lives have been sacrificed on this account!"[116]

Overall, White concluded that this war was protracted for several reasons: the lack of unity in the Northern army, pro-Southern sympathies in its leadership, military rivalry, a lack of resolve to defeat the enemy in battle, the unfeeling attitude of its leaders, and officers seeking guidance from spirit mediums. In White's mind, the entire enterprise was twisted: "This war is a most singular and at the same time a most horrible and heartsickening conflict." Other nations were "indignant" as they saw "such a determined effort to protract the war at an enormous sacrifice of life and money, while at the same time nothing" was "really gained," and it looked "to them like a strife to see which can kill the most men."[117]

Ultimately, for Ellen White, the spiritual lessons from this troubled war were paramount. She saw signs of the end in all of these events: "Everything is preparing for the great day of God. Time will last a little longer until the inhabitants of the earth have filled up the cup of their iniquity, and then the wrath of God, which has so long slumbered, will awake, and this land of light will drink the cup of His unmingled wrath. The desolating power of God is upon the earth to rend and destroy. The inhabitants of the earth are appointed to the sword, to famine, and to pestilence."[118]

As White brought this section of the *Testimony* on the war to an end, she lamented: "Blood has been poured out like water, and for nought. In every town and village there is mourning. Wives are mourning for their husbands, mothers for their sons, and sisters for their brothers. But notwithstanding all this suffering, they do not turn to God."[119]

Conclusion

As Otis Nichols, an Adventist believer, read through the latter part of this *Testimony*, much of it resonated with what he had read in the *Boston Evening Transcript*, a journal that repeatedly published comments about the Copperheads.[120] He penned a letter to James White that was later published in the *Review and Herald*. "It was a mystery," Nichols pondered,

> that the leading Democrats of the North, who were always in sympathy with the slave power of the South, should, after the fall of Ft. Sumpter [*sic*], unite with Mr. Lincoln's administration and fight against their Southern friends. But facts now show that their sympathy with the South never has changed. Their real object was to deceive and control the President and his cabinet, in the appointment of as many Democrats to power and trust, in the army, the navy, and the administration at Washington, as would favor the rebels. Hence the administration, and the army, especially of the Potomac, has been almost continually under the control of Northern traitors professing the Union and the constitution, in order to carry out their nefarious purposes in bringing the North under Southern dominion. But according to sister W.'s testimony they will not fully triumph over the Northern armies.[121]

Regardless of whether or not Nichols assessed the political situation accurately, he captured the ray of hope that White provided in the *Testimony*. Although the state of the Union was presently bleak and hopeless, she had assured readers that the North would not be defeated. "God," she said, "is not with the South, and He will punish them dreadfully in the end."[122] Additionally, "I saw that God would not give the Northern army wholly into the hands of a rebellious people, to be utterly destroyed by their enemies."[123] To Yankee Adventist readers, such as Nichols, who caught these rays of hope, this was encouraging given the backdrop of the slaughter at Fredericksburg, the marginal win at Stones River, and all the other problems facing the Northern armies during the winter of 1863.

Chapter in a nutshell

To many Adventists, the Militia Act of July 17, 1862, was the first tentative threat of a federal draft, and it spread fear throughout the community. This situation brought forth a twofold reaction from James White. First, he and other leading Adventists participated in meetings at Battle Creek to raise funds for bounties to pay volunteers to join the army and fight for the Union. This helped take the pressure off of Adventists to volunteer. Second, James White responded to the fear of the draft in his article "The Nation," which was published in the *Review and Herald on* August 12, 1862. An Adventist group in Iowa had overreacted and refused the draft and were branded as sympathizers with the South. In the article, James White stated that Adventists were antislavery and loyal to the Union but avoided participating in the war because it was not in harmony with their principles of Sabbath keeping and noncombatancy. In the case of the draft, the government assumes the responsibility of the violation of the law of God, he argued, and it would be madness to resist. This argument was tentative and more a response to the extremists in Iowa. The article created a firestorm of controversy, with Adventists taking both sides in the debate: join the army and fight, or stay out completely.

At this point, Ellen White entered the discussion with *Testimony for the Church, No. 9* and provided counsel on the controversy. Essentially, she stated that Adventists should avoid participation in this war because of the way it was being conducted at that time. They should obey the laws of the land as long as the laws are in harmony with the higher law of God. When there is a conflict between the two, Adventists should obey God rather than humans. Also, Adventists should keep a low profile, and if interrogated by a draft marshal, they should simply state the reasons for not engaging in the war and make it clear that they have no sympathy with the rebellion. These principles guided the Adventist people through the rest of the war. When the first national draft law was passed in March 1863, the Adventists worked with the government and eventually achieved noncombatant status as a church in September 1864. Additionally, White explained in this *Testimony* that the war was protracted because of problems in the Northern army, such as a lack of unity, pro-Southern officers, military rivalry, a lack of resolve to defeat the enemy in battle, and the unfeeling attitude of its leaders. In the midst of this depressing situation, she nevertheless offered a ray of hope that the North would not be defeated in the end.

1. *Review and Herald*, January 6, 1863, 48.

2. For more details on when this vision occurred, see the Introduction.

3. White, *Testimonies for the Church*, 1:355.

4. Ibid., 1:355, 356.

5. Ibid., 1:258.

6. Ibid., 1:356.

7. Robert E. Sterling, "Civil War Draft Resistance in the Middle West" (PhD diss., Northern Illinois University, 1974), 35.

8. William August Itter, "Conscription in Pennsylvania During the Civil War" (PhD diss., University of Southern California, 1941), 51, 52.

9. Basler, *The Collected Works of Abraham Lincoln*, 4:432.

10. Sterling, "Civil War Draft Resistance in the Middle West," 55.

11. Ibid., 56.

12. Samantha Jane Gaul, "Conscription, U.S.A.," in Heidler and Heidler, *Encyclopedia of the American Civil War*, 487.

13. Paul J. Springer, "Bounty System," in Tucker, *American Civil War: The Definitive Encyclopedia and Document Collection*, 1:204.

14. For a general overview on bounties, see Springer, "Bounty System," 1:204. For detailed discussions, see Eugene Converse Murdock, *Patriotism Limited, 1862–1865: The Civil War Draft and the Bounty System* (Kent, OH: Kent State University Press, 1967); Eugene Converse Murdock, *One Million Men: The Civil War Draft in the North* (New York: W. S. Hall, 1971), 197–304; and James W. Geary, *We Need Men: The Union Draft in the Civil War* (DeKalb, IL: Northern Illinois University Press, 1991), 12–21.

15. See Charles F. Howlett, "Conscription, CSA," in Tucker, *American Civil War: The Definitive Encyclopedia and Document Collection*, 1:421, 422.

16. Murdock, *Patriotism Limited*, 6.

17. For detailed discussion on the Militia Act, see Geary, *We Need Men*, 22–31.

18. "The Future of the War, the Government and the People," *New York Times*, August 4, 1862, quoted in Geary, *We Need Men*, 33.

19. Quoted in Geary, *We Need Men*, 38.

20. See Geary, *We Need Men*, 39; and Sterling, "Civil War Draft Resistance in the Middle West," 87.

21. Peter Brock, *Pacifism in the United States: From the Colonial Era to the First World War* (Princeton, NJ: Princeton University Press, 1968), 849.

22. McPherson and Hogue, *Ordeal by Fire*, 384.

23. James White, "The War Question," *Review and Herald*, October 14, 1862, 159.

24. As stated in the *Official Records of the Union and Confederate Armies*, ser. 3, vol. 2 (Washington, DC: Government Printing Office, 1899), 333.

25. W. C. White, D. E. Robinson, and A. L. White, "The Spirit of Prophecy and Military Service," 5, 6, in Ellen G. White Writings, accessed December 1, 2016, https://m.egwwritings.org/en/book/766.34.

26. Ibid., 6.

27. Ibid., 7.

28. E. S. W., "Another Good Example," *Review and Herald*, August 30, 1864, 112.

29. James White, "The Nation," *Review and Herald*, August 12, 1862, 84.

30. White, *Testimonies for the Church*, 1:356. James and Ellen White had recently been in Iowa and had observed a fanatical reaction to the draft issue that brought Adventists under suspicion of sympathizing with the rebels because they refused to fight. See Ron Graybill, "This Perplexing War: Why Adventists Avoided Military Service in the Civil War," *Insight*, October 10, 1978, 4.

31. Spalding, *Origin and History of Seventh-day Adventists*, 1:322.

32. James White, "The Nation," 84.

33. Ibid.

34. Ibid.

35. Ibid.

36. Ibid.

37. See White, *Testimonies for the Church*, 1:267.

38. James White, "The Nation," 100.

39. Ibid.

40. George R. Knight, *Lest We Forget: A Daily Devotional* (Hagerstown, MD: Review and Herald®, 2008), 180.

41. Ibid.

42. Joseph Clarke, "The Sword Vs. Fanaticism," *Review and Herald*, September 23, 1862, 135.

43. R. F. Cottrell, "Non-resistance," *Review and Herald*, October 14, 1862, 158; emphasis in the original.

44. James White, "The War Question," 159.

45. James White, "Letter to Bro. Carver," *Review and Herald*, October 21, 1862, 167.

46. White, *Testimonies for the Church*, 1:356.

47. Ibid.

48. Ibid., 1:356, 357.

49. B. F. Snook, "The War and Our Duty," *Review and Herald*, October 14, 1862, 159.

50. White, *Testimonies for the Church*, 1:357.

51. Ibid.

52. Stephen M. Kohn, *Jailed for Peace: The History of American Draft Law Violators, 1658–1985* (Westport, CT: Praeger, 1986), 20, 21.

53. White, *Testimonies for the Church*, 1:357.

54. Schwarz and Greenleaf, *Light Bearers*, 96.

55. White, *Testimonies for the Church*, 1:358, 359.

56. See "Ross, Alexander and Caroline," in Fortin and Moon, *The Ellen G. White Encyclopedia*, 501, 502.

57. White, *Testimonies for the Church*, 1:359.

58. Ibid.

59. Ibid., 1:360.

60. Ibid.

61. See "Ross, Alexander and Caroline," 501.

62. Ellen G. White to Mrs. T. M. Steward, Letter 7, 1862, quoted in Arthur White, *Ellen G. White*, 2:44.

63. Brock, *Pacifism in the United States*, 857.

64. White, *Testimonies for the Church*, 1:361.

65. Ibid., 1:361, 362.

66. See Neil Brody Miller, "Higher Law and Antislavery," Hinks and McKivigan, *Encyclopedia of Antislavery and Abolition*, 1:327–330.

67. White, *Testimonies for the Church*, 1:361.

68. For further discussion, see Arthur White, *Ellen G. White*, 2:49–52.

69. "Federal Conscription Act, March 3, 1863," in Mackey, *A Documentary History of the American Civil War Era*, 1:129–137. Quotation from §1.

70. White, Robinson, and White, "The Spirit of Prophecy and Military Service," 13.

71. McPherson, *Battle Cry of Freedom*, 606. For a detailed discussion on bounty jumpers, see Murdock, *Patriotism Limited*, 81–106; and Murdock, *One Million Men*, 218–254.

72. See Murdock's definitive study, *One Million Men*.

73. McPherson, *Ordeal by Fire*, 385.

74. For a general overview, see Samantha Jane Gaul, "New York City Draft Riots," in Heidler and Heidler, *En-*

cyclopedia of the American Civil War, 1414, 1415; and Martin K. Gordon, "New York City Draft Riots," in Tucker, *American Civil War: The Definitive Encyclopedia and Document Collection*, 1:1403–1405. For more detailed treatments, see Adrian Cook, *The Armies of the Streets: The New York City Draft Riots of 1863* (Lexington, KY: University of Kentucky Press, 1974); Iver Bernstein, *The New York City Draft Riots: Their Significance for American Society and Politics in the Age of the Civil War* (New York: Oxford University Press, 1991); and Barnet Schecter, *The Devil's Own Work: The Civil War Draft Riots and the Fight to Reconstruct America* (New York: Walker, 2005). For a challenge to the thesis that the riots were caused mainly by the commutation clause, see Geary, *We Need Men*, 105–108.

75. James McPherson provided an assessment of the first draft: "The Civil War draft has generally been accounted as a costly, sordid failure. Only 46,000 men were drafted directly into the Union army, and another 118,000 furnished substitutes. Taken together, these 164,000 men along with several thousand from earlier militia drafts constituted barely 8 percent of the Union soldiers. Thus conscription does indeed appear to have been a failure. But when one recalls that the real purpose of the draft was to stimulate volunteering, a different picture emerges. Nearly a million men enlisted or reenlisted voluntarily during the two years that the draft was in effect. Thus, despite its defects, the system did work. But it worked with such creaking inefficiency and apparent injustice that it became a model of how not to conduct a draft in future wars." McPherson, *Ordeal by Fire*, 385, 386.

76. Kevin Burton, a current doctoral student and former researcher at the Center for Adventist Research, has compiled a list of Seventh-day Adventist enlistees (about forty) and draftees (about ten) during the Civil War and will publish this research in the near future.

77. For discussion on all the noncombatant religious groups during the Civil War, see Edward Needles Wright, *Conscientious Objectors in the Civil War* (New York, NY: A Perpetua Book, 1961), 6–38; and Brock, *Pacifism in the United States*, 689–866.

78. See Wright, *Conscientious Objectors in the Civil War*, 121–131.

79. See ibid., 122–124; and John Nicolay and John Hay, *Abraham Lincoln: A History* (New York: Century, 1909), 6:328, 329.

80. Nicolay and Hay, *Abraham Lincoln: A History*, 6:327.

81. See Wright, *Conscientious Objectors in the Civil War*, 57–83.

82. Act of February 24, 1864, §17, quoted in ibid., 82, 83.

83. Schwarz and Greenleaf, *Light Bearers*, 97.

84. Wright, *Conscientious Objectors in the Civil War*, 84–86.

85. Schwarz and Greenleaf, *Light Bearers*, 97.

86. Knight, *Lest We Forget*, 181.

87. Ibid. For a detailed discussion on the events that took place in relation to Seventh-day Adventists, see White, Robinson, and White, "The Spirit of Prophecy and Military Service," 14–20; and Schwarz and Greenleaf, *Light Bearers*, 97–99.

88. White, *Testimonies for the Church*, 1:363.

89. McPherson, *Ordeal by Fire*, 319, 320. See also Weber, *Copperheads*, 68, 69.

90. McPherson, *Ordeal by Fire*, 295–297; and Weber, *Copperheads*, ix, 1–7.

91. Weber, *Copperheads*, 2.

92. Quoted in McPherson, *Ordeal by Fire*, 297.

93. See, e.g., Otis Nichols, "Letter From Brother Nichols," *Review and Herald*, March 10, 1863, 29.

94. White, *Testimonies for the Church*, 1:367.

95. Ibid., 1:363.

96. "Traitors in Our Army," *Review and Herald*, February 3, 1863, 74, 75.

97. White, *Testimonies for the Church*, 1:367.

98. Weber, *Copperheads*, 79–81; McPherson, *Ordeal by Fire*, 296, 297.

99. John W. Geary, quoted in Weber, *Copperheads*, 79.

100. William H. Gardiner II, quoted in Weber, *Copperheads*, 75.

101. Quoted in Weber, *Copperheads*, 83, 84.

102. Quoted in Weber, *Copperheads*, 84.

103. John W. Geary, quoted in Weber, *Copperheads*, 75.

104. White, *Testimonies for the Church*, 1:363.

105. Ibid., 1:365.

106. Ibid., 1:363.

107. Ibid., 1:366.

108. See Michael Burlingame and John R. Turner Ettlinger, eds. *Inside Lincoln's White House: The Complete Civil War Diary of John Hay* (Carbondale, IL: Southern Illinois University Press, 1997) 293, 294; and Tap, *Over Lincoln's Shoulder*, 131, 132. See especially Hennessy, *Return to Bull Run*, on McClellan, 238–242, and on Porter, 464, 465.

109. Sears, *The Civil War Papers of George B. McClellan*, 389. On McClellan's attitude expressed in letters to his wife, see Hennessy, *Return to Bull Run*, 240–242.

110. Sears, *The Civil War Papers of George B. McClellan*, 416.

111. Tap, *Over Lincoln's Shoulder*, 132.

112. Sears, *George B. McClellan: The Young Napoleon*, 254.

113. Edwin Bates, quoted in ibid., 254, 255.

114. White, *Testimonies for the Church*, 1:366.

115. Burlingame and Ettlinger, *Inside Lincoln's White House*, 37.

116. White, *Testimonies for the Church*, 1:366.

117. Ibid., 1:367.

118. Ibid., 1:363.

119. Ibid., 1:367.

120. See the following issues in the *Boston Evening Transcript*, February 5, 1863, 4; February 6, 1863, 4; February 17, 1863, 4; February 18, 1863, 4; February 19, 1863, 4; February 25, 1863, 4; and February 26, 1863, 4.

121. Nichols, "Letter From Bro. Nichols," 118.

122. White, *Testimonies for the Church*, 1:359.

123. Ibid., 1:365.

CHAPTER 13

OFFICERS AND THE SPIRITS

D id Union officers in Lincoln's army contact the spirits for guidance on the battlefield?[1] This is not a question one will find in the average Civil War book. But in light of the culture of that day, it is a question worth asking. This interesting subject was broached by Ellen White when she claimed that "many men in authority, generals and officers," acted "in conformity with instructions communicated by spirits."[2] She insisted that "the spirits of devils, professing to be dead warriors and skillful generals," had communicated "with men in authority" and controlled "many of their movements."[3] The present chapter will examine the historical setting of these interesting statements and determine their relevance in the Union army during the Civil War.

Ellen White's discussion on the officers and the spirits was published during the "heyday of spiritualism,"[4] a period when many Americans were captivated by the possibility of communicating with the dead. This movement, known by historians as Modern Spiritualism,[5] began in 1848 with the mysterious spirit rapping in Hydesville, New York, and flourished during the 1850s and the Civil War era. It declined after the war years but continued throughout the rest of the nineteenth century and found new forms of expression in the twentieth and twenty-first centuries. At its core was the belief "that two way communication is possible with specific spirit personalities through especially sensitive intermediaries called mediums."[6] The roots of Modern Spiritualism are most interesting and relevant to Ellen White's concern.

Roots of Modern Spiritualism

When Modern Spiritualism appeared on the American religious landscape during the late 1840s, it was not without its immediate historical antecedents. The occult practice of communicating with the spirits of the dead had figured prominently in many religions since ancient times. But several movements during the late eighteenth and early nineteenth centuries laid the foundation for the birth of Modern Spiritualism in 1848.[7] The most influential of these movements was Swedenborgianism.

Emanuel Swedenborg. Emanuel Swedenborg was a Swedish scientist and religion teacher who allegedly experienced a revelation in his late fifties from the spirit world, which changed the course of his life. During a trancelike state, he asserted that spirit beings gave him revelations of the true meaning of the Bible and the afterlife. He "bridged the gulf between life and death"[8] by speaking on a regular basis with departed spirits from this world, spirits from other worlds, and angelic beings. "I enjoy a perfect inspiration,"[9] he claimed and set forth his revelations of the spiritual sense of Scripture in his *Arcana Cœlestia*, an eight-volume commentary on Genesis and Exodus. The second coming of Christ was, to Swedenborg, a spiritual event manifested in his personal experience of disclosing the inner spiritual meaning of the Bible; that is, his writings *were* the Second Coming and thus products of divine dictation.[10]

During the last twenty-five years of his life, Swedenborg wrote voluminously on theological subjects revealed to him by the spirits.[11] "He believed that, like St. Paul, he had been taken into the spiritual realm while he was still alive in the natural world, and that his writings were an account of spiritual, rather than natural truths. They contained all previous truths and anticipated all future prophecies."[12] His influence on antebellum American society and culture was profound and could be found practically everywhere.[13] His alleged communication with spirit beings, trancelike states, and descriptions of the spirit world became influential factors in the development of American spiritualism.[14]

Animal magnetism and mesmerism. In addition to Swedenborgianism, belief in animal magnetism also helped lay the foundation for Spiritualism in America. In eighteenth-century Europe, various individuals believed that there was a magnetic fluid in the bodies of animals and humans that allowed for those with a large amount of this fluid in their systems to be put into a deep sleep, or "magnetic trance." During the trance, these individuals sometimes displayed supernatural characteristics, such as clairvoyant powers.[15] Experimentation with this theory became very popular and found its greatest exponent in the German physician Franz Anton Mesmer, who practiced in Paris and became well known for healing people of their ailments.[16]

Others built on Mesmer's theory and developed the practice of inducing a deep trance through staring intensely into the eyes of the patient, in combination with hand passes over the head and around the body (sometimes with a magnet). This induced trance state was eventually called mesmerism—known today as hypnotism.[17] The practice of mesmerism was introduced in America during the late 1820s, and the strange phenomenon spread across the East Coast, especially in the big cities such as Boston and New York.[18] By the early 1840s, lectures and public demonstrations of magnetism were immensely popular. According to Slater Brown, crowds thronged to the mesmerism displays, "and amateurs of all descriptions found that it was a simple matter to magnetize a subject."[19] The young Ellen White had her own encounters with mesmerists during the mid-1840s and considered any form of mind control to be a form of Spiritualism.[20]

Andrew Jackson Davis. The most direct historical link between mesmerism and Spiritualism occurred with Andrew Jackson Davis. As a young man, Davis was mesmerized in Poughkeepsie, New York, during the autumn of 1843. Traveling mesmerist J. Stanley Grimes had visited the little town and had captivated its citizens by mesmerizing people during public exhibitions at the town hall. Davis, a rather weak, anemic figure who worked for a local shoemaker, attended the meetings and volunteered one night to be mesmerized. Grimes failed to throw Davis into a mesmeric trance and sent him home because he was poor magnetic material. The people of Poughkeepsie, however, enthusiastically embraced the practice and began mesmerizing each other. One of these amateur mesmerizers successfully put Davis into a trance. "When magnetized and blindfolded, Davis could discern the inner organs of any invalid brought before him and was able to diagnose the patient's ailment or disability." Before long, Davis developed the reputation as an accomplished medical clairvoyant, and he attracted many patients from Poughkeepsie.[21]

On January 1, 1844, Davis experienced his first major vision, in which he flew through space and observed with "penetrating senses of the spirit" that "all Nature was radiant with countless lights, with atmospheres, with colors, with breathings, with emanations—all throbbing and pulsating with an indestructible life-essence— which seemed just ready to graduate and leap up into the human constitution!"[22] But it was not until March 6, 1844, that Davis received the vision that imparted his life calling and mission to the world. During this experience, Davis conversed with the spirits of Galen, the ancient Greek physician, and Emanuel Swedenborg. The climax of the vision was when Galen bestowed upon the young seer a magic staff that would provide guidance and comfort throughout his life's work.[23] In August 1847, Davis published his first major book, *The Principles of Nature, Her Divine Revelations, and a Voice to Mankind*; later that year he released the first edition of his periodical *Univercœlum and Spiritual Philosopher*. Davis's writings were thoroughly Swedenborgian in outlook and set forth the philosophical aspects of Spiritualism.[24]

The Shakers. Meanwhile, the group known as the Shakers had also been experiencing intense spiritualistic manifestations since 1837—eleven years before the advent of Modern Spiritualism. The Shaker movement began in the late 1740s as part of the Quaker revival in England and found its leadership in Ann Lee. Through visions, she led the group to America in 1774, where they established a colony near Albany, New York. Known for its unique style of worship that involved trembling and shaking (hence the term *shaker*), the sect attracted converts; after the death of Mother Ann Lee in 1784, Shaker communities spread across the Northeast. As the Shakers grew and developed in their religious experience, spirit visitations, allegedly from biblical prophets, were commonplace at their meetings.

In August 1837, a new era began in the Shaker colonies when several girls began to shake and twirl and subsequently went into a deep trance. They described traveling to heaven and talking with angels. As the experience spread throughout the community, it was apparent to the leaders that they were in a new era of spirit invasion and called it "Mother Ann's Second Appearing," or "Mother Ann's Work."[25] Mediums delivered messages from the spirits of the dead, including the spirit of Mother Ann; spirits visited the meetings and imparted songs for worship; people spoke in tongues; and revival ensued for years.[26] But the spirits began to withdraw in 1844 and were gone by 1846, leaving the sect in expectation of their return.[27] Some Shaker "instruments had prophesied, in fact, that similar manifestations would soon break forth in the world." When reports of the mysterious rappings in 1848 began to circulate, "the news did not come as a surprise."[28]

Thus, by 1848, the converging influence of Swedenborgianism, mesmerism, Andrew Jackson Davis, and the Shakers had laid the foundation for the birth of Modern Spiritualism.[29] While Jackson established the philosophical side of Spiritualism, the events that would transpire in the quaint little town of Hydesville, New York, birthed the more sensational and popular form of Spiritualism.

The birth and growth of Modern Spiritualism

During the night of Friday, March 31, 1848, the family of John D. Fox found no peace in their little Hydesville home. A strange knocking or rapping on the walls, under the floor, and around the beds kept the entire family awake. This rapping had first begun in 1844 at this house and returned with more intensity in 1847, accompanied by a cold presence felt by some members of the family and sightings of a strange man on the property.[30] The Fox family had already heard the rapping before, but this early spring night, blanketed with a light sheet of snow, was different. The rappings manifested intelligence.

Intelligent rapping sounds. According to Margaret Fox, John's wife, their two daughters, who slept in the same room with them, heard the noise "and tried to make a similar noise by snapping their fingers." As the youngest girl, Kate, snapped as fast as she could, "the sounds followed up in the room" and "made the same number of raps the girl did." When she stopped, the sounds stopped. The other girl, Margaretta (later known as Maggie), jokingly said to the rappings, "Now, do just as I do. Count one, two, three, four," while striking her hands on each number. The intelligence repeated her exactly. At this point, the girls were frightened. Mrs. Fox took over and asked the noise to count to ten. "It appeared to answer her by repeating every blow she made." Then she asked the ages of her "different children successively, and it gave the number of raps corresponding to the ages" of her children.[31]

Mrs. Fox eventually discovered, by communicating with the intelligence through rapping, that it was the spirit of a peddler who had been robbed and slain at the house. The family invited neighbors to come and hear the strange sounds, from which came personal knowledge known only to each visiting family.[32] By the spring and summer of 1848, hundreds of people had visited the Fox home and listened for communication from beyond the physical world. Before the end of the year, E. E. Lewis, an enterprising journalist, published the testimonies of those who heard the original raps in his forty-page pamphlet, titled *A Report of the Mysterious Noises Heard in the House of Mr. John D. Fox, in Hydesville, Arcadia, Wayne County, Authenticated by the Certificates, and Confirmed by the Statements of the Citizens of That Place and Vicinity.* The consensus was summed up by one witness who stated that he could not "account for it [the rappings] on any other ground than it is supernatural."[33] By the early months of 1849, the rappings were occurring in other homes throughout western New York, with hundreds of people believing in them as genuine voices from the spirit world. Some local newspapers published accounts of the rappings, and travelers spread stories, but the phenomenon was not yet known throughout the nation.[34]

Ellen White's response to the rappings. In August 1849, Ellen White published a warning about the rappings: "I saw that the mysterious knocking in N.Y. and other places, was the power of Satan; and that such things would be more and more common, clothed in a religious garb, to lull the deceived into more security."[35] Although other Protestant Christians attributed the rappings to a satanic origin, White appeared to be the only one who made this claim through a prophetic vision.

Three months after Ellen White published this statement, the Fox sisters, at the urging of the spirits, submitted their powers to an investigation before the public. Early in November, Eliab Wilkinson Capron, an itinerant newspaper writer and editor, took up the sisters' cause and orchestrated a series of committee investigations at Corinthian Hall in Rochester, New York. During each night of the investigation, the spirits manifested themselves before great crowds of people observing the proceedings. The *New-York Weekly Tribune* gave the meetings national attention in its columns and, before long, was flooded with articles and letters about the rappings.[36] Thus, the story of the Fox sisters' communication with the dead spread across the country and birthed Modern Spiritualism.

Rapid growth of Spiritualism. By the summer of 1850, mediums were showing up in sizable numbers in numerous places. In Auburn, New York, for instance, there were up to one hundred individuals who spoke with the spirits through rapping, clairvoyance, tongues, and other manifestations.[37] While in New York that spring, the Fox sisters sat down for an interview with a group of prominent figures, such as the novelist James Fenimore Cooper, the historian George Bancroft, and the poet William Cullen Bryant. The men could not account for the intelligence behind the raps, and they reported their findings to the public.[38] "Such candid statements," wrote Eliab Wilkinson Capron, "made on the authority of men eminent for their literary attainments and sense of honor, attracted very general attention."[39] Even the wife of Horace Greeley, the well-known editor of the *New-York Daily Tribune*, invited the girls to stay with them for a while and show their abilities. Although skeptical, Horace Greeley acknowledged that there were elements of the manifestations that were unexplainable, such as the responses to his questions of a "very remarkable character."[40] In 1888, the Fox sisters confessed that the rappings were created by artificial means (including the popping of knee and toe joints); however, they later recanted their confession.

Over the next several years, the movement grew and flourished at an astonishing rate across the North, especially in such big cities as New York, Boston, and Philadelphia. The manifestations moved beyond mere rapping when the spirits chose to speak through automatic writing, slate writing, control of the medium's voice, moving physical objects (table raising and levitating the bodies of the medium and others at a sitting), the playing of untouched musical instruments, and materializations of the spirits.[41]

The medium and the séance, or circle, were at the heart of the movement. The medium was the human channel through which the spirit communicated a message to those seated (sitters) in the séance (literally, "to sit").[42] Many of the mediums were women who, as historian Ann Braude documented, experienced through mediumship a social and political voice in their male-dominated society.[43] These séances often ended up being no more than a source of entertainment for many in the curious and thrill-seeking American audience. Unfortunately for the true believers, the movement was checkered with controversy, trickery, and fraud that perpetuated public skepticism over the years.[44] But there were enough manifestations that persuaded many to believe.

Throughout the 1850s, Spiritualist periodicals exploded off the press, new organizations formed, and mediums continued to multiply.[45] In 1857, the longest-lasting and most influential American Spiritualist journal rolled off the press in Boston—the *Banner of Light*. It reported on speakers and events and printed correspondence from across the country. Its publishers were avowed Spiritualists and mediums who conducted regular séances at the publishing office. The *Banner of Light* eventually became the "exponent of the Spiritual Philosophy of the Nineteenth Century"[46] and was a significant voice for the dead to speak to the living.[47] During the war, the

Banner of Light patriotically supported the Union and reported on Spiritualists participating in the war.

Many prominent political figures and government officials supported the movement as well: New York Congressman Augustus Porter Hascall, Senator Nathaniel P. Tallmadge, U.S. Supreme Court Justice John McLean, and Captain Abner Doubleday of the U.S. Army.[48] In 1854, when the Society for the Diffusion of Spiritual Knowledge was founded, it could count among its organizers several judges, successful businessmen, a former U.S. Senator and governor, and a military officer.[49]

The prominent New York lawyer George Templeton Strong observed the popularity of the Spiritualist movement and wrote in his journal on November 26, 1854, how surprised he was that "hundreds of thousands of people in this country would believe themselves able to communicate daily with the ghosts of their grandfathers." He was in disbelief that "ex-judges of the Supreme Court, senators, clergymen, professors of physical sciences, should be lecturing and writing books on the new treasures of all this."[50] By this time, the harmonial philosophy of Andrew Jackson Davis and the popular physical manifestations of the mediums had combined to form modern American Spiritualism.[51] "A new revelation, hostile to that of the Church and the Bible, finding acceptance on the authority of knocking ghosts and oscillating tables," wrote Strong, was "a momentous fact in history as throwing light on the intellectual caliber and moral tone of the age in which multitudes adopt it."[52]

After her initial warning about the rappings in 1849, Ellen White published two more warnings in 1850 and 1854, in which she reiterated her previous statements about the movement's satanic origins, rapid growth, and religious garb and then added several new insights and predictions.[53] By 1858, she published her book *Spiritual Gifts: The Great Controversy, Between Christ and His Angels, and Satan and His Angels*, which devoted an entire chapter to the subject of Spiritualism.[54] Over the years, as Spiritualism continued to grow, Adventist leaders published numerous pamphlets and books against the movement, warning readers of its dangers.[55]

As White predicted, Spiritualism took on a religious garb. Ministers in the Methodist, Universalist, and Quaker denominations, for example, experienced the rappings in their own residences and gave the manifestations their support.[56] Spiritualism especially appealed to the Unitarians and Universalists;[57] in some cases, entire Universalist congregations left their denomination to become Spiritualists.[58] Nearly all of the Spiritualists based their theology on Andrew Jackson Davis, who based his on Emanuel Swedenborg. They thus embraced a set of beliefs about man, God, death, and the spirit world with a distinctive religious character.[59] Although Spiritualism was anything but monolithic in terms of practice and belief,[60] scholars of the movement have still classified it as a religious movement—but with a heterodox belief system.[61] For example, some Spiritualists professed to be Bible-believing Christians, while others rejected the Bible. Many of the Spiritualists saw Jesus Christ as a medium clairvoyant, but their view of Christ could hardly be classified as an orthodox evangelical view.[62] Religious liberalism best describes how the Spiritualists viewed the Bible.[63] In short, Spiritualism "was a religion," wrote historian Molly McGarry, "that had no churches, no membership rolls, and no formal governing body until its waning years."[64]

Such was the historical context of Modern Spiritualism up to the time of the Civil War. By the mid-1850s, about "one million Americans—one out of every twenty-eight—believed in the spiritual nature of the manifestations and gave some support to the movement by buying publications, attending lectures, or patronizing mediums."[65] The *Spiritualist Register* for 1860 "estimated that there were one million, six hundred thousand spiritualists in the United States."[66] Although other estimates are slightly different, historians agree that Spiritualism was a substantial force in America by the end of the 1850s.[67] With such a significant history and presence of Spiritualism by the time of the Civil War, it should be no surprise that in the face of all the carnage and death, soldiers, officers, and civilians would appeal to the supernatural for comfort and guidance.

Spiritualism and the Civil War

After the height of its popularity in the mid-1850s, spiritual phenomena declined somewhat for the rest of the decade. "By the time war broke out, spiritualist notions were sufficiently common to influence and engage even those who were not formal adherents, and the war made spiritualist doctrines increasingly attractive."[68] Consequently, the Spiritualists' promise of connecting families with the spirits of deceased soldiers gave the movement a boost.

The *Banner of Light*, for example, began to publish messages from the spirits of deceased soldiers. Each message came through the *Banner of Light* medium, Mrs. J. H. Conant, who wrote "while in a condition called the Trance." Each message, claimed the *Banner of Light*, "was spoken by the spirit whose name it bears."[69] Thus,

Confederate and Union soldiers killed on the battlefield spoke from the spirit world and reported on their experience in the afterlife. Even Stonewall Jackson spoke from the grave and defended his reasons for supporting the Confederacy.[70]

Historian Drew Gilpin Faust discovered something interesting, however, when she searched on computer databases for the names of the disembodied spirits speaking through Mrs. Conant. Many of those names could not be found "in the database of 6.3 million records of 3.5 million soldiers that the National Park Service has compiled with the assistance of the tools of our computerized age." Faust concludes that "the *Banner of Light* did not present the story of any reader's actual kin; it did not provide accurate details of deaths and burials, the kind of information families sought as they flocked to battlefields or inundated the Sanitary Commission's Hospital Directory with tens of thousands of anxious inquires." Nevertheless, Faust explained, Spiritualism provided consolation "in its promise that there could and would be answers to these questions, even if it did not itself immediately provide them." Ultimately, "the Message Department of the *Banner of Light* . . . affirmed for its community of readers that individual soldiers were neither dead nor lost." As the departed spirits struggled "to reach out to those they had left behind in order to console them," they reassured the living with Spiritualism's core: "I Still Live."[71] Thus, Spiritualism made its impact on civilians in the face of so much death on the battlefield.

The Union army and Spiritualism

Ellen White's statements on the officers and spirits occur in the midst of *Testimony for the Church, No. 9*,[72] in which she discussed the issues of the draft debate among Adventists and the lack of unity in the Northern army. She framed this subject with a warning about the end of time. "Everything is preparing for the great day of God. Time will last a little longer until the inhabitants of the earth have filled up the cup of their iniquity, and then the wrath of God, which has so long slumbered, will awake, and this land of light will drink the cup of His unmingled wrath. The desolating power of God is upon the earth to rend and destroy. The inhabitants of the earth are appointed to the sword, to famine, and to pestilence."[73]

White and other Adventists believed that Christ was coming soon and that the war was a sign of His nearness. In her understanding, the "desolating power of God" was "upon the earth to rend and destroy" through the war then taking place. The last sentence of the paragraph alluded to a war beyond the present one in the United

States: "The inhabitants of the earth are appointed to the sword, to famine, and to pestilence." While this statement certainly found partial fulfillment in the two World Wars, it ultimately points to the time of the Second Coming, yet to come.

This paragraph was thus a fitting prelude to the manifestation of Spiritualism in the Union army. In White's view of the end times, Spiritualism was to play a large role in deceiving the world. As such, what took place in the Union army was part of Satan's snares "to deceive the world."[74]

After a prelude on the "great day of God," White penned. "Very many men in authority, generals and officers, act in conformity with instructions communicated by spirits."[75] That "very many" military leaders engaged in Spiritualism during the war is quite a bold claim. Because the context of the *Testimony* focused on the Union army, it is safe to assume that White meant mostly Northern "generals and officers." Spiritualism was a Northern phenomenon but had made some progress in the South during the antebellum years,[76] especially in the slave community and, in particular, New Orleans.[77]

The claim that many military leaders in the Union army engaged in Spiritualism probably came as no surprise to White's readers who had read J. H. Waggoner's 1858 book, *The Nature and Tendency of Modern Spiritualism*.[78] Waggoner had read through the Spiritualist literature of the time and confirmed White's earlier warnings about Spiritualism. But what evidence is there for White's claim that Spiritualism was widespread in the Union army?

The evidence

Historian Mark Lause pointed out in his book *Free Spirits: Spiritualism, Republicanism, and Radicalism in the Civil War Era* that Spiritualists were patriotic and thus supportive of the Union. After the shelling of Fort Sumter, for example, the *Banner of Light* rallied to the side of the Union and embraced war as the only cure for the rebellion in the South.[79] On August 16, 1861, Spiritualist and abolitionist Henry C. Wright spoke at the National Convention of Spiritualists on the subject "The Mission of Spiritualism in the present crisis of our country." He argued that Spiritualists should unite with their compatriots and take up "the great mission of our nation in maintaining the principles of the Declaration of Independence." He emphasized that Spiritualism claimed to be the best religion in the world and how its principles applied "to the needs of our Country."[80]

A NATION IN GOD'S HANDS

Judge John W. Edmonds, a leading Spiritualist, lawyer, and politician, admonished all Spiritualists: "Those of us who are strong and able may be called upon to do battle for Freedom, here, or on far off fields of carnage; and perhaps to perish in her cause." Then, "be it so!" he declared, for Spiritualists have no fear of death and should not be afraid to go into battle. Other Spiritualists should serve the sick and wounded with acts of kindness. "On the battle-field," Edmonds urged, "let the Spiritualist remember the forbearance and love which his faith teaches him."[81]

Spiritualists heeded these calls and generally threw themselves into the Union war effort. By November 1861, the *Banner of Light* wrote that "many a son is off with the troops, fighting battles for the government."[82] By December 1862, *Banner of Light* reported that much of its staff had left for the war and noted the military position that each one served.[83] There was also talk of a "regiment of Spiritualists," with the commander identified as a "well known Spiritualist and medium."[84] In response, Andrew Jackson Davis wrote an opinion piece that denounced the idea of a Spiritualist regiment and declared: "If Spiritualists cannot carry their glorious faith into any Regiment, and be sustained by it, they are not up to their own noble standards."[85] Apparently, the Spiritualist regiment idea never caught on, but Spiritualists could be found throughout many a regiment during the war.[86]

According to leading Spiritualist medium and historian Emma Hardinge in her history of the movement published in 1870, *Modern American Spiritualism*, "We doubt if the whole array of the vast [Northern] armies that marched to the fields of battle, should show a single regiment where one or more of this faith [Spiritualism] was not at the post of patriotic duty. When the peculiar idiosyncrasies of these raw and inexperienced forces began to be understood and appreciated by their leaders, Spiritualists were eagerly sought for as recruits, even by those who had no sympathy with their belief." The reasons she gave for this preference were "first, that the Spiritualists' total unconcern on the subject of death made them the bravest of soldiers; next, that their vital and peculiar faith rendered them amenable to command, gentle, subordinate, and exempt from most of the popular vices of the age, such as drinking, smoking, and profanity."[87]

Hardinge also noted that the war effort had depleted seats at the "rostrum, chair, hall and family altar" of the Spiritualist community. Those left at home provided funds for bounties, and lecturers gave their speaking "fees in aid of the country's suffering and wounded heroes." She claimed that Spiritualists could be found in every major aspect of the war effort: "The nurses in the hospitals, the surgeons in the ranks, the chaplains of the regiments, and the soldiers themselves, from the distinguished general officer to the humblest private of the ranks, numbered amongst them the ubiquitous Spiritualists."[88]

Lause estimates that throughout the war, "not a battle of any size was fought that did not claim the lives of spiritualists."[89] The *Banner of Light*, for example, printed obituaries of Spiritualist soldiers throughout the war.[90] Spiritualist physicians, nurses, and chaplains were also highlighted in the reporting on the war.[91] "As might be expected from the demographics of the movement," explained Lause, "numerous Federal officers were also ardent spiritualists."[92] Note the examples below of military personnel who were confirmed Spiritualists or had some connection to it. These names are not exhaustive, and the documentation is ongoing.

Union general. Ethan Allen Hitchcock was commissioned as a major general in 1862 and served on the president's War Board and later as the commissioner for the exchange of war prisoners.[93] He embraced the philosophic side of Spiritualism and believed that Swedenborg was "a High Mason" and that Jesus was a "poetic representation of the Truth" rather than a historical person.[94]

Officers. There are several examples of Union officers in the army who were either practicing Spiritualists or showed interest in it. Thomas Wentworth Higginson, a captain of the Fifty-First Massachusetts Infantry, was an avowed Spiritualist and abolitionist.[95] One example of a Confederate officer who had a history with Spiritualism is George Washington Rains, who served the Confederacy as a colonel and specialized in explosives.[96] He showed up frequently in the literature of Spiritualism during the 1850s.[97] Lause mentions several Northern officers who were obvious Spiritualists, such as Lieutenant William Berry, the copublisher of the *Banner of Light*, who died at Antietam, and Lieutenant Colonel Dorus M. Fox, the uncle of the Fox sisters.[98]

A more familiar example of an officer who probably believed in Spiritualism was Major Sullivan Ballou, who penned a letter to his wife before he died in the Battle of First Manassas that was featured in Ken Burns' 1990 documentary series *The Civil War*: "O Sarah! If the dead can come back to this earth and flit unseen around those they loved, I shall always be near you; . . . if there be a soft breeze upon your cheek, it shall be my breath, as the cool air fans your throbbing temple, it shall be my spirit passing by."[99]

Union soldiers. In the *Thirty-Third Regiment Illinois Veteran Volunteer Infantry,* the record shows a Jacob Miller (known as "Jake") from Abingdon, Illinois, who "was the guardian angel of Company H. If any one wanted to fuss with any of the H boys he had to first run up against Jake. After a 'seance' with him there was no more trouble."[100]

Union chaplains. Unitarian Spiritualist Arthur B. Fuller served in the Sixteenth Massachusetts and died at Fredericksburg. Another Unitarian Spiritualist, George H. Hepworth, ministered to the Forty-Seventh Massachusetts.[101] Ellen Elvira Gibson Hobart, the first female military chaplain, was an avowed Spiritualist who served the First Wisconsin Heavy Artillery.[102] John Pierpont served as the chaplain of the Twenty-Second Massachusetts and later as a clerk in the Treasury Department. He was a Universalist minister turned Spiritualist by the time of the war; while in the Treasury Department, he interacted with Mary Todd Lincoln in her quest to connect with her son in the spirit world.[103] Charles Spear, the brother of the flamboyant Spiritualist John Murray Spear, served as a hospital chaplain in the Washington area.[104]

Washington, D.C. In addition, Spiritualists flourished in Washington during the Civil War era.[105] Thomas Gales Forster, for example, served as a clerk in the War Department of the Union during the war and was a confirmed Spiritualist.[106] There was also Congressman Robert Dale Owen, who wrote *Footfalls on the Boundary of Another World*.[107] Lincoln's secretary of the Navy, Gideon Welles, and his wife, Mary Jane, supposedly consulted the spirits about their dead children, and some connected Edwin M. Stanton, the secretary of war, to Spiritualism because of his Spiritualist cousin.[108]

Mary Todd Lincoln and the president. From the beginning of his presidency, Abraham Lincoln received numerous communications from Spiritualists advising him on the conduct of the war. There is no evidence, however, that he responded to any of these communications.[109] When President and Mrs. Lincoln's son Willie died on February 20, 1862, however, both parents were susceptible to the Spiritualist's promise that their son could still speak with them. The president grieved deeply and intensely in the days following his son's death but eventually recovered enough to resume his presidential duties and conduct the war. Mary, however, sank into a period of intense mourning that lasted for months.[110]

As President Lincoln "read the Bible for comfort," Mrs. Lincoln "retreated into the spirit world and the society of spiritualists."[111] By the spring of 1862, she was found in regular attendance at the home of a well-known medium in Georgetown

Mary Todd Lincoln

who introduced her to Nettie Colburn (later Maynard due to marriage), a gifted trance medium. Colburn so impressed Mrs. Lincoln that she arranged for Colburn to stay in Washington, and she regularly utilized the young medium's services.[112] By November 1863, Mary Lincoln spoke of personal visitations from Willie's spirit without the use of a medium. "He lives," she divulged to her half-sister Emilie. "He comes to me every night, and stands at the foot of my bed with the same sweet, adorable smile he has always had; he does not always come alone; little Eddie is sometimes with him and twice he has come with our brother Alec." Mary exclaimed to Emilie: "You cannot dream of the comfort this gives me."[113]

During the war years 1862–1864, several séances were conducted in the White House, possibly as many as eight.[114] According to Nettie Colburn Maynard, who published her supernatural experiences at the White House in her 1891 book *Was Abraham Lincoln a Spiritualist?*, Lincoln attended several séances and actually participated. She claimed that at one séance, when a medium levitated a piano, Lincoln sat on it with his "legs dangling over the side" in an effort to hold it down. The President, she said, "expressed himself perfectly satisfied that the motion was caused by some 'invisible power.'"[115] In one of her trances, Maynard even drew lines on a battle map that conformed "to the plan agreed upon" by the president and his generals.[116]

Jay Monaghan provided a scholarly review of Nettie's book and concluded that, although some of the events may have occurred, the evidence that Lincoln embraced Spiritualism or heeded Maynard's words "is meager."[117] Lincoln scholars Don E. Fehrenbacher and Virginia Fehrenbacher believe Maynard's accounts of the president's attending her séances to be unauthentic.[118] "Evidence that Lincoln attended séances is weak," they argue, "depending almost entirely on the statements of spiritualists."[119] Civil War historian James M. McPherson agreed with the Fehrenbachers and stated that "no serious scholar" would take Maynard's account as authentic.[120] Accordingly, the major recent biographers of Lincoln, such as Benjamin Thomas, Stephen W. Sears, Allen C. Guelzo, Ronald C. White Jr., and Michael Burlingame do not even consider the claims of the Spiritualists worthy of mention in their well-received biographies.[121]

In his best-selling biography *Lincoln*, David Herbert Donald devotes a statement to the subject: "Perhaps as many as eight séances were held in the White House itself. Lincoln attended one, but he was not convinced."[122] The Rev. P. D. Gurley, whose church Lincoln attended, observed that "after his son's death," the President "was greatly annoyed by the report that he was interested in spiritualism." Lincoln told Gurley the "report originated from the fact that a medium had chanced to call on Mrs. Lincoln," and added, "a simple faith in God is good enough for me, and beyond that I do not concern myself with very much."[123] In the biographies of Mary Todd Lincoln, however, the topic of Spiritualism generally received attention because it is well documented that she involved herself in séances.[124]

When combined with the background of the Spiritualists' enthusiastic support for and involvement in the war, the above examples suggest that Spiritualism was not only present but fairly widespread throughout the Union army, as well as in Washington, DC. But is there any evidence that many Union military leaders utilized the occult skills of these Spiritualists before battle and, as White stated, acted in "conformity with instructions communicated by spirits"?[125]

Union officers utilizing Spiritualist mediums. It stands to reason that with so many Spiritualists in the military, commanding officers would at least have noticed their presence and considered using their skills as mediums on the battlefield. It is upon this point that Emma Hardinge made a most interesting comment in her history of American Spiritualism, which was published only five years after the Civil War ended:

> Numerous cases are recorded proving that kind spirits, through their mediums, have warned the officers of the proximity of danger, or the most advantageous course to pursue in positions of difficulty. As these spiritual interpositions were rarely openly acknowledged and never admitted into official reports, their record of course depends on the fidelity of personal narrative; hence we do not feel justified in making them more publicly known, than the chief actors therein themselves desired. Yet the truth of these ministrations and their value became at last so generally felt and admitted, that the presence of military Spiritualists, but especially mediums, was eagerly sought after in these desperate times.[126]

Several features of this significant statement are worth noting. First, Hardinge described a situation in which "kind spirits, through their mediums" gave helpful military guidance to officers on the battlefield. Second, Hardinge noted that "these spiritual interpositions were rarely openly acknowledged and never admitted into official reports" and the "chief actors" did not want their experience publicized. Seeking guidance from Spiritualist mediums was not considered good military strategy, and no officer spoke of it in *The War of the Rebellion: A Compilation of the Official Records of the Union and Confederate Armies*. Third, as Dee Morris observed, Hardinge must have reviewed correspondence that documented the "numerous cases" when military Spiritualists had advised their commanding officers during battles.[127] Unfortunately for researchers, however, she chose to keep confidential any names or details about these records, and so documentation for her claim is absent. Finally, Hardinge noted that these military mediums were "eagerly sought after in these desperate times." One can imagine situations in which officers were desperately seeking any advantage over their enemy in battle and thus turning to the supernatural for guidance.

This statement by Hardinge is most relevant to White's discussion. Both of them affirm that spirits guided officers in the Union army, but they represent two very different interpretations of this guidance by mediums. Hardinge saw Spiritualism in the army as a good thing. After all, the well-known medium believed that the spirits speaking with the officers were "kind spirits" that intended a positive outcome for the Union. White, however, took a polar opposite position on the spirits. She identified them as the "spirits of devils" and "lying spirits" that were leading the Union officers "to certain destruction." She lamented, "Instead of the leading men in this war trusting in the God of Israel, and directing their armies to trust in the only One who can deliver them from their enemies, the majority inquire of the prince of devils and trust in him."[128]

Although both the Hardinge and White statements on this subject are insightful, actual contemporary testimonial evidence of Union officers receiving guidance from spirits is still awaiting discovery. Nevertheless, the information above on the significant presence of Spiritualists in the Union army in various capacities does provide a framework for the believability of White's and Hardinge's claims.

How the spirits communicated with the officers

White explained how the spirits communicated with the officers. The spirits, she penned, speak as "dead warriors and skillful generals, [who] communicate with men in authority and control many of their movements." These "leaders in the army really believe that the spirits of their friends and of dead warriors, the fathers of the Revolutionary War, are guiding them." She noted that the military leaders recognized the "manners" and "peculiar traits of character" of the dead generals.[129] These phrases depicted the work of mediums while in a trance. Apparently, the spirits of military leaders who died earlier in the war and heroes of previous wars spoke through these mediums. The spirit of Revolutionary War father George Washington had already allegedly appeared and spoken through a medium before the war,[130] and messages from deceased Union and Confederate officers circulated in Spiritualist journals during and after the war.[131] If military officers experienced these kinds of spirit manifestations, they didn't admit it in their official reports, as Hardinge noted.

Assuming that White is correct, these military officers probably met with the mediums in their tents, most likely one-on-one or perhaps in the context of a séance. The spirits took control of the medium, who then spoke in the voice and mannerisms of the deceased military leader. Accordingly, the officers heard the voice of the dead military leader through the voice of the medium or recognized the physical form of the deceased person through materialization (the manifestation of a spirit that "appears to be solid by sight and touch" through the work of a medium) or transfiguration ("when the face of the medium transforms and transfigures into the face of a spirit entity").[132] Interestingly, in 1858, White had already noted that "Satan has power to bring the appearance of forms before us purporting to be our relatives and friends."[133]

To White, the satanic nature of the communications accounted for the inconsistent instruction: "One general has directions from these spirits to make special moves and is flattered with the hope of success. Another receives directions which differ widely from those given to the first. Sometimes those who follow the directions given obtain a victory, but more frequently they meet with defeat." At other times, the spirits give the "leading men an account of events to transpire in battles in which they are about to engage, and of individuals who will fall in the battle." When it comes to pass as the spirits said, the leaders believe in the "spiritual manifestations." But when the information from the spirit was incorrect, "the deceiving spirits make some explanation, which is received." In the end, "the deception upon minds is so great that many fail to perceive the lying spirits which are leading them on to certain destruction."[134]

It should be noted that White's explanation of this spirit guidance did not apply

Ellen White, about 1880
(egwwritings.org)

Emma Hardinge Britten in
1884

to every battle of the Civil War. Although she indicated that a large number of generals and officers ("very many") followed the counsel of the spirits, she also stated that there were generals "who are wholly devoted and seek to do all they can to stop this dreadful Rebellion."[135] So her discussion of spirit guidance does not apply to every Union military leader or every battle of the war.

Ultimately, White attributed all of the medium activity associated with the military leaders to satanic origins: "The great leading rebel general, Satan, is acquainted with the transactions of this war, and he directs his angels to assume the form of dead generals, to imitate their manners, and exhibit their peculiar traits of character." With a bit of satire, she stated, "If they were not under the strongest fascinating deception, they would begin to think that the warriors in heaven (?) did not manifest good and successful generalship, or had forgotten their famed earthly skill."[136]

The Union like Israel of old

Immediately following this dismal situation of officers seeking guidance from the spirits, White quoted an angel: "How can God prosper such a people? If they would look to and trust in Him; if they would only come where He could help them, according to His own glory, He would readily do it."[137] She then gave her readers a ray of hope: "I saw that God would not give the Northern army wholly into the hands of a rebellious people, to be utterly destroyed by their enemies."[138] With the background of the recent and devastating defeat at Fredericksburg, these words offered assurance that the Union would eventually turn to God and not be ultimately defeated. Yet the wording that the Northern army would not be given "wholly into the hands" of the enemy indicated that there would be plenty of death and destruction along the way to victory.

"I was referred to Deuteronomy 32:26-30," she wrote, and then she cited the entire text.[139] The context of this passage addressed a situation in which "the only thing that would prevent the Lord from permitting the complete destruction of his people would be concern that the adversaries employed in the divine judgment might claim for themselves the honor of victory over Israel." As Old Testament scholar Peter Craigie points out, "The poetic irony [in the passage] thus shows a brief hope, but not for any merit that could be found in Israel."[140] Apparently, White understood the Union as a nation like ancient Israel, with some hope in its war with the South—but not because of any merit in itself.

Last mention of the spirits

After Ellen White set forth the lack of mutual support among Union generals, White penned her last statement on the spirits: "Satan has, through his angels, communicated with officers who were cool, calculating men when left to themselves, and they have given up their own judgment and have been led by these lying spirits into very difficult places, where they have been repulsed with dreadful slaughter."[141] In this context, she emphasized Satan's love of carnage and death: "It suits his Satanic majesty well to see slaughter and carnage upon the earth. He loves to see the poor soldiers mowed down like grass." In the previous paragraph, she had probably alluded to the Second Battle of Bull Run. But here she possibly had in mind the "dreadful slaughter" at the Battle of Antietam in September 1862 (she received the vision in November 1862), in which "the poor soldiers" were clearly "mowed down like grass."[142] Her readers in January 1863 would have recalled the recent slaughter at Fredericksburg in December, as well as Antietam.

She continued her discussion on the battles: "I saw that the rebels have often been in positions where they could have been subdued without much effort; but the communications from spirits have led the Northern generals and blinded their eyes until the rebels were beyond their reach." One cannot help but think of General George McClellan during the summer and early fall of 1862 when he lost numerous opportunities to defeat the rebels. This famous general tended to sympathize with the South. "And some generals would rather allow the rebels to escape than to subdue them. They think more of the darling institution of slavery than of the prosperity of the nation."[143] One cannot say with absolute assurance that White had McClellan in mind. But Spiritualists have claimed him as one of their own despite the fact that there is no mention of Spiritualism in his biographies or in his writings—other than an alleged dream he experienced in 1861 in which the spirit of George Washington gave him military advice.[144] Whatever generals or officers to whom White's strong words applied, in her understanding, listening to and following the counsel of the spirits was one of the reasons "why the war is so protracted."[145]

Conclusion

In her 1858 book *Spiritual Gifts: The Great Controversy, Between Christ and His Angels, and Satan and His Angels*, Ellen White wrote, "Satan has power to bring the appearance of forms before us purporting to be our relatives and friends that now sleep in Jesus. It will be made to appear as if they were present, the words they uttered while here, which we were familiar with, will be spoken, and the same tone of voice which they had while living will fall upon the ear. All this is to deceive the world, and ensnare them into the belief of this delusion."[146]

These words reflected White's understanding that death is a state of unconsciousness until the resurrection[147] and provided the framework for her discussion, published early in 1863, of the officers and the spirits during the Civil War years. She then set forth an analogy relevant to the day that captured the swiftness in which the world would swallow the deception of Spiritualism:

I saw the rapidity with which this delusion was spreading. A train of cars was shown me, going with the speed of lightning. The angel bade me look carefully. I fixed my eyes upon the train. It seemed that the whole world was on board. Then he showed me the conductor, who looked like a stately fair person, whom all the passengers looked up to and reverenced. I was perplexed, and asked my attending angel who it was. Said he, It is Satan. He is the conductor in the form of an angel of light. He has taken the world captive. They are given over to strong delusions, to believe a lie that they may be damned. His agent, the next highest in order to him, is the engineer, and others of his agents are employed in different offices as he may need them, and they are all going with lightning speed to perdition.[148]

For the rest of her life, Ellen White would warn against the dangers of Spiritualism. The significance of the rapping at the Fox home in 1848 never faded from her mind. In the final book of the Conflict of the Ages series, titled *The Great Controversy*, White wrote, "The mysterious rapping with which modern spiritualism began was not the result of human trickery or cunning, but was the direct work of evil angels, who thus introduced one of the most of soul-destroying delusions."[149] This "soul-destroying" delusion, she explained, will continue to the end of time when it will reach the "full accomplishment" of Satan's "masterpiece of deception in the development of spiritualism."[150]

As she brought "The Rebellion" in *Testimony for the Church, No. 9* to a conclusion, White emphasized once more God's punishment on "both the South and the North,"[151] the subject to which we now turn in the final section of this book.

Chapter in a nutshell

In *Testimony for the Church, No. 9*, Ellen White stated that "Very many men in authority, generals and officers, act in conformity with instructions communicated by spirits." This interesting statement was published during the heyday of American Spiritualism, which found its roots in Emanuel Swedenborg, Andrew Jackson Davis, mesmerism, and the Shakers. These converging influences laid the foundation for the birth of Modern Spiritualism in 1848, when the Fox family heard strange rapping sounds in their house and discovered it was an intelligence communicating with them. The mysterious intelligent rapping sounds spread throughout the community and attracted many followers. During the decade of the 1850s, Spiritualist mediums flourished across the North and became a significant presence in American culture. By 1860, there were more than one million Spiritualists in America (one in twenty-eight Americans), and during the war many families turned to Spiritualism to communicate with their loved one who died in battle.

Spiritualists were patriotic and supportive of the Union. Once the war began, they rallied to the side of the Union and threw themselves into the war effort. They could be found throughout every aspect of the military: nurses in the hospitals, surgeons in the ranks, chaplains in the regiments, and the soldiers themselves. Based on the demographics of the movement, numerous officers were ardent Spiritualists. On historian estimates that "not a battle of any size was fought that did not claim the lives of spiritualists." While documentation is ongoing, numerous examples of military personnel involved in Spiritualism suggest that it was not only present but fairly widespread in the Union army.

It stands to reason that with so many Spiritualists in the Union army, commanding officers would at least have noticed their presence and considered using their occult skills on the battlefield. Spiritualist medium and historian Emma Hardinge claimed that officers did listen to the guidance of "kind spirits" and found them helpful in battle. Thus, both White and Hardinge affirm that spirits guided officers in the Union army, but they represent two very different interpretations of this medium guidance. For Hardinge, the "kind spirits" gave helpful guidance to officers; but for White, the spirits were "lying spirits" that led the officers to destruction. Presently, contemporary testimonial evidence of Union officers receiving guidance from spirits is still awaiting discovery. Nevertheless, the significant presence of Spiritualists in the Union army in various capacities does provide a framework for the believability of White's and Hardinge's claims. To the end of her life, White warned against the dangers of Spiritualism and never changed her view on the intensity of Spiritualist activity in the Union army during the Civil War.

1. Part of this chapter was first presented as a paper at the Fifth Biblical Conference at the University of Montemorelos, Montemorelos, Mexico, on July 8, 2016.

2. White, *Testimonies for the Church*, 1:363, 364.

3. Ibid., 1:364.

4. See Slater Brown, *The Heyday of Spiritualism* (New York: Pocket Books, 1972), which is an excellent, popular history of American Spiritualism.

5. For the most helpful studies on American Spiritualism, see, first of all, the following doctoral dissertations: Burton Gates Brown Jr., "Spiritualism in Nineteenth-Century America" (PhD diss., Boston University, 1972); Ernest J. Isaacs, "A History of Nineteenth-Century American Spiritualism as a Religious and Social Movement" (PhD diss., University of Wisconsin, 1975); Richard K. Silver, "The Spiritual Kingdom in America: The Influence of Emanuel Swedenborg on American Society and Culture: 1815–1860" (PhD diss., Stanford University, 1983); Lisa M. Lenker, "Haunted Culture and Surrogate Space: A New Historicist Account of Nineteenth-Century American Spiritualism" (PhD diss., Stanford University, 1998); Robert S. Cox, "Without Crucible or Scalpel: A Sympathetic History of American Spiritualism" (PhD diss., University of Michigan, 2002); Stephen D. Andrews, "Which Threatens to Tear Our Fabric Asunder: The Opposition to American Spiritualism, 1848–1860" (PhD diss., Stanford University, 2005); Laura Thiemann Scales, "Speaking in Tongues: Mediumship and American Narrative Voice" (PhD diss., Harvard University, 2006); Richard W. Fink II, "The Commercialization of the Afterlife: Spiritualism's Supernatural Economy, 1848–1900" (MA thesis, Temple University, 2010).

Second, see the following secondary studies: Frank Podmore, *Modern Spiritualism: A History and a Criticism*, 2 vols. (London: Methuen & Co., 1902); Nandor Fodor, *Encyclopedia of Psychic Science* (n.p.: University Books, 1966); Brown, *The Heyday of Spiritualism*; Howard Kerr, *Mediums, and Spirit-Rappers, and Roaring Radicals: Spiritualism in American Literature, 1850–1900* (Chicago: University of Illinois Press, 1972); R. Laurence Moore, *In Search of White Crows: Spiritualism, Parapsychology, and American Culture* (New York: Oxford University Press, 1977); Robert S. Ellwood Jr., *Alternative Altars: Unconventional and Eastern Spirituality in America* (Chicago: University of Chicago Press, 1979); Howard Kerr and Charles L. Crow, eds., *The Occult in America: New Historical Perspectives* (Chicago: University of Illinois Press, 1983); Bret E. Carroll, *Spiritualism in Antebellum America* (Bloomington, IN: Indiana University Press, 1997); Ann Taves, *Fits, Trances, and Visions: Experiencing Religion and Explaining Experience From Wesley to James* (Princeton, NJ: Princeton University Press, 1999); Braude, *Radical*

Spirits; John B. Buescher, *The Other Side of Salvation: Spiritualism and the Nineteenth-Century Religious Experience* (Boston: Skinner House Books, 2004); Barbara Weisberg, *Talking to the Dead: Kate and Maggie Fox and the Rise of Spiritualism* (San Francisco: HarperSanFrancisco, 2004); Cathy Gutierrez, ed., *The Occult in Nineteenth-Century America* (Aurora, CO: Davies Group, 2005); Todd Jay Leonard, *Talking to the Other Side: A History of Modern Spiritualism and Mediumship* (New York: iUniverse, 2005); Nancy Rubin Stuart, *The Reluctant Spiritualist: The Life of Maggie Fox* (Orlando, FL: Harcourt, 2005); Catherine L. Albanese, *A Republic of Mind and Spirit: A Cultural History of American Metaphysical Religion* (New Haven, CT: Yale University Press, 2007), especially chap. 4; Molly McGarry, *Ghosts of Futures Past: Spiritualism and the Cultural Politics of Nineteenth-Century America* (Berkeley, CA: University of California Press, 2008); Cathy Gutierrez, *Plato's Ghost: Spiritualism in the American Renaissance* (New York: Oxford University Press, 2009); Dee Morris, *Boston in the Golden Age of Spiritualism: Séances, Mediums, and Immortality* (Charleston, SC: History Press, 2014); and Lause, *Free Spirits*.

Finally, see the following selected primary sources: E. E. Lewis, *A Report of the Mysterious Noises Heard in the House of Mr. John D. Fox, in Hydesville, Arcadia, Wayne County, Authenticated by the Certificates, and Confirmed by the Statements of the Citizens of That Place and Vicinity* (Canandaigua, NY: E. E. Lewis, Shepherd and Reed, 1848); Eliab Wilkinson Capron and Henry D. Barron, *Singular Revelations: Explanation and History of the Mysterious Communion With Spirits, Comprehending the Rise and Progress of the Mysterious Noises in Western New York*, 2nd ed. (Auburn, NY: Capron and Barron, Cayuga Chief Press, 1850); Dellon M. Dewey, *History of the Strange Sounds or Rappings, Heard in Rochester and Western New-York, and Usually Called the Mysterious Noises!* (Rochester, NY: D. M. Dewey, Arcade Hall, 1850); Eliab Wilkinson Capron, *Modern Spiritualism: Its Facts and Fanaticisms, Its Consistencies and Contradictions* (New York: Partridge and Brittan, 1855); Emma Hardinge, *Modern American Spiritualism* (New York: Emma Hardinge, 1870); and Arthur C. Doyle, *The History of Spiritualism* (Amsterdam: Fredonia Books, 2003).

6. Brown, "Spiritualism in Nineteenth-Century America," iii.

7. There was a long history of supernatural phenomena in Europe and North America before the birth of Modern Spiritualism in 1848. See Arthur Versluis, "The 'Occult' in Nineteenth-Century America," in Gutierrez, *The Occult*, 12-14.

8. *Encyclopedia of Psychic Science*, 373.

9. Benjamin Worcester, *The Life and Mission of Emanuel Swedenborg* (Boston: Little, Brown, and Co., 1901), 386.

10. Ibid., 198ff.

11. For an annotated bibliography of Swedenborg's works, see Jonathan S. Rose, Stuart Shotwell, and Mary Lou Bertucci, eds., *Scribe of Heaven: Swedenborg's Life, Work, and Impact* (West Chester, PA: Swedenborg Foundation, 2005), 385–519.

12. Silver, "The Spiritual Kingdom in America," 29.

13. For a discussion of Swedenborg's enormous influence on American religion, Transcendentalism, Spiritualism, spiritual medicine, art, and education, see ibid, 1–305.

14. See ibid., 176–209. Most of the studies listed above in note 5 also identify Swedenborg as a major influence on American Spiritualism.

15. Brown, *The Heyday of Spiritualism*, 1–13.

16. On Mesmer's life and work, see Vincent Buranelli, *The Wizard From Vienna: Franz Anton Mesmer* (New York: Coward, McCann & Geoghegan, 1975); and James Wyckoff, *Franz Anton Mesmer: Between God and Devil* (Englewood Cliffs, NJ: Prentice-Hall, 1975).

17. For a helpful and concise overview of mesmerism, see *Encyclopedia of Psychic Science*, 239–241. For the development of mesmerism in France, see Robert Darnton, *Mesmerism and the End of the Enlightenment in France* (Cambridge, MA: Harvard University, 1968).

18. Brown, *The Heyday of Spiritualism*, 14–19. For the development of mesmerism in America, see Robert C. Fuller, *Mesmerism and the American Cure of Souls* (Philadelphia: University of Pennsylvania Press, 1982).

19. Brown, *The Heyday of Spiritualism*, 19.

20. See Michael D. Pearson, "Hypnotism and Mesmerism," in Fortin and Moon, *The Ellen G. White Encyclopedia*, 891, 892.

21. Brown, *The Heyday of Spiritualism*, 87. See also Andrew Jackson Davis, *The Magic Staff: An Autobiography of Andrew Jackson Davis* (New York: J. S. Brown & Co., 1857), 201–212.

22. Davis, *The Magic Staff*, 221, 223.

23. Ibid., 227–245, 248, 261–263.

24. For more information on Andrew Jackson Davis, see Robert W. Delp, "The Harmonial Philosopher: Andrew Jackson Davis and the Foundation of Modern American Spiritualism" (PhD diss., George Washington University, 1965); Robert W. Delp, "Andrew Jackson Davis: Prophet of American Spiritualism," *Journal of American History* 54 (1967): 43–56; and Robert W. Delp, "Andrew Jackson Davis's *Revelations*, Harbinger of American Spiritualism," *New York Historical Society Quarterly* 55 (1971): 211–234.

25. Edward Deming Andrews, *The People Called Shakers* (New York: Dover, 1963), 152.

26. See ibid., 153–172; and Henry C. Blinn, *The Manifestation of Spiritualism Among the Shakers, 1837–1847* (East Canterbury, NH: n.p., 1899), 76–88.

27. Andrews, *The People Called Shakers*, 175; and Blinn, *The Manifestation of Spiritualism Among the Shakers*, 77.

28. Andrews, *The People Called Shakers*, 175.

29. Scholars Howard Kerr and Charles L. Crow describe the history of the occult in America as "a historical hourglass in which the sands of witchcraft, popular ghostlore, mesmerism, Swedenborgianism, and scientism pour through the channel of spiritualism, then to disperse into Theosophy and parapsychology." Introduction to Kerr and Crow, *The Occult in America*, 4. Transcendentalism, with its roots in Swedenborgianism, was also part of the historical context in which Modern Spiritualism emerged. For discussion, see Ellwood, *Alternative Altars*, 92–94.

30. See Lewis, *A Report of the Mysterious Noises*, 32–38; and Capron, *Modern Spiritualism*, 33–38.

31. Lewis, *A Report of the Mysterious Noises*, 6; and Capron, *Modern Spiritualism*, 40.

32. Lewis, *A Report of the Mysterious Noises*, 7, 8; and Capron, *Modern Spiritualism*, 41, 42.

33. William Duesler, quoted in Lewis, *A Report of the Mysterious Noises*, 16.

34. Isaacs, "A History of Nineteenth-Century American Spiritualism," 65.

35. Ellen G. White, "Dear Brethren and Sisters," *Present Truth*, August 1849, quoted in *Earliest Seventh-day Adventist Periodicals*, Adventist Classic Library, ed. George R. Knight (Berrien Springs, MI: Andrews University Press, 2005), 21. See also White, *Early Writings*, 43.

36. Capron, *Modern Spiritualism*, 88–100; Isaacs, "A History of Nineteenth-Century American Spiritualism," 66–69.

37. Capron, *Modern Spiritualism*, 113, 114.

38. Ibid., 172–174.

39. Ibid., 175.

40. Horace Greeley, *The Autobiography of Horace Greeley; or, Recollections of a Busy Life* (New York: E. B. Treat, 1872), 235.

41. Kerr, *Mediums, and Spirit-Rappers*, 5; Moore, *In Search of White Crows*, 15, 16; and *Encyclopedia of Psychic Science*, s.v. "Spiritualism," 361.

42. Taves, *Fits, Trances, and Visions*, 177–180; Carroll, *Spiritualism in Antebellum America*, 120–151; Leonard, *Talking to the Other Side*, 103–135; and *Encyclopedia of Psychic Science*, s.vv. "Medium," "Séance," 232–238, 339–341.

43. Braude, *Radical Spirits*.

44. Isaacs, "A History of Nineteenth-Century American Spiritualism," 140–165. Interestingly, a Spiritualist's table on display at the Rochester, New York, Historical Society has a knocker beneath it in case the "spirits" didn't respond.

45. Brown, "Spiritualism in Nineteenth-Century America," 70–112.

46. "The Banner of Light," International Association for the Preservation of Spiritualist and Occult Periodicals, accessed December 6, 2016, http://www.iapsop.com/archive/materials/banner_of_light.

47. David K. Nartonis, "The Rise of 19th-Century American Spiritualism, 1854–1873," *Journal for the Scientific*

Study of Religion 49, no. 2 (June 2010): 361–373; and Morris, *Boston in the Golden Age of Spiritualism*, 22, 23.

48. See Lause, *Free Spirits*, 32, 33, which lists and documents these names and others as well.

49. Capron, *Modern Spiritualism,* 198–203. The military officer was Major George W. Rains, who would serve in the Confederacy during the Civil War (see, e.g., Boatner, *The Civil War Dictionary*, 676, 677).

50. Nevins and Thomas, *The Diary of George Templeton Strong*, 2:245.

51. See Isaacs, "A History of Nineteenth-Century American Spiritualism," 81–103.

52. Nevins and Thomas, *The Diary of George Templeton Strong*, 2:245.

53. White, *Early Writings*, 59, 86, 87. For discussion of White's visions on Spiritualism, see Roger W. Coon, *The Great Visions of Ellen G. White* (Hagerstown, MD: Review and Herald®, 1992), 49–60.

54. See White, *Spiritual Gifts*, 1:173–179.

55. See, e.g., J. H. Waggoner, *The Nature and Tendency of Modern Spiritualism* (Battle Creek, MI: Steam Press of the Review and Herald, 1858); and Uriah Smith, *Modern Spiritualism: A Subject of Prophecy and a Sign of the Times* (Battle Creek, MI: Review and Herald®, 1897). In a word search for "Spiritualism" in the "Words of the Pioneers" section of the *Ellen G. White Writings Comprehensive Research Edition* CD-ROM (Silver Spring, MD: Ellen G. White Estate), the term is found almost three thousand times. A search using the words "circle" or "circles," other names for séances, also reveals numerous discussions of concern for the growing participation in Spiritualism.

56. Isaacs, "A History of Nineteenth-Century American Spiritualism," 71, 72.

57. Braude, *Radical Spirits*, 46–49; Buescher, *The Other Side of Salvation*, 141–150.

58. See Braude, *Radical Spirits*, 48.

59. Isaacs, *A History of Nineteenth Century American Spiritualism,* 209-237.

60. See Moore, *In Search of White Crows*, 42, 43; and Laurence Moore, "Spiritualism," in Gaustad, *The Rise of Adventism*, 83–85.

61. McGarry, *Ghosts of Futures Past*, 44. See also Sydney E. Ahlstrom, *A Religious History of the American People*, 2nd ed. (New Haven, CT: Yale University Press, 2004), 489, 490; Isaacs, "A History of Nineteenth-Century American Spiritualism," 209–237; Gutierrez, *Plato's Ghost*, 3–10; Versluis, "The 'Occult' in Nineteenth-Century America," 14.

62. For a concise overview of Spiritualist views on Jesus Christ, see Taves, *Fits, Trances, and Visions*, 187, 188.

63. Moore, "Spiritualism," 88–93.

64. McGarry, *Ghosts of Futures Past*, 3.

65. Isaacs, "A History of Nineteenth-Century American Spiritualism," 137, 138.

66. Brown, "Spiritualism in Nineteenth-Century America," 113.

67. See Lause, *Free Spirits*, 14; and Albanese, *A Republic of Mind and Spirit*, 221.

68. Drew Gilpin Faust, *This Republic of Suffering: Death and the American Civil War* (New York: Vintage Civil War Library, 2008), 181.

69. "The Messenger," *Banner of Light*, October 19, 1861, 6.

70. "General 'Stonewall' Jackson," *Banner of Light*, July 2, 1864, 6, 7.

71. Faust, *This Republic of Suffering*, 184, 185.

72. White, *Testimonies for the Church*, 1:363–365.

73. Ibid., 1:363.

74. White, *Spiritual Gifts,* 1:173ff.

75. Ibid., 1:363, 364.

76. Brown, "Spiritualism in Nineteenth-Century America," 113, 114. See also Lause, *Free Spirits*, 16–19.

77. See Yvonne P. Chireau, *Black Magic: Religion and the African American Conjuring Tradition* (Berkeley, CA: University of California Press, 2003). See also Melissa Daggett, "Henry Louis Rey, Spiritualism, and Creoles of Color in Nineteenth-Century New Orleans" (MA thesis, University of New Orleans, 2009), http://scholarworks .uno.edu/cgi/viewcontent.cgi?article=1975&context=td.

78. Waggoner continued to engage the Spiritualist literature and revised the book several times until the fifth

edition. See J. H. Waggoner, *The Nature and Tendency of Modern Spiritualism*, 5th ed. (Battle Creek, MI: Review and Herald®, 1877).

79. Lause, *Free Spirits*, 49–54. I am indebted to Lause's research for various insights below.

80. "National Convention of Spiritualists, at Oswego, N.Y., Aug. 13 to 19, 1861," *Banner of Light*, September 14, 1861, 4.

81. " 'Spiritualism and the War': Judge Edmonds on 'The Times, and Our Duty in Regard to Them,' " *Banner of Light*, May 18, 1861, 8.

82. "Thanksgiving Day," *Banner of Light*, November 23, 1861, 4.

83. "Our War Register," *Banner of Light*, December 20, 1862, 4.

84. "The Regiment of Spiritualists," *Banner of Light*, November 2, 1861, 4. See also "The Spiritualist Brigade," *Banner of Light*, November 9, 1861, 5.

85. "The Regiment of Spiritualists," *Banner of Light*, November 30, 1861, 5.

86. For a discussion on the Spiritualist regiment that never became a reality, see Morris, *Boston in the Golden Age of Spiritualism*, 42, 43. Lause, however, suggested that such a regiment possibly existed and may have been the Fourteenth Massachusetts. Lause, *Free Spirits*, 181n36.

87. Emma Hardinge, *Modern American Spiritualism* (New York: Emma Hardinge, 1870), 493, 494. Scholars have noted that Hardinge's voluminous book is not always reliable in every detail. (See, e.g., Brown's assessment in *The Heyday of Spiritualism*, 276.) The same could be said about Arthur C. Doyle's *The History of Spiritualism* (Brown, *The Heyday of Spiritualism*, 275, 276). Nevertheless, Hardinge knew the field well and provided a wealth of quotations, detailed descriptions, and historical information that is still helpful to students of the Spiritualist movement. As a leading Spiritualist historian during the nineteenth century, her interpretation of Spiritualists' involvement in the war should not be ignored, as she was an eyewitness herself.

88. Hardinge, *Modern American Spiritualism*, 495.

89. Lause, *Free Spirits*, 58.

90. See, e.g., "Obituary Notices," *Banner of Light*, December 13, 1862, 5; "Passed to Spirit Life," *Banner of Light*, August 22, 1863, 7; and W. F. Jamieson, "Obituaries," *Banner of Light*, July 30, 1864, 7.

91. See Lause, *Free Spirits*, 183n44.

92. Ibid., 55.

93. *The Civil War Dictionary*, s.v. "Ethan Allen Hitchcock," 403; "Ethan Allen Hitchcock," in Heidler and Heidler, *Encyclopedia of the American Civil War*, 979, 980.

94. Ethan Allen Hitchcock, *Fifty Years in Camp and Field: Diary of Major-General Ethan Allen Hitchcock, U.S.A.*, ed. W. A. Croffut (New York: G. P. Putnam's Sons, 1909), 484.

95. Heidler and Heidler, *Encyclopedia of the American Civil War*, 970, 971. See Tilden G. Edelstein, *Strange Enthusiasm: A Life of Thomas Wentworth Higginson* (New Haven, CT: Yale University Press, 1968); Thomas Wentworth Higginson, *Army Life in a Black Regiment*, ed. Howard Mumford Jones (East Lansing, MI: Michigan State University Press, 1960). For his works on Spiritualism, see Thomas Wentworth Higginson, *The Rationale of Spiritualism: Being Two Extemporaneous Lectures Delivered at Dodworth's Hall, December 5, 1858* (New York: T. J. Ellinwood, 1859); and Thomas Wentworth Higginson, *The Results of Spiritualism: A Discourse Delivered at Dodworth's Hall, Sunday, March 6, 1859* (New York: S. T. Munson, 1859). Higginson is mentioned frequently in the literature about Spiritualism and abolitionism. See, e.g., Butler, *Awash in a Sea of Faith*, 255; and Braude, *Radical Spirits*, 28, 66, 73.

96. Heidler and Heidler, *Encyclopedia of the American Civil War*, 1599, 1600.

97. George W. Rains is listed as one of the vice presidents of the Society for the Diffusion of Spiritualism in 1854. Capron, *Modern Spiritualism*, 202. See also Ann Leah Underhill, *The Missing Link in Modern Spiritualism*, rev. ed. (New York: Thomas R. Knox, 1885), 258, 259.

98. Lause, *Free Spirits*, 55, 58. For more on Berry, see Morris, *Boston in the Golden Age of Spiritualism*, 45–47.

99. Lause, *Free Spirits*, 55. See also "Sullivan Ballou Letter," Civil War Trust, accessed December 6, 2016, http://www.civilwar.org/education/history/primarysources/sullivan-ballou-letter.html.

100. Virgil G. Way, comp., *History of the Thirty-Third Regiment Illinois Veteran Volunteer Infantry in the Civil War, 22nd August, 1861, to 7th December, 1865* (Gibson Hill, IL: Regimental Association, 1902), 162.

101. See John W. Brinsfield et al., eds., *Faith in the Fight: Civil War Chaplains* (Mechanicsburg, PA: Stackpole Books, 2003), 154, 162.

102. Ibid., 163. See also Robert C. Stroud, "The First Female Military Chaplain: Ellen Elvira Gibson Hobart," *Curtana: Sword of Mercy* 5, no. 1 (2014): 15–28.

103. Brinsfield et al., *Faith in the Fight*, 44, 185. Pierpont was seventy-six when he was commissioned in September 1861 and thus the oldest Union chaplain that served. Benedict R. Maryniak and John Wesley Brinsfield Jr., eds., *The Spirit Divided: Memoirs of Civil War Chaplains—the Union* (Macon, GA: Mercer University Press, 2007), 2n2. For a concise discussion of Pierpont's Spiritualist background, see Morris, *Boston in the Golden Age of Spiritualism*, 31–35. On the impact of Pierpont's Spiritualist poem "My Child," see Francis H. Underwood, *A Handbook of English Literature* (Boston: Lee & Shepard, 1889), 104; and Faust, *This Republic of Suffering*, 181, 182. On his interaction with Mary Todd Lincoln, see Daniel Mark Epstein, *The Lincolns: Portrait of a Marriage* (New York: Ballantine Books, 2008), 386.

104. See John Benedict Buescher, *The Remarkable Life of John Murray Spear: Agitator for the Spirit Land* (Notre Dame, IN: University of Notre Dame, 2006), 251, 252; and Buescher, *The Other Side of Salvation*, 93, 94.

105. See, for example, Noah Brooks, who claimed that spiritualism was all over Washington. *Washington in Lincoln's Time* (New York: The Century Co., 1895), 64–66.

106. For documentation that Forster served in the War Department, see *Register of Officers and Agents, Civil, Military, and Naval in the Service of the United States on the Thirtieth September, 1863* (Washington, DC: Government Printing Office, 1864), 126. For documentation that he was a Spiritualist, see Thomas Gales Forster, *What Is Spiritualism?* (Boston: William White, 1868); and Hardinge, *Modern American Spiritualism*, 494.

107. Robert Dale Owen, *Footfalls on the Boundary of Another World* (Philadelphia: Lippincott, 1860). For discussion on Owen's involvement in Spiritualism and the significance of his book, see Ahlstrom, *A Religious History of the American People*, 489.

108. See Lause, *Free Spirits*, 71; Jean H. Baker, *Mary Todd Lincoln: A Biography* (New York: W. W. Norton, 2008), 219; and Epstein, *The Lincolns: Portrait of a Marriage*, 380, 381, who list Gideon Welles and his wife, among others, who saw Spiritualists after their children died. See also Christopher Kiernan Coleman, *The Paranormal Presidency of Abraham Lincoln* (Atglen, PA: Schiffer Publishing, 2012), 106, 107. Although the documentation on Welles and others is not that strong, Spiritualism was flourishing all over Washington during the Civil War era. See, e.g., Noah Brooks, *Washington in Lincoln's Time* (New York: Century, 1895), 64–66.

109. See examples of spirit letters to Lincoln in *Abraham Lincoln and Religion: Spiritualist: Abraham Lincoln*, Files of the Lincoln Financial Foundation Collection, https://archive.org/details/abrahamlxxxxxxxx00linc; see also Richard N. Current, *The Lincoln Nobody Knows* (New York: McGraw-Hill Book Company, 1958), 66.

110. Burlingame, *Abraham Lincoln: A Life*, 298–300.

111. Epstein, *The Lincolns: Portrait of a Marriage*, 386.

112. For details on Mrs. Lincoln's encounters with spiritualists, see Baker, *Mary Todd Lincoln: A Biography*, 212–221; Catherine Clinton, *Mrs. Lincoln: A Life* (New York: Harper Perennial, 2009), 186–188; and Daniel Mark Epstein, *The Lincolns: Portrait of a Marriage*, 378–381, 384–387.

113. Katherine Helm, *The True Story of Mary, Wife of Lincoln* (New York: Harper & Brothers Publishers, 1928), 227. To put this remarkable statement in perspective, see Justin G. Turner and Linda Levitt Turner, *Mary Todd Lincoln: Her Life and Letters* (New York: Alfred A. Knopf, 1972), 123, 124.

114. See Baker, *Mary Todd Lincoln*, 221; "Lincoln's Attendance at Spiritualistic Séances," *Lincoln Lore*, January 1863, 1–4; and "Lincoln's Attendance at Spiritualistic Séances, Part 2," *Lincoln Lore*, February 1963, 1, 2.

115. Nettie Colburn Maynard, *Was Abraham Lincoln a Spiritualist? or Curious Revelations from the Life of a Trance Medium* (Philadelphia, PA: Rufus C. Hartranft, 1891), 90, 91.

116. Ibid., 165.

117. Jay Monaghan, "Was Abraham Really a Spiritualist?" *Journal of the Illinois State Historical Society* 34, no. 2 (June 1941): 209–232.

118. In Fehrenbacher and Fehrenbacher, *Recollected Words of Abraham Lincoln*, 311, they assign Maynard's statement an "E", which means it was "probably not authentic" (per the guide in the introduction on page liii).

119. Fehrenbacher and Fehrenbacher, *Recollected Words of Abraham Lincoln*, 311.

120. James M. McPherson, *This Mighty Scourge* (New York: Oxford University Press, 2007), 202. Lause, however, is more sympathetic to Maynard's book and believes that Lincoln was "a man of his age and circumstances" and that he participated in some Spiritualist events. Nevertheless, Lause acknowledges that, with regard to the sources claiming Lincoln's participation in spiritualist activities, "there are often multiple possible interpretations of their meaning" (Lause, *Free Spirits*, 69, 74, 76, 77). Several recent books that argue Lincoln was a Spiritualist are Michelle L. Hamilton, *"I Would Still Be Drowned in Tears": Spiritualism in Abraham Lincoln's White House* (La Mesa, CA: Vanderblumen Publications, 2013); Susan B. Martinez, *The Psychic Life of Abraham Lincoln* (Franklin Lakes, NJ: New Page Books, 2007); Christopher Kiernan, Coleman, *The Paranormal Presidency of Abraham Lincoln* (Atglen, PA: Schiffer Publishing, 2012). In my view, however, none of these three books provided convincing evidence that Lincoln was a Spiritualist. For a popularized version of Lincoln as a spiritualist, see, for example, Brian M. Thomsen, *Oval Office Occult: True Stories of White House Weirdness* (Kansas City, MO: Andrews McMeel Publishing, 2008), 69–99.

121. Benjamin P. Thomas, *Abraham Lincoln: A Biography* (Carbondale, IL: Southern Illinois University Press, 2008; 1952); Stephen B. Oates, *With Malice Toward None: A Biography of Abraham Lincoln* (New York: Harper Perennnial, 1994); Allen C. Guelzo, *Abraham Lincoln: Redeemer President* (Grand Rapids, MI: William B. Eerdmans, 1999); Ronald C. White Jr., *A. Lincoln: A Biography*; and Burlingame, *Abraham Lincoln: A Life.*, vol. 1-2.

122. David Herbert Donald, *Lincoln* (New York: Simon & Schuster Paperbacks, 1995), 427.

123. "Extracts From an Unfinished Manuscript of Rev. P. D. Gurley, D.D.," in Ervin Chapman, *Latest Light on Abraham Lincoln and War-Time Memories* (New York: Fleming H. Revell Company, 1917), 506; although not a member, Lincoln attended Gurley's New York Avenue Presbyterian Church. John Nicolay, Lincoln's personal secretary and biographer, was perhaps responding to the Maynard book when he wrote in a private letter to Jesse W. Weik (another biographer of Lincoln) on November 24, 1894: "I have not read either of the books you mention; but of course there will be no end to the extravagant stories invented and related about Mr. Lincoln. I never knew of his attending a séance of Spiritualists at the White House or elsewhere, and if he ever did it was out of mere curiosity, and as a manner of pastime, just as you or I would do. That he was in any sense a so-called 'Spiritualist' seems to me almost too absurd to need contradiction." Quoted in Jesse W. Weik, *The Real Lincoln: A Portrait*, ed. Michael Burlingame (Lincoln, NE: University of Nebraska Press, 2002), 370.

124. See the references in note 112.

125. White, *Testimonies for the Church*, 1:364.

126. Hardinge, *Modern American Spiritualism*, 494.

127. Morris, *Boston in the Golden Age of Spiritualism*, 43.

128. White, *Testimonies for the Church*, 1:364.

129. Ibid., 1:364.

130. Isaac Post, *Voices From the Spirit World, Being Communicatons From Many Spirits* (Rochester, NY: Charles H. McDonnell, 1852), 31–39, 49–54.

131. See, e.g., the messages of famed Confederate general Thomas "Stonewall" Jackson, who died in the Battle of Chancellorsville in May 1863, in "General 'Stonewall' Jackson," *Banner of Truth*, July 2, 1864, 6, 7. On the spirit of Colonel Edward D. Baker, a friend of Lincoln who was killed at the Battle of Ball's Bluff in October 1861, see John G. Jackson, "Remarkable Test in the Civil War," *Religio-Philosophical Journal*, May 21, 1881, 6. See also Rause, *Free Spirits*, 59, 60n51–53.

132. Leonard, *Talking to the Other Side*, 41, 119–122. See also *Encyclopedia of Psychic Science*, s.vv. "Materialization," "Transfiguration," 216–229, 391, 392.

133. White, *Spiritual Gifts*, 1:173; see also *Testimonies for the Church*, 1:297–299.

134. White, *Testimonies for the Church*, 1:364.

135. Ibid., 1:365.

136. White, *Testimonies for the Church*, 1:364.

137. Ibid., 1:364, 365.

138. Ibid., 1:365.

139. Ibid.

140. Peter C. Craigie, *The Book of Deuteronomy*, New International Commentary on the Old Testament (Grand Rapids, MI: Eerdmans, 1976), 385.

141. White, *Testimonies for the Church*, 1:366.

142. Ibid.

143. Ibid., 1:366, 367.

144. The written version of the dream was published by Wesley Bradshaw (not McClellan) on a broadside in 1861. It was circulated, e.g., in the *Portland (ME) Evening Courier*, March 8, 1862; and later in the *National Tribune*, December 1880. See "Bradshaw, Wesley (1837-1927) General M'Clellan's Dream," Gilder Lehrman Institute of American History, accessed December 7, 2016, https://www.gilderlehrman.org/collections /e23cd040-5dd9-4f0a-b163-710437719609. It also appeared in contemporary books, such as Brian M. Thomsen, *Oval Office Occult: True Stories of White House Weirdness* (Kansas City, MO: Andrews McMeel, 2008), 14–21, mostly from the article versions, and is taken as an authentic occurrence. The name "Wesley Bradshaw" was a pseudonym for author and publisher Charles Wesley Alexander, who capitalized on sensational publishing opportunities during the Civil War. He was known for such works as "Washington's Vision," "Jeff Davis' Confession! A Singular Document Found on the Dead Body of a Rebel!" and numerous other sensational stories. Alice Fahs, *The Imagined Civil War: Popular Literature of the North and South, 1861–1865* (Asheville, NC: University of North Carolina Press, 2001), 241. "General M'Clellan's Dream" was possibly fabricated by Alexander and not meant to be understood as authentic. McClellan never acknowledged it as an actual happening, and his son, George B. McClellan Jr., never heard his father mention it either. In fact, George B. McClellan Jr. was "very much surprised" that some people have accepted it as "an actual occurrence." See George B. McClellan Jr.'s letter in the *Journal of the American Society for Psychical Research* 9, no. 6 (June 1917): 354. Nevertheless, the general himself never denied it.

145. White, *Testimonies for the Church*, 1:367.

146. White, *Spiritual Gifts*, 1:173.

147. See Julius Nam, "Spiritualism," in Fortin and Moon, *The Ellen G. White Encyclopedia*, 1191.

148. White, *Spiritual Gifts*, 1:174, 175.

149. White, *The Great Controversy*, 553.

150. Ibid., 561. See also Edwin Reynolds, "Deception, Satan's Last," in Fortin and Moon, *The Ellen G. White Encyclopedia*, 761, 762.

151. White, *Testimonies for the Church*, 1:368.

PART VI

THE SCOURGE OF WAR (1864–1865): "GOD IS PUNISHING THIS NATION"

CHAPTER 14

JUDGMENT ON THE NATION

No people ever had more unmistakable evidences that they were guided and directed by an overruling Providence than have the people of the south since the commencement of their great struggle," declared a Confederate official early in the war.[1] This triumphant attitude was expressed in the Confederate national motto *Deo Vindice* ("With God as our defender").[2] Methodist minister William Seat claimed in *The Confederate States of America in Prophecy* that the Confederacy was ordained by God to fulfill a high destiny. "The one like the Son of man has appeared in the rise of the Confederate States of America," he trumpeted.[3] The evil powers in the North had conspired against the "final antitype" of the true Israel of God, but they would not prevail.[4] Even the Confederate constitution, unlike its federal counterpart, had explicitly invoked "the favor and guidance of Almighty God," which, the Confederates claimed, made them a uniquely Christian nation—the New Israel of God.[5] Their "cause" was a "just and holy" one, according to the Confederate president Jefferson Davis, and was protected with "Divine Power."[6]

The North equally claimed to be the "New Israel" and had previously adopted this rhetoric. America, they believed, was a "redeemer nation" that had entered into a special covenant with God.[7] Their just cause was the preservation of the Union. "It is not an anti-slavery war we wage," thundered A. L. Stone at the Park Street Church in Boston, "not a sectional war; not a war of conquest and subjugation; it is simply and solely a war for the maintenance of the Government and the Constitution."[8] This statement by and large represented the view of most Northern clergy.[9] God was on the side of the Union, and the South would not prevail. After witnessing a "massive military buildup" of Northern troops around Washington in the fall of 1861, Julia Ward Howe gained inspiration to write her famous poem "The Battle Hymn of the Republic," which employed biblical apocalyptic imagery throughout and confirmed that the North was fighting on God's side. As she put it, "He hath loosed the fateful lightning of His terrible swift sword: His truth is marching on."[10]

This religious conviction was indispensable to the war effort in both the North and the South. Each side invoked God's favor and believed, at least during the beginning of the war, that God was on its side and that its righteous armies marched into battle for a holy cause.[11] Thousands of Confederate and Union soldiers carried their Bibles and sought comfort from them on the eve of battles. On the home front, countless civilians sought the Lord for strength during the hardships of war.[12] According to historian George Rable, the Civil War was "the 'holiest' war in American history. Never before and likely never again would so many ministers, churches, and ordinary people turn not only to their Bibles but to their own faith to explain everything from the meanings of individual deaths, to the results of battles, to the outcome of the war itself."[13] Abraham Lincoln was right in his second inaugural address when he said of the North and South that "both read the same Bible, and pray to the same God."[14] Thus, as James McPherson wrote, "Religion was central to the meaning of the Civil War, as the generation that experienced the war tried to understand it."[15]

Ellen White's war *Testimonies* mirrored this religious sentiment during the Civil War but did so with a nuanced theological understanding. As the North and the South declared God was on their side, she declared God was on neither side: "God is punishing this nation for the high crime of slavery. . . . He will punish the South for the sin of slavery, and the North for so long suffering its overreaching and overbearing influence."[16] This theological statement was her first published statement on the war in August 1861, and it was published again in February 1862.[17] A year later, in her January 1863 *Testimony*, she declared, "God is punishing the North, that they have so long suffered the accursed sin of slavery to exist; for in the sight of heaven it is a sin of the darkest dye. God is not with the South, and He will punish them dreadfully in the end."[18] She concluded this last *Testimony* on the war by ending where she began: "I saw that both the South and the North were being punished."[19] Thus, from beginning to end in her Civil War *Testimonies*, White emphasized the theme that the entire war was a scourge to both sides for the sin of slavery, especially the South. Both were guilty, and both were being punished by the Almighty.

The framework for this view of judgment on the nation comes from the first part of her August 1861 article "Slavery and the War," also in *Testimony for the Church, No. 7*,[20] in which she provided a theological interpretation of the war from the perspective of God's judgment. Our discussion will focus on these judgment statements in the framework of the 1861 article and their fulfillment in both the North and the South, particularly during the last year of the war, 1864–1865.

The North and the sin of slavery

Interestingly, when Ellen White first penned her jeremiad in the August 27, 1861, issue of the *Review and Herald*, the North was still licking its wounds from the embarrassing defeat at the First Battle of Bull Run on July 21, 1861. The Northern clergy still believed that God favored the North but that besetting sins led Him to chastise His people. Some clergy pointed out that Bull Run took place on the Sabbath (Sunday),[21] and they saw in it "a timely warning against the tendency in the army to disregard the Sabbath." Profanity and drinking were also cited as besetting sins that contributed to the defeat.[22] But, according to White, the heart of God's chastisement was the "high crime of slavery." The North was being punished, she claimed, "for so long suffering its [slavery's] overreaching and overbearing influence."[23]

"At the Conference at Roosevelt, New York, August 3, 1861," White explained, "the brethren and sisters were assembled on the day set apart for humiliation, fasting, and prayer." Certainly, the war was on their minds as they sought the Lord for strength and guidance that day. "The Spirit of the Lord rested upon us, and I was taken off in vision and shown the sin of slavery, which has so long been a curse to this nation."[24] Her third son, Willie, seven at the time, was present, and he remembered this vision well. It was the "first one" he "witnessed as a little boy":

Father had given a short talk. Mother had given a short talk. Father prayed, Mother prayed, and as she was praying, I heard that shout, "Glory." There is nothing like it—that musical, deep shout of "Glory." She fell backward. My father put his arm under her.

In a little while her strength came to her. She stood up in an attitude of one seeing wonderful things in the distance, her face illuminated, sometimes bright and joyous. She would speak with that musical voice, making short comments upon what she saw. Then as she saw darkness in the world, there were sad expressions as she spoke of what she saw.

This continued ten or fifteen minutes. Then she caught her breath, and breathed several times deeply, and then, after a little season of rest, probably five or ten minutes, during which time Father spoke to the people, she arose, and related to the congregation some of the things that had been presented to her.[25]

According to her grandson Arthur White, Ellen White was shown a "broad diversification of subject matter" that can be found in volume 1 of *Testimonies for the Church*, pages 264–302.[26] She was shown scenes from the recent Battle of First Manassas (see chapter 5), as well as scenes relating to the curse of slavery. Based on her son's eyewitness statement above, the "sad expressions" on her face must have been prompted by the scenes related to the war and slavery. In fact, slavery was a major issue in her mind as she wrote out the vision—namely, "the sin of slavery, which has so long been a curse to this nation."[27]

Next she wrote, "The fugitive slave law was calculated to crush out of man every noble, generous feeling of sympathy that should arise in his heart for the oppressed and suffering slave."[28] As we saw in chapter 1, this law required Northern bystanders to join groups led by slave-catching marshals to help track down runaway slaves. White had already spoken out against this law two years before and had urged Adventists not to obey it.[29] The Fugitive Slave Law was in "direct opposition to the teaching of Christ," she declared.[30]

"God's scourge is now upon the North, because they have so long submitted to the advances of the slave power."[31] Two concepts stand out in this sentence: First, the term *scourge*, which was an instrument of punishment used to whip the slaves, indicated that the war was God's punishment on this nation. Second, the term *slave power* was, as noted in chapter 9, the social, economic, and political influence that the slaveholders exerted in the South and on the federal government during the antebellum years.

The next sentence continued the thought: "The sin of Northern proslavery men is great. They have strengthened the South in their sin by sanctioning the extension of slavery; they have acted a prominent part in bringing the nation into its present distressed condition."[32] These "proslavery men," or "doughfaces," were Northern politicians whose sympathies and votes were with the South, particularly on the issue of extending slavery into the territories. For forty years, the North had made numerous compromises with the slave power, from the Missouri Compromise of 1820, to the Compromise of 1850, to the last-minute attempts to broker compromise on the eve of secession and disunion (see chapter 1). These long years of compromise with slavery had, according to White, brought America "into its present distressed condition."

The next short paragraph refers to the late summer and early fall of 1861, when Northern morale was just beginning to experience an upsurge after the Manassas disaster in July. Even though there were some setbacks in the losses at Wilson's Creek and Ball's Bluff later that fall, General George McClellan was building a massive army just outside of Washington, and a feeling of optimism filled the hearts of Northerners and encouraged them to look for a decisive battle to end the war. Against this backdrop, White wrote, "I was shown that many do not realize the extent of the evil which has come upon us. They have flattered themselves that the national difficulties would soon be settled and confusion and war end, but all will be convinced that there is more reality in the matter than was anticipated. Many have looked for the North to strike a blow and end the controversy."[33] But the Battle of Shiloh in the spring of 1862 ended all hope of a short war (see chapter 4). The "evil" that had come upon the nation was the scourge of a long, bloody war because of slavery. Thus, "God's scourge is now upon the North, because they have so long submitted to the advances of the slave power."[34]

God's scourge upon the North

In what ways was God's "scourge," or punishment, manifested toward the North during the war? First, the human cost in terms of death was enormous. Of the approximately 2.2 million men who served the Union during the war, 360,000 died—110,000 from battle, and the rest dying from disease or accidents. This was a death rate of about one in six.[35] Although this was certainly not as high as the Confederacy's numbers, the 17.5 percent rate of Federal deaths is higher than the percentages in all other American wars.[36]

Second, the length of the war was long and punishing for the Northern people. At several points during the conflict, victory appeared to be in the Union's grasp but elusively slipped away. Consequently, the war went on and on, until Grant finally took command in the spring of 1864. Even then, however, ultimate victory did not come until a year later. Ellen White forecast this trend when she wrote that God "would not suffer victories to be gained faster than He ordained, and would permit no more losses to the Northern men than in His wisdom He saw fit, to punish them for their sins."[37]

Third, the war caused great emotional suffering at the Northern home front. The Civil War poet Walt Whitman best captured this suffering in the aftermath of war:

I saw the debris and debris of all the slain soldiers of the war, . . .
They themselves were fully at rest, they suffer'd not,
The living remain'd and suffer'd, the mother suffer'd,
And the wife and the child and the musing comrade suffer'd,
And the armies that remain'd suffer'd.[38]

Finally, some might consider the assassination of President Abraham Lincoln to be the culminating scourge upon the North for its sins. Ellen White never commented on this subject, but both the North and the South suffered in the death of Lincoln.

The South and the sin of slavery

After the First Battle of Bull Run, the South reveled in its surprising and sudden victory over the Union army. According to one Southern clergyman, it was an "answer to prayer" and proof of the "presence of God" with the Southern armies.[39] The wife of a Confederate colonel even wrote a Southern victory anthem, "The Battle of Manassas," that trumpeted God's hand in the South's victory and the North's humiliation.

"Now glory to the Lord of Hosts!" oh, bless and praise His name,
That He hath battled in our cause and brought our foes to shame,
And honor to our Beauregard, who conquered in His might,
And for our children's children won, Manassas' bloody fight.

Oh, let our thankful prayer ascend, our joyous praise resound,
For God—the God of victory, our untried flag hath crowned![40]

Ellen White's understanding was radically different: God "will punish the South for the sin of slavery."[41] In her August 1861 article, she likened Southern slavery to the biblical story of the Israelites in Egyptian bondage. "I was pointed back to ancient Israel, held in bondage by the Egyptians," she explained and then set forth the biblical story, emphasizing how Pharaoh "hardened his heart against his [God's] mighty wondrous works." This scene, she said, was given "to illustrate the selfish love of slavery, the desperate measures the South would adopt to cherish the institution, and the dreadful lengths to which they would go before they would yield."[42]

The South and slavery. This attitude was well illustrated in the South's reaction to the militant abolition activity of William Lloyd Garrison during the early 1830s. When Garrison's group sent petitions to Congress asking for emancipation in the District of Columbia and also sent abolitionist pamphlets to Southern communities, the South, highly sensitive to any outside interference with slavery, was infuriated. Southerners immediately struck back by holding meetings to protest the abolition publications. "In Charleston a group of irate citizens broke into the post office and burned the hated pamphlets." Several legislatures passed resolutions that affirmed slavery as central to the South. One U.S. senator from Tennessee "told the Senate that slavery was 'sacred' to the South." southerners, he declared, would never stand for "any outside meddling with slavery."[43]

Throughout the antebellum years, Southerners had considered slavery as the bedrock of their society, as historian William J. Cooper Jr. demonstrated:

Practically every white southerner agreed with Mississippi Governor John A. Quitman's assertion in his 1850 inaugural address: "This institution [slavery] is entwined with our political system and cannot be separated from it." Theresa Pulszky, accompanying Louis Kossuth on his southern tour in 1852, found slavery "so thoroughly interwoven with the life and habits of Southerners that it 'form[ed] a part of their existence.' " To the Savannah physician and politician Richard Arnold slavery was no abstract question: for southerners it "involve[d] life and property, safety and security." Slavery meant "life and death to the South," wrote Colonel Arthur Hayne of South Carolina in 1835 to his friend Andrew Jackson. In January 1849 the General Assembly of Florida resolved unanimously that no division existed in the South on questions involving "the institution of slavery." To a Little Rock audience in the summer of 1850 United States Senator Solon Borland described slavery as "underlying as a sort of substratum, and inseparably connected with, the structure of all our institutions." "It affects," Borland emphasized, "the personal interest of every white man."[44]

By 1860, slavery yielded a significant investment for the Southern economy. Some four million slaves populated the fifteen states that perpetuated the institution. According to Cooper, their value "totaled some three billion dollars, exceeding the combined sum of national investment in manufacturing and railroads plus bank capital by some 600 million dollars. In sum, by a wide margin slaves were the most valuable investment in the country."[45]

For Ellen White, all this was nothing more than the "selfish love of slavery" that was manifested in "the desperate measures which the South would adopt to cherish the institution."[46]

Hardened consciences of the slave masters. In her next sentence, White lamented that "the system of slavery has reduced and degraded human beings to the level of the brutes, and the majority of slave masters regard them as such."[47] Frederick Douglass described the impact of slavery on his own life in similar terms when he was the property of the cruel slave master Edward Covey: "My natural elasticity was crushed, my intellect languished, the disposition to read departed, the cheerful spark that lingered about my eye died; the dark night of slavery closed in upon me; and behold a man transformed into a brute!" He remembered spending his leisure time on Sundays in "a sort of beast-like stupor, between sleep and wake, under some large tree."[48] Once Douglass learned to read and became aware of his condition as a slave, he "envied" his "fellow-slaves for their stupidity." Reading, he said, had "opened my eyes to the horrible pit, but to no ladder upon which to get out."[49]

"The consciences of these masters have become seared and hardened, as was Pharaoh's," White charged, "and if compelled to release their slaves, their principles remain unchanged, and they would make the slave feel their oppressive power if possible."[50] Douglass remembered a kind woman who became his master: "a woman of the kindest heart and finest feelings." But once she tasted the "fatal poison of irresponsible power," everything about her changed dramatically. "That cheerful eye, under the influence of slavery, soon became red with rage; that voice, made all of sweet accord, changed to one of harsh and horrid discord; and that angelic face gave place to that of a demon."[51] Such was the searing and hardening of the masters' consciences.

Only God can end slavery. At this point in her *Testimony*, White reacted to the deeply entrenched nature of slavery in American culture as she saw it in vision: "It looked to me like an impossibility now for slavery to be done away."[52] At the time she wrote these words, the Lincoln administration was attempting to save the Union and leave slavery alone in the South. Nobody really knew how to end slavery. It was Jefferson's "wolf" that the nation could not safely hold on to or let go. Lincoln had articulated the nation's dilemma in 1854: "I should not know what to do, as to the existing institution."[53] From any human perspective, then, it appeared impossible to end human bondage in America.

All Ellen White knew in August 1861 with regard to how slavery would end was this: "God alone can wrench the slave from the hand of his desperate, relentless oppressor."[54] In the same article, she had already stated that God "has the destiny of the nation in his hands."[55] But she had no specifics to give on just how God would "wrench the slave from the hand of his desperate, relentless oppressor"—only that God would do it. As we look back on the Civil War today, we know the events in the war itself brought freedom to the slaves: Lincoln's Emancipation Proclamation, freed slaves fighting for the North, Grant's generalship, Sherman's march, Sheridan's victories, the North's ultimate victory, and the Thirteenth Amendment (see chapters 7, 8). As historian David B. Davis observed, "Given the economic growth and vitality of Southern slavery in 1860, it is difficult to imagine any other historical scenario that would have led to full and universal slave emancipation in the nineteenth or even early twentieth century."[56] From White's perspective, this was "God alone."

Cruelty of slavery. In the end, "all the abuse and cruelty exercised toward the slave is justly chargeable to the upholders of the slave system, whether they be Southern or Northern men."[57] According to this sentence, the slave power and those in the North who supported it would be held accountable for the pain and suffering inflicted upon the slaves.

Shortly before the outbreak of the Civil War, Frederick Law Olmsted traveled throughout the South on horseback and observed firsthand the nature of slavery. In one experience, he witnessed the horrible beating of a slave girl. An overseer of

An escaped slave named Gordon at the Baton Rouge Union camp
during his medical examination. Picture taken by Civil War photographer
Matthew Brady in March 1863.

slaves took the girl and "struck her thirty or forty blows across the shoulders with his tough, flexible, 'raw-hide' whip." Olmsted recalled that "at every stroke the girl winced, and exclaimed, 'Yes, sir!' or 'Ah, sir!" or 'Please, sir!' not groaning or scream-ing." Later the overseer had the girl lie down on her back with her garments up and flogged "her with the rawhide, across her naked loins and thigh, with as much strength as before. She now shrunk away from him, not rising, but writhing, grov-eling, and screaming, 'Oh, don't, sir! oh, please stop, master! please, sir! please, sir! oh, that's enough, master! oh, Lord! oh, master, master! oh, God, master, do stop! oh, God, master! oh, God, master!' "[58] Such tears, White believed, were "all bottled up in heaven," and as a result of such treatment of human beings, God's anger burns "against this nation."[59]

He will punish the South dreadfully in the end

"God is punishing the North, that they have so long suffered the accursed sin of slavery to exist; for in the sight of heaven it is a sin of the darkest dye. God is not with the South, and He will punish them dreadfully in the end."[60] This statement is one of Ellen White's strongest about the South and slavery. Slavery, she said, is "a sin of the darkest dye"—that is, the worst of sins. The phrase "in the sight of heaven" referred to God and the heavenly beings, as she stated in her 1858 jeremiad against slavery: "The cries and sufferings of the oppressed have reached unto heaven, and angels stand amazed at the hard-hearted, untold, agonizing, suffering, man in the image of his Maker, causes his fellow-man."[61]

"God is not with the South" was, most likely, a reference to the Confederacy and all those in the Southern states who supported its cause. This was a remarkable statement against the background of the Confederacy's claims that it was favored and blessed by God, as noted in the beginning of this chapter. Proslavery clergy taught that slavery was a "divine trust," in which the South was ordained by God "to perpetuate the institution of slavery" and function as "guardians of the slaves." As such, their cause was a holy and just one that God would never abandon.[62]

But Ellen White pulled no punches in her jeremiad and declared that God would punish the South "dreadfully in the end."[63] She had already warned against the evils and consequences of slavery before the war: "Agony, human agony, is car-ried from place to place, and bought and sold. God will restrain his anger but a lit-tle longer. His anger burns against this nation, and especially against the religious bodies who have sanctioned, and have themselves engaged in this terrible merchandise."[64] Additionally, "God's anger will not cease until he has caused the land of light to drink the dregs of the cup of his fury, and until he has rewarded unto Babylon double. Reward her even as she rewarded you, double unto her double according to her works: in the cup which she hath filled, fill to her double," which is an allusion to God's judgment on Babylon in Revelation 18:6.[65]

We can interpret this statement to mean that White believed God would visit His judgment "dreadfully" upon the institutions of the South, including its land, cities, personal property, social structure, and economy—all because of their unwillingness, like Pharaoh of old, to let the slaves go free.

It is significant that White noted this would happen "in the end." This particular statement was published early in 1863, shortly after Lincoln had issued his official draft of the Emancipation Proclamation. As we will see later, emancipation changed the way in which the Lincoln administration conducted the war. In the winter and spring months ahead, however, it would appear that the South still had the upper hand, with Lee's major victory in the Battle of Chancellorsville on April 30–May 6, 1863. Nevertheless, the divine wrath against the South for the institution of slavery would manifest itself with the *most intensity* "in the end" of the war, according to White, not at the beginning or middle. This period was apparently the last year of the war.

Fulfillment of the prediction: "Dreadfully in the end." How was the South punished "dreadfully in the end"? At the outset of the conflict in the spring of 1861, Union military policy toward Southern civilians was based upon conciliation, which was "the dominant Union policy for the first fifteen months of the war."[66] George McClellan articulated this view when he wrote to Lincoln, who had solicited his advice shortly after the defeat at Bull Run on July 21, 1861. McClellan said that the only way they could "hope for the permanent restoration of peaceful Union" (and he meant a Union with slavery still functioning in the South and left alone by the North) is "by thoroughly defeating their armies, taking their strong places, and pursuing a rigidly protective policy as to private property and unarmed persons."[67] This "rigidly protective policy" was the conciliation policy in a nutshell. Historian Mark Grimsley explained,

Initially the Federal government deliberately sought to exempt white Southerners from the burdens of war. Their constitutional rights were to be respected; their property was not to be touched. The Lincoln administration specifically renounced any intention of attacking slavery. The central assumption underlying the early policy was a faith that most white Southerners were lukewarm about secession, and if handled with forbearance, would withdraw their allegiance from the Confederacy once Union armies entered their midst. Not all Northern generals embraced this conciliatory policy, but most did, and it remained the dominant posture toward Southern civilians until the summer of 1862.[68]

As Grimsley noted, conciliation as a policy ended in the summer of 1862 after the Seven Days Battles of June 26–July 1, 1862, when Robert E. Lee's Army of Northern Virginia hammered McClellan's army and drove them away from the Confederate capital of Richmond. The Lincoln administration concluded that "harsher measures were necessary" to win the war and issued new orders that "encouraged Union armies to confiscate Southern property and live off the countryside whenever necessary."[69] During the months ahead, this new policy evolved and was transformed by Lincoln's Emancipation Proclamation.[70]

Once the war to save the Union was transformed into a war to save the Union *and* free the slaves, everything changed. Now blacks were encouraged to escape from their masters—a strike at the heart of the slave power. Moreover, blacks were allowed to join the Union army and fight for their freedom. But, most important, emancipation was "a symbol of Northern resolve, a touchstone of its intention to smash the slaveholding aristocracy that had spawned secession."[71] This "meant that the Lincoln administration would crush the rebellion by any means necessary."[72] And this means came to be known as "hard war."[73] Thus, the Union war policy toward Southern civilians changed from a limited war to hard war (some historians use the term *total war*), or, as Charles Royster put it in the title of his award-winning book, *The Destructive War.*[74]

General Grant and hard war. A vignette in Ulysses S. Grant's postwar memoir illustrated the nature of the hard-war policy in action. After defeating a rebel detachment in May 1863, Grant's army entered Jackson, Mississippi, and followed the general's orders to destroy the city's railroad connections and war factories. According to Grant, "Sherman and I went together into a manufactory which had not ceased work on account of the battle nor for the entrance of Yankee troops. Our presence did not seem to attract the attention of either the manager or the operatives, most of whom were girls. We looked on for a while to see the tent cloth which they were making roll out of the looms, with 'C. S. A.' woven in each bolt. There was an immense amount of cotton, in bales, stacked outside."[75] Grimsley re-created the scene: "In imagination, one can see the two travel-stained generals laconically chewing their ubiquitous cigars amid the din and bustle of production."[76] Then, Grant finally turned to his trusted general: "I told Sherman I thought they had done work enough. The operatives were told they could leave and take with them what cloth they could carry." The next matter-of-fact sentence captured the essence of hard war: "In a few minutes cotton and factory were in a blaze."[77]

While destruction of Confederate facilities and Southern property had already been taking place since the middle of 1862, "the year 1863 marked a significant watershed," according to Grimsley, "because during that year one can see the emergence of large-scale destruction carried out, in fairly routine fashion, by large bodies of troops."[78] The most dramatic manifestation of destructive war, however, came in the last full year of the Civil War when Grant was installed during March 1864 as lieutenant general of the entire Federal army. Once in charge, he implemented the hard-war policy as a grand strategy until the end of the war in April 1865. A significant part of this overall strategy was to "combine destruction of Southern armies with destruction of Southern war resources."[79] According to Grimsley, "Grant had a profound understanding of the fact that Civil War armies had become too large and too powerful to destroy in open combat. Their annihilation required not only military defeat but also the elimination of the foodstuffs, forage, ammunition, and equipage necessary to maintain them in the field."[80]

Such was the strategy of hard war, which seemed to fulfill White's prediction of the South's punishment "dreadfully in the end." It made its greatest impact during the last year of the war, 1864–1865.

General Sheridan and hard war. One of the two generals under Grant known for implementing total warfare was Philip H. Sheridan. During the early autumn of 1864, Sheridan's cavalry tore through the Shenandoah Valley, the "breadbasket of the Confederacy," and systematically destroyed the region's barns, crops, and livestock. One soldier, for example, "counted 167 barns ablaze at one time. By mid-October, Sheridan could report, 'I have destroyed over 2,000 barns filled with wheat, hay and farming implements; over 70 mills, filled with flour and wheat; have driven in front of the army over 4,000 head of stock, and have killed and issued to the troops not less than 3,000 sheep.' "[81] These operations in the valley adversely impacted Virginia civilians not only economically but psychologically as well. One Vermont soldier reported, "They see the grim determination of the North, and they begin to feel that to hold out longer is to fight against inevitable destiny." Sheridan informed Grant, "The people here . . . are getting sick of the war."[82]

General Sherman and hard war. The name most associated with hard, or destructive, warfare is Grant's right-hand general, William T. Sherman. In February of 1864, Sherman had led twenty-one thousand troops against the town of Meridian in east-central Mississippi, which stood at the intersection of two railroads and connected the Confederacy in an important way. "Destruction of this rail net would, in Sherman's words, 'close the door of rapid travel and conveyance of stores from Mississippi and the Confederacy east,' "[83] thus making it difficult for the rebels to conduct operations against the Federals on the Mississippi River. Additionally, Meridian was a stockpile of Confederate supplies and contained several important war factories that Sherman wanted to destroy. In five days, Sherman's troops meticulously dismantled Meridian's railroads and factories, during which time his men bent the rails in such a way that they were totally useless, calling them "Sherman's neckties." After the destruction was complete, Sherman reported, "Meridian, with its depots, store-houses, arsenal, hospitals, offices, hotels, and cantonments no longer exists."[84]

Grant approved of Sherman's Meridian operations, which became a prototype of his destruction in the South during the fall of 1864 and the winter and spring of 1865. After capturing Atlanta in September 1864 and ordering the city's population to evacuate, Sherman and his forces occupied the city until mid-November. Before they left, Federal engineers systematically destroyed the main railroad depot and its machine shops, various dry-good stores, theaters, fire stations, hotels, and slave markets, among other things. They set fires around the city that got out of control and devastated about two hundred acres. A large number of off-duty Federal soldiers also committed gratuitous acts of arson and vandalism.

March to the Sea. On November 15, Sherman's army left much of Atlanta in ruins and embarked on its famous March to the Sea. "Of all the operations of the American Civil War," wrote Grimsley, "this one was perhaps the most remarkable—and certainly the most famous example of hard war."[85] In his explanation to Grant on

Engraving of Sherman's March to the Sea

the effectiveness of such a march, Sherman declared, "I can make the march, and make Georgia howl!"[86] After mulling the proposition over, Grant persuaded Lincoln to approve it. Historian Allen C. Guelzo aptly summarized the march and its conclusion:

> Moving in four immense columns, Sherman swept aside the feeble resistance of the Georgia militia and burned a swath fifty miles wide across the state. He instructed his men to "forage liberally on the country during the march," an order they obeyed with gusto. "This is probably the most gigantic pleasure expedition ever planned," exclaimed one Illinois captain. "We had a gay old campaign," wrote another soldier. "Destroyed all we could not eat . . . burned their cotton & gins, spilled their sorghum, burned & twisted their R[ail] roads and raised Hell generally." On December 10 Sherman turned up outside Savannah, and on December 21 the Confederate defenders evacuated the city before Sherman could trap them inside. "I beg to present you, as a Christmas gift, the city of Savannah," Sherman telegraphed Lincoln, "with 150 heavy guns and plenty of ammunition, and also about 25,000 bales of cotton."[87]

When it was all said and done, Sherman estimated that his army did one hundred million dollars' worth of damage to the state of Georgia, with "about one-fifth 'inured to our advantage,' while 'the remainder is simple waste and destruction.' "[88] One Confederate noted that " 'the whole region stunk with putrefying carcasses' of all the cattle, hogs, mules, and horses slaughtered by the Federals, 'and earth and air were filled with innumerable turkey buzzards battening upon their thickly strewn death feasts.' "[89] In addition to wreaking havoc on the resources of the land, Sherman's accomplishments also had a damaging psychological impact on the Southern people. "We are not only fighting hostile armies, but a hostile people," he explained, "and must make old and young, rich and poor, feel the hard hand of war, as well as their organized armies. I know that this recent movement of mine through Georgia has had a wonderful effect in this respect."[90] This psychological dynamic of devastating Southern morale did more to bring the war to a conclusion than did the actual destruction of property.

March through the Carolinas. Sherman's March to the Sea was not total destruction of civilian lives and property. But the general could not control every soldier in his army, and the "bummers," as they were called, who worked along the fringes of the march, committed personal acts of pillage, robbery, and violence against Southern civilians and their homes.[91] But the worst was yet to come. When the soldiers learned that they were to march into the Carolinas, they felt a special sense of vengeance to get at South Carolina—the cradle of secession. "The truth is," Sherman explained to General Halleck, "the whole army is burning with an insatiable desire to wreak vengeance upon South Carolina. I almost tremble at her fate, but feel that she deserves all that seems in store for her."[92]

"Although the orders for the northward march remained the same as for the Savannah Campaign," explained Grimsley, "a number of soldiers believed they detected a different subtext. As one soldier wrote home, 'Shermans policy for South Carolina is understood to be destruction as we go.' 'Boys, this is old South Carolina,' boomed an 89th Ohio soldier as his regiment crossed the state line, 'lets give her h-ll.' " And this is precisely what happened. "In contrast to what had transpired in Georgia, entire towns were regularly put to the torch. One soldier, marching with his regiment in the wake of previous units, passed through Robertsville, 'a very nice little village but now there is nothing left to mark the place except about one hundred "monuments" (Chimnies) erected to the memory of Jefferson D.' "[93] The worst acts of destruction occurred in Columbia, South Carolina, in which much of the city was burned to the ground, homes pillaged, and slave women raped. The violence perpetrated on this city was the most controversial event in Sherman's marches through Georgia and the Carolinas.[94] One Union officer summed up the armies' vengeance on South Carolina: "The men 'had it in' for the State, and they took it out in their own way. Our track through the State is a desert waste."[95]

The South devastated. Such was the devastating effect of Sherman's marches through Georgia and the Carolinas. These types of raids, with their destruction of Southern war resources, were carried out by other Federal armies until the end of the war and contributed to the North's victory. Although officers issued orders against looting and indiscriminate violence, it still occurred. In the end, the entire Southern economy and much of its landscape was devastated. Historians William J. Cooper Jr. and Thomas E. Terrill describe the extent of this devastation at the end of the war:

Survivors in the South confronted devastation on a scale unprecedented in

American history. Major cities and important towns—Atlanta, Charleston, Richmond, Columbia, and Selma—lay in ruins. So did two-thirds of southern shipping and most of the 9,000 miles of the southern rail system. Rolling stock, roadbeds, and rails were in shambles, as were warehouses, depots, bridges, shops, water tanks, trestles, and switches. The small but important industrial sector of the South suffered from wear and tear, neglect, and destruction by the military. Worthless Confederate currency and bonds were bitter reminders of past hopes and present despair. Almost all other paper forms of exchange—banknotes, personal notes, state and local bonds—had little value. Not much more could be expected from rail and industrial stocks and bonds. The intricate credit system erected during the antebellum years had collapsed. Personal belongings and real property had in many cases been destroyed. The average value of all real property declined 50 percent; farm property, 70 percent. One-third of all livestock was gone, and $3 billion invested in slaves had been transferred from slaveholders to the former slaves, the largest single confiscation and transfer of private property in American history. Production of the principal southern crop—cotton—did not return to prewar levels until 1879. The South's share of the nation's wealth fell from 30 to 12 percent in the 1860s.[96]

Such was the demoralizing impact of the Union's total-war policy on the South. The transformation from a limited war of conciliation to a hard war of massive destruction shattered not only the Confederate government but also the economy, land, and, ultimately, the morale of the Southern people. It took decades for them to recover. From Ellen White's perspective, this was divine retribution for the sin of slavery: "He will punish them dreadfully in the end."[97]

Conclusion

Twice in her last *Testimony* on the war in January 1863, White stated that in vision she was referred to Deuteronomy 32, which dealt with the Song of Moses—a reminder to ancient Israel to be faithful to the covenant. Regarding the North, she wrote, "I saw that God would not give the Northern army wholly into the hands of a rebellious people, to be utterly destroyed by their enemies. I was referred to Deuteronomy 32:26–30."[98] She then quoted the passage with no comment. These particular verses spoke of God's judgment on Israel, His people, through other nations, with the hope of deliverance through affliction. The application of this passage to the North thus meant they would be afflicted by the war with the South, but not given "wholly" into rebel hands. Ultimately, God would deliver the North, as He had delivered ancient Israel from its enemies, but would teach it a lesson through its afflictions.

This understanding is reinforced by the way White applied the other verses in Deuteronomy 32 to the South: "In regard to the South, I was referred to Deuteronomy 32:35-37."[99] Again she quoted the passage with no comment. These verses refer to divine vengeance on Israel's enemies, whom God had used to punish His own people. The texts speak of the sudden destruction of the nations against Israel. White evidently meant that God would judge the South with calamity and destruction, which is a reinforcement of her earlier statement that the rebels would be punished "dreadfully in the end."[100]

It is noteworthy that she quoted these two passages of Scripture dealing with God's judgment on His people (Deuteronomy 32:26–30) and judgment on Israel's enemies (verses 35–37), and then she brought them together in her final statement on the war: "I saw that both the South and the North were being punished."[101] Thus, Ellen White's first published words on the war, in August 1861,[102] and her last published words on the war, in January 1863,[103] were declarations of judgment on the nation.

But at the heart of her message on the war was this assurance: "He has the destiny of the nation in His hands."[104] This indicated that in the end, God's purposes for the nation would prevail. The outcome of the war would be according to His divine will. This truth gradually dawned on Abraham Lincoln and found its fullest expression in his second inaugural address, delivered in the spring of 1865, which is the subject of the final chapter.

Chapter in a nutshell

In the context of the religious nature of the Civil War, Ellen White provided a theological interpretation from the perspective of God's judgment. She stated repeatedly in her war writings that God was punishing both the North and the South for the sin of slavery. In particular, she declared that God would punish the South "dreadfully in the end." This statement can be interpreted to mean that God would visit His

JUDGMENT ON THE NATION

judgment "dreadfully" upon the institutions of the South, its land, cities, properties, social structure, and economy, and this would happen with the most intensity toward the end of the war.

How was the South punished "dreadfully" in the end? After Lincoln issued the Emancipation Proclamation, the war took on a new strategy known as "hard war." Initially, the Union war effort was to save the Union only and leave the property of slave owners alone. But once the aim of the war was to free the slaves as well as save the Union, the Lincoln administration chose to crush the rebellion by any means necessary. During the last year of the war, General Grant implemented the hard-war policy in order to defeat the South. For example, General Sheridan tore through the Shenandoah Valley and destroyed the region's barns, crops, and livestock; and General Sherman devastated parts of the South in his famous march through Georgia and later through the Carolinas. At the end of the war, the Confederate government was gone, the South's great cities were in ruins, and its economy was shattered. Apparently, this was how God punished the South "dreadfully in the end."

1. James Williams, quoted in John Patrick Daly, *When Slavery Was Called Freedom: Evangelicalism, Proslavery, and the Causes of the Civil War* (Lexington, KY: University Press of Kentucky, 2002), 146.

2. The national motto was voted by the Confederate congress and formally introduced on the Confederacy's seal in 1863. See Ian Binnington, *Confederate Visions: Nationalism, Symbolism, and the Imagined South in the Civil War* (Charlottesville, VA: University of Virginia Press, 2013), 141–143; and Robert E. Bonner, *Colors and Blood: Flag Passions of the Confederate South* (Princeton, NJ: Princeton University Press, 2002), 115, 116.

3. W. H. Seat, *The Confederate States of America in Prophecy* (Nashville, TN: Southern Methodist Publishing House, 1861), 132.

4. Ibid., 141. Seat went on for hundreds of pages, exegeting Revelation and predicting total victory for the South and its reign during the millennium.

5. "Constitution of the Confederate States; March 11, 1861," Yale Law School, accessed December 8, 2016, http://avalon.law.yale.edu/19th_century/csa_csa.asp. For a comparison of the U.S. and Confederate constitutions, see Charles Robert Lee Jr., *The Confederate Constitutions* (Chapel Hill, NC: University of North Carolina

Press, 1963), 171ff. For elaboration on the Confederacy's religious convictions, see Stout, *Upon the Altar of the Nation*, 47–52.

6. Jefferson Davis, "Message of Jefferson Davis, April 29, 1861," in Moore, *The Rebellion Record*, 1:174, 175.

7. See Stout, *Upon the Altar of the Nation*, 38ff., who effectively explained the North's nationality in the theological concept of the "New Israel." See also Sean A. Scott, *A Visitation of God: Northern Civilians Interpret the Civil War* (New York: Oxford University Press, 2011), 46–49; Martin E. Marty, *Righteous Empire: The Protestant Experience in America* (New York: Dial Press, 1970), 35–56; and James H. Moorhead, *American Apocalypse: Yankee Protestants and the Civil War, 1860–1869* (New Haven, CT: Yale University Press, 1976), 42–81.

8. A. L. Stone, quoted in David B. Chesebrough, *"God Ordained This War": Sermons on the Sectional Crisis, 1830–1865* (Columbia, SC: University of South Carolina Press, 1991), 85.

9. See Chester Forrester Dunham, *The Attitude of the Northern Clergy Toward the South, 1860–1865* (Toledo, OH: Gray Company Publishers, 1842), 134–143.

10. Aamodt, *Righteous Armies, Holy Cause*, 82, 165, 166. For a helpful and concise analysis of Howe's poem, see ibid., 81–87.

11. For insightful discussion on the similarity between Northern and Southern attitudes on the apocalypse, see ibid., 3–15.

12. James McPherson, afterword to *Religion and the American Civil War*, edited by Randall M. Miller, Harry S. Stout, and Charles Reagan Wilson (New York: Oxford University Press, 1998), 408, 409; and Steven E. Woodworth, *While God Is Marching On: The Religious World of Civil War Soldiers* (Lawrence, KS: University Press of Kansas, 2001), 68ff.

13. Rable, *God's Almost Chosen Peoples*, 397.

14. Basler, *The Collected Works of Abraham Lincoln*, 8:333.

15. McPherson, afterword, 412. The editors of *Religion and the American Civil War* wrote, "Despite the uncontested and unrivaled centrality of the Civil War in American history, despite its importance for both the history of the South and the history of African Americans, and despite its nearly mythic place in the popular mind (as seen in the massive continuing interest in Abraham Lincoln and Robert E. Lee, as well as the huge popularity of the Ken Burns PBS series), surprisingly little attention has been devoted to the war as a religious experience and event." Randall M. Miller, Harry S. Stout, and Charles Reagan Wilson, introduction to *Religion and the American Civil War*, 3. Since this statement was printed in 1998, more studies have focused on this important topic, such as Mark A. Noll, *America's God: From Jonathan Edwards to Abraham Lincoln* (New York: Oxford University Press, 2002); Mark A. Noll, *The Civil War as a Theological Crisis* (Chapel Hill, NC: University of North Carolina Press, 2006); Stout, *Upon the Altar of the Nation*; Robert J. Miller, *Both Prayed to the Same God: Religion and Faith in the American Civil War* (Lanham, MD: Lexington Books, 2007); and especially, Rable, *God's Almost Chosen Peoples* (2010).

16. White, "Communication From Sister White: Slavery and the War," 100–101. Ellen White was not alone in this understanding, as others articulated a similar understanding. See, e.g., Scott, *A Visitation of God*, 40, 41, for a discussion of four sermons about slavery and the war delivered during the fall of 1861; and also abolitionist Lewis Tappan, "The War: Its Cause and Remedy." Nevertheless, this was a minority view early in the war.

17. See White, *Testimonies for the Church*, 1:264.

18. Ibid., 1:359.

19. Ibid., 1:368.

20. Ibid., 1:264–266.

21. See Scott, *A Visitation of God*, 39, 40.

22. See Stout, *Upon the Altar of the Nation*, 70.

23. White, *Testimonies for the Church*, 1:264.

24. Ibid.

25. William C. White, quoted in Arthur White, *Ellen G. White*, 1:471, 472.

26. Arthur White, *Ellen G. White*, 1:472.

27. White, *Testimonies for the Church*, 1:264.

28. Ibid.

29. Ibid., 1:202.

30. Ibid., 1:264.

31. Ibid.

32. Ibid.

33. Ibid.

34. Ibid.

35. Gallagher, *The American Civil War: Lectures 25–48*, 380; Davis, *Inhuman Bondage*, 300.

36. According to Gallagher, "As a percentage of those who served, the Civil War totals are also strikingly higher than in all our other wars. Thirty-seven to 39 percent for the Confederates, 17.5 for the Federals. Other wars: the revolution, between 4.2 and 5.7 percent of the soldiers died. In the War of 1812, 2.4 percent; the war with Mexico, 5.1 percent; the war with Spain, less than 1 percent; World War I, 5.4 percent; World War II, 5.8 percent. In Korea, about 2.5 percent, and in Vietnam, a shade more than 7 percent." Gallagher, *The American Civil War: Lectures 25–48*, 381.

37. White, *Testimonies for the Church*, 1:267.

38. Walt Whitman, "When Lilacs Last in the Door-yard Bloom'd," Walt Whitman Archive, accessed December 8, 2016, http://www.whitmanarchive.org/published/LG/1891/poems/193.

39. Stephen Elliott, *God's Presence With Our Army at Manassas!* (Savannah: W. Thorne Williams, 1861), 20, quoted in Aamodt, *Righteous Armies, Holy Cause*, 55.

40. Mrs. Clarke, "The Battle of Manassas," quoted in Aamodt, *Righteous Armies, Holy Cause*, 56.

41. White, *Testimonies for the Church*, 1:264.

42. White, "Communication From Sister White: Slavery and the War," 101. See also White, *Testimonies for the Church*, 1:264–266.

43. William J. Cooper Jr., *The South and the Politics of Slavery, 1828–1856* (Baton Rouge, LA: Louisiana State University Press, 1978), 58, 59.

44. Ibid., 59, 60.

45. Cooper, *We Have the War Upon Us*, 20.

46. White, *Testimonies for the Church*, 1:266.

47. Ibid.

48. Douglass, *Narrative of the Life of Frederick Douglass*, 58.

49. Ibid., 42.

50. White, *Testimonies for the Church*, 1:266.

51. Douglass, *Narrative of the Life of Frederick Douglass*, 36, 37.

52. White, *Testimonies for the Church*, 1:266.

53. Abraham Lincoln, "Speech at Peoria, Illinois," October 16, 1854, in Basler, *The Collected Works of Abraham Lincoln*, 2:255.

54. White, *Testimonies for the Church*, 1:266.

55. White, "Communication From Sister White: Slavery and the War," 100. See also White, *Testimonies for the Church*, 1:264.

56. Davis, *Inhuman Bondage*, 299.

57. White, *Testimonies for the Church*, 1:266.

58. Frederick Law Olmsted, *A Journey in the Back Country* (New York: Schoken Books, 1970), 85, 86.

59. White, *Spiritual Gifts*, 1:191.

60. White, *Testimonies for the Church*, 1:359.

61. White, *Spiritual Gifts*, 1:192.

62. See B. M. Palmer's sermon, "Slavery a Divine Trust," in *Fast Day Sermons; or, The Pulpit on the State of the Country* (New York: Rudd & Careton, 1861), 62, 65.

63. White, *Testimonies for the Church*, 1:359.

64. White, *Spiritual Gifts*, 1:191.

65. Ibid., 1:192, 193. Ellen White's jeremiad against slavery resonates with abolitionist and Protestant apocalyptic thought about slavery. See Moorhead, *American Apocalypse*, 109-112.

66. Mark Grimsley, *The Hard Hand of War: Union Military Policy Toward Southern Civilians, 1861–1865* (New York: Cambridge University Press, 1995), 23.

67. Sears, *The Civil War Papers of George B. McClellan*, 72.

68. Grimsley, *The Hard Hand of War*, 2, 3.

69. Ibid., 67. See also Charles Royster, *The Destructive War: William Tecumseh Sherman, Stonewall Jackson, and the Americans* (New York: Vintage Civil War Library, 1993), 79ff.

70. For a detailed discussion on the evolving nature of this new policy of total war, see Grimsley, *The Hard Hand of War*, 96–170.

71. Ibid., 141.

72. Ibid.

73. Ibid., 4, 5. Grimsley's *The Hard Hand of War* is the most thorough explanation of the transition from a limited conciliatory policy to a hard-war policy.

74. Royster, *The Destructive War*. Royster showed how the Confederacy planned for hard war as well, particularly in the war philosophy of Stonewall Jackson and his influence on other Confederate generals. See ibid., 34–78.

75. Grant, *Memoirs and Selected Letters*, 338.

76. Grimsley, *The Hard Hand of War*, 142.

77. Grant, *Memoirs and Selected Letters*, 338. After relating this story, Grant recalled, "The proprietor visited Washington while I was President to get his pay for this property, claiming that it was private. He asked me to give him a statement of the fact that his property had been destroyed by National troops, so that he might use it with Congress where he was pressing, or proposed to press, his claim. I declined." Ibid.

78. Grimsley, *The Hard Hand of War*, 143.

79. Ibid., 166. For discussion on Grant's "overall design," see ibid., 165, 166.

80. Ibid., 166.

81. Philip Sheridan, quoted in ibid., 168.

82. Quotations in Grimsley, *The Hard Hand of War*, 168.

83. William T. Sherman, quoted in Grimsley, *The Hard Hand of War*, 163.

84. Ibid., 164; on Sherman's neckties, see Agostino von Hassel and Ed Breslin, *Sherman: The Ruthless Victor* (Nashville, TN: Thomas Nelson, 2011), 35.

85. Grimsley, *The Hard Hand of War*, 169.

86. Sherman, quoted in ibid., 190.

87. Allen C. Guelzo, *Fateful Lightning: A New History of the Civil War and Reconstruction* (New York: Oxford University Press, 2012), 446.

88. William T. Sherman, quoted in Hattaway and Jones, *How the North Won*, 654.

89. Quoted in ibid.

90. Sherman, quoted in Hattaway and Jones, *How the North Won*, 655.

91. For a vivid account of examples, see Shelby Foote, *The Civil War: A Narrative,* vol. 3, *Red River to Appomattox* (New York: Random House, 1974), 644, 645.

92. William T. Sherman to General Halleck, December 24, 1864, *Official Records of the Union and Confederate Armies*, ser. 1, vol. 44 (Washington, DC: Government Printing Office, 1893), 799.

93. Grimsley, *The Hard Hand of War*, 201.

94. See John G. Barrett, *Sherman's March Through the Carolinas* (Chapel Hill, NC: University of North Carolina

Press, 1956); Lucas, *Sherman and the Burning of Columbia*; and McNeely, *Sherman's Flame and Blame Campaign*.

95. Major Connolly, quoted in Grimsley, *The Hard Hand of War*, 202.

96. William J. Cooper Jr. and Thomas E. Terrill, *The American South: A History*, vol. 2, 4th ed. (New York: Rowman & Littlefield, 2009), 411.

97. White, *Testimonies for the Church*, 1:359.

98. Ibid., 1:365.

99. Ibid., 1:368.

100. Ibid., 1:359.

101. Ibid., 1:368.

102. Ibid., 1:264.

103. Ibid., 1:368.

104. Ibid., 1:264.

CHAPTER 15

ABRAHAM LINCOLN:
A PROPHET TO THE NATION

braham Lincoln's religious experience is one of the great unknowns in American history. Enthusiasts and scholars alike have tried to unravel this mystery in the great president's life and have reached conflicting conclusions. Some have trumpeted that he was a born-again Christian, while others believe that he was an infidel. Different religious groups have claimed him as their own, including the Roman Catholics, Methodists, Quakers, Freemasons, and Spiritualists.[1] But Lincoln would not fit into any religious pigeonhole or denomination. He was a very spiritual man but not an orthodox Christian; he attended church services but never joined a church, prayed but was never baptized, read the Bible but said little about Christ.[2] His wife, Mary Todd, best captured the unique nature of her husband's spirituality: "He was not a technical Christian," yet "he was a religious man always."[3]

Although "we will never get to the bottom of Lincoln's private religious thought, or definitively weigh the competing claims about his personal piety," explained historian Richard Carwardine, "there are unmistakable signs that, from the time of his election, he attended to religion with growing seriousness, that his ideas about God's role in the universe sustained a marked change, and that these notions informed

President Lincoln in April 1861, taken by
Matthew Brady

President Lincoln in February 1865, taken by
Alexander Gardner

how he thought about his administration's purposes."[4] Early in the war Lincoln was struck with the immensity of national pain at so much spilt blood. He personally experienced the loss of close friends on the battlefield, such as Elmer Ellsworth and Edward Baker. The hardest blow was the death of his little son Willie from typhoid fever in February 1862. Both the president and his wife grieved deeply over this loss, leaving Mary on the verge of a nervous breakdown and Lincoln to pick up the pieces while trying to manage the war. According to William J. Wolf, "the erosion of these forces may be traced in the deepening facial lines of almost every subsequent photograph of Lincoln." The personal losses turned him "toward a deeper piety than he had known before," and the national crisis "inspired him to probe beneath the seeming irrationality of events for a prophetic understanding of the nation's history."[5]

As we have seen throughout this book and especially in the previous chapter, Ellen White claimed a prophetic understanding about the war and declared it as God's scourge on the nation for the sin of slavery. By the end of the war, Lincoln had reached the same conclusion, although not through any prophetic visions like White. His prophetic understanding was of a different nature. It evolved through his experience in the war and found its fullest expression in the second inaugural address on March 4, 1865. The following pages will examine the president's theological development, how it climaxed in his most significant speech, and the connection between his and White's message about the war.

Lincoln's spiritual experience in the White House

While in the White House, one of the ways the president pursued insight and wisdom was to read the Bible. Those closest to him noticed the marked change in his reading habits. His wife observed that he read the Bible "a good deal" as the war progressed into its later stages.[6] For example, while on a steamboat to Norfolk, Virginia, the president disappeared from his entourage and was later found in a secluded place "reading a dog eared *pocket* copy of the New Testament."[7]

Lincoln's closest friend, Joshua Speed, was with him at the Soldiers' Home one evening during the summer of 1864, when things were at an all-time low in the Union war effort. He walked into a room where the president was seated by a window "intently reading his Bible." Approaching Lincoln, Speed said, "I am glad to see you so profitably engaged."

"Yes," he said, "I am profitably engaged."

"Well," Speed remarked, "if you have recovered from your skepticism, I am sorry to say that I have not."

Lincoln gently placed his hand on the shoulder of his lifelong friend and peered earnestly into his face. "You are wrong Speed, take all of this book upon reason that you can, and the balance on faith, and you will live and die a happier and better man."[8] This statement best captured Lincoln's approach to the Bible during this critical phase in his life experience.

Commensurate with Lincoln's Bible reading was his reliance on God. Mary Todd noted that her husband "felt religious More than Ever about the time he went to Gettysburg."[9] Noah Brooks, a journalist who had daily contact with Lincoln during the last half of the war, observed that "there was something touching in his child-like and simple reliance upon Divine aid, especially when in such extremities as he sometimes fell into; then, though prayer and reading of the Scriptures was his constant habit, he more earnestly than ever sought that strength which is promised when mortal help faileth."[10] Carwardine rightly noted, though, that generally "those who felt they were close to Lincoln during the war saw no change of heart, and no evangelical-style conversion: rather, they thought his trials had released a latent interest in religion."[11] Lincoln himself best expressed his spiritual experience during his presidency when he said to a group of clergymen in late October 1863:

> I was early brought to a living reflection that nothing in my power whatever, in others to rely upon, would succeed without the direct assistance of the Almighty, but all must fail.
>
> I have often wished that I was a more devout man than I am.
>
> Nevertheless, amid the greatest difficulties of my Administration, when I could not see any other resort, I would place my whole reliance in God, knowing that all would go well, and that He would decide for the right.[12]

Lincoln's theological understanding

At the core of Lincoln's theological-philosophical beliefs were the concepts of fatalism and Calvinism. Fatalism—the idea that whatever happens will happen and there is nothing we can do to change it—remained a part of Lincoln's belief system for his entire life. "I have all my life been a fatalist," he stated while in the White

House. "What is to be will be."[13] When he was charged with being an infidel in 1846, he explained his fatalistic view in terms of the "doctrine of necessity," which, he explained, was the belief "that the human mind is impelled to action, or held in rest by some power, over which the mind itself has no control."[14] As Lincoln grew in his understanding, he expressed his fatalism more in religious terms and combined it with the Calvinistic view of God's will and divine providence. This "peculiar providentialism," or "Calvinized deism," as Allen C. Guelzo described it, would play a major role in Lincoln's approach to the war and slavery.[15]

The upshot of this hybrid religious faith was that when Lincoln entered the White House, he possessed a strong sense of destiny for the nation and for himself. When he said to the New Jersey Senate, while on his trip from Springfield, Illinois, to Washington, D.C., during February 1861, that "I shall be most happy indeed if I shall be an humble instrument in the hands of the Almighty," he was expressing a deep and profound conviction.[16] His belief in divine will, or the overruling providence of God, led him to believe that his destiny was controlled by that Higher Power and thus influenced how he approached his presidency throughout the war. To his fellow Kentuckian Albert G. Hodges, who asked him to explain why he changed his inaugural pledge of noninterference with slavery to the policy of emancipation, Lincoln replied on April 4, 1864, that "I claim not to have controlled events, but confess plainly that events have controlled me."[17]

Lincoln's evolving understanding about the war

At the beginning of the war, Lincoln interpreted his role as saving the Union only; ending slavery was not in the plan. But he "was wise enough to realize that terminating the Southern rebellion only to return the country to the unstable condition of 1860 would be senseless."[18] So the president began to press for gradual, compensated emancipation (a gradual emancipation of the slaves over the passage of years with financial compensation to the slaveholders). When this was rejected, he put into motion a more assertive plan that made emancipation a war necessity, which resulted in the Emancipation Proclamation on January 1, 1863.

It should be noted that Lincoln's initial strategy for emancipation was colonizing African Americans to another continent, as he had last stated in his annual message to Congress on December 1, 1862.[19] In August 1862, for example, he had met with a delegation of blacks to discuss the issue and had told them in a speech that "without the institution of Slavery and the colored race as a basis, the war could not have an existence." Thus, "it is better for us both, therefore, to be separated."[20] Frederick Douglass saw in the speech a "pride of race and blood," a "contempt for Negroes," and a "canting hypocrisy." He believed that the president's speech showed "no sincere wish to improve the condition of the oppressed" but only "the desire to get rid of them."[21] Some scholars believe that the president's continuing policy of colonization eighteen months into the war showed that he "remained a white supremacist and segregationist" up to that point and was not willing to wage a "war of racial liberation." He was genuinely antislavery but was not convinced of the equality of whites and blacks.[22]

But, as Carwardine observed, "the evolving purposes of the Union's war is also the story of Lincoln's personal development." How he understood his "moral obligations" and the "meaning of the conflict itself" underwent a transformation "under the grueling burden of leadership, the wider suffering of wartime, and personal grief." As we have noted already, there are aspects of the president's personal religious experience that we will never understand. But "there is every sign that his understanding of providential intervention both shaped the thinking by which he reached the most profound of his decisions, for emancipation, and—even more powerfully—steeled his nerve to stand by the implications of that decision once made."[23]

One of the implications of emancipation was the involvement of black troops in the Union effort. Initially, the president was not convinced that African Americans were capable of being good soldiers. A decided change took place in his attitude, however, when he saw how bravely and heroically these black soldiers fought at Port Hudson and Milliken's Bend on the lower Mississippi and at Fort Wagner on Morris Island off the coast of South Carolina.[24] Consequently, Lincoln, "who had on numerous occasions before the war asserted the superiority of the white race, suggested that white soldiers and black soldiers must be treated equally."[25] In various ways, he worked to ensure the equal treatment of both black and white troops until the end of the war. An evolution thus took place throughout the war in the president's "racial mind-set."[26] By 1864, he had dispensed with the idea of colonization[27] and believed that whites and blacks should learn to live together in the same nation.[28] The culmination of his effort to bring freedom to the blacks was his push for suffrage and the Thirteenth Amendment to the Constitution.

"Meditation on the Divine Will"

By the summer of 1864, when the casualties mounted and there was still no end in sight to the war, Lincoln endeavored to interpret it in light of his view of divine providence. All of his Bible reading, prayer, and theological pondering came into play as he penned one of the most profound soliloquies in American history, known as the "Meditation on the Divine Will."

This document is a small piece of writing that the president penned for himself only, with no intention of seeing it published. After Lincoln's death, his secretary, John Hay, found it among the president's papers and was struck with its significance. It was one of the many fragments of writing among Lincoln's papers, and it had no date. His habit was to write down his thoughts on paper, which, researchers discovered, would eventually show up in future speeches.[29] Hay titled this fragment "Meditation on the Divine Will," and it was eventually published in his biography of Lincoln.[30]

> The will of God prevails. In great contests each party claims to act in accordance with the will of God. Both *may* be, and one *must* be wrong. God cannot be *for*, and *against* the same thing at the same time. In the present civil war it is quite possible that God's purpose is something different from the purpose of either party—and yet the human instrumentalities, working just as they do, are of the best adaptation to effect His purpose. I am almost ready to say this is probably true—that God wills this contest, and wills that it shall not end yet. By His mere quiet power, on the minds of the now contestants, He could have either *saved* or *destroyed* the Union without a human contest. Yet the contest began. And having begun He could give the final victory to either side any day. Yet the contest proceeds.[31]

Most historians and biographers of Lincoln have used the date assigned to the piece by Nicolay and Hay, which was sometime in the late summer or early fall of 1862. But historian Douglas Wilson has provided compelling evidence that the piece was composed sometime in 1864, when "with a determined military and vastly superior resources, the Union forces were still unable to end the rebellion."[32] Perhaps the president wrote out his meditation during the summer when Grant's Overland Campaign in Virginia and Sherman's campaign for Atlanta were failing to break the enemy. He had high hopes for Grant's strategy for defeating the Confederacy and looked for a decisive victory that never came. It is impossible to be precise, but the contents of the meditation appear to fit this time frame.

In the "Meditation on the Divine Will," we have a snapshot of Lincoln's evolving theological understanding and interpretation of the war. Essentially, he concluded that God probably willed that this war should come upon the nation, that the war was not over and would continue, and that God's purpose in the war may be different from what either side imagined. In a letter to Eliza Gurney, a Quaker friend, he built upon and expanded his meditation when he said that the "purposes of the Almighty are perfect" and that the problem was not God's working but that human mortals failed to perceive what He was doing. In the meantime, humans needed to work in the best light that He gave, "trusting that so working still conduces to the great ends He ordains."[33] Surely, Lincoln believed, God intended some great good to come out of this "mighty convulsion."[34]

The outcome is that the meditation became the seed for Lincoln's future writings and speeches. According to Ronald White Jr., this was the process of Lincoln's thinking, writing, and speaking. "He took pleasure in working with an idea over time. He would turn ideas over and over in his mind in the course of months and even years. Only after he was satisfied that he had thought through his idea, chosen just the right words to express its many dimensions, and polished the grammar of its expression was he ready to share it with the public." This small meditation is an example of "Lincoln's private process of planting and watering that bore such a rich fruit in his public speaking."[35] It would form the basis for his most important speech—the second inaugural address.

The second inaugural address

As Inauguration Day, March 4, 1865, approached, the state of the war looked good for the Union.[36] The Confederacy was essentially shattered: Sherman was marching through the Carolinas, wreaking havoc on Confederate resources; Sheridan had almost finished off the remnants of the Confederacy in the Shenandoah Valley; and Grant was besieging Petersburg, Virginia, just twenty miles south of Richmond. After four years as a war president, Lincoln looked ahead to four years as a peace president.

People flocked to Washington for the festive occasion. Hotels were overflowing,

Abraham Lincoln stands in the center, with papers in hand, delivering
his second inaugural address as president of the United States, March 4, 1865.
(taken by Alexander Gardner)

Lincoln's Second Inaugural Address

At this second appearing to take the oath of the Presidential office there is less occasion for an extended address than there was at the first. Then a statement somewhat in detail of a course to be pursued seemed fitting and proper. Now, at the expiration of four years, during which public declarations have been constantly called forth on every point and phase of the great contest which still absorbs the attention and engrosses the energies of the nation, little that is new could be presented. The progress of our arms, upon which all else chiefly depends, is as well known to the public as to myself, and it is, I trust, reasonably satisfactory and encouraging to all. With high hope for the future, no prediction in regard to it is ventured.

On the occasion corresponding to this four years ago all thoughts were anxiously directed to an impending civil war. All dreaded it, all sought to avert it. While the inaugural address was being delivered from this place, devoted altogether to saving the Union without war, insurgent agents were in the city seeking to destroy it without war-seeking to dissolve the Union and divide effects by negotiation. Both parties deprecated war, but one of them would make war rather than let the nation survive, and the other would accept war rather than let it perish. And the war came.

One-eighth of the whole population were colored slaves, not distributed generally over the Union, but localized in the southern part of it. These slaves constituted a peculiar and powerful interest. All knew that this interest was somehow the cause of the war. To strengthen, perpetuate, and extend this interest was the object for which the insurgents would rend the Union even by war, while the Government claimed no right to do more than to restrict the territorial enlargement of it. Neither party expected for the war the magnitude or the duration which it has already attained. Neither anticipated that the cause of the conflict might cease with or even before the conflict itself should cease. Each looked for an easier triumph, and a result less fundamental and astounding. Both read the same Bible and pray to the same God, and each invokes His aid against the other. It may seem strange that any men should dare to ask a just God's assistance in wringing their bread from the sweat of other men's faces, but let us judge not, that we be not judged. The prayers of both could not be answered. That of neither has been answered fully.

The Almighty has His own purposes. "Woe unto the world because of offenses; for it must needs be that offenses come, but woe to that man by whom the offense cometh." If we shall suppose that American slavery is one of those offenses which, in the providence of God, must needs come, but which, having continued through His appointed time, He now wills to remove, and that He gives to both North and South this terrible war as the woe due to those by whom the offense came, shall we discern therein any departure from those divine attributes which the believers in a living God always ascribe to Him? Fondly do we hope, fervently do we pray, that this mighty scourge of war may speedily pass away. Yet, if God wills that it continue until all the wealth piled by the bondsman's two hundred and fifty years of unrequited toil shall be sunk, and until every drop of blood drawn with the lash shall be paid by another drawn with the sword, as was said three thousand years ago, so still it must be said "the judgments of the Lord are true and righteous altogether."

With malice toward none, with charity for all, with firmness in the right as God gives us to see the right, let us strive on to finish the work we are in, to bind up the nation's wounds, to care for him who shall have borne the battle and for his widow and his orphan, to do all which may achieve and cherish a just and lasting peace among ourselves and with all nations.

and buildings all over the city offered sleeping places, cramming people into every conceivable space. Each day the Washington newspapers provided a list of the notables who were arriving. All knew they were coming to witness a historic event. The idea had taken hold to make the inauguration a national holiday; throughout the North, festivities were planned. The president had earned the respect of the people and had proven himself to be a great leader in a time of war, argued some supporters. He deserved to crow a bit. Many anticipated a speech that would vindicate Lincoln's first four years and herald the impending victory over the enemy.

March 4 dawned with incessant rain, and the streets oozed with soft mud that locals described as a "black plaster." As the thousands of visitors made their way to the Capitol, many were streaked with mud from head to toe. The inaugural parade began to move by 11:00 A.M., and the rain suddenly ceased at 11:40, although the sky was still dark with angry clouds. As the service officially began at 12:00 P.M., the outgoing vice president, Hannibal Hamlin, gave his farewell speech, followed by the vice president elect, Andrew Johnson.

Johnson had been ill, and an hour before the ceremony, he drank some whiskey in order to feel better. But he evidently got carried away and drank three full glasses. As he rambled incoherently through his speech, it was obvious to all that he was drunk. The dignitaries at the occasion were mortified, and observers could see the expressions of shock and indignation on their faces. President Lincoln "closed his eyes, lowered his head in despair, and appeared to withdraw into himself."[37] After Johnson took the oath of office, he grabbed the Bible and said in a blaring voice, "I kiss this Book in the face of my nation of the United States," and followed his words with a drunken kiss. Lincoln bent over to a marshal for the inauguration and whispered, "Do not permit Johnson to speak a word during the exercises that are now to follow."[38]

After the ordeal with Johnson was over, Lincoln was escorted onto the wood platform extending from the east front of the Capitol. As he was introduced, the crowd erupted in loud cheers for several minutes. Noah Brooks, a friend of Lincoln and a correspondent for the *Sacramento Daily Union*, described what happened next: "Abraham Lincoln, rising, tall and gaunt, over the crowd about him, stepped forward to read his Inaugural Address, printed in two broad columns upon a half-sheet of foolscap. As he rose a great burst of applause shook the air and died far away on the outer fringes of the crowd like a sweeping wave upon the shore. Just then the sun, which had been obscured all day, burst forth in its unclouded meridian splendor and flooded the spectacle with glory and light."[39] Many who were there remembered the sudden light of the sun and commented on it years afterward.[40]

As Lincoln spoke, the noted Washington photographer Alexander Gardner recorded the event for posterity in a memorable picture, the only occasion in which the president was photographed while delivering a speech. Ironically, the picture captured Lincoln in the shadow of death. Up behind him on the right buttress stood John Wilkes Booth, the actor who seethed with hatred toward the president. He was hoping to do something heroic for the South and had come to hear what this "false president" would say.

In the crowd before him, Lincoln recognized the articulate Frederick Douglass, who had been dismayed at the president's first inaugural address and had found his words much too conciliatory toward the South. Douglass had visited with the president in the White House several times about issues concerning African Americans, and throughout the Civil War, he "had whipsawed back and forth from disgust to respect, and from despair to hope." But now Douglass was listening intently to the president's speech with the end of the war in view.[41]

The speech

Fellow-Countrymen:
At this second appearing to take the oath of the Presidential office there is less occasion for an extended address than there was at the first. Then a statement somewhat in detail of a course to be pursued seemed fitting and proper. Now, at the expiration of four years, during which public declarations have been constantly called forth on every point and phase of the great contest which still absorbs the attention and engrosses the energies of the nation, little that is new could be presented. The progress of our arms, upon which all else chiefly depends, is as well known to the public as to myself, and it is, I trust, reasonably satisfactory and encouraging to all. With high hope for the future, no prediction in regard to it is ventured.

On the occasion corresponding to this four years ago all thoughts were anxiously directed to an impending civil war. All dreaded it, all sought to avert it. While the inaugural address was being delivered from this place, devoted altogether to saving the Union without war, insurgent agents were in the city seeking to destroy it without war—seeking to dissolve the Union and divide effects by negotiation. Both parties deprecated war, but one of them would make war rather than let the nation survive, and the other would accept war rather than let it perish, and the war came.

One-eighth of the whole population were colored slaves, not distributed generally over the Union, but localized in the southern part of it. These slaves constituted a peculiar and powerful interest. All knew that this interest was somehow the cause of the war. To strengthen, perpetuate, and extend this interest was the object for which the insurgents would rend the Union even by war, while the Government claimed no right to do more than to restrict the territorial enlargement of it. Neither party expected for the war the magnitude or the duration which it has already attained. Neither anticipated that the cause of the conflict might cease with or even before the conflict itself should cease. Each looked for an easier triumph, and a result less fundamental and astounding. Both read the same Bible and pray to the same God, and each invokes His aid against the other. It may seem strange that any men should dare to ask a just God's assistance in wringing their bread from the sweat of other men's faces, but let us judge not, that we be not judged. The prayers of both could not be answered. That of neither has been answered fully.

The Almighty has His own purposes. "Woe unto the world because of offenses; for it must needs be that offenses come, but woe to that man by whom the offense cometh." If we shall suppose that American slavery is one of those offenses which, in the providence of God, must needs come, but which, having continued through His appointed time, He now wills to remove, and that He gives to both North and South this terrible war as the woe due to those by whom the offense came, shall we discern therein any departure from those divine attributes which the believers in a living God always ascribe to Him? Fondly do we hope, fervently do we pray, that this mighty scourge of war may speedily pass away. Yet, if God wills that it continue until all the wealth piled by the bondsman's two hundred and fifty years of unrequited toil shall be sunk, and until every drop of blood drawn with the lash shall be paid by another drawn with the sword, as was said three thousand years ago, so still it must be said "the judgements of the Lord are true and righteous altogether."

With malice toward none, with charity for all, with firmness in the right as

God gives us to see the right, let us strive on to finish the work we are in, to bind up the nation's wounds, to care for him who shall have borne the battle and for his widow and his orphan, to do all which may achieve and cherish a just and lasting peace among ourselves and with all nations.[42]

Lincoln's second inaugural address was one of the most eloquent and powerful speeches in American history, with a different focus from his well-known Gettysburg Address. Detailed analyses exist, so an in-depth evaluation will not be discussed here.[43] Only the essence of this speech, or sermon (because of its biblical and prophetic ethos), will be explicated. The address is unusually brief, a mere 701 words in five paragraphs that began with a straightforward, businesslike exposition that smoothly transitioned into "the color and cadence of poetry."[44] Lincoln's central aim was to prepare the American people for a generous reconstruction policy, but he chose not to do it by giving a litany of policy recommendations. Instead, he "sought to exorcise feelings of vindictiveness and self-righteousness" and "share his understanding of the nature of the war and the reasons for its long duration."[45]

In the first paragraph, he set forth reasons why an extended speech was not necessary. "The progress of our arms, upon which all else chiefly depends, is as well known to the public as to myself; and it is, I trust, reasonably satisfactory and encouraging to all." Reminiscent of his private meditation in which he wrote that the "will of God prevails," he added, "With high hope for the future, no prediction in regard to it is ventured." In the second paragraph, he summarized the events that had culminated in the war, acknowledging that "all dreaded it—all sought to avert it." But through the events that transpired, "the war came."

The third paragraph is where the tone changed and Lincoln got to the heart of his message. Now that he had explained *how* the war came, he proceeded to explain *why* it came. It came, he maintained, because of slavery. "One eighth of the whole population were colored slaves, not distributed generally over the Union, but localized in the Southern part of it. These slaves constituted a peculiar and powerful interest. All knew that this interest was, somehow, the cause of the war."[46] While some today do not believe that slavery was a major factor in causing the Civil War, Lincoln's words provide a helpful corrective. Slavery as the cause of the war is a crucial point for the rest of the address. "Neither anticipated that the *cause* of the conflict might cease with, or even before, the conflict itself should cease."

Then the president introduced the Bible and God into the second inaugural address, revealing his willingness to think theologically as well as politically. From this point on, the address took on a distinctly theological tone, reflecting the culmination of Lincoln's thought process about God and the war. "Both read the same Bible, and pray to the same God; and each invokes His aid against the other." This was a fact well known to both sides, and one that Lincoln had frequently observed in the soldiers of both sides.

He then appealed to the Bible itself: "It may seem strange that any men should dare to ask a just God's assistance in wringing their bread from the sweat of other men's faces." Here he invoked Genesis 3:19—"In the sweat of thy face shalt thou eat bread"—in which Adam and Eve were cast out of the Garden of Eden for disobeying God. Lincoln used those words, where God judged human beings, to begin his case for the judgment of slavery. But in the next part of that sentence, he invoked a text from the Sermon on the Mount, Matthew 7:1, and balanced judgment from the Old Testament with mercy from the New Testament: "But let us judge not that we be not judged." This was not an appeal to let the South off the hook, but an appeal to show mercy and compassion to the South, which he would capitalize on in the conclusion of the address.

Although both sides prayed to God for victory, "the prayers of both could not be answered; that of neither has been answered fully." Here we see the earlier private meditation coming to fruition in the second inaugural address. A comparison between the two writings reveals continuity in the ideas and that what had been speculative in the meditation had become more concrete and specific in the second inaugural address.[47]

At the rhetorical center of the address, Lincoln offered his major theological affirmation: "The Almighty has His own purposes." In the meditation, he had mused that "in the present civil war it is quite possible that God's purpose is something different from the purpose of either party." In the second inaugural address, Lincoln confirmed that God's purpose was different from either party's and clarified that that purpose was judgment: " 'Woe unto the world because of offenses! for it must needs be that offenses come; but woe to that man by whom the offense cometh!' "

By invoking this "fiery biblical quotation" from Matthew 18:7, explained Ronald C. White Jr., "Lincoln employed the sanction of scripture to initiate his indictment of slavery and his formal charges against the American people."[48] The context of Matthew

18 addresses how to treat others, particularly the "little ones," whose "angels do always behold the face of my Father which is in heaven" (verse 10). Verse 6 sets forth a severe punishment to those who "offend one of these little ones." Although the original Greek word for *offense* can be translated as "stumbling block," as White correctly noted, "whether or not Lincoln was aware of the larger context of this verse, he seems to have captured part of its essential spirit."[49] He believed that to hold one person in bondage to another was evil to its core and was thus a great offense.

"If we shall suppose that American Slavery is one of those offenses which, in the providence of God, must needs come, but which, having continued through His appointed time, He now wills to remove, and that He gives to both North and South, this terrible war, as the woe due to those by whom the offense came, shall we discern therein any departure from those divine attributes which the believers in a Living God always ascribe to Him?" In this loaded sentence, Lincoln identified "American Slavery," not Southern slavery, as "one of those offenses." In doing so, he indicted not only the South for the sin of slavery but also the North. In Lincoln's mind, God was the primary actor who had brought this offense to America and who "now wills to remove" it from the land.[50]

Most significantly, God was the one who "gives to both North and South, this terrible war, as the woe due to those by whom the offense came." Here the president suggested to the American people that this terrible war, with all of its carnage and suffering, may have come upon them because they were complicit in the sin of slavery. If so, then "shall we discern therein any departure from those divine attributes which the believers in a Living God always ascribe to Him?"

In the final section of the third paragraph, Lincoln used the most moving and graphic language to bring his point home: "Fondly do we hope—fervently do we pray—that this mighty scourge of war may speedily pass away. Yet, if God wills that it continue, until all the wealth piled by the bond-man's two hundred and fifty years of unrequited toil shall be sunk, and until every drop of blood drawn with the lash, shall be paid by another drawn with the sword, as was said three thousand years ago, so still it must be said 'the judgments of the Lord, are true and righteous altogether.' "

These words employed vivid imagery that set before the American people the intimate relationship between the sin of slavery and the judgment of God. Lincoln "brought the long dark night of slavery under an intense light that allowed his audience both to see and to understand the dimensions of this American '*offense*.' "[51]

"Instead of self-congratulation, he asked his fellow citizens for self-analysis." According to White, "No president, before or since, has so courageously pointed to a malady that resides at the very center of the American national family."[52]

The phrase "Fondly do we hope—fervently do we pray" conveyed the intensity of feeling for the war to come to an end. Although the phrase "mighty scourge" conjured up the image of a master whipping a slave, Lincoln's biblically literate audience would also associate "scourge" with divine chastisement. Thus, "this mighty scourge of war" conveyed the idea that God's punishment on the nation was the war itself, whose widespread affliction "would have affected almost every person in the audience that day."[53]

The "bond-man's two hundred and fifty years of unrequited toil" reached back beyond the nation's birth and reminded Lincoln's audience that American history was stained with the sin of slavery from its beginning. As the "judgments of the Lord" were uttered "three thousand years ago," so Lincoln applied the "judgments of the Lord" to America's "two hundred and fifty years" of practicing slavery. He wanted the nation to acknowledge that the war was the judgment of God for the offense of slavery. Furthermore, in linking "every drop of blood drawn with the lash" with "another drawn with the sword," Lincoln graphically portrayed an irrevocable connection between the punishment of slavery and the punishment of the war during the last four years of the nation's experience.

Lincoln said, "Yet, if God wills that it [the war] continue, . . . as was said three thousand years ago, so still it must be said 'the judgments of the Lord, are true and righteous altogether.' " Here Lincoln invoked his fourth and final biblical text, Psalm 19:9, which expressed his confidence in the judgments of God on the nation: for they "are true and righteous." White suggested that Lincoln spoke these words slowly and sorrowfully. At the end of this third paragraph, the president did not want to sound adversarial. "Quite the opposite. Lincoln the lawyer, now in this moment become pastor to the nation, seemed willing to rest his case on the 'judgments of the Lord.' "[54]

Lincoln later wrote that he expected the second inaugural address to "wear as well as—perhaps better than—any thing I have produced." But he also recognized that it was not popular with many, and he was right. "Men are not flattered by being shown that there has been a difference of purpose between the Almighty and them," he reflected soulfully.[55]

The last paragraph of the second inaugural address was a moving appeal for healing and reconciliation in the nation: "With malice toward none; with charity for all; with firmness in the right, as God gives us to see the right, let us strive on to finish the work we are in; to bind up the nation's wounds; to care for him who shall have borne the battle, and for his widow, and his orphan—to do all which may achieve and cherish a just, and a lasting peace, among ourselves, and with all nations." As Lincoln said these words, Noah Brooks observed that many eyes were moist with tears.[56]

Next, according to Brooks, "The President turned toward Chief Justice Chase, who held up his right hand, with his left upon the Book [Bible], held up by the Clerk of the Supreme Court, and administered the oath of office, the President laying his right hand upon the open page; then, solemnly repeating 'So help me God!' he bent forward and reverently kissed the Book, and rose inaugurated President of the United States for four years from March 4, 1865."[57] Brooks noted that Lincoln pressed his lips on Isaiah 5:27, 28: "None shall be weary nor stumble among them; none shall slumber nor sleep; neither shall the girdle of their loins be loosed, nor the latchet of their shoes be broken; whose arrows are sharp, and all their bows bent, their horses' hoofs shall be counted like flint, and their wheels like a whirlwind."[58]

A prophet to the nation

This chapter has briefly recounted Abraham Lincoln's spiritual and theological growth as a war president. In Lincoln's own understanding of divine providence, God had been preparing him for his task as "an humble instrument in the hands of the Almighty" during the greatest crisis in U.S. history. His lifelong familiarity with the Bible, his love for his country and its Constitution, his careful logic and keen intellect, his careful rhetorical skills, his personal suffering, his growing understanding of God's divine providence and of slavery and race, his efforts to interpret the war in light of God's purposes—all culminated in his greatest speech, the second inaugural address. God had been shaping Lincoln all of his life for his presidency and for this moment. The second inaugural address was his "last will and testament to the American nation."[59]

At its core, the second inaugural address was an indictment on the nation for the sin of slavery. Lincoln prosecuted not only the South but "both North and South" for their involvement in the crime of human bondage. The lengthy enigmatic third paragraph articulated a lament that cried out for God's justice and the atonement for the sin of "American Slavery." The war itself was that atonement, Lincoln said, the payment for sin. God gave this bloody war to the nation, and if He "wills that it continue," then His judgments are "true and righteous."

The second inaugural address was Lincoln at his finest as a writer and a statesman. But it was more than a speech. It was a jeremiad delivered in the tradition of the Puritans of New England, who, in the early years of the nation, condemned spiritual and social wrongs in the tradition of the biblical prophet Jeremiah. In these jeremiads, the Puritan preachers declared to their congregations the reasons for God's anger and set forth His judgment on sin. In the second inaugural address, Lincoln declared to the nation the reasons for God's anger and set forth His judgment on the American people.[60] He boldly declared that the Civil War was not just a war but "an act of judgment by an offended God—an act of judgment on the nation as a whole."[61]

After reflecting on the second inaugural address, the twentieth-century American theologian Reinhold Niebuhr stated that "Lincoln's faith is identical with that of the Hebraic prophets who first conceived the idea of a meaningful history." He "put the whole tragic drama of the Civil War in a religio-dramatic setting."[62] William J. Wolf argued that Lincoln was "one of the greatest theologians of America—not in the technical meaning of producing a system of doctrine, certainly not as the defender of some one denomination, but in the sense of seeing the hand of God intimately in the affairs of nations."[63] The second inaugural address, then, can be considered as Lincoln's theological interpretation of the war.

In this framework, Wolf claimed that "Lincoln stands among God's latter-day prophets," who "saw American history in the freshness of prophetic insight. He is the American Isaiah, or Jeremiah, or St. Paul."[64] Joe Wheeler agreed that Lincoln was "the prophet president,"[65] and Stephen Mansfield believed that the second inaugural address "was Lincoln as prophet pleading the case of God."[66] Although he made no claim to prophetic visions, the president's message was nevertheless prophetic in its orientation. In this sense, on March 4, 1865, Abraham Lincoln spoke as a prophet to the nation.

Abraham Lincoln and Ellen White

Ellen White and Abraham Lincoln never experienced any personal connection, but the two were joined in their theological messages about the nation. Both asserted that the war was God's scourge on the nation for the sin of slavery. The timing of their messages was different, though. White delivered her message during the first half of the war. Before the war, she warned with prophetic authority[67] that divine wrath was coming upon the land because of slavery.[68] Early in the war, she declared that "God is punishing this nation for the high crime of slavery" and would "punish the South for the sin of slavery, and the North for so long suffering its overreaching and overbearing influence."[69] Her last prophetic message midway through the war was the same: "I saw that both the South and the North were being punished."[70]

In contrast, Lincoln was not ready to declare that God was punishing the nation for slavery at the beginning of the war. He suspected that judgment might one day come, but he did not recognize the war as God's punishment for slavery. As the war progressed, protracted with mounting casualties, and took its toll on the nation, he reflected on it in light of divine providence and reached the same conclusion in his second inaugural address as Ellen White had earlier in the war. His religious experience and theological journey were different from hers, but his conclusion about slavery, God, and the nation were, in the end, the same.

Only in this sense—the message that the war was God's judgment—are the two connected. Ellen White was a prophet to the Adventist people and provided insight and encouragement during the war. She never sensed a calling to take her message to the nation; rather, Lincoln was the prophet to the nation. The message of judgment that she delivered to the Adventists[71] was the message that he would deliver later to the nation. Put differently, *Lincoln declared in his second inaugural address at the end of the war what Ellen White had declared in her* Testimonies *at the beginning of the war.* Thus, one could say that God spoke a message of judgment through both of them at the appropriate time.

The significance of the following statement by White early in the war should be noticed in its connection with Lincoln: "It looked to me like an impossibility now for slavery to be done away. God alone can wrench the slave from the hand of his desperate, relentless oppressor."[72] The irony in this statement is that at the time White published it in August 1861, Lincoln was working toward restoring the Union, with slavery still intact in the South. But, as we have seen throughout this chapter and others in this book, "God alone" transformed the same man into the Great Emancipator by the end of the war. "I claim not to have controlled events," Lincoln said, "but confess plainly that events have controlled me."[73]

Conclusion

Ellen White made no published comment about the president's second inaugural address. But a clue to her thinking about it may be found in the *Review and Herald*, where the climactic words of the third paragraph of the address were published on March 21, 1865, with the following remark preceding: "The following remarkable and noble sentiment was uttered by President Lincoln in his inaugural address March 4, 1865. It is an unequivocal acknowledgment that the scourge of war is a direct infliction of punishment upon this nation for the unparalleled crime of slavery. Such a declaration from such a source and on such an occasion will be hailed by many as most appropriate and timely."[74]

Frederick Douglass also appreciated those same words as well and often quoted them from memory later in life. After the inaugural ceremony, he went to the public reception at the White House to congratulate the president. After waiting in line for hours, he was blocked at the entrance by two police officers who told him that blacks were prohibited. Douglass assured them that there must be a mistake, "for no such order could have emanated from President Lincoln; and that if he knew I was at the door he would desire my admission." Eventually, Douglass got in but not without effort and patience. As he walked into the East Room, he must have felt out of place as a black man in a sea of white faces.

Then he saw the president:

> Recognizing me, even before I reached him, he exclaimed, so that all around could hear him, "Here comes my friend Douglass." Taking me by the hand, he said, "I am glad to see you. I saw you in the crowd to-day, listening to my inaugural address; how did you like it?" I said, "Mr. Lincoln, I must not detain you with my poor opinion, when there are thousands waiting to shake hands with you." "No, no," he said, "you must stop a little, Douglass; there is no man in the country whose opinion I value more than yours. I want to know what you think of it?" I replied, "Mr. Lincoln, that was a sacred effort." "I am glad you liked it!" he said.[75]

No one else could have encapsulated Lincoln's second inaugural address in better words than those chosen by Frederick Douglass.

The day after the inauguration, Lincoln commented to his friend Noah Brooks about the sudden light of the sun bursting through the cloudy sky at the moment he rose to speak. Lincoln said "he was just superstitious enough to consider it a happy omen."[76] With the war soon to end, perhaps the sunburst was a happy omen for the future as well as God's smile upon Lincoln's "sacred effort." But that same day was a mixture of sun, rain, and clouds.[77] If the sun was a happy omen, then perhaps the rain and clouds were a sad omen. For soon after celebrating the war's end, the faces of the Northern people were drenched with tears.

Chapter in a nutshell

President Abraham Lincoln's spiritual experience and theological understanding evolved throughout the war. His understanding of divine providence, his lifelong familiarity with the Bible, his love for his country and its Constitution, and his effort to interpret the war in light of God's purposes all culminated in his most significant speech, the second inaugural address, delivered on March 4, 1865. At its core, this speech was an indictment on the nation for the sin of slavery—a declaration that the war was God's judgment on the American people. In this important address, Lincoln spoke as a prophet to the nation, pleading the case of God. In this sense, his message was connected with Ellen White's declarations of judgment on America. She was a prophet to the Adventist people but never sensed a calling to take this message to the nation. The message that she delivered to the Adventist people was the message that he would later deliver to the nation. Thus, Lincoln declared in his second inaugural address at the end of the war what White declared in her *Testimonies* at the beginning of the war. Apparently, God spoke His message through both of them at the appropriate time.

1. See William E. Barton, *The Soul of Abraham Lincoln* (New York: George H. Doran, 1920), 225–243.

2. See Philip L. Ostergard, *The Inspired Wisdom of Abraham Lincoln: How Faith Shaped an American President—and Changed the Course of a Nation* (Carol Stream, IL: Tyndale House, 2008), who compiled Lincoln's use of the Bible in *The Collected Works of Abraham Lincoln*. On pages 257, 258, of his book, Ostergard provided a chart that shows the different names Lincoln used to describe Deity throughout his published writings. Lincoln quoted the Bible frequently but rarely mentioned Jesus Christ.

3. Douglas L. Wilson and Rodney O. Davis, eds., *Herndon's Informants: Letters, Interviews, and Statements About Abraham Lincoln* (Urbana, IL: University of Illinois Press, 1998), 360.

4. Richard Carwardine, *Lincoln: A Life of Purpose and Power* (New York: Vintage Books, 2006), 221.

5. William J. Wolf, *The Almost Chosen People: A Study of the Religion of Abraham Lincoln* (Garden City, NY: Doubleday, 1959), 115.

6. Wilson and Davis, *Herndon's Informants*, 360.

7. Ibid., 521 (emphasis in the original).

8. Joshua F. Speed, *Reminiscences of Abraham Lincoln and Notes of a Visit to California, Two Lectures* (Louisville, KY: John P. Morton, 1884), 32, 33. See also Fehrenbacher and Fehrenbacher, *Recollected Words of Abraham Lincoln*, 414. According to Ward Hill Lamon, Lincoln's bodyguard, Speed was Lincoln's lifelong best friend. "If he had on earth 'a bosom crony,' it was Speed, and that deep and abiding attachment subsisted unimpaired to the day of Mr. Lincoln's death." Ward H. Lamon, *The Life of Abraham Lincoln: From His Birth to His Inauguration as President* (Boston: James R. Osgood, 1872), 231, 232.

9. Wilson and Davis, *Herndon's Informants*, 360.

10. Michael Burlingame, ed., *Lincoln Observed: Civil War Dispatches of Noah Brooks* (Baltimore, MD: Johns Hopkins University Press), 1, 210.

11. Carwardine, *Lincoln*, 223.

12. Basler, *The Collected Works of Abraham Lincoln*, 6:535, 536.

13. Isaac N. Arnold, *The Life of Abraham Lincoln,* 11th ed. (Chicago: A. C. McClurg, 1909), 81.

14. Basler, *The Collected Works of Abraham Lincoln*, 1:382.

15. Allen C. Guelzo, *Abraham Lincoln: Redeemer President* (Grand Rapids, MI: Eerdmans, 1999), 447.

16. Basler, *The Collected Works of Abraham Lincoln*, 4:236.

17. Ibid., 7:282.

18. James Tackach, *Lincoln's Moral Vision: The Second Inaugural Address* (Jackson, MS: University of Mississippi, 2002), 78.

19. Basler, *The Collected Works of Abraham Lincoln*, 5:530. For details on Lincoln and colonization, see Burlingame, *Abraham Lincoln: A Life*, 2:354–367.

20. Basler, *The Collected Works of Abraham Lincoln*, 5:372.

21. Foner and Taylor, *Frederick Douglass*, 511, 513.

22. Tackach, *Lincoln's Moral Vision*, 90. See also George M. Fredrickson, *Big Enough to Be Inconsistent: Abraham Lincoln Confronts Slavery and Race* (Cambridge, MA: Harvard University Press, 2008), 84.

23. Carwardine, *Lincoln*, 193.

24. For an overview of the black soldiers' valor and bravery in these three battles, see Joseph T. Glatthaar, *Forged in Battle: The Civil War Alliance of Black Soldiers and White Officers* (New York: Free Press, 1990), 121–142.

25. Tackach, *Lincoln's Moral Vision*, 111.

26. Ibid., 115.

27. Lincoln's secretary, John Hay, noted in his diary on July 1, 1864, that the president had "sloughed off that idea of colonization," which was to Hay a "hideous & barbarous humbug." Burlingame and Ettlinger, *Inside Lincoln's Whitehouse*, 217. Lincoln had probably dismissed it a year earlier, according to Fredrickson, *Big Enough to Be Inconsistent*, 113.

28. See Tackach, *Lincoln's Moral Vision*, 115–120. Fredrickson provided the following caveat: "Whether Lincoln

ever went beyond being an antislavery white supremacist to become a true egalitarian—like the abolitionists and Radical Republicans—is a question that is difficult to resolve because of the paucity of evidence directly bearing on it and because of the fact that Lincoln's thinking about race may have been in flux at the time of his assassination." Fredrickson, *Big Enough to Be Inconsistent*, 117.

29. Ronald C. White Jr., *The Eloquent President: A Portrait of Lincoln Through His Words* (New York: Random House, 2005), 154, 155.

30. Hay and Nicolay also printed it in volume 8 of their *Complete Works of Abraham Lincoln* (New York: Lincoln Memorial University, 1894), 52.

31. Basler, *The Collected Works of Abraham Lincoln*, 5:403, 404 (emphasis in the original).

32. Douglas L. Wilson, *Lincoln's Sword: The Presidency and the Power of Words* (New York: Vintage Books, 2006), 256. For discussion on Wilson's evidence, see pages 329, 330.

33. Basler, *The Collected Works of Abraham Lincoln*, 7:535.

34. Ibid.

35. Ronald C. White, *The Eloquent President*, 155.

36. This section is indebted to Ronald C. White Jr., *Lincoln's Greatest Speech: The Second Inaugural* (New York: Simon & Schuster, 2002), 21–42. White set up the background to Lincoln's second inaugural address with considerable and interesting detail.

37. Burlingame, *Abraham Lincoln: A Life*, 2:766.

38. Andrew Johnson, quoted in ibid., 766. See also White, *Lincoln's Greatest Speech*, 38, 39.

39. Burlingame, *Lincoln Observed*, 168.

40. Ronald C. White, *Lincoln's Greatest Speech*, 42.

41. For these two paragraphs, see Ronald C. White, *Lincoln's Greatest Speech*, 40.

42. Basler, *The Collected Works of Abraham Lincoln*, 8:332, 333.

43. For the most detailed discussion, see the work of Ronald C. White, *Lincoln's Greatest Speech*; then Ronald C. White, *The Eloquent President*, 277–303; Wilson, *Lincoln's Sword*, 261–277; Tackach, *Lincoln's Moral Vision*, 125–146; Stout, *Upon the Altar of the Nation*, 425–428; and Rable, *God's Almost Chosen Peoples*, 370–374.

44. Wilson, *Lincoln's Sword*, 266.

45. Burlingame, *Abraham Lincoln: A Life*, 2:767.

46. Some think that Lincoln's use of the word *somehow* qualifies slavery as the cause of the war; i.e., he was not sure it was the cause. But this understanding doesn't fit with the words *peculiar and powerful interest*. So by "somehow," Lincoln suggested that he and his contemporaries may not have been sure exactly *how* slavery became the cause, but they had no doubt that it was the cause.

47. See Ronald C. White, *Lincoln's Greatest Speech*, 127, 128.

48. Ronald C. White Jr., "Abraham Lincoln's Sermon on the Mount: The Second Inaugural," in Harold Holzer and Sara Vaughn Gabbard, eds., *1865: America Makes War and Peace in Lincoln's Final Year* (Carbondale, IL: Southern Illinois University Press, 2015), 58.

49. Ronald C. White, *Lincoln's Greatest Speech*, 144.

50. Nicholas Parrillo noted that "Lincoln went further than ever before in his Calvinist conception of God." For the "very first time, he made it clear that providence caused slavery. Mortals had not initiated the offense; they were merely instruments 'by which the offense came.' " Parrillo, "Lincoln's Calvinist Transformation," 253. Ellen White attributed slavery to Satan, never to God, and would disagree with Lincoln on this issue.

51. Ronald C. White, *Lincoln's Greatest Speech*, 154 (emphasis in the original).

52. Ibid., 150.

53. See ibid., 154, 155.

54. Ibid., 163.

55. Basler, *The Collected Works of Abraham Lincoln*, 8:356.

56. Brooks, *Washington in Lincoln's Time*, 239. For discussion on the Northern clergy's reaction to the second

inaugural address, see Rable, *God's Almost Chosen Peoples*, 374–375.

57. Noah Brooks, quoted in Burlingame, *Lincoln Observed*, 168, 169.

58. Brooks, *Washington in Lincoln's Time*, 241. For an explanation on why Lincoln chose this text, see Ostergard, *The Inspired Wisdom*, 235, 236.

59. Ronald C. White Jr., "Lincoln's Sermon on the Mount," in Miller, Stout, and Wilson, *Religion and the American Civil War*, 209.

60. See Ronald C. White, *Lincoln's Greatest Speech*, 151–154.

61. Stephen Mansfield, *Lincoln's Battle With God: A President's Struggle With Faith and What It Meant for America* (Nashville, TN: Thomas Nelson, 2012), 167.

62. Reinhold Niebuhr, "The Religion of Abraham Lincoln," in Allan Nevins, ed., *Lincoln and the Gettysburg Address: Commemorative Papers* (Urbana, IL: University of Illinois Press, 1964), 75.

63. Wolf, *The Almost Chosen People*, 24.

64. Ibid., 24, 25.

65. Joe Wheeler, *Abraham Lincoln: A Man of Faith and Courage* (New York: Howard Books, 2008), 31. See also Wayne C. Temple, *Abraham Lincoln, From Skeptic to Prophet* (Mahomet, IL: Mayhaven, 1995), xiv; and Ostergard, *The Inspired Wisdom*, 236.

66. Mansfield, *Lincoln's Battle With God*, 185.

67. For discussion on Ellen White's prophetic authority in relation to the Bible's final authority, see Jud Lake, *Ellen White Under Fire: Identifying the Mistakes of Her Critics* (Nampa, ID: Pacific Press®, 2010), 132–178.

68. White, *Spiritual Gifts*, 1:191–193.

69. White, *Testimonies for the Church*, 1:264.

70. Ibid., 1:368.

71. It should be pointed out that Ellen White's message was not unique to her. Other abolitionists had also declared that God would punish the nation for the sin of slavery (see chap. 2). But she was the only one who claimed that her message came from prophetic visions, similar to that of the biblical prophets.

72. White, *Testimonies for the Church*, 1:266.

73. Basler, *The Collected Works of Abraham Lincoln*, 7:282.

74. *Review and Herald*, March 21, 1865, 128.

75. Douglass, *Life and Times of Frederick Douglass*, 803, 804.

76. Brooks, *Washington in Lincoln's Time*, 74.

77. According to some witnesses, just as the sun suddenly burst through the clouds when the president rose to speak, so it suddenly withdrew behind the clouds while he was still speaking.

Hundreds of thousands of brave men have entered the service," wailed James White in the January 31, 1865, issue of the *Review and Herald*, "and have suffered, and bled and died upon the field of battle, in hospitals, and in southern prisons. Oh! the sum total of human agony which has been wrung from the nation! This causeless rebellion of those whose hands were stained with the sin of slavery, has caused this tide of woe to flow onward for nearly four years! Great God! when will it cease?"[1]

Seventh-day Adventists, like many other Northerners, were weary of the war and desperately wanted the hostilities to end. Due to the high commutation fee, they were especially concerned over President Lincoln's recent call for three hundred thousand additional draftees to boost the war effort in 1865.[2] In response to this wave of the draft, a special season of humiliation and prayer was called by church leaders. "The present call for men, whether a draft takes place, or whether volunteers are raised by means of large bounties," declared the church leaders, "will cost the Battle Creek church more than the whole amount of their systematic benevolence for the past four years." They explained that the church would lose not only its means but also many members who would be drafted. Even worse, the church would lose its evangelistic purpose: "The mind of the nation is so absorbed in this dreadful contest that it is almost impossible to call attention to religious subjects."

If the war continued and periodic drafts were called, "the cause would be crushed." The bottom line was this: "If the war continues, we must stop." Either "the war must stop, or our work in spreading the truth must stop."[3]

"Which shall it be?" they asked. The answer: "Relying on God, and having confidence in the efficacy of prayer, and the indications of his prophetic word, we believe that the work of God must not be hindered." Thus, a call was extended to all the churches and scattered believers to "set apart four days commencing Wednesday, March 1, and continuing till the close of the following Sabbath, as days of earnest and importunate prayer" over the subject of the war coming to a speedy close.[4] As the believers prayed together during these four days, March 1–4, a spiritual revival ensued. As Lincoln delivered his second inaugural address on March 4, the Adventists were on their knees praying.

A month later Grant took Petersburg, and Richmond fell. Lincoln wired Edwin Stanton, his secretary of war, on April 3 from City Point, Virginia, and told him that since Richmond was in Union hands, he would pay the city a visit. "I think I will go there to-morrow," he said and added, to alleviate Stanton's concerns, "I will take care of myself."[5] On April 4, Lincoln entered the fallen Confederate capital. It was a dangerous venture. Buildings were on fire, and the streets were full of people. The president strode forth with only a small guard of soldiers behind and in front of him. He was holding the hand of his youngest son, Tad, whom he had brought along on his twelfth birthday. Some Southerners peered at the presidential party from their windows with anger and hate.[6]

Once the blacks heard that President Lincoln had been spotted, however, they flocked around him. "Hurrah! Hurrah! President Linkum hab come! President Linkum hab come!" they shouted. Many in the crowd exclaimed, "Glory to God!" and danced with joy. "God bless you, Massa Linkum," screamed a woman as she tossed her bonnet into the air. Charles Page of the *New-York Daily Tribune* reported that "the joy of the negro knew no bounds," and their joy "found expression in whoops, in contortions, in tears, and incessantly in prayerful ejaculations of thanks."[7] Another reporter noted Lincoln's response: "President Lincoln walked in silence, acknowledging the salutes of officers and soldiers and of the citizens, black and white! It was the man of the people among the people. It was the great deliverer meeting the delivered."[8]

Charles Carleton Coffin, a correspondent for the *Boston Journal*, who was among the crowd, remembered that as the president halted for a moment to rest from the long walk, an old black man approached him and said, " 'May de good Lord bless you, President Linkum.' " The man then removed his hat and bowed, with tears of joy streaming down his cheeks. "The President removed his own hat and bowed in silence: it was a bow which upset the forms, laws, customs, and ceremonies of centuries of slavery."[9] It was also a touching moment and a symbol of the healing that would take place between the two races and still continues today.

Several days later, on April 9, Lee surrendered the principal Confederate army to Grant. Once the news echoed across the North, the sounds of celebration were everywhere. Church bells rang, cannons fired, fireworks exploded, men threw their hats into the air, and parades marched in big cities and small towns. Many people wept with joy, others danced, and some chanted "John Brown!"[10] President Lincoln was serenaded several times the next day and requested one of the bands to play "Dixie," because he said it was "one of the best tunes I have ever heard."[11]

"While the loyal North is rejoicing in the downfall of Richmond," wrote Uriah Smith in the April 11, 1865, issue of the *Review and Herald*,

> the signal successes of the Union arms, and the apparent nearness of the complete overthrow of the rebellion, and the consequent peace, none have more reason to rejoice than the commandment-keeping people of God, and none can rejoice more understandingly than they. They see in the prospect not only the immediate effects that others see, the cessation of slaughter and bloodshed, a mitigation of the crying evils that center in camp life, the relief of the nation from the terrible pressure of war, and the opportunity for hundreds of thousands now ministering to military necessities, to turn their talents, their attention, and their means to other and peaceful pursuits, but they see in it, a fulfillment of prophecy, an answer to prayer, a bright token that the great Shepherd of Israel is going before his flock. We therefore thank God for the visible manifestation of his hand in our national affairs.[12]

On April 14, 1865, four years to the day after the surrender of Fort Sumter, Abraham Lincoln was shot by John Wilkes Booth in the presidential box at Ford's Theatre. After a nine-hour struggle for life, the sixteenth president of the United States succumbed to the assassin's bullet and was pronounced dead at 7:22 A.M. on April

15, 1865. There was silence in the small crowded room for a moment, and then the deceased president's son Robert began to sob uncontrollably. Stanton stood at the foot of the bed, and with tears streaming down his face, "paid tribute to his fallen chief: with a slow and measured movement, his right arm fully extended as if in a salute, he raised his hat and placed it for an instant on his head and then in the same deliberate manner removed it. 'Now,' he said, 'he belongs to the ages.' "[13]

The news of Lincoln's death spread rapidly across the nation. The *Berkshire Courier* extra in Great Barrington, Massachusetts, for example, published the news three hours after Lincoln was pronounced dead: "Terrible news! Lincoln Dead! He is Shot by an Assassin!"[14] The *New York Times* read, "AWFUL EVENT: PRESIDENT LINCOLN SHOT BY AN ASSASSIN. THE DEED DONE AT FORD'S THEATRE LAST NIGHT. THE ACT OF A DESPERATE REBEL."[15] The *New-York Daily Tribune* stated, "HIGHLY IMPORTANT! The President Shot! Secretary Seward Attacked."[16]

On April 19, the day of the president's funeral, Henry Lyman Morehouse, the pastor of the First Baptist Church in East Saginaw, Michigan, vividly depicted the nation's reaction upon hearing of the assassination:

Business stopped; hearts throbbed almost audibly; knots of men congregated on the streets; telegraph offices were thronged by anxious faces; and all were incredulous that such a stupendous, nefarious transaction had occurred in America. Oh! what moments of suspense were those! The nation held its breath alternating between hope and fear. Again the wires click: "President Lincoln is dead." Then it was the darkness of midnight. It is midnight yet. Laughter ceased. Trembling lips, tearful eyes, saddened countenances, and suppressed tones, evinced the unspeakable emotions of the soul. The heart of the nation had been pierced and every member became numb. Commercial life, social life, everything was stagnant; and then the nation went into mourning—"a day of gloom and darkness." Flags everywhere hung at half mast; bells everywhere tolled their mournful sounds; the land was hung in black—its homes, its places of business, its public buildings, its houses of worship. The bonfires of exultation which the night before lighted up the streets of many of our cities, as if in anticipation of the terrible event had left their ashes and blackened embers, emblems of mourning and disappointment, to be in readiness for the general sorrow. America mourns as she never mourned before.[17]

The Seventh-day Adventist reaction mirrored the nation's mood, as Uriah Smith, the editor of the *Review and Herald*, lamented that "the day of rejoicing over the fall of Richmond, and the surrender of Lee, and the apparent near end of the rebellion, April 14, had scarcely closed, ere the terrible announcement was flashed over the land that President Lincoln, and Secretary Seward had fallen by the hands of assassins." (The nation later learned that Seward was seriously wounded but had not died.) For Smith, "No tragedy in our nation has ever equaled this. It falls upon the country as a new development in the annals of crime. We have been wont to think of such scenes, as confined to the old world, and reserved for monarchs and tyrants. But the murder of our own humane and amiable President has scarcely a parallel in the dark annals of any nation."[18]

Lincoln was shot on Good Friday, and on Easter Sunday, April 16, Northern preachers put aside their Easter sermons and prepared new ones that addressed the tragic event. "He is risen" had been overwhelmed by "He is dead."[19] The church buildings were overflowing with unprecedented numbers of people wanting to attend, and many were turned away for lack of space. " 'Black Easter,' the people called it, for there were no flowers in the choir lofts, nor by the pulpits, nor near the altar—an Easter Sunday without flowers and, instead, with mourning draped from pew to pew."[20] For George Templeton Strong, it was "an Easter Sunday unlike any I have seen." On the way to church in downtown New York, he observed, "Nearly every building in Broadway and in all the side streets, as far as one could see, festooned lavishly with black and white muslin." During the church service, he remembered, "Men and women . . . were sobbing and crying bitterly all around. My own eyes kept filling, and the corners of my mouth would twitch now and then in spite of all I could do."[21]

Many a sermon that Black Easter Sunday began on a "note of sorrow" but ended in "raging damnations" against the South.[22] Phillips Brooks, the well-known rector of Holy Trinity Episcopal Church in Philadelphia, was representative of the response: "I charge this murder where it belongs, on Slavery."[23] As historian David B. Chesebrough explained, "In bitter terms the preachers attacked Southern character and enumerated previous alleged Southern atrocities that culminated in the assassination of the President." In their minds, "the South was responsible for Lincoln's murder" and deserved "swift, harsh, and uncompromising justice."[24] Uriah Smith expressed a similar notion about the president's assassination: "Nothing could exhibit in a more vivid light, the diabolical spirit that lies at the root of the rebellion." Then, adding an apocalyptic meaning to the event, he exclaimed: "No one act could show more clearly the perilous times that are upon us."[25]

On April 21, as the darkly draped funeral train of President Abraham Lincoln left for its journey across six states to its destination in Springfield, Illinois, several thousand soldiers positioned along the track stretching from the depot presented arms. One eyewitness described the departing scene: "A portion of the soldiers in line near the depot were two regiments of U.S. Colored Troops. They stood with arms reversed, heads bowed, all weeping like children at the loss of a father. Their grief was of such undoubted sincerity as to affect the whole vast multitude." Others standing by, "dignified Governors of States, grave Senators, and scar-worn army officers, who had passed through scenes of blood and carnage unmoved, lost their self control and were melted to tears in the presence of such unaffected sorrow."[26]

Ellen White had no published word to say about Lincoln's death. But her reaction was expressed collectively with her fellow Seventh-day Adventists in an official action at the Third Annual General Conference Session on May 17:

> *Whereas*, Abraham Lincoln, the noble-minded and upright chief magistrate of this nation, has fallen by the hand of an assassin.
>
> *Resolved*, That we hereby record our deep distress at the loss of this "prince and great man," 2 Sam. iii, 27–38, who was stricken down by his enemies at the very moment when he was studying how to forgive them all, and that we recognize in this most atrocious crime the true character of the slaveholders' rebellion.[27]

Northern preachers wrestled with God's providence in Lincoln's death and proclaimed differing views to their congregations. Some believed that Lincoln had finished the work God had given him to do. Others believed that Lincoln's death would expand his influence, unite the North in the postwar era, awaken the nation to the cruelty of slavery, or humble the North. Some preachers said that Lincoln's death was a punishment for the North's sins.[28] Ellen White and Adventists were silent on this issue. But if we follow White's interpretation of the war as a punishment on the entire nation for the sin of slavery, then it is possible to consider Lincoln's assassination as part of that punishment. James Tackach suggested that Lincoln had predicted his own death in the second inaugural address: "The blood drawn by the lash would be sunk with blood drawn by the sword. Lincoln, too, was guilty of allowing slavery to continue past God's appointed time. Lincoln's blood would have to be shed before slavery's debt was paid. Then the war would end."[29]

One can only wonder what the Reconstruction period would have been like if Lincoln had lived. His assassination changed everything. "The blast of the derringer at Ford's Theatre on the night of April 14, 1865," historian Martha Hodes perceptively noted, "was the first volley of the war that came after Appomattox—a war on black freedom and equality. That war still ebbs and flows in American history, a century and a half after the assassination of President Abraham Lincoln."[30]

Concluding remarks

Ellen White's relationship to the American Civil War can be summarized in the following observations: *First, she comprehended the issues of the war extraordinarily well.* Growing up in a New England Yankee Methodist home, she nurtured her abolitionist sentiments in a similar way that Harriet Beecher Stowe did in her Yankee Congregationalist home. By the time of White's in young adulthood, she understood slavery as a grievous sin and believed that God would bring judgment upon the nation because of it (chapters 1, 2). Thus, like many historians today, she understood slavery as central to the causation of the war.

She saw in the secession of South Carolina the beginning of the rebellion that would inevitability lead to war. She understood very early in the war that it would be long and bloody, when most thought it would be a short war, with only one or two major battles (chapters 3, 4). She also understood the proslavery influences in the Northern government, the lack of unity in the Federal military leadership, and the frustration that many soldiers faced regarding slavery early in the war (chapter 9). She grasped the truth that the North could be victorious over the South only when emancipation became a major component of the war effort (chapter 10). She recognized that if England went to war with the United States, the crisis would significantly impact the world stage (chapter 11). Finally, she viewed the war as a punishment from God on both sides, in full anticipation of Lincoln's analysis in his second inaugural address (chapters 14, 15).

Second, White provided several unique insights into the war based on her claim to visionary experience. She alone interpreted the sudden retreat of the Union troops at the First Battle of Bull Run as divine intervention by an angel who initiated the confusion and caused the Federals to leave the field and lose the battle. In her understanding, God was sparing the Union from a worse defeat at the hands of the Confederates by suddenly ending their first major battle. She viewed this supernatural occurrence as an example of how God would intervene in the battles of the entire war (chapter 5). In this context, she accurately prophesied the patterns of the Union's wins and losses and claimed that what would play out in the war was due to God's punishment of the North for its sin of compromising with slavery (chapters 6–8).

She also indicated that the Union would achieve ultimate victory in the war, but that it would be a long and protracted victory, involving much pain and loss of life (chapter 12). One of her more unique insights involved a claim that Union generals and officers sought guidance from Spiritualist mediums and that this played a role in battlefield disasters. At the present time, this cannot be proven from contemporary testimony, because officers would never state such a thing in their official reports. But in the context of the popularity that Modern Spiritualism was experiencing during the war and Spiritualists' involvement in the Northern war effort, White's claim is plausible (chapter 13).

Third, White provided her fellow Seventh-day Adventists with spiritual guidance throughout the war. It is important to note that she never predicted the winner or loser of any particular battle or any event such as the assassination of Abraham Lincoln. In fact, early in the war, she did not even know how slavery would ever end, except that "God alone"[31] would deliver the slaves from their bondage. There was nothing in her career, therefore, to suggest that she sought national publicity. Her counsels all focused on bracing the Adventist people for the crises of the war years, such as how to navigate through the national draft and how to stay faithful to God in the midst of great challenges. Ultimately, her message was to prepare for the soon coming of the Lord. When the war ended, White continued to teach the soon coming of Christ for the rest of her life.[32]

Fourth, White was silent on the war after January 1863.[33] Adventist historians have puzzled over this silence during the last half of the war. Eric Anderson, for example, correctly noted that after 1863, White "drops the subject, giving no evaluation of the Emancipation Proclamation, the employment of black troops, or the decisive victories of Grant and Sherman."[34] Did she become preoccupied with church matters and lose interest in the events of the war? This is certainly a valid question when one considers the momentous events that transpired toward the end of the war. Did she not have anything to say about the Thirteenth Amendment or Lincoln's assassination?

Apparently, White believed she had said all that needed to be said, based on her four visions during 1861–1863, and left it up to others to comment on events later in the war. For her, "God alone" would solve the terrible problem of slavery in the nation. At the time she wrote this statement in August 1861, it seemed "impossible" in her mind for slavery to ever end.[35] She thus waited for God to work through the events of the war to free the slaves, and, in the meantime, focused her writing on other theological and spiritual issues. Like most Northerners and fellow Adventists, she must have followed the war news carefully.[36] As she watched events unfold, it became clear how God would free the slaves. But she let others comment, such as her colleague, editor Uriah Smith, who in the *Review and Herald* on March 14, 1865, identified the Emancipation Proclamation, the Thirteenth Amendment, and the victories of Grant and Sherman as the work of God.[37]

Finally, White's comments offered a uniquely nuanced theological interpretation of the war. The heart of her interpretation of the war was articulated in her analysis of the First Battle of Bull Run after she saw the angel intervene. In that examination, she stated that "God had this nation in His own hand."[38] The idea behind this assertion, stated twice in her *Testimony*,[39] was that God would involve Himself in the battles of the war in such a way as to preserve the United States but would also punish it for the sin of slavery—hence the long, protracted war with massive loss of life on both sides, great suffering for the North, and utter destruction for the South.

This theological assertion seems to have a wider application than to just the Civil War period of American history. During the Revolutionary War period, for example, one could say that God blessed the patriots with military success and in His providence established the United States. Then decades later, when divine patience had reached its limit with American slavery, divine punishment came in the form of the Civil War. The nuanced idea is that God will bless or punish this nation as His providence deems best because He has its destiny in His hands.

Later in life, White articulated a fully matured Christian philosophy of history that embraced her earlier interpretation of the Civil War: "In the annals of human history the growth of nations, the rise and fall of empires, appear as dependent on the will and prowess of man. The shaping of events seems, to a great degree, to be determined by his power, ambition, or caprice. But in the word of God the curtain is drawn aside, and we behold, behind, above, and through all the play and counter-play of human interests and power and passions, the agencies of the all-merciful One, silently, patiently working out the counsels of His own will."[40]

Another subtle aspect of Ellen White's interpretation of the war was the idea that the great controversy between Christ and Satan, as depicted in the Bible, formed the background for this epic war on earth. The rebellion in the South was a mirror of Satan's rebellion in heaven; just as Satan and his hosts were cast out of heaven (Revelation 12), so slavery must be cast out of the nation for there to be any peace and hope for the future. While her war writings often manifest a somber mood, enough hints of hope were sprinkled throughout to give her readers confidence that God would prevail in this controversy and would work His good will through the horrors of war.

In the end, White's interpretation of the war was seen to be correct, and slavery as an institution was abolished in the Thirteenth Amendment to the Constitution. Her Civil War declaration that God "has the destiny of the nation in His hands"[41] remains a message of hope today for those who earnestly pray, "God bless the United States of America." But it also remains a message of warning, for if this nation violates God's law collectively, as it did with antebellum slavery, then divine wrath will strike again.

---

1. James White, "Non-combatants," *Review and Herald*, January 31, 1865, 76.
2. Basler, *The Collected Works of Abraham Lincoln*, 8:171, 172.
3. John Byington and James White, "The Time Has Come!" *Review and Herald*, February 21, 1865, 100.
4. Ibid.
5. Basler, *The Collected Works of Abraham Lincoln*, 8:385.
6. For a reliable narrative and primary source of this account, see Charles Carleton Coffin, *Four Years of Fighting:*

A Volume of Personal Observation With the Army and the Navy (Boston: Ticknor and Fields, 1866), 510–514. For the best contemporary discussion of the visit, see Masur, *Lincoln's Hundred Days*, 282–285.

7. Charles Page, quoted in Masur, *Lincoln's Hundred Days*, 283.

8. Charles Carleton Coffin, "Scenes in Richmond," in Harold Holzer, comp., *President Lincoln Assassinated!! The Firsthand Story of the Murder, Manhunt, Trial, and Mourning* (New York: Library of America, 2014), 7.

9. Coffin, *Four Years of Fighting*, 511, 512.

10. Martha Hodes, *Mourning Lincoln* (New Haven, CT: Yale University Press, 2015), 31, 32, 34. Nevins and Thomas, *The Diary of George Templeton Strong*, 3:578.

11. Basler, *The Collected Works of Abraham Lincoln*, 8:393.

12. Uriah Smith, "The Prospects of Peace," *Review and Herald*, April 11, 1865, 148.

13. Donald, *Lincoln*, 599. There are variations in reports of what Stanton said exactly, but it was close to Donald's version. See ibid., 686.

14. "Terrible News!" *Berkshire Courier*, April 15, 1865, quoted in Hodes, *Mourning Lincoln*, 52.

15. Holzer and Symonds, *The "New York Times": Complete Civil War, 1861–1865*, 424.

16. "Highly Important!" *New-York Daily Tribune*, April 15, 1865, 4.

17. Henry Lyman Morehouse, quoted in David B. Chesebrough, *"No Sorrow Like Our Sorrow": Northern Protestant Ministers and the Assassination of Lincoln* (Kent, OH: Kent State University Press, 1994), 3.

18. Uriah Smith, "The Nation's Appalling Calamity," *Review and Herald*, April 18, 1865, 156.

19. Rable, *God's Almost Chosen Peoples*, 377.

20. Lloyd Lewis, *Myths After Lincoln* (New York: Harcourt, Brace and Co., 1929), 68.

21. Nevins and Thomas, *The Diary of George Templeton Strong*, 3:585, 586.

22. Lewis, *Myths After Lincoln*, 79. For discussion on sermons that reacted to Lincoln's assassination, see Rable, *God's Almost Chosen Peoples*, 377, 387; and Stout, *Upon the Altar of the Nation*, 449–455.

23. Phillips Brooks, quoted in Chesebrough, *"No Sorrow Like Our Sorrow,"* xx.

24. Chesebrough, *"No Sorrow Like Our Sorrow,"* xx; see also 41–65.

25. Smith, "The Nation's Appalling Calamity," 156.

26. John Carroll Power, quoted in Robert M. Reed, *Lincoln's Funeral Train: The Epic Journey From Washington to Springfield* (Atglen, PA: Schiffer Publishing, 2014), 31.

27. Smith, "Report of the Third Annual Session of the General Conference of S. D. Adventists," 197.

28. For discussion of these interpretations and others, see Chesebrough, *"No Sorrow Like Our Sorrow,"* 66–78.

29. Tackach, *Lincoln's Moral Vision*, 146.

30. Hodes, *Mourning Lincoln*, 274.

31. White, *Testimonies for the Church*, 1:266.

32. For studies on Ellen White and the delay of Christ's coming, see the following studies: Ralph E. Neall, *How Long, O Lord?* (Washington, DC: Reivew and Herald®, 1988); Arnold Wallenkampf, *The Apparent Delay: What Role Do We Play in the Timing of Jesus' Return?* (Hagerstown, MD: Review and Herald®, 1994); Herbert Douglass, *Why Jesus Waits*, rev. ed. (Nampa, Idaho: Pacific Press®, 2001).

33. See White, *Testimonies for the Church*, 1:355–368.

34. Anderson, "War, Slavery, and Race," 263.

35. White, *Testimonies for the Church*, 1:266.

36. Ellen G. White to "Friends at Home," Letter 6a, Eagle Harbor, New York, July 26, 1861, provides an example of how Ellen White followed the "war news" early in the conflict.

37. Uriah Smith, "Can God Work?" *Review and Herald*, March 14, 1865, 116.

38. White, *Testimonies for the Church*, 1:267.

39. Ibid., 1:264, 267.

40. Ellen G. White, *Education* (Oakland, CA: Pacific Press®, 1903), 173.

41. White, *Testimonies for the Church*, 1:264.

FURTHER READING: FOR THOSE
WHO WANT TO KNOW MORE

For those who want to gain a basic working knowledge of the American Civil War, the following sources are a good place to start.

Internet

The Internet offers many Web sites on the American Civil War, and the best place to begin is the Civil War Trust's Web site at http://www.civilwar.org. Here one will find not only a wealth of information about battles and battlefields but also links to other helpful Web sites as well. Also try a Google search on any topic related to the American Civil War, and you will be amazed at what you can find.

Media documentaries

To get a basic knowledge of the American Civil War, there is no better documentary than Ken Burns's moving *The Civil War: A Film by Ken Burns* (re-released as Ken Burns: *The Civil War* 25th Anniversary Edition DVD; available at http://www.pbs .org/civilwar/). An excellent companion to Burns's documentary is the *Civil War:*

The Untold Story DVD (Silver Spring, MD: Athena, 2014). *The Civil War* provides a basic overview of the war, whereas *The Untold Story* focuses on the battles in the Western theater. There are plenty of other good media presentations, but these two documentaries give such a meaningful introduction to this great conflict that you will watch them repeatedly. These resources are great for families to watch and learn together.

If you are looking for a college-level course on the American Civil War without going back to college, then the lectures of renowned Civil War historian Gary W. Gallagher are perfect. His engaging and informative lectures are available at the Great Courses Web site and can be purchased in various media formats, including the transcript books. One can learn fascinating details about the war while driving in a car, cooking in a kitchen, or resting on a couch. *The American Civil War: Lectures 1–48* is one of the more popular courses offered at http://www.thegreatcourses.com, and each lecture is no more than thirty minutes long. If you want to understand the American Civil War from A to Z, this is a worthwhile investment.

Books

A classic one-volume treatment of the American Civil War is the Pulitzer Prize–winning *Battle Cry of Freedom: The Civil War Era* (New York: Oxford University Press, 1988), written by distinguished Civil War historian James M. McPherson. Read this engaging volume, and you will have the big picture with the important details. Another vital book is James M. McPherson and James K. Hogue's *Ordeal by Fire: The Civil War and Reconstruction*, 4th ed. (New York: McGraw-Hill, 2010). This is another comprehensive one-volume treatment of the American Civil War, but it adds discussion about the Reconstruction after the war. Although *Ordeal by Fire* has more of a textbook flavor than *Battle Cry of Freedom*, it is still highly readable—and a personal favorite.

The best nonfiction narrative histories of the American Civil War are found in the classic writings of Bruce Catton and Shelby Foote. Catton, who leaned toward the North, provided richly textured accounts of the war in his numerous books (for information on Catton and a list of his many books, see https://en.wikipedia.org /wiki/Bruce_Catton). My favorite Catton book is *This Hallowed Ground: A History of the Civil War* (1956; repr., New York: Vintage, 2012). If you are looking for a short, fast-paced, and exciting read on the American Civil War, this is the book for you.

Foote, who leaned toward the South, is well-known for his three-volume *The Civil War: A Narrative* (New York: Random House, 1958–1974). There is no other way to describe this massive accomplishment than as epic. With the combined skills of an imaginative novelist and a detailed historian, Foote paints unforgettable word pictures of this great conflict from beginning to end. Foote's work provides a singular reading experience worth having at least once in a lifetime. In short, both Catton and Foote make the American Civil War sizzle.

Two primary sources worth reading for the novice as well as the enthusiast are Robert Hunt Rhodes, ed., *All for the Union: The Civil War Diary and Letters of Elisha Hunt Rhodes* (New York: Vintage, 1985) and Frederick Douglass, *Frederick Douglass: Autobiographies* (New York: Library of America, 1994). Rhodes's diary is endlessly interesting and provides a soldier's eyewitness account of the war from First Bull Run to Appomattox. Rhodes survived the entire war and afterward shared his experiences. I cannot stress enough the importance of reading th autobiographies of Frederick Douglass. From escaped slave to the most famous black abolitionist in nineteenth-century America, Douglass provides moving insight into the horrors of slavery and the power of freedom in his personal narratives. The vigorous writing style and memorable word pictures bring the surrounding issues of the war to life and will keep you on the edge of your seat.

If you are looking for a reference book on the American Civil War, then my recommendation is Margaret E. Wagner, Gary W. Gallagher, and Paul Finkelman, eds., *The Library of Congress Civil War Desk Reference* (New York: Simon & Schuster, 2002). If all you want is one book that will give you any basic fact on the American Civil War when you need it, this is the one.

For books on individual battles and other detailed aspects of the American Civil War, the comprehensive endnotes in this volume provide a wealth of resources to study. For a wide-ranging bibliography of the American Civil War, you will find great help in Allen C. Guelzo's excellent book *Fateful Lightning: A New History of the Civil War and Reconstruction* (New York: Oxford University Press, 2012), 537–555.

A significant book that was published recently—too late to use in the research for this book—is Gary W. Gallagher and Joan Waugh's *The American War: A History of the Civil War Era* (State College, PA: Spielvogel Books, 2015). If you want only one book that provides a crisp and eloquent history of the American Civil War with the most recent scholarship and up-to-date bibliography at the time of this writing, this is it. I project that in the years ahead *The American War* will become a popular textbook for college-level classes on the subject.

Finally, the article by Adventist historian Douglas Morgan on the Civil War in the *Ellen G. White Encyclopedia* should be mentioned. This article is an effective and concise overview of Ellen White's comments relating to the American Civil War and provides the essence of this book in a nutshell. (See Douglas Morgan, "Civil War," in *The Ellen G. White Encyclopedia*, ed. Denis Fortin and Jerry Moon [Hagerstown, MD: Review and Herald®, 2013], 718–721.)